Cataloging and Classification

Cataloging and Classification

An Introduction

Fourth Edition

Lois Mai Chan and Athena Salaba

ROWMAN & LITTLEFIELD PUBLISHERS, INC.
Lanham • Boulder • New York • Toronto • Plymouth, UK

Published by Rowman & Littlefield
A wholly owned subsidiary of The Rowman & Littlefield Publishing Group, Inc.
4501 Forbes Boulevard, Suite 200, Lanham, Maryland 20706
www.rowman.com

Unit A, Whitacre Mews, 26-34 Stannary Street, London SE11 4AB

British Library Cataloguing in Publication Information Available

Library of Congress Cataloging-in-Publication Data

Names: Chan, Lois Mai, author. | Salaba, Athena, author.
Title: Cataloging and classification : an introduction / Lois Mai Chan and Athena Salaba.
Description: Fourth edition. | Lanham : Rowman & Littlefield, [2016] | Includes bibliographical references and index.
Identifiers: LCCN 2015028244 | ISBN 9781442232488 (cloth : alk. paper) | ISBN 9781442232495 (pbk. : alk. paper) | ISBN 9781442232501 (electronic)
Subjects: LCSH: Cataloging. | Classification—Books. | Resource description & access.
Classification: LCC Z693 .C437 2016 | DDC 025.3—dc23 LC record available at http://lccn.loc.gov/2015028244

∞™ The paper used in this publication meets the minimum requirements of American National Standard for Information Sciences—Permanence of Paper for Printed Library Materials, ANSI/NISO Z39.48-1992.

Printed in the United States of America

LOIS MAI CHAN, 1934–2014

This fourth edition of the classic *Introduction to Cataloging and Classification* represents Dr. Chan's final scholarly contribution after a long and distinguished career. She was a prolific author whose other major books include, *Library of Congress Subject Headings, Principles and Application*, *Dewey Decimal Classification: Principles and Application*, *A Guide to the Library of Congress Classification*, and *Fast: Faceted Application of Subject Terminology*. For over thirty years her works have made cataloging understandable to thousands of students and practicing librarians. Her scholarly contributions also include her extensive research and writing about cataloging issues and include more than sixty scholarly articles and numerous talks and lectures. Her prolific writing on subject analysis and other library issues shaped the modern view of information organization.

A native of China, she received an AB in foreign languages from National Taiwan University followed MA in English and a MS in library science from Florida State University. She was a cataloger at several academic libraries before earning her PhD in comparative literature from University of Kentucky. Dr. Chan joined the faculty at the University of Kentucky's School of Library and Information Science in 1970, where she shared her enthusiasm for cataloging and educated several generations of librarians on the art and science information organization. She contributed to the enhancement or creation of the major schemas for subject analysis as a consultant to the Library of Congress on the Library of Congress Subject Headings and the Library of Congress Classification and to OCLC on the Dewey Decimal Classification and the Facetted Application of Subject Terminology (FAST).

Dr. Chan was very involved in professional associations. She was member of the American Library Association since 1960 where she served on numerous committees including the Subject Analysis Committee, the International Relations Committee, and the Executive Committee of the Cataloging and Classification Section. She was active in the International Federation of Library Associations and Institutions where she was a member of the Classification and Indexing and Knowledge Management Standing Committees and the Working Group on the Functional Requirements for Subject Authority Records. In 1989, she was the recipient of the Margaret Mann Citation, the highest honor in cataloging bestowed by the American Library Association, and in 2006 the recipient of the Beta Phi Mu Award, presented to a library school faculty member or to an individual for distinguished service to education in librarianship.

Dr. Chan was a dedicated mother and grandmother, a loving wife, and an esteemed colleague. She is survived by her husband, S. K.; daughter, Jennifer; son, Stephen; daughter-in-law, Sol; and grandsons, Zachary and Isaac. She is greatly missed by her family and those who had an opportunity to work with her, particularly by those of us who also knew her as a valued friend.

Photo contributed by Dr. Ed O'Neill, retired from OCLC.

Contents

Preface

Since the publication of the third edition of *Cataloging and Classification: An Introduction*, the landscape, scope, and nature of bibliographic control in libraries have undergone enormous changes. In addition to their own print and non-print sources, libraries now rely heavily on external or remote sources available on the Internet and the Web, which have become important milieus for knowledge discovery. Libraries offer access to a range of digitized resources. Web resources, in particular, possess characteristics that are a far cry from those found among traditional library resources. The field of information organization has seen major developments this past decade. New ways of modeling today's bibliographic environment have been developed and, as a result, new standards for organizing resources have been created to accommodate the new information environment. Most notably, the functional requirements family models have been completed and released, resulting in the development of a new standard for describing information resources, the *Resource Description and Access* (RDA).

The adoption of the first three editions of this book by many library and information science programs as an introductory text for beginner in cataloging and classification, and by many cataloging departments as a training tool, has encouraged the preparation of the fourth edition. As in the case of the first three editions, the primary intended audience of the new edition consists of students in library and information science programs, beginning professionals working in the areas of resource description and organization, and public service librarians seeking a fuller understanding of the bibliographic control apparatus. It may also be useful to professionals in related fields who are concerned with knowledge organization, for example, indexers, abstractors, bibliographers, publishers, and information system designers. Individual chapters within the book may also be used separately in training or review classes dealing with information organization, storage, and retrieval. The scope of this new edition is the analysis and representation of methods used in describing, organizing, and providing access to resources made available in or through libraries, including both the materials owned by the library (mostly physical items such as books, journals, and nonprint materials) and external resources such as those in electronic form that are accessible through the library's portal. In other words, the frame of reference for the book is today's library environment and its emphasis is on the standards for bibliographic control that have been widely adopted in the library field. It reports on recent developments in the retrieval arena, but technical details, particularly with regard to online systems, have been excluded because they vary from system to system and are subject to rapid changes.

This edition retains the overall outline of the third edition, presenting the essence of library cataloging and classification in terms of three basic functions: descriptive cataloging, subject access, and classification. Many chapters have been reorganized internally to provide a more logical progression of ideas and factual details. Within this framework, all chapters have been rewritten to incorporate the changes that have occurred during the interval between the third and fourth editions. In each part, the historical development and underlying principles of the retrieval mechanism at issue are treated first, because these are considered essential to an understanding of cataloging and classification. Discussion and examples of provisions in the standards and tools are then presented in order to illustrate the operations covered in each chapter.

Recent decades have witnessed the tremendous impact that changes in technology have had on cataloging and classification. Because of the great variety and idiosyncrasies of various online systems, no attempt has been made to focus on any particular online catalog system. Thus, it is in broad and general terms that online catalogs are discussed in this edition, with cataloging examples taken from a number of online systems. In reference to the computer processing of cataloging information, it is the machine-readable cataloging (MARC) system that is illustrated in this book.

References to and discussion of MARC formats occur throughout the book. The MARC system and formats are introduced in chapter 1, and the development and architecture of MARC formats are discussed in more detail in chapter 3, with emphasis on their underlying structure and principles. In the chapters dealing with cataloging and classification operations, MARC tags and codes are given where appropriate.

Each part of the book begins with a list of the standards and tools used in the preparation and processing of that part of the cataloging record covered, followed by suggested background readings selected to help the reader gain an overview of the subject to be presented. The list includes many works considered to be classics in the field. For those who wish to pursue the subject in greater depth, additional works are listed in the bibliography.

In this book, an attempt has been made to reflect current practice. Part one, which consists of chapters 1 and 2, provides a general overview of description, organization, and access relating to library resources within the context of the information environment in general, followed by a brief preview of the basic functions of cataloging and classification, and an introduction to principles, conceptual models, and a historical account of cataloging standards development. Part two, consisting of chapters 3 and 4, covers record structures, encoding formats, and metadata standards.

Part three, *Resources Description and Access* (RDA), consists of chapters 5–9 and offers new content first introduced with this fourth edition, replacing the detailed discussion of Anglo-American Cataloguing Rules (AACR2) rules of previous editions of this book. It covers the principles of and guidelines for identifying works, expressions, manifestations and items, identifying persons, families, and corporate bodies, creating authorized access points for each entity respectively, plus the recording of relationships between entities.

Part four, consisting of chapters 10–14 on subject representation and access, begins with a general chapter on subject access and controlled vocabularies followed by chapters discussing major subject access systems, including Library of Congress Subject Headings and Sears List of Subject Headings. A brief introduction of a specialized system, Medical Subject Headings and the newer FAST (Faceted Application of Subject Terminology) is also included.

Part five, Organization, covers the classification and categorization of library resources, with emphasis on the two major systems: the Dewey Decimal Classification and the Library of Congress Classification. The discussion and examples pertaining to the Dewey Decimal Classification in part five are based on Edition 23 of the DDC full version. The discussion of, and examples from, the Library of Congress Classification system are based on the most recent editions of classes in Library of Congress Classification. Part five also includes a discussion of the National Library of Medicine Classification as well as brief discussions of a number of other classification systems. Some of the systems that are seldom used or no longer in use but not necessarily inferior to those in use are included for the purpose of exposing students to ideas that challenge current practice and helping to illustrate the principles and theory embodied in different manifestations. The chapters on individual subject headings systems and classification schemes have been designed so that they may be used as a whole or selectively. For example, chapter 13, on Sears List of Subject Headings, may be used without first studying chapter 11, on Library of Congress Subject Headings; and in chapter 16, the sections on the abridged edition of the Dewey Decimal Classification can be used without first studying the section on the full edition. As a result, certain over-lapping discussions or repetitions of similar points occurs in these chapters. This method of presentation is used because certain library science programs are designed for specific types of libraries (for example, school libraries and media centers) and generally do not cover all systems of subject cataloging or classification.

It should be pointed out that this text is intended to be an aid in the study of these operations and their attendant tools and not as a substitute for the tools themselves. In other words, one cannot prepare a bibliographic description of a resource without resorting to the *Resources Description and Access* (RDA) or classify an item without using a classification scheme. Therefore, the discussion concentrates on the essence of the rules and no attempt is made to replicate or reproduce the cataloging rules in the text.

A glossary containing common terms in cataloging and classification, updated to reflect recent developments and current literature, is included, as is a bibliography of cataloging tools and selected writings in the field.

Examples illustrating various cataloging operations consist of extracts mostly from Library of Congress cataloging records. Encoding-system-independent examples, based on standards of description RDA are given for a variety of resources and, in addition, complete records are included in the appendixes to show how the parts fit together in the final cataloging product using current practices in many libraries in the US. Throughout this edition, one set of examples, the authority record for G. Edward Evans and the bibliographic record for the third edition of his book on management basics, is used to illustrate the structure of and relationship between records and the various manifestations of the same records in different cataloging systems. Appendix A also contains a set of records showing the cataloging of different manifestations and expressions of a particular work, Jane Austen's *Pride and Prejudice*.

We wish to extend our gratitude to many individuals for their contributions to the contents of this book and assistance in the preparation of this edition. We also wish to extend our gratitude to those assisting with the previous editions on which this book builds. These include experts in the field, instructors of cataloging and classification, reviewers and editors of the manuscript, experts and graduate students assisting with editing, indexing, and proofreading. Last, our thanks goes to our families for their patience and support.

Part I

INTRODUCTION

Chapter 1

Information Resource Management

Description, Access, Organization

INTRODUCTION

The ways people look for information have changed enormously in the last fifty or sixty years. Up to the late 1940s, most people went to a library if they could not find what they wanted among their resources at home. There, besides finding a wealth of reference materials to consult, they could use the card catalog, whose brief, item-by-item records (organized by author, title, and subject) showed what the library had and where it could be found on the shelves. In those days, printed books made up the most substantial part of most library collections, with journals and their attendant abstracting and indexing vehicles making up a lesser part, except in special-subject libraries. As the last century wore on, however, more and more nonprint materials (sound recordings, visual materials, microforms, globes, dioramas, and so on) were gradually added. By late in the century, most library collections included a growing proportion of local-access electronic resources, and libraries began providing access to remote-access electronic resources as well.

Today, people have untold amounts of information available at their fingertips, whether at home, in school computer labs, in libraries, or anywhere else with Internet access. Collections, or the resources accessible to library users, are not necessarily housed in the library anymore. A large amount of information is digital. What has made the difference, fundamentally, is the use of computers in processing information for storage and retrieval. Technology has made a major difference to library operations, as it has in so many other sectors of today's world. One example is that card catalogs have morphed to online catalogs (previous called OPACs for "Online Public Access Catalogs") or electronic catalogs. Electronic catalogs offer access not only to local library holdings, but also to a wide range of distant information sources; among the examples of this are the full catalogs of major research libraries, the offerings of abstracting and indexing journals and other catalog-like services, digital libraries, and all of the resources available through the Internet. Most modern catalogs allow quite sophisticated search options to users who are trying to hone in on material of interest.

There is no question that the Internet dominates today's information environment. With so many home computers, with computer labs in most schools, with Internet access offered by most libraries, and with Internet access outside the home and libraries almost worldwide, it is often the Internet that is first approached for information seeking. The Internet is a vast information store, so vast that a person submitting a query may well be told, on being given an initial response list of twenty or thirty "hits," that there are thousands more. For many users, this may be sufficient; however, for many others, this may not be a satisfactory response because there is no mechanism for them to efficiently select the best or most useful information that the Internet can offer. Thus, there is a downside in having easy access to what is apparently an unlimited supply of information.

The primary focus of this book is the mechanisms the library sector of the information community has worked out for identifying—and thereby enabling others to find—the materials for which its sector is responsible.

In this context, it should be noted that traditional library catalogs, in whatever form, provided access to information at the level of a book or separately published document. Journals and other serials were listed under their titles, with information noting what volumes and issues their respective institutions held. However, users had to consult other tools to locate individual journal articles. Indexes to periodicals and journals, as well as abstracting services, were developed outside the library community to fill this need. Early periodical indexes were manually prepared and published in print versions. Almost all are now online, and are referred to collectively as the online database industry. Most are proprietary, but are available to the public, free or for a fee.

In the library community access to information is two-pronged. First, some sort of topical labeling is provided to help those who are trying to zero in on a subject. Second, enough information is given about the item at hand that a searcher can tell whether the item is a fair match for what he or she had in mind when formulating the search. These can be represented by the two sorts of information in traditional catalog records: (1) content information, such as subject headings, classification numbers, and, in some cases, content summaries; and (2) identification information, such as author and other responsible agents, title, publisher, place and date of publication, series membership, various control numbers, and so on.

When the power of the computer for search and retrieval first became apparent, there was some speculation in the library environment that, with the right programs, computers could greatly simplify, perhaps even take over, the somewhat tedious job of preparing items for search and retrieval. This was a heady prospect because constructing catalog records is a labor-intensive process requiring highly trained personnel, and is thus very expensive. However, early expectations regarding how much could be done automatically proved overly optimistic. Searching by subject in full-text search systems delivered fairly satisfactory results when the amount of available information was relatively small, but led to overwhelming retrieval sets as the amount of available information became enormous.

The information world of the first couple of decades of the twenty-first century is complex, with many independent agencies and factors contributing to the overall picture. The situation is perhaps made more easily understandable through the realization that information resources and activities can be grouped into three different sectors. One is represented by the Internet and the designers of its components, another by libraries and other traditional information agencies such as archives and museums, and the third by online information service providers. Each of these sectors is constantly searching for improved and cost-effective means of making information available to those who seek it.

It is the library sector of the information community that has the longest history in respect to bibliographic access systems. The chapters of this book presents an account of what has been done in that sector from early on to the present day. Such an account has been considered essential preparation in the past for those entering the library-based profession and has also served as a helpful text for those in the profession who feel they would benefit from a systematic and analytic review. The account may even be of help to the information community at large.

Of particular interest, of course, are changes in all aspects of information retrieval that have come about since the beginning of the 1950s, in what we may call the online age. Since then, most developments in the library and online database industry have rested on theoretical and practical developments in information technology—of which the most well-known and possibly the most significant are the Internet and the World Wide Web (WWW). It may therefore be instructive here to present parallel accounts of the milestones that each of the three sectors has passed on the road to their current positions. The Internet is featured here because it plays such an important role in current information-gathering activities. Developments in the online database service industry are grouped with those in the library sector because their retrieval mechanisms are similar in many respects.[1]

TIMELINES IN INFORMATION ACCESS

Foundations, Both Environments

The first rumblings of the approaching tectonic shift in information processing and retrieval were heard in Vannevar Bush's 1945 "Atlantic Monthly" article,[2] in which he posited the future possibility of an online interactive information-retrieval system he called Memex. Large computers, the necessary vehicles for such a system, were then in development. ENIAC (Electronic Numerical Integrator and Computer), the country's first electronic computer, was operative the following year at the University of Pennsylvania, and in 1948, Bell Laboratories developed the transistor. In 1951, Remington-Rand built UNIVAC (UNIVersal Automatic Computer), the first commercial general-purpose electronic computer. The same year, Mortimer Taube presented a paper on (computer-based) coordinate indexing, and two years later, proposed an indexing system based on what he called "uniterms," a concept that underlay the future practice of keyword indexing. The Atlantic cable, a requirement for efficient communication between Europe and the United States, was laid in 1956. In the late 1950s, Hans Peter Luhn showed how the computer could be used to enable keyword searching, sorting, and content analysis of written texts,[3] and from that time on, computer technology was applied almost universally in the field. In September 1956, IBM began shipping RAMAC (Random Access Memory Accounting System), the first hard drive—its capacity was 5 megabytes, it weighed a little over a ton, and it cost $50,000 (an estimated $350,000 today)—to lease for a year. From then on, its capacity increased as dramatically as its cost declined. By 2006, a gigabyte of storage on a 320 gigabyte, 3.5-inch hard drive cost less than 50 cents, and in 2013, three terabytes of storage became available with an average cost of less than 4 cents per gigabyte.[4]

1957–1970, the Internet Environment

In October 1957, the Union of Soviet Socialist Republic launched Sputnik, the world's first artificial satellite, a device the size of a basketball. The next month, it launched Sputnik II, with a considerably bigger payload including a dog named Laika. These launches may be considered the beginning of the space age and also of the space race. The US government reacted by funding programs aimed at regaining its former leading position in science and technology. An immediate step was establishing the National Aeronautics and Space Administration (NASA) in October 1958. Another was setting up the Advanced Research Projects Agency (ARPA) in the Department of Defense. One of ARPA's projects was designing a computer "interface message" system. With its first IMP (Interface Message Processor) delivery, ARPANET,[5] the progenitor of the Internet, became operable in August 1969.

1957–1970, the Library and Online Database Industry Environment

In the early 1960s, the Library of Congress (LC) began working on developing a coding system to enable computer manipulation of library catalog records. The result was MARC, an encoding language whose name is based on the words Machine-Readable Cataloging. LC began using it, and trial distribution of MARC tapes began in October 1966; by June 1968, approximately 50,000 coded records had been distributed to participating libraries. Libraries nationwide embarked on programs to convert their old catalog records in card form to ones that were machine-readable. Worldwide, many countries began developing their own MARC formats and cataloging-record conversion programs. In most libraries, early use of MARC was confined to printing catalog cards.

The early 1960s saw the emergence of various information databases run by corporations such as Lockheed Information Systems and the System Development Corporation (SDC) with support from government agencies such as NASA and the National Library of Medicine (NLM). Lockheed's RECON (later to become DIALOG) surfaced in 1965, and ERIC (Educational Resources Information Clearinghouse) in 1969. Throughout the 1960s, batch-processing of data was the rule for most of these systems.

Another important trend in the 1960s was growth in international cooperation on bibliographical matters. In 1961, the International Conference on Cataloguing Principles, a conference that resolved many country-to-country cataloging differences, was held in Paris. *Anglo-American Cataloging Rules* (AACR) was published in 1967, providing a set of rules that were drafted according to the Paris Principles and that governed how works were described and entered into a bibliographic database. In 1969, an international group began work on a standard order and content for describing monographic material, which led to the family of International Standard Bibliographic Descriptions known as ISBDs.

The 1960s also saw developments in indexing theory and practice. In 1961, Chemical Abstracts began regular publication of a KWIC (Key Word In Context) index to its *Chemical Titles*, and in 1964, the Institute for Scientific Information began producing a citation index for publications in science and technology.

1971–1980, the Internet Environment

1971 saw the first e-mail on ARPANET. University College of London connected with ARPANET in 1973 to make ARPANET's first international connection. In 1974, Vinton Cerf developed the basic architecture—TCP/IP (Transmission Control Protocol/Internet Protocol)—for a large complex network, and the same year saw the first published appearance of the term "Internet."

1971–1980, the Library and Online Database Industry Environment

One of the major developments in the 1970s was the emergence of shared library cataloging systems. Prominent examples include RLIN (Research Libraries Information Network), OCLC (Ohio Colleges Library Center, later named Online Computer Library Center), and WLN (Washington Library Network, later named Western Library Network).

Another important development was the emergence of dial-up access to specialized informational databases: MEDLINE, for the medical community, was the first, in 1971. Not to be ignored in this context is the importance of the development and subsequent wide availability of personal computers. Radio Shack's TRS-80 personal computer was first marketed in 1976, and Apple II in 1977.

Interest in indexing languages continued during the decade, with PRECIS (Preserved Context Index System) coming into use in England in 1974.

The MARC formats for encoding cataloging data were adopted as a national standard (American National Standards Institute [ANSI] Z39.2) in 1971, and as an international standard (International Organization for Standardization [ISO] 2709) in 1973. On the international front, the 1973 International Federation of Library Associations (IFLA) Conference adopted the goal of Universal Bibliographic Control, under which a publication would be cataloged at the time and place of issue, with cataloging data available worldwide.

Finally, a second edition of the cataloging code AACR, noted above, was published in 1978. The new edition reflected the fact that library collections had by that time come to include many types of items—computer files being one example—for which earlier rules for description and access were inadequate.

1981–1990, the Internet Environment

MS-DOS surfaced in 1981, and 1982 saw the first use of the term "cyberspace." The first domain name was registered in 1985, and the entity that was to become America Online also was founded that year. In 1986, The National Science Foundation's NSFNET merged with, and then replaced, ARPANET. 1989 saw the rise of Compuserve and also AOL's debut. In 1990, a new system was being developed at CERN (originally the Center for European Nuclear Research). It combined hypertext and Internet technologies, and was called the World Wide Web (WWW, as noted earlier).

1981–1990, the Library and Online Database Industry Environment

The 1980s saw the rounding-out of a trend that had begun somewhat earlier: the transformation of library catalogs from banks of catalog-card drawers to bibliographic databases accessed through personal computer screens. The new catalogs were known as OPACs. The first OPACs, now referred to as "first generation," allowed faster and easier searching, but were limited to on-site collections with search options not much beyond those of card or microfiche catalogs. Gradually, OPACs offered more and more sophisticated search options. By the late 1980s, OPACs had shown many improvements (including keyword searching with Boolean operations), which resulted in significantly improved access points. There were also provisions for truncation, index browsing, and more display options for search results. OPACs at this stage are generally referred to as the "second-generation" OPACs.

The online database industry also made great strides during this decade, with the creation of more databases and with search options becoming ever more sophisticated. There were also increasing efforts to provide additional end-user searching features.

1991–2000, the Internet Environment

In 1991, CERN released the WWW or Web, or W3, which began as a networked information project at CERN under the direction of Tim Berners-Lee, now Director of the World Wide Web Consortium [W3C].[6] The Web became immediately popular, with the potential offered by hyperlinks capturing the imagination of the information community. In 1993, MOSAIC, the first graphical Web browser, developed by the National Center for Supercomputing Applications (NCSA) at the University of Illinois, was released.

The United Nations went online in the same year. WebCrawler, the first full-text search engine, became operational in 1994, enabling the harvesting of Web content and the creation of searchable indexes.[7] Yahoo!, Netscape Navigator, and Lycos also emerged in 1994, all offering full-text searching on the content of their databases. In the same year, Cambridge (Massachusetts) and Lexington (Massachusetts) became the nation's first wired communities. In 1995, Amazon.com, the programming language JAVA, and eBay appeared; in addition, AOL and Compuserve began offering Internet access. AOL bought Netscape in 1998, the same year that Google surfaced. For a year or two before the turn of the century, there was widespread anxiety that there would be a massive disruption of computer systems worldwide at midnight on December 31, 1999, due to the century date change. Nothing happened. Nupedia, ancestor of Wikipedia, appeared in 2000.

1991–2000, the Library and Online Database Industry Environment

The 1990s saw several major developments. Those responsible for MARC made gains in expansion and consolidation. USMARC merged with CAN-MARC to become MARC 21 in 1999 and 2000.

Library OPACs continued improving, with many commercial companies being set up to develop and maintain them. With the development of the Web browsers, OPACs moved to the WWW and were sometimes called WebPACs. Web features such as hyperlinks and hypertext enabled many sophisticated features to be introduced into the Web-based OPACs, further enhancing search capabilities, access points, and display options.

On the theoretical front, an IFLA committee began work on developing a new base for determining the necessary factors for achieving optimum bibliographic retrieval: a study titled *Functional Requirements for Bibliographic Records* (FRBR) was published in 1998, its final report having been approved by the IFLA Section on Cataloguing in 1997.[8] Many new metadata schemas—special-purpose coding systems designed to cover different types of materials not well-served by existing schemas—appeared during this decade. A prominent and fairly general one is the Dublin Core (DC), developed at OCLC and aimed especially at Web materials. Work began on it in 1995.[9]

The DC schema calls for subject indicators, but traditional LC subject headings under their current rules for application are too cumbersome for that purpose. Accordingly, in 1998, OCLC began work on a subject-heading system called FAST, the initials standing for Faceted Application of Subject Terminology.[10] FAST is based on the terminology of Library of Congress Subject Headings (LCSH) but uses simpler application rules. It is designed to be easier to apply, to offer more access points, to be flexible, and to be interoperable across disciplines and access environments.

2000 on, the Internet Environment

In 2001, Wikipedia superseded Nupedia. The same year, the *New York Times* went on the Web, and Skype (an Internet phone service) was introduced. Google expanded over the next few years, offering Google Print, Google Earth, Google Scholar, and Google Knowledge Graph. In 2011, Google Art Project allowed users to take a virtual tour of the world's best museums and explore more than 1,000 works of art. In 2004, Google not only announced an IPO (Initial Public Offering) of stock in its company, but also began scanning, and making searchable, the contents of five major research libraries. In 2005, Yahoo! counted three million visitors a month, and the one-billionth Internet user went online. In April 2006, a Google-Earthlink team and the city of San Francisco agreed to sign a contract to install a WiFi (wireless fidelity) network for the whole city, to be free, or at very low cost, to users. At the same time, Earthlink was negotiating similar contracts with Philadelphia, Pennsylvania, Anaheim, California, New Orleans, Louisiana, and won several contracts, launching its first citywide WiFi network in Anaheim. In 2012, the company upgraded its network infrastructure by adding next-generation optical transport capabilities and significantly expanding its nationwide IP footprint.

2000 on, the Library Environment

By 2002, AACR2 had undergone yet another revision. The consensus of the information community was that a new code was called for, a code that would include provisions for rapidly developing information items and packages and that would incorporate the conceptual framework set forth in the document, FRBR.[11] The Joint Steering Committee for the Revision of AACR (JSC) began work on such a code in 2005; their work was initially released in June 2010 as "*RDA: Resource Description and Access*" in the RDA Toolkit,[12] which was meant to replace AACR2. In March 2013, the LC started full implementation of RDA cataloging, and several other national libraries announced their plans to implement RDA in 2013, including the British Library, Library and Archives Canada, National Library of Australia, and Deutsche Nationalbibliothek.

By 2013, OCLC's WorldCat contained over 290 million bibliographic records and more than two billion holding records for items from more than 170 countries and in 470 languages.

As time progresses, online database providers continue to increase the contents of their databases and improve searching capabilities, with Web interfaces providing multiple options for users of differing degrees of skill and sophistication. Attempts are also being made to link search results to holdings of particular libraries.

Future Prospects

In 2006, OCLC made a bold move to provide free access to its vast WorldCat database (hitherto accessible to OCLC members only) through its Open WorldCat program.[13] This program enables Web users of popular Internet search, bibliographic, and bookselling sites such as Google, Yahoo! and Bing to identify and locate library materials. For example, through Google Books,[14] a partner site in the OCLC Open WorldCat program, users can search for all sorts of library materials, retrieve bibliographic data based on cataloging records, and locate copies in OCLC libraries by city, region, and country. Google Books has partnered with publishers through the Partner

Project and with libraries through the Library Project to connect Web users to books.

By 2013, Linked Open Data (LOD) initiatives were starting to publish data on the Web. Information providers such as OCLC and the LC have made data available as linked data, and many libraries and other information agencies publish their data, including resource metadata as linked data. Linked data provide a set of simple rules that allow representation of any conceptual thing on the Web, using unique resource identifiers (URIs). Linked data provide information that describes conceptual things and also indicate explicit relationships to other conceptual things that also have URIs. Linked data will allow library systems and library users to explore data related to a resource not only based on library metadata, but on many other sources of data as well. Other Web search engines already use linked data to connect searchers to many authoritative sources, including library catalogs.

Because most people start their information searches on the Web, the result of these initiatives is a convergence of access to both library and Web resources. Libraries are thus much more visible on the Web than they were before. These recent developments represent the first steps toward the vision of integrating library catalogs with open Web discovery tools.[15]

LIBRARY AND INTERNET ACCESS PROVISIONS

The trends revealed in the accounts above can be summarized as follows:

The Internet environment shows an accelerating increase in technological advances, coverage, and services, with no sign of slackening on any front. It has been international in scope and participation since the beginning. Services offered are mainly proprietary, a fact that means that little or no information is available about what methods the various search services use to produce their results.

The library environment, with a much longer history, took steps to enter the online age at its beginning, through its development of MARC and MARC-like coding systems. The online age continued the trends that had previously been in effect, working toward consistency on the one hand and expanded coverage on the other. The latter, in particular, focused on the types of materials that cataloging rules and coding systems are designed to handle. International cooperation on all fronts increased steadily over the fifty-year period at issue. Control mechanisms for names, for surrogate design and content, and for topic designators are still strong. OPACs, and more recently WebPACs, with their increasingly sophisticated access provisions and search options, have replaced card and book catalogs in almost all libraries.

It is appropriate here to consider information-retrieval results from Internet and library or library-like search systems. At the end of a subject search on the Internet using full-text searching—the most common Internet search mode—the user is presented with a list of the leading documents within a much longer list of links to information sources that contain his or her query term. There is no mechanism to inform that user of other documents on the same topic whose authors use a synonym for the submitted term. Furthermore, the number of these other documents in a list of all retrieved documents is often at least in the thousands. Internet name searches may deliver many matches with little or nothing to differentiate them, with many in the list being the wrong fit for the wanted entity or individual.

Searches in bibliographic databases designed on the pattern of library catalogs result in a smaller number of hits and a higher on-target rate. There are two main reasons for such precision. One is that such databases store brief representations of documents, representations drawn up by trained catalogers who have studied the documents to which the representations apply. The other is that modern systems such as OPACs are likely to have embedded synonym control, ensuring that a user wanting material about eyeglasses will get all the system has to offer even if his or her query term is "spectacles." If a given system lacks embedded controls, it at least presents users with *see* and *see also* references. Modern systems do the same thing for names, so that users searching for an author's works will get all the material that author wrote, whether they search on the author's real name or a pseudonym. Synonym control also acts as a filter, using qualifiers for distinguishing ambiguous terms. Thus, users are not presented with material on both submitted terms and on their homographs, for example, on both waterfalls and eye-lens conditions in response to a search on "cataracts."

Why do the two systems deliver such different results? The key concept is "bibliographic control," a term in use for decades among librarians. Behind the phrase "bibliographic control" lie two other concepts: *recall* and *precision.* A system is said to have good recall if a search delivers almost everything in its collection or database that matches a submitted query. And it is said to have good precision if the search delivers almost nothing else. Although very few library systems rate a perfect score on these two measures, many come close.

BIBLIOGRAPHIC CONTROL

As a prelude to discussing the concept of bibliographic control with all its ramifications, it is useful to describe the role that adherence to standards has played in the library sector of the information community. Even late in the nineteenth century, librarians began to realize the advantages of standardizing practice and fostering cooperation among libraries. The need for codification of cataloging practice became particularly apparent as the use of cooperative or shared cataloging increased. Economically, shared cataloging is a boon for libraries, greatly reducing cataloging costs. However, libraries can benefit from shared cataloging only if the records in the catalogs of different libraries are compatible. One reason for aiming for a high level of compatibility was the observation that user searches are more successful when document surrogates are consistent with others in the same system. Another is the fact that many practical aspects of library management are more efficient if records are consistent. Such consistency is especially important among records in a union catalog (i.e., a catalog of multiple collections) or in a union database with records coming from different sources. Only if participating libraries follow the same cataloging rules and practices can optimum compatibility of records be obtained.

Particularly since the late nineteenth century, numerous standards for bibliographic control have been developed. There are separate standards for bibliographic description, for subject and nonsubject access, and for classification. For bibliographic description, the primary standard used in library catalogs in English-speaking countries until 2013 has been the AACR, first published in 1967 and revised every few years since until 2005. RDA is expected to replace AACR. For specific types of materials, such as archives and electronic resources, additional standards—called metadata schema—including Encoded Archival Description (EAD) and DC have emerged. For access, AACR and RDA include rules for designating and formulating nonsubject access points through names of persons, corporate bodies, families, titles, etc. Subject access points are determined by other standards such as LCSH, *Sears List of Subject Headings*, and *Medical Subject Headings* (MeSH). For organization, the most commonly used schemes are the *Library of Congress Classification* (LCC) and the *Dewey Decimal Classification* (DDC). These standards are discussed in detail in the following chapters.

A library or other information system can keep its collection under bibliographic control when it follows these standards appropriately for the situation at hand. To understand why the provisions of various standards were designed as they are, one needs to consider the functions of bibliographic control mechanisms—in other words, what bibliographic control is supposed to achieve. Various thinkers over the years have written on this subject. A synopsis of the most influential statements follows.

FUNCTIONS OF BIBLIOGRAPHIC CONTROL

Among the earliest articulation of the functions of bibliographic control was Charles A. Cutter's statement of the "objects of the catalog" and the means for attaining them, as found in his cataloging code, *Rules for a Dictionary Catalog*; these functions are[16]

Objects

1. To enable a person to find a book of which any of the following is known:
   a. the author
   b. the title
   c. the subject
2. To show what the library has in terms of the following:
   d. a given author
   e. a given subject
   f. a given kind of literature
3. To assist in the choice of a book with respect to the following:
   g. its edition (bibliographically)
   h. its character (literary or topical)

Means

1. Author entry with the necessary references (for 1a and 2d)
2. Title entry or title reference (for 1b)
3. Subject entry, crossreferences, and classed subject table (for 1c and 2e)
4. Form entry and language entry (for 2f)
5. Giving edition and imprint, with notes when necessary (for 3g)
6. Notes (for 3h)

In the mid-twentieth century, the notable articulation of cataloging principles and theory came from Seymour Lubetsky. Lubetsky was a librarian at the LC and later a professor at the School of Library Services at the University of California, Los Angeles. His primary interest was descriptive cataloging, the functions of which he posited as the following:[17]

1. To describe the significant features of the book that will serve (a) to distinguish it from other books and other editions of the book, and (b) characterize its contents, scope, and bibliographical relations; and
2. To present the data in an entry that will (a) fit well with the entries of other books and other editions of this book in the catalog, and (b) respond best to the interests of the majority of readers.

Lubetsky was a prolific writer. His work underlay the deliberations of the International Conference on Cataloguing held in Paris in 1961. The Statement of Principles, also known as the Paris Principles, adopted by the Conference includes the following "Functions of the Catalogue":[18]

> The catalogue should be an efficient instrument for ascertaining
>
> 2.1 whether the library contains a particular book specified by
> (a) its author and title, *or*
> (b) if the author is not named in the book, its title alone, *or*
> (c) if author and title are inappropriate or insufficient for identification, a suitable substitute for the title; and
>
> 2.2 (a) which works by a particular author and
> (b) which editions of a particular work are in the library.

This statement in turn laid the basis for the code that dominated the second half of the century: AACR.

In 1998, FRBR redefined the requirements for bibliographic records in relation to the following generic tasks that are performed by users when searching and making use of national bibliographies and library catalogs:[19]

- using the data to find materials that correspond to the user's stated search criteria (e.g., in the context of a search for all documents on a given subject, or a search for a recording issued under a particular title);
- using the data retrieved to identify an entity (e.g., to confirm that the document described in a record corresponds to the document sought by the user, or to distinguish between two texts or recordings that have the same title);
- using the data to select an entity that is appropriate to the user's needs (e.g., to select a text in a language the user understands, or to choose a version of a computer program that is compatible with the hardware and operating system available to the user);
- using the data in order to acquire or obtain access to the entity described (e.g., to place a purchase order for a publication, to submit a request for the loan of a copy of a book in a library's collection, or to access online an electronic document stored on a remote computer).

As a follow-up on the development of FRBR, IFLA published the *International Cataloguing Principles* in 2009, with its main focus being to guide the development of cataloging codes. Section 4 of the statement includes the revised objectives and functions of a catalog, which should enable the user[20]

> 1. to find bibliographic resources in a collection as the result of a search using attributes or relationships of the resources:
> 1.1. to find a single resource
> 1.2. to find sets of resources representing
> all resources belonging to the same work

all resources embodying the same expression
all resources exemplifying the same manifestation
all resources associated with a given person, family, or corporate body
all resources on a given subject
all resources defined by other criteria

2. to identify a bibliographic resource or agent
3. to select a bibliographic resource that is appropriate to the user's needs
4. to acquire or obtain access to an item described or to access, acquire, or obtain authority data or bibliographic data;
5. to navigate within a catalogue and beyond.

Similarly, RDA states that its objectives for responsiveness to user needs are to guide data creation that will enable users to[21]

- *find* resources that correspond to the user's stated search criteria;
- *find* all resources that embody a particular work or a particular expression of that work;
- *find* all resources associated with a particular person, family, or corporate body;
- *find* all resources on a given subject;
- *find* works, expressions, manifestations, and items that are related to those retrieved in response to the user's search;
- *find* persons, families, and corporate bodies that correspond to the user's stated search criteria;
- *find* persons, families, or corporate bodies that are related to the person, family, or corporate body represented by the data retrieved in response to the user's search;
- *identify* the resource described (i.e., confirm that the resource described corresponds to the resource sought, or distinguish between two or more resources with the same or similar characteristics);
- *identify* the person, family, or corporate body represented by the data (i.e., confirm that the entity described corresponds to the entity sought, or distinguish between two or more entities with the same or similar names, etc.);
- *select* a resource that is appropriate to the user's requirements with respect to the physical characteristics of the carrier and the formatting and encoding of information stored on the carrier;
- *select* a resource appropriate to the user's requirements with respect to form, intended audience, language, etc.;
- *obtain* a resource (i.e., acquire a resource through purchase, loan, etc., or access a resource electronically through an online connection to a remote computer);
- *understand* the relationship between two or more entities;
- *understand* the relationship between the entity described and a name by which that entity is known (e.g., a different language form of the name); and
- *understand* why a particular name or title has been chosen as the preferred name or title for the entity.

BIBLIOGRAPHIC CONTROL THROUGH SURROGATES

We now turn to a discussion of the various ways those in charge of different types of bibliographic systems operate their databases. Managers of large bibliographic systems, for the most part, employ two different ways of setting up items of database content for efficient storage and retrieval. One is to store the full text of whatever is posted or submitted and conduct searches of that. Most Internet and Web searches are on full text, and search engines such as Google and Bing apparently base their results on calculations involving term frequencies and links. (As noted above, the retrieval mechanisms most search engines use are trade secrets, so outsiders cannot know just how they work. Informal surveys, however, indicate that user satisfaction is high.) The other way to manage storage and retrieval for a collection of documents or other book-like materials is to construct and store *brief representations* of what is in the collection. This is what has been done for centuries, and is still being done, in the library environment. There, before the advent of computers, the only way to go directly to the full text of books or journals was to go to library or bookstore shelves, scan for a promising item, then pick it up and flip through its pages. Such a process was neither efficient nor ultimately satisfying for those who wanted to do systematic searches for information. Accordingly, throughout the history of bibliographic lists or catalogs, those in charge of a collection have created brief descriptions conveying the salient facts about the items they hold. Booksellers at the medieval Frankfurt book fairs drew up such descriptions, mostly in the form of brief-title listings. Librarians have done the same since the early days of the field, drawing up (and setting up for searching) descriptions that are referred to either as document surrogates or as bibliographic records—terms that are used interchangeably in the paragraphs that follow.

Surrogates present essential information about documents and other cataloged items: in brief, the responsible agent's name, title of work, publisher, date, content, and so on, to the extent that those elements apply. Surrogates are constructed by human catalogers or indexers based on the actual content of the resource, and now follow a standard, internationally recognized pattern for at least part of their content. (Internationally, the pattern for description is the ISBD[22]; in the Anglo-American cataloging environment, it is AACR[23] and RDA.)

A more comprehensive account of surrogates is that they carry information on authors or other responsible agents, on coauthors if any, on other contributors such as illustrators or translators, on title (and subtitle if any), on edition, and on publisher, place of publication, and copyright. They also show series membership, if any, and provide notes on anything unusual about the edition. Furthermore, they carry subject headings reflecting topical coverage, and classification numbers showing where the item can be located in a physical collection as well as how the item's topic fits into a hierarchical portrayal of human knowledge. In the United States, most subject headings are chosen from LCSH, a huge list of continuously updated headings that incorporates synonym control and suggests related, broader, and narrower terms as well. (In some situations, catalogers use headings from a smaller, somewhat simplified, subject-headings list known as the *Sears List of Subject Headings.*) Again in the United States, most records carry classification numbers from both DDC and LCC. In individual library collections, class numbers are followed by *book numbers,* or *item numbers*, to sequence the item to which the record pertains among others in the same class position (and therefore in the same area of the shelves). Finally, records also carry other control numbers, such as the item's International Standard Book Number (ISBN) and its LC control number. (It should be noted here that surrogates carrying all the information detailed above are not appropriate to all storage and retrieval situations. A bookstore with a stock of a few thousand titles does not need surrogates to carry all the information that a library of millions or many hundreds of thousands requires in its surrogates.)

Another, and older, term for a document surrogate is a bibliographic record. Bibliographic records are the building blocks of a bibliographic file. Each bibliographic record pertains to an item in the collection represented in the file, and contains two primary kinds of information: first, enough data for the item to be identifiable in the context of the file, and, second, at least one assigned "access point." Names of authors are access points, as are titles and subject terms, as well as other entities, such as performers. In addition, there may be any number of computer-extracted words that also serve as access points. Broadly defined, a bibliographic record could be an entry in an index, in a bibliography, in a library catalog, or in any other text-based file. The amount and nature of information included in a record depend on the purposes for which the file is prepared. In some bibliographic files, such as scientific periodical indexes or catalogs of highly specialized libraries, it is appropriate that records provide extensive subject and/or descriptive information; in others, such as a short-title catalog of items published at a given place and time, very little information per item is often sufficient. Creating records of the kind just described requires highly trained personnel if the work is to be done well. One of the issues facing library-oriented information professionals at the present time is to determine whether current practice is cost-effective, and if not, how it might be made so.

An important factor in the cost of surrogate production stems from a long-held library-world tenet: name and synonym control. One of the principles behind the design of library-oriented retrieval mechanisms is that material on the same topic should be tagged with the same subject heading, not disbursed in an alphabetical array, as happens if some materials on timekeeping devices are labeled clocks, some watches, some timepieces, some chronographs, and so on. The same principle holds for names, whether personal, geographic, corporate, or named entities such as the Flatiron Building or a work such as the *Iliad*. To achieve a system reflecting the one-term-per-entity principle, catalogers had to work out a mechanism to show what terms or names should be preferred. The result for topical terms, built over more than a century, is LCSH, a list of preferred terms with directions on what references should be made to broader terms, to narrower terms, and to related terms at the same hierarchical level, such as near-synonyms. The list also carries alternates to preferred terms called lead-in terms with references to the preferred term. (Lead-in terms are words searchers might use in looking for the topics denoted by the preferred term.) A similar mechanism exists for names, and a preferred-term list exists for them also. Constructing such lists, called authority lists because they are lists of authorized terms, is a highly labor-intensive undertaking because it takes extensive checking into both popular and professional or scientific literature to ascertain the most effective term to authorize or establish. The procedure involved is called authority work; it must be done whenever new terms or names are added to preferred lists and also whenever terms or names already in the list are changed. Authority work, needed in keeping subject and name lists up to date as well as in dealing with new terms and names, is therefore the most costly aspect of the cataloging operation.

Another part of the cataloging operation, ubiquitous since computers first became an important factor in library work, is coding surrogates for computer manipulation; in other words, making them machine-readable. The LC began work on a workable coding system when it first became apparent that computers would be playing a significant role in library matters. The resulting system was MARC, which went into use in the late 1960s. Its current version, called the MARC 21 formats, is the standard encoding system for library materials, and is widely used all over the world.

In recent years, a new concept and product has entered the information-retrieval arena, the *metadata schema*. A rigorous definition of metadata is "structured data about data." Thus, a metadata schema provides a structure or standard format for recording data that bring out the essential characteristics of an information item or object. Although, in a broad sense, the term *metadata records* includes what are traditionally called catalogs and indexes, the term is used primarily for files designed to accommodate material that is not suited to standard cataloging rules and coding systems. Examples include archeological relics as well as various types of electronic resources.

Bibliographic files exist in many forms and, within each form, one file may differ considerably from another in type of bibliographical material covered, the pattern followed in drawing up its records, amount of information provided per record, how records are organized, and how records may be retrieved. Bibliographic databases, which are bibliographic files in electronic form, show even more variation than manually prepared files because of the versatility and power of today's computers in handling bibliographic data and allowing different designs of online systems. It is through this power that bibliographic databases are able to offer users many more search and display options than were available in static systems.

Later chapters in this book discuss these various operations and tools in some detail, with copious examples.

SURROGATE PRODUCTION

The bibliographic control methods used for centuries to help library users find information consist of three distinct but related operations: description, access-point provision, and arrangement. *Description* refers to the preparation of a surrogate or a brief representation containing essential elements of the original resources, thereby creating a bibliographic or metadata record. *Access-point provision* refers to designating selected elements in the representation that the user can use as means to gain "entry" to the representation. (In a card catalog or online or static browsing list, access points are the headings under which records appear.) Both of these operations are carried out in accordance with established standards, AACR and RDA in English-speaking countries. *Arrangement* or *organization* refers to the method of arranging both surrogates and physical resources, also according to established orders, alphabetic (in most browsing lists or files), alpha-numeric (in LC classification order), or numeric (DDC order).

Description

In a broad sense, *resource description* refers to the process and the product of presenting, in a record, the essential facts concerning an information item, which are drawn up according to established standards. The resulting record in turn serves as the surrogate in the file or catalog for the full item itself. The purpose of resource description is to tell what the resource is, in enough detail to distinguish it from other items with similar descriptions, such as other editions or versions of the same work.

Different levels of description are appropriate for different situations. For some books, for instance, the title, the name of the author, and the location of the item are all that is needed in a description. On the other hand, descriptions in a rare-book dealer's sales list or catalog must be extensive and detailed. Furthermore, the sorts of information needed in descriptions vary according to what is being cataloged: the descriptions of museum items and other realia must include different elements than descriptions of books. The same is true for descriptions of most nonbook items (including films and sound recordings) and especially for electronic resources.

Various user communities have drawn up metadata schemas that provide frameworks for resource description in which the details of the content elements are defined according to the needs of their communities. Therefore, metadata descriptions vary in content and in extent. When such factors apply, the most common elements of a metadata description include most of the elements specified in standard rules for description in addition to the community-specific elements for which the schemas were designed.

Conventions for bibliographic description have remained relatively steady, but not static, over the past several decades. To accommodate changes in the information environment, description standards have been revised on an ongoing basis. The unusually rapid proliferation of electronic resources, especially those available on the Web, has necessitated a reexamination of the way individual items are described for the discovery and retrieval of information. Standards for description are changing considerably. The many new metadata schemas that have already emerged are part of this change.

Methods of displaying bibliographic records have also varied over the years, from early manuscript (handwritten) catalogs to OPACs. To enable the display of records electronically, the elements within the records are encoded according to one or another encoding scheme, such as the MARC formats, HTML (Hypertext Markup Language), XML (Extensible Markup Language), and so on. MARC, the coding system widely used in the library environment—and in many others—is first presented at the end of this chapter and is discussed in detail in chapter 3 of this book. Many other encoding schemes, including those just mentioned, either are or can be made compatible with MARC.

Access

A catalog or a bibliographic database contains a collection of bibliographic records. Sizes of catalogs or databases vary greatly from hundreds to thousands to millions. To aid retrieval in *surrogate-based databases*, the record elements that are most frequently used by users to identify resources have traditionally been designated as access points. Typical access points include subject terms and nonsubject elements such as the title and the name of the author(s), editors, translators, and suchlike. To ensure consistency, standards concerning the designation or assignment of access points are followed.

Arrangement

The growing volumes of a library collection or a virtual collection of electronic resources require efficient methods of organization. Early on, for library collections, elaborate classification schemes were devised for shelf arrangement, with the aim of enabling easy browsing and retrieval. Many such schemes are still in use, particularly, in the United States, the DDC and the LCC. The same schemes also are often used for listing entries in a catalog or bibliography. A case can be made that electronic resources must also be organized in some logical and easy-to-navigate fashion if search and retrieval are to be made easier and more efficient. To date, for resources on the Web, relatively simple classification or categorical schemes are being used in some systems to guide users to desired subjects. In fact, the name of the search engine Yahoo! is said to reflect the phrase "Yet Another Hierarchically Organized Operating system." Hierarchical schemes have also been used in Web directories to display search results or to organize the links between and among retrieved items. These links are typically URIs.

Methods of displaying bibliographic records may or may not reflect how they are organized or sequenced *within* a bibliographic database. In manually maintained systems and in the early OPACs, what users saw reflected the internal organization of the system. In fully electronic systems, internal organization is hidden from users; however, in most modern systems, users are offered many options for how they want search results displayed.

LIBRARY CATALOGS

General Characteristics

A library catalog is a kind of bibliographic file. It differs from a bibliography or a periodical index in that all of its records pertain to items in one or more libraries and carry information on where the items can be found. Most library catalogs represent a single institution's holdings (which may be distributed in many branches). Other catalogs show the holdings of several libraries or collections; these are called *union catalogs*.

A library catalog consists of a set of records that, like the records in other bibliographic files, provide data about the items in the collection or collections the catalog represents. The data on each record include, at least (1) a bibliographic description giving the identification, publication, and physical characteristics of the resource; and, (2) for a physical item, a call number (consisting of the classification number, based on the subject content, and an item number, based on the author, the title, or both) that indicates the physical location of the item in the collection. Most records also include subject terms, which state succinctly the subject content of the resource.

Almost all library catalogs are *multiple-access* files. This means that they offer many ways, or *access points*, to retrieve a particular record. In most card catalogs, there were often several cards for the same item, each filed under a heading that represented a different access point. This way of providing information about items in a collection—multiple-access points to records that provide sufficient details for identification plus characterization of content—helps users locate particular items or select items they judge to be relevant to the subject they are pursuing.

In library cataloging, it has long been the practice to designate one of the access points as the chief access point, or *main entry*. In most cases, the main entry is based on the author if such can be determined. Otherwise, the main entry is based on either the title or the corporate body responsible for the content or the title. There are two reasons for main entry practice. First, it is the most efficient way to manage lists that are maintained manually. In the days of manually prepared cards, it was the convention to record all needed information on one card and to include only brief descriptions on other cards (called added entries) for the same item. In online situations, the original justification for designating a main entry no longer holds. But even for computer-stored lists, it remains helpful to have a standard convention for the way a bibliographic item should be cited. The main entry pattern (in other words, author/title) is the usual way of referring to a work, a fact that adds to its effectiveness as a consistent citation standard. The terminology has changed with RDA, which instructs catalogers to record relationships between a resource and persons, families, or corporate bodies, at a minimum, as elements for the *creator* and *other person, family,* or *corporate body* associated with the resource. RDA does not use the term primary access point or main entry, but its use of MARC to encode RDA data carries the MARC 1XX field definitions as main entry fields.

Forms of Catalogs

When catalog records were manually produced—handwritten, typed, or typeset—there were only a few options for physical form: books, cards, and, to a limited extent, microforms. Within these forms, considerations of cost and bulk placed a severe limit on the amount of information that could be included in a given record and on the number of access points that could be provided for it. As it did with access points, the advent of catalog automation made a major difference in the potential forms catalogs could take and in the variety of features an individual catalog could exhibit. In particular, automation removed the limits on record length that had prevailed in the manual environment.

The following brief account treats major catalog forms both historically and as they exist today.

Book Catalogs

The book catalog is a list in book form of the holdings of a particular library collection or group of collections, with the cataloging records displayed in page format. This is the oldest form of library catalog. Its items may be recorded by handwriting as in a manuscript catalog, by typing, or by a printing process. The oldest manuscript catalog goes back as far as the Pinakes compiled by Callimachus for the ancient Alexandrian library. The book form catalog was the predominant form of library catalog until the late nineteenth century, when use of the card catalog began to spread. Even so, manually prepared book catalogs continued to be issued in small numbers for many years. Also, for a period around the middle of the last century, several major libraries published their whole catalogs in book form, with their pages made up of photographs of their catalog cards, sequenced as they appeared in the catalog. Online catalogs, accessible from anywhere, eliminated the market for such publications.

Card Catalogs

In card catalogs, cataloging entries were recorded on 3" by 5" cards, one entry per card or set of cards. Each entry could then be revised, inserted, or deleted without affecting other entries. Before the card catalog, most library catalogs were in book form, either printed or looseleaf. When the card catalog was first introduced in the latter part of the nineteenth century, its advantage in ease of updating was immediately perceived, and libraries throughout the United States began adopting this form. The fact that, in 1901, readymade sets of card catalogs were being distributed by the LC to subscribing libraries contributed significantly to the widespread use of card catalogs. For nearly a century, the card catalog was the predominant form of catalog in the United States. It was catalog automation that eventually changed the picture, but not for well over a decade after its introduction: early catalog databases were used primarily to print sets of catalog cards.

Microform Catalogs

The microform catalog was a variant of the book catalog, and served in many situations as an interim device between card and online catalogs. It contained cataloging records in microimage and required the use of a microform reader for viewing. The prevalent form of microform catalog was on microfiche, updated (that is, replaced by a new set of fiche showing additions and changes) on a regular basis, usually quarterly. The need for a microform reader, the handling of the fiche or film, and the display image all proved major psychological barriers for many users. For the early, not-always-dependable online catalogs, however, the microform catalog provided a viable backup.

Online Catalogs

When a library's users can retrieve catalog records directly from a computer database, the library is said to have an online catalog, usually called an OPAC. The usual mode of display in an online catalog is through a computer terminal. In this mode, individual cataloging records or parts thereof are retrieved by means of access points or search keys and are displayed instantly on a monitor. Many OPAC terminals are accompanied by printers. Users gain numerous advantages from online catalogs, including instant feedback during the retrieval process and the availability of more access points than any manual catalog can offer. Furthermore, OPACs allow remote access so that the user does not have to be physically present in a library in order to search its catalog. Modern OPACs, sometimes called WebPACs, allow users to get to the Web and Internet and avail themselves of many of the features that search engines offer.

An online catalog can be integrated with other library operations such as cataloging, acquisitions, and circulation, resulting in an integrated online system. With an integrated system, the user is able not only to identify an item but also to ascertain whether the item is currently available for browsing or circulation. In some integrated systems, it is also possible to find out whether a particular item is on order.

MARC records form the basic units of an online catalog. For a cataloging record to be machine-readable, it must not only be input into a computer, but also its various elements must be tagged or labeled in such a way that they can be stored, manipulated, and eventually retrieved in all the ways that are appropriate for technical and reference services in libraries. In the early 1960s, in consultation with other major libraries, the LC began work on developing a protocol for coding bibliographic records. The emerging protocol was called the MARC format. Although there are other protocols for coding various kinds of records for computer storage and retrieval, MARC is the system that has prevailed for library records in the United States and in many other countries. As noted earlier, the MARC format is briefly explained at the end of this chapter and is presented in greater detail in chapter 3.

Compact Disk-Read Only Memory (CD-ROM) Catalogs

A related catalog form is sometimes referred to as an online catalog, although it is much less flexible. This is the CD-ROM catalog. For CD-ROM catalogs, a catalog database is periodically—usually quarterly—copied onto compact disks, which can be accessed through stand-alone microcomputers.

Displaying Cataloging Records

In a manually prepared book or card catalog, how the records or entries were arranged determined how they could be retrieved and displayed. There were two primary ways in which individual bibliographic entries could be assembled to form a coherent file: alphabetic and classified (or systematic). In a classified catalog, the entries were arranged according to a chosen system of classification, resulting in subject collocation. This is a form of catalog arrangement that was popular in the nineteenth century but which, as a public tool, has become all but extinct in American libraries. In an alphabetical catalog or dictionary catalog, entries are organized in alphabetical sequence, with author, title, and subject headings interfiled. This form was introduced in the latter part of the nineteenth century and soon became predominant in the United States.

How records in an online catalog are arranged internally is a matter of system design, and affects end users only in the sense that one system may be easier to use and may apparently deliver more satisfactory results than another. But how retrieved items appear on the screen also depends on system design, and here, end users should be aware that many more options are open to them when compared to a manual catalog. Results of a search are usually displayed in a default order, by date or by name, but in most systems the list may be re-sorted according to users' preferences.

CATALOGING OPERATIONS

One cannot discuss cataloging in today's library environment without acknowledging that catalogers in local libraries make heavy use of bibliographic records prepared elsewhere, a practice called *copy cataloging*. Sources of such records are the LC and, for those that are members of shared-cataloging networks or consortia, records prepared by other members. A *network* or *consortium* is an association of libraries with the main purpose of sharing resources including cataloging information. It maintains a cataloging database of contributed records that also includes records from the LC MARC database. Member libraries have direct online access to the database, and may use its records for verification of items to be purchased, for identification of items for interlibrary loan purposes, or for producing records for the local catalog. The largest network in this country is OCLC, which has absorbed two other major networks, WLN and RLIN. OCLC's WorldCat, containing over 290 million bibliographic records, is now the largest cataloging database in the world.

Despite the large role that copy cataloging plays in local libraries today, all professional catalogers have to be able to do full cataloging for an item—a process that is called *original cataloging*. During a cataloging department workday, many items may show up for which no cataloging copy exists. For these, after a reasonable wait, one must rely on original cataloging.

Cataloging Files

The catalog consists of two major files: the bibliographic file and the authority file. The bibliographic file contains cataloging records. This is the file that a library user interacts with. The authority file, on the other hand, is a cataloging tool that records the standardized forms of names and topical terms that have been authorized as headings, that is, as access points, along with their associated cross-references. The need for an authority file and the work that goes into building one are described briefly below under the section "Authority work," as well as in greater detail in chapters 7 and 8. In manual systems, authority files were often maintained separately, one authority file for names and another for subject headings. In online catalog systems, they may either be one or two separate files; either way, they may or may not be integrally linked to the bibliographic file.

Cataloging Procedures

Several distinct cataloging procedures are part of preparing an individual bibliographic record for a library: (1) resource description, the preparation of bibliographic descriptions and the determination of bibliographic access points; (2) subject analysis (often referred to as subject cataloging), the operation of assigning subject headings; (3) classification, the assignment of classification numbers and book numbers; and (4) authority work, the determination of the standardized forms of subject terms and names. For those doing online cataloging, an additional procedure is MARC tagging. Each of these activities is the focus of one or more later chapters in this book. Only a brief account of these activities is given in this introductory chapter.

The record resulting from the first three steps is called a *bibliographic record*. The result of authority work is referred to as the *authority record*.

Resource Description

Resource description, also called descriptive cataloging, consists of:

(1) drafting information that includes the resource title, the agent responsible for the content (most often the author), the edition, the place and date of publication, the publisher, a physical description, series membership if any, and any appropriate notes (such as "Includes index" or "Sequel to . . .");
(2) deciding what elements in the description should be the basis for access points, and including relationships linking to other entities; and
(3) determining the proper form for the names and titles selected as authorized access points. (This last component is called authority work, which is described below.)

Descriptive cataloging in the United States, and indeed in much of the world, is carried out according to accepted standards. The standards that have prevailed over the years are described in part 2 of this book. AACR was the standard used in most English-speaking countries for descriptive cataloging until 2013, when it was replaced by its successor, RDA.

Subject Analysis

For each bibliographic record, appropriate subject headings representing the "aboutness" of a resource's intellectual content are chosen from an authorized list. Most general libraries in this country use one of two authorized lists, the LCSH for large libraries, and the *Sears List of Subject Headings* for smaller ones. For specialized libraries, special subject-headings lists, such as MeSH, may be used. In some libraries, subject headings under which there are local listings are registered in a local subject authority file.

Traditionally, subject headings have been assigned from authorized lists only. In online catalogs, subject terms not derived from an authorized list are sometimes assigned to augment, or to take the place of, the authorized terms.

Classification

Classification requires fitting the primary topic of a work to the provisions of whatever classification scheme is being used. Most American libraries use either the LCC or the DDC. Specialized libraries often use subject-oriented systems such as the NLM classification. After the appropriate class number has been chosen, an item number is added to form a call number. This too is done according to standard patterns, somewhat different for each system. The act of classifying also calls for adjusting the numbers indicated in the standards to fit the new item into the shelf array of existing items in each collection.

Authority Work

Authority work entails a procedure that spans both descriptive and subject cataloging. In order to fulfill the objective of the catalog as a tool for retrieving all works by a given author or all works on a given subject, the access points to bibliographic records are normalized and standardized. In other words, all works by a given author or on a given subject are listed under a uniform access point for that author or subject. To this end, each author's name or each subject's name is "established" when used for the first time, and the decision is recorded in a record called the *authority record*. Furthermore, to allow access through variant names and different forms of a name or a subject, cross-references to a given heading are provided in the catalog and also recorded in the authority record for that heading. The same is true for references between related headings. A fact worth noting is that while each bibliographic record represents a physical item or group of items in a collection, each authority record represents a person, corporate body, common title, or subject that may appear in any number of bibliographic records. The activities of authority control include both integrating standardized authority records into the local system and preparing authority records for those names and subjects not available from standard authority files.

When a new authority record must be made, considerable checking in references and other sources, as well as considerable consultation, is often required to arrive at the decisions that are ultimately registered in it. Authority work, therefore, has long been regarded as the most time-consuming and costly aspect of cataloging.

MARC Tagging

In an automated cataloging environment, the cataloger also must supply the codes and other information needed for computer processing. In MARC records, for instance, there is considerably more information relating to the item than is called for in a standard bibliographic description. This added information includes various computer tags as well as codes for language, type of publication, and other attributes of the item being cataloged. Records are set up according to the various MARC formats, the most common being the MARC 21 formats, a set of related standards for handling different kinds of bibliographic and authority data records developed and maintained by the LC in cooperation with other libraries and organizations. For a more detailed discussion of the MARC 21 formats, see chapter 3 of this book.

A MARC record is made up of three parts. The first two, called *leader* and *directory*, contain information that aids in processing the record and are not the direct responsibility of catalogers; in modern installations, this information is "system supplied." It is the data in the main part of a MARC record that catalogers must learn how to create. This part of a MARC record is organized into fields and, for most fields, into component subfields. Each field is identified by a three-digit numerical code called a *field tag*, and each subfield is identified by an alphabetic or numeric *subfield code*. Certain fields contain two *indicators* bearing values (in the form of numeric characters or blanks) that interpret or supplement the data in the field, for example, whether a personal name includes a surname or what kind of title is presented.

In more recent years, there have been numerous discussions about moving from MARC to using an XML-based encoding system for cataloging records. This may be necessary for the exchange of library cataloging information with nonlibrary environments such as Web search engines, the publishing industry, and other information agencies that create non-MARC metadata.

In 2012, the LC announced that it had contracted with Zepeira to help launch the Bibliographic Framework Initiative (BIBFRAME). The initiative's goal is to create a Linked Data model to translate MARC21 data into linked data.

Examples of Cataloging Records

Introduction

The following examples of cataloging and authority records present an overview of the cataloging procedures and their overall structures. The remaining chapters in the book provide details regarding individual components of the records.

The Bibliographic Record

The record shown below (Figure 1.1), pertaining to a one-volume monographic work by William A. Evans, illustrates the creation of bibliographic records.

A Coded Bibliographic Record

To make the cataloging data machine-readable, each of the elements shown above must be coded. The example below (Figure 1.2) shows the bibliographic record for the Evans book from the OCLC WorldCat, with codes for the variable fields as defined in the MARC bibliographic format. (Examples in this chapter carry the codes for the fields only; for a detailed discussion of other details relating to the MARC 21 formats, see chapter 3.)

To understand this MARC record, it is necessary to look at it in conjunction with Table 1.1 and its accompanying explanation. Table 1.1 shows the major MARC field tags for a bibliographic record. Individual fields are illustrated by a coded record example, which is also explained in turn.

(1) Classification data:	
Class number and item number:	Z678 .E9 2013 *(based on Library of Congress Classification)*
Class number:	**025.1** *(based on Dewey Decimal Classification)*
(2) Descriptive data:	
(A) Bibliographic description:	
Title:	Management basics for information professionals
Statement of responsibility:	G. Edward Evans, Camila A. Alire
Edition statement:	Third edition
Publication:	Chicago: Neal-Schuman, an imprint of the American Library Association, 2013
Physical description:	xvii, 577 pages ; 23 cm
Note:	Contents: Operating environment—Legal issues and library management—The planning process—Power, accountability, and responsibility—Delegating—Decision making—Communicating—Changing and innovating—Assessment, quality control, and operations—Marketing—Motivating—Leading—Building teams—Addressing diversity—Staffing—Managing money—Managing technology—Managing and planning physical facilities—Ethics—Planning your career.
Note:	Includes bibliographical references and index.
Standard numbers:	9781555709099 (acid-free paper) 1555709095 (acid-free paper)
(B) Bibliographic access points:	
Creator(s):	Evans, G. Edward, $d 1937- Alire, Camila A.
Title:	Management basics for information professionals
(3) Subject cataloging data:	
Subject heading:	Library administration—United States *(based on Library of Congress Subject Headings)*
Subject heading:	Information services—United States—Management *(based on Library of Congress Subject Headings)*

Figure 1.1 Labeled bibliographic record.

Explanation of Table 1.1

In a MARC record, all of the field tags are three digits long. The various kinds of fields are often referred to as the 00X fields, the 0XX fields, the 1XX, 2XX fields, etc.

The information ordinarily thought of as cataloging data is recorded in that part of the MARC structure called the variable fields. The variable fields, in turn, comprise two additional types: (1) control fields and (2) data fields.

The control fields (00X) contain either a single-data element or a series of fixed-length data elements. Such data play an important role in computer processing of MARC records.

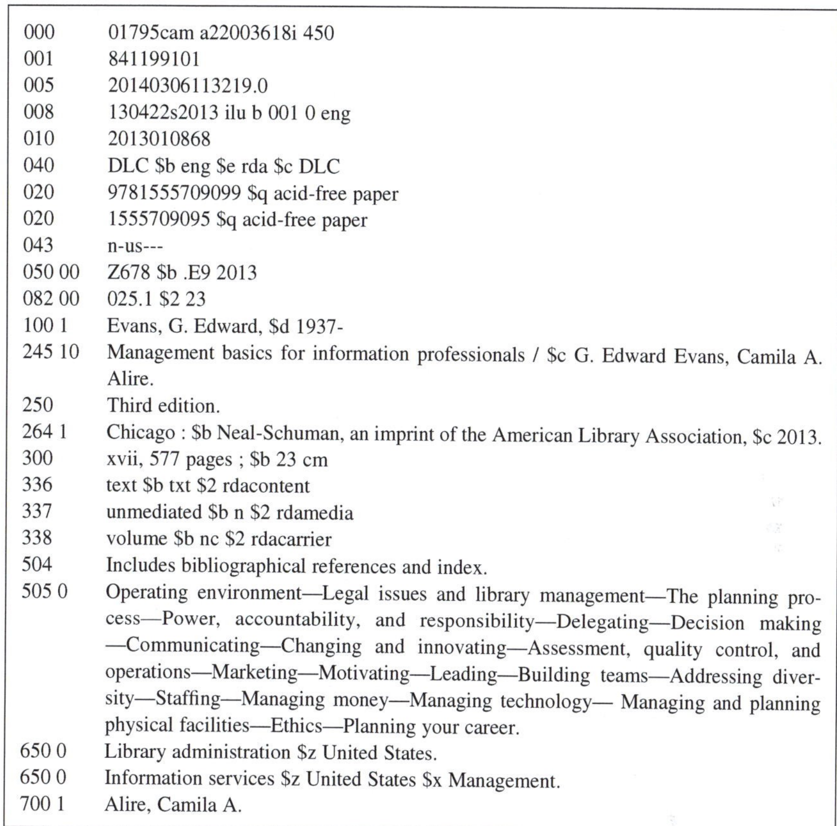

000	01795cam a22003618i 450
001	841199101
005	20140306113219.0
008	130422s2013 ilu b 001 0 eng
010	2013010868
040	DLC $b eng $e rda $c DLC
020	9781555709099 $q acid-free paper
020	1555709095 $q acid-free paper
043	n-us---
050 00	Z678 $b .E9 2013
082 00	025.1 $2 23
100 1	Evans, G. Edward, $d 1937-
245 10	Management basics for information professionals / $c G. Edward Evans, Camila A. Alire.
250	Third edition.
264 1	Chicago : $b Neal-Schuman, an imprint of the American Library Association, $c 2013.
300	xvii, 577 pages ; $b 23 cm
336	text $b txt $2 rdacontent
337	unmediated $b n $2 rdamedia
338	volume $b nc $2 rdacarrier
504	Includes bibliographical references and index.
505 0	Operating environment—Legal issues and library management—The planning process—Power, accountability, and responsibility—Delegating—Decision making —Communicating—Changing and innovating—Assessment, quality control, and operations—Marketing—Motivating—Leading—Building teams—Addressing diversity—Staffing—Managing money—Managing technology— Managing and planning physical facilities—Ethics—Planning your career.
650 0	Library administration $z United States.
650 0	Information services $z United States $x Management.
700 1	Alire, Camila A.

Figure 1.2 MARC-coded bibliographic record.

The data fields (01X-8XX) contain cataloging data. (These are shown line by line in Figure 1.1.) Fields 010–082 contain numbers and codes, such as standard book number, LC control number, and call numbers. Fields 100-8XX contain bibliographic and subject cataloging data: elements of a bibliographic description, main and added access points, and subject headings.

We can see that some of the field tags fall into groups. The 1XX fields are for different categories of main entry. The 490 and 8XX fields pertain to series. The 5XX fields are for notes. The 6XX and 7XX fields are for subject added entries and name and title added entries, respectively. Field 856, a field added since the advent of electronic resources, holds information relating to electronic location and access.

Most fields are divided into subfields, identified by alphabetic or numeric codes preceded by a delimiter (represented by the symbol ǂ [a dagger], | [a vertical bar], or $ [a dollar sign, as used in this text], e.g., $b, $2, etc.).

Table 1.1 MARC Tags for Frequently Occurring Data Fields in a Bibliographic Record

Tag	*Name*
008	Coded control information
010	Library of Congress Control Number
020	International Standard Book Number
040	Cataloging Source
043	Geographic Area Code
050	Library of Congress Call Number
082	Dewey Decimal Classification Number
090	Local call numbers
100	Main Entry—Personal Name
110	Main Entry—Corporate Name
111	Main Entry—Meeting Name
130	Main Entry—Uniform Title
245	Title Statement
246	Variant title
250	Edition Statement
264	Publication, Production, Distribution, Manufacture, & Copyright
300	Physical Description
336	Content Type
337	Media Type
338	Carrier Type
490	Series Statement
500	General Note
504	Bibliography, etc. Note
505	Formatted Contents Note
600	Subject Added Entry—Personal Name
610	Subject Added Entry—Corporate Name
611	Subject Added Entry—Meeting Name
650	Subject Added Entry—Topical Term
651	Subject Added Entry—Geographical Name
653	Index Term—Uncontrolled
655	Index Term—Genre/Form
700	Added Entry—Personal Name
710	Added Entry—Corporate Name
730	Added Entry—Uniform Title
740	Added Entry—Uncontrolled Related/Analytical Title
800	Series Added Entry—Personal Name
810	Series Added Entry—Corporate Name
811	Series Added Entry—Meeting Name
830	Series Added Entry—Uniform Title
856	Electronic Location and Access

Generally, the first element in a field is subfield "$a," followed by other subfields. For instance, in the publication details field (264), "$a" is for place of publication, "$b" is for publisher, and "$c" is for date; in the DDC number field (082), "$a" is for classification number, "$b" is for item number, and "$2" is for edition number (i.e., the number of the edition of DDC from which the classification number is taken). Some subfield codes have mnemonic value, for instance, "$d" in fields 100, 700, and 800, for personal name entry, is for date of birth or birth/death dates, and "$*l*" in fields 1XX, 4XX, and 7XX is for language of work. Table 1.1 does not show subfield codes, but some are shown in Figure 1.1, the coded Evans record. (In some systems, the "$a" subfield code is often implicit and does not show in the record display.)

Explanation of Figure 1.2

Figure 1.2 shows the "full" MARC record for the Evans book. "Full" here refers to the fact that virtually all elements and codes contained in the record are displayed. It is primarily library personnel who need to see coded records; in most cases, users of online catalogs are offered abbreviated or full but noncoded displays. Although some of what appears in the Evans MARC record has no obvious relation to what the user normally finds in the library catalog, most of what is shown in the MARC record is simply a different manner of displaying standard catalog information, with each element showing the codes that enable the data to be processed by the computer. The following explanation goes through the Evans MARC record element by element.

The first four lines (000–008) contain control data, such as the length, status, and type of the record, date of publication, illustrations, language, and so on. Although most of the control data are of no direct interest to end users and often not displayed in the public catalog, this coded information is essential to efficient record processing, especially in systems that allow searchers to specify such things as "English language material only," or "only if there are illustrations," or "only if published since 2010."

The remaining lines of the record (data fields 010–700) present what many would call the heart of the MARC record. The three-digit number at the beginning of each line is its MARC field tag. Field by field, the Evans MARC record shows the following:

010	LC control number
040	Cataloging sources, for example, DLC for the LC
020	ISBN, 13-digit
020	ISBN, 10-digit
043	Geographic area associated with the resource, in this case based on the subjects
050	LC call number (class number is first subfield; subfield b is for the item number)
082	Dewey class number
100	Personal name primary access point for Evans (subfield d is for date of birth)

- 245 Title and statement of responsibility (the latter is subfield c; if there were a subtitle, it would be subfield b)
- 250 Edition statement
- 264 Place of publication, publisher (subfield b), and date of publication (subfield c)
- 300 Number of volumes or pages (for a one-volume work) and size (subfield c)
- 336 Type of content, text in this case
- 337 Medium required to access the content, none required (unmediated) in this case
- 338 Type of carrier where the content is stored, volume in this case
- 504 Bibliography and index note
- 505 Contents note for the titles of each of the chapters
- 650 First topical subject heading
- 650 Second topical subject heading
- 700 Personal name added access point for Alire, the second author

The numerals 0 and 1 that appear between some field tags and the first subfield are *indicators*, the meanings of which are defined uniquely for each field. They are not shown in the analysis above; for details, consult chapter 3 of this book and *MARC 21 Concise Formats*.[24]

Once coded, the information contained in the MARC record can be manipulated by the computer to produce various cataloging products such as online catalog records, acquisitions lists, and suchlike. While the layout of a catalog card is standardized, online display of records varies from system to system. Within a particular system, records may also be displayed in long or short formats.

Further examples of bibliographic records are shown in appendix A.

The Authority Record

An authority record contains essentially the following elements: the preferred form for the name of a person, a corporate body, a place, or a preferred title of a resource (i.e., the standardized title for a work that has appeared under different titles; for a fuller discussion see chapter 7 of this book), or a subject authorized for use as access points in bibliographic records; cross-references from other names, titles, or terms not used for the preferred access points, and to and from related headings; information associated with the person, for example, affiliation, occupation, associated language, and so on; and, the sources used in establishing the heading.

For example, the name authority record for G. Edward Evans includes the following data:

Authorized access point: **Evans, G. Edward, 1937-**
Variant access point: Evans, Gayle Edward, 1937-

Sources used:

Introduction to technical services for library technicians,1971: (G. Edward Evans)

The influence of book selection agents upon book collection . . . 1969: t.p. (Gayle Edward Evans, B.A., Univ. of Minnesota, 1959; M.A. (Anthro.), Univ. of Minnesota, 1961; M.A. (Lib.Sc.), Univ. of Minnesota, 1963) vita (b. Jan. 5, 1937 in Huntington, Pa.)

Management basics for information professionals, 2013: ECIP t.p. (G. Edward Evans) data view (b. 1937; G. Edward Evans is an administrator, researcher, teacher, and writer; he holds several graduate degrees in anthropology and library and information science; as a researcher he has published in both fields, and held a Fulbright (librarianship) and National Science Foundation (anthropology) Fellowship; his teaching experience has also been in both fields in the U.S. and the Nordic countries; most of his administrative experience has been in private academic libraries--Harvard and Loyola Marymount Universities; retired from full-time work as Associate Academic Vice president for Libraries and Information Resources; author of numerous books, he consults for and volunteers at the Museum of Northern Arizona library and archives and Flagstaff City, Coconino Country Library System)

A Coded Authority Record

In the MARC 21 formats, the codes used vary according to the type of headings and on whether the heading appears in the authority record or is used as a main or added entry or a subject access point in the bibliographic record. Table 1.2 lists the tags for frequently occurring variable data fields in an authority record in the MARC 21 format (for details regarding the structure of MARC 21 formats, see chapter 3).

Figure 1.3 shows the name authority record, coded with the field tags based on the MARC 21 format, for the heading for G. Edward Evans.

Table 1.2 MARC Tags for Frequently Occurring Data Fields in an Authority Record

Tag	*Name*
008	Coded control information
010	Library of Congress Control Number
040	Cataloging Source
046	Special Coded Dates
050	Library of Congress Call Number
100	Heading—Personal Name
110	Heading—Corporate Name
111	Heading—Meeting Name
130	Heading—Uniform Title
150	Heading—Topical Term
151	Heading—Geographic Name
155	Heading—Genre/Form Term
336	Content Type
368	Other Attributes of Person or Corporate Body
370	Associated Place
372	Field of Activity
374	Occupation
375	Gender
377	Associated Language
380	Form of Work
400	See From Tracing—Personal Name
410	See From Tracing—Corporate Name
411	See From Tracing—Meeting Name
430	See From Tracing—Uniform Title
450	See From Tracing—Topical Term
451	See From Tracing—Geographic Name
455	See From Tracing—Genre/Term
500	See Also From Tracing—Personal Name
510	See Also From Tracing—Corporate Name
511	See Also From Tracing—Meeting Name
530	See Also From Tracing—Uniform Title
550	See Also From Tracing—Topical Term
551	See Also From Tracing—Geographic Name
555	See Also From Tracing—Genre/Term
663	Complex See Also Reference—Name
664	Complex See Reference—Name
670	Source Data Found
675	Source Data Not Found
678	Biographical or Historical Data
680	Public General Note

000	01679cz a2200193n 450
001	2814732
005	20130422200912.0
008	781206n| azannaabn |a aaa
010	n 78091996 $z no2010002167
040	DLC $b eng $e rda $c DLC $d DLC
046	$f 19370105
100 1	Evans, G. Edward, $d 1937-
400 1	Evans, Gayle Edward, $d 1937-
670	Introduction to technical services for library technicians,1971: $b (G. Edward Evans)
670	The influence of book selection agents upon book collection . . . 1969: $b t.p. (Gayle Edward Evans, B.A., Univ. of Minnesota, 1959; M.A. (Anthro.), Univ. of Minnesota, 1961; M.A. (Lib.Sc.), Univ. of Minnesota, 1963) vita (b. Jan. 5, 1937 in Huntington, Pa.)
670	Management basics for information professionals, 2013: $b ECIP t.p. (G. Edward Evans) data view (b. 1937; G. Edward Evans is an administrator, researcher, teacher, and writer; he holds several graduate degrees in anthropology and library and information science; as a researcher he has published in both fields, and held a Fulbright (librarianship) and National Science Foundation (anthropology) Fellowship; his teaching experience has also been in both fields in the U.S. and the Nordic countries; most of his administrative experience has been in private academic libraries—Harvard and Loyola Marymount Universities; retired from full-time work as Associate Academic Vice president for Libraries and Information Resources; author of numerous books, he consults for and volunteers at the Museum of Northern Arizona library and archives and Flagstaff City, Coconino Country Library System)

Figure 1.3 Coded authority record.

In Figure 1.3, the first four lines (numbered 000–008) show control data. The remaining lines, containing data fields, are analyzed below:

010	LC name authority control number
040	Record originated with LC and modified by other libraries
046	Coded Date for Evans' birth date
100	Authorized personal name access point for G. Edward Evans, with his birth date
400	Form of name not used as an authorized access point for Evans, from which a *see* reference would be made to the preferred access point
670	One of the sources in which the chosen form of Evans' name was found
670	A second source used in establishing Evans' name
670	A third source used in establishing Evans' name

The authority record shows the standardized heading to be used as an access point in the catalog and also provides data for generating cross-references that link variant names and forms to the authorized heading. The cross-references may be displayed in different ways in the online catalog.

Further examples of name authority records are shown in appendix B.

As was the case with the coded Evans bibliographic record shown in Figure 1.1 and the table of MARC 21 bibliographic tags (see Table 1.1 above), the coded Evans authority record can be best understood in conjunction with Table 1.2, which shows the major fields and field tags in the MARC 21 Format for Authority Data. Some of the fields in the authority format parallel those in the format for bibliographic data: the control fields and 1XX fields (with the authorized headings reflecting different types of names: 100 personal, 110 corporate, 111 meeting, etc.). Others are quite different: the 4XX fields show *see* references; the 5XX fields are for *see also* references; and the 6XX fields are variously defined, including complex references, history notes, source for name choice, and notes identifying other sources used in establishing the heading.

In **authority** records (NR = not repeatable; R = repeatable):

100 Heading—Personal name (NR)
110 Heading—Corporate name (NR)
111 Heading—Meeting name (NR)
130 Heading—Uniform title (NR)
151 Heading—Geographic name (NR)

400 *See from* tracing—Personal name (R)
410 *See from* tracing—Corporate name (R)
411 *See from* tracing—Meeting name (R)
430 *See from* tracing—Uniform title (R)
451 *See from* tracing—Geographic name (R)

500 *See also from* tracing—Personal name (R)
510 *See also from* tracing—Corporate name (R)
511 *See also from* tracing—Meeting name (R)
530 *See also from* tracing—Uniform title (R)
551 *See also from* tracing—Geographic name (R)

In **bibliographic** records:

100 Main entry—Personal name (NR)
110 Main entry—Corporate name (NR)
111 Main entry—Meeting name (NR)
130 Main entry—Uniform title (NR)

600 Subject added entry—Personal name (R)
610 Subject added entry—Corporate name (R)
611 Subject added entry—Meeting name (R)

630 Subject added entry—Uniform title (R)
651 Subject added entry—Geographic name (NR)

700 Added entry—Personal name (R)
710 Added entry—Corporate name (R)
711 Added entry—Meeting name (R)
730 Added entry—Uniform title (R)

800 Series added entry—Personal name (R)
810 Series added entry—Corporate name (R)
811 Series added entry—Meeting name (R)
830 Series added entry—Uniform title (R)

Record Display

The same MARC record can be displayed in various formats and in different degrees of fullness in the catalog for users, depending on the type of library and user needs. The following examples show a typical full-record display and a typical brief-record display of the Evans book from a library catalog. In the public display, the MARC tags are replaced by labels that are easily recognized.

Full-record display:

Type of Material:	**Book (Print)**
Personal Name:	**Evans, G. Edward, $d 1937-** **Alire, Camila A.**
Main Title:	**Management basics for information professionals**
Edition Information:	**Third edition**
Published/Created:	**Chicago : Neal-Schuman, an imprint of the American Library Association, 2013.**
Description:	**xvii, 577 pages ; 23 cm**
ISBN:	**9781555709099 (acid-free paper)** **1555709095 (acid-free paper)**
Contents:	**Operating environment—Legal issues and library management—The planning process—Power, accountability, and responsibility—Delegating—Decision making—Communicating—Changing and innovating—Assessment, quality control, and operations—Marketing—Motivating—Leading—Building teams—Addressing**

	diversity—Staffing—Managing money—Managing technology—Managing and planning physical facilities—Ethics—Planning your career
Notes:	**Includes bibliographical references and index.**
Subjects:	**Library administration—United States** **Informationservices—UnitedStates—Management**
LC Classification:	**Z678 .E9 2013**
Dewey Class No.:	**025.1**

Brief-record display:

Type of Material:	**Book (Print)**
Personal Name:	**Evans, G. Edward, $d 1937-**
Main Title:	**Managementbasicsforinformationprofessionals**
Edition Information:	**Third edition.**
Published/Created:	**Chicago : Neal-Schuman, an imprint of the American Library** **Association, 2013.**
Description:	**xvii, 577 pages ; 23 cm**
ISBN:	**9781555709099 (acid-free paper)** **1555709095 (acid-free paper)**

CONCLUSION

This chapter has attempted to set the framework for a study of bibliographic control in the library environment, particularly in a general library. It began with an account of the difference between today's information world and that of two generations ago, briefly describing advances in the Internet along with parallel advances in the library environment and in the online database industry. It proceeded with discussions of the devices the library world has used to provide the best information services within its resources, taking into account how much impact technology has had on all phases of library and library-like operations. It attempted to show the general picture, defining bibliographic control and noting the various ways of achieving it in all environments where it is used—showing, at the same time, how its demands vary according to the nature of the material to be brought under control.

The discussion then turned to library catalogs. It proceeded to the major operations entailed in producing and maintaining a library catalog and its subsidiary files: description, access, and organization. All of these topics are treated in extensive detail in subsequent chapters. Their order reflects the order of activities in producing a bibliographic record: drafting a description, deciding on access points and forms of names, assigning subject headings, and classifying. Emphasis is on standard North American cataloging practice, but along the way alternative means and tools are also discussed. Examples showing a bibliographic record and an authority record are included and briefly explained in order to present a comprehensive picture of the cataloging process. The MARC structure is also introduced; in-depth considerations of the MARC formats and other encoding schemes are discussed in chapter 3.

NOTES

1. Major sources used in drafting the following timelines include the following:

Bourne, C. P., and Hahn, T. B. (2003). *A History of Online Information Services, 1963–1976*. Cambridge, MA: MIT Press.

Hahn, T. B. (1998). Pioneers of the online age. In T. B. Hahn and M. Buckland (Eds.), *Historical Studies in Information Science* (pp. 116–31). Medford, NJ: Information Today.

Kanellos, M. (September 11, 2006). The hard drive at 50: Half a century of hard drives, *CNET News.com*. Retrieved from http://www.zdnet.com/news/a-half-century-of-hard-drives/149491.

Meadow, C. (1988). Online database industry timeline. *Database, 11*(5), 23–31. Retrieved from http://www.infotoday.com/.

Tedd, L. (1994). OPACs through the ages. *Library Review, 43*(4), 27–37. Retrieved from http://www.emeraldinsight.com/loi/lr.

Richmond, P. (1981). *Introduction to PRECIS for North American Usage*. Littleton, CO: Libraries Unlimited.

Joint Steering Committee for Development of RDA. (n.d.). *RDA: Resource Description and Access: Background*. Retrieved from http://www.rda-jsc.org/rda.html#background.

Hardy, Q. (March/April 2006). Can we know everything? *California [UC Berkeley Alumni Magazine], 117*(2). Retrieved from http://alumni.berkeley.edu/california-magazine/march-april-2006-can-we-know-everything/can-we-know-everything.

2. Bush, V. (1945). As we may think. *The Atlantic Monthly, 176*(1), 101–08. Retrieved from www.theatlantic.com/unbound/flashbks/computer/bushf.htm.

3. Chu, H. (2003). *Information Representation and Retrieval in the Digital Age*. Medford, NJ: Information Today.

4. McCallum, J. C. (February 23, 2013). *Disk Drive Prices*. Retrieved from http://jcmit.com/diskprice.htm.

5. Hauben, M., and Hauben, R. (1998). Behind the Net: The untold history of the ARPANET and computer science. *First Monday, 8*(3). Retrieved from http://firstmonday.org/index.

6. Laughead, G., Jr. (2008). *WWW-VL: History: Internet & W3 World-Wide Web.* Retrieved from http://vlib.iue.it/history/internet/.

7. WebCrawler. (2006). *About WebCrawler.* Retrieved from www.webcrawler.com/info.wbcrwl/search/help/about.htm.

8. IFLA Study Group on the Functional Requirements for Bibliographic Records. (1998). *Functional Requirements for Bibliographic Records: Final Report* (UBCIM Publications, New Series Vol. 19). München, Germany: K. G. Saur. Retrieved from http://www.ifla.org/publications/functional-requirements-for-bibliographic-records.

9. Dublin Core Metadata Initiative. (2014). *History of the Dublin Core Metadata Initiative.* Retrieved from http://dublincore.org/about/history/.

10. O'Neill, E. T., and Chan, L. M. (2003). "FAST (faceted application of subject terminology): simplified vocabulary based on the Library of Congress subject headings. *IFLA Journal, 29*(4), 336–42.

11. IFLA Study Group on the Functional Requirements for Bibliographic Records, 1998.

12. Joint Steering Committee for Development of RDA, n.d.

13. Online Computer Library Center. (2014). *OCLC World Cat.* Retrieved from www.oclc.org/worldcat/open/.

14. Google. (2012). *Google Books.* Retrieved from http://books.google.com/.

15. Calhoun, K. (2006). *The Changing Nature of the Catalog and its Integration with Other Discovery Tools* (Prepared for the Library of Congress). Retrieved from www.loc.gov/catdir/calhoun-report-final.pdf.

16. Cutter, C. A. (1953). *Rules for a Dictionary Catalog* (4th ed. rewritten). London, England: The Library Association (Original work published 1876) (p. 12).

17. Lubetzky, S. (1985). Principles of descriptive cataloging. In M. Carpenter and E. Svenonius (Eds.), *Foundations of Cataloging: A Sourcebook* (pp. 104–12). Littleton, CO: Libraries Unlimited (Original work published 1946).

18. International Conference on Cataloguing Principles. (1961). *Statement of Principles Adopted by the International Conference on Cataloguing Principles.* Retrieved from http://www.nl.go.kr/icc/paper/20.pdf.

19. IFLA Study Group on the Functional Requirements for Bibliographic Records, 1998.

20. IFLA Cataloguing Section and IFLA Meetings of Experts on an International Cataloguing Code. (2009). *Statement of International Cataloguing Principles.* München, Germany: K. G. Saur. Retrieved from http://www.ifla.org/publications/statement-of-international-cataloguing-principles.

21. American Library Association, Canadian Library Association, Chartered Institute of Library and Information Professionals (Great Britain), & Joint Steering Committee for Development of RDA. (2010). *RDA: Resource Description & Access.* Chicago, IL: American Library Association.

22. International Federation of Library Associations. (1974). *ISBD (M): International Standard Bibliographic Description for Monographic Publications* (1st standard ed.). London, England: IFLA Committee on Cataloguing. (And subsequent editions.)

23. Joint Steering Committee for Revision of AACR (A committee of the American Library Association, the Australian Committee on Cataloguing, the British

Library, the Canadian Committee on Cataloguing, Chartered Institute of Library and Information Professionals, & the Library of Congress). (2002). *AngloAmerican Cataloguing Rules* (2nd ed.). Chicago, IL: American Library Association.

24. Network Development and MARC Standards Office, Library of Congress. (2008). *MARC 21 Concise Formats*. Retrieved from http://www.loc.gov/marc/concise/.

Chapter 2

Foundations, Principles, Conceptual Models, and Standards of Resource Description

BIBLIOGRAPHIC DESCRIPTION AND SURROGATE RECORDS

In the print environment, keyword searching of texts was not an option; to help identify and choose relevant information items, users relied on brief descriptions of books and other library materials for indications of their characteristics and content. Each brief description contained what were considered to be essential attributes of a given item and served as its surrogate in the library's catalog.

In the early days of library service, cataloging was largely an individual activity for each library. Different libraries developed their own policies and practices in formulating surrogate records and in organizing them to form the catalogs they deemed most suitable for their purposes. Thus, cataloging records were presented in forms and styles that varied from library to library. Chapter 1 described how American librarians in the early part of the twentieth century came to value standardization of cataloging practice, and how various schemes and sets of rules merged to facilitate standardization. This chapter discusses the principles underlying the standards that emerged.

CONTRIBUTIONS TO CATALOGING THEORY

Over the past hundred years or so, many individuals and organizations have contributed to the development of standards and codes for bibliographic description, particularly by articulating basic tenets or principles and by setting standards. Early efforts at codifying cataloging practice were often the results of individual labors. As time went on, such efforts became more communal. Some of the most influential cataloging concepts and principles, along with their proponents and their impacts, are discussed briefly below.

Panizzi's Principles

Sir Anthony Panizzi (1797–1879), who worked as a cataloger and later became the Principal Librarian of the British Museum Department of Printed Books, was responsible for formulating ninety-one rules to be used in compiling the catalog of the British Museum. These rules are hailed as "the ancestor of all modern library cataloging codes."[1] Some of the underlying principles of the rules were articulated in a letter, "Mr. Panizzi to the Right Hon. the Earl of Ellesmere. —British Museum, January 29, 1848."[2] Although some of the ideas and principles embodied in the rules and in his letter do not seem relevant to the current environment, many others, such as the objectives of a library catalog, the requirement for normalization of names (personal and corporate), the status of works modified or adapted from differing originals, and the requirement for uniformity in application of cataloging rules still resonate in today's cataloging codes and practices.[3]

Jewett's Principles

Charles C. Jewett (1816–1868) was appointed Librarian and Assistant Secretary at the Smithsonian Institution soon after its establishment in Washington, DC, in 1846. He embarked on an effort to establish a great national library, one that would incorporate within it a union catalog of the holdings of all public libraries in the United States. He envisioned the union catalog as the first step in a course that would lead eventually to a "universal catalog."[4] To realize this vision, Jewett proposed two courses of action. The first was the use of entries embossed on separate stereotype plates in order to facilitate the production of such a catalog and, in addition, to drastically reduce the cost of catalog production and maintenance—particularly in preparing new editions of the book catalog that was the predominant catalog form in his time. Jewett's second proposal was cooperative cataloging, a development he saw as necessary to building a universal catalog. Jewett's union catalog and cooperative cataloging ideas reverberated in later developments in library practice.

Cutter's Principles

Charles Ammi Cutter (1837–1903), a librarian at Harvard College who was later appointed as the librarian of the Boston Athenaeum, was responsible for compiling *Rules for a Dictionary Catalog*, in which he claimed to "set forth rules in a systematic way or to investigate what might be called the first principles of cataloging."[5] These rules first appeared in 1976 as an adjunct to a government publication on the state of American libraries. Two statements from Cutter's *Rules* that have been widely quoted in the literature and later cataloging codes are worthy of particular note. The first, "The convenience of the public is always to be set before the ease of the cataloger,"[6] placed the focus of catalog design squarely on the user. The second is the statement cited in chapter 1 of this book concerning the objectives of the catalog and the means for attaining them.[7]

Lubetzky's Principles

During the mid-twentieth century, Seymour Lubetzky (1898–2003), a librarian at the Library of Congress and later a faculty member of the School of Library Services at the University of California, Los Angeles, played an important role throughout his career in shaping the future direction of cataloging codes. He was a prolific writer and produced many publications about cataloging. Particularly influential are the following:

Studies of Descriptive Cataloging (1946)[8]
Cataloging Rules and Principles (1953)[9]
Code of Cataloging Rules (1960)[10]
Principles of Cataloging (1969)[11]

Paris Principles

In 1961, one of the most important events in the evolution of cataloging codes took place. The International Conference on Cataloguing Principles was held in Paris, from October 9 to October 18, 1961, under the auspices of the IFLA. There were delegations from fifty-three countries and twelve international organizations. The discussion of cataloging principles was based on a draft statement circulated before the meeting. As a result of the conference, a statement of principles that has become known as the "Paris Statement" or the "Paris Principles" was issued. It drew heavily upon Seymour Lubetzky's 1960 draft cataloging code, although its scope was limited to choice of entry and forms of headings. The work opens with a statement of the functions of the catalog, which in essence is a restatement of Lubetzky's and Cutter's objectives. The principles that follow rest logically on these objectives and are stated in specific terms and in considerable detail.

The Paris Statement represented a great step forward toward international agreement. One frequently cited feature of this document is its endorsement of corporate entry and natural, rather than grammatical, arrangement of titles, which removes the major differences between the Anglo-American and the Germanic traditions of cataloging. (In German catalogs, titles were filed under their first substantive word.)

Since its appearance, the Paris Principles has served as a set of principles for the development of cataloging standards, and many such codes have been revised or developed according to its provisions, notably the AACR, the German Code (*Regeln für die alphabetische Katalogisierung* [RAK]), and the Swedish and Danish codes. The RAK represented a major revolution in Germanic cataloging in that the concept of corporate entry was introduced and use of the literal title (rather than the grammatical title) was accepted.

International Cataloguing Principles Statement

In early 2000s, IFLA held a series of meetings of international cataloging experts to develop a new set of cataloging principles that would guide the development of cataloging standards or content standards, which include guidelines and rules for the content of resource descriptions. The series of meetings, called IFLA Meetings of Experts on an International Cataloguing Code, took place between 2003 and 2007, and resulted in the statement of International Cataloguing Principles, published in 2009.[12]

As principles for the development of cataloging standards, the International Cataloguing Principles place highest emphasis on the convenience of the user and aim at being defensible and not arbitrary, which means that in cases where the principles contradict each other, one should find a defensible and practical solution. These international cataloging principles are the following:

1. Convenience of the user. Decisions taken in the making of descriptions and controlled forms of names for access should be made with the user in mind.
2. Common usage. Vocabulary used in descriptions and access should be in accord with that of the majority of users.
3. Representation. Descriptions and controlled forms of names should be based on the way an entity describes itself.
4. Accuracy. The entity described should be faithfully portrayed.
5. Sufficiency and necessity. Only those data elements in descriptions and controlled forms of names for access that are required to fulfill user tasks and are essential to uniquely identify an entity should be included.
6. Significance. Data elements should be bibliographically significant.
7. Economy. When alternative ways exist to achieve a goal, preference should be given to the way that best furthers overall economy (i.e., the least costly or the simplest approach).
8. Consistency and standardization. Descriptions and construction of access points should be standardized as far as possible. This enables greater consistency, which in turn increases the ability to share bibliographic and authority data.

9. Integration. The descriptions for all types of materials and controlled forms of names of all types of entities should be based on a common set of rules, insofar as it is relevant.

International Standard Bibliographic Description (ISBD)

After the Paris Conference, the next step toward greater international agreement was taken at the International Meeting of Cataloguing Experts, which was held in Copenhagen in 1969. At this meeting, an international working group was established for the purpose of developing a standard order and content for describing monographic material. The objectives of the new format for bibliographic description were defined as follows:

> First, that records produced in one country or by the users of one language can be easily understood in other countries and by the users of other languages; second, that the records produced in each country can be integrated into files or lists of various kinds containing also records from other countries; and third, that records in written or printed form can be converted into machinereadable form with the minimum of editing.[13]

To fulfill these requirements, the order of bibliographic elements in a record was standardized and a special punctuation pattern distinguishing these elements was prescribed.

A document entitled *ISBD (M): International Standard Bibliographic Description (for Single Volume and Multi-Volume Monographic Publications)* was issued in 1971. In the following years, this format was accepted and adopted by many national bibliographies. As often happens, the course of its application revealed many ambiguities and a need for more details in some areas. These deficiencies were discussed at the IFLA conference held in Grenoble, France, in 1973. After this conference, two documents were published: the first standard edition of ISBD(M) and a set of recommendations for ISBD(S) (for serial publications). The first standard edition of ISBD(S) was published in 1977.

After the development of ISBD(M) and ISBD(S), it was considered desirable to develop a general ISBD that could serve as the framework for specific ISBDs. *ISBD(G): International Standard Bibliographic Description (General)* was published in 1977. Since then, other ISBDs have also been developed. The family of ISBDs now includes the following:

ISBD (A): International Standard Bibliographic Description for Older Monographic Publications (Antiquarian).

ISBD (CF): International Standard Bibliographic Description for Computer Files.

ISBD (CM): International Standard Bibliographic Description for Cartographic Materials.

ISBD(CR): International Standard Bibliographic Description for Serials and Other Continuing Resources.

ISBD (ER): International Standard Bibliographic Description for Electronic Resources.

ISBD (G): General International Standard Bibliographic Description.

ISBD (M): International Standard Bibliographic Description for Monographic Publications.

ISBD (NBM): International Standard Bibliographic Description for Non-Book Materials.

ISBD (PM): International Standard Bibliographic Description for Printed Music.

ISBD (S): International Standard Bibliographic Description for Serials.

After the publication of the Final FRBR Report, it was decided to merge the format-specific ISBDs. The consolidated edition merges specialized ISBDs into a single document. The preliminary consolidated edition was published in 2007 and the completed consolidated edition was published in 2011. The ISBD (2007 consolidation) was incorporated into RDA (Appendix D) as one of the options for data presentation.

Universal Bibliographic Control (UBC)

The theme of the thirty-ninth IFLA meeting in 1973 was the ideal of UBC; this concept was adopted as a goal for ultimate international cooperation.

The ideal of UBC was first articulated at the International Meeting of Cataloguing Experts:

> Efforts should be directed towards creating a system for the international exchange of information by which the standard bibliographic description of each publication would be established and distributed by a national agency in the country of origin.[14]

The basic idea of UBC is having each document cataloged only once, as near to the source of publication as possible, and making basic bibliographic data on all publications, issued in all countries, universally and promptly available in a form that is internationally acceptable.[15]

The fact that such a dream was even conceivable was due to the many encouraging developments toward international cooperation and standardization that had occurred in the field of cataloging in the preceding decades. The Paris Conference and the International Meeting of Cataloguing Experts in Copenhagen were two milestones on the road toward achieving the goal of

UBC. The standards and agreements produced by these conferences played an important role in the revision of cataloging rules around the world.

Functional Requirements for Bibliographic Records (FRBR)

Another important occurrence was the development of FRBR by an IFLA study group in the mid-1990s. FRBR is a conceptual model for viewing the entities and relationships of bibliographic and authority records. Based on the four tasks performed by users when using catalogs or bibliographies—to find, to identify, to select, and to obtain a bibliographic entity—the study group formulated a model consisting of three groups of entities[16]:

- Group 1 entities consist of rigorous definitions and relationships among bibliographic entities called *work, expression, manifestation*, and *item.*
- Group 2 entities consist of *person* and *corporate body* that are related to Group 1 entities in terms of their roles with respect to *work, expression, manifestation*, and *item.*
- Group 3 entities concern the subjects of works, including concepts, objects, events, places, and any of the Group 1 or Group 2 entities.

Group 1 entities are defined as follows:

- *Work* is a distinct intellectual or artistic creation.
- *Expression* is the intellectual or artistic realization of a *work* in the form of alpha-numeric, musical, or choreographic notation, sound, image, object, movement, etc., or any combination of such forms.
- *Manifestation* is the physical embodiment of an *expression* of a *work* and
- *Item* is a single exemplar of a *manifestation.*

Group 2 entities relate to bibliographic access points (discussed in part 3 of this book), and Group 3 entities relate to subject access points (discussed in part 4 of this book).

Work on Group 1 entities has been completed and has resulted in the publication *Functional Requirements for Bibliographic Records, Final Report.*[17] Work on Group 2 and Group 3 entities has been completed and has resulted in the publications *Functional Requirements for Authority Data (FRAD): A Conceptual Model*[18] and *Functional Requirements for Subject Authority Data (FRSAD): A Conceptual Model,*[19] respectively. IFLA groups are continuing to work on the review and harmonization of the three conceptual models and, in addition, are collaborating to bridge conceptual models from different environments for more effective and interoperable information sharing.

Concepts brought forward in FRBR continue to provide an important approach to the development of cataloging codes and practice. A more detailed discussion of FRBR, FRAD, and FRSAD is included in later chapters of this book.

METADATA SCHEMAS

The rapid growth of the Internet and the proliferation of electronic resources have created a crushing need for better methods of describing and organizing these resources for efficient retrieval. Interest in such methods extends beyond the library community. Outside of the library community, cataloging standards are not well understood or widely applied. Even within the library profession, many feel that current cataloging rules are not only too complex for coping with electronic resources, but may also be inadequate in other ways. In addition, current cataloging standards are not always suitable for describing and representing various types of resources such as archival, geospatial, or visual resources, nor are they attuned to the needs of different user communities, such as those in the educational, publishing, government, and commercial sectors.

Over the course of ten years, beginning in the mid-1990s, numerous metadata schemas were developed by various communities and groups concerned with managing electronic resources. Chapter 4 of this book contains a brief discussion of some of the more widely used metadata schemas.

DEVELOPMENT OF STANDARDS

Since the middle of the nineteenth century, many cataloging codes, reflecting the principles discussed above, have been developed and published. Most of the earlier codes represented the efforts of individuals, but later ones result from corporate undertakings. The following is a brief discussion of the development of standards for library resource description.

British Museum Cataloguing Rules (BM; 1839)

> British Museum, Department of Printed Books. (1936). *Rules for Compiling the Catalogues of Printed Books, Maps and Music in the British Museum* (rev. ed.). London, England: British Museum.

The BM, also known as Panizzi's ninety-one rules, was drafted as a guide for the compilation of the British Museum catalogs. The rules, published in

1841 as part of the introductory matter for the British Museum's printed book catalog, with a revised edition published in 1936, reflect the functions of the catalog as an inventory list and finding list.

This set of rules is considered to be the first major cataloging code ever produced and is recognized as having had a substantial influence on later codes.

Jewett's Rules (1853)

Jewett, C. C. (1853). *Smithsonian Report on the Construction of Catalogues of Libraries, and their Publication by Means of Separate, Stereotyped Titles, with Rules and Examples* (2nd ed.). Washington, DC: Smithsonian Institution.

Charles C. Jewett was responsible for developing the code for the catalog of the Smithsonian Institution. The code contains thirty-three rules,[20] which were largely based on Panizzi's rules. Jewett advocated stringent and detailed rules that left little to the individual judgment of the cataloger.

A matter of particular interest is that Jewett's discussion of subject headings represents the earliest call for the codifying of subject-heading practice.

Cutter's Rules (1876)

Cutter, C. A. (1953). *Rules for a Dictionary Catalog* (4th ed. rewritten). London, England: Library Association.

The first edition of this work appeared in 1876 with the title *Rules for a Printed Dictionary Catalogue*, which formed Part II of the US Bureau of Education Publication, *Public Libraries in the United States*. It contains 369 rules covering descriptive cataloging, subject headings, and filing.

Cutter's purpose was to "investigate what might be called the first principles of cataloging." His code has had enormous influence on subsequent codes and cataloging practice in the United States. It became the basis for the dictionary catalog, which was to emerge as the predominant form of catalogs in general libraries in the United States.

AA (1908)

American Library Association. (1908). *Catalog Rules: Author and Title Entries* (American ed.). Chicago, IL: American Library Association.

AA (1908) represented the first joint effort between American and British librarians in developing a cataloging code. However, the two groups did not reach full agreement on all details and the code was published in two editions (English and American).

AA (1908) reflected the influence of previous codes—British Museum and Cutter—and, to a large extent, the then-current practice of the LC, which had begun distributing printed cards in 1902. It owed a great deal to Cutter's rules; however, it did not include Cutter's statements of objects and means, and also omitted any rules for subject headings. The major aim of the code was to meet the requirements of larger academic and research libraries. To a considerable extent, this focus has set the tone of subsequent codes, which have been drawn up primarily to respond to the needs of such libraries. In AA (1908), the particular needs of smaller libraries are only occasionally recognized through alternative rules.

Prussian Instructions (PI)

> *The Prussian Instructions: Rules for the Alphabetical Catalogs of the Prussian Libraries* (translated from the 2nd ed., authorized August 10, 1908, with an introduction and notes by A. D. Osborn). (1938). Ann Arbor, MI: University of Michigan Press.

Originally developed as a standardized system of cataloging for Prussian libraries, the PI was adopted by many libraries in Germanic and Scandinavian countries.

The rules reflected two major differences in cataloging between the Germanic and the Anglo-American traditions. PI preferred entry under title instead of corporate entry. The second major difference was that grammatical arrangement of title is preferred over natural or mechanical arrangement.[21]

Vatican Code

> Vatican Library (Biblioteca Apostolica Vaticana). (1948). *Rules for the Catalog of Printed Books* (translated from the 2nd Italian ed. by the Very Rev. T. J. Shanahan, V. A. Schaefer, and C. T. Vesselowsky). W. E. Wright (Ed.). Chicago, IL: American Library Association.

The Vatican rules were developed for the purpose of compiling a general catalog of the printed books in the Vatican Library after its reorganization in the 1920s. The persons responsible were either Americans or American-trained local librarians. Therefore, American influence is evident, to the extent that it has been called an "international code with a definite American bias."[22] Its significance for American librarians lies in the fact that, for many years, the Vatican code was, as Wyllis Wright states in the Foreword to the

English translation, "the most complete statement of American cataloging practice."[23]

Probably the most comprehensive and best-structured code at the time, the Vatican code contained rules for entry, description, subject headings, and filing, with ample examples throughout.

American Library Association (ALA; 1941 Draft)

American Library Association. (1941). *ALA Catalog Rules: Author and Title Entries* (preliminary American 2nd ed.). Chicago, IL: American Library Association.

During the early 1930s, there was a general feeling that the Anglo-American cataloging code needed revision. A Catalog Code Revision Committee under the ALA was established for this purpose. Although the plan was to cooperate with the Library Association of Great Britain and other national library associations, this intention was not fully realized because of the eruption of World War II.

The draft code was completed in 1941. The 88-page pamphlet AA (1908) had blossomed into a 408-page document. The reason for the elaboration, as stated in the Preface, was the need for standardization required by centralized and cooperative cataloging. The committee felt that elaborate and precise detail was the means to accomplish this end. The code consists of two parts, one dealing with entry and headings and the other with description. Again, the rules for subject headings were omitted.

The 1941 draft code was dealt a heavy blow in June 1941 by Andrew D. Osborn's article entitled "The Crisis in Cataloging."[24] Osborn criticized the code for attempting to provide a rule for every situation or question that might come up, an approach he referred to as "legalistic." The consequence, Osborn maintained, was unnecessary multiplication of rules.

Library of Congress (LC; 1949)

Library of Congress. (1949). *Rules for Descriptive Cataloging in the Library of Congress Adopted by the American Library Association*. Washington, DC: Library of Congress.

Because of the extensive use of LC-printed catalog cards by libraries in the United States, the LC decided to publish its descriptive cataloging rules, which were not fully compatible with the AA rules.

In 1946, the LC published its *Studies of Descriptive Cataloging: A Report to the Librarian of Congress by the Director of the Processing Department*, which advocated simplification of cataloging details. As noted earlier, it was

Lubetzky who was responsible for the studies. The LC responded favorably to the report and took its tenets into consideration as it proceeded to complete the work on the rules for description. A preliminary edition appeared in 1947, and the final edition in 1949 (LC 1949).

The rules cover bibliographic description only, excluding choice of entries (i.e., of access points) and forms of headings. Many types of materials are considered: monographs, serials, maps, relief models, globes and atlases, music, facsimiles, photocopies and microfilms, and incunabula.

American Library Association (ALA; 1949)

> American Library Association. (1949). *ALA Cataloging Rules for Author and Title Entries* (2nd ed.) C. Beetle (Ed.). Chicago, IL: American Library Association.

Because the LC was revising its rules for description at the time, the ALA decided, in revising the 1908 ALA code, to omit the descriptive portion of the rules from the 1941 draft and include only the provisions for entry and heading in the new ALA rules. This decision was made partly because individual libraries had been following LC practice (due to the availability of LC-printed cards) and partly because that portion of ALA (1941) had not been very well received. As a result, the rules in ALA (1949) covered entry and headings only, and had to be used in conjunction with LC (1949). Osborn's criticism of the 1941 draft code did not seem to have much effect on ALA (1949). The rules in this code, in the opinion of many, were as pedantic, elaborate, and often arbitrary as those in the preliminary edition of 1941. Together, ALA (1949) and LC (1949) served as the standards for descriptive cataloging for American libraries until the appearance of the AACR in 1967.

Anglo-American Cataloging Rules (AACR; 1967)

> American Library Association, Library of Congress, Library Association, & Canadian Library Association. (1967). *Anglo-American Cataloging Rules* (North American text). Chicago, IL: American Library Association.

The strongest criticism of ALA (1949) was voiced in Lubetzky's *Cataloging Rules and Principles*,[25] which included a thorough and penetrating analysis of ALA (1949). Lubetzky criticized ALA (1949) for being unnecessarily long and confusing because it provided duplicate and overlapping rules to meet identical conditions. Related rules were scattered, he maintained, and there was a lack of logical arrangement and organization.

Lubetzky's report was received favorably, and another ALA Catalog Code Revision Committee, with Wyllis Wright as the chair, was established for the purpose of drafting a new code. In 1956, Lubetzky was appointed the editor of the new code.

In 1960, Lubetzky's *Code of Cataloging Rules, Author and Title Entry: An Unfinished Draft*[26] appeared. It begins with a statement of objectives, followed by specific rules developed on the basis of these objectives. Although not completed, the draft code gives an indication of what can be accomplished by basing specific rules on basic principles. One major departure from previous codes is the determination of entry based on conditions of authorship rather than on types of work.

Lubetzky's work was exciting but also raised concerns among those involved in cataloging. It presaged a new era for cataloging, yet many were concerned about the costs that its drastic changes would incur. This concern was to become a major factor in ensuing code revision work.

Lubetzky resigned as editor of the new code in 1962 and was succeeded by C. Sumner Spalding. Code revision proceeded on the basis of the work already done under Lubetzky and the Paris Principles. Cooperation between the American and British Library associations was also initiated. The new code AACR appeared in 1967. Because the British and the American communities failed to reach complete agreement on some of the details, two texts of the code were published: British Text and North American Text.

It was decided that the new code should include rules for both entry and description. Since the Paris Principles dealt with the problems of entry and headings only, and since there were yet no international guidelines for the development of the rules for description, LC (1949) was used as the basis for description of monographs and serials, as well as for the rules for cataloging nonprint materials in the North American text.

AACR (1967) was received with mixed feelings. Its logical arrangement and its emphasis on the conditions of authorship rather than on types of work were considered to be great improvements over previous codes. However, some critics lamented the compromises made in the face of practical considerations as well as the code's inadequate handling of nonprint materials.

Anglo-American Cataloging Rules, 2nd Edition (AACR2; 1978)

American Library Association, British Library, Canadian Committee on Cataloguing, Library Association, & Library of Congress. (1978). *Anglo-American Cataloguing Rules* (2nd ed.). M. Gorman and P. W. Winkler (Eds.). Chicago, IL: American Library Association.

By 1973, it was felt that the appropriate time had come for an overhaul of the Anglo-American cataloging code. Certain significant developments since the publication of AACR in 1967 pointed to the desirability of a revision.[27] First, rapid progress toward the formulation of international standards for the description of monographs, serials, and other media indicated the need to redraft the AACR provisions for bibliographic description so that the code would facilitate the effort to promote international exchange of bibliographic data. Second, the rules for nonprint materials in AACR (1967) had been considered inadequate from the beginning, which resulted in the proliferation of various cataloging codes for such materials. Only a complete revision of the rules for nonprint media could provide the standardization needed in this area. Third, the points of divergence between the separate North American and British texts of AACR had been gradually reconciled, leading to the prospect of a unified code. Furthermore, because there had been numerous piecemeal revisions and changes in the rules since 1967, the code had become rather inconvenient to use. Finally, the ideal of UBC and the development of the ISBDs were further important forces behind the revision of AACR (1967).

Michael Gorman and Paul W. Winkler were appointed editors of the second edition of AACR. In the revision, the JSC decided to conform to international agreements and standards, particularly the Paris Principles and the ISBD. As a result, in the second edition of AACR, the ISBDs formed the basis for Part I, which covers the rules for bibliographic description, and the Paris Principles underlie Part II, which contains the rules for access points. For the first time, rules for both description and access rested on international agreement. Furthermore, differences between the North American and the British texts of the first edition were reconciled, resulting in a single text.

Anglo-American Cataloging Rules, 2nd Edition, 1988 Revision (AACR2R; 1988)

> Joint Steering Committee for Revision of AACR (American Library Association, Australian Committee on Cataloguing, British Library, Canadian Committee on Cataloguing, Library Association, & Library of Congress.) (1988). *Anglo-American Cataloguing Rules* (2nd ed., 1988 revision). M. Gorman and P. W. Winkler (Eds.). Chicago, IL: American Library Association.

In the early 1980s, three supplements containing revisions to AACR2 (1978) were issued. In addition, revisions that had yet to be published were also approved by the JSC. Furthermore, a draft revision of the rules for computer files was prepared and published in 1986 in response to the ever-changing nature of computer files. With these changes, it was considered appropriate to issue a revised edition of AACR2. The JSC decided to call the new version *Second Edition 1988 Revision* instead of the "third edition," perhaps because of the "anguished howls and monumental upheaval that greeted the advent of the original *AACR2* in 1978,"[28] or the fact that "the rules have not been radically recast [nor was there] basic rethinking."[29]

Michael Gorman and Paul W. Winkler again served as the editors of the revised edition, which was published in 1988.

Anglo-American Cataloging Rules, 2nd Edition, 1998 Revision (AACR2R; 1998)

> Joint Steering Committee for Revision of AACR (American Library Association, Australian Committee on Cataloguing, British Library, Canadian Committee on Cataloguing, Library Association, & Library of Congress). (1998). *Anglo-American Cataloguing Rules* (2nd ed., 1998 revision). M. Gorman and P. W. Winkler (Eds.). Chicago, IL: American Library Association.

By the late 1990s, sufficient additions, deletions, and changes had accumulated since the 1988 revision to warrant a new issue of the second edition. A new revision of AACR2R containing the rules of the 1988 revision and subsequent updates was issued in 1998.

Anglo-American Cataloging Rules, 2nd Edition, 2002 Revision (AACR2R; 2002)

> Joint Steering Committee for Revision of AACR (American Library Association, Australian Committee on Cataloguing, British Library, Canadian Committee on Cataloguing, Chartered Institute of Library and Information Professionals, & Library of Congress). (2002). *Anglo-American Cataloguing Rules* (2nd ed., 2002 revision). Chicago, IL: American Library Association.

AACR2R (2002) contains changes and additions since 1998, particularly with regard to the treatment of electronic resources.

Anglo-American Cataloging Rules, 2nd Edition, 2005 Revision (AACR2R; 2005)

> Joint Steering Committee for Revision of AACR (American Library Association, Australian Committee on Cataloguing, British Library, Canadian Committee on Cataloguing, Chartered Institute of Library and Information Professionals, & Library of Congress). (2005).

*Anglo-American Cataloguing Rules (*2nd ed., 2005 revision). Chicago, IL: American Library Association.

AACR2R (2005) contains changes and additions since the 2002 revisions, particularly with regard to cataloging of cartographic materials. The JSC is no longer maintaining AACR2, due to its replacement by RDA.

The Concise AACR2 (2004)

Gorman, M. (2004). *The Concise AACR2* (4th ed.). Chicago, IL: American Library Association.

For libraries that do not need the details embodied in the full edition of AACR, a concise version prepared by Michael Gorman (one of the editors of AACR) has been published at appropriate intervals since 1981. The current edition accompanies AACR2R (2002). The intent of the concise version, as stated in the General Introduction to the latest edition, is "to convey the essence and basic principles of the second edition of the *Anglo-American Cataloguing Rules* (*AACR2*) without many of that comprehensive work's rules for out-of-the-way and complex materials."

Resource Description and Access (RDA)

American Library Association, Canadian Library Association, & CILIP: Chartered Institute of Library and Information Professionals. (2010–). *RDA Toolkit: Resource Description and Access*. Available from www.rdatoolkit.org

Joint Steering Committee for Development of RDA (American Library Association, Australian Committee on Cataloguing, British Library, Canadian Committee on Cataloguing, CILIP: Chartered Institute of Library and Information Professionals, & Library of Congress). (2010–). *RDA: Resource Description and Access*. Chicago, IL: American Library Association.

In the early 2000s, discussion began on a new edition of AACR. In 2004, work on the new edition started, and Tom Delsey was appointed as the editor. In 2005, a new title was adopted, "RDA: Resource Description and Access," along with a new approach for the standard. RDA is based on the conceptual models FRBR and FRAD, provides a flexible framework to describe all bibliographic resources (with special attention to digital resources), and allows for better efficiency for organizations that use emerging database technologies. A full draft of RDA was first made available in November 2008, and the new standard was released in 2010 in the RDA Toolkit as an integrated online resource. The RDA content standard is regularly updated with new releases of the RDA Toolkit. Print versions of RDA are also available. RDA has been translated into other languages, among them Chinese, French, German, and Spanish. The French, German, and Spanish translations have been integrated into the RDA Toolkit.

The Joint Steering Committee for Development of RDA is responsible for overseeing revision work. This is an international organization, with representatives from ALA, Australian Committee on Cataloguing, The British Library, Canadian Committee on Cataloguing, CILIP: Chartered Institute of Library and Information Professionals, Deutsche Nationalbibliothek, and the LC.

Chapter 5 of this book offers an overview of FRBR, FRAD, and ISBN, as well as an introduction to RDA. Chapter 6 discusses and gives examples of the guidelines and instructions for description contained in RDA. Descriptive—that is, nonsubject—access points based on the RDA guidelines and instructions are discussed in chapters 7 through 9 of this book.

NOTES

1. Panizzi, A. (1985). Rules for the compilation of the catalogue. In M. Carpenter and E. Svenonius (Eds.), *Foundations of Cataloging: A Sourcebook* (pp. 3–14). Littleton, CO: Libraries Unlimited (Original work published 1841).

2. Panizzi, A. (1985). Mr. Panizzi to the Right Hon. the Earl of Ellesmere—British Museum, January 29, 1848. In M. Carpenter and E. Svenonius (Eds.), *Foundations of Cataloging: A Sourcebook* (pp. 18–47). Littleton, CO: Libraries Unlimited (Original work published 1850).

3. Carpenter, M. (1985). Editor's introduction: "Mr. Panizzi to the Right Hon. the Earl of Ellesmere." In M. Carpenter and E. Svenonius (Eds.), *Foundations of Cataloging: A Sourcebook* (pp. 15–17). Littleton, CO: Libraries Unlimited.

4. Svenonius, E. (1985). Editor's introduction: "Smithsonian catalogue system [by] Charles C. Jewett." In M. Carpenter and E. Svenonius (Eds.), *Foundations of Cataloging: A Sourcebook* (p. 49). Littleton, CO: Libraries Unlimited.

5. Cutter, C. A. (1904). *Rules for a Dictionary Catalog* (4th ed. rewritten). Washington, DC: Government Printing Office (p. 3).

6. Cutter, 1904, p. 6.

7. Cutter, 1904, p. 12.

8. Lubetzky, S. (1985). Principles of descriptive cataloging. In M. Carpenter and E. Svenonius (Eds.), *Foundations of Cataloging: A Sourcebook* (pp. 104–12). Littleton, CO: Libraries Unlimited (Original work published 1946).

9. Lubetzky, S. (2001). Cataloging rules and principles: A critique of the A.L.A. rules for entry and a proposed design for their revision. In E. Svenonius and D. McGarry (Eds.), *Seymour Lubetzky: Writings on the Classical Art of Cataloging* (pp. 78–139). Englewood, CO: Libraries Unlimited (Original work published 1953).

10. Lubetzky, S. (1960). *Code of Cataloging Rules: Author and Title Entry*. Chicago, IL: American Library Association.

11. Lubetzky, S. (1969). *Principles of Cataloging. Final Report. Phase I: Descriptive Cataloging*. Los Angeles, CA: Institute of Library Research, University of California.

12. IFLA Cataloguing Section and IFLA Meetings of Experts on an International Cataloguing Code. (2009). *Statement of International Cataloguing Principles*. München, Germany: K. G. Saur. Retrieved from http://www.ifla.org/publications/statement-of-international-cataloguing-principles.

13. International Federation of Library Associations. (1974). *ISBD (M): International Standard Bibliographic Description for Monographic Publications* (1st standard ed.). London, England: IFLA Committee on Cataloguing (p. vii).

14. International Federation of Library Associations, 1974.

15. Anderson, D. (1974). *Universal Bibliographic Control: A Long Term Policy, A Plan for Action*. Pullach/Munich, Germany: Verlag Dokumentation (p. 11).

16. Tillett, B. B. (2003). FRBR (Functional Requirements for Bibliographic Records). *Technicalities*, *23*(5), 1, 11–13. Retrieved from: www.loc.gov/cds/FRBR.html.

17. IFLA Study Group on the Functional Requirements for Bibliographic Records. (1998). *Functional Requirements for Bibliographic Records: Final Report* (UBCIM Publications, New Series Vol. 19). München, Germany: K. G. Saur. Retrieved from http://www.ifla.org/publications/functional-requirements-for-bibliographic-records.

18. Patton, G. E. (2009). *Functional Requirements for Authority Data: A Conceptual Model* (IFLA Series on Bibliographic Control Vol. 34). München, Germany: K. G. Saur. Retrieved from http://www.ifla.org/publications/functional-requirements-for-authority-data.

19. Zeng, M. L., Žumer, M., and Salaba, A. (Eds.). (2011). *Functional Requirements for Subject Authority Data (FRSAD): A Conceptual Model* (IFLA Series on Bibliographic Control Vol. 43). Berlin/München, Germany: De Gruyter Saur. Retrieved from http://www.ifla.org/publications/ifla-series-on-bibliographic-control-43.

20. Jewett, C. C. (1961). *Smithsonian Report on the Construction of Catalogues of Libraries, and their Publication by Means of Separate, Stereotyped Titles, with Rules and Examples* (2nd. ed.). Ann Arbor, MI: University Microfilms (Original work published 1853).

21. Dunkin, P. S. (1969). *Cataloging U.S.A.* Chicago, IL: American Library Association (p. 11).

22. Bakewell, K. G. B. (1972). *A Manual of Cataloguing Practice*. Oxford, England: Pergamon Press (p. 32).

23. Biblioteca Apostolica Vaticana (Vatican Library). (1948). *Rules for the Catalog of Printed Books*. W. E. Wright (Ed.). (The Very Rev. T. J. Shanahan, V. A. Schaefer, and C. T. Vesselowsky, Trans.) Chicago, IL: American Library Association (p. v).

24. Osborn, A. D. (October 1941). The crisis in cataloging. *Library Quarterly, 11*(4), 393–411. Available from http://www.jstor.org/.

25. Lubetzky, 2001 [1953].

26. Lubetzky, 1960.

27. AACR 2: Background and summary. (October 20, 1978). *Library of Congress Information Bulletin 37*, 640–52. Retrieved from http://babel.hathitrust.org/cgi/pt?id=mdp.39015036838459;view=1up;seq=1.

28. Maxwell, M. F. (1989). AACR2R: Anglo-American Cataloguing Rules. *Library Resources & Technical Services, 33*(2), 179–81.

29. Gorman, M. (1989). AACR2R: Editor's Perspective. *Library Resources & Technical Services, 33*(2), 181–86.

Part II

RECORD PRODUCTION AND STRUCTURE, ENCODING FORMATS, AND METADATA RECORDS

STANDARD AND TOOLS

Network Development and MARC Standards Office, Library of Congress. (n.d.). *BIBFRAME.* Retrieved from http://www.loc.gov/bibframe/

Network Development and MARC Standards Office, Library of Congress. (December 4, 2007). *MARC 21 Specifications for Record Structure, Character Sets, and Exchange Media.* Retrieved from http://www.loc.gov/marc/specifications/

Network Development and MARC Standards Office, Library of Congress. (April 24, 2008). *MARC 21 Lite Bibliographic Format.* Retrieved from http://www.loc.gov/marc/bibliographic/lite/

Network Development and MARC Standards Office, Library of Congress. (April 13, 2012). *MARC Records, Systems and Tools.* Retrieved from http://www.loc.gov/marc/marcservice.html

Network Development and MARC Standards Office, Library of Congress. (June 11, 2013). *MADS: Metadata Authority Description Schema.* Retrieved from http://www.loc.gov/standards/mads/

Network Development and MARC Standards Office, Library of Congress. (April 28, 2014). *MARC 21 Format for Classification Data.* Retrieved from http://www.loc.gov/marc/classification/

Network Development and MARC Standards Office, Library of Congress. (May 21, 2014). *MARCXML: MARC 21 XML Schema.* Retrieved from http://www.loc.gov/standards/marcxml/

Network Development and MARC Standards Office, Library of Congress. (October 20a, 2014). *MARC 21 Format for Authority Data.* Retrieved from http://www.loc.gov/marc/authority/

Network Development and MARC Standards Office, Library of Congress. (October 20b, 2014). *MARC 21 Format for Bibliographic Data.* Retrieved from http://www.loc.gov/marc/bibliographic/

Network Development and MARC Standards Office, Library of Congress. (October 20c, 2014). *MARC 21 Format for Holdings Data*. Retrieved from http://www.loc.gov/marc/holdings/

Network Development and MARC Standards Office, Library of Congress. (November 24, 2014). *MODS: Metadata Object Description Schema*. Retrieved from http://www.loc.gov/standards/mods/

Network Development and MARC Standards Office, Library of Congress. (December 18, 2014). *MARC Standards*. Retrieved from http://www.loc.gov/marc/

RECOMMENDED READING

Alemu, G., Stevens, B., Ross, P., and Chandler, J. (May 24, 2012). *Linked Data for Libraries: Benefits of a Conceptual Shift from Library-Specific Record Structures to RDF-based Data Models*. Paper presented at the 78th IFLA General Conference and Assembly, August 11–17, 2012, Helsinki, Finland (Meeting 92—New Futures for Bibliographic Data formats: Reflections and Directions—UNIMARC Core Activity). Retrieved from http://conference.ifla.org/past-wlic/2012/92-alemu-en.pdf

Avram, H. D. (1975). *MARC: Its History and Implications*. Washington, DC: Library of Congress.

Library of Congress. (November 21, 2012). *Bibliographic Framework as a Web of Data: Linked Data Model and Supporting Services*. Retrieved from http://www.loc.gov/bibframe/pdf/marcld-report-11-21-2012.pdf

Library of Congress. (July 2014). *RDA in MARC*. Retrieved from http://www.loc.gov/marc/RDAinMARC.html

MARC Development Office, Library of Congress. (1974). *Information on the MARC System* (4th ed.). Washington, DC: Library of Congress.

Network Development and MARC Standards Office, Library of Congress. (November 1996). *The MARC 21 Formats: Background and Principles*. Retrieved from http://www.loc.gov/marc/96principl.html

Network Development and MARC Standards Office, Library of Congress. (September 9a, 2013). *Understanding MARC Authority Records: Machine-readable Cataloging*. Retrieved from www.loc.gov/marc/uma/

Network Development and MARC Standards Office, Library of Congress. (September 9b, 2013). *Understanding MARC Bibliographic: Machine-readable Cataloging*. Retrieved from www.loc.gov/marc/umb/

OCLC. (2015). *OCLC Online Computer Library Center*. Retrieved from www.oclc.org/

Taylor, A. G. (2006). *Introduction to Cataloging and Classification* (10th ed.). Westport, CT: Libraries Unlimited (Chapter 3, pp. 19–20).

Chapter 3

Records and Encoding Schemas

INTRODUCTION

Resource descriptions and other metadata—such as information regarding a controlled subject term or a person's name, including the preferred form of, and variations of, that name—have always been stored in some type of records, physical or digital. Records can be produced in-house or can be copied from another agency that produced them. To set up such records for computer manipulation, for printing or browsing, or for any of the myriad other things a computer can do with its data, elements in or pertaining to the records must be coded according to a standard format or markup language. The one markup language commonly used in the library community is MARC. In the Web environment, other encoding schemas based on SGML (Standard Generalized Markup Language) and XML also come into play. More recently, libraries have been exploring ways to encode their library data for the semantic Web and linked-data environment. A new model for expressing and connecting bibliographic data has been developed for these purposes, the BIBFRAME.

CATALOGING RECORDS

In cataloging any given item, there are two ways to proceed. The first, called *copy cataloging,* is to make the fullest possible use of records prepared elsewhere—records that are called *cataloging copy*. The second, called *original cataloging*, is to do the cataloging in-house, from scratch. In any given library with a general collection, it is typical to find a mix of both, with fully original cataloging restricted to items for which no outside record is available.

The more specialized the library or indexing agency, of course, the fewer outside records are likely to be suitable, if any can be found at all.

In strict copy cataloging, a local cataloging record is based on an outside record with minimum modification to fit the item being cataloged. Nonetheless, in many cases of copy cataloging, a high level of professional judgment may be needed once a candidate outside record is found: first, to be sure that the record in question matches the item at hand; second (if it does match), to determine whether the item was adequately cataloged by the originating agency; and third, to alter, add, or delete cataloging elements to suit local needs. Thus, there are elements of original cataloging even in what is usually considered copy cataloging. In general libraries, nevertheless, most local cataloging departments stay as close as possible to strict copy cataloging because doing so has been found to bring about a large increase in the productivity of cataloging staff.

Where do outside records come from? Where can they be found? Two facets of the cataloging process come into play here: *centralized cataloging* and *shared cataloging*. Centralized cataloging describes the situation in which cataloging records are prepared by one agency and made available to subscribers; shared cataloging describes the situation in which cataloging records are contributed by two or more libraries or agencies to a central database and made generally available.

In the history of cataloging in the United States, the LC has played a major role in both centralized and shared cataloging. Beginning with the Library's printed card service in 1902 (which, for many years, simply amounted to distributing duplicates of catalog cards prepared by its own staff for its own use), libraries around the country have made use of LC cataloging records or data in their own catalogs.

By the middle of the 1950s, even LC could not keep up with its current cataloging load, so it began welcoming cataloging records prepared by other major libraries. It used these records to supplement its own cataloging and also made them available to other libraries. Shared cataloging has been a major force in American cataloging ever since.

Besides shared bibliographic records, there is another kind of cataloging information that the library community benefits from sharing. The LC has been making its subject authority list available since early in the twentieth century, publishing it as LCSH. In 1986, LCSH became available in machine-readable form, first on magnetic tape as the *Subject Authorities*, and later on CD-ROM as *CDMARC Subjects*. In 1974, the LC began issuing its name authority records, first serially in book form,[1] then on microfiche, and finally on magnetic tape as the *Name Authorities* and on CD-ROM as *CDMARC Names*. Currently, the authorities' databases are accessible from the library's web site (http://authorities.loc.gov), and as part of Cataloger's Desktop and Classification Web, both of which are online tools developed and maintained by the LC.

At first, LC was effectively the only agency involved in the large-scale collection and distribution of cataloging records. Now, spurred by the use of computer technology to facilitate library operations, there are many others, particularly the cooperatives called *bibliographic networks* or *bibliographic utilities*.

Bibliographic utilities are agencies with large cataloging databases that provide a wide range of bibliographic services to members or subscribers. Some are networks in which members contribute their original cataloging records to be shared with other members. There are also many commercial and government-supported processing centers that provide precataloged books and other resources to libraries. Some of them create their own cataloging records; others adapt cataloging copy and either make it directly available to libraries or use it in their own products. Such processing centers offer a variety of services often tailored to individual libraries' needs. Many provide cataloging data to be integrated into online catalogs of member libraries, along with library materials ready to circulate.

MAJOR SOURCES OF CATALOGING COPY

Cataloging records—both bibliographic records and authority records—are available through subscriptions offered by the LC, and through bibliographic utilities. These records are also searchable for free on LC's web sites: Library of Congress Online Catalog (http://catalog.loc.gov) for bibliographic records and *Library of Congress Authorities* (http://authorities.loc.gov) for authority records.

The Library of Congress (LC)

The LC has a long history of making cataloging data available (through several different vehicles) under the direction of the Cataloging Distribution Service (CDS; formerly the Card Distribution Service). In 1942, LC began publishing *The Library of Congress Catalog: A Cumulative Catalog of Books Represented by Library of Congress Printed Cards*, which made available, en masse, the author- or main-entry cataloging records of the vast holdings of the Library. In 1953, the title was changed to *National Union Catalog* (NUC), and the scope was enlarged to include cataloging records of contributing North American libraries with holdings information for many items. In 1983, the LC discontinued the print version of NUC and began issuing it on microfiche.

Since March 1969, LC has been distributing cataloging data in machine-readable form, coded according to the MARC format. Currently, the MARC Distribution Service (MDS), a part of CDS, offers a service in which MARC bibliographic and authority records in hundreds of languages (including non-Roman alphabet languages in their original scripts) are available through subscription. These records encompass a variety of resource types, including books, serials, electronic resources, maps, music, and visual materials. They can be transmitted via File Transfer Protocol (FTP), the protocol for exchanging files over the Internet.

Program for Cooperative Cataloging (PCC)

An important component of the cooperative cataloging activities worldwide is the PCC, which is "an international cooperative effort aimed at expanding access to library collections by providing useful, timely, and cost-effective cataloging that meets mutually accepted standards of libraries around the world."[2] PCC, an initiative of the Cooperative Cataloging Council (CCC), began work in 1992. Currently, PCC has four components:

NACO: the Name Authority Cooperative
SACO: the Subject Authority Cooperative
BIBCO: the Monographic Bibliographic Record Program
CONSER: the Cooperative Online Serials Program.

Member libraries contribute to the various programs by creating authority and bibliographic records based on mutually agreed-upon standards and then submitting them to the LC, which coordinates the activities of PCC. The LC also provides training and documentation for such activities. The resulting authority records are made available through the authority databases maintained by the LC, and the bibliographic records are made available through the Library of Congress Online Catalog and OCLC's WorldCat.

Cataloging-in-Publication (CIP)

The LC established the CIP program in 1971, with the objectives of cataloging books prior to publication and including cataloging data inside individual publications themselves. The program represents a cooperative effort between the LC and publishers, with the majority of American trade publishers participating. Selected federal government documents are also included. The introduction of the Electronic CIP (ECIP) program in 1999 allowed for widespread partnerships, which led to the development of the ECIP Cataloging Partnership Program. In addition, the CIP program has more recently developed a process to provide CIP data for materials that are simultaneously published as e-books and print books.

Publishers submit galleys of their books to the CIP Office at LC, where the material is processed through regular cataloging channels. The CIP information is then returned to the publisher for inclusion in the resource itself. For books, for example, the CIP information appears on the verso of the title page. Librarians or library assistants working with the item in hand can then prepare a complete cataloging record by filling in whatever else is needed, such as other title information, edition, publication information, physical description, and local call number.

Bibliographic Utilities

Over the last four decades, bibliographic utilities have been playing an increasingly larger role in distributing cataloging data. A bibliographic utility is an organization that offers bibliographic resources and services to subscribing libraries at much lower cost than preparing the same records in-house.

Most of the bibliographic utilities began as cooperative arrangements among small groups of participating libraries. Some of them have become enormous operations involving many libraries and have extended their services beyond the United States. Examples of bibliographic utilities include OCLC, begun in 1967 as the Ohio College Library Center and later expanded to serve libraries in the United States and abroad, and RLIN (pronounced Arlin), begun in 1974 as a partnership between three universities, Columbia, Harvard, and Yale. WLN was serving libraries in the state of Washington in the early 1970s, and later expanded to serve many libraries outside the state. Both RLIN and WLN have merged with OCLC, with WLN in 1999, and RLIN in 2006.

Online Computer Library Center (OCLC)

Among the utilities, OCLC is the largest in scale and service. In 2014, its WorldCat (a union catalog of MARC records contributed by member libraries, including LC MARC records) totaled over 330 million records. It affords an apt example of what a bibliographic utility can do for member libraries.

OCLC was founded by Frederick G. Kilgour in 1967 as a consortium of forty-nine academic libraries in the state of Ohio. Its principal objectives were resource sharing and reduction of per-unit library costs.[3] It began operation in 1971 with its first subsystem, cataloging. Other subsystems, including serials control, online acquisitions, and online interlibrary loan requests, were implemented as time went on. Since 1973, access to its union catalog and services has been extended to libraries in states outside of Ohio and eventually abroad, an important step toward making OCLC the largest online bibliographic network in the world. To reflect its expanded scope, the name Ohio College Library Center was changed to OCLC Online Computer Library Center in 1977. OCLC Pacific was formed in 1976 to provide training and support to West Coast OCLC members, and in 1999 OCLC Pacific merged with WLN. The result was the OCLC/WLN Pacific Northwest Service Center, now called OCLC Western.

OCLC's cataloging subsystem consists of an online union catalog set up as a shared cataloging operation. Early use of the network leaned heavily toward off-line catalog card production using MARC tapes from the LC. Now, libraries with proper equipment can download or import OCLC records directly to their own online catalog.

Since 1985, United Kingdom's MARC records have also been incorporated into WorldCat. The LC Name Authority File was loaded as a separate file in 1984; and in 1987, the LC Subject Authority File was also added. These authority files are kept current as new and corrected data are received. With millions of bibliographic records and a large number of authority records available online, member libraries have been able to reduce cataloging costs considerably.

An important feature of WorldCat is that each bibliographic record has corresponding holdings records, giving each library's holdings information. As of 2014, WorldCat contains more than 330 million bibliographic records, with over two billion holdings records in hundreds of languages, for a wide variety of library materials, ranging from stone tablets to electronic books, wax recordings to MP3s, DVDs, and web sites.

In 2005, OCLC launched its OCLC Open WorldCat program, making the records in WorldCat visible and freely accessible to Web users through popular Internet search sites such as Yahoo! and Google, and through its worldcat.org interface. In early 2006, OCLC incorporated the RLG Union Catalog (discussed in the next section) containing more than 48 million titles and more than 150 million holdings records. Early OCLC cataloging systems allowed retrieval of records by only a limited number of search keys, none of which afforded subject access.

Over the years, OCLC has implemented very sophisticated searching options as well as a number of progressively effective systems with enhanced features and capabilities for online cataloging operations. The current cataloging interface is called Connexion, which is based on an Oracle platform for its databases and which uses the Web as its communications platform. In addition to online cataloging services, OCLC provides a number of metadata services, including open bibliographic data, discovery services, and resource-sharing services.

Other Networks and Services

There are a number of other networks and agencies that provide bibliographic services to libraries. Some networks are nationwide or regional. Some serve special types of libraries. A prominent example is Research Libraries Group (RLG),[4] which, like OCLC, was a not-for-profit organization. Its membership consisted of over 150 research libraries, archives, museums, and other cultural memory institutions. RLG was founded in 1974 by Columbia, Harvard, and Yale universities and the New York Public Library. One of its products was the RLG Union Catalog, a database containing bibliographic records covering a wide range of subjects and material types in almost 400 languages. Its major clientele consisted of academic and research libraries. Its RLIN21 Web interface offered sophisticated search and navigation capabilities supported by Web browsers. On July 1, 2006, RLG merged with OCLC, and RLG's programs continue to operate as a new unit of OCLC.

In addition to networks such as OCLC, many commercial companies also offer bibliographic services, supplying completely processed library materials, both print and nonprint, with bibliographic records ready to be downloaded to local library systems. It is a fairly common practice among libraries, particularly small libraries, to outsource their cataloging operations to commercial companies. For example, Yankee Book Peddler, Inc. (YPB) is a participant of the OCLC WorldCat Cataloging Partners (formerly PromptCat) service, whereby libraries receive complete MARC records from OCLC's WorldCat along with materials purchased from the vendor.[5]

ONLINE CATALOGING

In working with online catalogs, reference librarians as well as catalogers and collection development and acquisitions personnel need to know about how cataloging records are coded. For reference librarians, such knowledge is an important factor in effectiveness when using the catalog as a retrieval tool.

Even with the computer playing a significant role in the cataloging operations, the intellectual part of the cataloging process is still largely performed by human catalogers and is completed before the computer plays its part. This is true no matter how little fully original cataloging is done, because cataloging copy has to be screened and often altered before it can be used.

Online Cataloging Activities

The availability of facilities for the online processing of cataloging records has proven to be extremely helpful to libraries, not only in terms of catalog cost savings but also in terms of reducing the time between an order request and the appearance of the purchased item on the shelves. The following discussion describes some of the processes involved in online cataloging.

Searching

For catalogers, the main purpose of searching is to ascertain whether there is a record in the database that can serve as cataloging copy. The most common search keys used in this regard are name, title, name-title, subject heading, LC control number, ISBN, ISSN (International Standard Serial Number), and a special control number in the database. These are elements that appear in cataloging records. The last, the special control number, is unique to a given record, barring keying mistakes. Using the others will frequently call up more than one record, because the computer will respond with all the records containing the same search key. In such a case, the system displays brief descriptions, and the searcher then decides which particular record is to be displayed in full.

Once it is ascertained that a particular record is in the database, that record can then be used as needed. For cataloging, the next step is to compare the record with the item being cataloged. If their descriptions are a full match, the record then can be processed and downloaded for local use. However, if the record varies in certain details from what fits the item being cataloged, or if it differs from local cataloging norms, it can be modified to suit the item. The modifying process is called *editing*.

Editing

Editing can be performed online. One great advantage of online cataloging is its instant feedback. In editing, changes are made directly on the screen and the modified or edited record will be shown instantly, allowing the cataloger to ensure that all necessary modifications have been made.

Deriving Records

Frequently, there may be a record in the database for the same work but in a different format from the item being catalogued. For example, the searcher may locate a record created for a book in the database that matches the item being cataloged, but that is in microform or electronic form. The source record can then be adapted by editing the details with regard to physical description and adding appropriate notes to fit the item in hand.

Inputting Cataloging Records

To store original cataloging data in machine-readable form in a database, records must be input in coded form. When there is no record in the database that can be used as a cataloging copy for the item in hand, the cataloger creates an original cataloging record, adding all additional data and tags called for in the MARC format. This newly created record is then input into the database. The inputting process is made relatively easy in online cataloging systems because a MARC worksheet or workform, showing the most frequently used field tags needed in a typical record, is displayed on the screen. Cataloging data are then entered in the appropriate fields.

Downloading and Transporting Records

After records have been created and verified, the next step is to transport them to the local system. For members of a cooperative such as OCLC, records can be efficiently exported to local systems via the Internet. Because the online systems in different libraries are likely to differ in system requirements and needed protocols, some adjustments may be needed before imported records can be used. Downloading of records can be done on a one-by-one or multiple/batch basis.

Retrospective Conversion

Before online catalogs came into being, the catalogs of most libraries were in card form, with some card sets produced in-house and some imported. With the advent of the online age, it was naturally considered desirable that the information on those cards be made machine-readable. The term *retrospective conversion* refers to the process of converting manually produced records to MARC records, a necessary step in a library's transition from the manual to the automated cataloging environment and in the implementation of an online catalog. It is a time-consuming task, in part because, during conversion, it is desirable to update old records, particularly their access points, to reflect current practice. Fortunately, most libraries have completed the conversion process; some may still have small portions of the catalog not completely converted. Many bibliographic utilities and commercial companies offer retrospective conversion services. Use of such services is often the most cost-effective means for a library to effect its transition to an online catalog.

Catalog Maintenance

Maintenance refers to the process of correcting errors and updating cataloging records to keep them compatible with current standards. Maintenance is an ongoing and highly labor-intensive process. For example, when a subject heading is revised, the authority record and all bibliographic records bearing the heading should be revised to conform to the current heading.

Maintenance is a never-ending process because a catalog is dynamic; it not only grows but changes as cataloging standards are refined and as the technology of cataloging is improved. The most important objective in catalog maintenance is ensuring the quality of the catalog so that it can best serve the needs of its users. A secondary goal is to contain cataloging costs.

RECORD STRUCTURE

In computer science and database design, a record is a structure that holds data. A record includes a set of elements (also known as fields), which describe one or more units that are treated as an entity.[6] In other words, a record is a collection of fields that constitute a complete set of information about an entity (e.g., a set of fields that provide complete information about an author). Each record is typically identified by a serial number or an identifier (ID number). A collection of records constitutes a file. A system may have one or more files. Figure 3.1 shows a record structure in relation to the larger context of a system.

In MARC formats, the terms *record structure* and *record format* are sometimes used interchangeably, although record format is a broader concept representing record structure, record designation, and record content.[7] Following is a discussion of MARC formats for data on resources in library collections, with the record structures defined for different types of records.

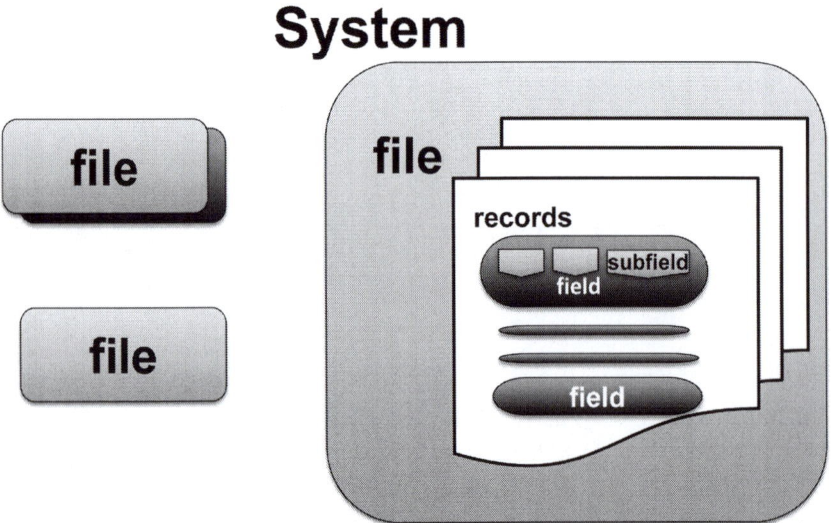

Figure 3.1 Record structure in system file context.

MARC FORMATS AND OTHER ENCODING STANDARDS

Machine-Readable Cataloging 21 (MARC 21)

A MARC format contains codes for labeling individual areas, elements, subelements, and other pertinent data in a given cataloging record. MARC formats began to emerge in the 1960s. Initially, individual countries developed their own; examples include USMARC for American libraries, UKMARC for British libraries, and CANMARC for Canadian libraries. Not much later, the IFLA developed an international schema called UNIMARC. In the interest of exchanging and sharing cataloging data internationally, and also because of the cost of maintaining such formats, many countries have since decided to adopt or convert to UNIMARC or USMARC. In 1999, USMARC and CANMARC were harmonized to become MARC 21, the name chosen in honor of the approaching new century. Minimal information on MARC was presented in the first chapter of this book. In this chapter, the formats are discussed in considerable detail, in terms of both their historical background and their basic structure.

MARC 21: History

The MARC 21 formats are a set of standards developed for the purpose of representing and communicating machine-readable descriptive metadata about information items—particularly, but not solely, bibliographic items.[8] Work on the formats started in the mid- to late 1950s, when the LC began investigating the possibility of automating its internal operations. In the early 1960s, the Council on Library Resources provided financial support for two exploratory studies. One examined the feasibility of applying automated techniques to the LC's internal operations. The other considered possible methods of converting the data on LC catalog cards to machine-readable form in order to print bibliographic products by computer. These studies generated a great deal of interest and enthusiasm. As a result, a pilot project, called MARC, was initiated in January 1966 to test the feasibility and utility of having LC distribute machine-readable cataloging data on tape to user libraries. For the pilot project, sixteen libraries of different types and geographic locations were chosen to receive MARC tapes. Trial distribution began in October 1966. By June 1968, approximately 50,000 cataloging records for English-language book materials had been converted to machine-readable form and distributed to the participating libraries. (By comparison, in 2014, the number of records in OCLC's WorldCat came to more than 300 million.) The results of the MARC pilot project were sufficiently encouraging for LC to proceed on a full-scale basis. The original MARC book format was refined and became the MARC II format for monographs.

It is the Network Development and MARC Standards Office of the Library of Congress that is responsible for the development and maintenance of the MARC 21 formats. The MARC Distribution Services, a part of LC's Cataloging Distribution Service, was established in March 1969 to disseminate MARC records to subscribing libraries and institutions. Initially, the cataloging data being distributed were limited to records for currently cataloged English-language monographic material,[9] but, over the years, coverage has been broadened to include a range of types of material, in many languages.

The MARC structure was adopted as a national standard (ANSI standard Z39.2)[10] in 1971 and as an international standard (ISO standard 2709)[11] in 1973. Also in 1973, the ALA committee working on machine-readable forms of bibliographic information became a MARC advisory committee working with LC on changes and refinements in MARC formats. The MARC Advisory Committee is known by its acronym, MAC (previously MARBI). Other representatives from the American library and bibliographic community and national libraries also participate in the continuing development of MARC. In 1982, a set of principles was prepared and published.[12] The LC continues to hold principal responsibility for the maintenance and publication of the MARC 21 formats, but all proposed changes are discussed at MAC meetings and published after approval.

Initially, the MARC formats were intended as communications formats for the purpose of transmitting machine-readable data from the LC to users in the library community. But with wide adoption and use, LC MARC became known as USMARC and later, beginning in 1999, as MARC 21.

The MARC 21 formats have been translated in various degrees of fullness into many different languages. Many libraries worldwide use the English versions and their equivalents in other languages.

Types of MARC 21 Formats

There are currently five types of MARC 21 formats; these are for (1) bibliographic data, (2) authority data, (3) classification data, (4) holdings data, and (5) community information. The first four types are used for bibliographic information, while the fifth is for structuring information relating to individuals, organizations, programs or services, events, and other such entities. These formats have been published in separate volumes. It is the first four types of MARC 21 formats that are used in creating and maintaining bibliographic and authority records.

(1) *MARC 21 Format for Bibliographic Data*[13] is designed to cover bibliographic information for various types of materials, including books, maps, music, sound recordings, visual materials, continuing resources,

electronic resources, and mixed materials. Initially, separate formats were prepared for different media—books, serials, etc.—and there were differences in the provisions for each medium, differences that were soon seen to cause problems in application.[14] For example, bibliographic items that fall into more than one category, such as nonprint materials in serial form, could not fit adequately into one format. Although bibliographic items in many media may be issued in serial form, provisions for serial publications or products were inconsistent among the various formats. Furthermore, comparable elements in different formats were not always handled consistently. In practice, the multiplicity of formats made maintenance and systems support difficult and cumbersome. As a result, in the early 1990s, the various medium-specific formats were rationalized and integrated into a single format.

(2) *MARC 21 Format for Authority Data*[15] is intended for use by persons who create and maintain authority records. It contains specifications for encoding and identifying data elements in authority records, including those for name headings, name/title headings, uniform or preferred title headings, topical term headings, extended headings (i.e., headings with subdivisions), and references to headings.

(3) *MARC 21 Format for Classification Data*[16] is designed for identifying data elements in classification records. In effect, a classification record is an "authority record" for a class number. It is intended for use by persons who (a) create and maintain classification records, (b) arrange the publication of classification schemes from machine-readable data, and (c) design and maintain systems for processing classification records and entering them into the appropriate database.

(4) *MARC 21 Format for Holdings Data*[17] is designed for identifying the data elements in MARC holdings reports (i.e., reports indicating the holdings of individual libraries). As such, it contains provisions for recording copy-specific information of any particular resource, plus information that is peculiar to the holding library. It is designed to allow the potential use of the format to interface with automated control systems such as union catalogs, automatic serials claiming, and interlibrary loan systems. It is intended for use by those who create and maintain MARC 21 holdings information.

Levels of MARC 21 Formats

To accommodate the needs of different types and sizes of libraries and different levels of use, MARC 21 is issued in three levels according to fullness of detail: full, concise, and "LITE." The full and concise versions contain all format types, while MARC 21 LITE is limited to the bibliographic format only. MARC 21 Concise has all data elements contained in the full version but with less explanatory detail. MARC 21 LITE, on the other hand, contains fewer data elements and even fewer explanatory details. The LITE format is extensible; if more details are needed than defined in each format, details from the full format may be added selectively.

MARC 21 Full

The full versions are the most inclusive in respect to details.

MARC 21 Concise

For those who do not need the elaborate explanatory details in the individual formats, a concise version including all formats, entitled *MARC 21 Concise Formats,* has also been published.[18] The nature and purpose of this version are stated as the following:

The *MARC 21 Concise Formats* contains abridged descriptions of every data element, along with examples. Descriptions of subfield codes and coded values are given only when their names may not be sufficiently descriptive. Examples are included for each field. (www.loc.gov/marc/concise/concise.html)

MARC 21 LITE

In 2001, an even simpler version for bibliographic data, called *MARC LITE,* was developed for use in simple cataloging and metadata records. The nature and purpose of this version are stated as the following:

"The *MARC 21 LITE Bibliographic Format* is a subset of the markup defined in the full MARC 21 Bibliographic Format. It includes all essential data elements to create bibliographic records." The created records using only the elements in this MARC 21 LITE format, are valid MARC records and may be integrated with fuller records without changes later on. If needed, elements from the full format can be added to LITE records. (http://www.loc.gov/marc/bibliographic/lite/genintro.html)

Availability of MARC 21 Formats

The MARC 21 formats are available in various publication types and are also found in many cataloging tool packages. The formats are also available on the LC web site (www.loc.gov/marc/), along with other MARC-related documents and tools.

The full version of MARC 21 is also included in Cataloger's Desktop, which is available by subscription from the Cataloging Distribution Service of the Library of Congress.

Architecture of MARC 21 Formats

The general architecture of the various formats is much the same for all formats. The separately published formats, which include instructions on application as well as the format definitions and provisions themselves, are enormously complex and detailed. For beginners and those interested in an overview of the formats, the concise version offers essential details sufficient for an understanding of MARC architecture.

It is helpful to consider the basic structure of the MARC 21 formats in three perspectives: what is the overall structure, what is included, and how is all the content organized? One should bear in mind that a MARC record in the communications format consists of a sequential string of characters, with a blank space counting as a character. For example, the sequence "MARC format" equals eleven characters. A typical coded bibliographic record consists of hundreds of such sequences. (The MARC records taken from the LC online catalog and from OCLC's WorldCat shown throughout this book have been reformatted for easy reading.)

Certain control characters used in the MARC record are given arbitrary graphic representation in various displays of MARC records. For example, in different contexts or systems, the subfield limiting character may be represented by the dollar sign ($), the vertical bar (|), or by the dagger (‡). The field and record terminators are often omitted from record displays, but never from the actual record.

In this text, the following graphics are used:

  blank (indicating a positive or fixed value, e.g., in the indicator)
$ subfield limiting character
@ field terminator
% record terminator

Figure 3.2 shows a cataloging record in the MARC communications format (along with a field-by-field analysis) as it stands before individual elements are formatted for display.

Structural Components of the MARC 21 Format

Three elements form the basis of the MARC 21 format: record structure, content designators, and data content:

(1) The record structure is the overall framework for the MARC record.
(2) The content designators are a set of symbols by which data in the record are identified and manipulated; these include field tags, indicators, and subfield codes (see explanation below).

(a)

01795cam#a22003618i#450000100130000000030004000130050017000170080041000340100001
500075020003700090020003400127040002300161043001200184050002000196082
00140021610000290023024500940025925000190035326400860043930000300046
9336002600499337002800525338002700553504005100580505047200631650004
301103650005301146700002201199###841199101#@DLC@20140306113219.0@
130422s2013#ilu#b#001#0#eng##@ ##$a2013010868@ ##$a9781555709099#$q#acid-free
paper@ ##$a1555709095#$q#acid-free paper@ ##$aDLC$beng$erda$cDLC@ ##$an-us---@
00$aZ678#$b.E9#2013@ 00$a025.1$223@ 1#$aEvans, G.#Edward,$d1937@ 10$aManag
ement#basics#for#information#professionals#/#$cG.#Edward#Evans,# Camila#A.#Alire.@
##$aThird#edition.@ #1$aChicago#:#$bNeal-Schuman,#an#imprint#of#the#American#Libra
ry#Association,#$c2013.@ ##$axvii,#577#pages#;#$c23#cm@ ##$atext$btxt$2rdacontent@
##$aunmediated$bn$2rdamedia@ ##$avolumebnc2rdacarrier@ ##$aIncludes bibliographical
references and index.@ ##$aOperating#environment#--#Legal#issues#and#library#managem
ent#-- #The#planning#process#--#Power,#accountability,#and#responsibility#--#Delegating#-
-#Decision#making#--#Communicating#--#Changing#and#innovating#--#Assessment,#quali
ty#control,#and#operations#--#Marketing#--#Motivating#--#Leading#--#Building #teams#--
#Addressing#diversity#--#Staffing#--#Managing#money#--#Managing#technology#--#Managi
ng#and#planning#physical#facilities#--#Ethics#--#Planning#your#career.@#0$aLibrary#admi
nistration$zUnited#States.@ #0$aInformation#services$zUnited#States$xManagement.@ 1#$a
Alire,#Camila#A.@

(b)

Leader	01795cam#a22003618i#4500
Directory entries	001001300000
	003000400013
	005001700017
	008004100034
	010001500075
	020003700090
	020003400127
	040002300161
	043001200184
	050002000196
	082001400216
	100002900230
	245009400259
	250001900353
	264008600439
	300003000469
	336002600499
	337002800525
	338002700553
	504005100580
	505047200631
	650004301103

Figure 3.2 MARC record in the communications format for Evans, G. Edward. (2013). *Management Basics for Information Professionals*. 3rd ed.: a bibliographic record (a) and a field-by-field analysis (b), with $ = delimiter, @ = field terminator, % = record terminator, and # = blank.

```
              650005301146
              700002201199
Data fields  ###841199101#@DLC@20140306113219.0@
             130422s2013#ilu#b#001#0#eng##@
             ##$a2013010868@
             ##$a9781555709099#$q#acid-free paper@
             ##$a1555709095#$q#acid-free paper@
             ##$aDLC$beng$erda$cDLC@
             ##$an-us---@
             00$aZ678#$b.E9#2013@
             00$a025.1$223@
             1#$aEvans,@G.#Edward,$d1937-@
             10$aManagement#basics#for#information#professionals#/#$cG.#Edward#Evans,#
               Camila#A.#Alire.@
             ##$aThird#edition.@
             #1$aChicago#:#$bNeal-Schuman,#an#imprint#of#the#American#Library
               #Association,#$c2013.@
             ##$axvii,#577#pages#;#$c23#cm@
             ##$atext$btxt$2rdacontent@
             ##$aunmediated$bn$2rdamedia@
             ##$avolume$bnc$2rdacarrier@
             ##$aIncludes bibliographical references and index.@
             ##$aOperating#environment#--#Legal#issues#and#library#management#--
               #The#planning#process#--#Power,#accountability,#and#responsi
               bility#--#Delegating#--#Decision#making#--#Communicating#--
               #Changing#and#innovating#--#Assessment,#quality#control,#and
               #operations#--#Marketing#--#Motivating#--#Leading#--#Building
               #teams#--#Addressing#diversity#--#Staffing#--#Managing#money#--
               #Managing#technology#--#Managing#and#planning#physical#facilities#--
               #Ethics#--#Planning#your#career.@
             #0$aLibrary#administration$zUnited#States.@
             #0$aInformation#services$zUnited#States$xManagement.@
             1#$a Alire,#Camila#A.@
```

Figure 3.2 *Continued*

(3) The data content is field-by-field record-specific information (bibliographic data, authority data, classification data, etc.). Data content is what is usually thought of as "catalog information," and is usually defined by standards outside the formats, such as cataloging rules, classification schemes, subject vocabularies, code lists, and so on.

Units in a MARC 21 Record

Another way to look at what constitutes a MARC record is in terms of units. The term "unit" here refers to an item of MARC-tagged information. Any MARC record consists of the following units:

(1) *Data element*: This is the lowest unit of information. It may be only one character long, for example, the code for record status. It may be a numeric string, such as an ISBN, a copyright date, or an LC control number, or it may be a character string, such as an author's full name. Also, it may be of fixed or variable length:
   (a) *Fixed-length element*: This is an element that is always expressed by the same number of characters, for example, the coding of a language is always three characters long.
   (b) *Variable-length element*: This is an element (such as an author's name, a series title, an edition statement, etc.) the length of which cannot be predetermined.
(2) *Field*: A field is a collection of data elements, such as a main entry that consists of the data elements for the person's name and possibly a title of nobility or the dates of his or her birth and death. Some fields consist of only one data element, such as the LC control number. All of the fields in a MARC record end with a field terminator, which is often not shown in a record display. Each field terminator indicates that the next character in the MARC string begins a new field.
(3) *Record*: A record is a collection of fields treated as a unit, for example, a bibliographic record, an authority record, or a classification record. In a string of records, each one ends with a record terminator (not always shown in record displays), indicating that the next character in the MARC string begins a new record.

MARC 21 Record Structure

A final way to look at what makes up a MARC record is to consider how its distinct parts are organized. There are three main sections: the leader, the directory, and the fields. Table 3.1 shows the three-part structure.

(1) The *leader*, fixed at twenty-four characters (positions 0–23), is the first field in a MARC record. It provides particular information for processing the ensuing record, data such as total length, status (e.g., new, deleted, or corrected), type (e.g., books, maps, sound recordings, or name authority or subject authority), base address of data, and encoding level (full, minimal, complete, incomplete, etc.). Each specific bit of leader information is entered at a prescribed position in the leader. The leader does not need a field terminator because its length is fixed: the system is set up to "realize" that position 24 is where the directory begins.

Table 3.1 MARC 21 Record Structure

Leader	Directory	Data Fields

Table 3.2 Outline of Directory Entries

Tag	Field Length	Starting Character Position

(2) The *directory* is a computer-generated index to the locations of the control and data fields within a record. It is similar to the table of contents in a book. It begins at record position 24 and lists the various data fields in the record, giving their respective locations by starting character position. Directory data are system-computed after a record is entered—the cataloger does not have to supply them. The directory consists of a series of fixed-length (twelve characters each) entries, one for each of the fields that contain data presented later in the record. The elements in each directory entry are: the field tag (such as 100 for a personal name main entry); the field length (how many characters—letters, numbers, punctuation marks, subfield codes, and blanks—are in that field); and its starting character position in the record. A record's directory has as many of these twelve-character entries as there are fields in the record. It ends with a field terminator. Table 3.2 shows the outline of a directory entry.

(3) The *fields* contain the essence of the record, that is, cataloging, authority, classification, or holdings data. Each field is identified by a three-character numeric tag stored in the directory. The field tag identifies the nature of each field in the record: personal name main entry, corporate name main entry, title, subject, and so on. At the end of each field is a field terminator. There are two types of fields: *control fields* and *data fields.*

Control fields are numbered 00X (e.g., 001, 005, 008); they contain either a single data element or a series of fixed-length data elements identified by relative character position.

Data fields are numbered 01X–8XX; most of the fields in the range of 010–09X are for various numbers or codes (e.g., 020 for ISBN, 050 for LC call number, 082 for DDC number), while the ones in the range of 100–8XX are for bibliographic, subject, and linking information (in other words, what is usually considered cataloging information). The 9XX fields contain local data.

Two kinds of content designators are used within data fields: *indicators* and *subfield codes.* The indicators are two one-character positions containing values that interpret or supplement the data found in the field.

Not every field uses indicators; those which have not been defined are kept as blanks in the string. The subfield codes identify the data elements within the field that require separate manipulation. Each subfield code is an alphabetic or a numeric character that is preceded by a character ($ in this text) called a *delimiter*; for example, $d or $2, respectively. Each subfield delimiter and code is followed by the appropriate data, defined independently for each field.

Tables 3.3 and 3.4 show an example of a data field and its corresponding directory entry in a bibliographic record. Some fields, such as the 100 (main entry), occur only once in each record. Others, such as those for subject headings or index terms, may be repeated. Similarly, some subfields are also repeatable. The repeatability (R) or nonrepeatability (NR) of each field and subfield is indicated in the MARC 21 formats.

(a)

Table 3.3 A Variable Data Field in a Bibliographic Record

Indicators	*Subfield Code*	*Data*	*Subfield Code*	*Data*	*Field Terminator*
1 #	$a	Evans, G. Edward,	$d	1937–	@

(b)

Table 3.4 The Corresponding Directory Entry for the Variable Data Field in Table 3.3

Field Tag	*Field Length*	*Starting Character Position*
100	0029	230

What a given content designator means varies considerably from one MARC 21 format to another. This is shown in the contrast between the two tables included in the first chapter for bibliographic and authority data, respectively. Nevertheless, there are similar patterns. The schemas below, for bibliographic data, illustrate the sort of things that may be found in other formats. Fields in the *bibliographic record* are grouped into blocks identified by the first character of the tag, which normally indicates the function of the data within the record.

0XX Control information, identification and classification numbers, etc.
1XX Main entry fields
2XX Titles and title-related fields (title, edition, imprint)
3XX Physical description, etc. fields
4XX Series statement fields
5XX Note fields
6XX Subject access fields
7XX Added entry fields other than subject or series; linking fields
8XX Series added entry fields, holdings, location, etc. fields
9XX Reserved for local implementation

Within the 100, 400, 600, 700, and 800 blocks, the type of information (e.g., personal name, corporate name, uniform title, and geographic name) is often identified by the second and third characters of the tag.

X00 Personal names
X10 Corporate names
X11 Meeting names
X30 Uniform titles
X40 Bibliographic titles
X50 Topical terms
X51 Geographic names

Indicators and subfield codes are defined individually for each field. For example, the main entry personal name field (tag 100) in a bibliographic record uses the first indicator position to specify the type of personal name according to the following codes:

0—Forename
1—Surname
3—Family name

The second indicator, left as a blank, is undefined. If the main entry is in the form of a personal name, the most commonly used subfield codes are the following:

Code	*Subfield*
$a	Personal name
$b	Numeration
$c	Titles and other words associated with a name
$d	Dates associated with a name

For example, see Table 3.3. Wherever feasible, parallel content designation is used in the various formats. For example, the same subfield codes shown above are used in fields containing personal names in both the bibliographic and authority formats.

It is the coding in a MARC record that allows it to be processed by the computer for various uses and various types of display. There are many circumstances when library personnel need to see and work with fully coded records. Catalog maintenance is one, but other sectors of the library often need them too. OPAC records can be displayed in various formats and levels of detail. They do not show MARC coding, but it is the codes that make such variety possible. It is also the codes that enable many of the sophisticated search options available in today's OPACs. Thus, it can be seen that the same cataloging information, once coded, can be tailored for use in different environments and for different purposes—online catalogs, acquisitions lists, circulation records, etc. The flexibility is great: the design of each online catalog system determines what can be done with the coded catalog data.

MARC-RELATED FORMATS

In addition to the three levels of MARC 21 formats, a number of other formats have been developed by the LC to facilitate the use of MARC records in different environments. All of these standards have been developed and are maintained by the Network Development and MARC Standards Office of the Library of Congress with input from MARC and from users.

Three of these standards—MARCXML, Metadata Object Description Schema (MODS), and Metadata Authority Description Schema (MADS)—are discussed below. Because these standards are encoded in XML, a brief introduction to the markup languages used to process electronic data is in order.

Standard Generalized Markup Language (SGML)

A markup language is used to indicate how a document or text has to be structured and presented. The term has its origin in the publishing field. Before a book or journal is published, a copyeditor or "markup" person goes through the manuscript and writes instructions on the margins regarding the font, type, size, etc. for the typesetter. SGML was developed to process digital data. SGML is derived from IBM's Generalized Markup Language (GML), developed in the 1960s by Charles Goldfarb, Edward Mosher, and Raymond Lorie. By 1986, GML had been adopted by the ISO and was promulgated as "ISO 8879:1986 Information Processing—Text and office systems—Standard Generalized Markup Language (SGML)." The standard, which is rather complex, was adopted by agencies that require tremendous amounts of data to be processed from text files, notably the US Department of Defense and the Association of American Publishers. SGML is not a markup language itself but it is a meta-language that is used to define markup languages. By 1992, experiences in using markup had led researchers at the Centre européen pour la recherché nucléaire (or European Organization for Nuclear Research, now commonly referred to as the European Laboratory for Particle Physics, or just "CERN") to create the HTML, an application of SGML. HTML is a markup language designed for displaying documents on Web browsers.

SGML also serves as a meta-meta-language, which means that meta-languages can be created based on SGML. XML is an example of such an implementation of SGML.

Extensible Markup Language (XML)

XML, an instantiation or implementation of part of SGML, was developed and maintained by the W3C.[19] An important feature of XML is that it allows documents to contain data about themselves *within* the document, the same way that MARC records contain the directory. This means the data carry with them specifications that guide their processing, independent of any specific software application. XML was initiated mainly to serve as a simpler and easier-to-implement meta-markup language than SGML, with all of the necessary concepts embodied within it. The first version of XML specification was published in 1996. The current version of XML specification is version 1.1. The XML Recommendation (http://www.w3.org/TR/xmlschema11-1/) contains a set of specifications that guide the creation of XML-tagged records of information resources.

Today, XML has grown into an all-purpose and all-pervasive way to insert structure into text documents and to create flexible surrogates, or metadata, for text and other objects. The use of XML has become so pervasive that it led Catherine Ebenezer to declare: "Every serious Web technology is now expected to define its relationship to XML."[20] The characteristics of XML can be summarized briefly as follows:

- XML is a simplified implementation of SGML;
- XML consists of a subset of SGML specifications;
- Like SGML, XML is a meta-markup language for text documents;
- Unlike HTML, XML is not a markup language for indicating display options.

In other words, XML tags assign meaning to the data (e.g., <title>**Paradise Lost** </title>), while HTML tags indicate how the data are to be displayed (e.g., <b>**Paradise Lost**). Elliotte Rusty Harold and W. Scott Means summarize the purposes and benefits of XML as follows[21]:

Flexibility: XML allows users to invent the elements based on their needs.

Syntax: The XML Recommendation defines a grammar for XML documents that indicates where tags may be placed, what they must look like, which element names are legal, how attributes are attached to elements, etc.

Semantics: The markup in an XML document describes the structure of the document, that is, the document's semantics. That is, XML supports a structural and semantic markup language.

Extensibility: XML can be extended and adapted to meet many different needs.

Interoperability: Individuals or organizations may agree to use only certain tags, forming tag sets called XML applications. As a result, XML documents based on the same XML application are interoperable.

Portability: XML is a simple, well-documented, straightforward data format, offering the possibility of cross-platform, long-term data formats. XML documents are text-based and can be read with any tool that can read a text file.

Similar to HTML tags, XML tags are indicated by angled brackets “<”and “>.” Tags are case sensitive (e.g., <B> is not the same as <b>), and each starting tag (e.g., <b>) must have a corresponding ending tag (e.g.,).

Document-Type Definition and XML Schema

As mentioned earlier, XML is a meta-language. The application of XML in a particular domain, such as in libraries, is called an XML application; similarly, an XML document is a realization of an XML application. An XML application is a formal definition for a document type that conforms to the XML specification. In each XML application, the elements (tags), attributes, and structural rules that are permitted in an XML document must be specified.

There are several ways of creating an XML application. The languages for creating such applications are Document-Type Definitions (DTDs) and the XML Schema. The terms DTD or XML Schema are often used to refer to XML applications as well as to the schemas themselves. In general, the XML Schema Language provides a more precise grammar than does the DTD format. Thus, using the XML Schema is preferred in situations that require quite sophisticated rules or controls governing the elements and attributes of what is being coded. In an XML application, a formal grammar specifies which elements can be used, how those elements can be used, and what contents and attributes are valid.

Details regarding XML applications are beyond the scope of this book. Rather, the primary focus here is on XML *documents*, in other words, on instances of XML applications. By definition, an XML document is a document combining content data and an XML grammar specified in a particular XML application.

Two simple examples of XML documents are shown below. These documents contain the same content, but the first illustrates the use of a DTD, while the second shows the use of an XML Schema. The following is an example of an XML document using a DTD:

```
<?xml version “1.0” encoding “ISO-8859-1”?>
<!DOCTYPE record SYSTEM “simpleRecord.dtd”>
<record>
<title> Cataloging and classification </title>
<author>
<first_name> Lois </first_name>
<middle_name> Mai </middle_name>
<last_name> Chan </last_name>
<edition> third edition </edition>
```

```
10 <subject> cataloging </subject>
11 <subject> classification </subject>
12 </record>
```

An XML document is divided into two parts: XML *declaration* and XML *content*. In the declaration, a variety of external information, such as XML version, encoding scheme, or validation, is stated. In the example above, the first two lines constitute the declaration. The first line indicates the currently used version of XML (1.0) and the encoding schema (ISO-8859-1 character set). The second line indicates that this document is written in conformance with the syntax of the DTD described in a file called *simple Record.dtd*, and that the DTD file is located within the same directory as the XML document.

Lines 3–12 contain a mix of document content and a set of valid elements and attributes written according to the grammar described in the *simpleRecord.dtd* file in the example. Every XML document must have a single root element that contains all document content. In this example, the content begins with the third line where the root element <record> of the XML document is declared. Under the root element, four nested elements (*title, author, edition,* and *subject*) are declared. Under the *author* element, there is another nested hierarchical structure showing the subelements *first_name*, *middle_name*, and *last_name*. There are two instances of the *subject* element. Each element must be enclosed within a pair of opening and closing tags, for instance, the pair of <title> as an opening tag and </title> as a closing tag, with the element content given between the tags. An element name indicates what the element content is. For example, the *title* element contains the title "cataloging and classification."

The following shows the same XML document using an XML Schema:

```
<?xml version "1.0" encoding "ISO-8859-1"?>
<record>
xmlns:xsi "http://www.w3.org/2001/XMLSchema-instance"
xsi:noNamespaceSchemaLocation "book.xsd">
<title> Cataloging and classification </title>
<author>
<first_name>Lois </first_name>
<middle_name> Mai </middle_name>
<last_name> Chan </last_name>
<edition> third edition </edition>
<subject> cataloging </subject>
<subject> classification </subject>
</record>
```

In this example, the first line indicates that this is an XML document conforming to XML version 1.0 and that the encoding schema is the ISO-8859-1. According to the XML Schema Recommendation ("http://www.w3.org/2001/XMLSchema"), all possible sets of elements and attributes for an XML application should be predefined and predeclared in *namespaces*, and the links between these elements and attributes and their corresponding namespaces must be explicitly or implicitly stated in the XML document. (A namespace is the equivalent of the name of a table in relational databases. The namespace, among other things, guides computer programs parsing the record to know the correct XML Schema for a given element. This is useful because once an XML Schema has been created, it is then easy to share it.) Such links, with the prefix *xsi,* indicate which namespace is to be used for which element and/or attribute. The XML Schema Language specifies two special namespaces: in the first one ("http://www.w3.org/2001/XMLSchema"), all standard schema elements are defined; and in the other ("http://www.w3.org/2001/XMLSchema-instance"), four attributes are defined. For example, the "noNamespaceSchemaLocation" attribute in Line 4 is one of the four attributes.

In the example above, two attributes are specified in the top element *record*, as shown in Lines 3 and 4. Line 3 begins with the term *xmlns*. "xmlns" stands for "XML Namespace."

The combination of "xmlns:xsi" is a reserved word in the XML Schema Language for referencing a namespace specified in the ensuing URI, in this case "http://www.w3.org/2001/XMLSchema-instance." This reference means that all four attributes specified in the particular namespace can be used within the record element or any attributes prefixed *xsi*. In Line 4, the "noNamespaceSchemaLocation" attribute is declared, which gives the location of the XML Schema to be used in this document. More specifically, it means that the designated XML Schema (*book.xsd*) is to be used for elements that are not included in any namespace. In this example, since no other XML Schema is declared anywhere else for the five different elements (record, title, author, edition, and subject), the file *book. xsd* will be used for the attributes of the elements.

More recently, DTDs have been replaced by XML Schemas because they are considered more powerful and richer than DTDs, they are written in XML, and they support data types and namespaces.

To summarize, SGML is a set of abstract specifications for creating markup languages, such as XML for marking up the *structure* of the data and HTML for marking up the *presentation* of data. Since it does not contain fixed sets of terms (elements and attributes) or their relationships, the creators of SGML applications can build selected sets of elements and attributes for their particular domains. This has led to numerous SGML/XML applications for different domains. The flexibility of SGML-based applications enables documents to be encoded in unlimited ways. There is no reason why, for instance, an XML Schema for literature could not have both a tag called "<protagonist>" for adult readers and a tag called "<main_character>" for young adult readers. XML provides a flexible and adaptive means of storing, structuring, and identifying information, without prescribing how the information is displayed or used. Additional tools, such as eXtensible Stylesheet Language (XSL) and Cascading Style Sheets (CSS), are used for processing and manipulating XML data and for handling the proper display of XML-tagged data.

The main features of XML include the following:

- XML is hierarchical, with a root element and parent and child elements.
- An XML Schema is usually stored in a separate file and then is associated with XML documents by references to namespaces.
- There is no fixed or standard set of valid elements and attributes for an XML application; the developer can create them.
- XML is an open standard (nonproprietary), sharable by all.
- Data to be encoded in an XML document can be of any type.
- Data encoded in XML are valid and well-formed.
- The syntax of XML is easily processed by software and machines, because many programming languages, especially Java, include resources (called "libraries") for computer programs to parse XML records.
- Natural language tags make XML understandable to humans.
- Record content data are completely separate from presentation or display instructions.
- Creating and using shared XML Schemas increases interoperability (sharing) of the data.

XML in Library Applications

XML makes it possible to update legacy XML-based cataloging and metadata records and to create new XML-based text records that can be searched across various database systems. Furthermore, the well-structured text in XML-coded records makes catalog and metadata records amenable to full-text parsing and other techniques found in information-retrieval systems.

Integrated Library Systems (ILS) can integrate access to all sorts of materials and resource types. Since the record structure of an XML-coded record is open and available (i.e., the schema itself is available along with any records that have been tagged following its provisions), it is possible to create metasearch systems and to incorporate data based on multiple metadata schemes within a single record. For instance, OCLC's WorldCat accepts both MARC and DC tags.

In the end, the power of XML enables librarians to convert MARC data to be used in an XML environment and to adjust document content to adapt to new devices and new user needs. Use of XML also facilitates the easy transfer of data between systems.

The following sections discuss the application of SGML and XML to standards for structuring and processing catalog and metadata records.

MARCXML

XML, originally designed to meet the challenges of large-scale electronic publishing, is now also playing an important role in the exchange of a wide variety of cataloging data and metadata on the Web. To enable MARC users to work with MARC data in the Web environment and in ways specific to their needs, the Network Development and MARC Standards Office of the Library of Congress has developed a framework called MARCXML, by casting MARC data in an XML framework. Based on XML, MARCXML enables the representation of MARC 21 data in an XML environment. It allows users to work with MARC data in ways specific to their needs. The framework itself includes many components such as schemas, stylesheets, and software tools. Along with the MARCXML schema, LC also provides a variety of XML tools, including stylesheets for transforming and displaying the data.[22] The tools LC provides also permit libraries to convert their old MARC records to MARCXML, to MODS, or to DC or other metadata records.

The MARCXML schema retains the semantics of MARC 21. However, some structural elements in MARC 21, such as the length of field and starting position of field data in directory entries, are not needed in an XML record. MARC's leader and the control fields are treated as data strings, and its fields are treated as subelements. Nevertheless, all of the essential data in a MARC record can be converted and expressed in XML. Figure 3.3 shows the same work encoded in the MARC 21 bibliographic format and in MARCXML. Figure 3.3(a) is the complete MARC 21 record for Evans' *Management Basics for Information Professionals*. Figure 3.3(b) is the MARCXML record for the same work. (As all XML records are required to do, the first line of the XML record, <?xml version "1.0" encoding "UTF-8" ?>, declares the XML version and the encoding schema. Line 2 indicates that the root of this record is "record." The second part of this line gives information about the XML Namespace: http://www.loc.gov/MARC21/slim.)

Metadata Object Description Schema (MODS)

The MODS[23] is a metadata schema for creating original resource description records that consist of selected data from the MARC 21 Bibliographic Format. For encoding, it uses XML.

(a)

```
000     01795cam a22003618i 450
001     841199101
005     20140306113219.0
008     130422s2013 ilu b 001 0 eng
010     2013010868
040     DLC $b eng $e rda $c DLC
020     9781555709099 $q acid-free paper
020     1555709095 $q acid-free paper
043     n-us---
050 00  Z678 $b .E9 2013
082 00  025.1 $2 23
100 1   Evans, G. Edward, $d 1937-
245 10  Management basics for information professionals / $c G. Edward Evans, Camila
        A. Alire.
250     Third edition.
264 1   Chicago : $b Neal-Schuman, an imprint of the American Library Association, $c
        2013.
300     xvii, 577 pages ; $b 23 cm
336     text $b txt $2 rdacontent
337     unmediated $b n $2 rdamedia
338     volume $b nc $2 rdacarrier
504     Includes bibliographical references and index.
505 0   Operating environment -- Legal issues and library management -- The planning
        process -- Power, accountability, and responsibility -- Delegating -- Decision
        making -- Communicating -- Changing and innovating -- Assessment,
        quality control, and operations -- Marketing -- Motivating -- Leading -- Building
        teams -- Addressing diversity -- Staffing -- Managing money -- Managing
        technology -- Managing and planning physical facilities -- Ethics -- Planning
        your career.
650 0   Library administration $z United States.
650 0   Information services $z United States $x Management.
700 1   Alire, Camila A.
```

(b)

```
<?xml version=”1.0” encoding=”UTF-8” standalone=”no”?>
<record xmlns=”http://www.loc.gov/MARC21/slim”>
<leader>00000cam a2200000 i 4500</leader>
<controlfield tag=”001”>841199101</controlfield>
<controlfield tag=”008”>130422s2013 ilua b 001 0 eng </controlfield>
<datafield ind1=” “ ind2=” “ tag=”010”>
<subfield code=”a”> 2013010868</subfield>
</datafield>
<datafield ind1=” “ ind2=” “ tag=”020”>
<subfield code=”a”>9781555709099 (alk. paper)</subfield>
</datafield>
<datafield ind1=” “ ind2=” “ tag=”020”>
<subfield code=”a”>1555709095 (alk. paper)</subfield>
</datafield>
```

Figure 3.3 Evans, G. Edward. (2013). *Management Basics for Information Professionals.* 3rd ed.: a MARC 21 record (a) and MARCXML record (b).

```
<datafield ind1=”1” ind2=” “ tag=”100”>
<subfield code=”a”>Evans, G. Edward,</subfield>
<subfield code=”d”>1937-</subfield>
</datafield>
<datafield ind1=”1” ind2=”0” tag=”245”>
<subfield code=”a”>Management basics for information professionals /</subfield>
<subfield code=”c”>G. Edward Evans, Camila A. Alire.</subfield>
</datafield>
<datafield ind1=” “ ind2=” “ tag=”250”>
<subfield code=”a”>Third edition.</subfield>
</datafield>
<datafield ind1=” “ ind2=”1” tag=”264”>
<subfield code=”a”>Chicago :</subfield>
<subfield code=”b”>Neal-Schuman, an imprint of the American Library Association,</subfield>
<subfield code=”c”>2013.</subfield>
</datafield>
<datafield ind1=” “ ind2=” “ tag=”300”>
<subfield code=”a”>xvii, 577 pages :</subfield>
<subfield code=”b”>illustrations ;</subfield>
<subfield code=”c”>23 cm</subfield>
</datafield>
<datafield ind1=”0” ind2=” “ tag=”505”>
<subfield code=”a”>Operating environment -- Legal issues and library management -- The planning process -- Power, accountability, and responsibility -- Delegating -- Decision making -- Communicating -- Changing and innovating -- Assessment, quality control, and operations -- Marketing -- Motivating -- Leading -- Building teams -- Addressing diversity -- Staffing -- Managing money -- Managing technology -- Managing and planning physical facilities -- Ethics -- Planning your career.</subfield>
</datafield>
<datafield ind1=” “ ind2=”0” tag=”650”>
<subfield code=”a”>Library administration</subfield>
<subfield code=”z”>United States.</subfield>
</datafield>
<datafield ind1=” “ ind2=”0” tag=”650”>
<subfield code=”a”>Information services</subfield>
<subfield code=”z”>United States</subfield>
<subfield code=”x”>Management.</subfield>
</datafield>
<datafield ind1=”1” ind2=” “ tag=”700”>
<subfield code=”a”>Alire, Camila A.</subfield>
</datafield>
</record>
```


Figure 3.3 *Continued*

MODS consists of a subset of twenty bibliographic elements based on the MARC 21 Format for Bibliographic Data, selected specifically for supporting the description of electronic resources and objects. As such, it is a rich, library-oriented XML metadata schema. Yet, although it is a simpler schema than the MARC 21 Bibliographic Format, it retains compatibility with MARC 21. It also provides multiple linking functions.

For encoding, MODS uses language-based tags rather than numeric ones. The top-level MODS elements include the following:

titleInfo
name
typeOfResource
genre
originInfo
language
physicalDescription
abstract
tableOfContents
targetAudience
note
subject
classification
relatedItem
identifier
location
accessCondition
part
extension
recordInfo

There are a great number of subelements and attributes for MODS listed on the LC' web site (www.loc.gov/standards/mods/). Figure 3.4 contains the MODS record for Evans' *Management Basics for Information Profes sionals.*

The following example, based on the title field (MARC tag 245) only, shows the parallel and coordination among MARC, MARCXML, and MODS:

MARC

245 14$a**The heart of Midlothian** / $c **Sir Walter Scott**

MARCXML

<datafield tag "'245" ind1 "1" ind2 "'4">
<subfield code "a">**The heart of Midlothian**</subfield>
<subfield code "c">**Sir Walter Scott**</subfield>
</datafield>

```
<mods xmlns:xlink=”http://www.w3.org/1999/xlink” xmlns:xsi=”http://www.w3.org/2001/
XMLSchemainstance” xmlns=”http://www.loc.gov/mods/v3”version=”3.5”xsi:schemaLocation=
”http://www.loc.gov/mods/v3 http://www.loc.gov/standards/mods/v3/mods-3-5.xsd”>
<titleInfo>
<title>Management basics for information professionals /</title>
<name type=”personal” authorityURI=”http://id.loc.gov/authorities/names” valueURI=”http://
id.loc.gov/authorities/names/n78091996”>
<namePart> Evans, G. Edward, </namePart>
<namePart type=”date”>1937-</namePart>
<role>
<roleTerm type=”text”>creator</roleTerm>
</role>
</name>
<name type=”personal” authorityURI=”http://id.loc.gov/authorities/names” valueURI=”http://
id.loc.gov/authorities/names/n85829996 “>
<namePart> Alire, Camila A.<namePart>
<role>
<roleTerm type=”text”>creator</roleTerm>
</role>
</name>
<typeOfResource>text</typeOfResource>
<originInfo eventType=”publication”>
<place>
<placeTerm authority=”marccountry” type=”code” authorityURI=”http://id.loc.gov/vocabulary/
countries”valueURI=”http://id.loc.gov/vocabulary/countries/ilu”>ilu</placeTerm>
</place>
<place>
<placeTerm type=”text”>Chicago</placeTerm>
</place>
<publisher> Neal-Schuman, an imprint of the American Library Association,</publisher>
<dateIssued>2013</dateIssued>
<dateIssued encoding=”marc”>2013</dateIssued>
<issuance>monographic</issuance>
</originInfo>
<language>
<languageTerm authority=”iso639-2b” type=”code” authorityURI=”http://id.loc.gov/vocabulary/
iso639-2” valueURI=”http://id.loc.gov/vocabulary/iso639-2/eng”>eng</languageTerm>
</language>
<physicalDescription>
<form authority=”marcform”>print</form>
<extent> xvii, 577 pages : illustrations ; 23 cm</extent>
</physicalDescription>
<note type=”statement of responsibility”> G. Edward Evans, Camila A. Alire.</note>
<note type=”bibliography”>Includes bibliographical references and index.</note>
<tableOfContents> Operating environment -- Legal issues and library management -- The
planning process -- Power, accountability, and responsibility -- Delegating -- Decision making
-- Communicating -- Changing and innovating -- Assessment, quality control, and operations
-- Marketing -- Motivating -- Leading -- Building teams -- Addressing diversity -- Staffing --
```


Figure 3.4 MODS record for Evans, G. Edward. (2013). *Management Basics for Information Professionals*. 3rd ed.

```
Managing money -- Managing technology -- Managing and planning physical facilities -- Ethics
-- Planning your career.
</tableOfContents>
<subject authority="lcsh" authorityURI="http://id.loc.gov/authorities/subjects">
<topic valueURI="http://id.loc.gov/authorities/subjects/sh85076655"> Library administration</
topic>
<geographic valueURI="http://id.loc.gov/authorities/names/n78095330">United States</geo-
graphic>
</subject>
<subject authority="lcsh" authorityURI="http://id.loc.gov/authorities/subjects">
<topic valueURI="http://id.loc.gov/authorities/subjects/sh00006253"> Information services </
topic>
<geographic valueURI="http://id.loc.gov/authorities/names/n78095330">United States</geo-
graphic>
<topic valueURI="http://id.loc.gov/authorities/subjects/sh2002007911"> Management</topic>
</subject>
<classification authority="lcc"> Z678 .E9 2013</classification>
<classification edition="23" authority="ddc">025.1 </classification>
<identifier type="isbn">9781555709099 acid-free paper</identifier>
<identifier type="isbn">1555709095 $q acid-free paper</identifier>
<identifier type="lccn">2013010868</identifier>
<recordInfo>
<descriptionStandard>rda</descriptionStandard>
<recordContentSource>DLC</recordContentSource>
<recordCreationDate encoding="marc">20130422</recordCreationDate>
<recordChangeDate encoding="iso8601">20140306113219.0</recordChangeDate>
<recordIdentifier>841199101</recordIdentifier>
</recordInfo>
</mods>
```

Figure 3.4 *Continued*

MODS

<titleInfo>
<nonSort>**The**</nonSort><title>**heart of Midlothian**</title>
</titleInfo>
<note type "statementOfResponsibility">**Sir Walter Scott**</note>

Metadata Authority Description Schema (MADS)

MADS[24] is an XML Schema for an authority element set that may be used to provide metadata about agents (people, organizations), events, and terms (topics, geographics, genres, etc.). MADS records may also include elements such as topical, temporal, genre, geographic, or occupation.

MADS is compatible with the MARC 21 Authorities format. It was intended to be a companion to MODS, and thus was designed to be as

```
<mads:mads xmlns:mads=”http://www.loc.gov/mads/v2” xmlns:xlink=”http://www.
w3.org/1999/xlink” xmlns:xsi=”http://www.w3.org/2001/XMLSchema-instance”version=”2.0”
xsi:schemaLocation=”http://www.loc.gov/mads/v2 http://www.loc.gov/standards/mads/mads-2-
0.xsd”>
<mads:authority geographicSubdivision=”not applicable”>
<mads:name type=”personal” authority=”naf”>
<mads:namePart> Evans, Edward G.</mads:namePart>
<mads:namePart type=”date”>1916</mads:namePart>
</mads:name>
</mads:authority>
<mads:note type=”source”>nuc86-76260: Reimer, B. Teaching the experience of music, 1973 $b
(hdg. on OOxM rept.: Evans, Edward G., 1916- ; usage: Edward G. Evans, Jr.)</mads:note>
<mads:note type=”source”>Washington post, 6/7/91 (Stan Getz, 64; b. 2/2/27, Philadelphia; d.
6/6/91, Los Angeles)
</mads:note>
<mads:note type=”source”>LC data base, 3/4/87 $b (hdg.: Evans, Edward G., 1916- ; usage:
Edward G. Evans, Jr.)</mads:note>
<mads:identifier type=”lccn”>n 87812300</mads:identifier>
<mads:gender>
<mads:genderTerm>male</mads:genderTerm>
</mads:gender>
</mads:extension>
<mads:recordInfo>
<mads:recordContentSource authority=”marcorg”>DLC</mads:recordContentSource>
<mads:recordChangeDate encoding=”iso8601”> 19870319120758.3</mads:recordChangeDate>
<mads:recordIdentifier source=”DLC”>n87812300</mads:recordIdentifier>
<mads:languageOfCataloging>
<mads:languageTerm authority=”iso639-2b” type=”code”>eng</mads:languageTerm>
</mads:languageOfCataloging>
<mads:descriptionStandard>aacr2</mads:descriptionStandard>
</mads:recordInfo>
</mads:mads>
```


Figure 3.5 MADS record for a personal name heading.

consistent and compatible with MODS as possible. The relationship between MADS and MARC 21 Authorities parallels that between MODS and MARC 21 Bibliographic.

MADS also uses language-based tags. A MADS record contains the same basic components as found in a MARC authority record:

Authorized heading
Related heading(s) (see also reference(s))—attributes:

- earlier
- later
- parentOrg
- broader

```
<mads:mads xmlns:mads=”http://www.loc.gov/mads/v2” xmlns:xlink=”http://www.
w3.org/1999/xlink” xmlns:xsi=”http://www.w3.org/2001/XMLSchema-instance”version=”2.0”
xsi:schemaLocation=”http://www.loc.gov/mads/v2 http://www.loc.gov/standards/mads/mads-2-
0.xsd”>
<mads:authority>
<mads:topic authority=”lcsh”>Management</mads:topic>
</mads:authority>
<mads:related type=”other”>
<mads:topic>Industrial relations</mads:topic>
</mads:related>
<mads:related type=”other”>
<mads:topic> Organization</mads:topic>
</mads:related>
<mads:variant type=”other”>
<mads:topic> Administration</mads:topic>
</mads:variant>
<note>subdivision Management under types of industries, industrial plants and processes,
special activities, resources, etc. and under names of corporate bodies, including individual gov-
ernment agencies, galleries, museums, parks, etc.; also subdivision Administration under types of
institutions and names of individual institutions, especially libraries, health and social services,
etc.; also subdivision Politics and government under names of countries, cities, etc.; and phrase
headings for specific types of management or administration, e.g. Industrial management; Police
administration</note>
<note>Here are entered works on the principles of management as a discipline. Works on the
application of systematic, logical, and mathematical methods and techniques to the solution of
problems of management are entered under Management science.</note>
<note>Note under Management science</note>
<mads:identifier type=”lccn”>sh 85080336</mads:identifier>
<mads:recordInfo>
<mads:recordContentSource authority=”marcorg”>DLC</mads:recordContentSource>
<mads:recordChangeDate encoding=”iso8601”>19890524110202.3</mads:recordChangeDate>
<mads:recordIdentifier source=”DLC”>sh85080336</mads:recordIdentifier>
</mads:recordInfo>
</mads:mads>
```

Figure 3.6 MADS record for a subject heading.

narrower
etc.

Variant heading(s) (see reference(s))—attributes:
equivalent
acronym
abbreviation
translation
etc.

Other elements (e.g., notes, affiliation, url, identifier, etc.)

Examples of MADS records are shown in Figures 3.5 and 3.6.

Bibliographic Framework (BIBFRAME)

With the implementation of FRBR family models and the new RDA description standard, many saw several limitations in MARC 21, and discussions on the future of MARC called for the development of a new way to represent and exchange bibliographic data. The new way would have to be oriented toward the Web and linked-data environment, use enhanced linking and semantic Web standards, allow for easy integration of catalog data into Web tools (including Web search engines), and allow the use and reuse of bibliographic data by other applications that use Web technologies. As a response to this call, the Network Development and MARC Standards Office of the Library of Congress launched the Bibliographic Framework Initiative in May 2011; a year later, it contracted Zepheira, an independent company, to review other related initiatives, explore the translation of bibliographic data into linked data, develop tools and services, and design a model that will allow alternative approaches to bibliographic data representation. The proposed new model, BIBFRAME goes beyond a simple replacement of the MARC format or an alternative encoding system.[25] It is designed to differentiate between conceptual content and physical/digital manifestations, identify entities without ambiguity, and place emphasis on relationships between and among entities.

Four high-level classes or entities are defined in the BIBFRAME Model: Work, Instance, Authority, and Annotation. The BIBFRAME Vocabulary is a set of defined classes and properties that function like the defined elements and attributes of MARC. Classes identify types of BIBFRAME resources, similar to a MARC field. Properties allow further description of a resource, like MARC subfields, and more specifically identify aspects of the concept described in a field. As of this writing, BIBFRAME is still in the experimental phase of development and testing, with a small group of libraries joining the Early Experimenters group to test and provide feedback on the BIBFRAME Implementation Testbed initiative.[26]

Figure 3.7 is a BIBFRAME transformation of the MARCXML record for Evans' *Management Basics for Information Professionals* (see Figure 3.3[b]), using the MARC to BIBFRAME Transformation Service.[27]

```
<rdf:RDF>
<bf:Work rdf:about=“http://bibframe.org/resources/Hbh1422331522/841199101”>
    <rdf:type rdf:resource=“http://bibframe.org/vocab/Text”/>
    <bf:authorizedAccessPoint>Evans, G. Edward, 1937- Management basics for information
    professionals</bf:authorizedAccessPoint>
    <bf:workTitle rdf:resource=“http://bibframe.org/resources/Hbh1422331522/841199101title5”/>
```

Figure 3.7 BIBFRAME resource.

```
    <bf:creator rdf:resource="http://bibframe.org/resources/Hbh1422331522/841199101person6"/>
    <bf:contributor rdf:resource="http://bibframe.org/resources/Hbh1422331522/841199101per
    son7"/>
    <bf:language rdf:resource="http://id.loc.gov/vocabulary/languages/eng"/>
    <bf:subject rdf:resource="http://bibframe.org/resources/Hbh1422331522/841199101topic9"/>
    <bf:subject rdf:resource="http://bibframe.org/resources/Hbh1422331522/841199101topic10"/>
    <bf:derivedFrom rdf:resource="http://bibframe.org/resources/Hbh1422331522/841199101.
    marcxml.xml"/>
    <bf:authorizedAccessPoint xml:lang="x-bf-hash">alirecamilaaevansgedward1937managem
    entbasicsforinformationprofessionalsengworktext</bf:authorizedAccessPoint>
</bf:Work>
<bf:Instance rdf:about="http://bibframe.org/resources/Hbh1422331522/841199101instance14">
    <bf:title>Management basics for information professionals (alk. paper)</bf:title>
    <bf:isbn10 rdf:resource="http://isbn.example.org/1555709095"/>
    <bf:isbn13 rdf:resource="http://isbn.example.org/9781555709099"/>
    <rdf:type rdf:resource="http://bibframe.org/vocab/Monograph"/>
    <bf:instanceTitle rdf:resource="http://bibframe.org/resources/Hbh1422331522/841199101
    title20"/>
    <bf:publication><bf:Provider><bf:providerName><bf:Organization><bf:label>Neal-Sc
    human, an imprint of the American Library Association</bf:label></bf:Organization></
    bf:providerName>
    <bf:providerPlace><bf:Place><bf:label>Chicago</bf:label></bf:Place></bf:providerPlace>
    <bf:providerDate>2013</bf:providerDate></bf:Provider></bf:publication>
    <bf:modeOfIssuance>single unit</bf:modeOfIssuance>
    <bf:dimensions>23 cm</bf:dimensions>
    <bf:illustrationNote>illustrations ;</bf:illustrationNote>
    <bf:titleStatement>Management basics for information professionals</bf:titleStatement>
    <bf:edition>Third edition.</bf:edition>
    <bf:providerStatement>Chicago : Neal-Schuman, an imprint of the American Library Asso-
    ciation, 2013.</bf:providerStatement>
    <bf:contentsNote>Operating environment -- Legal issues and library management -- The
    planning process -- Power, accountability, and responsibility -- Delegating -- Decision
    making -- Communicating -- Changing and innovating -- Assessment, quality control, and
    operations -- Marketing -- Motivating -- Leading -- Building teams -- Addressing diversity
    -- Staffing -- Managing money -- Managing technology -- Managing and planning physical
    facilities -- Ethics -- Planning your career.</bf:contentsNote>
    <bf:lccn><bf:Identifier><bf:identifierValue>2013010868</bf:identifierValue><bf
    :identifierScheme rdf:resource="http://id.loc.gov/vocabulary/identifiers/lccn"/></
    bf:Identifier></bf:lccn><bf:derivedFrom rdf:resource="http://bibframe.org/resources/
    Hbh1422331522/841199101.marcxml.xml"/><bf:instanceOf rdf:resource="http://bibframe.
    org/resources/Hbh1422331522/841199101"/>
</bf:Instance>
<bf:Annotation rdf:about="http://bibframe.org/resources/Hbh1422331522/841199101annotation13">
    <bf:derivedFrom rdf:resource="http://bibframe.org/resources/Hbh1422331522/841199101.
    marcxml.xml"/>
    <bf:descriptionConventions rdf:resource="http://id.loc.gov/vocabulary/descriptionConven-
    tions/isbd"/>
    <bf:generationProcess>DLC transform-tool:2015-01-16-T11:00:00</bf:generationProcess>
    <bf:annotates rdf:resource="http://bibframe.org/resources/Hbh1422331522/841199101"/>
</bf:Annotation>
```

Figure 3.7 *Continued*

```
<bf:Title rdf:about="http://bibframe.org/resources/Hbh1422331522/841199101title5">
    <bf:titleValue>Management basics for information professionals</bf:titleValue></bf:Title>
    <bf:Person rdf:about="http://bibframe.org/resources/Hbh1422331522/841199101person
    6"><bf:label>Evans, G. Edward, 1937-</bf:label><bf:authorizedAccessPoint>Evans, G.
    Edward, 1937-</bf:authorizedAccessPoint><bf:hasAuthorityrdf:resource="http://id.loc.
    gov/authorities/names/n78091996"/></bf:Person>
    <bf:Person rdf:about="http://bibframe.org/resources/Hbh1422331522/841199101person
    7"><bf:label>Alire, Camila A.</bf:label><bf:authorizedAccessPoint>Alire, Camila A.</
    bf:authorizedAccessPoint>
    <bf:hasAuthority rdf:resource="http://id.loc.gov/authorities/names/n85829996"/></
    bf:Person>
    <bf:Topic rdf:about="http://bibframe.org/resources/Hbh1422331522/841199101topic9">
    <bf:authorizedAccessPoint>Library administration--United States</
    bf:authorizedAccessPoint> <bf:label>Library administration--United States</bf:label>
    <bf:hasAuthority rdf:resource="http://id.loc.gov/authorities/subjects/sh2009129720"/></
    bf:Topic>
    <bf:Topic rdf:about="http://bibframe.org/resources/Hbh1422331522/841199101to
    pic10"> <bf:authorizedAccessPoint>Information services--United States--Management</
    bf:authorizedAccessPoint> <bf:label>Information services--United States--Manage-
    ment</bf:label> <bf:hasAuthority><madsrdf:Authority><rdf:type rdf:resource="http://
    www.loc.gov/mads/rdf/v1#ComplexSubject"/> <madsrdf:authoritativeLabel>In
    formation services--United States--Management</madsrdf:authoritativeLabel>
    <madsrdf:isMemberOfMADSScheme rdf:resource="http://id.loc.gov/authorities/sub-
    jects"/></madsrdf:Authority></bf:hasAuthority></bf:Topic>
    <bf:Title rdf:about="http://bibframe.org/resources/Hbh1422331522/841199101title20">
    <bf:titleValue>Management basics for information professionals</bf:titleValue></bf:Title>
</rdf:RDF>
```

Figure 3.7 *Continued*

OTHER METADATA RECORDS ENCODED IN SGML AND XML

SGML and XML are also used to encode metadata records. The content definitions of some of the widely used metadata schemas are given in chapter 4. The following examples show metadata records encoded in SGML or XML.

Dublin Core (DC)

The example in Figure 3.8, extracted from OCLC's Connexion, shows the XML version of the unqualified DC record for Evans' *Management Basics for Information Professionals*. In this application, the prefix "rdf: RDF xmlns:rdf" is used as the reference to the URI of the namespace.

Encoded Archival Description (EAD)

Figure 3.9 contains an example of a fully encoded <eadheader> element.[28]

```
<?xml version=”1.0”?>
<rdf:RDF xmlns:rdf=”http://www.w3.org/1999/02/22-rdf-syntax-ns#”
xmlns:dc=”http://purl.org/dc/elements/1.0/”
xmlns:dcq=”http://purl.org/dc/qualifiers/1.0/”>
<rdf:Description about=”2013010868”>
<dc:title>Management basics for information professionals /</dc:title>
<dc:coverage>n-us---</dc:coverage>
<dc:creator>Evans, G. Edward, 1937-</dc:creator>
<dc:format>xvii, 577 pages : illustrations ; 23 cm</dc:format>
<dc:contributor>Alire, Camila A.</dc:contributor>
<dc:date>2013</dc:date>
<dc:description>Third edition.</dc:description>
<dc:description>Operating environment -- Legal issues and library management -- The planning
process -- Power, accountability, and responsibility -- Delegating -- Decision making -- Commu-
nicating -- Changing and innovating -- Assessment, quality control, and operations -- Marketing
-- Motivating -- Leading -- Building teams -- Addressing diversity -- Staffing -- Managing money
-- Managing technology -- Managing and planning physical facilities -- Ethics -- Planning your
career.</dc:description>
<dc:identifier>2013010868</dc:identifier>
<dc:identifier>9781555709099 (alk. paper)</dc:identifier>
<dc:identifier>1555709095 (alk. paper)</dc:identifier>
<dc:language>eng</dc:language>
<dc:subject> <rdf:Description> <dcq:subjectQualifier>class</dcq:subjectQualifier>
<rdf:value>Z678 .E9 2013</rdf:value> </rdf:Description> </dc:subject>
<dc:subject> <rdf:Description> <dcq:subjectQualifier>class</dcq:subjectQualifier>
<rdf:value>025.1</rdf:value> </rdf:Description> </dc:subject>
<dc:subject> <rdf:Description> <dcq:subjectQualifier>topical</dcq:subjectQualifier>
<rdf:value>Library administration--United States.</rdf:value> </rdf:Description> </dc:subject>
<dc:subject> <rdf:Description> <dcq:subjectQualifier>topical</dcq:subjectQualifier>
<rdf:value>Information services--United States--Management.</rdf:value> </rdf:Description>
</dc:subject>
<dc:type>Text data</dc:type>
</rdf:Description>
</rdf:RDF>
```

Figure 3.8 Encoded Dublin Core record.

```
<ead xmlns=”urn:isbn:1-931666-22-9” xmlns:xsi=”http://www.w3.org/2001/XMLSchema-
instance” xsi:schemaLocation=”urn:isbn:1-931666-22-9 http://www.loc.gov/ead/ead.
xsd” id=”mferd56e2”>
   <eadheader repositoryencoding=”iso15511
   countryencoding=”iso3166-1” scriptencoding=”iso15924” dateencoding=”iso8601”langencod
   ing=”iso639-2b” id=”mferd56e3”>
   <eadid mainagencycode=”US-DLC” countrycode=”US” identifier=”hdl:loc.mss/eadmss.ms01
   3115”encodinganalog=”856$u”>http://hdl.loc.gov/loc.mss/eadmss.ms013115</eadid>
   <filedesc>
```

Figure 3.9 Encoded EAD header.

```
<titlestmt>
  <titleproper>Hayes, Hollister, and Kelman Families Papers</titleproper>
  <subtitle>A Finding Aid to the Collection in the Library of Congress</subtitle>
  <author>Prepared by Laura J. Kells with the assistance of Tammi Taylor</author>
</titlestmt>
<publicationstmt>
  <publisher>Manuscript Division, Library of Congress</publisher>
  <address>
    <addressline>Washington, D.C.</addressline>
  </address>
  <date normal=”2013” era=”ce” calendar=”gregorian”>2013</date>
</publicationstmt>
<notestmt>
  <note>
    <p>Contact information: <extref xmlns:xlink=”http://www.w3.org/1999/
    xlink” xlink:type=”simple” xlink:show=”new” xlink:actuate=”onRequest”xlink:hre
    f=”http://hdl.loc.gov/loc.mss/mss.contact”>http://hdl.loc.gov/loc.mss/mss.contact</
    extref></p>
  </note>
  <note id=”lccnNote”>
    <p>Catalog Record:
    <extref xmlns:xlink=”http://www.w3.org/1999/xlink” xlink:href=”http://lccn.loc.gov/
    mm2012085747” xlink:actuate=”onRequest”xlink:title=”MARC record for collec-
    tion” xlink:type=”simple”>http://lccn.loc.gov/mm2012085747</extref></p>
  </note>
</notestmt>
</filedesc>
  <profiledesc>
    <creation>Finding aid encoded by Library of Congress Manuscript Division,
    <date normal=”2013” era=”ce” calendar=”gregorian”>2013</date>
    </creation>
  <langusage>Finding aid written in <language>English.</language></langusage>
  </profiledesc>
</eadheader>
…
</ead>
```

Figure 3.9 *Continued*

```
<Product>
  Record metadata
  Product numbers
  <DescriptiveDetail>
    Product form
    Product parts (for multipleitem products)
    Collection
    Product title
    Authorship
```

Figure 3.10 Encoded ONIX record.

Conference detail
Edition
Language
Extents
Illustrations and ancillary content
Subject
Audience
</DescriptiveDetail>
Text content
Cited content
Supporting resources
Prizes
</CollateralDetail>
<ContentDetail>
Content item detail
</ContentDetail>
<PublishingDetail>
Imprint and publisher
"Global" publishing status and copyright
Sales rights and restrictions
</PublishingDetail>
<RelatedMaterial>
Related works
Related products
</RelatedMaterial>
<ProductSupply>
Market Group
Market publishing status
Supply detail: availability and price within market
</ProductSupply>

Figure 3.10 *Continued*

Online Information Exchange

Figure 3.10 shows a portion of an Online Information Exchange (ONIX) record using ONIX Release 3.0, the product record, containing bibliographic information about a book.[29]

NOTES

1. Library of Congress. (1974–1983). *Library of Congress Name Headings with References*. Washington, DC: Library of Congress.
2. Program for Cooperative Cataloging (PCC). (n.d.). *About the PCC*. Retrieved from http://www.loc.gov/aba/pcc/about/.
3. Kilgour, F. G. (1977). Ohio College Library Center. In A. Kent, H. Lancour, and J. E. Daily (Eds.), *Encyclopedia of Library and Information Science* (Vol. 20, pp. 346–47). New York, NY: Marcel Dekker.

4. OCLC. (2015). *History of the OCLC Research Library Partnership*. Retrieved from http://www.oclc.org/research/partnership/history.html.

5. OCLC. (2015). *WorldCat Cataloging Partners*. Retrieved from https://www.oclc.org/cataloging-partners.en.html.

6. Library of Congress. (2000). *MARC 21 Specifications for Record Structure, Character sets, and Exchange Media*. Retrieved from http://www.loc.gov/marc/specifications/spechome.html.

7. OCLC. (n.d.). *OCLC-MARC Records: Record Structure*. Retrieved from http://www.oclc.org/content/dam/support/worldcat/documentation/records/subscription/1/1.pdf.

8. Avram, H. D. (1975). *MARC: Its History and Implications*. Washington, DC: Library of Congress; Crawford, W. (1989). *MARC for Library Use: Understanding Integrated USMARC*. Boston, MA: G. K. Hall & Co. (pp. 203–41).

9. MARC Development Office, Library of Congress. (1974). *Information on the MARC System* (4th ed.). Washington, DC: Library of Congress (p. 1).

10. American National Standards Institute. (1971). *American National Standard Format for Bibliographic Information Interchange on Magnetic Tape (ANSI Z39.2-1971)*. New York, NY: ANSI, 1971; current edition: National Information Standards Organization. (2014). *Information Interchange Format (ANSI/NISO Z39.2-1994* [R2009]). Retrieved from http://www.niso.org/apps/group_public/download.php/12590/z39-2-1994%28r2009%29.pdf.

11. International Organization for Standardization. (1973). *Documentation: Format for Bibliographic Information Interchange on Magnetic Tape: ISO 2709*. Geneva, Switzerland: International Organization for Standardization; current edition: International Organization for Standardization. (2011). *Information and Documentation: Format for Information Exchange: ISO 2709:2008*. Geneva, Switzerland: International Organization for Standardization.

12. Attig, J. (June 1982). The USMARC formats—Underlying principles. *Information Technology and Libraries, 1*(2), 169–74.

13. Library of Congress, Library and Archives Canada, National Library of Canada, & British Library. (1999–). *MARC 21 Format for Bibliographic Data: Including Guidelines for Content Designation*. Washington, DC: Cataloging Distribution Service, Library of Congress.

14. Crawford, W. (1989). *MARC for Library Use: Understanding Integrated USMARC*. Boston, MA: G. K. Hall & Co. (pp. 221–22).

15. Library of Congress & National Library of Canada. (1999–). *MARC 21 Format for Authority Data: Including Guidelines for Content Designation*. Washington, DC: Cataloging Distribution Service, Library of Congress.

16. Library of Congress & National Library of Canada. (2000–). *MARC 21 Format for Classification Data: Including Guidelines for Content Designation*. Washington, DC: Cataloging Distribution Service, Library of Congress.

17. Library of Congress, Library and Archives Canada, British Library, & National Library of Canada. (2000–). *MARC 21 Format for Holdings Data: Including Guidelines for Content Designation*. Washington, DC: Cataloging Distribution Service, Library of Congress.

18. Network Development and MARC Standards Office, Library of Congress. (July 27, 2004). *MARC 21 Concise Formats*. Retrieved from http://www.loc.gov/marc/archive/2000/concise/.

19. W3C. (January 26, 2015). *Extensible Markup Language (XML)*. Retrieved from www.w3.org/XML/.

20. Ebenezer, C. (2003). Trends in integrated library systems. *VINE, 32*(4), 19–45.

21. Harold, E. R., and Means, W. S. (2004). *XML in a Nutshell* (3rd ed.). Sebastopol, CA: O'Reilly (pp. 4, 6).

22. Network Development and MARC Standards Office, Library of Congress. (May 21, 2014). *MARCXML: MARC 21 XML Schema*. Retrieved from http://www.loc.gov/standards/marcxml/.

23. Network Development and MARC Standards Office, Library of Congress. (November 24, 2014). *MODS: Metadata Object Description Scheme*. Retrieved from http://www.loc.gov/standards/mods/.

24. Network Development and MARC Standards Office, Library of Congress. (June 11, 2013). *MADS: Metadata Authority Description Schema*. Retrieved from http://www.loc.gov/standards/mads/.

25. Library of Congress. (November 21, 2012). *Bibliographic Framework as a Web of Data: Linked Data Model and Supporting Services*. Retrieved from http://www.loc.gov/bibframe/pdf/marcld-report-11-21-2012.pdf.

26. Bibliographic Framework Initiative. (n.d.). *BIBFRAME.org*. Retrieved from http://bibframe.org/.

27. Bibliographic Framework Initiative. (n.d.). *BIBFRAME.org Tools*. Retrieved from http://bibframe.org/tools/.

28. Library of Congress. (May 26, 2006). *Encoded Archival Description Tag Library, Version 2002: EAD Elements: <eadheader> EAD Header*. Retrieved from http://www.loc.gov/ead/tglib/elements/eadheader.html.

29. Editeur. (2009). *ONIX for Books* (ONIX 3.0). Retrieved from http://www.editeur.org/11/Books/.

Chapter 4

Metadata Schemas

METADATA

The term "metadata" has been used by different communities to mean different things. Within the information community, it has been used since the early 1990s to mean data about other data. More elaborate definitions of metadata have been offered by various user communities. Some examples follow:

> Metadata is structured information that describes, explains, locates, or otherwise makes it easier to retrieve, use, or manage an information resource. Metadata is often called data about data or information about information.[1]
>
> Metadata are structured, encoded data that describe characteristics of information-bearing entities to aid in the identification, discovery, assessment, and management of the described entities.[2]
>
> [Metadata is] anything used to describe and or to organize electronic, and primarily Web, resources (born digital and digitized) for management and/or retrieval.[3]
>
> Metadata is . . . used to mean structured information about an information resource of any media type or format.[4]
>
> Metadata is structured information that describes the attributes of information packages for the purposes of identification, discovery, and sometimes management.[5]
>
> [M]etadata encapsulates the information that describes any document or object in both digital and traditional formats.[6]

Broadly defined, cataloging information, as data about data, can be considered a type of metadata. In most cases, however, the term metadata is used in reference to data, recorded in electronic records, that is created to describe or represent resources. The term *metadata schema* refers to a set of elements designed with specific types of resources or user communities in mind.

During the past couple of decades, numerous metadata standards or schemas have emerged. With regard to function, there are three main types of metadata:[7]

- *Descriptive Metadata* describe a resource for purposes such as discovery and identification. These can include elements such as title, abstract, author, and keywords.
- *Structural Metadata* indicate how compound objects are put together, for example, how pages are ordered to form chapters.
- *Administrative Metadata* provide information to help manage a resource, such as when and how it was created, file type and other technical information, and who can access it.

This chapter focuses on descriptive metadata. Among existing metadata schemes, Dublin Core (DC) has emerged as the most widely used worldwide. The following sections of this chapter present brief discussions (with examples) of the DC and a number of other metadata schemas.

DUBLIN CORE (DC)

Introduction

On a cost-effectiveness basis, cataloging codes, with their extensive and detailed rules and their focus on material traditionally held by libraries, are not a satisfactory vehicle for characterizing the content of Internet and Web resources. Cataloging rules are costly to apply, in part because it takes professional training to use them well and in part because the per-item time required for them is relatively lengthy. They are also much more detailed than is needed for the bibliographical control of most Web resources.

Accordingly, a group of information professionals met in 1995 at OCLC in Dublin, Ohio, to consider the matter. This meeting led to a new metadata schema aimed particularly at electronic resources such as those on the Web. This new schema came to be called the Dublin Core (DC). Another offshoot of the initial and subsequent Dublin meetings was the Dublin Core Metadata Initiative (DCMI), an open forum that oversees the continuing development of the DC and promotes other interoperable metadata standards. DCMI's activities include not only annual global conferences, workshops, and working groups organized around specific problem domains, but also both standards liaison and educational efforts to promote widespread acceptance of metadata standards and practices. Since the first DC meeting, which was sponsored by OCLC and the National Center for Supercomputing Applications (NCSA), was held in Ohio, there have been annual workshops held in different countries in the world, including Australia, Canada, China, Finland, Germany, Japan, Mexico, Spain, the United Kingdom, and the United States.

The original objective of the March 1995 Metadata Workshop held in Dublin, Ohio, was to define a set of descriptive elements simple enough for noncatalogers, including the authors themselves, to describe Web resources.[8] It began with thirteen elements and later, with the addition of the elements Description and Rights, was expanded to fifteen.

Since its inception, DC has been well received by many different information communities worldwide. In 2001, the Dublin Core Metadata Element Set (DCMES) version 1.1 was approved by the National Information Standards Organization as ANSI/NISO Standard Z39.85-2001.[9] In 2003, it was approved as an international standard, ISO Standard 15836-2003 (February 2003).[10] In 2007, DCMES version 1.1 was revised and approved as NISO Z39.85-2007.

DC Element Set

The DC contains a set of fifteen core elements.[11] These are listed below:

Element Name: title
Label: Title
Definition: A name given to the resource.
Comment: Typically, a Title will be a name by which the resource is formally known.

Element Name: creator
Label: Creator
Definition: An entity primarily responsible for making the content of the resource.
Comment: Examples of a Creator include a person, an organization, or a service. Typically, the name of a Creator should be used to indicate the entity.

Element Name: subject
Label: Subject
Definition: The topic of the resource.
Comment: Typically, the Subject will be expressed as keywords, key phrases, or classification codes. Recommended best practice is to use a controlled vocabulary.

Element Name: description
Label: Description
Definition: An account of the resource.
Comment: A Description may include, but is not limited to, an abstract, table of contents, a graphical representation, or a free-text account of the resource.

Element Name: publisher
Label: Publisher
Definition: An entity responsible for making the resource available.
Comment: Examples of a Publisher include a person, an organization, or a service. Typically, the name of a Publisher should be used to indicate the entity.

Element Name: contributor
Label: Contributor
Definition: An entity responsible for making contributions to the resource.
Comment: Examples of a Contributor include a person, an organization, or a service. Typically, the name of a Contributor should be used to indicate the entity.

Element Name: date
Label: Date
Definition: A point or period of time associated with an event in the lifecycle of the resource.
Comment: A Date may be used to express temporal information at any level of granularity. Recommended best practice is to use an encoding scheme, such as the W3CDTF profile of ISO 8601 [W3CDTF].

Element Name: type
Label: Type
Definition: The nature or genre of the resource.
Comment: Recommended best practice is to select a value from a controlled vocabulary such as the DCMI Type Vocabulary [DCMITYPE]). To describe the file format, physical medium, or dimensions of the resource, use the Format element.

Element Name: format
Label: Format
Definition: The file format, physical medium, or dimensions of the resource.

Comment: Examples of dimensions include size and duration. Recommended best practice is to use a controlled vocabulary such as the list of Internet Media Types [MIME].

Element Name: identifier
Label: Identifier
Definition: An unambiguous reference to the resource within a given context.
Comment: Recommended best practice is to identify the resource by means of a string or number conforming to a formal identification system.

Element Name: source
Label: Source
Definition: A related resource from which the present resource is derived.
Comment: The described resource may be derived from the related resource in whole or in part. Recommended best practice is to reference the resource by means of a string conforming to a formal identification system.

Element Name: language
Label: Language
Definition: A language of the resource.
Comment: Recommended best practice is to use a controlled vocabulary such as RFC 4646 [RFC4646].

Element Name: relation
Label: Relation
Definition: A related resource.
Comment: Recommended best practice is to identify the related resource by means of a string conforming to a formal identification system.

Element Name: coverage
Label: Coverage
Definition: The spatial or temporal topic of the resource, the spatial applicability of the resource, or the jurisdiction under which the resource is relevant.
Comment: Spatial topic and spatial applicability may be a named place or a location specified by its geographic coordinates. Temporal topic may be a named period, date, or date range.

A jurisdiction may be a named administrative entity or a geographic place to which the resource applies. Recommended best practice is to use a controlled vocabulary such as the Thesaurus of Geographic Names [TGN]. Where appropriate, named places or time periods can be used in preference to numeric identifiers such as sets of coordinates or date ranges.

Element Name: rights
Label: Rights
Definition: Information about rights held in and over the resource.
Comment: Typically, rights information includes a statement about various property rights associated with the resource, including intellectual property rights.

Although the original intention was to develop a simple and concise schema for describing Web resources, the DC has been used to describe other types of resources as well. In different applications, some users require more descriptive details than others. Thus, there are two different views with regard to the implementation of DC: the minimalist view supporting a minimum of elements and simple semantics and syntax, and the structuralist view supporting greater extensibility through finer semantic distinctions. These different views first led to two approaches to the implementation of DC: the simple (unqualified) DC, consisting of the original fifteen elements, and the qualified DC with finer details allowed within each element.[12] Today, the term qualifiers has been replaced by refinements. For example, the element DATE may be refined to indicate the type of event associated with the date (i.e., created, available, copyrighted, etc.) and the encoding schema (W3CDTF) of the value.

The DCMI recognizes two broad classes of refinements[13]:

Element Refinement. These refinements make the meaning of an element narrower or more specific. A refined element shares the meaning of the simple element, but with a more restricted scope. A client that does not understand a specific element refinement term should be able to ignore the refinement and treat the metadata value as if it were a simple (broader) element. The definitions of element refinements must be publicly available.

Encoding Scheme. These qualifiers identify schemes that aid in the interpretation of an element value. These schemes include controlled vocabularies and formal notations (or parsing rules). A value expressed using an encoding scheme will thus be a token selected from a controlled vocabulary (e.g., a term from a classification system or set of subject headings) or a string formatted in accordance with a formal notation (e.g., "2000-01-01" as the standard expression of a date). If an encoding scheme is not understood by a client or agent, the value may still be useful to a human reader. The definitive description of an encoding scheme for qualifiers must be clearly identified and available for public use.

In 2003, all refinements were declared as terms, and have since been maintained as part of the DCMI Metadata Terms document.[14] The elements, refinements, and encoding schemes for the fifteen DCMI Metadata Terms are shown in Table 4.1:

Table 4.1 Dublin Core Summary Refinement and Scheme Table

DCMI Element	*Element Refinement(s)*	*Element Encoding Scheme(s)*
Title	Alternative	—
Creator	—	—
Subject	—	LCSH MeSH DDC LCC UDC
Description	Table of Contents Abstract	—
Publisher	—	—
Contributor	—	—
Date	Created Valid Available Issued Modified Date Accepted Date Copyrighted Date Submitted	W3C-DTF
Type	—	DCMI Type Vocabulary
Format	—	IMT
	Extent	—
	Medium	—
Identifier	—	URI
	Bibliographic Citation	—
Source	—	URI
Language	—	ISO 639-2 RFC 3066
Relation	Is Version of has Version Is Replaced by Replaces Is Required by Requires Is Part of has Part is Referenced by References Is Format of has Format Conforms to	URI
Coverage	Spatial	DCMI Point ISO 3166 DCMI Box TGN
	Temporal	DCMI Period W3C-DTF
Rights	Access Rights	—
	License	URI

Source: DCMI Metadata Terms, http://dublincore.org/documents/dcmi-terms (May 30, 2013).

In addition to the fifteen core elements and their refinements, the DCMI Metadata Terms include new elements and element refinements. New elements (such as accrualMethod, accrualPeriodicity, accrualPolicy, audience, provenance, instructionalMethod, and rightsHolder) and new element refinements (such as mediator for audience) reflect the need of different communities to have additional information in their metadata. These additions require approval of the DC Usage Board before being registered in the DC Terms namespace.

Following are examples of DC Metadata records with refinements from OCLC's WorldCat:

(1) An electronic book:

Title:	Trained capacities : John Dewey, rhetoric, and democratic practice /
Identifier.ISBN:	9781611173192 (electronic bk.)
Identifier.ISBN:	1611173191 (electronic bk.)
Identifier.incorrect.ISBN:	9781611173185
Identifier.incorrect.ISBN:	1611173183
Identifier.URI:	http://search.ebscohost.com/login.aspx?direct=true&scope=site&db=nlebk&db=nlabk&AN=654805
Identifier.URI:	http://alltitles.ebrary.com/Doc?id=10827211
Type:	Electronic books.
Contributor.namePersonal:	Jackson, Brian, 1932- editor of compilation.
Contributor.namePersonal:	Clark, Gregory, 1950- editor of compilation.
Date.issued.MARC21-Date:	2014
Description.tableOfContents:	Dewey and democratic practice : science, pragmatism, religion. Dewey on science, deliberation, and the sociology of rhetoric / William Keith and Robert Danisch -- John Dewey, Kenneth Burke, and the role of orientation in rhetoric / Scott R. Stroud -- Minister of democracy : John Dewey, religious rhetoric, and the great community / Paul Stob -- Dewey and his interlocutors : Thomas Jefferson, Jane Addams, W. E. B. Du Bois, Walter Lippmann, James Baldwin. Dewey on Jefferson : reiterating democratic faith in times of war / Jeremy Engels -- John Dewey and Jane Addams debate war / Louise W. Knight -- John Dewey, W. E. B. Du Bois, and a rhetoric of education / Keith

	Gilyard -- Walter Lippmann, the indispensable opposition / Jean Goodwin -- "All safety is an illusion" : John Dewey, James Baldwin, and the democratic practice of public critique / Walton Muyumba -- Dewey as teacher of rhetoric. Rhetoric and Dewey's experimental pedagogy / Nathan Crick -- The art of the inartistic, in publics digital or otherwise / Brian Jackson, Meridith Reed, and Jeff Swift -- Dewey's progressive pedagogy for rhetorical instruction : teaching argument in a nonfoundational framework / Donald C. Jones -- Afterword: the possibilities for Dewey amid the angst of paradigm change / Gerard A. Hauser.
Format.extent:	1 online resource.
Language.ISO639-2:	eng
Relation.isPartOfSeries.MARC21-490:	Studies in rhetoric/communication
Relation.isPartOfSeries.MARC21-830:	Studies in rhetoric/communication.
Subject.class.LCC:	B945.D44 T58 2014eb
Subject.class.NALcategories:	PHI 016000
Subject.class.DDC:	191
Subject.namePersonal.LCSH:	Dewey, John, 1859-1952.
Subject.topical.LCSH:	Rhetoric • Philosophy.
Subject.topical.LCSH:	Democracy • Philosophy.
Subject.namePersonal:	Dewey, John, 1859-1952.

(2) A sound recording:

Title:	Zachary Preucil, cello.
Contributor.namePersonal:	Preucil, Zachary, 1990- performer.
Contributor.namePersonal:	Lam, Wing Yan Evelyn, 1991- performer.
Date.issued.MARC21-Date:	2014-2014
Description.note:	Title from disc label.
Description.note:	Candidate for the degree of Master of Music.
Description.note:	Recording master produced as .wav file and housed at Eastman

	School of Music's Technology & Media Production Department.
Description.tableOfContents:	Adagio and allegro, op. 70 / Robert
Schumann (8:44)	-- Suite for cello and piano (1933)
/ Edward Collins (25:00) --	Sonata no. 1 in E minor, op. 38 /
Johannes Brahms (26:10).	
Format.extent:	1 audio disc : CD audio; 4 3/4 in.
Language.ISO639-2:	zxx
Relation.isPartOfSeries.MARC21-490:	Program / Eastman School of Music, University of Rochester; 2013-14
Relation.isPartOfSeries.MARC21-810:	Eastman School of Music. Program; 2013-14.
Subject.topical.LCSH:	Cello and piano music, Arranged.
Subject.topical.LCSH:	Suites (Cello and piano)
Subject.topical.LCSH:	Sonatas (Cello and piano)

OTHER METADATA STANDARDS FOR RESOURCE DESCRIPTION

In addition to the DC, numerous other metadata schemas for resource description have also been developed and/or adopted by various information communities, such as libraries, museums, archives, art institutions, and so on. Following is a brief description of some of the more widely used metadata schemas:

Metadata Object Description Schema (MODS)

MODS,[15] developed by the Library of Congress Network Development and MARC Standards Office in 2002, is a schema for a bibliographic element set that may be used for a variety of purposes, particularly for library applications. It consists of a subset of MARC fields (see discussion in chapter 3), is cataloging code independent, uses language-based tags (in XML) rather than numeric ones, and uses attributes to refine elements. MODS is continually revised by the MODS Editorial Committee. The top-level MODS elements include the following:

titleInfo	note
name	subject
typeOfResource	classification
genre	relatedItem

originInfo	identifier
language	location
physicalDescription	accessCondition
abstract	part
tableOfContents	extension
targetAudience	recordInfo

The following examples show the top elements in two MODS records:

(1) Carl Sandburg's *Arithmetic* (a book):

titleInfo	**Arithmetic**
name	**Sandburg, Carl, 1878-1967**
name	**Rand, Ted**
typeOfResource	**text**
originInfo	**San Diego, Harcourt Brace Jovanovich, c1993**
language	**eng**
physicalDescription	**1v. (unpaged) : ill. (some col.); 26 cm.**
abstract	**A poem about numbers and their characteristics. Features anamorphic, or distorted, drawings which can be restored to normal by viewing from a particular angle or by viewing the image's reflection in the provided Mylar cone.**
targetAudience	**juvenile**
note	**illustrated as an anamorphic adventure by Ted Rand.**
note	**One Mylar sheet included in pocket.**
subject	**Arithmetic**
subject	**Juvenile poetry**
subject	**Children's poetry, American**
classification	**PS3537.A618 A88 1993**
classification	**811/.52**
identifier	**isbn: 0152038655**
identifier	**lccn: 92005291**

(2) *Campbell County, Wyoming* (a map):

Title Information	**Campbell County, Wyoming**
Name:Corporate	**Campbell County Chamber of Commerce (Wyo.)**
Type of Resource	**cartographic**
Genre (MARC)	**map**
Origin Information	**[Gillette, Wyo.] : Campbell County Chamber of Commerce**

Date Issued	**1982**
Issuance	**monographic**
Language	**eng**
Physical Description	**1 map; 33 × 15 cm.**
Note	**this map reproduced by Campbell County Chamber of Commerce.**
Note	**In lower right corner: Kintzels-Casper.**
Subject (LCSH)	**Campbell County (Wyo.)—Maps**
Classification (LCC)	**G4263.C3 1982 .C3**
Record Information	**DLC** **830222** [Record Creation Date] **19830426000000.0** [Record Change Date]
Record Identifier	**5466714**

For more details and encoding of MODS records, see chapter 3.

Text Encoding Initiatives (TEI)

Text Encoding Initiatives (TEI; http://www.tei-c.org/) is an international standard providing guidelines for the preparation and interchange of electronic texts of literary and linguistic textual materials, such as fiction, drama, and poetry, for scholarly research in the humanities.

Originally sponsored by the Association of Computers in the Humanities (ACH), the Association for Computational Linguistics (ACL), and the Association of Literary and Linguistic Computing (ALLC), TEI is now maintained by the TEI Consortium.

The TEI's *Guidelines for Electronic Text Encoding and Interchange* (TEI P4), first published in April 1994 in print form, has undergone several revisions. The latest version is available online (http://www.tei-c.org/Guidelines) and is updated in a six-month cycle. A simplified version, called TEI Lite (http://www.tei-c.org/Lite/), is a specific customization designed for the core TEI constituency.

TEI Header

All TEI encoded texts have two main elements, a TEI header and the transcription of the text. The TEI header contains a bibliographic description (i.e., metadata about the work), an encoding description, a nonbibliographic description, and a revision history. It is an "electronic title page," similar to the title page of a printed work. The tags used to label individual parts of the TEI header follow the SGML convention of using brackets to enclose element tags. (For more details about SGML, see chapter 16.)

The header is introduced by the element <teiHeader> and has four major parts:

File description: <fileDesc> contains a full bibliographic description of an electronic file.
Encoding description: <encodingDesc> documents the relationship between an electronic text and the source or sources from which it was derived.
Profile description: <profileDesc> provides a detailed description of nonbibliographic aspects of a text, specifically the languages and sublanguages used, the situation in which it was produced, and the participants and their setting.
Revision description: <revisionDesc> summarizes the revision history for a file.

The <fileDesc> element is mandatory. It contains a full bibliographic description of the file with the following elements:

<titleStmt>
groups information about the title of a work and those responsible for its intellectual content.
<editionStmt>
groups information relating to one edition of a text.
<extent>
describes the approximate size of the electronic text (as stored on some carrier medium) or of some other object, digital or nondigital, specified in any convenient unit.
<publicationStmt>
groups information concerning the publication or distribution of an electronic or other text.
<seriesStmt>
groups information about the *series*, if any, to which a publication belongs.
<notesStmt>
collects together any notes providing information about a text additional to that recorded in other parts of the bibliographic description.
<sourceDesc>
describes the source from which an electronic text was derived or generated, typically a bibliographic description in the case of a digitized text, or a phrase such as "born digital" for a text that has no previous existence.

A minimal header has the following structure shown here with SGML coding:

<teiHeader>
<fileDesc>

```
    <titleStmt> ... </titleStmt>
    <publicationStmt> ... <publicationStmt>
    <sourceDesc> ... <sourceDesc>
  </fileDesc>
</teiHeader>
```

The <encodingDesc> element specifies the methods and editorial principles that governed the transcription of the text. Its use is highly recommended. It may be prose description, and may contain elements from the following list:

<projectDesc>
: describes in detail the aim or purpose for which an electronic file was encoded, together with any other relevant information concerning the process by which it was assembled or collected.

<samplingDecl>
: contains a prose description of the rationale and methods used in sampling texts in the creation of a corpus or collection.

<editorialDecl>
: provides details of editorial principles and practices applied during the encoding of a text.

<refsDecl>
: specifies how canonical references are constructed for the text.

<classDecl>
: contains one or more taxonomies defining any classificatory codes used elsewhere in the text.

Examples of <projectDesc> and <samplingDesc>:

```
<encodingDesc>
  <projectDesc>
    <p>Texts collected for use in the Claremont Shakespeare Clinic,
       June 1990.
    </p>
  </projectDesc>
</encodingDesc>
```

```
<encodingDesc>
  <samplingDecl>
    <p>Samples of 2000 words taken from the beginning of the text.
    </p>
  </samplingDecl>
</encodingDesc>
```

The <profileDesc> element enables information characterizing various descriptive aspects of a text to be recorded within a single framework. It has three optional components:

<creation>
contains information about the creation of a text.
<langUsage>
describes the languages, sublanguages, registers, dialects, etc., represented within a text.
<textClass>
groups information which describes the nature or topic of a text in terms of a standard classification scheme, thesaurus, etc.

Example:
<creation>
<date value="1992-08">**August 1992**</date>
<name type="place">**Taos, New Mexico**</name>
</creation>

The <revisionDesc> element provides a change log in which each change made to a text may be recorded. The log may be recorded as a sequence of <change> elements, each of which contains a brief description of the change. The attributes @when and @who may be used to identify when the change was carried out and the agency responsible for it.

Example:
<revisionDesc>
<change when="1991-03-06" who="#EMB">**File format updated**
</change>
<change when="1990-05-25" who="#EMB">**Stuart's corrections entered**</change>
</revisionDesc>

The TEI header is usually placed at the beginning of the electronic resource that it describes. It can also function in detached form as a surrogate record in a separate list or catalog. Some libraries use TEI headers to derive MARC records for inclusion in their catalogs. Following is an example of a TEI header bibliographic information (fileDesc):[16]

<teiHeader>
<fileDesc>
<titleStmt>

```
<title>Shakespeare: the first folio (1623) in electronic form</title>
<author>Shakespeare, William (1564–1616)</author>
<respStmt>
<resp>Originally prepared by</resp>
<name>Trevor Howard-Hill</name>
</respStmt>
<respStmt>
<resp>Revised and edited by</resp>
<name>Christine Avern-Carr</name>
</respStmt>
</titleStmt>
<publicationStmt>
<distributor>Oxford Text Archive</distributor>
<address>
<addrLine>13 Banbury Road, Oxford OX2 6NN, UK</addrLine>
</address>
<idno type="OTA">119</idno>
<availability>
<p>Freely available on a non-commercial basis.</p>
</availability>
<date when="1968">1968</date>
</publicationStmt>
<sourceDesc>
<bibl>The first folio of Shakespeare, prepared by Charlton Hinman
(The Norton Facsimile, 1968)</bibl>
</sourceDesc>
</fileDesc>
</teiHeader>
```

Encoded Archival Description (EAD)

The EAD is a standard for describing and encoding finding aids for archival materials. Finding aids are tools such as inventories, registers, indexes, and other documents created by archives, libraries, museums, and manuscript repositories for both managing and providing access to their collections.[17] Records for finding aids are different from cataloging records in that they are much longer and contain extensive narrative and explanatory information, which is structured hierarchically.[18] EAD is used by many academic and research libraries, archives, historical societies, and museums to describe the finding aids for their special collections.

The EAD began in 1993 at the University of California, Berkeley. The goal was to create a standard for machine-readable finding aids used in archival work. At the same time, the original investigators wanted to include in EAD records information that went beyond what was found in traditional MARC records. As the EAD site states, the requirements for this project "included the following criteria: (1) ability to present extensive and interrelated descriptive information found in archival finding aids, (2) ability to preserve the hierarchical relationships existing between levels of description, (3) ability to represent descriptive information that is inherited by one hierarchical level from another, (4) ability to move within a hierarchical informational structure, and (5) support for element-specific indexing and retrieval."[19]

An EAD record typically contains a header similar to a TEI header. It describes the finding aid itself and contains a description of the archival collection as a whole, as well as more detailed information about the records or series within the collection. In other words, the EAD header carries metadata about the finding aid itself.

The current version, maintained by the LC and the Society of American Archivists, is EAD DTD Version 2002.[20]

The EAD header contains the following elements:

```
<eadheader>
  <eadid>
  <filedesc>
    <titlestmt>
      <titleproper>
      <subtitle>
      <author>
      <sponsor>
    <editionstmt>
    <publicationstmt>
      <addresses>
      <date>
      <num>
      <p>
      <publisher>
    <seriesstmt>
    <notestmt>
  <profiledesc>
    <creation>
    <language>
  <revisiondesc>
```

The following excerpt is based on an example of an EAD header from the EAD Tag Library, Version 2002:[21]

```
<eadheader>
   <eadid>Mildred Davenport Dance Programs and Dance School
   Materials, MS-P29
   </eadid>
   <filedesc>
      <titlestmt>
         <titleproper>Guide to the Mildred Davenport Dance Programs
         and Dance School Materials</titleproper>
         <author>Processed by Adrian Turner; machine-readable find-
         ing aid created by Adrian Turner</author>
      </titlestmt>
      <publicationstmt>
            <date>2001</date>
            <p>The Regents of the University of California. All rights
            reserved.</p>
      </publicationstmt>
      <notestmt><note> <p>
            <subject source="cdl">Arts and Humanities--Dance--Dance
            Performance</subject>
            <subject source="cdl">Arts and Humanities--Dance--Dance
            History and Criticism</subject>
            <subject source="cdl">Area, Interdisciplinary, and Ethnic
            Studies--African American Studies</subject> </p>
            </note>
      </notestmt>
   </filedesc>
   <profiledesc>
      <creation>Machine-readable finding aid derived from MS Word.
      Date of source: <date>2001.</date>
      </creation>
      <langusage>Description is in <language>English.</language>
      </langusage>
   </profiledesc>
</eadheader>
```

Visual Resources Association Core Categories

Visual Resources Association (VRA; http://www.vraweb.org/projects/vra-core4/) is a standard for the cultural heritage community. VRA Core Categories is designed for describing visual works of art, architecture, and artifacts or structures from material, popular, and folk culture, as well as the images that document them. Its purpose is to facilitate the sharing of information among visual resources collections about *works* and *images*. The standard is based on the DC, with modifications. Some of the VRA elements are based on the DC elements such as title, creator, subject, and relation. Other elements—such as measurements, material, and technique—are added to enable a richer description of artworks. The VRA standard is a result of a collaboration between The Network Development and MARC Standards Office of the Library of Congress and the VRA.

Core Element Set

The VRA Core 4.0 Element Description (VRA Core, Version 4.0, 2007) (http://www.vraweb.org/vracore3.htm) contains nineteen elements,[22] each of which may contain one or more attributes or subelements to allow further specifications within the element:

WORK, COLLECTION, or IMAGE
Attributes: id
  Definition: A choice of one of three elements, Work, Collection, or Image, defines a VRA 4.0 record as describing a Work (a built or created object), a Collection (an aggregate of such objects), or an Image (a visual surrogate of such objects).

AGENT
Subelements:
 name
  Attributes: type
 culture
 dates
  Attributes: type
  earliestDate
  latestDate
 role
 attribution
  Description: The names, appellations, or other identifiers assigned to an individual, group, or corporate body that has contributed to the design, creation, production, manufacture, or alteration of the work or image.

CULTURAL CONTEXT
Attributes: none
  Description: The name of the culture or people (ethnonym), or the adjectival form of a country name, from which a Work, Collection, or Image

originates, or the cultural context with which the Work, Collection, or Image has been associated.

DATE
Attributes: Type
Subelements:
earliestDate
latestDate
Description: Date or range of dates associated with the creation, design, production, presentation, performance, construction, or alteration, etc., of the work or image. Dates may be expressed as free text or numericals.

DESCRIPTION
Attributes: None
Description: A free-text note about the Work or Image, including comments, description, or interpretation, which gives additional information not recorded in other categories.

INSCRIPTION
Subelements:
author
position
text
Attributes: type
Description: All marks or written words added to the object at the time of production or in its subsequent history, including signatures, dates, dedications, texts, and colophons, as well as marks, such as the stamps of silversmiths, publishers, or printers.

LOCATION
Attributes: type
Subelements:
name
Attributes: type
refid
Attributes: type
Description: The geographic location and/or name of the repository, building, or site-specific work or other entity whose boundaries include the Work or Image.

MATERIAL
Attributes: type

Description: The substance of which a Work or an Image is composed.

MEASUREMENTS
Attributes:
type
unit
Description: The physical size, shape, scale, dimensions, or format of the Work or Image. Dimensions may include such measurements as volume, weight, area, or running time. The unit used in the measurement must be specified.

RELATION
Attributes:
type
relids
Description: Terms or phrases describing the identity of the related work and the relationship between the work being cataloged and the related work or image. Use this element to relate work records to other work or collection records, or to relate image records to work or collection records.

RIGHTS
Attributes: type
Subelements:
rightsHolder
text
Description: Information about the copyright status and the rights holder for a Work, Collection, or Image.

SOURCE
Subelements:
name
Attributes: type
refid
Attributes: type
Description: A reference to the source of the information recorded about the work or the image. For a work record, this may be a citation to the authority for the information provided. For an Image, it can be used to provide information about the supplying agency, vendor, or individual. In the case of copy photography, it can be a bibliographic citation or other description of the image source. In all cases, names, locations, and source identification numbers can be included.

STATE EDITION
Attributes:
type (state, edition, or impression)
num (state number or edition number)
count (number of known states, known editions, or number of impressions in an edition)
Subelements
name (name of state or edition)
description (descriptive note)
Description: The identifying number and/or name assigned to the state or edition of a work that exists in more than one form, and the placement of that work in the context of prior or later issuances of multiples of the same work. For published volumes, such as books, portfolios, series, or sets, the edition is usually expressed as a number in relation to other editions printed. In other cases, a scholar may have identified a series of editions, which have then been numbered sequentially.

STYLE PERIOD
Attributes: none
Description: A defined style, historical period, group, school, dynasty, movement, etc., whose characteristics are represented in the Work or Image. Cultural and regional terms may be combined with style and period terms for display purposes.

SUBJECT
Subelements
term
Attributes: type
Description: Terms or phrases that describe, identify, or interpret the Work or Image and what it depicts or expresses. These may include proper terms that describe and the elements that it comprises, terms that identify particular people, geographic places, narrative and iconographic themes, or terms that refer to broader concepts or interpretations.

TECHNIQUE
Attributes: none
Description: The production or manufacturing processes, techniques, and methods incorporated in the fabrication or alteration of the work or the image.

TEXTREF
Subelements:

name
Attributes: type
refid
Attributes: type
Description: Contains the name of a related textual reference and any type of unique identifier that text assigns to a Work or Collection that is independent of any repository. "Refid" examples include exhibition and catalog raisonné numbers, or identification numbers assigned to works of art in the scholarly literature that are commonly included in scholarly discussion to further identify a work, such as Bartsch or Beazley numbers.

TITLE
Attributes: type
Definition: The title or identifying phrase given to a Work or an Image. For complex works or series the title may refer to a discrete unit within the larger entity (a print from a series, a panel from a fresco cycle, a building within a temple complex) or may identify only the larger entity itself. For an Image record, this category describes the specific view of the depicted Work or Collection.

WORK TYPE
Attributes: type
Definition: Identifies the specific type of WORK, COLLECTION, or IMAGE being described in the record.

Examples of VRA:[23]

(1) A record for a work of architecture:

agent =	**Henry Bacon (American architect, 1866-1924)**
culturalContext =	**American**
date =	**1911-1912 (design); 1914-1922 (creation)**
description =	**Design was chosen by competition. The chosen design was influenced by the Greek Parthenon. Built into the design are symbols of the Union like the 36 exterior Doric columns representing the 36 states in the Union at the time of Lincoln's death.**
inscription =	**Inscribed above the statue: IN THIS TEMPLE / AS IN THE HEARTS OF THE PEOPLE / FOR WHOM HE SAVED THE UNION / THE MEMORY OF ABRAHAM LINCOLN / IS ENSHRINED FOREVER; [the northern wall contains an inscription of**

	Lincoln's second inaugural speech, the southern wall contains an inscription of the Gettysburg address]
location =	**Washington, District of Columbia, United States**
material =	**Exterior: Colorado Yule marble; tripods: Pink Tennessee marble; interior walls and columns: Indiana limestone; ceiling: Alabama marble saturated with paraffin for translucency; floor and wall base: Pink Tennessee marble**
measurements =	**30.18 m (height, building)**
relation	
rights	
source =	**Core 4 Sample Database (VCat) [source, description] Longstreth, Richard , ed.; Mall in Washington, 1791-1991, Hanover and London: University Press of New England, 1991 (0894681389)**
stateEdition	
stylePeriod =	**Twentieth century**
subject =	**rulers and leaders; Lincoln, Abraham, 1809-1865; commemoration; Union (United States); temples; Doric order; columns; states (political divisions); Mall, The (Washington, D.C.)**
technique =	**carving (processes); construction (assembling)**
textref	
title =	**Lincoln Memorial [en, cited, preferred]**
worktype =	**buildings; memorials; built works; monuments**

(2) A record for a slide:

agent =	**G. [Gaston] Massiot et Compagnie (French photographic firm, active ca. 1899-1940) [agent note] Abbreviated G. Massiot & Cie; also Radiguet & Massiot (from 1899-1905)**
culturalContext =	**French**
date =	**ca. 1899-before 1909 (creation)**
description =	**An aerial view taken by an unknown photographer before 1909, therefore probably taken from a hot air balloon, not an airplane.**
inscription =	**Title on slide label: Nice, France - Panorama.**
location =	**University of Notre Dame, Architecture Library (South Bend, Indiana, United States)[repository] Nice, Provence-Alpes-Côte d'Azur, France [creation]**
material =	**black and white film; glass**
measurements =	**4 in (height) x 3.25 in (width)**

relation = **partOf Historic architectural views [lantern slide collection]**
rights = **publicDomain**
source = **Core 4 Sample Database (VCat)**
stateEdition =
stylePeriod = **Nineteenth century; Twentieth century**
subject = **architectural exteriors; cityscapes; Aerial photography in city planning; City planning; Housing; balloons (aircraft)**
technique = **photography**
textref =
title = **Aerial topographic view of Nice, France [lantern slide] [en, descriptive, preferred] Nice, France - Panorama [en, repository, alternate]**
worktype = **photographs; lantern slides; photographs; positives (photographs); black-and-white transparencies; topographical views**

Online Information Exchange (ONIX)

ONIX is an international metadata standard designed specifically to support electronic commerce applications. It was developed by publishers among the book industry trade groups in the United States and Europe and was designed to capture the images, cover blurbs, reviews, and other promotional information that can be used to enhance book sales. The main purpose of ONIX is to enable publishers to supply "rich" product information to Internet booksellers, and its major objective is to publicize and promote publishers' products by means of content-rich metadata.

Three bodies are involved in the development and maintenance of ONIX: Book Industry Communications (BIC) based in London, the Book Industry Study Group (BISG) based in New York, and EDItEUR (http://www.editeur.org/, an international steering group that is responsible for the maintenance of the ONIX standard). ONIX for Books was the first and most widely adopted ONIX standard. ONIX for Books release 1.0 was published in 2000. ONIX for Books release 3.0 (published in 2009) reflects the need for revision to handle digital products.[24]

An ONIX record contains bibliographic information as well as trade information. Libraries and information agencies have found the ONIX descriptions useful as starting points or as enhancements for resource descriptions for their own materials. Because much of this information is also included in library catalog records, ONIX records provide a source for ordinary cataloging information and for additional information, such as tables of contents, that is sometimes useful for enhancing cataloging records.

ONIX metadata can also be used as the beginning of a cataloging record to save money and effort in original cataloging. To facilitate this use, the LC initiated the Bibliographic Enrichment Advisory Team (BEAT) project to explore the feasibility of converting ONIX information for bibliographic use. The team created a crosswalk that maps elements between ONIX for Books and MARC 21;[25] it includes a mapping table in ONIX data element order and a record builder for creating MARC 21 records from ONIX data. The LC ONIX to MARC 21 mapping is based on ONIX release 2.1. More recently, OCLC developed comprehensive mappings from ONIX 3.0 to MARC.[26] Another approach to enriching cataloging records is to include hyperlinks in MARC records to ONIX information relating to the authors' or contributors' biographical information, and to the tables of contents and summaries contained in the ONIX records. ONIX Release 3.0 supported formal definitions in three formats, DTD, XML Schema Definition (XSD), and RELAX NG (RNG).

In the ONIX system, publishing data are organized in "ONIX messages" for transmission across networks and the Internet. The ONIX message contains data elements defined by XML tags, conforming to the ONIX DTD. A single ONIX message may contain data about multiple publications and therefore consist of one or more product records.

The ONIX DTD contains a set of over two hundred data elements in four groups:

(1) The ONIX message header—containing information concerning the message being transmitted.
(2) Main Series Record (optional)—consisting of seven main elements with subelements, describing a series or "top level" of a series or subseries.
(3) Subseries Record—consisting of eight main elements with subelements, describing a subseries.
(4) Product Record—consisting of twenty-six main elements with subelements, describing an individual publication, such as a book.

The ONIX for Books message has a header, which identifies the sender of the message and some additional optional information about the sender, followed by a number of product records.

```
<?xml version="1.0"?>
<ONIXMessage release="3.0">
  <Header>..............</Header>
  <Product>..............</Product>
  <Product>..............</Product>
  <Product>..............</Product>
</ONIXMessage>
```

The Product Record is the basic unit within an ONIX Product Information message. The following are the main elements in the Product Record using ONIX Release 3.0:[27]

<Product>
Record metadata
Product numbers
<DescriptiveDetail>
Product form
Product parts (for multipleitem products)
Collection
Product title
Authorship
Conference detail
Edition
Language
Extents
Illustrations and ancillary content
Subject
Audience
</DescriptiveDetail>
Text content
Cited content
Supporting resources
Prizes
</CollateralDetail>
<ContentDetail>
Content item detail
</ContentDetail>
<PublishingDetail>
Imprint and publisher
"Global" publishing status and copyright
Sales rights and restrictions
</PublishingDetail>
<RelatedMaterial>
Related works
Related products
</RelatedMaterial>
<ProductSupply>
Market Group
Market publishing status
Supply detail: availability and price within market
</ProductSupply>

Following is an example showing the part of an ONIX record that contains bibliographic and biographical information relating to a book:

Product Title	**British English, A to Zed**
Authorship	**Schur, Norman W.**
BiographicalNote	**A Harvard graduate in Latin and Italian literature, Norman Schur attended the University of Rome and the Sorbonne before returning to the United States to study law at Harvard and Columbia Law Schools. Now retired from legal practise, Mr Schur is a fluent speaker and writer of both British and American English**
Edition	**REV**
EditionNumber	**3**
Language	**eng**
Extents	**493** [Pages]
Descriptions and other Text	**BRITISH ENGLISH, A TO ZED is the thoroughly updated, revised, and expanded third edition of Norman Schur's highly acclaimed transatlantic dictionary for English speakers. First published as BRITISH SELF-TAUGHT and then as ENGLISH ENGLISH, this collection of Briticisms for Americans, and Americanisms for the British, is a scholarly yet witty lexicon, combining definitions with commentary on the most frequently used and some lesser known words and phrases. Highly readable, it's a snip of a book, and one that sorts out – through comments in American – the "Queen's English" – confounding as it may seem.** **Norman Schur is without doubt the outstanding authority on the similarities and differences between British and American English. BRITISH ENGLISH, A TO ZED attests not only to his expertise, but also to his undiminished powers to inform, amuse and entertain. – Laurence Urdang, Editor, VERBATIM, The Language Quarterly, Spring 1988**

Publisher	
Publisher Name	**Facts on File Inc**
PublicationDate	**1987**
Dimensions	
Measurement	**9.25 in**
Measurement	**6.25 in**
Measurement	**1.2 in**

NOTES

1. National Information Standards Organization (U.S.). (2004). *Understanding Metadata*. Bethesda, MD: NISO Press. Retrieved from www.niso.org/standards/resources/UnderstandingMetadata.pdf (p. 1).
2. Association for Library Collections & Technical Services, Committee on Cataloging: Description & Access, Task Force on Metadata. (June 16, 2000). *Final Report* (CC:DA/TF/Metadata/5). Retrieved from www.libraries.psu.edu/tas/jca/ccda/tf-meta6.html.
3. Intner, S. S., Lazinger, S. S., and Weihs, J. (2006). *Metadata and Its Impact on Libraries*. Westport, CT: Libraries Unlimited (p. 6).
4. Caplan, P. (2003). *Metadata Fundamentals for all Librarians*. Chicago, IL: American Library Association (p. 3).
5. Taylor, A. G. (2004). *The Organization of Information* (2nd ed.). Englewood, CO: Libraries Unlimited (p. 139).
6. Zeng, M. L., and Qin, J. (2008). *Metadata*. New York, NY: Neal-Schuman Publishers (p. 7).
7. National Information Standards Organization (U.S.), 2004, p. 1.
8. National Information Standards Organization (U.S.), 2004, p. 3.
9. National Information Standards Organization (U.S.). (2001). *The Dublin Core Metadata Element Set* (ANSI/NISO Z39.85-2001). Bethesda, MD: NISO Press. Retrieved from http://www.niso.org/apps/group_public/download.php/6578/The%20Dublin%20Core%20Metadata%20Element%20Set.pdf.
10. International Organization for Standardization. (2003). *Information and Documentation—The Dublin Core Metadata Element Set* (ISO 15836: 2003). Available from http://www.iso.org/iso/iso_catalogue/catalogue_tc/catalogue_detail.htm?csnumber=37629.
11. National Information Standards Organization (U.S.), 2001.
12. Hillmann, D. (November 7, 2005). *Using Dublin Core*. Retrieved from http://dublincore.org/documents/2005/11/07/usageguide/.
13. Dublin Core Metadata Initiative. (November 7, 2005). *Using Dublin Core—Dublin Core Qualifiers*. Retrieved from http://dublincore.org/documents/2005/11/07/usageguide/qualifiers.shtml.
14. DCMI Usage Board. (June 14, 2012). *DCMI Metadata Terms*. Retrieved from http://dublincore.org/documents/dcmi-terms/.

15. Library of Congress. (n.d.). *MODS: Metadata Object Description Schema*. Retrieved from www.loc.gov/standards/mods/.

16. Text Encoding Initiative. (September 16, 2014). *Example: <teiHeader> (TEI Header)*. Retrieved from http://www.tei-c.org/release/doc/tei-p5-doc/en/html/examples-teiHeader.html.

17. Library of Congress. (December 2002a). *Development of the Encoded Archival Description DTD*. Retrieved from www.loc.gov/ead/eaddev.html.

18. National Information Standards Organization (U.S.), 2004, p. 6.

19. Library of Congress, 2002a.

20. Library of Congress. (2002b). *Encoded Archival Description: Version 2002*. Retrieved from www.loc.gov/ead/.

21. Library of Congress. (2002c). *Encoded Archival Description Tag Library, Version 2002. Appendix C: Encoded Examples*. Retrieved from http://www.loc.gov/ead/tglib/appendix_ca.html.

22. Visual Resources Association Data Standards Committee. (April 5, 2007). *VRA Core 4.0 Element Description and Tagging Examples*. Retrieved from http://www.loc.gov/standards/vracore/.

23. Visual Resources Association Data Standards Committee. (2007). *VRA Core Cataloging Examples*. Retrieved from http://www.loc.gov/standards/vracore/schemas.html.

24. Editeur. (2009). *ONIX for Books, Release 3.0*. Retrieved from http://www.editeur.org/12/Current-Release/.

25. Network Development and MARC Standards Office, Library of Congress. (May 3, 2005). *ONIX to MARC 21 Mapping*. Retrieved from www.loc.gov/marc/onix2marc.html.

26. Godby, C. J. (2012). *A Crosswalk from ONIX Version 3.0 for Books to MARC 21*. Dublin, OH: OCLC Research. Retrieved from http://www.oclc.org/research/publications/library/2012/2012-04.pdf.

27. Editeur. (2009). *ONIX for Books: Product Information Format Specification, Release 3.0*. Retrieved from http://www.editeur.org/11/Books/.

Part III

RESOURCE DESCRIPTION AND ACCESS (RDA)

Chapter 5

RDA and Its Foundations

INTRODUCTION

Chapter 2 provided an introduction to the principles of resource description and an historical overview of the development of standards for description. Chapters 3 and 4 provided an overview of records in an online environment and of the different ways to encode the data created by them using description standards to represent resources. The chapters in Part Three will take a more detailed look at current resource description guidelines for the creation of descriptive bibliographic data using RDA.

RDA: *Resource Description and Access*[1] is the new standard providing guidelines for description and access to different types of information resources and is available in a variety of formats. It was intended as a replacement for AACR2. The history of the development of this standard has been given in chapter 2. Even though it was developed by the library community, the standard is designed for wider applicability in the linked-data environment of the semantic web.

RDA is based on the foundations established by the *Anglo American Cataloguing Rules* (AACR), and therefore often continues the practices and traditions influenced by the application of AACR. RDA does not provide guidelines for the presentation of data in a record structure, nor does it specify the use of an encoding schema for electronic record coding. RDA's Appendix D provides a link to the mappings of RDA elements to ISBD: *International Standard Bibliographic Description*, including its respective punctuation specifications, and RDA Toolkit's "RDA Mappings" provides mappings to MARC 21 Format for Bibliographic Data fields. This is due to the fact that libraries have traditionally used ISBD as a standard for data presentation and MARC 21 as a standard for encoding.

Major differences between AACR and RDA are due to RDA's foundation in other conceptual models, the Functional Requirements for Bibliographic Records (FRBR) and the Functional Requirements for Authority Data (FRAD). These two models, and especially FRBR, provide RDA with the framework that underlies its scope. According to the RDA documentation,[2] RDA provides three major benefits:

- A structure based on the conceptual models of FRBR and FRAD to help catalog users find the information they need more easily.

  RDA's objective to be responsive to the needs of the users means that the guidelines instruct those who create resource description to include attributes and relationships that will connect the user to resources matching their search criteria and to their desired resources. With the FR models as the foundation for the guidelines, RDA places emphasis on the user tasks defined in the conceptual models. RDA is structured so that each section provides guidelines for recording attributes and relationships as they relate to finding, identifying, selecting, and obtaining tasks. The data produced allow users to find all embodied works using several different attributes, find resources based on attributes of persons, corporate bodies, and families. Such data also allow users to find links to related resources through recorded relationships between works and persons responsible for them, and resources and corporate bodies responsible for their production. In addition, RDA provides instructions to record attributes and relationships, which will make it possible to identify and differentiate resources from other similar resources. Users should be able to select resources based on considerations such as language, physical characteristics (such as dimensions), and whether the content of a work is stored in a print volume or an electronic file. Users should also be able to obtain the resource from the collection, for example, by borrowing the resource or accessing the content online. Last, RDA aims to help the user understand the relationships that exist between entities and the names used to identify the entities, such as a person and the name or names of a person. Therefore, the guidelines instruct us to record any information that provides a rationale for the titles, names, or forms of names chosen as preferred access points.
- A flexible framework for content description of digital resources that also serves the needs of libraries organizing traditional resources.

  Unlike AACR2, which was structured to provide guidelines for specific resource formats (e.g., separate guidelines for monographic print volumes, for electronic resources, for sound recordings, etc.), RDA guidelines are independent of the format of a resource. Also, the guidelines are not written for a specific record structure, record format, or encoding system. AACR2 had a tradition of focusing on the card catalog record. RDA's instructions are based on attributes and relationships and not created on a record-specific format.

- A better fit with emerging database technologies, enabling institutions to introduce efficiencies in data capture and storage retrievals.

  We should be able to store new data in existing databases and integrate with existing records (e.g., with AACR2 records); but also be flexible enough for future systems, be represented in new encoding and data representation systems, and be retrieved in an efficient and effective way. RDA-created data should be easily expressed as linked data and should fit well with and use semantic technologies to retrieve and link all relevant data.

The introduction of the FRBR entities, relationships, and user tasks has shaped the RDA's structure, terminology, and basic approach to resource description guidelines. RDA elements are aligned, for the most part, with the attributes of the entities and the relationships among the entities defined in FRBR and FRAD. An overview of FRBR, FRAD, and ISBD, as well as an introduction to RDA, is offered in this chapter. The RDA guidelines are discussed in more detail in chapters 6 through 9.

Functional Requirements for Bibliographic Records (FRBR)

Functional Requirements for Bibliographic Records (FRBR),[3] developed by the International Federation of Library Associations (IFLA) Working Group on Functional Requirements for Bibliographic Records (FRBR), was first published in 1998. FRBR is not a description standard; it does not instruct nor provide guidelines on how to describe a resource, but rather offers a conceptual model. More specifically, it is an entity-relationships (ER) model, implementing a modeling method often used in conceptual modeling of relational databases. In order to cover all types of information included in bibliographic systems, a set of three models was developed, known as the FR family models. These models include FRBR, with its focus on the bibliographic data of a system, FRAD,[4] with its focus on authority data included in a bibliographic system, and the *Functional Requirements for Subject Authority Data* (FRSAD),[5] with its focus on authority data for subject terms and other subject or classification expressions to be used to represent what a resource is about.

The FRBR conceptual model defines entities and relationships in relation to the main user tasks performed by users when interacting with a bibliographic retrieval system. Major user tasks defined in FRBR include the following:

- to **find** entities: users should be able to find a resource or a set of resources based on information entered in a bibliographic system (e.g., the title of a work, an ISBN number);

- to **identify** an entity: users should be able to confirm that what they were looking for is what they found in the system based on a number of resource characteristics; users should also be able to identify differences in characteristics among similar resources found in the system;
- to **select** an entity: users should be able to select resources that match their needs by reviewing the attributes and relationships included in bibliographic description, such as the date of publication, a particular translator, and so on; and
- to **acquire or obtain** access to the entity described: users should be able to find out how they can access the resources themselves and their content, whether through loan, purchase, Internet links, or other means.

FRBR identifies three groups of entities. Group 1 entities are the products that result from creative or intellectual activities; typically, these are the content resources we add in our collections, describe in our bibliographic descriptions, and provide access to through bibliographic systems. *Work*, *expression*, *manifestation*, and *item* are the four entities identified in Group 1. Those entities responsible for the creation, production, sponsorship, etc., of Group 1 entities are gathered together in Group 2. These include *person*, *corporate body*, and *family* (family was not included in the original FRBR model). The third group of FRBR entities includes any entity that can serve as the subject of a product of intellectual and artistic activity. FRBR defines *concept*, *object*, *event*, and *place* as Group 3 entities, but specifies that any entity from Group 1 and Group 2 can also serve as the topic of a resource.

The major focus of the FRBR model is on the entities, relationships, and attributes among works, expressions, manifestations, and items (Group 1 entities) as they relate to FRBR-defined user tasks. FRBR Group 1 is defined as the "products of intellectual or artistic endeavor" and consists of the following entities:

- *work:* a distinct intellectual or artistic creation;
- *expression:* the intellectual or artistic realization of a *work* in the form of alpha-numeric, musical, or choreographic notation, sound, image, object, movement, etc., or any combination of such forms;
- *manifestation:* the physical embodiment of an *expression* of a *work*; and
- *item:* a single exemplar of a *manifestation*.

As an ER model, FRBR also defines entities, relationships, and attributes of persons, corporate bodies, and families (Group 2 entities) and objects, events, places, and concepts (Group 3 entities); however, the other two conceptual models in the FR family created consequently, FRAD and FRSAD, further develop Group 2 and Group 3 entities, respectively. Connections between

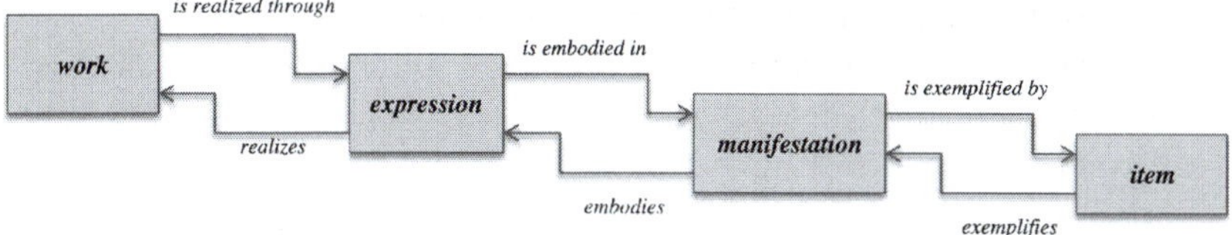

Figure 5.1 FRBR Group 1 entity relationships.

FRBR and RDA, as they relate to *works, expressions, manifestations,* and *items* (the Group 1 entities), are shown in Figures 5.1 to 5.3 and discussed in chapter 6. Group 2 entities are briefly discussed under the section on FRAD, although RDA's coverage of attributes and relationships for Group 2 entities was influenced more by FRBR than by FRAD, and given in more detail in chapters 7 and 8.

Figure 5.2 shows the relationships between Group 1 entities, using as an example Darwin's work on the origins of species.

- The *work* is an abstract entity representing the intellectual content of Darwin's work.
- This content is presented in a variety of ways and in a number of different languages. It is *realized* through different *expressions*, as an English text (E1), a translated German text (E2), a translated Greek text (E3), and English spoken word (E4).
- Each of these presentations is either published as a print book or produced as a sound recording. In FRBR terms, the *expressions* are *embodied* in one or more *manifestations*. For example, E1, the English text, has been embodied in a manifestation (or published as a book) entitled *On the Origins of Species by Means of Natural Selection*. This manifestation was published in London by Murray in 1859 (M1). The same expression was embodied (published) in a manifestation (book) entitled *The Origin of Species*. This particular manifestation was published in New York by Gramercy in 1995 (M2). Similarly, expressions E2, E3, and E4 have been embodied in different manifestations.
- A publication of a particular book is made available as one copy or a large number of copies. In FRBR terms, a manifestation may be *exemplified* by one or multiple *items*. Mass-produced manifestations, such as publications, result in large numbers of items. Items can be *owned* by individuals or institutions. In the example from Figure 5.2, we see that one item (a copy) of M1 is held by a local public library; a second item is held by the local rare books collection. A copy of a particular publication (item) may have unique information or item-specific information such as an autograph on

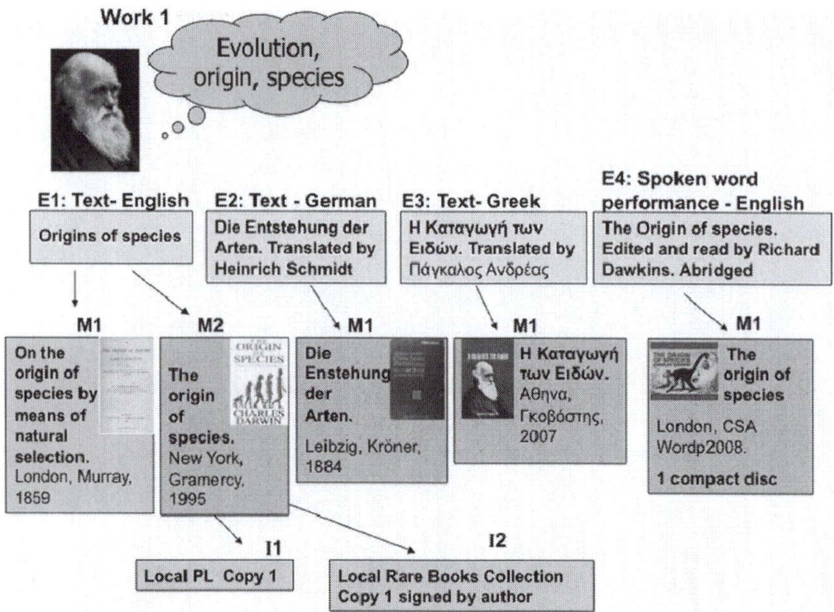

Figure 5.2 Example of Group 1 entities for Darwin.

the title page, which is not shared by all copies (items) of a publication (manifestation) of an expression.

Based on traditions influenced by AACR and MARC 21 structure, it is typical that the cataloging process starts with the item, because it is the item a collection acquires. Cataloging in most American libraries is done in a way that facilitates copy cataloging and, therefore, the description includes those features of the item that are expected to apply to all copies of the manifestation. Information that only applies to a single item is often not shared and is only stored in the local catalog record, although FRBR suggests looking at the entities and their attributes and relationships in a different way. Based on current practices, bibliographic descriptions shared through a network often reflect work, expression, and manifestation information. RDA's "composite description" allows the combination of some elements identifying the work and/or expression embodied in a manifestation with the description of that manifestation.

Two broad categories of entity characteristics, or attributes, are defined in FRBR: those that are inherent in each entity and those that are supplied for each entity from external sources. Inherent attributes are typically determined by examining the entity itself; attributes that are supplied usually require reference to an external source. It is not necessary that all defined attributes apply to all instances of an entity.

Examples of FRBR attributes include the following:

Work attributes
- title of the work
- form of work
- date of the work
- other distinguishing characteristics
- intended termination
- intended audience
- context for the work
- medium of performance (musical work)
- numeric designation (musical work)
- key (musical work)
- coordinates (cartographic work)
- equinox (cartographic work)

Expression attributes
- title of the expression
- form of expression
- date of expression
- language of expression
- other distinguishing characteristic
- extensibility of expression
- revisability of expression
- extent of the expression
- summarization of content
- context for the expression
- critical response to the expression
- use restrictions on the expression
- sequencing pattern (serial)
- expected regularity of issue (serial)
- expected frequency of issue (serial)
- type of score (musical notation)
- medium of performance (musical notation or recorded sound)
- scale (cartographic image/object)
- projection (cartographic image/object)
- presentation technique (cartographic image/object)
- representation of relief (cartographic image/object)
- geodetic, grid, and vertical measurement (cartographic image/object)
- recording technique (remote sensing image)
- special characteristic (remote sensing image)
- technique (graphic or projected image)

Manifestation attributes
- title of the manifestation
- statement of responsibility
- edition/issue designation
- place of publication/distribution
- publisher/distributor
- date of publication/distribution
- fabricator/manufacturer
- series statement
- form of carrier
- extent of the carrier
- physical medium
- capture mode
- dimensions of the carrier
- manifestation identifier
- source for acquisition/access authorization
- terms of availability
- access restrictions on the manifestation
- typeface (printed book)
- type size (printed book)
- foliation (hand-printed book)
- collation (hand-printed book)
- publication status (serial)
- numbering (serial)
- playing speed (sound recording)
- groove width (sound recording)
- kind of cutting (sound recording)
- tape configuration (sound recording)
- kind of sound (sound recording)
- special reproduction characteristic (sound recording)
- colour (image)
- reduction ratio (microform)
- polarity (microform or visual projection)
- generation (microform or visual projection)
- presentation format (visual projection)
- system requirements (electronic resource)
- file characteristics (electronic resource)
- mode of access (remote access electronic resource)
- access address (remote access electronic resource)

Item attributes
- item identifier

fingerprint
provenance of the item
marks/inscriptions
exhibition history
condition of the item
treatment history
scheduled treatment
access restrictions on the item

Figure 5.3 shows a sampling of FRBR attributes and their related content (i.e., the values for each attribute) as they apply to the example of Darwin's English expression published in 1859 by Murray, as depicted in Figure 5.2.

Chapter 6 of the FRBR Report links the attributes of each entity and ER with relevant user tasks. It also indicates the relative value of each attribute or relationship in supporting a specific user task. For example, the attribute "form of work" is of moderate value in finding a work and identifying it, but is of high value in selecting a work; the attribute "title of manifestation" is of high value in finding and identifying a work, expression, or manifestation, of moderate value in selecting a work, expression, or manifestation, and of high value in obtaining a manifestation. This information could aid those developing description standards to identify which attributes and relationships should be mandatory or core in order to facilitate user tasks.

Since the FRBR attributes and relationships serve as the basis for the RDA elements and relationships, these will be defined and discussed in more detail in the chapters that follow.

Functional Requirements for Authority Data (FRAD)

The second model of the FR model family, the *Functional Requirements for Authority Data* (FRAD),[6] was developed by the IFLA Working Group on Functional Requirements and Numbering of Authority Records (FRANAR), and was published in 2009. Its scope was to expand the work of FRBR to define the functional requirements of authority records necessary to support functions of a bibliographic system. The premises of this model are that bibliographic entities are known by names or identifiers, that these names are the basis for the controlled access points used in bibliographic descriptions, and that all decisions about them are recorded as authority data. For example, a person is known by a name or set of names, and this name or set of names becomes the basis for the access point we use in bibliographic descriptions to provide access to resources by this particular person. Information on the name(s) and decisions about the composition of the controlled access point (authority data) is recorded in an authority record.

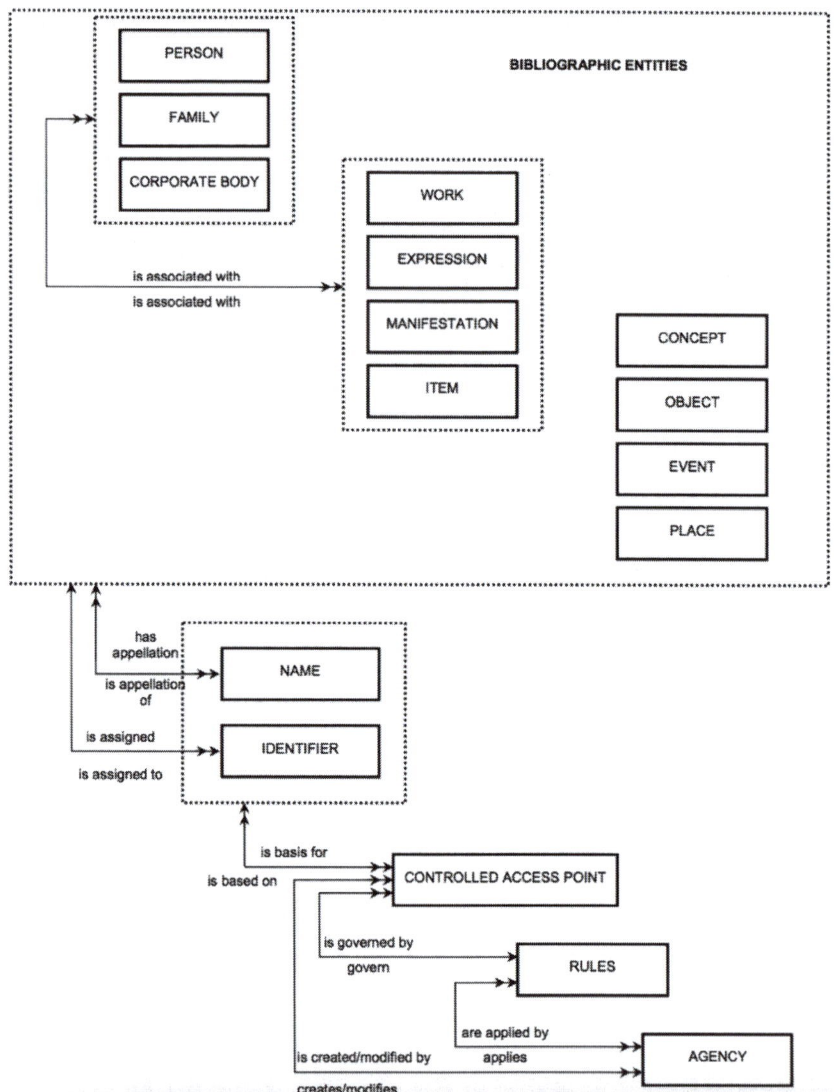

Figure 5.3 Bibliographic entities and relationships in FRAD.

Placing this model in the context of Darwin's *The Origins of Species* from Figure 5.2, one sees the following:

- The *work* "origins of species" is associated with a *person*.
- This *person* is an appellation or is known by a *name* (e.g., Charles Darwin).
- This *name* is used as the basis for composing a *controlled access point* (e.g., Darwin, Charles, 1809–1882).

- This *controlled access point* is governed by, or formulated according to, guidelines from a set of *rules* (e.g., RDA), and
- These *rules* are applied by an *agency* (e.g., the Library of Congress).

Proceeding in reverse order, an *agency* applies *rules* to govern the formulation of a *controlled access point,* which is based on the *name* by which a *person* is known.

FRAD expands the initial FRBR entities by introducing name, controlled access point, identifier, rules, and agency as additional entities. FRAD defines the following entities and attributes (only select attributes are listed):

Entity	Attributes
Person	Dates associated with the person Title of person Gender Place of birth Place of death Country Place of residence Affiliation Address Language of the person Field of activity Profession/occupation Biography/history Other information associated with the person
Family	Type of family Dates of family Places associated with family Language of family Field of activity History of family
Corporate body	Place associated with the corporate body Dates associated with the corporate body Language of the corporate body Address Field of activity History Other information associated with the corporate body
Work	\
Expression	\ See FRBR section and discussion in chapters that follow

Manifestation	/
Item	/
Concept	\
Object	\ No attributes defined in FRAD
Event	/
Place	/
Name	Type of name
	Name string
	Scope of usage
	Dates of usage
	Language of name
	Script of name
	Transliteration scheme of name
Identifier	Type of identifier
Controlled access point	Type of controlled access point
	Status of controlled access point
	Designated usage of controlled access point
	Undifferentiated access point
	Language of base access point
	Language of cataloguing
	Script of base access point
	Script of cataloguing
	Transliteration scheme of base access point
	Transliteration scheme of cataloguing
	Source of controlled access point
	Base access point
	Addition
Rules	Citation for rules
	Rules identifier
Agency	Name of agency
	Agency identifier
	Location of agency

FRAD has defined its own user tasks, with users of authority data being creators of authority data as well as those who use authority data in a bibliographic system. These users perform four major tasks when interacting with authority data:

- **Find** an entity or entities based on a set of criteria.
- **Identify** an entity based on a set of criteria or validate the form of a name to be used as a controlled access point.

- **Contextualize** or place a person, corporate body, work, etc., in context, and
- **Justify** or document the authority data creator's reason for choosing the name or form of name on which a controlled access point is based.

Similar to FRBR, FRAD maps entities and relationships to FRAD user tasks.

Since the FRAD attributes and relationships serve as the basis for the RDA elements and relationships, these will be defined and discussed in more detail in the chapters that follow.

Functional Requirements for Subject Authority Data (FRSAD)

The third and last model in the FR model family, the *FRSAD*, was developed by the IFLA Working Group on Functional Requirements for Subject Authority Records (FRSAR), and was published in 2011. Its scope was to provide a framework of entities relating to the aboutness of works and for sharing and communicating subject authority data. The premise of this model is that works have a subject or are about a subject matter. The focus of FRSAD is in the relationship that exists between a work and its subject matter. In FRSAD (Figure 5.4), two entities are introduced, *thema*, defined as any entity used as a subject of a work, and *nomen*, defined as any sign or sequence of signs that a *thema* is known by or referred to.

Placing this model in the context of Darwin's *The Origins of Species* from Figure 5.2, one sees the following:

- The *work The Origins of Species*" has as subject a *thema*, and
- This *thema* has an appellation or is known by a *nomen* (e.g., evolution).

FRSAD introduces a more abstract-level modeling of subject data to accommodate any types of vocabularies or other knowledge-organization systems used to represent aboutness. In FRSAD, FRBR's *objects, events, places, and concepts* can be considered types of *themas*. Table 5.1 lists the entities and attributes defined in the FRSAD conceptual model:

FRSAD has defined its own user tasks, with users of subject authority data including information professionals who create and maintain subject authority data, information professionals who create and maintain metadata,

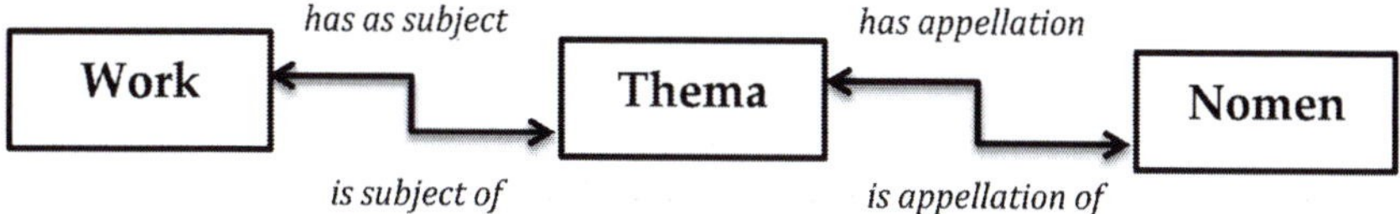

Figure 5.4 Subject entities and relationships in FRSAD.

Table 5.1 Example of FRBR Attributes for Darwin's Work

Entity	*Attribute*	*Value for Darwin*
work	title of work	origins of species
	form of work	essay
expression	language of expression	English
	form of expression	alpha-numeric nation, text
manifestation	title of the manifestation	on the origins of species by means of natural selection
	publisher/distributor	John Murray
	date of publication/ distribution	1859
	form of carrier	volume
item	condition of the item	covers and spine are not in good condition

intermediaries and end users who search for information to fulfill information needs. These users perform four major tasks when interacting with authority data:

- **Find** one or more subjects and/or their appellations, that correspond(s) to the user's stated criteria, using attributes and relationships.
- **Identify** a subject and/or its appellation based on its attributes or relationships.
- **Select** a subject and/or its appellation appropriate to the user's needs, and
- **Explore** relationships between subjects and/or their appellations.

Most subject authority data are created during the development and organization systems. Contributions to subject authority data are also made during the metadata creation, when describing information resources and vocabularies are used to select appropriate subject terminology. A detailed discussion of this model, its entities, and attributes is out of the scope of this book.

Since the publication of the individual FR family models, the IFLA FRBR Review Group has reviewed and maintained the FR family of conceptual models and has been working on special projects like the preparation of an object-oriented formulation of FRBR (FRBRoo) as a compatible extension of the CIDOC-CRM conceptual reference model, or as a general data model for museums. The FRBR Review Group is also working on the consolidation of the three FR family conceptual models into one library reference model (LRM).

International Standard Bibliographic Description (ISBD)

In 1969, the IFLA Committee on Cataloguing sponsored an International Meeting of Cataloguing Experts to start work on the development of guidelines that would standardize the content and format of bibliographic descriptions and increase the sharing and exchange of bibliographic data.[7] The resulting standard was the ISBD, with the first ISBD being the 1971 *International Standard Bibliographic Description for Monographic Publications* (ISBD(M)). The International Standard Bibliographic Description (General), developed by agreement between the IFLA and the Joint Steering Committee for Revision of AACR (JSCAACR), was first published in 1977, and served as a framework for the description of all types of publications in all types of media, thereby ensuring a uniform approach in bibliographic description. The current edition of ISBD is the consolidated edition, published in 2011. ISBDs standardize content and format of bibliographic descriptions by identifying and defining areas of description (elements), the order these areas should appear in a bibliographic record, and a set of prescribed punctuation used to indicate the content of a bibliographic description (this serves as a way to identify/code the areas that appear in a description). A number of ISBDs were developed and maintained over the years, each focusing on a particular type of resource, in addition to the general ISBD. The list of ISBDs published over the years includes the following:

- ISBD (A): *International Standard Bibliographic Description for Older Monographic Publications* (Antiquarian); 1980; 2nd rev. ed. 1991;
- ISBD (CF): *International Standard Bibliographic Description for Computer Files*; 1990;
- ISBD (CM): *International Standard Bibliographic Description for Cartographic Materials*; 1977; rev. ed. 1987;
- ISBD (CR): *International Standard Bibliographic Description for Serials and Other Continuing Resources*; 2002;
- ISBD (ER): *International Standard Bibliographic Description for Electronic Resources*; 1997;
- ISBD (G): *General International Standard Bibliographic Description*; 1977; rev. ed. 1992; 2004 ed.;
- ISBD (M): *International Standard Bibliographic Description for Monographic Publications*; 1974; 1st standard ed. rev., 1978; rev. ed. 1987; 2002 rev.;
- ISBD (NBM): *International Standard Bibliographic Description for Non-Book Materials*; 1977; rev. ed. 1987;
- ISBD (PM): *International Standard Bibliographic Description for Printed Music*; 1980; 2nd rev. ed. 1991;
- ISBD (S): *International Standard Bibliographic Description for Serials*; 1974; 1st standard ed. 1977; rev. ed. 1988;

After the publication of the Final FRBR Report, it was decided to merge the format-specific ISBDs into one. The consolidated edition merges seven specialized ISBDs (for books, maps, serials, sound recordings, computer files and other electronic resources, etc.) into a single text. A new area 0 for content form and media type was introduced in the 2011 consolidated edition. The preliminary consolidated edition was published in 2007 and was incorporated into RDA (Appendix D) as one of the options for data presentation.

A mapping of the ISBD major provisions, including areas, subareas, and prescribed punctuation and mapping to RDA elements, is shown in Table 5.2.

The ISBD consolidated edition introduced a new area of description (Area 0, Content form and media type area) currently not included in the RDA mapping to ISBD (linked from Appendix D of RDA). Subareas and punctuation for Area 0 include the following:

0. Content Form and Media Type area
    0.1 Content form
. Subsequent content form in same media type
\+ Subsequent content form in different media type
( ) 0.1.1 Content qualification
; Subsequent content qualification
: 0.2 Media type

ISBD Punctuation

One of the unique features of the ISBDs is prescribed punctuation marks. Their most prominent feature is using spaces before and after most of them—the exceptions are noted in the list below under "Space." A prescribed punctuation mark precedes each element in the description and signifies the nature of that element. The reason that ISBD-prescribed punctuation marks

Table 5.2 FRSAD Entities and Attributes

Entity	*Attributes*
Thema	Type of thema Scope note
Nomen	Type of nomen Scheme Reference source of nomen Representation of nomen Language of nomen Script of nomen Script conversion Form of nomen Time of validity of nomen Audience Status of nomen

differ considerably from standard prose punctuation is that they were selected to function as a signal or recognition device for the individual areas and elements in the bibliographic description; this serves as a markup language for humans. A person faced with a bibliographic record in an unknown language, for instance, can identify its statement of responsibility because it follows the format of space-slash-space after the title.

The use of ISBD punctuation is incorporated in and required by AACR2, which has often resulted in controversial discussions among catalogers.[8,9,10] Unlike AACR2, RDA does not require the use of ISBD punctuation, but does offer a mapping between ISBD areas of description and their prescribed punctuation and RDA elements in a document-linked form Appendix D, also available through IFLA's web site.[11] This serves as a guideline for the presentation of RDA data according to ISBD specifications, including the order of the elements that are presented in a bibliographic record. Even though it is not required by RDA, the majority of cataloging agencies still follow ISBD punctuation, especially when using the MARC structure. Examples in this text include ISBD punctuation.

RDA BASICS

The development of the RDA guidelines and instructions has been informed by the IFLA *Statement of International Cataloguing Principles.*[12] The principles governing RDA guidelines include the following:

- *Differentiation*: Data used in a description should differentiate one resource from the other. To support this principle, RDA encourages the addition of data beyond the core when it is necessary for identification of resources and the differentiation among similar resources. The guidelines also provide for the addition of notes related to an attribute if the information included in the element associated with an attribute is not considered sufficient.
- *Sufficiency*: Sufficient data should be provided to meet the needs of the user. As explained earlier under the discussion of the objective for responsiveness to users, RDA allows for more granular description by including elements for content, for carriers of content, for details on illustrations, language, presentation of the content, and more.
- *Relationships*: Enough data should be provided to indicate relationships between entities. Due to its connection to the conceptual models of FRBR and FRAD, RDA places much more emphasis on relationships than earlier content standards, like AACR2, did. Not only does RDA have guidelines to record relationships, but it also has guidelines for the use of relationship designators that clearly identify the type of relationships that exist. For

example, for the relationship between a resource and the person responsible for the work, RDA guidelines specify whether the relationship is that of an "author," a "translator," or an "illustrator."

- *Representation*: Data used in the description should truly represent the resource. One of the major differences with AACR2 is that RDA often instructs us to take the information as it appears on the resource itself. Examples of this include guidelines to transcribe the edition information as it appears on the resource (e.g., "second revised edition") instead of altering this information into abbreviated edition statements (e.g., 2nd rev. ed.)
- *Accuracy*: Description data should accurately represent the resource. RDA provides guidelines for the accurate representation of a resource in cases where there is erroneous or ambiguous information, whether when recording the element information or in an explanatory note for elements where transcription of information as it appears on the resource is required.
- *Attribution*: Data should reflect attributes, whether correct or not. For example, in the case of a fictitious character identified by the resource as being responsible for it, RDA instructs us to record such a relationship, despite its fictional nature.
- *Common usage or practice*: Data that are not transcribed should reflect common usage in the language and script chosen for recording the data. Unlike AACR2, which often made use of Latin terminology, RDA guides toward using terminology most commonly employed by the users of the data; currently, this applies mostly to English-speaking users, but as more translations of RDA are made available, this principle will extend to all users. Examples include the use of "publisher not identified" versus "s.n." for *sine nomine* (without a name).
- *Uniformity*: Data should promote uniformity in the presentation of resource descriptions or entity descriptions. RDA separates the recording of information from how the information is displayed. To ensure uniformity, through various appendices for capitalization, order of elements, punctuation, presentation of information, etc., it relates to best practices and use of standards such as ISBD and MARC.

RDA is based on the conceptual models FRBR and FRAD, which can be seen as reflected in its structure. The RDA standard was released in 2010 in the RDA Toolkit, an integrated online resource, and is also available in print. RDA content is grouped in ten sections based on FRBR, FRAD entities and relationships. Sections 4, 7, and 10 (mostly Section 7), relating mostly to the subject relationship for a work, based on FRSAD, have been the most recent additions to RDA guidelines. More specifically, RDA includes the following:

Chapter number: Chapter title:

0. Introduction

Section 1: Recording Attributes of Manifestation & Item

1. General Guidelines on Recording Attributes of Manifestations and Items
2. Identifying Manifestations and Items
3. Describing Carriers
4. Providing Acquisition and Access Information

Section 2: Recording Attributes of Work & Expression

5. General Guidelines on Recording Attributes of Works and Expressions
6. Identifying Works and Expressions
7. Describing Content

Section 3: Recording Attributes of Person, Family, & Corporate Body

8. General Guidelines on Recording Attributes of Persons, Families, and Corporate Bodies
9. Identifying Persons
10. Identifying Families
11. Identifying Corporate Bodies

Section 4: Recording Attributes of Concept, Object, Event, & Place

12. General Guidelines on Recording Attributes of Concepts, Objects, Events, and Places
13. Identifying Concepts
14. Identifying Objects
15. Identifying Events
16. Identifying Places

Section 5: Recording Primary Relationships Between Work, Expression, Manifestation, & Item

17. General Guidelines on Recording Primary Relationships

Section 6: Recording Relationships to Persons, Families, & Corporate Bodies

18. General Guidelines on Recording Relationships to Persons, Families, and Corporate Bodies Associated with a Resource
19. Persons, Families, and Corporate Bodies Associated with a Work

20. Persons, Families, and Corporate Bodies Associated with an Expression
21. Persons, Families, and Corporate Bodies Associated with a Manifestation
22. Persons, Families, and Corporate Bodies Associated with an Item

Section 7: Recording Relationships to Concepts, Objects, Events, & Places
23. General Guidelines on Recording the Subject of a Work

Section 8: Recording Relationships between Works, Expressions, Manifestations, & Items
24. General Guidelines on Recording Relationships between Works, Expressions, Manifestations, and Items
25. Related Works
26. Related Expressions
27. Related Manifestations
28. Related Items

Section 9: Recording Relationships between Persons, Families, & Corporate Bodies
29. General Guidelines on Recording Relationships Between Persons, Families, and Corporate Bodies
30. Related Persons
31. Related Families
32. Related Corporate Bodies

Section 10: Recording Relationships between Concepts, Objects, Events, & Places
33. General Guidelines on Recording Relationships between Concepts, Objects, Events, and Places
34. Related Concepts
35. Related Objects
36. Related Events
37. Related Places

Additional guidelines and instructions are offered in the appendices:
A. Capitalization
B. Abbreviations and Symbols
C. Initial Articles
D. Record Syntaxes for Descriptive Data

E. Record Syntaxes for Access Point Control
F. Additional Instructions on Names of Persons
G. Titles of Nobility, Terms of Rank, Etc.
H. Dates in the Christian Calendar
I. Relationship Designators: Relationships between a Resource and Persons, Families, and Corporate Bodies Associated with the Resource
J. Relationship Designators: Relationships between Works, Expressions, Manifestations, and Items
K. Relationship Designators: Relationships between Persons, Families, and Corporate Bodies
L. Relationship Designators: Relationships Between Concepts, Objects, Events, and Places
M. Relationship Designators: Subject Relationships

RDA ELEMENTS AND ACCESS POINTS

Most FR family model entity attributes and relationships are defined in RDA as elements, defined in the RDA Glossary as a "word, character, or group of words and/or characters representing a distinct unit of bibliographic information." For each entity, some elements used to describe are identified as "core elements." Often, the indication of "core" applies to the entire element or just to a subelement, or an element subtype, or only under certain conditions. Core elements are typically associated with the *find* and *identify* user tasks of FRBR and FRAD, and the *find*, *identify*, and *explore* user tasks of FRSAD.

In addition to defining elements for the description of entities, RDA provides guidelines for the construction of access points—authorized and variant—representing works, expressions, persons, families, and corporate bodies. Access points are names, codes, terms, etc. that are used to represent an entity, whereas elements are data used to describe an entity. An authorized access point is the standard access point reprinting the entity. A variant access point is an alternative to the authorized access point representing the entity, but not considered the standardized access point. RDA Chapter 6 provides guidelines for the construction of authorized access points representing works and expressions; these are discussed in chapter 7 of this book. RDA Chapters 9 through 11 provide guidelines for the construction of authorized access points to represent persons, families, and corporate bodies; these are discussed in chapter 8 of this book. Relationships between entities, an important feature introduced in RDA (compared to AACR2), are often recorded through the use of authorized access points in bibliographic records. Recording relationships are discussed in chapter 9 of this book.

Standardization through authorized access points ensures consistency in the representation of an entity, such as identical, and ideally unique, text strings to represent an entity (work, expression, person, family, or corporate body) in all relevant records. Consistent representation of these entities also helps facilitate user tasks. As hinted in this paragraph, text strings may not always result in a unique representation and identification of an entity. Identifiers, recorded in RDA elements such as "identifier for the work," or "identifier for the person," may provide a more unique identification, but not all entities have assigned identifiers.

Throughout the RDA guidelines, we see instructions to either record certain information as separate elements or as part of an authorized or variant access point representing the entity. Agencies may determine whether an element will be recorded as a separate element, as part of an access point, or both ways, based on policies, practices, and other standards such as encoding schemas used to create and store bibliographic information.

In addition to authorized access points, RDA provides guidelines for the use of titles (such as the title proper of a manifestation) as access points. Other elements can be used as access points, but RDA does not specifically provide guidelines for other data elements to be used as access points. Which elements will be used as additional access points is determined by cataloging agencies or data management systems based on the needs of their users.

RDA AND MARC

Although RDA guidelines do not specify a record structure or an encoding system for bibliographic descriptions, the majority of American libraries currently use MARC 21 to encode bibliographic records, using RDA for the creation of resource descriptions. In the following chapters, discussions on RDA are accompanied by examples to illustrate the guidelines. These examples use MARC 21 to illustrate current encoding practices. Examples of MARC representations may include additional contextual information, with relevant information being highlighted. Often, only a portion of the MARC record is included in the examples. Chapter 3 offers a more detailed discussion of MARC 21.

Use of RDA as the cataloging standard is indicated in a MARC 21 record by the use of the code "rda" in subfield $e (description conventions) of field 040 (cataloging source). In the past, Leader position 18 (labeled as "Desc" in OCLC fixed-field display) of a bibliographic record was used to identify the cataloging standard for the creation of the description included in each bibliographic record. This position was redefined and currently is used primarily to identify whether and how the ISBD standard is applied in the record. A value of "i" indicates that the descriptive portion of the record follows ISBD punctuation conventions. A value of "c" in this position indicates that ISBD punctuation is omitted. A value of "a" indicates use of ISBD punctuation as it is incorporated in AACR2, and a value of blank (#) indicates non-ISBD descriptive cataloging form. Records in this text use "i" for this Leader position, as it is the most common current practice in American libraries, including the Library of Congress–Program for Cooperative Cataloging (LC/PCC).

Cataloging Standard Indication (RDA) in a MARC Bibliographic Record
<begin list here>

Books	Rec Stat c	Entered 20130208		Replaced 20140131093421.8		
Type a	ELvl	Srce	Audn	Ctrl	Lang	eng
BLvl m	Form	Conf 0	Biog	MRec	Ctry	txu
	Cont b	GPub	LitF 0	Indx 1		
Desc i	Ills a	Fest 0	DtSt s	Dates 2013,		

010	2013002241
040	DLC $b eng **$e rda** $c DLC $
020	9781602588219 (hbk. : alk. paper)
020	160258821X (hbk. : alk. paper)
050 00	HM831 $b .R6293 2013
082 00	302.23 $2 23
100 1	Robinson, Brett T., $d 1975-
245 10	Appletopia : $b media technology and the religious imagination of Steve Jobs / $c Brett T. Robinson.
264 1	Waco, Texas : $b Baylor University Press, $c [2013]
300	xi, 147 pages : $b illustrations ; $c 23 cm
336	text $2 rdacontent
337	unmediated $2 rdamedia
338	volume $2 rdacarrier
504	Includes bibliographical references (pages 129-142) and index.
650 0	Social change.
650 0	Mass media $x Technological innovations $x Social aspects.
650 0	Mass media $x Influence.
600 10	Jobs, Steve, $d 1955-2011.
610 20	Apple Computer, Inc.

<end list here>

In addition to the information recorded in bibliographic records, some of the data created using RDA are recorded in authority records, such as information regarding titles of works and expressions, and names of persons, families, and corporate bodies. Similar to MARC bibliographic records, MARC authority records use fixed-field 008, position 10 (labeled as "Rules" in OCLC fixed-field display), value "z" for "other" and the code "rda" in subfield $e (description conventions) of field 040 (cataloging source) to identify RDA as the set of rules used to establish the entity's preferred title or name, appearing in field 1xx of the authority record.

Cataloging Standard Indication (RDA) in MARC Authority Records
<begin list here>

Rec stat n	Entered 20130227	Replaced	20130227104416.0
Type z	Upd status a	Enc lvl n	Source
Roman	Ref status n	Mod rec	Name use a
Govt agn	Auth status a	Subj a	Subj use a
Series n	Auth/ref a	Geo subd n	Ser use b
Ser num n	Name a	Subdiv tp n	Rules

010 n 2013010398
040 DLC $b eng $c DLC $e **rda**
046 $f 1975
100 1 Robinson, Brett T., $d 1975-
670 Appletopia, 2013: $b eCIP t.p. (Brett T. Robinson) data view screen (b. 1975)
<end list here>

<begin list here>

Rec stat c	Entered 19960112	Replaced	20130107162211.0
Type z	Upd status a	Enc lvl n	Source c
Roman	Ref status a	Mod rec	Name use a
Govt agn	Auth status a	Subj a	Subj use a
Series n	Auth/ref a	Geo subd n	Ser use b
Ser num n	Name a	Subdiv tp n	Rules **z**

010 no 96001744
040 CoU $b eng $e **rda** $c CoU $d DLC
100 1 Darwin, Charles, $d 1809-1882. $t On the origin of species. $l Spanish
377 spa
400 1 Darwin, Charles, $d 1809-1882. $t Origen de las especies
670 His El origen de las especies, 1953.
<end list here>

Although the examples used to illustrate RDA element guidelines provide MARC-coded examples, it is not the purpose of this text to discuss in detail MARC 21 coding. For each field used in the examples, the official MARC documentation, available at www.loc.gov/marc, should be consulted. Additional examples, explanations, and specific information applicable to OCLC WorldCat members and available at www.oclc.org/bibformats should also be reviewed.

The following chapters cover RDA guidelines in more detail, each illustrating how to record information in RDA elements representing attributes and relationships. Chapter 6 covers identifying manifestations and items (RDA Chapters 1–4), chapter 7 covers identifying works and expressions (RDA Chapters 5–7), chapter 8 covers attributes for identifying persons, corporate bodies, and families (RDA Chapters 8–11), and chapter 9 covers recording relationships.

NOTES

1. American Library Association, Canadian Library Association, Chartered Institute of Library and Information Professionals (Great Britain), & Joint Steering Committee for Development of RDA. (2010). *RDA: Resource Description & Access*. Chicago, IL: American Library Association.

2. RDA Toolkit. (2010). *RDA Background*. Retrieved from http://www.rdatoolkit.org/background.

3. IFLA Study Group on the Functional Requirements for Bibliographic Records, International Federation of Library Associations and Institutions. (2009). *Functional Requirements for Bibliographic Records, Final Report*. München, Germany: K. G. Saur. Retrieved from http://www.ifla.org/files/assets/cataloguing/frbr/frbr_2008.pdf.

4. IFLA Working Group on Functional Requirements and Numbering of Authority Records (FRANAR), International Federation of Library Associations and Institutions. (2013). *Functional Requirements for Authority Data: A Conceptual Model*. München, Germany: K. G. Saur. Retrieved from http://www.ifla.org/files/assets/cataloguing/frad/frad_2013.pdf.

5. IFLA Working Group on the Functional Requirements for Subject Authority Records (FRSAR), International Federation of Library Associations and Institutions. (2011). *Functional Requirements for Subject Authority Data (FRSAD): A Conceptual Model*. Berlin, Germany: De Gruyter Saur. Retrieved from http://www.ifla.org/files/assets/classification-and-indexing/functional-requirements-for-subject-authority-data/frsad-final-report.pdf.

6. IFLA Working Group on Functional Requirements and Numbering of Authority Records (FRANAR), International Federation of Library Associations and Institutions. (2013). *Functional Requirements for Authority Data: A Conceptual Model*. München, Germany: K. G. Saur. Retrieved from http://www.ifla.org/files/assets/cataloguing/frad/frad_2013.pdf.

7. IFLA Cataloguing Section and ISBD Review Group, International Federation of Library Associations and Institutions. (2011). *International Standard Bibliographic Description (ISBD)* (Consolidated ed.; IFLA series on bibliographic control, Vol. 44). München, Germany: De Gruyter Saur. Retrieved from http://www.ifla.org/publications/international-standard-bibliographic-description.

8. Berman, S. (1977). The cataloging shtik. *Library Journal, 102*(11), 1251–53.

9. Freedman, M. J. (1977). Public libraries, the Library of Congress, and the National Bibliographic Network. *Library Journal, 102*(19), 2211–19.

10. Gorman, M. and Hotsinpiller, J. (1979). ISBD: Aid or barrier to understanding? *College & Research Libraries, 40*(6), 519–26.

11. Dunsire, G. and IFLA Cataloguing Section's ISBD Review Group. (2015). *Alignment of ISBD with RDA, 17 February 2015. Version 3.1. Alignment of the ISBD: International Standard Bibliographic Description Element Set with RDA: Resource Description & Access Element Set.* Retrieved from http://www.ifla.org/files/assets/cataloguing/isbd/OtherDocumentation/isbd2rda_alignment_v3_1.pdf.

12. IFLA Cataloguing Section and IFLA Meetings of Experts on an International Cataloguing Code, International Federation of Library Associations and Institutions. (2009). *Statement of International Cataloguing Principles.* Retrieved from http://www.ifla.org/files/cataloguing/icp/icp_2009-en.pdf.

Chapter 6

Resource Description and Access

Identifying Manifestations and Items

Building upon the RDA basics covered in the previous chapter, this chapter discusses the guidelines as laid out in the web-based version of *RDA*,[1] available through the RDA Toolkit. Sections I and II of RDA contain guidelines on bibliographic description: in other words, they provide instructions on how to represent the bibliographic and physical characteristics of the resources being cataloged. More specifically, Section I of RDA contains guidelines on how to identify and record attributes of manifestations and items, and Section II contains guidelines on works and expressions. All core elements and other major elements and subelements are discussed here and illustrated with examples. Elements associated with Group 2 entity attributes and the relationships among Group 1 and Group 2 entities are discussed in chapter 8.

ORGANIZATION OF THE DESCRIPTION

A bibliographic description includes information about the characteristics or properties of an entity. For example, a film has a time duration, a map has a scale, a toy is made up of different materials, or an object is produced by a manufacturer. These characteristics are identified as attributes (e.g., materials) and relationships (e.g., object is produced by) in FRBR. In RDA, these attributes and relationships are represented as elements recorded in a bibliographic description. RDA uses the following description units, each including elements used to represent attributes for manifestations and items first, and for works and expressions second, to guide the metadata creator or cataloger. Here, minimum requirements for elements, defined as core elements in RDA, are listed under each grouping:

- Recording Attributes of Manifestation & Item
    - General guidelines
    - Identifying Manifestations and Items:
        - Title
        - Statement of responsibility
        - Edition statement
        - Numbering of serials
        - Production statement
        - Publication statement
        - Distribution statement
        - Manufacture statement
        - Copyright date
        - Series statement
        - Identifier for the manifestation
    - Describing Carriers:
        - Carrier type
        - Extent
    - Providing Acquisitions and Access information
- Recording Attributes of Works & Expressions
    - General guidelines
    - Identifying Works and Expressions:
        - Preferred title of the work
        - Identifier of the work
        - Signatory to a treaty, etc.
        - Identifier for the expressions
        - Content type
        - Language of expression
    - Describing Content:
        - Horizontal scale of cartographic content
        - Vertical scale of cartographic content

Additionally, elements can be further defined into subelements or element subtypes, which may vary according to the type of material in hand. The remainder of this chapter discusses descriptive areas and elements pertinent to a wide range of materials.

CORE ELEMENTS IN RDA

It was Charles A. Cutter, in his *Rules for a Dictionary Catalog*,[2] who first proposed the idea of three different levels of cataloging (short, medium, and full) to accommodate the different needs of libraries of different sizes and purposes. The first edition of AACR (1967) and the preceding ALA codes were each designed to respond to the needs of general research libraries, and made only occasional alternative provisions for other types of libraries. AACR2 (1978) remedied this situation by providing three levels of bibliographic description, reflecting Cutter's ideals of a flexible code. This provision continued in *AACR2R*.[3] The first level, also known as minimal-level cataloging, contains at least the elements that basically identify the resource without providing any detailed description. The second level, also known as standard-level cataloging, provides all applicable elements to uniquely identify all copies of a manifestation. The third level represents full description and contains all elements set forth in the rules that are applicable to the item being described.

RDA does not define levels of description but identifies a number of elements as core elements based on the FRBR assessment of the value of each attribute and relationship in supporting the general user tasks defined in FRBR as *find*, *identify*, *select,* and *obtain*. RDA guidelines (0.6.1) specify that, at a minimum, a resource description should include all applicable and readily ascertainable core elements. In addition to core elements, all elements necessary to differentiate the resource described from other similar resources should also be included. It is under the discretion of cataloging agencies to either establish policies and guidelines for the use of all other specific elements or allow individual cataloger judgment to decide the level of detail included in a resource description. For example, both LC and PCC have identified additional elements as core requirements.

The example below shows the applicable RDA core elements in comparison to all applicable RDA elements and relationships, as shown in Figure 3.1 for the same resource.

RDA Core Elements in MARC:

020	9781602588219 (hbk.: alk. paper)
020	160258821X (hbk.: alk. paper)
245 10	Appletopia: $b media technology and the religious imagination of Steve Jobs / $c Brett T. Robinson.
264 1	Waco, Texas: $b Baylor University Press, $c [2013]
300	xi, 147 pages
336	text $2 rdacontent
338	volume $2 rdacarrier

ALTERNATIVES AND OPTIONS

RDA contains a number of alternatives and options, indicated by *Alternative, Optional Addition, Optional Omission*, or *Exception*. These allow individual libraries or cataloging agencies to make decisions based on individual considerations in cases where two or more provisions are equally valid. Each library or cataloging agency must decide on whether or not to use each optional provision by either establishing a local policy on the application of the optional provision or allowing individual catalogers to use their judgment (preferably having users in mind). Libraries using LC cataloging data will most likely conform to LC practice.

LIBRARY OF CONGRESS-PROGRAM FOR COOPERATIVE CATALOGING POLICY STATEMENTS (LC-PCC PS)

In its own use of RDA, the LC has made a number of guideline interpretations and/or application decisions of optional provisions. Similarly, the international PCC has made a number of mutually acceptable decisions regarding the application of RDA guidelines. To ensure consistency in application, these LC-PCC PS are made available as part of the RDA Toolkit. Libraries and other information agencies that make use of LC cataloging data consult LC-PCC PS regularly in order to achieve consistency between their own cataloging and that of LC and most other libraries.

LC-PCC PS is also included in Cataloger's Desktop, an integrated online system that also contains other cataloging tools. Desktop is produced by the Library of Congress Cataloging Distribution Service and available as a subscription product on the Web.

TRANSCRIPTION AND RECORDING

A number of RDA elements have been identified as transcription elements, which means that they should be copied exactly as they appear on the specified places of the resource, such as the title page of a book, or the title screens of a moving image. This emphasis on transcription is in line with the representation principle of the *International Cataloging Principles,*[4] which recommends content standards to include guidelines to represent a resource the way it represents itself. Stated in more simple words, transcription is also referred to as "take what you see." In RDA, and more generally in cataloging, these specified places of a resource where certain information is to be taken from are identified as sources of information. Transcription of these elements, along with some exceptions, is discussed in RDA 1.7. In applying RDA 1.7, several guidelines are included for capitalization, punctuation, diacritical marks, symbols, letters or words intended to be read more than once, abbreviations, and inaccuracies. For elements that are not transcribed, RDA instructs us to "record" information instead of transcribing the information.

For recorded elements, the information found on the resource may be adjusted or taken from another source, outside the resource itself. For example, information may be copied from a source, but exact wording, as it appears on the source may not necessarily be preserved.

The guidelines for capitalization (RDA 1.7.2) point to Appendix A, where different cases are described in detail, including capitalization of information in English and select other languages. The following example illustrates the most common practice in American libraries for English, which instructs us to basically follow *The Chicago Manual of Style*: for English titles, capitalize the initial letter of the first word of the title proper, alternative title, parallel title, or quoted title, and the initial letter of each word of any proper name (RDA A.4 and A.10).

Title page:
ERIK BRYNJOLFSSON
ANDREW McAFEE

THE SECOND MACHINE AGE
Work, Progress, and Prosperity
in a Time of Brilliant Technologies

Transcription as it is represented in RDA elements:

Title proper:	**The second machine age**
Other title information:	**work, progress, and prosperity in a time of brilliant technologies**
Statement of responsibility:	**Erik Brynjolfsson, Andrew McAfee**

Transcription as it is represented in MARC 21, grouped onto one field (245):

245 14 $a **The second machine age**: $b **work, progress, and prosperity in a time of brilliant technologies** / $c **Erik Brynjolfsson, Andrew McAfee**.

From this example, we see that the *title* element for a manifestation consists of three units of data (subelements) that are transcribed from the source of information (title page of the book). These include the *title proper*, the main title of the manifestation, *other title information*, in this case the subtitle, and the *statement of responsibility*, or information about those responsible for the resource. In the transcription, the information is taken as it appears on the source, but not necessarily in the order it appears on the title page (those responsible for the resource appear before the title, but in the transcription, we start with the main title) or with the same capitalization of the words transcribed. So, although we take information as it is on the resource, we closely but not exactly copy this information following RDA guidelines.

LANGUAGE AND SCRIPT

In creating a resource description, one needs to consider the language of the resource—most specifically, the language(s) and the script of the given resource's main source of information, as well as the language and the script preferred by the cataloging agency. RDA 1.4 identifies a number of elements that should be transcribed in the language and script as they appear on the sources from which this information is taken. These elements include the title, statement of responsibility, edition statement, numbering of serials, production, publication, distribution, and manufacture statements, and series statement. An alternative is to record the transliterated form if it is not possible to record the information in the script used on the source itself.

Title page:
ΕΛΕΝΗ ΣΚΟΤΕΙΝΙΩΤΟΥ
Φώτης Κόντογλου
Η γραφή του ως διακείμενο
Εκδόσεις Σοκόλη

Language and script as it appears on the resource:
245 10 $a Φώτης Κόντογλου: $b η γραφή του ως διακείμενο / $c Ελένη Σκοτεινιώτη.
264 1 $a Αθήνα: $b Εκδόσεις Σοκόλη, $c 2009.
300 $a 255 pages; $c 24 cm
336 $a text $2 rdacontent
337 $a unmediated $2 rdamedia
338 $a volume $2 rdacarrier
504 $a Includes bibliographical references (pages [247]-255).

Alternative in transliterated form (Latin script):
245 10 $a **Phōtēs Kontoglou**: $b **hē graphē tou hōs diakeimeno** / $c **Helenē Skoteiniōtē.**
264 1 $a **Athēna**: $b **Ekdoseis Sokolē**, $c c2009.
300 $a 255 pages; $c 24 cm
336 $a text $2 rdacontent
337 $a unmediated $2 rdamedia

338 $a volume $2 rdacarrier
504 $a Includes bibliographical references (pages [247]-255).

RDA allows for an optional addition of the element in the transliterated form when the information is already recorded in the script and language appearing on the source.

Language and script as they appear on the resource with optional addition in transliterated form (Latin script):

245 10 $6880-02 $a Φώτης Κόντογλου: $b η γραφή του ως διακείμενο / $c Ελένη Σκοτεινιώτη.
880 10 $6245-02 a **Phōtēs Kontoglou**: $b **hē graphē tou hōs diakeimeno** / $c **Helenē Skoteiniōtē**.

TYPES OF DESCRIPTION

Based on the type of the resource and the purpose of the description (RDA 1.5), RDA defines three different ways an information agency may choose to describe a resource: comprehensive description, analytical description, and hierarchical description.

Comprehensive Description (RDA 1.5.2)

A comprehensive description is used to describe a resource as a whole. This resource can be a single unit, a multipart monograph, a serial, an integrating resource, or a collection of two or more resources gathered by an individual or an agency.

Analytical Description (RDA 1.5.3)

An analytical description is used to describe part of a larger resource. This part can be a single unit contained within the larger unit, part of a multipart monograph, part of a serial, part of an integrating resource, or part of a collection gathered by an individual or an agency. Details about the larger unit or other parts of the resource should be recorded either as series statements or relationships.

Hierarchical Description (RDA 1.5.4)

A hierarchical description combines a comprehensive description of a whole resource and analytical descriptions of its parts. LC-PCC PS 1.5.4 instructs us not to create hierarchical descriptions.

CHANGES REQUIRING NEW DESCRIPTION

The guidelines in RDA 1.6 instruct us to create new descriptions when there are major changes in three main categories of resources: multipart monographs, serials, and integrated resources. More specifically, these include changes in the following:

- Mode of Issuance of a multipart monograph (e.g., change to a serial)
- Media Type changes of a multipart monograph (e.g., change from print, unmediated, to electronic)
- Mode of Issuance of a serial (e.g., change to an integrated resource)
- Carrier Characteristics of a serial (e.g., from print to electronic)
- Title Proper (major) of a serial
- Responsibility of a serial (e.g., change that requires different identification of the work)
- Edition of a serial, indicating change in the scope or coverage of the serial
- Mode of Issuance of an integrated resource (e.g., change to a serial or multipart monograph)
- Media Type of an integrated resource (e.g., print to electronic)
- Base volumes of an integrated resource (e.g., change in how the pages are indicated)
- Edition of an integrated resource, indicating a change in scope or coverage of the integrating resource

IDENTIFYING GROUP 1 ENTITIES

On a broad level, RDA guidelines are organized in sections dealing with attributes (Sections 1–4) and those dealing with relationships (Sections 5–10). RDA guidelines within sections are organized based on the entities and user tasks defined in FRBR. RDA Chapters 2 through 4 (Section 1) include instructions on attributes of manifestations and items, with Chapter 2 relating to the FRBR user task *identify*, Chapter 3 to *select*, and Chapter 4 to *obtain.* Chapters 5 through 7 (Section 2) include guidelines on attributes of works and expressions, with Chapter 6 relating to the FRBR user task *identify*, and Chapter 7 to *select.*

Bibliographic and authority information is covered by different RDA sections but is not necessarily identified as such. Neither does RDA specify record structures for each section's elements. The remainder of this chapter covers what is traditionally defined as descriptive bibliographic data, which includes Recording Attributes of Manifestation & Item and Recording Attributes of Work & Expression.

IDENTIFYING MANIFESTATIONS AND ITEMS

RDA Chapters 2 through 4 provide guidelines for the description of a "resource," which typically refers to a manifestation. Resources can be issued in different forms. They can be one discrete unit that is tangible or intangible (one sound recording, or one letter printed on a piece of paper). They can also be a series of units that together form a resource, an aggregate of entities, or a component of an entity. A resource can then be issued as a single unit (single-unit monograph), a multipart monograph, or a serial or integrating resource. This categorization is recorded as Mode of Issuance. In addition, guidelines for the description items are also included.

When identifying or describing a manifestation or item, all applicable core elements should be included at the minimum, if applicable and readily ascertainable. RDA 1.3 identifies the following core manifestation and item elements:

- Title
  - Title proper
- Statement of responsibility
  - Statement of responsibility relating to title proper (if more than one, only the first recorded is required)
- Edition statement
  - Designation of edition
  - Designation of a named revision of an edition
- Numbering of serials
  - Numeric and/or alphabetic designation of first issue or part of sequence (for first or only sequence)
  - Chronological designation of first issue or part of sequence (for first or only sequence)
  - Numeric and/or alphabetic designation of last issue or part of sequence (for last or only sequence)
  - Chronological designation of last issue or part of sequence (for last or only sequence)
- Production statement
  - Date of production (for a resource in an unpublished form)
- Publication statement
  - Place of publication (if more than one, only the first recorded is required)
  - Publisher's name (if more than one, only the first recorded is required)
  - Date of publication
- Distribution statement

Place of distribution (for a published resource, if place of publication not identified; if more than one, only the first recorded is required)
Distributor's name (for a published resource, if publisher not identified; if more than one, only the first recorded is required)
Date of distribution (for a published resource, if date of publication not identified)
Manufacture statement
Place of manufacture (for a published resource, if neither place of publication nor place of distribution identified; if more than one, only the first recorded is required)
Manufacturer's name (for a published resource, if neither publisher nor distributor identified; if more than one, only the first recorded is required)
Date of manufacture (for a published resource, if neither date of publication, nor date of distribution, nor copyright date identified)
Copyright date
Copyright date (if neither date of publication nor date of distribution identified)
Series statement
Title proper of series
Numbering within series
Title proper of subseries
Numbering within subseries
Identifier for the manifestation
Identifier for the manifestation (if more than one, prefer an internationally recognized identifier if applicable)
Carrier type
Carrier type
Extent
Extent (only if the resource is complete or if the total extent is known)

Sources of Information

When we create a description to represent a resource, we determine from where to take the data that will be included in the description. The location from where we take the data is referred to as source of information. Having guidelines for sources of information is imperative for the creation of consistent and interoperable metadata. The RDA principle of representation emphasizes the need for the data describing a resource to be a true representation of the resource itself, and therefore identifying attributes that are inherent in the resources is very useful. RDA identifies preferred sources of information and other sources of information. For most elements, RDA specifies the preferred source of information to be used for that particular element but also allows the use of other sources (or "any source"), if the information is not available in the preferred source or the preferred source is not available for that particular resource. Other sources are typically listed in order of preference. For example, a typical book may have its title printed on its spine, the front cover, the back cover, and the title page. There are cases, where variations in the title appear in these locations of the book. When the information for the RDA element *title proper*, a core element of the manifestation, has to be transcribed, follow RDA's instruction of using the title page of the book as the preferred source of information. If the book does not have a title page, then we are instructed to first look at the cover or jacket of the book to take the title information; if the cover or jacket is not available either, use the caption as the source, and so on. If the resource is a video game, the title frame(s) or title screen(s) are the preferred sources for the *title proper*.

Not all elements have a preferred source of information. For example, information can be taken from any source when providing information for the element *note on manifestation*.

RDA 2.1 instructs us to choose an appropriate source of information based on the type of description that will be created (comprehensive or analytical) and the mode of issuance of the resource. The current discussion focuses on comprehensive description, a description of the resource as a whole, which is more commonly used than analytical description.

In general, the basic guideline is to use a source of information that identifies a resource as a whole. More specifically, when creating a comprehensive resource that is issued as a nonintegrating single unit (e.g., one volume, one video recording), we choose a source of information that identifies the resource as a whole; if there are multiple works in the resource, then we choose the one that has a collective title.

When describing a resource that has more than one part, we choose, as appropriate, from the following:

a. If the set of parts are unnumbered or the numbering does not establish an order, choose the source that identifies the resource as a whole, with preference to the one that has a collective title.
b. If the parts or issues are sequentially numbered, choose the source with the lowest numbered part or issue.
c. If the parts or issues are unnumbered or the numbering does not establish an order, choose the issue or part with the earliest date of issue.

d. If there is no source that identifies the resource as a whole, choose the source that has a title that identifies the predominant content or the resource, and
e. If none of the above, treat the sources identifying the individual parts as a collective source of information or whole resource.

If the source of information is not the first issue or part, the issue or the part that serves as the basis for the description should be identified in a note (RDA 2.20.13.3)

When creating a comprehensive description for an integrating resource, choose a source of information that identifies the most current version of the resource as a whole, no matter how many parts it has. In a note, identify the basis of the description.

Once the various sources of information are identified and selected (which source), the cataloger can use the detailed guidelines to choose the preferred source of information (where in the source) to look for the information to transcribe or record in the various elements of the bibliographic description. Often, information relating to the same element appears in more than one place in the resource itself. For example, a title proper may appear on the title page, the front cover, spine, back cover, title page verso, or colophon, and it may not always be exactly the same. RDA 2.2.2 guides the cataloger in the choice of the preferred source.

Resources consisting of one or more pages, leaves, sheets, or cards (or images of pages, leaves, sheets, cards) (RDA 2.2.2.2): If the resource is any type of general printed material, such as a book, images of printed material, such as microform, the preferred source of information is the title page, title sheet, or title card. If there is no title page, sheet, or card, choose as preferred source of information the first of the following that includes a title:

a. A cover or jacket that is part of the resource.
b. A caption: a page that has the title and typically is also the first page of text or music.
c. A masthead: a statement near the beginning of a serial publication that includes the title, editors, and other details.
d. A colophon: a page at the end of the resource that may include the title, author, publication information, printing information, or other additional information.

If none of the above has a title, choose any part of the resource that includes the title, preferably one that has a formal presentation of the title.

Resources consisting of moving images (RDA 2.2.2.3): For moving images, such as film reels, a videodisc or video file, use the title frame (area at the beginning or end of a film where the title, director, casts, etc. are included), or the title screen (same information presented in a digital resource) as the preferred source of information. Always prefer the title frames or title screens that formally present a collective title when the moving image consists of individual contents that form parts of the resource. As an alternative, RDA allows the use of a label that is permanently printed or affixed to the resource itself (not its container or accompanying material) if it includes title and other information. For resources without title frames or screens, use the alternative label permanently affixed on the resource or the embedded textual metadata that contain title information. Furthermore, for online resources, RDA instructs us to use the place between the textual content and embedded metadata where the title appears first. For tangible resources, RDA instructs us to use the title from the first source as it appears between the label on the resource, a supplemental resource that is accompanying the resource itself (e.g., the title page of a print booklet that comes with the resource), and a place within the source itself (opening menu in the disc).

Other Types of Resources (RDA 2.2.2.4): For all other resources, not covered in RDA 2.2.2.2–2.2.2.3, use as the preferred source of information the first of the following that includes title information, or collective title information (in case of works with individual titled contents): textual source of the resource itself, label permanently affixed to the resource (not the container or accompanying material), internal source such as the title screen, or a container or accompanying material that is issued with the resource, when dealing with tangible resources; textual content or embedded metadata in textual form that contain title information, when dealing with online resources. If none of these sources has title information, use another source forming part of the resource that formally presents the title information.

Other Sources of Information (RDA 2.2.4): If there is no title information on the resource itself or a source forming part of the resource, use another source from the following (in order of precedence): accompanying material, other published descriptions of the resource, a container not issued with the resource, or any other source. Indication of the source of information is made typically as a note, except when the resource itself does not normally carry identifying information (e.g., photographs, natural objects, archival collections). More specifically, RDA instructs us to indicate the source of information if not available from the preferred source for the manifestation elements of title, statement of responsibility, edition statement, numbering of serials, production, publication, distribution, and manufacture statements, and series statement.

MANIFESTATION ATTRIBUTES

Manifestation attributes are often used to identify a resource. This is similar to information publishers would use to identify their product, such as its title. The elements covered in this section are associated with manifestation attributes, but not all of them will be applicable to all manifestations. If applicable, at a minimum, all elements and subelements identified as core should be included in the description of the resource. Additions to the core elements should be provided if necessary for the identification of a resource and to ensure differentiation among similar resources.

Title (RDA 2.3)
Core element: *title proper*
[MARC field 245 and 246]

Title is defined as one or more words and/or characters that name the resource or the work contained in the resource. The following titles are identified in RDA: (1) title proper, (2) parallel title proper; (3) other title information; (4) parallel other title information; (5) variant title; (6) earlier title proper; (7) later title proper; (8) key title; and (9) abbreviated title. The title proper is a core element; other titles are optional.

Recording titles (RDA 2.3.1.4): Titles are transcribed based on RDA 1.7. If a title is very lengthy, it is possible to abridge the title, as long as there is no loss of essential information and no omission of the first five words of the title. Omission of words is indicated by the use of ellipses (. . .). A general title, especially title proper, is not abridged, and it is only in rare occasions that words from the title are omitted.

Title page:

Members of the Ancient and Honorable Artillery Company in the colonial period, 1638-1774; and, Members of the General Court of Massachusetts Bay (1638), comprising the governor, the governor's council, and deputies to the General Court and clergymen who preached annual election sermons (1638-1774).

RDA 2.3.1.4 Title abridgement:

245 10 $a **Members of the Ancient and Honorable Artillery Company in the colonial period, 1638-1774 . . .** / $c originally compiled by Maude Roberts Cowan.
250 $a Revised edition / $b Mrs. William Homer Watkins.

264 1 $a [Washington, D.C.]: $b National Society Women Descendants of the Ancient & Honorable Artillery Co., $c 1989.

Names of Persons, Families, and Corporate Bodies as titles (RDA 2.3.1.5): Transcribe the title as it appears on the preferred source of information, even if it is just the name of a person, family, or corporate body. If a name is included in the title and is an integral part of the title, transcribe it as it appears in the title. However, if the name precedes or follows the title and is not an integral part of it, do not include it in the transcription of the title.

Title page:
Bergin and Garfield's handbook of psychotherapy and behavior change

Names or Persons as part of the title:
245 00 $a **Bergin and Garfield's handbook of psychotherapy and behavior change** / $c edited by Michael J. Lambert.
250 $a 6th edition.
264 1 $a Hoboken, N.J.: $b John Wiley & Sons, $c 2013.

Introductory words (RDA 2.3.1.6): Introductory words that are not intended to be part of the title should not be included in the transcription of the title. This is more common in moving pictures, sound recordings, or web sites, where we see statements like "Warner Brothers Presents . . ." preceding a title.

Audio disc label:
Warner Brothers presents
MONTROSE!

Introductory words:
245 10 $a **Montrose!**
264 0 $a Burbank, Calif.: $b Warner Bros., $c [1990?], 1973.
264 2 $a Scarborough, ON: $b Distributed by WEA Music of Canada Ltd., $c 1990.
300 $a 1 audio disc: $b digital; $c 4 3/4 in.

Title Proper (RDA 2.3.2)
Core element
[MARC field 245, subfield $a]

The title proper is defined as the chief name of a resource. In other words, it is the main title of a resource, the title typically used to cite a resource. Title proper includes any alternative titles and is transcribed as it appears on the preferred source of information, following its wording, order, and spelling, though not necessarily the punctuation and capitalization (see above discussion on transcription, RDA 1.7). An alternative title is a second title, typically preceded by "or" in English (or equivalent in other languages). As a second title, the first letter of the initial word is capitalized (RDA A.4.1). In print materials, the title proper is usually readily identifiable. It is more difficult to determine the title proper of a web site or web page.

Title proper: **The American Bar Association legal guide for women**
MARC21: 245 04 $a **The American Bar Association legal guide for women**

Title proper: **An Introduction to the complete Dead Sea scrolls**
MARC21: 245 13 $a **An introduction to the complete Dead Sea scrolls** / $c Geza Vermes.

Title proper: **Oroonoko, or, The royal slave**
MARC21: 245 10 $a **Oroonoko, or, The royal slave** / $c Aphra Behn; edited by Catherine Gallagher with Simon Stern.

Title proper: **Women, equality, and the French Revolution**
MARC 21: 245 10 $a **Women, equality, and the French Revolution** / $c Candice E. Proctor.

Title proper: **The hobbit, or, There and back again**
MARC21: 245 14 $a **The hobbit, or, There and back again** / $c by J.R.R. Tolkien.

Title proper: **3D home design suite deluxe 4.0**
MARC21: 245 00 $a **3D home design suite deluxe 4.0**

Title proper: **3 sonatas of the English Baroque**
MARC21 245 00 $a **3 sonatas of the English Baroque**: $b for treble recorder (flute) and basso continuo = 3 englische Barock-Sonaten: für Altblockflöte (Querflöte) und Basso continuo / $c William Turner, William Topham, Robert Valentine; edited by Hugo Ruf.

If the resource described has a source of information that includes both a collective title and titles of individual contents, use the collective title in the transcription of the title proper when creating a comprehensive description (RDA 2.3.2.6).

Title page:
The
OVERSOUL SEVEN
Trilogy

THE EDUCATION OF OVERSOUL SEVEN
THE FURTHER EDUCATION OF OVERSOUL SEVEN
OVERSOUL SEVEN AND THE MUSEUM OF TIME

Collective title:

245 14 $a **The Oversoul Seven trilogy** / $c Jane Roberts; cover art by Robert F. Butts.

505 0_ $a The education of Oversoul Seven—The further education of Oversoul Seven—Oversoul Seven and the Museum of Time.

If an analytical description is created for any of the parts of the resource, then the title of that particular part as it appears on its source of information is transcribed.

Other Elements as Part of the Title Proper (RDA 2.3.2.8)

Music resources often have a generic title such as "Symphony" or "Piano concerto" indicating the type of composition. Such resources end up with lengthy titles proper partly because there are a number of elements that are added to distinguish them from other resources with the same generic titles. If the title of the resource includes a term indicating the type of composition, transcribe as part of the title proper any information included that identifies a medium of performance (e.g., "for two pianos"), a key (e.g., "A minor"), the date of composition (e.g., "[1876]"), or a number (e.g., "opus 5").

Title proper: **Sonate für Klavier und Viola Es-Dur, Opus 5 Nr. 3**

MARC21: 245 10 $a **Sonate für Klavier und Viola Es-Dur, Opus 5 Nr. 3** = $b Sonata for piano and viola in E♭ major, op. 5 no. 3 / $c Johann Nepomuk Hummel; herausgegeben von Ernst Herttrich; Fingersatz der Klavierstimme von Klaus Schilde; mit zusätzlicher bezeichneter Violastimme von Tabea Zimmermann.

If the title of the music resource is not a generic term that indicates the type of composition, transcribe the additional information included on the preferred source of information as part of the other title information (subfield b), not in the title proper.

Title proper: **They who hunger**
MARC21: 245 10 $a **They who hunger**: $b for piano and strings / $c by Jan Swafford.

Cartographic materials (maps, atlases, etc.) often include information about the scale in their title. If such statement is included in the title proper as it appears on the preferred source of information, transcribe the scale as part of the title proper. Scale information is also a separate element, covered in RDA 7.25.

Title proper: **London AZ super scale 9" to 1 mile street map**
MARC21: 245 10 $a **London AZ super scale 9" to 1 mile street map**: $b one way streets, selected car parks, over 8,000 streets . . . sports facilities.

Resource Lacking a Collective Title (RDA 2.3.2.9)

Resources that contain more than one individual work typically have a collective title that represents the collection of all works included in the resource. Sometimes, there is no collective title present, but individual titles are listed, with or without their respective creators, on the preferred source of information. There are also cases where there is no one preferred source of information and titles are listed individually on separate title pages (or other locations) throughout the resource. According to RDA 1.5, there are two choices: (a) create a comprehensive description for the resource as a whole; or (b) create individual analytical descriptions for each of the parts contained in the resource.

If a comprehensive description is created for a resource lacking a collective title, transcribe the titles proper for each part contained in the resource as they appear on the source of information as a whole, or as they appear in the individual title pages, in the order they appear in the resource, if there is no one collective title page for the entire resource.

For a resource lacking a collective title, with one source of information listing all titles of parts:

Title proper: **The clouds; The birds; Lysistrata; The frogs**
MARC21: 245 14 $a The clouds; $b The birds; Lysistrata; The frogs / $c Aristophanes; translated by James H. Mantinband.

Note that all works are by the same person, and, therefore, the titles are separated by a semicolon (;). The ISBD punctuation and only the first title is included in MARC subfield $a. The remaining titles are listed in subfield $b.

For a resource lacking a collective title, with individual title pages for each part:

Title proper:	**Ground zero**	
Title proper:	**Guide for the apoplexed**	
MARC21:	100 1_	$a Lysymy, Paul.
	245 10	$a **Ground zero** / $c by Paul Lysymy. **Guide for the apoplexed** / by Herman Gnuticks.
	264 1	$a Pittsburgh: $b SterlingHouse, $c 2000.
	300 __	$a 146, 62 pages; $c 23 cm
	500 __	$a Guide for the apoplexed is a fictional work by Lysymy writing under the pseudonym Herman Gnuticks and is the subject of Ground zero.
	500 __	$a Issued with individual title pages and inverted paging.
	710 12	$a Lysymy, Paul. $t Guide for the apoplexed.

Note that each work has a different creator, and, therefore, each title is listed separately and associated with its statement of responsibility. Note that there is no MARC subfield encoding in Field 245 to indicate the separate statements for the title and associate responsibility for additional works.

Resources with No Title (RDA 2.3.2.10)

The title proper is a core element in RDA. If a resource has no title, the cataloger has to either find the title of the resource in a different source or devise a title if one cannot be found. A title found in another source should be recorded in the title proper as found, and the source of the title should be indicated in a note (MARC 500 field), if the resource would normally bear a title (e.g., a printed book). It is a typical practice to indicate that a title is taken from outside the resource itself by enclosing it in square brackets.

Title proper:	**[Manuscripts in the libraries of the Greek and Armenian patriarchates in Jerusalem]**	
MARC21:	245 10	$a **[Manuscripts in the libraries of the Greek and Armenian patriarchates in Jerusalem]**
	500	$a Title from index.
	500	$a Accompanied by an index prepared under the direction of Kenneth W. Clark:

Checklist of manuscripts in the libraries of the Greek and Armenian Patriarchates in Jerusalem.

Devising Titles (RDA 2.3.2.11)

If there is no title on the resource and one cannot be found in other sources, RDA 2.3.2.11 allows the cataloger to devise a title that describes the nature or the subject of a resource, or both.

If the resource would normally bear a title, enter the title proper enclosed within square brackets and indicate the source in a note:

Title proper:	**[Music from Symphony in black, Reminiscing in tempo, and New world a comin']**	
MARC21:	245 10	**[Music from Symphony in black, Reminiscing in tempo, and New world a comin']** / $c [Duke Ellington]
	264 0	[2013]
	300	16 folders (scores + parts (258 leaves)) in 1 container; $c 28 cm.
	336	notated music $2 rdacontent
	337	unmediated $2 rdamedia
	338	volume $2 rdacarrier
	500	From the Smithsonian National Museum of American History Archives: Duke Ellington collection, 1927-1988. Series 1, Box 371, Folders 15-17 (Ducky wucky, Jealuous, and Saddest tale from Symphony in black); Box 305, Folders 1-5 (Reminiscing in tempo); and Box 243, Folders 1-8 (New world a comin').
	546	$b **Staff notation.**

If the resource would normally not bear a title, enter the title proper without square brackets:

Title proper:	**Tobacco bowl.**	
MARC21:	245 10	$a Tobacco bowl.
	264 0	$c [1920?].
	300	a 1 container with lid: $b woven straw and lacquer; $c approx. 13 cm. and 11 cm. in diameter.

500 $a Dark brownish black colored woven bowl. Lid has design with sea shells and small crab.

When devising a title for a number of resources that require additional elements in the title, include applicable information necessary to distinguish them from other similar resources. For example, for music, include any applicable medium of performance, numeric designation, key, or other distinguishing characteristics of the work and expression; for cartographic resources, include the area covered and subject portrayed; for moving images, include the product name (and note that the word "advertisement" is a product advertisement); and for archival resources and collections, include applicable names of creators, collectors, or source.

Title proper:	**Richard W. Etulain Papers**	
MARC21:	100 1	Etulain, Richard W. $e creator
	245 10	Richard W. Etulain Papers
	300	0.2 linear feet. $a (1 folder)
	336	text $2 rdacontent
	337	unmediated $2 rdamedia
	338	sheet $2 rdacarrier
	506	There will be a published version of the manuscript with the University of Oklahoma Press which will be different from the copy in the MHS archives.
	520 2	Richard W. Etulain Papers (2014). This collection consists of an unpublished version of Etulain's "Calamity Jane: a Life and Legends" that was published by the University of Oklahoma Press. The manuscript in this collection contains end notes and bibliography.
	524	Richard W. Etulain Papers, (n.d.), Montana Historica Society Research Center
	541	Richard W. Etulain, $b Clackamas, Oregon $d December 2013 $e AC2014-01.
	545 0	Richard W. Etulain is the author or editor of more than fifty books, including Conversations with Wallace Stegner on Western History and Literature, Beyond the Missouri: The Story of the American West, and Lincoln Looks West: From

the Mississippi to the Pacific. A Professor Emeritus of History at the University of New Mexico, he lives in Clackamas, Oregon.

Changes in the Title Proper (RDA 2.3.2.12 and RDA 2.3.2.13)

RDA 1.6 lists a number of changes that require the creation of a new description, among them changes in the title proper. This question is also based on whether the changes are such that the resource is not considered a new work, expression, or manifestation, or whether the changes are minor and do not require a new description. In these cases, relevant guidelines that should be consulted include RDA 1.6 and 6.1.3.

Major changes in the title proper of subsequent parts of a multipart monograph that would affect identification or access should be recorded as later title proper.

Major changes in the title proper of subsequent issues or parts of a serial (RDA 2.3.2.13) should be treated as new resources, and, therefore, a new description should be created. The two works should be treated and linked as related works (RDA 25.1). If the changes in the title proper are minor, but important enough for identification and access, record the later title as later title proper. Major changes in the title proper of serials include changes in the first five words of the title proper; changes in the meaning of the title or changes in the subject matter of the content; and changes in any corporate body name included in the title proper. Minor changes in the title proper of a serial include differences in representation of any word in the title (e.g., spelled-out numbers or symbols); changes in articles, prepositions, and conjunctions included in the title; changes in the name of the same corporate body included in the title; changes in the order of titles in different languages; changes in title words associated with the numbering of a serial; changes in words that are not considered significant to change the subject matter of the content; and changes in title words indicating the type of resource (e.g., journal).

Parallel Title Proper (RDA 2.3.3) [MARC field 245, subfield $b]

The title proper of a resource is often given in multiple languages. The title appearing first on the preferred source of information is considered the title proper. The remaining titles, equivalent in meaning to the title proper, are treated as parallel titles. A parallel title is the title proper in another language and/or script. It should not be confused with an alternative title or other title information, which are not equivalent in meaning to the title proper. Parallel titles are recorded using the same guideline as the title proper (RDA 2.3.1) and in the order they appear on the resource. Also, current MARC encoding practice is to record the parallel title in MARC field 246 for direct access to the title.

Title proper: The one hundred new tales
Parallel title: **Les cent nouvelles nouvelles**
MARC21: 245 14 $a The one hundred new tales = $b **Les cent nouvelles nouvelles**
246 31 $a Cent nouvelles nouvelles

Title proper: She doesn't want the worms
Parallel title: **Ella no quiere los gusanos**
MARC21: 245 10 She doesn't want the worms = $b **Ella no quiere los gusanos** / $c by Karl Beckstrand; illustrated by David Hollenbach.
246 30 Ella no quiere los gusanos

Title proper: International travel maps, Beijing, China, scale 1:20,000 (City), 1:100,000 (Region)
Parallel title: **Guo ji lü you di tu, Beijing, bi li 1:20,000 (Beijing Cheng), 1:100,000 (Beijing Shi)**
MARC21: 245 10 $a International travel maps, Beijing, China, scale 1:20,000 (City), 1:100,000
(Region) = $b **Guo ji lü you di tu, Beijing, bi li 1:20,000 (Beijing Cheng), 1:100,000 (Beijing Shi)**
246 31 $a Guo ji lü you di tu, Beijing, bi li 1:20,000 (Beijing Cheng), 1:100,000 (Beijing Shi)

Often, parallel titles are followed by parallel statements of responsibility. In such cases, based on ISBD ordering, elements of the same language are kept together.

Title proper: Likovna Baština obitelji Pejačević
Parallel title: **Tre art Heritage of the Pejačević family**
MARC21: 245 10 Likovna Baština obitelji Pejačević: $b studijsko-tematska izložba katalog izložbe = **Tre art Heritage of the Pejačević family**: a study and thematic exhibition catalogue of the exhibition / $c Jasminka Najcer Sablijak, Silvija Lučevnjak.

Other Title Information (RDA 2.3.4) [MARC field 245, subfield $b]

Other title information includes any title other than the title proper, the parallel, or series title(s), and any phrase appearing in conjunction with the title proper. Subtitles, avanttitres, and phrases indicative of the character and contents of the item or the motives for, or occasion of, its production or publication, all fall into this category. RDA instructs us not to supply other title information that does not appear on the preferred source of information, except possibly for cartographic materials (when area covered or subject is not included in the title proper or other title information) and moving images (for trailers of a larger movie but not indicated as such).

Other Title Information:
Title page:
MARBLED PAPER
ITS HISTORY, TECHNIQUES,
AND PATTERNS
With Special Reference to the Relationship of
Marbling to Bookbinding in Europe and
the Western World

RICHARD J. WOLFE

Title proper:	Marbled paper
Other title information:	**its history, techniques, and patterns**: **with special reference to the relationship of marbling to bookbinding in Europe and the Western world**
MARC21	245 10 $a Marbled paper: $b **its history, techniques, and patterns: with special reference to the relationship of marbling to bookbinding in Europe and the Western world** / $c Richard J. Wolfe.
Title proper:	Autism and creativity
Other title information:	**is there a link between autism in men and exceptional ability?**
MARC21:	245 10 $a Autism and creativity: $**b is there a link between autism in men and exceptional ability?** / $c Michael Fitzgerald.

Parallel Other Title Information (RDA 2.3.5) [MARC 245, subfield $b]

Parallel other title information is the other title information in a language or script different from the title proper and the other title information. The same instructions as for all other titles (RDA 2.3.1) apply for the recording of the parallel other title information. The source of information is the same as the corresponding parallel title proper source.

Title proper:	Likovna Baština obitelji Pejačević
Other title information:	studijsko-tematska izložba katalog izložbe
Parallel title:	Tre art Heritage of the Pejačević family
Parallel other title information:	**a study and thematic exhibition catalogue of the exhibition**
MARC21:	245 10 Likovna Baština obitelji Pejačević: $b studijsko-tematska izložba katalog izložbe = Tre art Heritage of the Pejačević family: **a study and thematic exhibition catalogue of the exhibition** / $c Jasminka Najcer Sablijak, Silvija Lučevnjak.

Variant Title (RDA 2.3.6) [MARC field 246]

A variant title is the title associated with the resource that serves as a main title, but is different from the title proper (or other title, parallel title, parallel other title, earlier or later title, key title, or abbreviated title). Variant titles may

- appear in the resource itself (cover, spine, title screen, etc.), on the container, dust jackets, or accompanying materials;
- be found in reference sources;
- be assigned by an agency preparing the resource description;
- be assigned by the creator, owner, or custodian of the resource;
- be correction to what appears on the resource itself;
- be a portion of the title appearing on the resource; and may
- be variations of other titles, for example, other title information, parallel, title, and so on.

Variant titles are recorded in MARC field 246 or 740, omitting initial articles. LC provides best practices for variant titles in LC-PCC PS 2.3.6.3. Cataloger's judgment is required in many cases.

Title proper:	101 things that changed the world
Variant title (alternate form):	**One hundred and one things that changed the world.**
MARC21:	245 00 $a 101 things that changed the world. 246 3_ $a **One hundred and one things that changed the world.**

Title proper:	Backroad mapbook, central Alberta
Other title information:	outdoor recreation guide
Variant title (portion):	**Central Alberta:** $b **outdoor recreation guide**
MARC21:	245 10 $a Backroad mapbook, central Alberta: $b outdoor recreation guide / $c writer, Trent Ernst. 246 30 $a **Central Alberta**: $b **outdoor recreation guide**

Title proper:	The Bad Seeds jukebox
Variant title (container)	**Mojo presents The Bad Seeds jukebox**
MARC21:	245 04 The Bad Seeds jukebox. 246 18 Title from container spine: $a **Mojo presents The Bad Seeds jukebox**

Indicators in MARC field 246 allow automatic note generation. Indicator 1 specifies whether a note should be generated (e.g., indicator value 1 specifies indexing the title and generating a note; 3 is for indexing the title without generating a note). The second indicator specifies the type of variant title (e.g., 0 for "Portion of title:", or 4 for "Cover title:", etc.)

Key Title (RDA 2.3.9) and Abbreviated Title (RDA 2.3.10)

Key title is specific to serial publications, assigned at the same time as the ISSN. A key title found on the resource is recorded in MARC field 222. An abbreviated title of the key title is often provided and is recorded in MARC field 210. Both key title and abbreviated title are assigned by the agency assigning ISSNs, and, therefore, catalogers record them if they are available; they do not supply these.

Title proper:	Asian scientist magazine
Key title:	**Asian scientist magazine**
Abbreviated title:	**Asian sci. mag.**
MARC21:	210 1_ $a **Asian sci. mag.**
	222 _0 a **Asian scientist magazine**
	245 00 a Asian scientist magazine

Statement of Responsibility (RDA 2.4.2)
Core element: *first statement relating to title proper*
[MARC field 245, subfield $c]

The statement of responsibility names the person or persons responsible for the intellectual or artistic content of the resource being described, the corporate body or bodies from which the content emanates, or the persons or corporate bodies responsible for the performance of the content. The persons named may include writers, editors, compilers, adapters, translators, revisers, illustrators, reporters, composers, artists, photographers, cartographers, collectors, narrators, performers, producers, directors, and investigators. The statement relating to the title proper that appears first is the preferred source of information for an RDA core element (required). Other statements of responsibility are optional, allowing for cataloger's judgment to record based on what is important for identification of the resource and access to it. Using RDA 1.7 as the overarching guidelines, the statement or statements of responsibility are recorded as they appear on the source (RDA 2.4.1.4). One does not need to add the words "by" or "and" to make a grammatically correct statement; however, if they do appear on the source, they should be recorded (do not change "&" to "and"). A single statement of responsibility may include one or more persons, families, or corporate bodies, and such statements should be recorded as a single statement of responsibility.

Do not abbreviate words or correct inaccuracies. Do not omit words or abridge statements. If you choose to follow the optional provision to abridge a statement of responsibility without loss of essential information, do not use a mark of omission (. . .). If clarification of the role of a person, family, or corporate body is necessary, add a word or brief phrase in square brackets to indicate that it was taken from outside the resource (RDA 2.4.1.7). Noun phrases associated with the statement of responsibility are recorded as part of the statement. Statements of responsibility can be taken from anywhere in the resource itself, without the need to use square brackets.

Statement of responsibility:	**Jonathan Ames**
MARC21:	245 10 $a Wake up, **sir!**: $b a novel / $c **Jonathan Ames**
Statement of responsibility:	**by Anne Baker**
MARC21:	245 10 $a From biplane to Spitfire: the life of Air Chief Marshal **Sir** Geoffrey Salmond / $c **by Anne Baker**
Statement of responsibility:	**David Coombs, Minnie Churchill**
MARC21:	245 10 $a **Sir** Winston Churchill paintings / $c **David Coombs, Minnie Churchill**
Statement of responsibility:	**Robin Prior and Trevor Wilson**
MARC21:	245 10 $a Command on the Western Front: $b the military career of **Sir** Henry Rawlinson 1914-18 / $c **Robin Prior and Trevor Wilson**
Statement of responsibility:	**[editors in chief,] Joseph E. Shigley, Charles R. Mischke, Thomas H. Brown, Jr.**
MARC21:	245 00 $a Standard handbook of machine design / $c **[editors in chief,] Joseph E. Shigley, Charles R. Mischke, Thomas H. Brown, Jr.**
Statement of responsibility:	**developed by the National Information Standards Organization**
MARC21:	245 10 $a Information retrieval (Z39.50): $b application service definition and protocol specification: an American national standard / $c **developed by the National Information Standards Organization**
Statement of responsibility:	**The Diagram Group, Victoria L. Chapman & David Lindroth**
MARC21:	245 10 $a The 20th century / $c **The Diagram Group, Victoria L. Chapman & David Lindroth**

If there is more than one statement of responsibility, record additional statements in the order they appear on the source of information (RDA 2.4.1.6), separated by the ISBD space-semicolon-space punctuation.

Statement of responsibility:	**project editors, Joanna Callihan, Lindsay Ann Mizer; art director, Robert Sanford; interior design and production, Christopher Fowler, Suzanne Reinhart**
MARC21:	245 00 $a Sculpting & drama / $c **project editors, Joanna Callihan, Lindsay Ann Mizer; art director, Robert Sanford; interior design and production, Christopher Fowler, Suzanne Reinhart**
Statement of responsibility:	**Sir David Gibbons, a.k.a. Grandpa; with Allison Moir-Smith**
MARC21:	245 10 $a Life of an optimist / $c **Sir David Gibbons, a.k.a. Grandpa; with Allison Moir-Smith**
Statement of responsibility:	**Saint Thomas More**
Statement of responsibility:	**by William Roper; edited by John F. Thornton and Susan B. Varenne; preface by Joseph W. Koterski**
MARC21:	245 10 $a Selected writings / $c **Saint Thomas More**. Together with, The life of Sir Thomas Moore / **by William Roper; edited by John F. Thornton and Susan B. Varenne; preface by Joseph W. Koterski**
Statement of responsibility:	**by Sir Arthur Conan Doyle; edited, with a foreword and notes by Leslie S. Klinger; introduction by John le Carré; with additional research by Patricia J. Chui**
MARC21:	245 10 $a The new annotated Sherlock Holmes / $c **by Sir Arthur Conan Doyle; edited, with a foreword and**

notes by Leslie S. Klinger; introduction by John le Carré; with additional research by Patricia J. Chui

If a statement is taken from outside the resource, record it within square brackets:

Statement of responsibility:	**[compiled by Mrs. Roy Dean Burk]**
MARC21:	245 00 $a Oak Grove Cemetery, Nacogdoches, Texas / $c **[compiled by Mrs. Roy Dean Burk]**

Recording all statements of responsibility is a major change from previous cataloging rules, more specifically the AACR2 "rule of three," which instructed that up to three names be recorded in one statement of responsibility when more than three were listed on the source of information.

In RDA, transcribing all statements of responsibility is the default guideline. RDA guidelines provide an optional omission of multiple statements of responsibility if more than three performing the same function are named (RDA 2.4.1.5). In such cases, the first name (person, family, corporate body) is always listed as an RDA core requirement, and any additional statements are recorded or omitted in the language of the cataloging agency, summarizing what was omitted.

Title page:
AIRPORT COOPERATIVE RESEARCH PROGRAM
ACRP REPORT 104
Defining and Measuring
Aircraft Delay and Airport
Capacity Thresholds

TransSolutions
Fort Worth, TX

Futterman Consulting
St. Petersburg, FL

Harris Miller & Hanson, Inc.
Herndon, VA

Jasenka Rakas
Berkley, CA

Statement of responsibility:	**TransSolutions . . . [and three others]**
MARC21:	245 00 Defining and measuring aircraft delay and airport capacity thresholds / $c **TransSolutions . . . [and three others]**

Edition Statement (RDA 2.5)
Core element: *edition designation* subelement
[MARC field 250]

RDA defines "edition statement" as the statement identifying the edition to which a resource belongs. In terms of a traditional definition, edition is "all copies of a book, pamphlet, fascicle, single sheet, etc., printed from the same typographic image and issued by the same entity in the same format at one time or at intervals without alteration. An edition may consist of several impressions in which the text and other matter are not substantially changed."[5] Sometimes, a new edition is required due to changes in the content relating to the expression (e.g., in an abridged edition). RDA associates the edition statement with a phrase appearing on a manifestation.

The edition statement is a transcription element following RDA 1.7 guidelines, and, therefore, is recorded exactly as it appears on the resource. One has to be careful to distinguish the edition statement from the generic use of the word edition by publishers and printers to mean impression or printing (e.g., 10th printing)—a distinction that is generally ignored. Music resources often use "edition" to indicate an arrangement. Electronic resources often use the terms version, update, or release to indicate edition.

If there is no edition statement associated with the resource, you should not assume it is the "first edition." An identified or named edition is not simply a sequence of the publication history of a resource; such histories often convey information about content changes and are indicators of when we have a new manifestations of an existing work.

Edition Designation (RDA 2.5.2)

An edition designation is the first part of the edition statement, and often the only part available. Additional parts include parallel edition statements and statements of responsibility relating to the edition and parallel edition statements. The preferred source for edition statement information is the source of the title proper, but any location within the resource itself serves as the source of information. If the edition statement comes from outside the resource itself, it should be recorded within square brackets. If there is a named revision of an edition, record both the edition and revision, separated by a comma. The edition designation and the designation of a named revision are core elements. The remaining edition statement subelements are optional.

Edition statement: **First edition**
MARC21: 250 $a **First edition.**

Edition statement: **2005 edition**
MARC21: 250 $a **2005 edition.**

Edition statement: **3rd ed.**
MARC21: 250 $a **3rd ed.**

Edition statement: **Tax release 3**
MARC21: 250 $a **Tax release 3.**

Edition statement: **Version**
MARC21: 250 $a **Version 2.**

Edition statement: **Preliminary ed.**
MARC21: 250 $a **Preliminary ed.**

Edition statement: **2e édition**
MARC21: 250 $a **2e édition.**

Edition statement: **1. Auflage**
MARC21: 250 $a **1. Auflage.**

Edition statement: **2nd edition, 2002 revision**
MARC21: 250 $a **2nd edition, 2002 revision.**

If an edition statement consists of a letter or letters and/or a number without an associated word, add an appropriate word for the type of edition within square brackets to indicate that the word is taken from outside the resource itself (RDA 2.5.2.3).

Edition statement: **Second [edition]**
MARC21: 250 $a **Second [edition]**

If the edition statement is part of the title proper, other title information, statement of responsibility or an integral part of other elements, record it with the element with which it appears and do not add a separate edition statement.

Title proper:	John Colet on the ecclesiastical hierarchy of Dionysius
Other title information:	a **new edition** and translation with introduction and notes
MARC21:	245 10 $a John Colet on the ecclesiastical
hierarchy of Dionysius:	$b a **new edition** and translation with introduction and notes / $c introduction, annotations, and edited text by Daniel T. Lochman; translation and comments on Colet's Latin by Daniel J. Nodes.

If the edition designation appears in more than one language, record the edition statement in the language of the title proper. If there are parallel edition designations, use cataloger's judgment to decide whether parallel edition statements will be recorded, as this is not an RDA core element, and, therefore, not required.

Edition statement:	**2. Auflage**
Parallel edition statement:	**2a edizione**
MARC21:	250 $a **2. Auflage** = $b **2a edizione.**

Statement of Responsibility Relating to the Edition (RDA 2.5.4)

Sometimes, an edition designation has a statement of responsibility associated with the particular edition. A statement of responsibility relating to an edition designation, and not associated with the title proper, is recorded in the edition statement, following the edition designation.

Edition statement:	Revised ed. / **Mrs. William Homer Watkins**
MARC21:	250 $a Revised ed. / $b **Mrs. William Homer Watkins.**

Numbering of Serials (RDA 2.6)
Core element
[MARC field 362]

For serial publications, numeric, alphabetic, and/or chronological designations of issues or parts are identified, typically relating to the first and last (if the serial is completed) issues. The numeric and/or alphabetic designation of first issue or part of sequence, chronological designation of first issue or part of sequence, numeric and/or alphabetic designation of last issue or part of sequence, and chronological designation of last issue or part of sequence, if available, are core elements. Even though core, the designations for the last issue, part, etc. are not recorded until the serial is complete (available). Other numbering information is optional.

Numbers are recorded based on RDA 1.8, which states that they should be recorded in the form preferred by the agency creating the data, which could be as it appears on the resource itself or in a specified form, for example, always using Arabic numerals. Other words or characters associated with the numbering of serials are recorded as they appear on the resource.

The subelements of the numbering of serials include the following:

- The numeric/alphabetic designation of the first part
- The chronological designation of the first part
- The numeric/alphabetic designation of the last part
- The chronological designation of the last part

Title proper:	**American journal** of applied sciences
Numbering of serial:	
designation of the first part:	**Vol. 1, no. 1**
chronological desig. of first part:	**Jan./Mar. 2004**
MARC21:	362 1 $a **Vol. 1, no. 1 (Jan./Mar. 2004)-**

Title proper:	Air repair
Numbering of serial:	
designation of the first part:	**Vol. 1, no. 1**
chronological desig. of first part:	**July 1951**
designation of the first part:	**v. 4, no. 4**
chronological desig. of first part:	**Feb. 1955**
MARC21:	362 $a **Vol. 1, no. 1 (July 1951)-v. 4, no. 4 (Feb. 1955)**

Title proper:	Progress in tumor research
Numbering of serial:	**in 2014**
designation of the first part:	**Began with vol. 41**
chronological desig. of first part:	**in 2014**
MARC21:	362 1 $a **Began with vol. 41 in 2014.** 588 $a Description based on: Vol. 41 (2014); title from title page. 588 $a Latest issue consulted: Vol. 41 (2014).

If this information is not available to the cataloger, it is normally omitted (although many catalogers add this information in a note). For a number of subelements, RDA (2.5.2–2.6.5) gives the option to add a note rather than record the information in the numbering of serials element. LC and PCC often follow the alternative to make a note (using RDA 2.20.5).

Production Statement (RDA 2.7)
Core element: *Date of production* subelement
[MARC field 264, Indicator 1 = 0]

The production statement is used for unpublished resources and its main purpose is to identify the place of production, name of producer, and date of production, which are the three subelements of the production statement element. Unfortunately, RDA does not define published and unpublished resources, and, therefore, cataloger's judgment may be required to determine when a resource is unpublished; the exception to this is RDA 2.8.1.1, which instructs us to consider all online resources as published. Only the date of production is core.

Place of Production (RDA 2.7.2)

Transcribe the place of production as it appears on the resource. If the place of production is taken from a source outside the resource, it should be recorded within square brackets. Not being a core element, the place of production is often omitted.

Place of production:	**Madison, WI**
MARC21	264 0 $a **Madison, WI**

Producer's Name (RDA 2.74)

If the name of the producer of an unpublished resource is given, record it as it appears on the resource. If it is taken from outside the resource, it should be recorded within square brackets. Producer's name is not a core element, and, therefore, it is often omitted.

Producer's name:	**John Marinos**
MARC21:	264 0 $a Madison, WI: $b **John Marinos**, $c 2010

Date of Production (RDA 2.7.5)

The date of production of unpublished resources is a core; therefore, it is required. Often, a date is the only subelement included in the production statement. This is true in most descriptions of archival collections, where the date of production of the collection (single date or a range of dates) is recorded. Note that the date of production can be taken from any source, and, therefore, use of square brackets is not required if the date is taken from outside the resource.

Date of production:	**1991-2011**
MARC21:	100 1 Adams, Irene, $e creator.
	245 10 Irene Adams papers.
	264 0 $c **1991-2011**.
	300 1 carton $a (1 linear ft.)
	300 1 half box $a 0.25 linear ft.)

Publication Statement (RDA 2.8)
Core element
[MARC field 264, Indicator 1 = 1]

The publication statement records information about the place of publication, publisher's name, and date of publication of all published resources. This information is very important in the identification, differentiation, and verification of the resource sought, and, therefore, all three subelements are core, and recording each of them is required. Information is recorded as it appears on the source of information.

Place of Publication (RDA 2.8.2)
[MARC field 264, subfield $a]

Information about the place of publication can come from anywhere on the resource, with preference given to the source where the publisher's name is found. If place of publication is not found on the resource, a place of publication found outside the resource is recorded within square brackets. If no place can be found, the cataloger should supply a place (city, but, if not possible, then country). If the cataloger is not sure about the supplied place, then the supplied place is followed by a question mark. If it is impossible to supply a place of publication, the phrase "Place of publication not identified" is recorded in the place of publication subelement.

The place of publication is recorded in the form in which it appears on the source of information, and, therefore, should not be abbreviated, unless it appears so on the resource. The name of the country, state, province, etc. is added to the name of a local place if it is considered necessary for identification, or for the purpose of distinguishing the place from others of the same name. The name of the country, state, province, etc. is enclosed in brackets if it does not appear on the source of information.

Place of publication: **New York**
MARC21: 264 1 $a **New York**: $b Simon & Schuster, $c 2014.

Place of publication: **Singapore**
MARC21: 264 1 $a **Singapore**: $b Asian Scientist Publishing Pte Ltd, $c 2014-

Place of publication: **Philadelphia, Pennsylvania**
MARC21: 264 _1 $a **Philadelphia, Pennsylvania**: $b Elsevier Saunders, $c [2014]

Place of publication: **Athens [Greece]**
MARC21: 264 1 $a **Athens [Greece]**: $b Technological Educational Institute of Athens, $c 2007-

Place of publication: **[Athens, Greece?]**
MARC21: 264 1 $a **[Athens, Greece?]:** $b Polyphone Records, $c [1979]

Place of publication: **[Place of publication not identified]**
MARC21: 264 1 $a **[Place of publication not identified]**: $b Match Books, LLC. , $c 2013.

Place of publication: **[Washington, D.C.]**
MARC21: 264 1 $a **[Washington, D.C.]**: $b [U.S. Government Printing Office], $c [2014]

If the resource being described lists two or more places of publication, or names of publishers, the firstnamed place of publication and the corresponding publisher's name are recorded. Only the first place of publication is core.

Source of information:

Springer
Heidelberg New York London
Springer © 2012

Place of publication: **Heidelberg**
MARC21: 264 1 $a **Heidelberg**: $b Springer, $c [2012]

As a core element, the first place of publication must be recorded. Any other place and name can be recorded or omitted.

Place of publication: **Heidelberg; New York; London**
MARC21: 264 1 $a **Heidelberg; New York; London**: $b Springer, $c [2012]
Place of publication: **Heidelberg; New York**
MARC21: 264 1 $a **Heidelberg**; **New York**: $b Springer, $c [2012]

Publisher's Name (RDA 2.8.4)
[MARC field 264, subfield $b]

The publisher's name is transcribed as it appears on the source of information, without any abbreviations or shortening. RDA 2.8.1.4 offers the cataloger the option to omit "levels in a corporate hierarchy that are not required to identify the publisher" without having to add the omission mark (. . .). LC-PCC policy statement recommends no omission of hierarchical levels. The source of information for the publisher's name is the entire resource, but preference is given to the source where the title proper is found. If the publisher's name is found outside the resource, the information is recorded within square brackets.

Publisher's name: London: **Penguin**, 1994
MARC21: 264 1 $a London: **$b Penguin**, $c 1994.

Publisher's name: Washington, DC: **American Institute of Architects**, 2008
MARC21: 264 1 $a Washington, DC: **$b American Institute of Architects**, $c 2008.

Publisher's name: Chico, CA: **Department of Health and Community Services, California State University**, [2003]
MARC21: 264 1 $a Chico, CA: **$b Department of Health and Community Services, California State University**, $c [2003]

Publisher's name: [Hollywood, California]**: Americana, the Institute for the Study of American Popular Culture**, 2011
MARC21: 264 1 $a [Hollywood, California]**:** $b **Americana, the Institute for the Study of American Popular Culture**, $c 2011.

Publisher's name: Piggyback Interactive Limited
MARC21: 264 _1 $a [London]: $b **Piggyback Interactive Limited**, $c [2014]

Title page:
Howard Books
a Division of Simon & Schuster

Publisher's name: **Howard Books**
MARC21: 264 1 $a New York: $b **Howard Books**, $c 2013.

If there is more than one publisher listed on the resource, record all names in the order they appear on the resource. If there are multiple places associated with the multiple publishers, record each publisher with its associate place. Only the first publisher's name is core and required to be recorded.

Publisher's name: **M. Witmark & Sons**
Publisher's name: **Josef Weinberger**
Publisher's name: **Allan & Co.**
Publisher's name: **Canadian-American Music**
MARC21: 264 1 $a New York; $a Chicago; $a London; $a San Francisco: $b **M. Witmark & Sons**; $a Leipzig; $a Vienna: $b **Josef Weinberger**; $a Melbourne, Australia: $b **Allan & Co.**; $a Toronto: $b **Canadian-American Music**, $c 1905.

If no publisher is found on the resource or can be found outside the resource, the phrase "Publisher not identified" is recorded.

Publisher's name: **[Publisher not identified]**
MARC21: 264 1 $a [Germany]: $b **[publisher not identified],** $c [1889]

Date of Publication (RDA 2.8.6) [MARC field 264, subfield $c]

Date of publication is the year or range of years of publication, release, or issuing of the resource. Copyright dates and printing dates are not considered publication dates, but a resource may have the same publication and copyright date, for example. The preferred sources for the date of publication are, in order of preference, the source of the title proper, any source within the resource itself, or any other source specified in RDA 2.2.4 and discussed earlier in this chapter under Sources of Information. When cataloging a book, most commonly, dates of publication can be found on the title page, the title page verso, and the colophon. If no date of publication is found in the resource and one is supplied from outside the resource itself or inferred, enter the date within square brackets. If the date appearing on the resource is known to be incorrect, make a note giving the correct date.

For recording numbers including dates using RDA 1.8.2, the date of publication is recorded in the preferred form of the cataloging agency. Alternatively, if the date is not in numerals, it can be transcribed (as it is on the resource itself), and the equivalent date using numerals can be added within square brackets, following the transcribed date. This is also the LC policy (LC-PCC PS 1.8.2).

Date of publication:	**2004**	
MARC21:	264 1	$a London: $b Penguin, $c **2004**
Date of publication:	**2011**	
MARC21:	264 1	$a New York: $b Little, Brown and Co., $c **2011**
Date of publication:	**MDCCCLXXXIX [1889]**	
MARC21:	264 1	$a New York: $b Anson D.F. Randolph, $c **MDCCCLXXXIX [1889]**

When cataloging multipart monographs, serials, and integrating resources, record the date of publication of the first part and the date of publication of the last part. If publication is not yet complete, the earliest date followed by a hyphen (called an open entry) is given. If the dates of the first and last parts are not found on the first and last parts themselves, record dates found elsewhere within square brackets.

Publication date:	**19691973**
MARC21:	264 1 $a New York: $b Academic Press, $c **19691973**
Publication date:	**2011-**
MARC21:	264 1 $a New York: $b Random House, $c **2011-**
Publication date:	**[2013]-**
MARC21:	264 1 $a [Thousand Oaks, CA]: $b Sage on behalf of: The American Orthopaedic Society for Sports Medicine, $c **[2013]-**

If the date of publication is not found on the resource or outside the resource, the date of publication for a single-part resource can be inferred. This is done because it provides important information about the age of the content (in most cases, as the date of publication does not always mean date of expression or work creation) and because the date of publication is often used to limit searches. By not having a date at all, these resources or their records will not be retrieved in a limited search of date of publication. Most libraries will infer missing publication date from the copyright date. It is then optional to record both the inferred date of publication and the date of copyright.

Date of publication:	**[2011]**
MARC21:	264 1 $a Thousand Oaks: $b SAGE Publications, $c **[2011]**
Copyright date:	©2011
MARC21:	264 4 $c ©2011

Other supplied dates of publication can be recorded based on instructions in RDA 1.9.2, as follows:

unknown year:

Date of publication:	**[2013]**
MARC21:	264 1 $a Chicago: $b American Library Association, $c **[2013]**

either one of two consecutive dates:

Date of publication:	**[1994 or 1995]**
MARC21:	264 1 $a New York, N.Y.: $b Palgrave Macmillan, $c **[1994 or 1995]**

probable year:

Date of publication:	**[1963?]**
MARC21:	264 1 $a [Nacogdoches, Tex.]: $b Nacogdoches Historical Commission, $c **[1963?]**

probable range of years:

Date of publication:	**[between 1963 and 1975?]**
MARC21:	264 1 $a [Draper, UT]: $b Live Your Truth Press, $c **[between 1963 and 1975?]**

earliest and/or latest possible date known

Date of publication:	**[not before 1932]**
MARC21:	264 1 $a Sydney: $b Angus & Robertson, $c **[not before 1932]**

Date of publication:	**[not after 1943]**
MARC21:	264 1 $a New York $b Simon and Schuster, $c **[not after 1943]**

Date of publication: **[between December 12, 1994 and March 17, 1999]**
MARC21: 264 1 $a Geneva, Switzerland: $b World Health Organization, $c **[between December 12, 1994 and March 17, 1999]**

If no information can be found about the date of publication or inferred date, enter the phase "date of publication not identified" within square brackets. In this case, the date of distribution becomes core and should be recorded. If both dates of publication and distribution are not identified, the copyright date becomes core.

Publication date: **[date of publication not identified]**
MARC21: 264 1 $a New York: $b Random House, $c **[date of publication not identified]**

Distribution Statement (RDA 2.9)

Core element only for publications with no publication information
[MARC field 264, Indicator 1 = 2]

The distribution statement records information about the place of distribution, distributor's name, and date of distribution in the three defined subelements. The subelements are not core unless one of the publication information subelements is missing, in which case the relevant distribution subelement becomes core, if available. Guidelines for recording distribution information are similar to the guidelines for recording publication information.

Place of distribution: **Boston**
Distributor's name: **distributed in the U.S. by Random House**
Date of distribution: **1998**
MARC21: 264 2 $a **Boston**: $b **distributed in the U.S. by Random House**, $c **1998**

Manufacture Statement (RDA 2.10)

Core element for publications with no publication or distribution information
[MARC field 264, Indicator 1 = 3]

The manufacture statement records information about the place of manufacture, manufacturer's name, and date of manufacture. These three subelements are not core unless one of the publication and distribution information subelements is missing or there is no copyright date, in which case the relevant manufacture subelement becomes core, if available. Guidelines for recording manufacture information are similar to the guidelines for recording publication information.

Place of distribution:	**Lexington, Ky**	
Distributor's name:	**[manufacturer not identified]**	
Date of distribution:	**2014**	
MARC21:	264 3 $a	**Lexington, Ky**.: $b **[manufacturer not identified]**, $c **2014**

Place of distribution:	**[Bristol]**	
Distributor's name:	**J. Sage**	
Date of distribution:	**[approximately 1830]**	
MARC21:	264 3	$a **[Bristol]**: $b **J. Sage**, $c **[approximately 1830]**

Copyright Date (RDA 2.11)
Core element for publications with no publication or distribution dates
[MARC field 264, Indicator 1 = 4, $c]

The date associated with the claim of the rights to the resource under copyright law or similar regulations constitutes the copyright date. Copyright also includes phonogram date, which is the date associated with the rights of an audio recording. Copyright date becomes a core if no publication or distribution dates are available. In practice, we see that a copyright date is recorded if the publication date is different from the copyright date or inferred from the copyright date.

The copyright date can appear in different forms on the resource, such as "copyright 1984," "©2013," "Copyright by Random House 1974," among others. Similarly, the phonogram date may follow the symbol "℗" or a phrase. Copyright and phonogram dates are always recorded in numeric form and are preceded by the copyright or phonogram symbol, regardless of how they appear on the source of information (RDA 2.11.1.3). If there are multiple dates that apply to different aspects of the resource (e.g., text, illustrations, etc.), record all that are considered important for identification and selection in repeated elements (MARC fields). If a resource is issued in several parts and there are different copyright dates for the parts, record the range of copyright dates (first-last) in one element (MARC field).

Place of publication:	Sydney
Publisher's name:	Studio Canal
Date of publication	

(inferred):	[2013]
MARC21:	264 1 $a Sydney: $b Studio Canal, $c [2013]
Copyright date:	**©2013**
MARC21:	264 4 $c **©2013**

Place of publication:	Chicago, IL
Publisher's name:	Bloodshot Records
Date of publication	
(inferred):	[2014]
MARC21;	264 _1 $ a Chicago, IL: ‡b Bloodshot Records, $c [2014]
Copyright date:	**℗2014**
MARC21:	264 _4 $c **℗2014**

Series Statement (RDA 2.12)
Core element
[MARC field 490]

RDA defines a series as a "statement identifying a series to which a resource belongs and the numbering of the resource within the series." A series may or may not be numbered. A resource may belong to one or more than one series. The series statement contains the following subelements:

Title proper of series (RDA 2.12.2)
Parallel title proper of series (RDA 2.12.3)
Other title information of series (RDA 2.12.4)
Parallel other title information of series (RDA 2.12.5)
Statement of responsibility relating to series (RDA 2.12.6)
ISSN of series (RDA 2.12.8)
Numbering within series (RDA 2.12.9)

In addition, the same subelements for a subseries are also included (RDA 2.12.10–RDA 2.12.17).

The series statement is transcribed according to the corresponding guidelines in the title proper and statement of responsibility elements (RDA 1.7), exactly as it appears on the resource in terms of the wording and spelling, but not necessarily in terms of capitalization and punctuation. Numbering of the series is recorded as it appears on the source of information (including the caption preceding the series number). A series is considered a separate work (FRBR and RDA), and, therefore, the series as an authorized access point (MARC 8XX), as discussed in chapter 9, under the section on recording relationship between works.

Often, phrases that look like series titles appear on resources and typically serve as a publisher's category designation or as a guide for organizing materials in various settings, for example, "A Touchstone Book." The LC (LC-PCC PS 2.12) considers these as series-like phrases, often to be recorded in a note.

Resources sometimes belong to more than one series, and, therefore, multiple series statements may be required (RDA 2.12.1.5), each recorded in a separate element (MARC field 490). A subseries is not a separate series and should be recorded in the same element as the main series.

Title proper of series:	**Mark Twain and his circle series**
MARC21:	490 1 $a **Mark Twain and his circle series**

Title proper of series:	Harvard-Yenching Institute monograph series
Numbering within series:	**58**
MARC21:	490 1 $a Harvard-Yenching Institute monograph series; $v **58**

Title proper of series:	Series in machine perception and artificial intelligence
Numbering within series:	**volume 7**
MARC21:	490 1 $a Series in machine perception and artificial intelligence; $v **volume 7**

Title proper of series:	Series of Slovak Academy of Sciences
Numbering within series:	**Band 5**
MARC21:	490 0 $a Series of Slovak Academy of Sciences; $v **Band 5**

Title proper of series:	Humanprojekt
Other title information of series:	**Interdisziplinäre Anthropologie**
ISSN of series:	**1868-8144**
MARC21:	490 1 $a Humanprojekt: **Interdisziplinäre Anthropologie**, $x **1868-8144**

If the resource belongs to a subseries that is named in the resource along with the main series, both series are recorded within the same series statement, with a period separating the two titles proper.

Title proper of series:	Dear dragon
Title proper of subseries:	**New series**
MARC21:	490 1 $a Dear dragon. **New series**

Series with subseries and parallel series statements:

Title proper of series:	Europäische Hochschulschriften
Title proper of subseries:	**Reihe XXIV, Ibero-romanische Sprachen und Literaturen**
ISSN of series:	0721-3565
Numbering within series:	Bd. 88
Parallel title proper:	**Publications universitaires Européennes**
Parallel subseries title:	**Série 24, Lenguas y literaturas Iberorománicas**
Numbering within series:	Vol. 88
Parallel title proper:	**European university studies**
Parallel subseries title:	**Series 24, Ibero-Romance languages and literature**
Numbering within series:	Vol. 88
MARC21:	490 1 $a Europäische Hochschulschriften. **Reihe XXIV, Ibero-romanische Sprachen und Literaturen**, $x 0721-3565; $v Bd. 88 = $a **Publications universitaires Européennes. Série 24, Lenguas y literaturas Iberorománicas**; $v Vol. 88 = $a **European university studies. Series 24, Ibero-Romance languages and literature**; $v Vol. 88

More than one series:

Title proper of series 1:	**LEA's organization and management series**
MARC21:	490 1 $a **LEA's organization and management series**
Title proper of series 2:	**Series in applied psychology**
MARC21:	490 1 $a **Series in applied psychology**
Title proper of series 1:	**Bulletin**
Statement of resp. of series:	American School of Prehistoric Research
Numbering within series 1:	no 47

MARC21:	490 1 $a **Bulletin** / American School of Prehistoric Research; $c no. 47
Title proper of series 2:	**Dolnovestonické studie**
Numbering within series 2:	vol. 10
MARC21:	490 1 $a **Dolnovestonické studie**; $c vol. 10

Mode of Issuance (RDA 2.13)
Core element
[MARC leader byte 07, Bibliographic level; OCLC fixed-field display BLvL]

Mode of issuance identifies whether a resource is issued in one or more parts, how it is updated, and when the addition of new or revised content will stop. Four types of mode of issuance are defined in RDA 2.13.1.3): single unit (single monograph), multipart monograph, serial, and integrated resource. Mode of issuance is not an RDA core, but a core for LC and PCC (LC-PCC PS 2.13). In a MARC environment, this information is entered as coded information in the MARC bibliographic Leader 07 position, defined as bibliographic level. In OCLC, this is equivalent to the fixed-field display "BLvL."

Mode of issuance:	**single unit**
MARC21 Leader/07 or BLvL:	**m**
Mode of issuance:	**multipart monograph**
MARC21 Leader/07 or BLvL:	**m**
Mode of issuance:	**serial**
MARC21 Leader/07 or BLvL:	**s**
Mode of issuance:	**integrating resource**
MARC21 Leader/07 or BLvL:	**i**

Mode of issuance—single unit:

Type a	ELvl 8	Srce	Audn	Ctrl	Lang eng
BLvl m	Form	Conf 0	Biog	MRec	Ctry bcc
Cont	GPub	LitF 0	Indx 1		
Desc i	Ills ab	Fest 0	DtSt s	Dates 2014,	

007 a $b d $d c $e a $f n $g z $h n

040	NLC $b eng $e rda $c NLC
016	20149014422
020	9781926806532 (pbk.)
020	1926806530 (pbk.)
043	n-cn-ab

055 _0 G1167 C46E63 $b E76 2014
082 04 796.5097123 $2 23
100 1_ Ernst, Trent, $e author.
245 10 Backroad mapbook, central Alberta: $b outdoor recreation guide / $c writer, Trent Ernst.
246 30 Central Alberta: $b outdoor recreation guide
250 4th edition.
264 _1 Coquitlam, British Columbia: $b Mussio Ventures Ltd., $c 2014.
300 1 atlas.
336 text $b txt $2 rdacontent
336 cartographic image $b cri $2 rdacontent
337 unmediated $b n $2 rdamedia
338 volume $b nc $2 rdacarrier

Mode of issuance—serial:

Type a	ELvl I	Srce d	GPub	Ctrl	Lang eng
BLvl s	Form	Conf 0	Freq q	MRec	Ctry si
S/L 0	Orig	EntW	Regl r	Alph a	
Desc i	SrTp p	Cont	DtSt c	Dates 2014, 9999	

040 SINAP $b eng $e rda $c SINAP $d OCLCO $d SINLB
022 2345-7333
082 04 505 $2 23
210 1_ Asian sci. mag.
222 _0 Asian scientist magazine
245 00 Asian scientist magazine
260 Singapore: $b Asian Scientist Publishing Pte Ltd, $c 2014-
300 volumes: $b illustrations (some color); $c 26 cm.
310 Four no. a year
336 text $b txt $2 rdacontent
337 unmediated $b n $2 rdamedia
338 volume $b nc $2 rdacarrier
362 0_ Vol. 1, issue 1, January 2014-

Frequency (RDA 2.14) [MARC 310; 321; leader byte 01, Frequency; OCLC fixed-field display Freq]

Frequency identifies how often and at what intervals, the parts of a serial or integrating resource are issued. Frequency is not a core element in RDA, but it is a core for LC and PCC (LC-PCC PS 2.2.14). The information for the frequency can be taken from any source. RDA 2.14.1.3 requires the use of a predetermined frequency term from the list provided in the guidelines. If none of the listed terms is appropriate for the resource described, a note should be given, detailing the frequency, following RDA 2.20.12.3. The RDA frequency terms include the following:

daily
three times a week
biweekly
weekly
semiweekly
three times a month
bimonthly
monthly
semimonthly
quarterly
three times a year
semiannual
annual
biennial
triennial
irregular

Changes in frequency of a serial or integrating resource should also be given in a note, following RDA 2.20.12.4.

In a MARC environment, this information is entered as coded information in the MARC bibliographic Leader 01 position, defined as frequency. In OCLC, this is equivalent to the fixed-field display "Freq," which spans MARC field 310 for current frequency and 321 for earlier frequency.

Frequency:	**weekly**
MARC21 "Freq":	**w**
MARC21:	310 $a **Weekly**
Frequency (current):	**monthly, 2013-**
MARC21 "Freq":	**m**
MARC21:	310 $a **Monthly,** $b **<2013->**
Frequency (earlier):	**semimonthly (except Aug.), 1993**
MARC21:	321 $a **Semimonthly (except Aug.),** $b **1993–**

Identifier for the manifestation (RDA 2.15)
Core element
[MARC fields 020 (ISBN), 022 (ISSN), URN]

An identifier is an alpha-numeric string that uniquely identifies and differentiates a manifestation from other manifestations. Identifiers for manifestations can be registered international standard identifiers. Most commonly used standards are the ISBN, the ISSN, or a URI. They may also include identifiers issued by publishers and distributors, music publishers' numbers, plate numbers, early printed resource fingerprints, and the International Standard Music (ISMN). Identifiers for the manifestation can be taken from any source.

If there is a specified display formatting for an identifier, record it as specified. If there is no specified display format, record the identifier as it appears on the source of information, preceding it by a trade name or the issuing agency name. Resources are often associated with more than one identifier.

Identifier for the manifestation: **ISBN 031610924X**
MARC21: 020 $a **031610924X**

Identifier for the manifestation: **ISSN 1544-5402**
MARC21: 022 $a **1544-5402**

A brief qualification is given if the item bears two or more identifiers of the same type (RDA 2.15.1.7). Qualification may also be added for the type of binding, if a resource is a "loose-leaf," or a designation of the part of a resource associated with the identifier, in cases where the parts of a resource have their own identifiers.

Identifier for the manifestation: ISBN 0-444-88812-8 **(set)**
MARC21: 020 $a 0444888128 $q **set**

Identifier for the manifestation: ISBN 0-444-88242-1 **(v. 1)**
MARC21: 020 $a 0444882421 $q **v. 1**

A publisher's music number is a designation assigned by a music publisher and usually appears on the title page, the cover, or the first page of the published music.

Identifier for the manifestation
(music publisher's number): **RP086**
MARC21 (first indicator = 3) 028 32 $a **RP086** $b Rondo Publishing

024 2 M007140144
024 3 9790007140144
028 30 CV 31.106/03 b Carus
028 30 31.106/03 $b Carus
028 22 Carus 31.106/03 $b Carus
041 1 ger $a eng $n ger $g ger $g eng $m ger
048 va01 $a vc01 $a vd01 $a vf01 $a ka01
050 4 M2023 $b .B1183 no.106 2013
072 7 M $2 lcco
100 1 Bach, Johann Sebastian, $d 1685-1750, $e composer.
245 10 Gottes Zeit ist die allerbeste Zeit: $b BWV 106: Actus tragicus (Trauermusik): für

	Sopran, Alt, Tenor, Bass, 2 Altblockflöten, 2 Violen da Gamba und Basso continuo = Actus tragicus (funeral music): for soprano, alto, tenor, bass, 2 alto recorders, 2 viole da gamba and basso continuo / $c Johann Sebastian Bach; neu herausgegeben von Peter Thalheimer; English version by Jean Lunn.
246 3	Actus tragicus
246 3	Trauermusik
246 3	Funeral music
250	Klavierauszug = $b Vocal score / Paul Horn.
264 1	Stuttgart: $b Carus, $c [2013]
264 4	$c ©2013
300	1 vocal score (32 pages); $c 27 cm.
336	notated music $b ntm $2 rdacontent
337	unmediated $b n $2 rdamedia
338	volume $b nc $2 rdacarrier

In addition, a music publisher may assign a plate number for music. Record the plate number for music as it appears, including an abbreviation, word, or phrase identifying the publisher preceding the plate number.

Notes on Manifestation (RDA 2.17) [MARC fields 5XX]

Useful descriptive information that cannot be presented in the other elements is given in notes. The notes may be based on information taken from any suitable source. Notes are not core elements in RDA and can be recorded in any order.

Some notes supplement or clarify information given in other elements; others provide additional bibliographic information. Traditionally, many notes follow a particular structure and may be highly stylized. For example, notes relating to a particular element (discussed above) use similar prescribed punctuation. When quotations from the item or from other sources are used as notes, they are enclosed in quotation marks.

Some types of manifestation notes, but not all, are illustrated below with examples.

Notes on Titles (RDA 2.17.2)

Notes on titles are typically used to provide information on the source of the title, title variations, date a title was last viewed, inaccuracies, and other information relating to the title.

Note on title: **Title from cover**
MARC21: 500 $a **Title from cover**

Note on title: **Title from PDF file as viewed on 2/9/2006**
MARC21: 500 $a **Title from PDF file as viewed on 2/9/2006**

Note on title: **Cover title: Biochemistry crash course**
MARC21: 246 14 $a **Biochemistry crash course**

Note on title: **Spine title: Volkmann Collection of the Zamorano 80**
MARC21: 246 18 $a **Volkmann Collection of the Zamorano 80**

Note on title: **Parallel title on back of container insert: Tinagong paraiso**
MARC21: 246 1# $i **Parallel title on back of container insert** $a **Tinagong paraiso**

Note on Statement of Responsibility (RDA 2.17.3)

This note is used for information relating to the persons, families, or corporate bodies not listed in the statement of responsibility.

Note on statement of responsibility: **Compiled by Pete Heywood**
MARC21: 500 $a **Compiled by Pete Heywood**
Note on statement of responsibility: **A project of the Society of Satellite Professionals International, hosted by: the Institute for Telecommunications Studies, Ohio University**
MARC21: 500 $a **A project of the Society of Satellite Professionals International, hosted by: the Institute for Telecommunications Studies, Ohio**

Note on Edition Statement (RDA 2.17.4)

This note is available to provide additional information relating to the edition statement, ranging from information on the source of the edition statement or any information on parts of the resource that may differ from the edition statement for the entire resource, to changes in the edition statement, to any other detailed information that is deemed important for the identification of the resource.

Note on edition statement: **Vol. 3 lacks an edition statement**
MARC21: 500 $a **Vol. 3 lacks an edition statement**

Note on Numbering Serials (RDA 2.17.5)

This note is a less formal way to record information about the numbering of serials, and can be used instead of RDA 2.6 to record this information.

Note on numbering serials: **Vol. 3, no. 4 omitted**
MARC21: 515 $a **Vol. 3, no. 4 omitted**

Note on Publication Statement (RDA 2.17.7)

Often it is necessary to add a note about the publication statement in order to clarify or help identify and access a resource.

Note on publication statement: **Co-published simultaneously as Science & technology libraries, volume 23, number 4, 2003**
MARC21: 500 $a **Co-published simultaneously as Science & technology libraries, volume 23, number 4, 2003**

Note on publication statement: **First published in Great Britain by Little, Brown and Company, 2004**
MARC21: 500 $a **First published in Great Britain by Little, Brown and Company, 2004**

Note on Series Statement (RDA 2.17.11)

This note is used to provide information on complex series, incorrect series numbering, or any changes in the series statement.

Note on series: Series **statement from jacket**
MARC21: 500 $a Series **statement from jacket**

Note on series: **Third in a series of four**

MARC21: 500 $a **Third in a series of four**

Note on Frequency (RDA 2.17.12)

This note is used to provide more information on the frequency of the parts of a series or integrating resource.

Note on frequency: **Began with vol. 41 in 2014**
MARC21: 362 1_ $a **Began with vol. 41 in 2014**

Date of Viewing of an Online Resource (RDA 2.17.13.5)

When describing an online resource, record the date the resource was viewed for the creation of the description.

Date viewing online resource: **Viewed on March 25, 2012**
MARC21: 500 $a **Viewed on March 25, 2012**

ITEM ATTRIBUTES

Items are specific copies of manifestations, and, therefore, any item-specific characteristic applies only to the description of the particular copy. Therefore, item elements are not typically included in shared bibliographic descriptions. Most of item attributes are recorded as notes in a bibliographic record (especially when using a MARC structure). Because of the uniqueness of these notes relating only to the specific item, as a best practice, it is preferable that the note identifies the collection to which this item belongs.

Custodial History of Item (RDA 2.18)

This element is used to record a brief history of the ownership or custody of a resource. It is more commonly seen in rare book and archival resource descriptions.

Immediate Source of Acquisition of Item (RDA 2.19)

The source from which the particular item was acquired is recorded in this element.

Identifier for the Item (RDA 2.20)

Typically, a string of characters uniquely identifying the item and differentiating the item from all other items of the same manifestation.

Notes on Item (RDA 2.21)

This element is used to provide additional notes for details relating to the item attributes not included in the previous item-specific elements.

For an additional item-related note, see also "Note on item-specific carrier characteristic" under the following section "Describing Carriers."

DESCRIBING CARRIERS

A resource's intellectual content is typically stored in or on a carrier, defined in RDA as a "physical medium in which data, sound, images, etc., are stored." Resources may be stored in one or more carrier and these carriers can be of the same or different types. Text, for example, may be stored in one print and bound volume or multiple volumes, or a portion of the content can be stored in a volume and other portions of the content can be stored in a DVD or electronic file, or on a poster, and other material. Therefore, "physical" medium does not necessarily mean tangible object, but any medium where data can be stored.

Sources of Information: When describing the carrier or carriers of a resource, information is taken from the resource itself, any resource that accompanies it, or any other source (RDA 3.1.1).

Manifestations Available in Different Formats: When a work's manifestations, from the same expression, are available in different formats, follow RDA 3.1.2, which instructs us to describe the carrier of the manifestation at hand. In other words, when descriptions are stored in MARC records, separate bibliographic records are to be created for manifestations in different formats, such the same text manifested in a print format, electronic format as PDF, and electronic format as HTML web content. Recording the relationships of these manifestations is described in RDA 27.1.

Resources With More than One Carrier Type: When a resource (one complete manifestation) consists of different types of carriers, RDA 3.1.4 provides three options for describing the carriers:

a. record only the "carrier type" and "extent" of each carrier (details on these elements follow below). For example, a resource consisting of one volume, one poster, and one stuffed animal would be described as the following:

Carrier type: **volume**
Extent: **210 pages**

Carrier type: **sheet**
Extent: **1 poster**
Carrier type: **object**
Extent: **1 stuffed frog**
MARC21: 300 $a **210 pages**
338 $a **volume**
300 $a **1 poster**
338 $a **sheet**
300 $a **1 stuffed frog**
338 $a **object**

b. record the carrier type, extent, and other characteristics of each carrier. The same resource is described as the following:

MARC21: 300 $a **208 pages**: $b illustrations, reproduction pages; $c **30 cm**
300 $a **1 poster;** $c **36 × 61 cm**
300 $a **1 stuffed frog**: $b green; $c **23 × 19 × 27 cm**
338 $a **volume**
338 $a **sheet**
338 $a **object**

c. record the predominant carrier type and extent in general terms. The predominant carrier of the same resource is described as the following:

MARC21: 300 $a **1 kit**: $b binder with pages, handouts, poster, stuffed animal, contained in a backpack.
338 $a **object**

The carrier type "online resource" is recorded for all online resources, and extent is recorded when the resource is complete or the total extent is known (RDA 3.1.5):

Carrier type: **online resource**
Extent: **1 online resource (xxiii, 204 pages)**

MARC21: 300 $a **1 online resource (xxiii, 204 pages)**
338 $a **online resource**

A number of elements have been defined in RDA to describe carriers. Not all elements are applicable to all types of carriers or types of resources. The majority of elements defined in RDA are described in the following section, but this is not an exhaustive coverage of all RDA carrier elements.

Media Type (RDA 3.2) [MARC field 337]

This element describes what type of device may be necessary to access or use the content of the resource. A list of terms to be used for this element is available in RDA 3.2.1.3 (the source code "rdamedia" is recorded in MARC when the RDA terms are used). Even though not an RDA core element, it is a core for LC/PCC (LC-PCC PS 3.2), and, therefore, a common practice among libraries. If more than one type of media is necessary to use the content of a resource, all types are recorded. Alternatively, RDA allows the recording of the media type for the predominant section or majority of the content. If no medium is necessary, the term "unmediated" is recorded in the media type element.

Media type: **video**
MARC21: 337 $a **video** $b v $2 rdamedia
Media type: **unmediated**
MARC21: 337 $a **unmediated** $c rdamedia
Media type: **computer**
MARC21: 337 $a **computer** $b c $2 rdamedia

Carrier Type (RDA 3.3)—Core Element [MARC field 338]

Carrier type, an RDA core element, describes the format of the container or the storing device and housing of the container, and is dependent on the media type. Each carrier type is a subcategory of one of the media types. A list of terms to be used in the element carrier type is available in RDA 3.3.1.3. This list is recorded as the source of the carrier type term as "rdacarrier" in MARC field 338, subfield 2. If the resource content is stored in more than one type of carrier, all types are recorded. Alternatively, RDA allows the recording of the carrier type for the predominant section or majority of the content.

The following examples illustrate the combination of media and carrier type:

Sound recording of performed music:
Media type: audio
Carrier type: **audio disc**
MARC21: 337 $a audio $2 rdamedia
338 $a **audio disc** $2 rdacarrier

Map printed on a sheet of paper:
Media type: unmediated
Carrier type: **sheet**
MARC21: 337 $a unmediated $b n $2 rdamedia
338 $a **sheet** $b nb $2 rdacarrier

Electronic text:
Media type: computer
Carrier type: **computer disc**
MARC21: 337 $a computer $b c $2 rdamedia
338 $a **computer disc** $b cd $2 rdacarrier

Recorded concert, CD, and DVD:
Media type: audio
Carrier type: **audio disc**
Media type: video
Carrier type: **video disc**
MARC21: 337 $a audio $2 rdamedia
337 $a video $2 rdamedia
338 $a audio disc $2 rdacarrier $3 CD
338 $a videodisc $2 rdacarrier $3 DVD

Media type and Carrier type are related elements because each Carrier type is a subtype of a particular Media type term.

Extent (RDA 3.4)—Core Element [MARC field 300, subfield $a]

Extent is a statement identifying the units or subunits and how many of them make up a resource. For example, a printed text is made up of one volume or more, or of a number of pages or leaves, a cartographic resource is made up of one or more maps, and so on. The extent element is an RDA core element and is required when describing a manifestation, unless the content of the resource was incomplete at the time the description was created.

Extent is recorded by giving the number of units or subunits and a term for the unit or subunit. The term is chosen from the list of carrier types in RDA 3.3.1.3. If no appropriate term is found in the list or if the agency creating the description prefers the use of a different term, terms outside the list can be used.

Carrier type: volume
Extent: **xv, 379 pages**
MARC21: 300 $ a **xv, 379 pages**

Carrier type: online resource
Extent: **1 online resource**
MARC21: 300 $a **1 online resource**

If the number of subunits is easily ascertainable and it is deemed necessary to aid in the identification or selection of the resource, the extent using subunits is recorded within parentheses, following the extent using the unit.

Carrier type: online resource
Extent: **1 online resource (ix, 126 pages)**
MARC21: 300 $a **1 online resource (ix, 126 pages)**

If the resource is not complete or the total number of units is unknown, follow RDA, which instructs us to either record the term for the unit without the number or not record the extent at all (another option).

Carrier type: volume
Extent: **volumes**
MARC21: 300 $a **volumes**

If the number of units is not easily ascertained, but estimated, RDA allows the use of the term "approximately" in front of the estimated number of units, for example, stated as "approximately 400 pages."

The extent of a resource may be very different for different formats, and, therefore, RDA offers a number of guidelines for different types of resource carriers.

Collections: When describing a collection (archival or other) in its entirety, RDA offers three options: (a) to use number of items, containers, or volumes, with the option to specify number of items within parentheses; (b) to use the amount of space the collection occupies, with the option to specify number of items within parentheses; and (c) use the number and term of unit for each type.

Carrier type: sheet
Extent: **68 items**
MARC21: 300 $a **68 items**

Carrier type: sheet
Carrier type: volume
Extent: **25 linear ft.**
MARC21: 300 $a **25 linear ft.**

Carrier type: volume
Extent: **12 linear ft. (approximately 340 items)**

MARC21: 300 $a **12 linear ft. (approximately 340 items)**

Carrier type: sheet
Extent: **32 photographs**
MARC21: 300 $a **32 photographs**

Analytical description: When describing a resource that is part of a larger resource, record the number and units of the part or record the location of the part within the larger resource.

Carrier type: volume
Extent: **65 pages**
MARC21: 300 $a **65 pages**

Carrier type: volume
Extent: **pages 120-185**
MARC21: 300 $a **pages 120-185**

Cartographic resources (RDA 3.4.2)—Core element: The extent is a core element for cartographic materials if the resource is complete or the total extent is known. To describe the extent, record the number of units and an appropriate term from the list available in RDA 3.4.2.2. If there is more than one cartographic unit on one or more sheets and the number of units does not correspond to the number of sheets (e.g., 4 maps on 2 sheets), record the number and unit term, and then add "on . . ." the number and the term "sheet(s)." It is also possible to have one unit appearing on more than one sheet. For example,

Carrier type: sheet
Extent: **4 maps**
MARC21: 300 $a **4 maps**

Carrier type: sheet
Extent: **4 maps in 3 sheets**
MARC21: 300 $a **4 maps on 3 sheets**

Carrier type: sheet
Extent: **1 map on 2 sheets**
MARC21: 300 $a **1 map on 2 sheets**

When describing the extent of atlases, follow RDA 3.4.2.5 instruction to include the number of volumes or pages in addition to the number of atlases:

Carrier type: volume
Extent: **1 atlas (210 pages)**
MARC21: 300 $a **1 atlas (210 pages)**

Notated music (RDA 3.4.3)—Core element: The extent is a core element for notated music if the resource is complete or the total extent is known. To record extent, use the number of units and a term for the unit from the list included in 7.20.1.3. If more than one type of unit is used, record the number and term for each as specified in 7.20.1.3. Specify the number and unit term for volumes, pages, leaves, or columns, in addition to the main type of unit.

Carrier type: volume
Extent: **1 score (v, 24 pages)**
MARC21: 300 $a **1 score (v, 24 pages)**

If a score consists of a set of parts, omit the number of volumes, pages, and so on of the part; record the number of parts:

Carrier type: volume
Extent: **4 parts**
MARC21: 300 **$a 4 parts**

Carrier type: volume
Extent: **1 score and 3 parts (28 pages)**
MARC21: 300 $a **1 score and 3 parts (28 pages)**

Still images (RDA 3.4.4)—Core element: The extent is a core element for still images such as photographs, paintings, drawings, and other images, if the resource is complete or the total extent is known. To record extent, use the number of units and a term for the unit from the list included in RDA 3.4.4.2.

Carrier type: sheet
Extent: **134 photographs**
MARC21: 300 $a **134 photographs**

Carrier type: sheet
Extent: **1 painting**
MARC21: 300 $a **4 1 painting**

Carrier type: sheet
Extent: **4 drawings in 2 sheets**
MARC21: 300 $a **4 drawings in 2 sheets**

Text (RDA 3.4.5)—Core element: The extent is a core element for text printed or manuscript appearing in volumes, sheets, portfolios, or cases, if the resource is complete or the total extent is known. Text appearing in other media is discussed in the respective media RDA guideline. A major distinction is made among text consisting of a single unit and text consisting of more than one unit. Guidelines for a number of special cases are available in RDA. Only some of them are covered below.

Single volume with numbered pages, leaves, or columns (RDA 3.4.5.2): If a resource consists of a single volume, record the extent in terms of the numbered subunit, whether these are pages, leaves, or columns (if more than one column appears in each page) following the sequence used for each type. If a resource consists of a mix of numbered pages and numbered leaves, or numbered columns, record each sequence separately.

If more than one numbering sequence is present, record each numbered or lettered sequence using the number from the last numbered page, leaf, or column in each sequence, and the appropriate term for the unit. Here, one has to be cautious to make sure that the sequences are indeed different. For example, if there is a sequence of pages numbered using roman numerals up to "vi" followed by a page numbered with an Arabic numeral "7," then it is apparent that there is one continuous sequence but two numbering systems. If the initial numbering ends in "vi" and the next numbering starts over with "1" (printed on the page or assumed), then it is apparent that there are two sequences, using two different numberings.

Extent: **462 pages**
MARC21: 300 $a **462 pages**

Extent: **84 leaves**
MARC21: 300 $a **84 leaves**

Extent: **348 columns**
MARC21: 300 $a **348 columns**

Extent: **vii, 533 pages**
MARC21: 300 $a **vii, 533 pages**

Extent: **xi, 46 pages, 570 leaves**
MARC21: 300 $a **xi, 46 pages, 570 leaves**

Early printed resources are an exception to the above guidelines, using the exact form presented in the resource and recording in the extent all information, including blank pages or leaves.

Extent: **2 unnumbered pages, 265, 140 pages, 3 unnumbered pages, 144-168, 2 unnumbered leaves, 10 pages**
MARC21: 300 $a **2 unnumbered pages, 265, 140 pages, 3 unnumbered pages, 144-168, 2 unnumbered leaves, 10 pages**

Single volume with unnumbered pages, leaves, or columns. (RDA 3.4.5.3): RDA suggests three options for single volumes with no numbered pages, leaves, or columns. First, one can count and record the extent by giving the number followed by "unnumbered" and the term pages, leaves, or columns (e.g., 35 unnumbered leaves). Second, one can record an approximate number followed by the appropriate terms (e.g., approximately 200 columns). Third, one can just record the main units as "1 volume (unpaged)." LC practice is to follow the third option (LC-PCC PS 3.4.5.3).

Extent: **28 unnumbered pages**
MARC21: 300 $a **28 unnumbered pages**

Extent: **approximately 300 pages**
MARC21: 300 **$a approximately 300 pages**

Extent: **1 volume (unpaged)**
MARC21: 300 **$a 1 volume (unpaged)**

Incomplete volume (RDA 3.4.5.6): If the resource consists of one volume and this volume is incomplete (last part is missing or it is not easy to ascertain the total extent), record the number appearing on the last page, leaf, or column, followed by the appropriate term and "(incomplete)." This information should also be recorded in an item-specific carrier characteristic note.

Extent: **xii, 282 pages (incomplete)**
MARC21: 300 $a **xii, 282 pages (incomplete)**

Pages and so on numbered as part of a larger sequence (RDA 3.4.5.7): If the resource described is numbered as part of a larger resource, record the first and last numbers preceded by an appropriate term. If both a numbering of a larger resource and additional numbering for the resource itself are used, record the numbering for the resource itself.

Extent: **pages 23-123**
MARC21: 300 $a **pages 23-123**

Complicated or irregular numbering (RDA 3.4.5.8): Sometimes, resources have complicated or irregular page numbering. In such cases, RDA instructs to either (a) record total number of pages, leaves, or columns, followed by "in various pagings," "in various foliations," or "in various numberings"; (b) record the main sequences and add the total number of remaining various sequences; or (c) record "1 volume (various pagings)," which is the preferred LC practice (LC-PCC PS 3.4.5.8).

Extent: **986 pages (in various pagings)**
MARC21: 300 $a **986 pages (in various pagings)**

Extent: **269 pages, 46 unnumbered pages, 27, 52 pages**
MARC21: 300 $a **269 pages, 46 unnumbered pages, 27, 52 pages**

Leaves or pages of plates (RDA 3.4.5.9): Pages or, more often, leaves of plates are leaves that contain illustrations without text, and that are not part of the main numbering sequence. Unnumbered pages or leaves of plates are recorded all together after the last numbered sequence, whether they are together in the resource or not.

Extent: **347 pages, 12 pages of plates**
MARC21: 300 $a **347 pages, 12 pages of plates**

Single sheet (RDA 3.4.5.14): If the resource consists of one sheet, then record in the extent "1 sheet." A folded sheet can fit one or more laid-out pages. In this case, record "1 folded sheet" followed by the number of laid-out pages within parentheses.

Extent: **1 folded sheet (16 pages)**
MARC21: 300 $a **1 folded sheet (16 pages)**

More than one volume (RDA 3.4.5.16): The extent of resources consisting of more than one volume is recorded with the use of the number of volumes followed by the term "volumes." If the volumes use one continuous page numbering, record the number of volumes followed by the term "volumes" and the numbering of subunits (pages, leaves, or columns), with the appropriate term within parentheses.

Extent: **2 volumes (ix, 900 pages)**
MARC21: 300 $a **2 volumes (ix, 900 pages)**

Extent of three-dimensional form (RDA 3.4.6)—Core element: The extent of three-dimensional resources is a core element if the resource is complete or the total extent is known. Record the number of units followed by an appropriate term from the list available in RDA 3.4.6. When deemed appropriate, the number and terms for subunits can be recorded within parentheses in addition to the main unit.

Extent: **2 jigsaw puzzles**
MARC21: 300 $a **2 jigsaw puzzles**

Extent: **1 game (200 cards, 4 dice, 10 reward cards)**
MARC21: 300 $a **1 game (200 cards, 4 dice, 10 reward cards)**

Dimensions (RDA 3.5) [MARC field 300, subfield $c]

The size of the carrier and sometimes the size of the container of a manifestation is one of the elements recorded in the description of a manifestation. Dimensions may include the measurements of the height, width, depth, length, gauge, or diameter. Use the resource itself as the source for dimension information and any source for any additional information. The majority of dimensions are recorded in centimeters, always rounded up to the next whole centimeter, followed by "cm," the centimeter symbol. LC practice is to use inches for discs and any audio carrier (LC-PCC PS 3.5.1.3). RDA Appendix B lists abbreviated terms for other units of measurements that may be preferred by the cataloging agency. As symbols, "cm" and "mm" do not end with a period (full stop).

Guidelines for different types of carriers are included in RDA. The following are a few examples of how the dimensions of different carriers are recorded:

Cards: height × width   Dimensions: **10 × 18 cm**
MARC21: 300 $a 25 flash cards; $c **10 × 18 cm**

Cartridges: length × height (for audio), length of the side inserted in a computer (computer cartridges), gauge (for film, video, etc.)

Cassettes: length × height
Disc: diameter
Filmstrips: gauge or width

Sheets: height × width of the sheet; add the dimensions of folded sheet
Slides: height × width
Volumes: height of volume Dimensions: **29 cm**
MARC21: 300 $a vi, 242 pages; $c **29 cm**

With the exception of cases where the width of the volume is less than half the height or greater than the height, record only the height. In such exceptional cases, record the height × width.

If a resource comes in a container and the container is deemed important to include, the dimensions of the container may be used instead of the carrier measurements or in addition to the measurements of the carrier.

Dimensions: **31 × 52 cm in box 10 × 14 cm**
MARC21: 300 $a 1 jigsaw puzzle; $c **31 × 52 cm in box 10 × 14 cm**

For resources consisting of more than one carrier of one type for which all carriers are of the same dimensions, record the dimensions of one carrier. If the carriers are same type, but have different sizes, record the dimensions of the smallest and those of the largest carriers.

If a resource is housed in more than one container of one size, record only the dimensions for the container; if they are of various sizes, record the range of container measures by entering the size of the smallest and the size of the largest containers.

Dimensions of maps are given in the measurements of the face of the map in height **3** width. If two different sheets are used for a map, record the dimensions of the two sheets; if more sheets are used that differ in size, record the largest sheet height 3 the largest width, followed by "or smaller."

Dimensions: **sheets 20 × 30 cm and 35 × 60 cm**
MARC21: 300 $a 2 maps; $c **sheets 20 × 30 cm and 35 × 60 cm**

Dimensions: **sheets 30 × 60 cm or smaller**
MARC21: 300 $a **5 maps; $c sheets 30 × 60 cm or smaller**

For folded maps, record both the dimensions of the folded map sheet and the sheet.

Dimensions: **120 × 80 cm, folded to 30 × 10 cm**
MARC21: 300 $a 1 map; $c **120 × 80 cm, folded to 30 × 10 cm**

When a resource is a sheet containing a drawing, painting, photograph, print, etc., record dimensions by giving height × width, diameter or other appropriate dimension. If the sheet is other than a rectangle, indicate the shape.

Dimensions: **20 × 25 cm**
MARC21: 300 $a 2 photographic prints: $b gelatin silver; $c **20 × 25 cm**

Dimensions: **30 × 43 cm**
MARC21: 300 $a 7 sheets of plans; $c **30 × 43 cm**

Base Material (RDA 3.6)
[MARC field 340, subfield $a; 300, subfield $b; 500]

Base material is the physical material composition of a resource, typical of two-dimensional or three-dimensional objects. Base material is recorded if it is considered an important characteristic. Appropriate terms for base material can be selected from the list available in RDA 3.6.1.3. Some examples include "canvas" or "glass" for a painting and "marble" for a sculpture.

Base material: **gelatin silver**
MARC21: 300 $a 2 photographic prints: $b **gelatin silver**; $c 20 × 25 cm

Base material: **marble**
MARC21: 340 $a **marble**

An additional list of terms is provided for microfiche, microfilm, and film (RDA 3.6.2).

Applied Material (RDA 3.7)
[MARC field 340, subfield $c; 300, subfield $b; 500]

The materials (chemical or physical) applied to the base material may also be recorded if considered important. If more than one material is applied, but only one is predominant, then record only the predominant material. If more than one is applied, but none is predominant and considered important, select all applicable terms from the list of appropriate terms available in RDA 3.7.1.3. If not all are identifiable, use the term "mixed materials."

Applied material: **watercolour, pen and ink** on artist board
MARC21: 300 $a 1 drawing: $b **watercolour, pen and ink** on artist board; $c 23.7 × 23.6 cm

In this case, the materials watercolour, pen, and ink have been applied to the base material.

Mount (RDA 3.8)
[MARC field 340, subfield $e; 300, subfield b; 500]

Base material is often mounted on some other physical material for support. This information is recorded if it is considered important for the identification and selection of a resource.

Mount: **wood**
MARC21: 340 $a canvas $b 30 × 57 cm. $c watercolor $e **wood**

In the above example of a painting, the base material is the canvas, with applied material on the canvas being watercolor, and mount to support the canvas being the wood.

Production Method (RDA 3.9)
[MARC field 340, subfield $d; 300, subfield $b; 500]

The method of production or process used to produce a resource may be recorded if important. When describing art prints, the production method is always considered important. RDA provides a list of production method terms in RDA 3.9.1.3.

Production method: **molded**
MARC21: 340 $d **molded $2 rda**

Production method: **engraving**
MARC21: 300 $a 1 print: $b **engraving**; $c 30 × 22 cm

Generation (RDA 3.10)
[MARC field 340, subfield $j; 300, subfield, $b; 500]

Generation information is recorded to indicate the relationship between the original carrier and the carrier for the reproduction made from the original. Examples include duplicate, master printing, second generation, and so on. This information is most often relevant to audio, digital, microform, film, and video carriers. Instructions for each of these types of recording generations are included in RDA 3.10-2–3.10.6.

Generation: **original master**
MARC21: 340 $j **original master** $2 rda

Generation: **first generation**
MARC21: 340 $j **first generation** $2 rda

Layout (RDA 3.11) [MARC field 340, subfield $k; 300, subfield, $b; 500]

Layout is the arrangement of the text, images, and so on, and is recorded if considered important for the identification and selection of a resource. Terms are listed in RDA 3.11.1.3. For example, a cartographic material, like a map, would be recorded having a "both sides" layout when the map continues from one side of the sheet to the other, or "back to back" when the same map image is printed on both sides, but in different languages. Text printed on both sides is recorded as "double-sided."

Layout: **double sided**
MARC21: 340 $k **double sided** $2 rda

Book Format (RDA 3.12) [MARC field 340, subfield $m; 300, subfield $b; 500]

Book format describes the result from folding a printed sheet to produce a book. It is also known as the makeup of the signatures or gatherings in a book. If, for example, a sheet is folded once, it produces four pages in two leaves, if it is folded three times it produces sixteen pages on eight leaves, and so on. This information is often recorded when describing early printed books or rare and special-collection books. A list of book format terms is provided in RDA 3.12.1.3.

Books format: **8vo**
MARC21: 340 $m **8vo** $a rda
500 $a Collation: **8vo**: [1]^4 2-51^4 [$$1 signed]; 204 leaves, pages [i-v] vi-vii [viii] [9] 10-90 [91-93] 94-314 [315] 316-387 [388] 389-395 [396] 397-408 + frontispiece.

Font Size (RDA 3.13) [MARC field 340, subfield $n; 300; 500]

Font size is recorded if it is considered important for identification and selection of a resource. For example, it is important to record the fact that a book is printed in "large print." A list of three terms is provided in RDA: giant print, large print, and jumbo braille. Other terms not included on the RDA list may be used if necessary.

Font size: **large print**
MARC21: 340 $n **large print**
MARC21: 300 $a 238 pages (large print); $c 23 cm

Polarity (RDA 3.14)
[MARC field 340, subfield $o; 300, subfield $b; 500]

The colors and tones of an image are described in the polarity RDA element. An image may have a positive polarity (normal image), negative polarity (inverse tones and colors so that light tones become dark, and dark become light), or mixed. Polarity is often important to record when describing any type of film.

Polarity: **positive**
MARC21: 340 $o **positive** $2 rda

Sound Characteristic (RDA 3.16)
[MARC field 344; 300, subfield $b; 500]

Technical details about the sound encoding of a resource are recorded in the RDA sound characteristic element. Among the information included in the sound characteristics are the

- **type of recording** (RDA 3.16.2): the terms digital or analog are provided in RDA;
- **recording medium** (RDA 3.16.3): the RDA terms magnetic, magneto-optical, and optical are used;
- **playing speed** (RDA 3.16.4):expressed typically in revolutions per minute (rpm) for analog, meters per second (m/s) for digital discs, and centimeters per second (cm/s) for analog tapes;
- **groove characteristic** (RDA 3.16.5): the RDA terms coarse groove and microgroove are available for analog discs, and the terms fine and standard are available in RDA for analog cylinders;
- **track configuration** (RDA 3.16.6): centre track or edge track are used for sound-track film;
- **tape configuration** (RDA 3.16.7): the number of tracks on a tape that are recorded for tape cartridges, cassettes, and reels;
- **configuration of playback channels** (RDA 3.16.8): the number of sound channels used to make the sound recording, which can be mono, stereo, surround, and quadrophonic; and
- **special playback characteristic** (RDA 3.16.9): refers to any special characteristic such as equalization, and noise reduction, used in the audio recording. A list of terms is included in RDA 3.19.9.3.

These details are recorded if they are considered important for identification and selection of a sound recording.

Type of recording:	**digital**
Recording medium:	**optical**
Configuration playback:	**surround**
Special playback characteristic:	**Dolby digital 5.1**
MARC21:	344 $a **digital** $b **optical** $g **surround** $h **Dolby digital 5.1** $2 rda
Type of recording:	**digital**
Recording medium:	**optical**
Special playback characteristic:	**Dolby digital**
MARC21:	344 **digital** $b **optical** $h **Dolby digital** $2 rda
Type of recording:	**digital**
Recording medium:	**optical**
Configuration playback:	**surround**
Special playback characteristic:	**Dolby digital 5.1**
Special playback characteristic:	**DTS digital surround**
MARC21:	344 **digital** $b **optical** $g **surround** $h **Dolby digital 5.1**
	344 **digital** $b **optical** $g **surround** $h **DTS digital surround**
	300 2 audio discs: $b CD audio, **digital**; $c 4 3/4 in.

Video Characteristic (RDA 3.18) [MARC field 346]

The technical specifications of the encoding of a video resource is described in the video characteristic element of RDA if they are considered helpful for identification and selection. The two characteristics identified in RDA are video format and broadcast standard.

Video Format (RDA 3.18.2) refers to the standard used to encode the analog video content. A list of terms appropriate for the format is available in RDA 3.18.2.3. Additional terms can be used if the list does not include a specific term needed to identify the video format.

Broadcast standard (RDA 3.18.3) is the system used to broadcast a video for television. RDA instructs us to use the terms HDTV, NTSC, PAL, and SECAM as terms for the standard.

Video format: **VHS**
Broadcast standard: **NTSC**
MARC21: 346 $a **VHS** $b **NTSC** $2 rda
Broadcast standard: **NTSC**
MARC21: 346 $b **NTSC** $2 rda

Video format: **laser optical**
Broadcast standard: **NTSC**
MARC21: 346 $a **laser optical** $b **NTSC** $2 rda

Video format: **VHS**
Broadcast standard: **PAL, NTSC, SECAM**
MARC21 346 $a **VHS** $b **PAL**, **NTSC**, **SECAM** $2 rda

Digital File Characteristic (RDA 3.19) [MARC field 347]

This element is used for technical specifications for the encoding of any type of digital data. Characteristics included in this element are file type, encoding format, file size, resolution, regional encoding, and encoded bitrate.

File type (RDA 3.19.2) is the general type of data encoded in a computer file. A list of terms is offered in RDA 3.19.2.3, which includes audio, data, image, program, text, and video file.

Encoding format (RDA 3.19.3) is the standard or schema used to encode the digital content in a resource. A list of terms is available in RDA 3.19.3.3, which includes HTML, PDF, TIFF, MP3, and others.

File size (RDA 3.19.4) is the number of bytes of a file. Record the number followed by "KB" for kilobytes, "MB" for megabytes, "GB" for gigabytes, and so on.

Resolution (RDA 3.19.5) is the clarity of detail in a digital image measured in number of pixels.

Regional encoding (RDA 3.19.6.3) is the regional encoding used, and affects where a video can be used or what equipment can play a video. This information is often used, especially when considered important for identification and selection.

File type: **audio file**
Encoding format: **CD audio**
MARC21: 347 $a **audio file** $b **CD audio** $2 rda

File type: **image file**
Encoding format: **TIFF**
File size: **12 MB**
Resolution: **8 megapixels**
MARC21: 347 $a **image file** $b **TIFF** $c **12 MB** $d **8 megapixels** $2 rda

File type: **image file**
Encoding format: **JPEG**
File type: **audio file**
Encoding format: **MP3**
Encoding format: **FLAC**
MARC21: 347 **image file** $b **JPEG** $2 rda
347 **audio file** $b **MP3** $b **FLAC** $2 rda
Resource includes content: 336 performed music $b prm $2 rdacontent
336 still image $b sti $2 rdacontent

Equipment or System Requirement (RDA 3.20) [MARC field 538]

This element is used to record any equipment or system that is required for use in playback (to access the content) of a resource.

Equipment or:
System requirement: **PlayStation 3; 7 MB required hard drive space; HD video output 480p/720p/1080i/1080p; DualShock 3; Blu-ray disc**
MARC21: 538 $a System requirements: **PlayStation 3; 7 MB required hard drive space; HD video output 480p/720p/1080i/1080p; DualShock 3; Blu-ray disc.**

Equipment or:
System requirement: **Blu-ray, widescreen; 1080p High Definition 16x9 presentation; Dolby True-HD**

	5.1 (new English soundtrack), 2.0 (original English soundtrack) or mono (original Japanese soundtrack); Region A, B.
MARC21:	538 $a **Blu-ray, widescreen; 1080p High Definition 16x9 presentation; Dolby True-HD 5.1 (new English soundtrack), 2.0 (original English soundtrack) or mono (original Japanese soundtrack); Region A, B.**

Note on Carrier (RDA 3.21) [MARC field 500]

This element is used for "a note providing information on attributes of the carrier or carriers of the manifestation." This note is used for any information about the carrier that has not been recorded in one of the carrier attributes, such as notes relating to the extent of the manifestation, dimensions of the manifestation, and changes in carrier characteristics.

Note on carrier:	**Printed on durable stencil paper**
MARC21:	500 $a **Printed on durable stencil paper**

Note on Item-specific Carrier Characteristic (RDA 3.22) [MARC field 590 or 500]

This element is used to provide any additional information about the carrier characteristics specific to an item that were not included in the note of carrier element (RDA 3.21). This note is usually a local note, since the information does not apply to other copies (items) of the same manifestation. Since most cataloging records are shared through bibliographic networks, this note needs to clarify that the information has limited applicability.

Information recorded in this element includes autograph and inscription information, damage to the carrier, carrier condition, etc.

Note on item-specific carrier characteristic::	**Autographed by author**
MARC21:	590 $a **Autographed by author.**

Note on item-specific carrier characteristic:	**Library's copy lacks pages 89-92**
MARC21:	590 $a **Library's copy lacks pages 89-92**.

PROVIDING ACQUISITION AND ACCESS INFORMATION

Chapter 4 of RDA includes a number of manifestation and item attributes that relate to acquisition, access, and availability of resources, and, therefore, support the FRBR *obtain* user task. It is important to users to find, identify, and select the resource that best matches their information need or the resource they sought, and to be able to know how to obtain the resource itself or access the resource and therefore its intellectual content.

Terms of Availability (RDA 4.2) [MARC field 020, subfield c]

This element is defined as conditions under which a publisher will supply a resource or the price of a resource. This element was frequently used to record the retail price of a resource in the past, but current LC and PCC practice is not to use this element due to price changes and LC's decision not to use this element (LC-PCC PS 4.2.1.3).

Contact Information (RDA 4.3) [MARC field 270]

Recorded here is the contact information for the organization that makes a resource available for use. This element is more frequently used for descriptions of archival collections and materials.

Contact information:	**Johns Hopkins University, 5457 Twin Knolls Road, Columbia MD**
MARC21:	270 $a **Johns Hopkins University** $a **5457 Twin Knolls Road** $b **Columbia** $c **MD**

Restrictions on Access (RDA 4.4) [MARC field 506]

In this element, any information relating to restrictions placed by the holding agency on access to the resource is recorded. This element is often used to indicate that there are no restrictions, if users expect a resource to be restricted.

Restrictions on access:	**Unrestricted**
MARC21:	506 $a **Unrestricted**.
Restrictions on access:	**Access to parts of this collection may be restricted**

MARC21: 506 $a **Access to parts of this collection may be restricted.**

Restrictions on Use (RDA 4.5) [MARC field 506]

Often, a resource may not have restrictions on access, but it may have restriction on use. RDA 4.5 guides the recording restriction on access information.

Restrictions on use: **Collection is open for research. Materials must be used on-site; advance notice suggested. Access to parts of this collection may be restricted under provisions of state or federal law.**
MARC21: 506 $a **Collection is open for research. Materials must be used on-site; advance notice suggested. Access to parts of this collection may be restricted under provisions of state or federal law.**

Uniform Resource Locator (RDA 4.6) [MARC field 856]

A URL is the address of an Internet or remote-access resource, but may also include addresses for local resources available in an agency's network. Using a URL for a local resource may not be a best practice if the records are shared and include a link to a local resource not available outside the agency's network. The most common use of this element is for World Wide Web site addresses.

Uniform resource locator: **www.worldcat.org**
MARC21: 856 4 $u **www.worldcat.org**
Uniform resource locator: **http://lcweb2.loc.gov/diglib/ihas/loc.natlib.ihas.200199289/**
MARC21: 856 41 $3 Online version: $u http://lcweb2.loc.gov/diglib/ihas/loc.natlib.ihas.200199289/

SUMMARY

The elements covered in the current chapter are a major portion of what is considered the description of a resource or the descriptive data created during the process of describing a resource for access. The majority of this information is recorded in MARC21 fields 2xx-5xx for bibliographic data. Additional information is provided for resources, mostly considered as authority data, which relate to identifying works and expressions, as covered in chapter 7.

NOTES

1. *RDA: Resource Description and Access*. (2010–). Developed in a collaborative process led by the Joint Steering Committee for Development of RDA (JSC). Chicago: American Library Association.
2. Cutter, C. A. (1904). *Rules for a Dictionary Catalog* (4th ed., rewritten). Washington, DC: Government Printing Office (p. 11).
3. Joint Steering Committee for Revision of AACR, American Library Association, Canadian Library Association, and Chartered Institute of Library and Information Professionals (Great Britain). (2002). *AngloAmerican Cataloguing Rules* (2nd ed., 2002 revision). Chicago, IL: American Library Association (pp. 14–15).
4. IFLA Cataloguing Section and IFLA Meetings of Experts on an International Cataloguing Code. (2009). *Statement of International Cataloguing Principles*. München, Germany: K. G. Saur. Retrieved from http://www.ifla.org/publications/statement-of-international-cataloguing-principles.
5. Reitz, J. M. (2004–2014). *ODLIS: Online Dictionary for Library and Information Science*. Retrieved from www.abc-clio.com/ODLIS/searchODLIS.aspx.

Chapter 7

Resource Description and Access

Identifying Works and Expressions

RDA Section 2, Chapters 5 through 7, provides guidelines for identifying works and expressions and for describing the content of a resource. The FRBR definitions of the terms work and expression are used in RDA. "Work" is defined as the distinct intellectual or artistic content of a resource, and "expression" is defined as the realization of a work in a particular form or combination of forms. These forms may include alpha-numeric characters, notation for music or choreography, images, sound, objects, and others. Works and expressions can be individual entities, aggregates, or components of an entity.

Although most RDA terminology for attributes comes from the FRBR and FRAD models, RDA terms for elements may be different from terms used in the models and may have specific technical meanings; therefore, it is necessary to explain some of the terminology here before we discuss the guidelines in more detail.

Title: terms used for different titles associated with a work, including title of the work, preferred title for the work, and variant title for the work.

Title of the work is a character or string of characters forming a word or words by which a work is known. A work may be known by more than one title, and, therefore, there may be more than one title of a work or more than one forms of the title of the work. For example, a work may be known by the titles "On the Origin of Species by Means of Natural Selection," "Preservation of Favoured Races in the Struggle for Life," or "Origin of Species."

Preferred title for the work is the title of the work or the form of the title of the work selected to identify the work, and is the basis for the title used as the access point for the work. In the above example, the title "On the Origin of Species" is selected as the preferred title, and forms the basis of the authorized access point that represents this work.

Variant title for the work is the title or the form of the title of the work that is different from the title or the form of the title that is selected as the preferred title of the work. The title "Preservation of Favoured Races in the Struggle for Life" is a variant title for the work illustrated in the above example.

Access point: three terms are used for a name, title, etc., to represent an entity, a work, or an expression in this case. The three terms defined in RDA are access point, authorized access point, and variant access point.

Access point is a title, a name, a code, or any other term that represents a particular entity. One form of the access point is standardized to become the authorized access point.

Authorized access point is the access point that has been established as the standardized form of an access point that represents an entity. The authorized access point is typically formed using the name of the entity responsible for the work (if applicable), the title of the work, and possibly additional elements. Continuing with our example, the combination of the author's name, Charles Darwin, and the preferred title, "On the Origin of Species," was selected as the access point for the work. In our example, the name of the work's creator is standardized based on RDA guidelines as "Darwin, Charles, 1809-1882," and is combined with the standardized form of the preferred title of the work "On the Origin of Species" into "Darwin, Charles, 1809-1882. On the origin of species" as the authorized access point of the work.

Variant access point is an access point that is not selected as the authorized access point. A variant access point is formed using the authorized access point for the entity responsible for the work, the variant title of the work, and additional elements, if necessary. The form of the access point not used as the authorized access point, "Darwin, Charles, 1809-1882. On the origin of species," is a variant access point.

It is necessary to identify all known forms of a title or a name for an entity and to record them as authority data so that we can connect the users with the resource they are looking for, no matter which form of a name, title, or other identifier they use in their search.

Two principles are used in RDA guidelines (included in RDA Chapters 6 and 7) for identification and description of works and elements: the principle of *differentiation* and the principle of *representation*. The principle of differentiation guides identification of works and expressions as unique entities that are differentiated from other works or expressions. In other words, users of resource descriptions should be able to uniquely identify an entity and differentiate it from other similar entities. The principle of representation guides the selection of the title or the form of the title of a work, namely, the preferred title of the work, which is used to identify the work in resource description. The title chosen to serve as the preferred title of the work should be based on the most frequently appearing title in original embodiments (manifestations), namely in the original language, if a language material, the title most frequently found in reference sources, or be based on the most frequent title appearing in any other embodiments (manifestations) of the work. Other titles, not chosen as the preferred title of a work, should be recorded as variant titles of the work. Both principles of differentiation and representation facilitate the following functional objectives, which are variations of a number of user tasks identified in the FRBR model family. The functional objectives state that a user should be able to

- *find* works and expressions corresponding to their search criteria;
- *identify* the work or expression described in the search results, including uniquely identifying it and confirming it is, indeed, the one sought, and that it can be differentiated from other similar ones;
- *understand* the relationship between the title used to represent the work and any other title used to refer to the particular work (e.g., variations of the title due to different language expressions or embodiments, such as publications by different publishers);
- *understand* why a particular title has been recorded as a preferred or variant title; and
- *select* a work or expression matching the user's content characteristics' requirements, including the form, language, and so on.

CORE ELEMENTS

RDA defines core elements for each entity based on the FRBR and FRAD attributes and relationships identified as supporting the user tasks.[1] Agencies can identify additional RDA elements as core for their own cataloging. For example, the LC, through its LC-PCC PS, identifies a number of elements as LC core that have not been defined as core in RDA.

Works

At the minimum, the following two elements are included when identifying a work:

Preferred title of the work
Identifier of the work.

In differentiating a preferred title of a work, it may be necessary to associate it with the name of the person, corporate body, or family by preceding the preferred title of the work with the authorized access point form of the name. If it is necessary to differentiate the preferred title of a work due to its similarity with other work titles and associated names responsible for the creation of the work, as many as necessary of the following elements should be recorded:

Form of work
Date of work
Place of origin of the work
Other distinguishing characteristic of the work.

Musical works: When identifying musical works, record as many of the following elements as necessary to identify works with no distinctive titles or to differentiate works that have distinctive titles but are similar to the titles of other works:

Medium of performance
Numeric designation
Key

Expressions

At the minimum, record the following elements, as applicable, when describing an expression:

Identifier for the expression
Content type
Language of expression

If necessary to differentiate expressions of the same work, record the following additional elements:

Date of expression
Other distinguishing characteristic of the expression

Cartographic expressions: When describing cartographic expressions, record the following elements, as applicable:

Horizontal scale of cartographic content
Vertical scale of cartographic content

In addition to the core work and expression elements, RDA allows the inclusion of elements based on agency policies or cataloger's judgment. Although not required, these elements may be included either due to best practices or because the cataloger considers them important for the support of user tasks.

LANGUAGE AND SCRIPT

RDA 5.4 instructs to record titles of works in the language and script as they appear on the sources from which they are taken. As an alternative, RDA instructs that the transliterated title of the work be recorded to serve as a substitute for or in addition to the title appearing on the source.

Other identifying elements of works and expressions should be recorded in the language and script specified in the respective RDA Chapter 6 guidelines. For descriptive elements covered in RDA Chapter 7, use the language preferred by the cataloging agency.

LC-PCC PS specifies LC and PCC practice to follow the alternative guidelines and record the transliterated form of the title of works and expressions in authorized access points, using the ALA-LC Romanization Tables, and to allow the recording of the title the way it appears on the source as an optional variant access point.

STATUS OF IDENTIFICATION

This element is intended specifically to indicate the status of an authorized access point. MARC authority 008, position 33, Level of establishment is used in an MARC 21 authority record to indicate whether an access point (appearing in the 1xx field of the record) is fully established, provisional (due to insufficient data), or preliminary (resource is not available, and information is taken from an external source), based on the terminology provided in RDA 5.7. This element is considered core for LC-PCC.

SOURCES CONSULTED

In the process of authority work, one may consult a number of resources to determine the title of a work or other identifying elements of a work or expression. These consulted sources are cited in an authority record based on the guidelines in RDA 5.8.1.3. In a MARC 21 record structure, they are entered in MARC fields 670 and 675. This element is considered core for LC-PCC.

Example:

670 $a Empire and resistance, 2010: $b t.p. (Conrad) p. 15 (Jozef Tedor Konrad Nalecz Korzeniowsky; b. 1857, d. 1924)

670 $a Wikipedia, web site viewed 26 June 2012 $b (Joseph Conrad; bornk Józef Teodor Konrad Korzeniowski; b. 3 December 1857, Berdichev, Ukraine; d. 3 August 1924, Bishopsbourne, England; Polish novelist who wrote in English after settling in England; wrote stories predominantly with a nautical setting; great English novelist)

670 $a Encyc. Brit. $b (Wright, Frank Lloyd; b. 6/8/1867; d. 4/9/59)

670 $a Encyc. Amer. $b (Wright, Frank Lloyd; b. 6/8/1869; d. 4/9/59; Note: year of birth in dispute, Wright himself maintained 1869, his sister, 1867)

CATALOGER'S NOTES

In addition to sources consulted, those creating authority data may add a note with information deemed helpful to the user of the authority data. Such information may include instructions on the use of the access point, justifying decisions, or providing specific guidelines and information not included in any other element. MARC field 677 is used to record a cataloger's note. This element is considered core for LC-PCC.

Example:

667 $a Do not use as main entry for Homeric hymns or Battle of the frogs and mice, which should normally be entered under a uniform title. For these and other works attributed to "Pseudo-Homer" or otherwise once attributed to Homer, make an added entry for Homer.

Below are two examples of MARC 21 authority records, including data for work and expression. Notice that in the first example, the work is not associated with a person, corporate body, or family responsible for the content of the work. In the second example, the authorized access point consists of a combination of the authorized access point for the person responsible for the work (Kander) and the preferred title of the work (Zorba), with the addition of other identifying elements for the work and expression.

Authority record 1:

Rec stat c	Entered 19900320	Replaced	20130108073233.0
Type z	Upd status a	Enc lvln	Source
Roman	Ref status a	Mod rec	Name use a
Govt agn	Auth status a	Subj a	Subj use a
Series n	Auth/ref a	Geo subd n	Ser use b
Ser num n	Name n	Subdiv tp n	Rules z

010	$a n 88008741
040	DNLM ‡b eng ‡e rda ‡c DLC ‡d DLC
130 _0	$a Diane Rehm show (Radio program)
380	$a Radio program
500 1_	$a Rehm, Diane
670	$a State of the art in medical computers [SR] 1985: ‡b label (D. Rehm show) narration (Diane Rehm show)
670	$a WAMU radio Web site, viewed Apr. 16, 2007: ‡b (Diane Rehm show)

Authority record 2:

Rec stat c	Entered 20110616	Replaced	20130326125931.0
Type z	Upd status a	Enc lvl n	Source
Roman	Ref status a	Mod rec	Name use a
Govt agn	Auth status a	Subj a	Subj use a
Series n	Auth/ref a	Geo subd n	Ser use b
Ser num n	Name a	Subdiv tp n	Rules z

010	$a n 2011040925
040	DLC $b eng $e rda $c DLC $d DLC
100 1	$a Kander, John. $t Zorbá (Musical). $k Selections; $o arranged
400 1	$a Kander, John. $t Music from the Broadway hit Zorbá
400 1	$a Kander, John. $t Zorbá (Musical). $k Selections; $o arr. $w nnea
670 $a	Music from the Broadway hit Zorbá [SR], 1968.

In both of the above examples, we see that field 040, subfield $e rda indicates that the RDA guidelines were used in determining what authority data to include and in making decisions regarding the authorized and variant access points. As access points in a MARC bibliographic record describing a resource, authorized access points of works and expressions appear in different fields and often not in the combined form as they appear in the authority record:

Authority record:

100 1 $a Blake, Wendon. $t Figures in oil
400 1 $a Blake, Wendon. $t Portrait and figure painting book. $n Pt. 3, $p Figures in oil $w nna
670 $a His Figures in oil, c1980.

Bibliographic record:

100 1 $a Blake, Wendon, $e author.
245 10 $a Figures in oil / $c by Wendon Blake; paintings by George Passantino.
500 $a Originally published as pt. 3 of the author's The portrait and figure painting book.

Bibliographic record:

100 1 $a Blake, Wendon.
240 10 $a Figures in oil. $l Spanish
245 13 $a El desnudo al óleo / $c Wendon Blake, George Passantino.

Although RDA does not specify a particular record structure and does not differentiate between bibliographic data (information relating to the resource description) and authority data (information relating to named entities), this chapter indicates current practice by identifying which elements are typically recorded in a bibliographic record and which elements are typically recorded in an authority record, with the addition of respective MARC bibliographic or authority fields.

In current practice of recording work and expression elements in MARC records, we see that the majority of the elements described in RDA Chapter 6 appear in authority records (although some also appear in bibliographic records). The majority of the elements described in RDA Chapter 7 (describing content) appear in bibliographic records. This chapter will cover the elements in the order they appear in RDA, and not in the order of their appearance in a MARC record structure; whether bibliographic or authority records, the MARC record, although the current practice in most US libraries, is just an implementation of a particular record structure and encoding schema and is not necessarily applicable to all environments or future practices.

GENERAL GUIDELINES

To describe works and expressions, RDA uses two separate chapters: Chapter 6, "Identifying Works and Expressions," and Chapter 7, "Describing Content."

The focus of these chapters is on recording information for works and expressions, and not necessarily on how to formulate access points for works and expressions. In RDA Chapter 6, a discussion on all elements is followed by a section on constructing access points to represent works and expressions.

To determine the elements necessary to construct an authorized access point that represents a work or expression is to determine what combination of author, title, and preferred title will be used. Typically, these elements include the preferred title of the work (covered in RDA 6.2.2), any additions to the preferred title (RDA 6.27.1.9), and the authorized access point for the entity responsible for the content, most often the author, who can be a person, a family, or a corporate body (RDA 19.2). Elements in, and construction of, authorized access points for persons, families, and corporate bodies are covered in chapter 8 of this book.

When describing works, one needs to take into account whether the content of the work is complete or whether it is being developed over time. FRBR's "intended termination" attribute of a work describes whether a work's content has a finite end or continues indefinitely. When a work continues indefinitely, the content and other characteristics change over time. Therefore, some changes are considered important and they affect how a work is identified. These are changes in the title of the work and changes in the responsibility for the work. RDA 6.1.3 distinguishes between a change that is significant enough to constitute a new and different work and a change that is not as significant, and, therefore, should be treated as part of the original work. Considerations are different for multipart monographs, serials, or integrating resources (see mode of issuance in chapter 6 or RDA 2.13).

Multipart monographs: When a monographic resource is issued in multiple parts, it is possible to have some changes in the responsibility as new parts are released. This change alone is not significant enough, per RDA 6.1.3.1, to consider this as a new work. The original author is still considered responsible for the work, and, therefore, all parts are included in the same description of the work.

If, in addition to the change of responsibility, there is a change in the mode of issuance or a change in media type—for example, a change from a multipart monograph to an integrating resource or from a textual volume to sound recording—then, based on RDA 6.1.3.1, this change is significant enough to constitute a new work, and, therefore, a new work description will be created and a new access point will be used.

Example (bibliographic record):
100 1 $a Paull, E. T., $d 1858-1924, $e composer, $e arranger of music.

245 10 $a Say "au revoir" but not good bye / $c the most beautiful ballad ever written by Harry Kennedy; revised, rewritten and rearranged by E.T. Paull.
500 $a "Words and music by Harry Kennedy; revised and rearranged by E.T. Paull; French version by Jacques H. Caliche"--Caption.
700 1 $i Revision of: $a Kennedy, Harry. $t Say "Au revoir" but not "Good-bye."

Serials: When a work is issued as a serial, either a change in the responsibility or a major change in the title of the serial is considered significant enough to treat the serial as a new work. Changes in the responsibility include changes in the authorized access point representing a person, family, or corporate body that is used as part of the authorized access point representing the serial work.

In current practice, relationships to new serial works due to changes in title works are commonly recorded in bibliographic records and are not recorded as authority data for the authorized access point for the work. In the following example, we see that the *Journal of Nurse-Midwifery* was previously published as *Bulletin of the American College of Nurse-Midwives*, and later on its title was changed to *Journal of Midwifery & Women's Health*.

Example (bibliographic record):
130 0 $a Journal of nurse-midwifery (Online)
780 00 $t Bulletin of the American College of Nurse-Midwives
785 00 $t Journal of midwifery & women's health (Online)

In an authority record for the work *Journal of Nurse-Midwifery*, this information would be recorded as:
022 1879-1565
130 0 Journal of nurse-midwifery (Online)
530 0 $w r $i Continues (work): $a Bulletin of the American College of Nurse-Midwives
530 0 $w r $i Continued by (work): $a Journal of midwifery & women's health (Online)

Integrating resource: When a work is issued as an integrating resource—for example, an updating web site or an updating loose-leaf publication—and there is either a change in the responsibility or a change in the title of the resource, such a change is not considered significant enough to treat the work as a new work. Instead, the authorized access point in the description of the original work is revised to reflect the change in the name of the creator or the preferred title of the work.

WORK ATTRIBUTES

FRBR work entity is defined as "a distinct intellectual or artistic creation."[2] As an abstract entity, it does not have an object that we can use to describe the work, and, therefore, it is usually through references to its expressions and sometimes through the manifestations of an expression that we may base our work descriptions, as the guidelines will instruct us.

RDA provides guidelines on elements to be used, either as core (indicated as "core" below) or as optional additions for the identification of works (indicated as "differentiating core" below). Core elements are necessary to identify a work, but in some cases the guidelines will instruct us to treat an element as core only if it is necessary to differentiate between two works with the same title or with similar names as other entities. It is also a good practice to include elements, whether core under the differentiation condition or noncore, if it is determined that this information would be helpful to users.

The following work elements are discussed in more detail below:

- Title of work
  - Preferred title of work *[core]*
  - Variant title of the work
- Form of work *[core if needed to differentiate]*
- Date of work *[core if needed to differentiate]*
- Place of origin of work *[core if needed to differentiate]*
- Other distinguishing characteristics of work *[core if needed to differentiate]*
- History of work
- Identifier of work *[core]*

Additional work elements are discussed that are applicable to special cases, such as musical, legal, and religious works.

Title of the Work (RDA 6.2)
Core Element: *Preferred title of the work*

Works are typically identified by the title of the work, which can be taken from any source of information. Two types of work titles are considered when identifying a work, the preferred title of the work and the variant title of the work, both of which were defined earlier in this chapter. In the case where a work has a creator, a relationship exists between the work entity and the person, family, or corporate body entity. RDA Chapter 19 covers the recording of the relationship between the work and its creator or creators and also additional collaborative relationships.

When a work is associated with a creator, the authorized access point for the work is recorded in the authority record (MARC) as a combination of the creator's authorized access point, followed by the preferred title of the work (field 1XX, subfield $a for creator's name, subfield $t for preferred title of work, with additional subfields as required). Some works are not associated with a creator, either because they are the result of collaborative work, or the creator is unknown, or they fall under a condition where the creation relationship is distributed in a way that no one can be considered responsible for the work. In such cases, the preferred title of the work is the authorized access point and is recorded in the MARC authority field 130.

Capitalization of the title of the work (RDA 6.2.1.4) follows the instructions in RDA Appendix A.3, which provides different instructions for different languages. For example, for English work titles, capitalize the initial letter of the first word of the title and any proper name that may be included in the title; for German work titles, capitalize all nouns; and so on.

Example:
Work title on source of information: FOOD52 GENIUS RECIPES
Recording of preferred title of work: Food52 genius recipes

Additional instructions on dealing with premodern forms of letters, such as in Latin titles (e.g., use of "v" on the resource for either "u" or "v"; use of "I" for "i" or "j") are discussed in LC-PCC PS 6.2.2.8.

Initial articles (RDA 6.2.1.7) are included when recording the title of a work. LC-PCC PS policy is to follow the alternative guideline to omit the initial article, unless the title of the work is indexed and accessed under the article as an integral part of a name (*Las* Vegas, *Le* Blank, etc.). In a way, this is the common practice among libraries creating MARC records, due to their limitations in terms of handling initial articles of works.

Example:
Work title: The glorious game Alternative guideline: Glorious game
An acceptable time Acceptable time

RDA Appendix C provides lists of initial articles in various languages.

Spacing of Initials and Acronyms (RDA 6.2.1.8) guidelines instruct that space should not be included or added between initials or between an initial and a full stop.

Examples:
Title on source: A C T FLASH Cards
Work title: ACT flash cards

Abbreviations (RDA 6.2.1.9) guidelines direct that the title of a work should be transcribed, and, therefore, no words are to be abbreviated. Abbreviated words included in the work title are transcribed in the abbreviated form they appear.

Example:
Title on source: INDONESIA, ETC.
Work title: Indonesia, etc.

Tile on source: Etcetera
Work title: Etcetera

Preferred Title of the Work (RDA 6.2.2)
Core Element
[MARC authority field 130, or field 100, 110, 111 subfield t]

As a core element, the preferred title of the work is required and serves as the basis for the authorized access point for the work. Guidelines for all works are given here, but there are also additional guidelines for the treatment of musical works (RDA 6.14–6.18), legal works (RDA 6.19–6.21), religious works (RDA 6.23–6.25), and official communications (RDA 6.26).

Based on the principle of representation, sources of information for selecting the preferred title are discussed in relation to when they were created.

For **works created after 1500**, select the title in the original language in which the work became known. This means, of course, that one is able to know the language of the work, but often the language is not known until a work is expressed.

If no original language is known, use the title by which the work is most commonly known. Again, in this type of case, "most commonly known" is assumed to be the original language of the work. Often, reference sources are consulted to determine the original language and the most commonly known title.

Examples (authority record):
Preferred title of work: **Babar en famille**
MARC21: 100 1 $a Brunhoff, Jean de, $d 1899-1937. $t **Babar en famille**

Preferred title of work: **Guide to jobs & working on cruise ships**
MARC 21: 100 1 $a Divel, Fred. $t **Guide to jobs & working on cruise ships**

Preferred title of work: **Fredegarii chronicon**
MARC 21: 130 0 $a **Fredegarii chronicon**

This becomes more challenging when describing nonlanguage materials, like works of art. For example, what is the original language among the four versions of a work by Munch? He named his painting *Der Schrei der Natur* (*The Scream of Nature*), but it is most commonly known as "The Scream." LCC-PC PS 6.2.4–5 instructs that English-language reference sources (including books and articles written about a work of art) be consulted as the source for selecting the preferred title of the work in these cases. In accordance with this practice, the preferred title of Munch's 1895 work in the LC authority record (note the reference sources cited) appears as the following:

Preferred title of work: **Scream**
100 1 $a Munch, Edvard, $d 1863-1944. $t **Scream** (1895)
670 $a Work cat.: Temkin, Ann. The scream, c2012: $b t.p. (Scream) p. 5, etc. (Scream, 1895; pastel on paper on cardboard, 32 × 23 1/4»; private collection; other versions in the Munch Museum in Oslo, pastel drawing created in 1893 and tempera and oil on cardboard, 1910?, the National Museum in Oslo, painting on cardboard, 1893, and a 1895 lithograph)
670 $a New York Times (via Internet), Sept. 12, 2012 $b (Edvard Munch's 1895 version of "The Scream";
Munch made four versions from 1893 to 1910)

If there is doubt about the original title of the work, use the title proper appearing in the manifestation of the original edition (see RDA 2.3.2).

RDA instructs to omit any alternative title, if included as part of the title of the work. An alternative title is the second portion of a title, typically connected with the first portion of the title with the use of the word "or."

For **works created before 1501**, use modern reference sources to identify the most commonly known title appearing in the original language of the work, if possible. Preference is given to reference sources published after 1500. Many works created prior to 1501 have no known creator. This means that there is no relationship to a person, family, or corporate body responsible for the work, and, therefore, that the preferred title of the work will be recorded in field 130 of the MARC authority record.

Examples (authority records):

Preferred title of work:	**Gilgamesh**
MARC 21:	130 0 $a **Gilgamesh**
	. . .
	670 $a Brill's new Pauly online, 3 March 2011 $b (Gilgamesh, Gilgamesh epic; Gilgamesh is mentioned in non-literary sources as early as 2700 BC, but the written form of the Epic of Gilgamesh was produced in Sumerian during the 21st century BC; an Akkadian version arose in the 19th/18th centuries BC)
Preferred title of work:	**The Canterbury tales**
MARC 21:	100 1 $a Chaucer, Geoffrey, $d -1400. $t **Canterbury tales**
	400 1 $a Chaucer, Geoffrey, $d -1400. $t Caxton's Chaucer
	670 $a Caxton's Chaucer, 2003?

There is an exception for **classical and Byzantine Greek works**. If the work was written in classical Greek or if it was created before 1453, then select a well-established title in the language of the cataloging agency as the preferred title of the work.

Example of classical Greek work (authority records):

Title of work:	Βατραχομυομαχία
Preferred title of work:	**Battle of the frogs and mice**
MARC 21:	130 0 $a **Battle of the frogs and mice**

Example of Byzantine Greek work (authority records):

Title of work:	Θεογονία
Preferred title of work:	**Theogony**
MARC 21:	100 0 $a Hesiod. ǂt **Theogony**
	400 0 $a Hesiod. ǂt Theogonia
	. . .

Similarly, when an anonymous work is created before 1501 and the original is not written in Greek or in the language of the cataloging agency, select a well-established title in the language of the cataloging agency as the preferred title of the work.

Preferred title of work:	**Arabian nights**
MARC 21:	130 0 $a **Arabian nights**
	430 0 $a Hikajat 1001 malem
	430 0 $a a Thousand and one nights
	430 0 $a One thousand and one nights
	. . .

The guidelines for recording the preferred title of the work are divided into (a) single work and compilation of works by one person, family, or corporate body; (b) single part or two or more parts of a work; (c) compilations of works by one person, family, or corporate body; and (d) compilations of two or more works.

Single work (RDA 6.2.1 and 6.2.2): Recording the preferred title of a single work has been covered earlier in this chapter.

Single part (RDA 6.2.2.9.1): Recording the preferred title of one part of a work follows the same guidelines as those for a single work, using the title of the part, if the part has a distinctive title.

Preferred title of larger work:	The lord of the rings
Preferred title of part:	**The fellowship of the ring**
MARC 21 (authority):	100 1 $aTolkien, J. R. R. $q (John Ronald Reuel), $d 1892-1973. $t **Fellowship of the ring**
MARC 21 (bibliographic):	100 1 $aTolkien, J. R. R. $q (John Ronald Reuel), $d 1892-1973. 245 14 $a **The fellowship of the ring**: $b being the first part of The lord of the rings / $c by J.R.R. Tolkien.

In case the part does not have a distinctive title, a general term is used, such as “book,” “chapter,” or a general division such as “preface.” The following is an example of this:

Preferred title of larger work:	De occulta philosophia
Preferred title of part:	**Book 4**
MARC 21 (authority):	100 1 $a Agrippa von Nettesheim, Heinrich Cornelius, $d 1486?-1535. $t De occulta philosophia. $n **Book 4**

MARC21 (bibliographic):	100 1 $a Agrippa von Nettesheim, Heinrich Cornelius, $d 1486?-1535.
240 10	$a De occulta philosophia. $n **Book 4.** $l English
245 14	$a The fourth book of occult philosophy / $c Henry Cornelius Agrippahis; edited with introduction and commentary by Stephen Skinner; translated into English by Robert Turner.

Guidelines on how to construct the authorized access point representing one part of a work are included in RDA 6.27.2.2. An exception is made for serials and integrating resources; in such cases, RDA 6.2.2.9.1 instructs that both the title and the designation of the part for the preferred title of the part be used if both are identified:

Preferred title of larger work:	Advances in consciousness research
Title of part:	Research in progress
Preferred title of part:	**Series B. Research in progress**
MARC 21 (authority):	130 0 $a Advances in consciousness research. $n **Series B**, $p **Research in progress**

Two or more parts (RDA 6.2.2.9.2): When identifying consecutively numbered parts of a work identified by a general term and a numeral, record the term and the numbered sequence as the preferred title of the parts. For unnumbered parts or parts that are numbered nonconsecutively, use the preferred title for each part. LCC-PC PS 6.2.2.9.2 states that the LC practice is to follow the option of recording the term "Selections," described as a conventional collective title, instead of identifying each part by its individual preferred title. This practice does not allow identification of, and eventually access to, a particular part of a work.

Preferred title of work:	Odyssey
Title of the part:	**Book 19-20**
	Book 21-22
MARC 21 (authority):	100 0 $a Homer. $t Odyssey
MARC 21 (authority):	100 0 $a Homer. $t Odyssey. $n **Book 19-20**
MARC 21 (authority):	100 0 $a Homer. $t Odyssey. $n **Book 21-22**

Compilations of works of one person, family, or corporate body (RDA 6.2.2.10): If a compilation of a body of works is known by a title used in manifestations, use that title as the preferred title. When no distinctive title is used for the compilation of works, use an appropriate term as follows:

(1) *Works*: a compilation that includes the complete works of a person, corporate body or family:

MARC 21 (authority): 100 1 $a Cavalcanti, Guido, $d -1300. $t Works

(2) A term appropriate representing a particular form, such as "poems," "correspondence," "short stories," etc.:

MARC 21 (authority): 100 1 $a Diepenbrock, Alphons, $d 1862-1921. $t Songs

For other compilations of two or more works, record the preferred title of each work when the compilation includes not all works of a particular form, or when the compilation includes not all works various forms. LC-PCC PS 6.2.2.10.3 states that the LC and PCC practice is to follow the alternative guideline to use the conventional collective title for the particular form, followed by the term "Selections":

Preferred title of individual sonnets in a compilation:

MARC 21 (authority): 100 1 $a Hejda, Jiří. $t Mirov
100 1 $a Hejda, Jiří. $t Leopoldov
100 1 $a Hejda, Jiří. $t Kartouzy

MARC 21 (bibliographic): 100 1 $a Hejda, Jiří
245 10 $a Sonety / $c Jiří Hejda
700 12 $a Hejda, Jiří. $t Mirov
700 12 $a Hejda, Jiří. $t Leopoldov
700 12 $a Hejda, Jiří. $t Kartouzy

Alternative, using conventional collective terms:

MARC 21 (authority): 100 1 $a Hejda, Jiří. $t Sonnets. $k Selections.

MARC 21 (bibliographic): 100 1 $a Hejda, Jiří
240 10 $a Sonnets. $k Selections
245 10 $a Sonety / $c Jiří Hejda
505 0 $a Mírov—Leopoldov—Kartouzy

Variant Title of the Work (RDA 6.2.3) [MARC authority field 430, or field 400, 410, 411 subfield t]

Often, works are known by a number of different titles, or different forms of the same title, mostly due to variation in expressions and because different titles appear in the various embodiments (manifestations) of a work. The variant title of the work is defined as the title (or titles) of the work that is (or are) different from the preferred title of the work or that has (or have) a different form from that of the chosen preferred title of the work. For example, Chaucer's work appears as "Canterbury tales" and as "Caxton's Chaucer." The work title "Canterbury tales" has been selected as the preferred title of the work, and, therefore, "Caxton's Chaucer" is the variant title of the work. In a MARC 21 authority record structure, the preferred title of the work is recorded as part of the authorized access point in field 1XX, and all variant titles of a work are recorded as part of variant access points in field 4XX in a way similar to how the preferred title of the work is recorded in field 1XX (following RDA 6.2.1 and 6.2.2).

Preferred title of the work:	Canterbury tales
MARC 21 (authority):	100 1 $a Chaucer, Geoffrey, $d -1400. $t Canterbury tales
Variant title of the work:	**Caxton's Chaucer**
MARC 21 (authority):	400 1 $a Chaucer, Geoffrey, $d -1400. $t **Caxton's Chaucer**

Variant titles are important parts of the syndetic structure of a catalog, providing links (cross-references) from variant titles to the preferred titles to enable the user to find all variations of a work under the same preferred title of the work. Typically, an information system, such as a library catalog, will display this link for the above work by Chaucer as the following:

Chaucer, Geoffrey, -1400
  Caxton's Chaucer
    see under Canterbury tales

This will allow any user entering "Caxton's Chaucer" in a search box to refine his or her search to use the preferred access point. Often, many information systems are designed to skip the display of the above linking information and, by default, retrieve and display the results for the preferred access point.

RDA 6.2.3.3 instructs that a variant title of a work should be recorded only if it is significantly different from the preferred title of the work and if there is reasonable expectation that a user may look for the work under that variant title. Variant titles of a work created due to a translation in a language different from that of the original work are recorded in the description of the expression (separate description recorded in an authority record other than that for the work).

Alternative linguistic forms of the work title (RDA 6.2.3.4) may be recorded as variant titles. This may seem contradictory to the previous instruction of RDA 6.2.3.3 to not include titles in different languages due to translation of the work. However, work titles often have linguistically variant forms because the work was created in more than one language. In this case, the variant title of the work is recorded. Also, because the preferred title of the work is not always in the language of the original (e.g., classical and Byzantine Greek), the title in the original language would be considered an alternative linguistic form of the title of the work.

MARC authority record:

Preferred title of work:	Children of Heracles
MARC authority:	100 0 $a Euripides. $t Children of Heracles
Variant title of work:	Ηρακλεῖδαι
MARC authority:	400 0 $a Euripides. $t Ηρακλεῖδαι

User display as a cross reference:
Euripides.
Ηρακλεῖδαι
see under Children of Heracles

MARC authority record:

Preferred title of work:	130 0 $a Arabian nights
Variant title of work:	**Hikajat 1001 malem**
MARC authority:	430 0 $a **Hikajat 1001 malem**

User display as a cross-reference:
Hikajat 1001 malem
see under Arabian nights

The alternative linguistic form may include the title in a different script (see example for Euripides' *Children of Heracles*) or for nonlanguage materials known differently in various languages. These linguistic variations may be recorded as variant titles of the title of the work.

Preferred title of work:	Mona Lisa
Variant—Alternative linguistic form:	**Dzhokonda**
	Gioconda
	Τζοκόντα

MARC authority record:
100 0 $a Leonardo, $c da Vinci, $d 1452-1519. $t Mona Lisa
400 0 $a Leonardo, $c da Vinci, $d 1452-1519. $t **Dzhokonda**
400 0 $a Leonardo, $c da Vinci, $d 1452-1519. $t **Gioconda**
400 0 $a Leonardo, $c da Vinci, $d 1452-1519. $t Τζοκόντα

Other variant titles of the work (RDA 6.2.3.5) can be recorded if the cataloger deems them helpful for users, with the exception of titles for translations covered in RDA 6.2.3.3. The examples below illustrate different cases where the recording of the variant title of the work would be helpful to the user, and, therefore, should be included.

Preferred title of work:	Bagman's story
Variant title of work:	**Pickwick papers. Bagman's story**
MARC authority:	100 1 $a Dickens, Charles, $d 1812-1870. $t Bagman's story 400 1 $a Dickens, Charles, $d 1812-1870. $t **Pickwick papers.** $p **Bagman's story**

Dickens, Charles, $d 1812-1870.
Pickwick papers. Bagman's story
see under Bagman's story

Preferred title of work:	130 0	$a Double falsehood
Variant title of work:	430 0	$a **Double falshood**
	430 0	$a **Distrest lovers**

Distrest lovers
see under Double falsehood
Double falshood
see under Double falsehood

Preferred title of work:	130 0	$a Agriculture information bulletin
Variant title of work:	430 0	$a **AIB (Series)**
	410 1	$a United States. $b Dept. of Agriculture. $t Agriculture information bulletin

AIB (Series)
see under Agriculture information bulletin
United States. Dept. of Agriculture. Agriculture information bulletin
see under Agriculture information bulletin

Other Identifying Attributes of Works

A number of additional elements are used to identify a work, some of which are core elements under certain conditions.

Form of Work (RDA 6.3)
Core Element (if needed for differentiation)
[MARC authority field 380]

Form of work is defined as the class or genre of the work. This element is considered core when it is necessary to distinguish a work from another work that has a similar title or to distinguish it from the name of a person, family, or corporate body. It can also be recorded if a cataloger judges that it is helpful for users to find, identify, or select a resource that best fits their needs. The form of the work may be part of the authorized access point or may be a separate element. A list of terms is included as examples in RDA 6.3.1.3. As a best practice, appropriate terms from the LCSH, the Art and Architecture Thesaurus (AAT), and the Library of Congress Genre/Form Terms (LCGFT) are considered among the most common vocabularies that can be used to identify the form of work. Note that $2 of MARC field 380 below indicates the vocabulary used as the source for the form of work term. Also note that more than one term for form of work can be recorded.

Example:
Form of work: **Novels**
Form of work: **Fantasy fiction**
MARC 21 authority: 100 1 $aAlexander, Lloyd. $t Black cauldron
380 $a **Novels** $2 aat
380 $a **Fantasy fiction** $2 lcsh

Example where the form of work is part of the authorized access point and a separate element:

Form of work (LCSH): **motion pictures**
Form of work (LCGFT): **biographical films**
historical films
feature films
MARC 21 authority: 046 $k 2013
130 0 $a 12 years a slave (**Motion picture**)
380 $a **Motion pictures** $2 lcsh
380 $a **Biographical films** $a **Historical films** $a **Feature films** $2 lcgft

430 0 $a Twelve years a slave (Motion picture)
670 $a 12 years a slave, 2013.
670 $a Internet Movie Database, January 30, 2014 $b (12 years a slave (2013); director, Steve McQueen; screenplay by John Ridley, based on Twelve years a slave by Solomon Northup; genres: biography, drama, history)

Date of Work (RDA 6.4)
Core Element
[MARC authority field 046 subfield k]

Date of work is defined as the earliest date associated with a work. The element is core for treaties. For other works, the date of work is core if it is necessary to differentiate it from other works with the same title or from the name of a person, family, or corporate body. The date of work may also be recorded if a cataloger deems it helpful to include the date of work.

Some may consider it impossible to know the date a work was created, due to the abstract nature of the work. Therefore, if no date of creation is associated with the work, use the earliest date associated with a manifestation, the earliest embodiment of the work.

The calendar preference of the cataloging agency determines how a date of work is recorded. The date of work may be part of the authorized access point of a work and it may also be a separately recorded element. Instructions on recording the date as part of the authorized access point of the work can be found in RDA 6.28.1 for musical works and in RDA 6.29.1 for legal works.

In a MARC authority record, the date of work is recorded in subfield "k" of field 046. A year or a range of years alone is recorded for works other than treaties. For treaties, the year, month, and day are recorded (RDA 6.20.3.3).

Example:

Date of work:	**1972**
MARC 21 authority:	046 $k **1972** 100 1 $a Adams, Richard, $d 1920- $t Watership Down 380 $a Novels $2 aat 380 $a Adventure stories $2 lcsh 530 0 $i Adapted as motion picture (work): $a Watership down (Motion picture) $w r 670 $a Adams, Richard. La colina de Watership, 1977.

670 $a Wikipedia, 18 July 2014 $b (Watership Down; adventure novel written by Richard Adams, first published in 1972)

Note in the example above that the date of the work is based on the date the novel was first published (field 670).

Place of Origin of the Work (RDA 6.5) Core Element (if needed for differentiation) [MARC authority field 370 subfield g]

Place of origin of the work is defined as the place, country, or other jurisdiction where the work originated. This element is core when it is necessary for distinguishing from other works or names of people, families, etc. The place of origin of the work can also be recorded if considered helpful to users.

Record the name of the place as instructed in RDA Chapter 16 on identifying places and, if applicable, abbreviate the names of places according to RDA Appendix B.11. The place of origin of the work can be recorded as a separate element or as part of the authorized access point for the work.

In MARC 21 authority records, the element place of the origin of the work is recorded in subfield "g" of field 370. One or more places may be recorded if necessary.

Example:

Place of origin of the work:	**Paris, France**
MARC 21 authority:	046 $k 1825
	100 1 $a Bonington, Richard Parkes, $d 1801-1828. $t Anne Page and Slender
	370 $g **Paris, France**
	380 $a Oil paintings

It is not as common to have and record a place associated with the creation of a work. More often, it is used to distinguish a series from other series, when the preferred title of the series is the same. Other common cases where this element is typically recorded and helpful involve works of art (see example above).

Other Distinguishing Characteristic of the Work (RDA 6.6) [MARC authority field 381 subfield a, 373]

A characteristic of a work—other than the form, date, and place of origin of the work, discussed above—can be recorded as a distinguishing characteristic of the work if it serves to differentiate two works with the same title or form of the name of a person, corporate body, or family. Special instructions for other distinguishing characteristics of legal works are covered in RDA 6.21. When this information is necessary to distinguish works with the same title of from the name of people, families, or corporate bodies, the element is considered core. These distinguishing characteristics may be part of the authorized access of the work or may be recorded as a separate element.

Example:
Other distinguishing characteristic
Of work: **Douglas**
MARC 21 authority: 130 0 $a Harlow (Motion picture: 1965: **Douglas**)
381 $a **Douglas**

History of the Work (RDA 6.7) [MARC authority field 678, 365]

The definition of this element is simply any known history of the work, such as information about its creation and any other information that would be helpful to the user. This element may become the basis for a public display of a history of the work. Information should follow best practices of notes, to be succinct. The element is mapped to MARC 21 fields 678 and 665; the former is most commonly used for biographical and historical data, as 665 is used for historical reference.

Identifier for the Work (RDA 6.8) Core Element [MARC authority field 010, 016, 025, 035]

Identifier of the work is a string of characters that is uniquely associated with the work or its surrogate (record describing the work, such as an authority record) and helps differentiate the work from other works. The element is core, and, therefore, should be recorded. Often in a database environment, a unique identifier of the surrogate is automatically assigned or recorded when a new record is created. Authority record number is, for example, recorded in MARC field 010 for all authority records created by LC. Field 001 is used in OCLC's WorldCat to record the authority record number of each authority record in the database.

Example:
Identifier for work: **n2013065743**

MARC21 authority
010 **n2013065743**
040 DLC $b eng $e rda $c DLC

046 $k 1948
100 1 Jacobi, Frederick, $d 1891-1952. $t Ode to Zion
382 mixed voices $n 4 $a harp $n 2
670 Ode to Zion, for mixed chorus and 2 harps, 1948
670 New Grove online, Nov. 5, 2013 $b (Ode to Zion (J. Halevi), 4vv, 2 hp, 1948)

EXPRESSION ATTRIBUTES

FRBR defines expression as the "intellectual or artistic realization of a work in the form of alpha-numeric, musical, or choreographic notation, sound, image, object, movement, etc., or any combination of such forms."[3] In other words, it is the form it takes any time a work is realized or expressed. Distinct expressions exist: (a) for different forms of expression; (b) for different content versions, usually indicated by the Date of expression element; (c) for versions in different languages; and (d) for other differences, such as performances. More than one of these facets may apply to a given expression, for example, a translation of a revised edition of a text.

All work attributes also apply to each particular expression, but additional attributes are defined that are specific to each expression. RDA guidelines are provided for the following expression elements, which are identified here as core or differentiating core:

Content type [core]
Date of expression [core if differentiation is needed]
Language of expression [core]
Other distinguishing characteristic of expression [core if differentiation is needed]
Identifier of expression [core]

Note that, although title of expression is an attribute in FRBR, RDA does not provide an element for title of expression.

Additional expression elements are discussed that are applicable to musical, legal, and religious works.

As explained earlier in this chapter, expression information is considered authority data. In current practice, some expression elements are recorded in authority records and others are recorded in bibliographic records. Examples included in this section of the chapter illustrate the elements as they appear in authority records. Based on current practice, we see that not all of these elements or occurrences of elements are currently recorded in authority records.

Often, these data are included in bibliographic records as authorized access points, using the guidelines, without the creation of an authority record for the authorized access point for the particular expression. For example,

> Authorized access points for expressions of the work *Origin of Species* by Charles Darwin in different languages, found in WorldCat's authority file are the following:
>
> 100 1 Darwin, Charles, $d 1809-1882. $t On the origin of species. $l English
>
> 100 1 Darwin, Charles, $d 1809-1882. $t On the origin of species. $l Danish
>
> 100 1 Darwin, Charles, $d 1809-1882. $t On the origin of species. $l French
>
> 100 1 Darwin, Charles, $d 1809-1882. $t On the origin of species. $l Norwegian
>
> 100 1 Darwin, Charles, $d 1809-1882. $t On the origin of species. $l Russian
>
> 100 1 Darwin, Charles, $d 1809-1882. $t On the origin of species. $l Spanish
>
> 100 1 Darwin, Charles, $d 1809-1882. $t On the origin of species. $l Swedish
>
> Authorized access points for expressions of *Origin of Species* by Charles Darwin in different languages, found in WorldCat's bibliographic file are the following:
>
> 100 1 Darwin, Charles, $d 1809-1882, $e author.
>
> Work: 240 10 $a On the origin of species
>
> Language of text expressions:
>
> Chinese
> German
> English
> French
> Greek
> Korean
> Nepali
> Norwegian
> Polish
> Portuguese
> Slovenian
> Spanish
> Suomi
> Etc.

Content Type (RDA 6.9)
Core Element
[MARC authority field 336]

Defined as a term representing the fundamental form of communication in which the content of a work is expressed and the senses a human needs to use to perceive the content. In cases such as images, the number of spatial dimensions, that is, two-dimensional or three-dimensional, is part of the content type specification. This element corresponds to FRBR's expression attribute "form of expression."

Content type is a core element, and, therefore, must be recorded. RDA Table 6.9.1, under RDA 6.1.3 guidelines, provides a list of controlled terms that are appropriate as values for content type. RDA instructs that all terms applicable for a particular resource be recorded, but by using only those terms listed in Table 6.1. If none of these terms is applicable, the guidelines instruct that the term "other" should be recorded as the content type. If the content type is not easily identified, RDA instructs using the term "unspecified."

Examples:
Content type: **two-dimensional moving image**
MARC authority: 336 $a **two-dimensional moving image** $2 rdacontent

Content type: **text**
MARC authority: 336 $a **text** $b txt $2 rdacontent

Content type: **still image**
MARC authority: 336 $a **still image** $2 rdacontent

Content type: **cartographic image**
MARC authority: 336 $a **cartographic image** $2 rdacontent

Content type: **notated music**
MARC authority: 336 $a **notated music** $2 rdacontent

More than one content type may be present in one expression:

100 1 $a Schalansky, Judith, $d 1980- $t Atlas der abgelegenen Inseln. $l English
336 $a **cartographic image** $2 rdacontent
336 $a **text** $2 rdacontent

Note that in MARC authority field 336, subfield 2 is used to identify the source from which the term in subfield a (content type) is taken. In such cases, "rdacontent" is the MARC code for the RDA-controlled vocabulary for content type (RDA Table 6.1). The same field is defined in MARC bibliographic for content type.

Date of Expression (RDA 6.10)
Core Element (for differentiation)
[MARC authority field 046]

Date of expression is defined as the earliest date associated with an expression. This element is core if it is necessary to differentiate between expressions of the same work. The date of expression can be recorded as a separate element or as part of the authorized access point for the expression (covered in RDA 6.27.3).

Examples:

Date of expression:	**1997**	
MARC authority:	046	$k **1997**
	100 1	$a Rowling, J. K. $t Harry Potter and the philosopher's stone
Date of expression:	**1999**	
MARC authority:	046	$k **1999**
	130 0	$a Thomas Crown affair (Motion picture: 1999)

Language of Expression (RD4A 6.11)
Core Element
[MARC authority field 377]

The language in which a work is expressed is recorded in the element language of expression. This is a core element, and, therefore, should be recorded using appropriate terms in the language of the cataloging agency. The language of expression may be recorded as a separate element or as part of the authorized access point for the expression. Per LC-PCC PS 6.11.1.3, LC practice is to use the name of the language from the *MARC Code List for Languages*, including special instructions on how to record the languages from the code list, when recorded in a MARC record. Record all languages if an expression incudes more than one language.

Examples:

Language of expression:	English
MARC authority:	377 $a eng
Language of expression:	Italian
Language of expression:	French
MARC authority:	377 $a ita
MARC authority:	377 $a fre

The same LC-PCC PS instructs that the term "Greek" be used for expressions in attic, ancient, and modern Greek, unless there are translations from one form of Greek to another or if the text includes more than one form of Greek, in which case the more specific parenthetical terms should be recorded (e.g., "Greek (Ancient Greek)" for ancient Greek). A similar practice is recommended to record "Norwegian" for texts expressed in Bokmål Norwegian or Nynorsk Norwegian.

In a bibliographic record, the language of the expression is recorded in MARC field 008, positions 35–38 and field 041. For example,

Language of expression:	Russian
MARC bibliographic:	008 Lang (35-38): rus

The following example illustrates the recording of language of expression as authority and bibliographic data, both as separate elements and as part of the authorized access point (covered in RDA 6.27.3).

Language of expression:	Greek
	Latin
MARC authority:	377 $a grc
	377 $a lat
MARC bibliographic:	008 Lang (35-38): grc
	041 0 $a grc $a lat

Other Distinguishing Characteristic of the Expression (RDA 6.12) Core Element (for differentiation) [MARC authority field 381 or 373]

This element is used when it is necessary to differentiate between two expressions of the same work, and includes expression characteristics other than the content type, language, or date of an expression. Examples of such additional characteristics include the version, translator, editor, publisher, and other details.

The following are examples of different English translations of *Beowulf*, distinguished by the translator:

Distinguishing characteristic of expression: **Alexander**
MARC authority: 130 0 $a Beowulf. $l English $s (Alexander)
377 $a eng
381 $a **Alexander**

Distinguishing characteristic of expression: **Chickering**
MARC authority: 130 0 $a Beowulf. $l English $s (Chickering)
377 $a eng
381 $a **Chickering**

Distinguishing characteristic of expression: **Crossley-Holland**
MARC authority: 130 0 $a Beowulf. $l English $s (Crossley-Holland)
377 $a eng
381 $a **Crossley-Holland**

Distinguishing characteristic of expression: **Garmonsway and Simpson**
MARC authority: 130 0 $a Beowulf. $l English $s (Garmonsway and Simpson)
377 $a eng
381 $a **Garmonsway and Simpson**

Identifier for the Expression (RDA 6.13)
Core Element
[MARC authority field 010, 016, 024, 035]

As a core element, the identifier of the expression should be recorded. The identifier is a character string uniquely identifying the expression or a record representing the expression (e.g., an authority record).

Examples:
Identifier for the expression: VIAF ID: **303689140** (Expression)
MARC authority: 035 $a (VIAF)**303689140** (Expression)

Identifier for the expression: LCCN: **no2014100184**
MARC authority: 010 $a **no2014100184**

SPECIAL CASES—WORK & EXPRESSION ELEMENTS

Although the initial principles guiding RDA were to adhere to the Statement of International Cataloguing Principles, which holds that guidelines for descriptions will be created to apply to all types of materials and that controlled forms of all types of entities should be based on a common set of guidelines, it was decided that there was a need to have additional guidelines for certain types of works. Therefore, additional RDA elements were defined, with guidelines providing instructions on how to provide information that is specific to musical works, legal works, treaties, and official communications. Each of these sets of elements is briefly discussed here. Note that the fact that these types of works are treated separately here does not mean that all elements needed to describe them are covered here. For example, all elements discussed under the general guidelines for all works also apply to musical works; those described here serve as additional elements or additional guidelines for musical works. For elements that appear both under the special cases and also under general guidelines, follow the special guidelines. For elements that are not specific to these works, follow the general guidelines.

MUSICAL WORKS

Additional elements defined for musical works include medium of performance, numeric designation of a musical work, key, and other distinguishing characteristic of a musical work. Also, special guidelines are provided for the title of a musical work and how to record the preferred title of a musical work.

Title of a Musical Work (RDA 6.14)
Core Element

The title of a musical work is defined as a string of characters or words by which the work is known. A known title of a musical work can be selected as either the preferred title or the variant title of the musical work. Preferred titles of musical works are covered in RDA 6.14.2, and variant titles are covered in RDA 6.14.3. When recording the titles, the same guidelines as for the general title of the work, covered in RDA 6.2.1, apply.

Preferred Title of a Musical Work (RDA 6.14.2)
Core Element
[MARC authority 130, 1XX subfield t]

This core element is defined as the title or the form of the title selected to identify a musical work and to serve as the basis for the authorized access point representing the musical work. To select the preferred title of a musical work (RDA 6.14.2.2–6.14.2.3) that was created after 1500, consult embodiments of the work (manifestations) or reference sources. For works created prior to 1501, consult reference sources. In most cases, the preferred title of a musical work will be the original title given by the composer, but if there is a better-known title in the same language, it should be selected as the preferred title. If the title of the musical work is very long, select first a brief title by which the work is commonly known. If a reference source is necessary for the selection of the preferred title of a musical work, use well-known reference sources specializing in the particular genre.

Examples:
Carl Phillip Emanuel Bach
Known titles of work: Du bist unser Zuflucht für und für
Herr Gott, du bist unser Zuflucht
Herrn Pastors Schäffer Einführungsmusik
Einführungsmusik Schäffer
Preferred title of work: **Herrn Pastors Schäffer Einführungs-musik**

Gloria Coates
Known titles of work: WW II poems for peace
Voices of women in wartime
Cantata de requiem
Preferred title of work: **Cantata de requiem**

If one were to apply the general rules about recording preferred titles of work, it would often be difficult to uniquely identify the work. Due to the nature of musical works, special guidelines are given in RDA 6.14.2.4 for the recording of a preferred title of a musical work. When a preferred title for a musical work is selected, according to RDA 6.14.2.3, the following steps are needed:

1. Removal of any statement of the medium of performance, regardless of how it appears on the title.

Example:
Preferred title selected: Symphony for five instruments, piano solo, violin, viola, cello, bassoon
Preferred title after removal: **Symphonies**
MARC 21 authority:
100 1 $a Gold, Ernest, $d 1921-1999. $t **Symphonies**, $m piano, violin, viola, cello, bassoon
380 $a Symphonies $2 lcsh
382 $a piano $a violin $a viola $a cello $a bassoon
670 $a Gold, E. Symphony for five instruments, piano solo, violin, viola, cello, bassoon, 1980, ©1952.

2. Removal of the "key" name.

   Example:
   Preferred title selected: Flute quartet in F major
   Preferred title after removal: **Quartet**

3. Removal of the serial, opus, and thematic index number.

   Example:
   Preferred title selected: WoO 26, Romanze, B-Dur, für Violine und Klavier
   Preferred title after removal: **Romances**

4. Removal of other numbers, unless they are an integral part of the title.

   Example:
   Preferred title selected: Three Donald Hall songs
   Preferred title after removal: **Donald Hall songs**

5. Removal of the date of composition.

   Example:
   Preferred title selected: Dream music no. 1 for piano solo, 1965
   Preferred title after removal: **Dream music**

6. Removal of adjectives and epithets that are not part of the original title of the work.

   Example:
   Preferred title selected: The famous solo
   Preferred title after removal: **Solos**

One exception to RDA 6.14.2.3, and consequently to RDA 6.14.2.2, is for titles that include type of composition, which is also cited in its own numbered sequence of the composer's list of works. In this case, the type of composition is selected as the preferred title for a musical work instead of the specific title of the work.

Example:
Joseph Haydn
Preferred title selected: Paukenschlag-Sinfonie
Numbered sequence listed as: Symphony no. 94
Resulting preferred title: **Symphonies**

As we can see by a number of examples above, often, once the preferred title of a musical work is selected and all the elements listed in RDA 6.14.2.4 are removed, all that is left for the preferred title of a musical work is a single name of the type of composition, for example, "Romances," "Symphonies," "Quartet," and others. In this case, RDA 6.14.2.5 instructs that the resulting preferred title be recorded in the language preferred by the cataloging agency (English for LC-PCC PS and all US libraries) and in plural form, unless the composer wrote only one work of this particular type of musical work.

Examples:

Eugen Albert
Preferred title selected: Konzert für Violoncello und Orchester C-Dur, op. 20
Preferred title after removal: **Symphony**

Joseph Haydn
Preferred title selected: Symphony no. 92 in G
Preferred title after removal: **Symphonies**

This guideline may not be the easiest to apply because it requires some research (possibly extensive) on the part of the cataloger. One has to know that the composer created only one work of a particular type. This also creates a maintenance issue, as it is possible that at the time the preferred title of a musical work is established according to RDA 6.14.2.5, only one work of this type existed, but the composer may have subsequently created additional works of the same type. Thus, the LC (and PCC) practice, per LC-PCC PS 6.14.2.5.2, holds that when cataloging for the first time a particular type of composition of a work by a specific composer, select the preferred title's singular or plural form based on whether the composer is still alive or deceased. If the composer is deceased, one should consult reference sources and select the appropriate plural or singular form based on whether this is the composer's only work of this particular type of composition. If the composer is living and only one work of the particular type of composition exists, select the singular form, unless there is a serial number associated with the title of the work (e.g., Symphony no. 1), in which case one can assume that the composer intends to write additional works of the same type. In this case, the plural form is used.

Preferred title for a part or parts of a musical work (RDA 6.14.2.7) is used when only part of the work, instead of the entire musical work, is described.

In the case of one part only being described (RDA 6.14.2.7.1), if the part is identified by a number, then the number is recorded as the preferred title of the part of a musical work. If the part is identified by a title, this title is recorded as the preferred title of the part. When a part is identified both by a number and a title, preference typically is given to the title, with a number of exceptions covered in RDA 6.14.2.7.1.3–6.14.2.7.1.4.

In a MARC record structure, the preferred title of a part of a musical work is entered in the same field as the preferred title of the musical work, in subfield $n (for number) or $p (for name of part) of field 1XX.

Example:
Beethoven's Christus am Ölberge, part Schlusschor der Engel

Preferred title of work:	Christus am Ölberge
Preferred title of part:	**Schlusschor der Engel**
MARC 21 authority:	100 1 $a Beethoven, Ludwig van, $d 1770-1827. $t Christus am Ölberge. $p **Schlusschor der Engel**

In the case where two or more parts are described (RDA 6.14.2.7.2), record the preferred titles of the parts, following the guidelines in RDA 6.14.7.1, as described above for a single part. An alternative option is to use the term "Selections" as the preferred title of the parts, unless the parts are called "suite" by the composer, in which case, the term "suite" is recorded as the preferred title of the parts.

Examples (MARC authority):
100 1 $a Brahms, Johannes, $d 1833-1897. $t Ungarische Tänze. $k **Selections**
100 1 $aBrower, Russell. $t World of Warcraft. $p **Suite**

Compilations of musical works (RDA 6.14.2.8) follow the same guidelines for recording the preferred title of a compilation of musical works as with the preferred titles of musical works (RDA 6.2.2). One exception is the use of a variety of conventional collective titles, as listed in RDA 6.14.2.8. Collective titles include examples of one medium title (e.g., piano music, string quartet music, etc.) or medium (e.g., concertos, operas, sonatas, etc.).

Variant Title of a Musical Work (RDA 6.14.2) [MARC authority 430, 4XX subfield t]

Variant title of a musical work is defined as the title or form of title of a musical work that has not been selected as the preferred title of the musical work. The recording of variant titles of musical works follows exactly the same guidelines as the recording of variant titles of all other works, as described in RDA 6.2.3.

Examples:

Preferred title of a musical work:	World of Warcraft
Variant title of a musical work:	**Suite from World of Warcraft**
MARC 21 authority:	100 1 $a Brower, Russell. $t World of Warcraft. $p Suite 400 1 $a Brower, Russell. $t **Suite from World of Warcraft**

Preferred title of a musical work:	Trinity concerto
Variant title of a musical work:	**Byzantium after Byzantium**
MARC 21 authority:	100 1 $aGrigoriu, Theodor. $t Trinity concerto 400 1 $a Grigoriu, Theodor. $t **Byzantium after Byzantium**, $n no. 1

Medium of Performance (RDA 6.15)
Core Element (if needed for differentiation)
[MARC authority 382]

The medium of performance of a musical work is defined as the instrument(s), voice(s), etc., for which a musical work was originally composed. The element is core when it is necessary to differentiate between works with the same title or when the title of work is not distinctive enough for identification. In addition, inclusion of this element regardless of the need for differentiation is useful information for users. This information may be recorded as a separate element or as part of the authorized access point for the musical work. RDA 6.15.1.3 instructs that the following information be included in this element: instrumental music for one performer; instruments; accompanying ensembles with one performer to a part; instrumental music for orchestra, string orchestra, or band; solo instruments and accompanying ensemble; solo voices; choruses; and indeterminate medium of performance. RDA 6.15.1.6 lists a number of instruments that may be used for this element. LC-PCC PS instructs that the English term be used for instruments whenever possible, and also lists some preferred instrument terms, such as cello, English horn, contrabassoon, and timpani.

Examples (MARC authority):

382 0 $b **violin** $n 1 $a orchestra $n 1 $2 lcmpt
382 0 $a **cello** $n 1 $a orchestra
382 $a **violin** $a **piano accompaniment**

382 0 $a **guitar** $n 1 $2 lcmpt
382 $a **mezzo-soprano** $n 1 $a **piano** $n 1 $a **flute** $n 1 $a **clarinet** $n 1 $a **violin** $n 1 $a **cello** $n 1
382 $b **soprano voice** $n 1 $a **harpsichord** $n 1 $a **flute** $n 1 $a **cello** $n 1 $s 4 $2 lcmpt
382 $b **tenor voice** $n 1 $p **soprano voice** $n 1 $a **piano** $n 1 $s 2 $2 lcmpt

In the above examples, "lcmpt" in subfield $2 indicates the source of the terms used in 382, which is the *Library of Congress Medium of Performance Thesaurus for Music* (LCMPT).

Numeric Designation of a Musical Work (RDA 6.16) Core Element (if needed for differentiation) [MARC authority field 383]

The numeric designation of a musical work is defined as a serial number, opus number, or a thematic index number assigned to a musical work by a composer, publisher, or musicologist. This element is core when it is necessary to differentiate works with the same title and also to help identify a musical work when its title is not distinctive enough. Inclusion of this information is helpful to users regardless of the need for differentiation. The term used as a prefix to the number is abbreviated based on the list offered in RDA Appendix B.7–10

Serial number (RDA 6.16.1.3.1) is a number within a sequence of a particular type of compositions by the same composer, in the same medium of performance.
Opus number (RDA 6.16.1.3.2) is a number used for numbering a composer's works.
Thematic index number (RDA 6.16.1.3.3) is a number used in a numbered bibliography of a composer's works. Best practice, as instructed in LC-PCC PS 6.16.1.3.3, is to use the thematic catalog codes and abbreviations developed by the Music Library Association (MLA) and adopted by the Library of Congress and NACO.[4]

Examples (MARC authority):
383 $b **op. 17**
383 $a **no. 2** $b **op. 24**
383 $c **LW A68 $c S. 451** $c **R. 284** $c **C. 262** $c **G. 451**
383 ‡c **BWV 75** ‡d Schmieder ‡2 mlati

Key (RDA 6.17)
Core Element (if needed for differentiation)
[MARC authority field 384]

Key is defined as the set of pitch relationships that establish the tonal center of a work. The key is usually indicated in terms of pitch name (B, C, etc.) and mode (major or minor). Not all works have an identifiable key. The element is core when differentiation is necessary. Record the key when it is commonly identified in reference sources, when it appears on the composer's original title, and when it is apparent from the resource described. Key can be recorded as a separate element or as part of the authorized access point of the musical work.

Examples (MARC authority):
384 0 $a **D major**
384 0 $a **G major**
384 0 $a **A minor**
384 0 $a **F♯ minor**

Other Distinguishing Characteristic of the Expression of a Musical Work (RDA 6.18)
Core Element (if needed for differentiation)
[MARC authority field 381]

Other distinguishing characteristic of the expression of a musical work is defined as a characteristic used to differentiate an expression of a musical work from another expression of the same work. Typical information includes arrangements, transcriptions, versions, settings, sketches, and vocal and chorus scores. The element is core when it is necessary for differentiation.

Example (MARC authority):
381 $a **arranged**

LEGAL WORKS

Similar to musical works, describing legal works follows the same general guidelines as other works. RDA 6.19–6.22 covers some special guidelines that are specific to legal works. Any other element used to describe legal works should follow the general guidelines.

Title of a Legal Work (RDA 6.19)

Defined as any character, word, or group of words and/or characters by which a legal work is known, the title of a legal work can be categorized as its preferred title or its variant title.

Preferred Title of a Legal Work (RDA 6.19.2)
Core Element
[MARC authority 130, 1XX subfield t]

The same guidelines apply here for the selection of the preferred title of a legal work. For works created after 1500, consult the best-known title resources embodying the work or reference source to select the preferred title. For works created before 1501, consult modern reference sources. The guidelines are the same as the general guidelines for selecting the preferred title and for recording this element (RDA 6.2). The major difference is in the treatment of "Laws" and "Treaties."

Laws are divided into modern laws, ancient, medieval, and other laws, and treaties.

In discussing modern laws, the guidelines treat single laws separately from compilations of laws. When the work is a compilation of all or part of the laws of a jurisdiction or a compilation of all laws on a subject, use the phrase "Laws, etc." as the preferred title of the legal work. Using such a phrase allows the description of all these different aggregations of legal works to be entered under the same title, but to be differentiated by other elements that follow the preferred title of the work, such as the date of the legal work or other distinguishing characteristics. For legal works on a particular subject that has a citation title, use the citation title as the preferred title of the work.

Examples (MARC authority):
110 1 $a Great Britain. $t **Laws, etc.** (Statutes at large: 1762)
110 1 $a Papua New Guinea. $t **Laws, etc.** (Selected laws of Papua New Guinea)
110 1 $a West Virginia. $t **Laws, etc.**

When recording the preferred title of a single law, use the title of the law (official or unofficial) and the title of the enactment, preferably a short title or citation title, which could also be the title proper and any other official designation (RDA 6.19.2.5.2)

Examples (MARC authority):
110 1 $a United States. $t **Act to Amend the Manufacturing Clause of the Copyright Law**

110 1 $a Enugu State (Nigeria). $t **Customary Court of Appeal Law**
110 1 $a Great Britain. $t **Immigration Act 1971**

A treaty is an agreement between two or more governments. It is typical for each treaty to have different versions, since each body creates its own version for approval by its own governing body. For a treaty between two national governments, international intergovernmental bodies, or the Holy See, record as the preferred title of the legal work the official title of the treaty, a short title or a citation title, or any other designation the treaty is known by. For compilations of treaties, record the phrase "Treaties, etc." as the preferred title of the work. If the compilation of treaties is known by a collective title, use this title as the preferred title for the compilation of treaties.

Examples (MARC authority):
130 0 $a **Antarctic Treaty** $d (1959 December 1)
130 0 $a **Egyptian-Israeli Peace Treaty** $d (1979 March 26)

Variant Title of a Legal Work (RDA 6.19.3) [MARC authority 430, 4XX subfield t]

Variant title of a legal work is the title or form of the title a legal work is known by, but it is not selected as the preferred title of the legal work. For the variant title of a legal work record the title by which it is cited in reference sources and the transliterated title, linguistic variants of the preferred title, and any other variant title. When a conventional collective title is used as the preferred title of a legal work, record the proper title of the manifestation or the title found in a reference source as variant titles.

Examples (MARC authority):

Preferred title:	110 1 $a Alabama. $t Laws, etc.
Variant title:	410 1 $a Alabama. $t **Revised code of Alabama**
Preferred title:	110 1 $a Malaysia. $t Income Tax Act 1967
Variant title:	410 1 $a Malaysia. $t **Laws of Malaysia, Act 53**
Preferred title:	110 1 $a Canada. $t Canada Labour Code
Variant title:	410 1 $a Canada. $t **Code canadien du travail**

Date of a Legal Work (RDA 6.20) Core Element [MARC authority 046]

The earliest date associated with a legal work is recorded in this element. Date of legal work is core when describing a treaty. It is also core when necessary for differentiating a legal work from another work with the same title or from the name of a person, corporate body, or family. The date of a legal work can be recorded as a separate element and also as part of the authorized access point for the work.

Two specific examples of dates are described in RDA 6.20: the "date of promulgation of law, etc." and the "date of a treaty." To record the date of promulgation, use the calendar preference of the cataloging agency (RDA Appendix H covers the Christian calendar).

According to RDA 6.20.3.3, use the form [year] [month] [day] to record the date of a treaty.

In MARC 21 authority records, field 046 is defined as special coded dates, with subfield $k used for "beginning or single date created." This subfield is currently used to enter the date of a legal work, but in a coded formatting following ISO 8601, which is not the same as the formatting in the RDA guidelines. The dates used in the authorized access point for a legal work (RDA 6.29.1.29–30) and recorded in MARC authority field 1XX follow the RDA formatting.

Examples (MARC authority):
046 $k **19960910**
130 0 $a Comprehensive Nuclear-Test-Ban Treaty $d (**1996 September 10**)

046 $k **19660622**
110 1 $a United States. $t Bail Reform Act of 1966

046 $k **19910701**
110 1 $a California. $t Probate Code

Other Distinguishing Characteristic of a Legal Work (RDA 6.21) Core Element (if needed for differentiation) [MARC authority 381]

Other distinguishing characteristic of a legal work is any characteristic other than the form, date, or place of origin of a legal work. This element is core if needed for differentiation between works with the same title or from a name, family, or corporate body. Other characteristics can be recorded as a separate element or as part of the authorized access point of the work. Recording of this information follows the same general guidelines for recording other distinguishing characteristics of works (RDA 6.6).

This element is used when no other information can truly be used to differentiate a legal work from another. Information that could be used as other distinguishing characteristic includes a word or words of the title proper of the manifestation, a commonly used brief title, the name of the editor, name of publisher, etc.

RELIGIOUS WORKS

Again, similar to musical and legal works, the description of religious works follows the same general guidelines for all works. Some additional instructions are offered for the description of religious works in RDA 6.23, mostly about the title of religious works, which differ somewhat from titles of other works. For any other elements not covered here, follow the general guidelines for identifying works.

Title of a Religious Work (RDA 6.23)

The title of a religious work is defined as a character, word, or group of words and/or characters by which a religious work is known. As with all works, this title can be a preferred title or variant title.

Preferred Title of a Religious Work (RDA 6.23.2)
Core Element
[MARC authority 130, 1XX]

The title chosen to identify a religious work is the preferred title of the work, and is used as the basis for constructing the authorized access point for the work. The preferred title of the work is a core element.

Due to the complex nature of religious works, a set of guidelines is offered on how to select and record the preferred titles of different types of religious works. In general, recording the preferred title of a religious work follows the same guidelines as other works, with the exception of capitalization in some cases. For example, RDA Appendix A covers capitalization rules, but A.17.6 and A.17.8 instruct us to capitalize all nouns, adjectives, verbs, etc., in the title of sacred scriptures, creeds, and confessions.

RDA has specific guidelines for sacred scriptures, apocryphal books, theological creeds, confessions of faith, etc.

A brief overview of the preferred title of each of these types of religious works is given here.

Selecting and Recording the Preferred Title for Sacred Scriptures

A sacred scripture is typically the authoritative text of a religious body. Often, the religious body canonizes this text. Per RDA 6.23.2.5, select as the preferred title a title that appears in a reference source dealing with the particular religious group and that is phrased in the language of the cataloging agency. The respective LC-PCC PS provision states that LC's practice is to use an English language reference source. Examples of sacred scriptures include the Bible, Talmud, Vedas, Avesta and Qur'an, to name a few.

Examples of preferred title of religious works and MARC authority:
Bible 130 0 $a **Bible**
Qur'an 130 0 $a **Qur'an**
Tripiṭaka 130 0 $a **Tripiṭaka**

Recording parts of the Bible (RDA 6.23.2.9)**.** The Bible is a collection of works considered sacred by a number of religious bodies. RDA provides guidelines for the description of not only particular works within the collection of Bible works, but also for parts of these works, which are all added terms to the preferred title "Bible."

For testaments (RDA 6.23.2.9.1), record "Old Testament" or "New Testament" as a subdivision to the preferred title "Bible." For particular books (RDA 6.23.2.9.2), add a brief citation of the name of the book, record the number as an ordinal number after the name of the book, the chapter in roman numerals, and the verse in Arabic numerals, if necessary. The parts recorded after the preferred title are separated by a comma.

Examples (MARC authority):
130 0 $a **Bible**. $p **Old Testament**
130 0 $a **Bible**. $p **New Testament**
130 0 $a **Bible**. $p **Corinthians, 1st**
130 0 $a **Bible**. $p **Epistle of John, 3rd**
130 0 $a **Bible**. $p **Genesis, VI, 9-XI, 32**
130 0 $a **Bible**. $p **Luke**

You will note that if you locate a record created using the AACR2, the abbreviated form of the individual book name was used (e.g., O.T. and N.T. for Old Testament and New Testament, respectively). Not using abbreviations is one of the major changes in describing the titles of religious works.

A list of groups of books can also be recorded. The preferred title of the group of books is recorded as a subdivision of "Bible." A list of acceptable group names is provided in RDA 6.23.2.9.3, in Table 6.2.

Examples (MARC authority):
130 0 $a **Bible**. $p **Thessalonians**

130 0 $a **Bible**. $p **Epistles of John**

Selecting and Recording the Preferred Title for Apocrypha

An apocryphal book is presented as a sacred scripture, but not all religious bodies recognize it as such. The preferred title of apocryphal books is selected from reference sources in the language of the cataloging agency.

Add "Apocrypha" as a subdivision of "Bible," and further subdivide it by the name of the individual apocryphal book.

Examples (MARC authority):
130 0 Bible. $p **Apocrypha**. $p **Baruch**.
130 0 Bible. $p **Apocrypha**. $p **Ecclesiasticus**

Selecting and Recording the Preferred Title for Bible selections

If a single selection is to be described, and if it has a distinctive title, record the name of the part. If no distinctive name is used to identify the selection, record chapters and verse numerals (RDA 6.23.2.9.5).

Examples (MARC authority):
Luke, I, 68-79
Use distinctive title for selection: 130 0 $a **Benedictus Dominus Deus Israel**

Ecclesiasticus XLIV-L
Use chapter numerals for selection without distinctive title:
130 0 $a Bible. $p Apocrypha. $p **Ecclesiasticus XLIV-L**

For more than one selection from the Bible, with each part having its own preferred title, identify each selection separately (RDA 6.23.2.9.6). For other selections from the Bible, RDA 6.23.2.9.7 instructs that the most specific title appropriate for the selections be used, followed by the collective title "Selections."

Examples (MARC authority):
130 0 Bible. $p Ephesians. $k **Selections**
130 0 Bible. $p Daniel, VII. $k **Selections**
130 0 Bible. $p Hagiographa. $k **Selections**

Selections of parts for other sacred scriptures follow the same guidelines as those for the Bible, recording the title of the part immediately after the title of the scripture.

Selecting and Recording the Preferred Title for Theological Creeds, Confessions of Faith, and other Similar Works. (RDA 6.23.2.7)

A well-established title in English is used as the preferred title of these types of works.

Selecting and Recording the Title of liturgical works (RDA 6.23.2.8)

Select the preferred title of a liturgical work based on a well-established title in the language of the cataloging agency. In general, the preferred title of a liturgical work is recorded under the authorized access point for the church of the denomination the work applies to. Therefore, the language of the preferred title and the language of the preferred name of the religious body sanctioning the liturgical work should be the same.

Examples (MARC authority):
110 2 Armenian Church. $t **Surb Patarag**
110 2 Catholic Church. $t **Liturgy of Saint John Chrysostom**

In recording a part of a liturgical work, use a well-known title of the part (observance, group of observances, extracted text, etc.). Record the term "Mass" or "Office," followed by the appropriate title for the office or the mass for that particular day.

Examples (MARC authority):
110 2 Catholic Church. $t **Mass, Christmas (Pre-Vatican II: In nocte)**
110 2 Catholic Church. $t **Office, Saint Benedict (Pre-Vatican II)**

Variant Title of a Religious Work (RDA 6.23.3) [MARC 430, 4XX subfield t]

A variant title of a religious work is a title by which a work is known, but it is not selected as the preferred title for the religious work. Record the variant titles following the general guidelines in RDA 6.2.1. Titles or forms of titles, which are different from the preferred title and appear in reference sources, and those titles resulting from transliteration of the original title should be recorded as variant titles. Use a manifestation title as a variant title only if it is significantly different from the work title and if it is useful to the users. Also include the alternative linguistic form if a preferred title is used as a variant title.

Examples (MARC authority):

Preferred title:	110 2 $a Church of Scotland. $t Book of common order
Variant titles:	410 2 $a Church of Scotland. $t **Booke of the common order**
	410 2 $a Church of Scotland. $t **Euchologion**
	410 2 $a Church of Scotland. $t **John Knox's Book of common order**
Preferred title:	130 0 $a Bible. $p Old Testament
Variant titles:	430 0 $a **Antico Testamento**
	430 0 $a Bible. $p **Antico Testamento**
	430 0 $a Bible. $p **Hebrew Bible**
	430 0 $a Bible. $p **Hebrew Scriptures**
	430 0 $a Bible. $p **Kitve-ḳodesh**
	430 0 $a Bible. $p **Miḳra**

Date of Expression of a Religious Work (RDA 6.24) Core Element (if needed for differentiation) [MARC 046]

The earliest date associated with an expression of a religious work is recorded in this element. If the date of expression is not known, use the date of the earliest manifestation of this expression. This element is core when it is necessary to differentiate between expressions of the same religious work.

In general, record the date of an expression of a religious work by following the general guidelines in RDA 6.10. For the date of an expression of the Bible and part of the Bible, record the year of publication of the resource.

Example (MARC authority):
046 $k **1990**
130 0 $a Bible. $p Ephesians. $l English. $s Lincoln. $f **1990**

Other Distinguishing Characteristic of the Expression of a Religious Work (RDA 6.25) Core Element (if needed for differentiation) [MARC 381]

Any expression characteristic of a religious work other than its content type, language of expression, or date of expression can be added in the description of a work, if necessary for identification or if deemed useful for users. An example of such a characteristic for the Bible or parts of the Bible is the named version (except when the resource is in three or more languages). In addition, the name of the translator (brief name) can be used as a distinguishing characteristic of the expression. If more than two translators are listed on the resource, name the first, followed by "and others." Other information that is typically used as another distinguishing characteristic of the expression may include the name of the manifestation, the name of the person responsible for the expression, or the name used to identify the particular expression.

This element is core if it is needed to differentiate between expressions or from a name for a person, family, or corporate body.

Example (MARC authority):
046 $k 1900
130 0 $a Bible. $p Apocrypha. $l English. $s **Brenton**. $f 1900
377 $a eng
381 $a **Brenton**
670 $a Septuagint version of the Old Testament and Apocrypha with an English translation
046 $k 2007
130 0 $a Blade runner (Motion picture: $s **Final cut**)
381 $a **Final cut** $a 25th anniversary edition $a 2007 final cut $a Definitive version $a 2007 version

OFFICIAL COMMUNICATIONS

Official communications is a special category of work created by a person when serving in an official capacity, for example, as the head of a church, official of a government, and so on. Details about official communications are mostly concerned with the construction of authorized access points to represent official communication, which are covered in RDA 6.31. As it will be described later this chapter, in the section on constructing authorized access points, when describing an official communication, the work is not considered as the creation of an individual (a person), but as the creation of the office, title, or position held by that person. Examples include communications of a pope, a governor, a president, or prime minister of a government, among others.

Title of an Official Communication (RDA 6.26)
Core Element

The title of an official communication is defined as a character, word, or groups of words by which an official communication is known. The general guidelines on capitalization, numbers, etc. of RDA 6.2.1 should be followed when recording the title of an official communication.

Preferred Title of an Official Communication (RDA 6.26.2) Core Element [MARC authority field 130, 1XX subfield $t]

The preferred title of an official communication follows the same general guidelines of any other type of work, as described in RDA 6.2.2.3–6.2.2.7. Two types of work that receive special attention in this section, and that are exceptions to the general guidelines, are official communications of a pope and official communications of Roman curia. This element is a core element.

For the preferred title of an individual work for which a pope is considered as creator, select the brief title by which the work is known and cited in the language of the original (typically Latin). The short title of an official communication of Roman curia, for example, communications of tribunals, congregations, etc., can also be selected as the preferred title.

Examples:
Preferred title of official communication: **Evangelii Gaudium**
MARC authority: 110 2 Catholic Church. $b Pope (2013-: Francis). $t **Evangelii Gaudium**

Variant Title of an Official Communication [MARC authority field 430, 4XX subfield $t]

Recording the variant title of an official communication follows the general guidelines of RDA 6.2.1. Record a variant title that a work was issued or cited under or a varying title that is a result of different transliterations of the title.

ACCESS POINTS: CONSTRUCTING AUTHORIZED ACCESS POINTS REPRESENTING WORKS AND EXPRESSIONS

In the FRBR conceptual model, the user task to find, identify, and select resources associated with a particular work are facilitated by the attributes and relationships. Links through relationships would connect a work to the name representing its creator, the manifestation of the work and its creator, the manifestation to the work via the preferred title of work, the expression to the name representing the translator, and so on. Currently, most library systems that are based on MARC record structures are not designed to handle relationships and to link the data in such meaningful ways. The current practice is to create authorized access points using authority data. These access points are recorded or added to each bibliographic record associated with these entities. The presence of authorized access points, like the authorized access point for a person, is what links associated resources when a user is searching by that particular name.

This means that having consistency in access points is imperative, and also that formulating unique or differentiated authorized access points is very important. For example, RDA 0.4.3.1 explains how important it is that the data describing a work and the relationship to its creator differentiates this work from any other work with the same title. When a conflict exists in terms of having two different works with the same preferred title, additional information is necessary to differentiate the two. This is why we often see RDA guidelines defining elements as core if they are deemed necessary for differentiation between works with the same title. For example, works that have the same preferred title are differentiated by their creator. If the works have the same preferred title and creator, they are differentiated by other elements such as the form of the work, the place of origin of the work, the date of the work, and so on.

RDA provides instructions on how to construct authorized and variant access points that represent works, expressions, persons, corporate bodies, and families. Additional access points are identifiers, such as the title proper of a manifestation, the parallel title of manifestation, and others.

RDA also includes guidelines for the construction of access points to record relationships between work, expression, and manifestation, known as primary relationships, relationships between a resource and a person, corporate body, or family associated with the resource, relationship between works, expressions, manifestations, and items, and the relationships between persons, families, and corporate bodies.

Guidelines on other elements that may be used to access resources, for example, if one wants to find resources published in 2014, are not covered in RDA. Each retrieval system or agency has to decide which additional elements should be indexed, and, therefore, are available to be used as means to access information representing the collection resources.

The next section of this chapter discusses how to construct authorized access points representing works and expressions. When and how to record relationships associated with a work, expression, manifestation, or item is covered in RDA, Chapters 19 through 22, and will be discussed in chapter 9 of this text.

General Guidelines for Constructing Authorized Access Points

As a general rule, when formulating an access point for a work of an expression, a combination of the authorized access point for the entity responsible for the content of the work, whether a person, a family, or a corporate body, and the preferred title of the work is used. Guidelines on authorized access points of persons, families, and corporate bodies are covered in RDA 6.27.1.2–6.27.8. Guidelines for the preferred title of a work are covered in RDA 6.2.2. Not all works have an associated person, family, or corporate body recognized as responsible for the content of the work. Therefore, some authorized access points for works and expressions may only have a preferred title of the work as the basis of the authorized access point.

In order to differentiate between two or more works that have the same or similar access points, additional identifying elements are included in the formulation of the authorized access point. To create an authorized access point for an expression, RDA instructs that elements identifying the specific expression be added to the authorized access point of the work.

> Example:
> Preferred title of the work: *On the origin of species*
> Authorized access point for author: *Darwin, Charles, 1809-1882*
> Authorized access point of the work: Darwin, Charles, 1809-1882. *On the origin of species*

Information on how to establish an authorized access point for a person, corporate body, or family is covered in chapter 8. The authorized access point for a person, corporate body, or family is provided in the examples of this chapter, when necessary, to illustrate its use in work and expression elements.

General Guidelines for Constructing Variant Access Points

The variant title of a work (RDA 6.2.3) is used as the basis to formulate the variant access point. If the authorized access point for the work is formulated by combining a person, family, or corporate body with a preferred title of the work, use the authorized access point for the person, family, or corporate body in combination with the variant title of the work to formulate the variant access point. In this case, the authorized access point representing the person, family, or corporate body precedes the variant title of the work.

If considered important for identification, additional elements for the access points representing a work or authorized access points of expressions may be included (see RDA 6.27.1.9 and 6.27.3).

> Example:
> Preferred title of the work: *On the origin of species*
> Variant title of the work: *Origin of species*
> Authorized access point for author: *Darwin, Charles, 1809-1882*

Variant access point of the work: Darwin, Charles, 1809-1882. Origin of species

In addition to the access points for the work and expression, part of the authority data includes information about the process of establishing an authorized access point. RDA provides guidelines on the inclusion of the status of identification, sources consulted, and cataloger's note as part of the authority data.

AUTHORIZED ACCESS POINTS REPRESENTING WORKS [MARC authority 100, 110, 111, 130]

When constructing the authorized form of an access point for a single work, one has to first decide whether this work, or a new creation or a new work based on another existing work, is the work of one person, family, or corporate body or the result of a collaboration between two or more persons, families, or corporate bodies.

In addition, there are resources that are considered as compilations of works, where two or more works by different persons, families, or corporate bodies are combined.

RDA 6.27.1 discusses the construction of authorized access points for the above cases, for adaptations and revisions, for when new content is added to an existing work, and for when the origin of a work is uncertain or unknown. For details on LC-PCC policies on punctuation and spacing of access points recorded in authority and bibliographic record, consult LC-PCC PS 1.7.1.

In most cases, you will be instructed to combine a work title with the authorized access point of a person or persons, a family or families, or a corporate body or bodies. Guidelines for the construction of an authorized access point for a person are found in RDA 9.19.1, for a family in RDA 10.11.1, and for a corporate body in RDA 11.13.1. Chapter 8 of this text discusses these guidelines.

In general, authorized access points for a work are constructed by combining the name of the creator and the preferred title of the work. If this does not produce a differentiated authorized access point for the work, that is, because there is more than one work with the same preferred title or the same combination of creator and preferred title, then additional elements are included in the construction of the authorized access point.

Works Created by One Person, Family, or Corporate Body (RDA 6.27.1.2)

If one person, family, or corporate body is considered responsible for the creation of a work, based on RDA 19.2.1.1 (see chapter 9 of this text), construct the authorized access point for work by combining one of the following:

- Authorized access point representing the person + preferred title of work
- Authorized access point representing the family + preferred title of work
- Authorized access point representing the corporate body + preferred title of work.

A period separates the authorized access point of the person, family, or corporate body and the preferred title of the work, unless the authorized access point of the creator ends in an open date. For more details on LC-PCC policies on punctuation and spacing of access points recorded in authority and bibliographic records, consult LC-PCC PS 1.7.1.

Examples:

Authorized access point of work:	**Darwin, Charles, 1809-1882. On the origin of species.**
MARC authority:	100 1 $a Darwin, Charles, $d 1809-1882. $t On the origin of species.
Authorized access point of work:	**Eisler, Barry. Fault line.**
MARC authority:	100 1 $a Eisler, Barry. $t Fault line.
Authorized access point of work:	**Bank for International Settlements. Eighth annual report.**
MARC authority:	110 2 $a Bank for International Settlements. $t Eighth annual report.
Authorized access point of work:	**Arnberg, Lenore, 1947- Raising children bilingually**
MARC authority:	100 1 $a Arnberg, Lenore, $d 1947- $t Raising children bilingually

Collaborative Works (RDA 6.27.1.3)

If two or more persons, families, or corporate bodies are responsible for the creation of a work based on RDA 19.2.1.1, construct the authorized access point of the work by combining one of the following:

- Authorized access point of person with principal responsibility + preferred title of work
- Authorized access point of family with principal responsibility + preferred title of work

- Authorized access point of corporate body with principal responsibility + preferred title of work.

Per RDA 19.2.1.1, in a collaborative work, principal responsibility may be given to the main creator of the work. This is typically indicated by a statement following the first-named responsible body, such as "with assistance by" or "in collaboration with," and similar terms. Often in collaborations, the main creator is not identified and equal responsibility among creators is assumed. In this case, the creator named first is considered the principal creator.

Examples:

Responsibility:	Clive Cussler and Thomas Perry.
Authorized access point of work:	**Cussler, Clive. Mayan secrets.**
MARC authority:	100 1_ $a **Cussler, Clive**. $t **Mayan secrets.**
Responsibility:	Paul W. Kroll with the assistance of William G. Boltz, David R. Knechtges, Y. Edmund Lien, Antje Richter, Matthias L. Richter, Ding Xiang Warner.
Authorized access point of work:	**Kroll, Paul W., $d 1948- A student's dictionary of Classical and Medieval Chinese**
MARC authority:	100 1 $a **Kroll, Paul W., $d 1948**- $t **Student's dictionary of Classical and Medieval Chinese**
Responsibility:	John Kwoka with contributions by Daniel Greenfield and Chengyan Gu.
Authorized access point of work:	**Kwoka, John E. Mergers, merger control, and remedies.**
MARC authority:	100 1 $a **Kwoka, John E.** $t **Mergers, merger control, and remedies**

An alternative, not followed in the LC-PCC practice, allows for the combination of the authorized access points of all creators of the work and the preferred title of the work.

Example:

Creators: Clive Cussler and Thomas Perry.

Authorized access point of work: **Cussler, Clive; Perry, Thomas. Mayan secrets.**

This would require a revision of MARC 21 authority fields 100, 110, and 111 to allow for multiple subfields $a, which is currently a nonrepeatable subfield.

As an exception to these guidelines, if there is a collaboration of one or more corporate bodies and one or more persons or families who are all considered creators of the work according to RDA 19.2.1.1, RDA instructs that the corporate body be considered as the principal creator and that the authorized access point of the work be constructed by combining the authorized access point for the principal corporate body and the preferred title if the work.

Example:

Responsibility:	Committee on Investing in Health Systems in Low- and Middle-Income Countries, Board on Global Health, Gillian J. Buckley, John E. Lange, and E. Anne Peterson, editors, Institute of Medicine of the National Academies.
Authorized access point of work:	**Institute of Medicine (U.S.). Committee on Investing in Health Systems in Low- and Middle-Income Countries. Investing in global health systems.**
MARC authority:	110 2 $a **Institute of Medicine (U.S.).** $b **Committee on Investing in Health Systems in Low- and Middle-Income Countries.** $t **Investing in global health systems.**

For moving images, construct the authorized access point of the work by recording the preferred title of the work only:

Responsibility: Paramount Pictures and Indian Paintbrush present; a Right of Way/Mr. Mudd production; a film by Jason Reitman; produced by Lianne Halfon, Russell Smith, Jason Reitman, Helen Estabrook.
Authorized access point of work: **Labor Day**
MARC authority: 130 0 $a **Labor Day** (Motion picture)

The most likely rationale for this policy is that there is no one responsibility that would be significant enough to be considered the principal responsibility for the creation of a moving image. If the moving image is the creation of one person, family, or corporate body, then the general guidelines for a work by one creator would apply.

Compilation of Works by Different Creators (RDA 6.27.1.4)

A work that contains works by different persons, families, or corporate bodies is treated separately from each individual work it contains. In the case of a work described in a compilation of different works created by different persons, families, or corporate bodies with a title identifying the compilation, RDA 6.27.1.4 instructs that the preferred title for the compilation of works be used as the authorized access point of the compilation.

Example:
Responsibility: Readings compiled by Kurt Spellmeyer and Richard E. Miller
Preferred title of work: **New humanities reader**
MARC authority: 130 0 $a **New humanities reader**

If there is no collective title to identify the compilation of works, separate authorized access points are constructed for each work included in the compilation. An option is for a cataloger to devise a collective title to identify the compilation of works, but the LC does not recommend this practice in its LC-PCC PS 6.14.1.4.

Example:

Compilation of:	Jacques de Decker's The magnolia, Serge Goriely's The sorcerers, and Jean-Marie Piemme's Patriot's café
Authorized access points:	**Decker, Jacques de. The magnolia.** **Goriely, Serge. The sorcerers.** **Piemme, Jean-Marie. Patriot's café.**
MARC authority:	100 1 $a Decker, Jacques de. $t Magnolia 100 1 $a Goriely, Serge. $t **Sorcerers**. 100 1 $a Piemme, Jean-Marie. $t **Patriot's café**

Adaptations and Revisions (RDA 6.27.1.5)

RDA 6.27.1.5 covers revisions or adaptations of works by a person, family, or corporate body, but it is up to the cataloger to judge whether the revisions or changes are significant enough to constitute new works.

In the cases where it is deemed that the changes are considered significant enough to treat the resulting work as a new work, the authorized access point for the work is constructed using the authorized access point of the person, family, or corporate body responsible for the changes (i.e., the creator of the resulting work, not the original work) and the preferred title of the new work. If the changes are considered simple revisions that do not result in a new work, then the authorized access point is the same as the original work, which is a combination of the authorized access point of the creator and the preferred title of the original work.

In addition to the one clue of "significant changes" for consideration, RDA instructs that if the work presents itself as an edition of a previous work, treat it as an expression of the original work and not as a new work, as instructed in RDA 6.27.3 and discussed below.

Example (same work):

Original work:	Hilary Mantel's Wolf Hall
Adaptation:	Wolf Hall, a stage adaptation by Mike Poulton from the novel by Hilary Mantel
Authorized access point:	**Mantel, Hilary, 1952- Wolf Hall**
MARC authority:	100 1 $a **Mantel, Hilary**, $d **1952-** $t **Wolf Hall**

Example (different work):

Original work:	Victor Hugo's Les Misérables
Adaptation:	Les miserable, a manga adaptation of the story for screen and stage by Crystal Silvermoon
Authorized access point:	**Silvermoon, Crystal. Misérables**
MARC authority:	100 1 $a **Silvermoon, Crystal**. $t **Misérables**

Changes transposing a work into a new medium are considered a new work, according to RDA 6.27.1.5.

Commentary, Annotations, Illustrative Content, Etc., Added to a Previously Existing Work (RDA 6.27.1.6)

There are cases in which commentary, notes, illustrations, and other content are created for an existing work and the new content could be considered a work on its own. If such additions of content to an existing work by a person, family, or corporate body are presented with the original work and this work is presented as the work of the person, family, or corporate body responsible for the additions, then treat it as a new work. The authorized access point is constructed as a combination of the authorized access point of the creator of the comments, and other content, and the preferred title of the commentary, and these additions

Example:

Original work:	Plato's Phaedrus
Commentary:	Plato's Phaedrus, a commentary for Greek readers by Paul Ryan, including the original Greek text
Authorized access point:	**Ryan, Paul, 1929- Plato's Phaedrus**
MARC authority:	100 1 $a **Ryan, Paul, $d 1929-** $t **Plato's Phaedrus**

If the resource presents itself simply as an edition of the original work, treat it as an expression of that work and create an authorized access point based on the original work.

Different Identities for an Individual (RDA 6.27.1.7)

Sometimes, an individual uses different identities for the creation of different works. This often occurs when a person creates work in different genres or forms. For example, a person may create fictional text using one identity and compose music using a different identity. In this case, the creator is consistently using the same identify for each particular work.

RDA 6.27.1.7 provides guidelines for cases where there is no consistency on how an individual is identified on resources embodying a particular work. In such an instance, the guidelines instruct that the authorized access point of the identity most frequently appearing on embodiments of this work be combined with the preferred title of the work in the construction of the authorized access point for the work. If the most frequent identity cannot be determined, RDA instructs that the identity appearing in the most recent embodiment of the work be used.

Works of Uncertain or Unknown Origin (RDA 6.27.1.8)

All works have creators, but they are not always known, and sometimes it is not possible to identify the creator with certainty.

If there is uncertainty that the probable person, family, or corporate body is the creator of a work, then construct the authorized access point for the work by using only the preferred title of the work. If reference sources indicate that this person, family, or corporate body is probably the creator, then use the combination of the authorized access point of the body probably responsible and the preferred title of the work as the authorized access point for the work.

Examples:

The work *Libri Carolini* was composed on the command of Charlemagne but it is uncertain who the creator of the work is

Authorized access point: **Libri Carolini**

MARC authority: 130 0 $a **Libri Carolini**

The work *Aurora consurgens* is commonly attributed to Thomas Aquinas

Authorized access point: **Thomas, Aquinas, Saint, 1225?-1274. Aurora consurgens**

MARC authority: 100 0 $a **Thomas**, $c **Aquinas, Saint, $d 1225?-1274**. $t **Aurora consurgens**

Additions to Access Points Representing Works (RDA 6.27.1.9)

In order to construct unique authorized access points for a work, it is often necessary to add information that will differentiate the authorized access points representing different works, if the combination of creator and preferred title of the work, or just the preferred title of the work alone, does not create a differentiated access point. It may also be necessary to differentiate an authorized access point of a work from the name of a person, family, or corporate body. In this case, the authorized access point of the work is formulated by the following combination:

Authorized access point for the creator + preferred title of work + addition(s)

Additions to the authorized access point of a work include one or more of the following: the form of the work, the date of the work, the place of origin of the work, or another distinguishing characteristic of the work. Guidelines for recording these elements (RDA 6.3–6.6) have been discussed under the respective sections of this chapter. The number of additions depends on the number of elements needed to create a differentiated authorized access point.

Examples:
130 0 $a 21 Jump Street (**Television program**)
130 0 $a 21 Jump Street (**Motion picture**)
130 0 $a 101 Dalmatians (**Motion picture**: **1996**)
130 0 $a Animal jam (**Game**)
130 0 $a 101 (**Series**: **Rome, Italy**)

Part or Parts of a Work (RDA 6.27.2)

The construction of an authorized access point for a part or parts of a work follows the same guidelines as for the construction of an authorized access point of a work. In other words, when there is a person, family, or corporate body responsible for the creation of the work, the authorized access point of the part is constructed by combining the authorized access point for the creator, followed by the preferred title of that part of the work (as instructed in RDA 6.2.2.9 and discussed in the respective sections of this text).

Examples:
100 1 $a Alberione, James, $d 1884-1971. $t Brevi meditazioni per ogni giorno dell'anno. $k **Selections**
100 0 $a Apollonius, $c of Perga. $t Conics. $n Book 1-3
100 1 $a Dunkelman, Stephan, $d 1956- $t Dreamlike shudder in an airstream. $n Part 1, $p **For a crumpled woman**
100 1 $a Glass, Philip. $t Music in twelve parts. $n **Part 1-2**

AUTHORIZED ACCESS POINTS REPRESENTING EXPRESSIONS

[MARC authority 100, 110, 111, 130]

The authorized access point for an expression of a work, a part of a work, or parts of a work is constructed using the following combinations:

Authorized access point of the work + expression element
Authorized access point of a part or parts of a work + expression element

Expression elements added to the authorized access point of a work, and so on, include any of the following: content type, date of expression, language of expression, or other distinguishing characteristic of the expression. Guidelines for the recording of these elements are included in RDA 6.9–6.11 and are discussed under the "Expression Attributes" section of this chapter.

Examples:
100 0 $a Aeneas, $c Tacticus, $d active 4th century B.C. $t Peri tou pōs chrē poliorkoumenous antechein. $l **English** $s **(Illinois Greek Club)**
100 0 $a Aeneas, $c Tacticus, $d active 4th century B.C. $t Peri tou pōs chrē poliorkoumenous antechein. $l **French** $s **(Bon)**
100 0 $a Aeneas, $c Tacticus, $d active 4th century B.C. $t Peri tou pōs chrē poliorkoumenous antechein. $l **Greek** $s **(Bettalli)**
100 1 $a Camus, Albert, $d 1913-1960. $t Works. $k Selections. $l **English**. $f **1984**

VARIANT ACCESS POINTS REPRESENTING WORKS AND EXPRESSIONS

[MARC authority 400, 410, 411, 430]

Variant access points of works and expressions are constructed in the same way as the authorized access points of works and expressions are, with the exception that the variant titles of works or expressions, and not the preferred titles of works or expressions, are used.

Variant access points are recorded as authority data, and serve as pointers to the authorized forms of access points. Therefore, in current practice of creating MARC records, no variant access points are recorded in bibliographic records.

Although there is no title of an expression based on RDA, the title of an expression that is a translation of an original work is the most commonly recorded variant title for a work's title.

Examples:

Authorized access point:	Gershkovich, Aleksandr Abramovich. Teatr na Taganke, 1964-1984. English
Variant access point:	Gershkovich, Aleksandr Abramovich. **Theater of Yuri Lyubimov**
MARC authority:	100 1 $a Gershkovich, Aleksandr Abramovich. $t Teatr na Taganke, 1964-1984. $l English 400 1 $a Gershkovich, Aleksandr Abramovich. $t **Theater of Yuri Lyubimov**
Authorized access point:	Tolkien, J. R. R. $q (John Ronald Reuel), 1892-1973. Two towers
Variant access point:	Tolkien, J. R. R. $q (John Ronald Reuel), 1892-1973. Lord of the rings. **2, Two towers**
MARC authority:	100 1 $a Tolkien, J. R. R. $q (John Ronald Reuel), $d 1892-1973. $t Two towers 400 1 $a Tolkien, J. R. R. $q (John Ronald Reuel), $d 1892-1973. $t Lord of the rings. $n 2, $p **Two towers**
Authorized access point:	ACIAR proceedings
Variant access point:	Australian Centre for International Agricultural Research. **ACIAR proceedings** **ACIAR proceedings series (Canberra, A.C.T.)**
MARC authority:	130 0 $a ACIAR proceedings 410 2 $a Australian Centre for International Agricultural Research. $t **ACIAR proceedings** 430 0 $a **ACIAR proceedings series (Canberra, A.C.T.)**

Authorized access point: 21 grams (Motion picture)
Variant access point: **Twenty one grams (Motion picture)**
21 gramos (Motion picture)
Veintiun gramos (Motion picture)
MARC authority: 130 0 $a 21 grams (Motion picture)
430 0 $a **Twenty one grams (Motion picture)**
430 0 $a **21 gramos (Motion picture)**
430 0 $a **Veintiun gramos (Motion picture)**

Similarly, the construction of variant titles for a part or parts of works, compilations of works, and their expressions follows the same RDA guidelines as for the construction of authorized forms for these access points. This includes guidelines for additions to works or expressions.

AUTHORIZED ACCESS POINTS FOR SPECIAL CASES

Like the general categories of works and expressions, the construction of authorized and variant access points for musical works, legal works, and religious works and their expressions follows the pattern of combining the authorized access point of the creator, when one is associated with the work, and the preferred title of the work.

Authorized Access Points for Musical Works and Expressions (RDA 6.28)

Musical works follow the same guidelines for the construction of authorized access points, but, due to the fact that many musical works are aggregate works, RDA provides some additional guidelines. A number of these special guidelines are very briefly discussed below.

Musical Works with Lyrics, Libretto, Text, Etc. (RDA 6.28.1.2). When a musical work includes music and words, such as a libretto, lyrics, text, and so on, construct the authorized access point of the musical work by combining the authorized access point for the composer and the preferred title of the musical work.

Example:
The postman and the poet; music by Michael Jeffrey; lyrics by Eden Phillips; book by Trevor Bentham & Eden Phillips

Authorized access point: 100 1 $a **Jeffrey, Michael**, $d **1966-** $t **The postman and the poet**

Musical Works Composed for Choreographic Movement (RDA 6.28.1.4). When a musical work is composed for choreographic movement, construct the authorized access point representing the musical work by combining the authorized access point of the composer and the preferred title of the work.

Example:
Phonurgia; includes music, performance notes, technical notes and stage plan, choreography and lighting directions
Authorized access point: 100 1 $a **Wilkins, Caroline**, $d **1953**- $t **Phonurgia**

Adaptations of Musical Works (RDA 6.28.1.5). The guidelines here list a number of adaptations and revisions of musical works that would constitute new works. Examples include arrangements of music that result in a change of harmony or musical style from the original, paraphrases of works of other composers, etc. In this case, the authorized access point for the adapter and the preferred title of the adaptation are used to construct the authorized access point of the new work.

Example:
Bach's piano music improvisations; Francis Poulenc
Authorized access point (authority): 100 1 $a **Poulenc, Francis**, $d **1899-1963**. $t **Piano music**. $k **Selections**

Additions to Access Points Representing Musical Works (RDA 6.28.1.9). To differentiate authorized access points of musical works with the same tile, add one or more of the following: medium of performance, numeric designation, or key.

Example:
100 1 $a Beethoven, Ludwig van, $d 1770-1827. $t Symphonies, $n no. 7, op. 92, $r A major. $s **Performed music (London Symphony Orchestra)**

Add the medium of performance or another distinguishing characteristic to the authorized access point of musical works with distinctive titles.

Example:
100 1 $a Abeliovich, L. $q (Lev), $d 1912-1985. $t Aria, $m **violin, orchestra**

Authorized Access Points Representing Musical Expressions (RDA 6.28.3). In addition to the general instruction regarding musical expressions, RDA offers guidelines for the construction of authorized access points for the following types of expressions: arrangements, added accompaniments, sketches, vocal and chorus scores, and translations.

Examples:
100 1 $a Gabriel, Wolfgang. $t Ballade, $m clarinet, piano, $n op. 23; $o **arranged**
100 1 $a Bartók, Béla, $d 1881-1945. $t Works. $k Selections **(Sketches)**
100 1 $a Nabokov, Nicolas, $d 1903-1978. $t Love's labour's lost. $s **Vocal score.** $l German

LC-PCC PS 6.28.3 states that LC practice is not to add other distinguishing characteristics to differentiate an expression not already represented by a name authority record. Instead, information included in bibliographic records can be used for differentiation (e.g., do not add anything to Berlioz's arrangements to differentiate one from the other).

Variant Access Points for Musical Works and Expressions

Using the variant title of a musical work, construct the variant access point by combining the authorized access point of the creator and the variant tile. If necessary, make additions to variant titles as instructed in RDA 6.28.1.9–6.28.1.11, when applicable.

Examples:

Authorized access point:	100 1 $a Nabokov, Nicolas, $d 1903-1978. $t Love's labour's lost. $s Vocal score. $l German
Variant access point:	400 1 $a Nabokov, Nicolas, $d 1903-1978. $t **Verlor'ne Liebesmüh'** $s **Vocal score**
Authorized access point:	100 1 $a Lecocq, Charles, $d 1832-1918. $t Fille de Madame Angot. $p Couplets de Clairette; $o arranged
Variant access point:	400 1 $a Lecocq, Charles, $d 1832-1918. $t **Couplet Clairette**

400 1 $a Lecocq, Charles, $d 1832-1918. $t **Fille de Madame Angot**. $p **Couplet Clairette**

Authorized Access Points Representing a Legal Work and Expression (RDA 6.29)

Construction of authorized access points for legal works follows the same general guidelines as those for the construction of authorized access points for other works and expressions. A combination of the principal creator and the preferred title of the work is the basis for the authorized access points of works and expressions. When a legal work is composed of laws, decrees, legislation, constitutions, treaties, etc., the principal creator is the jurisdiction governed by these laws.

Laws Governing One Jurisdiction (RDA 6.29.1.2). Construct the authorized access point by combining the authorized access point for the jurisdiction and the preferred title of the legal work.

Example:
110 1 $a **Texas**. $t **Labor code**
110 1 $a **Japan**. $t **Minji soshōhō**
110 1 $a **Ohio**. $t **Laws, etc.**

Treaties (RDA 6.19.1.15). The authorized access point of a treaty between two nations is usually constructed by using the preferred title of the treaty as the authorized access point. To make additions to the authorized access point of a treaty, follow the guidelines in RDA 6.29.1.30.1.

Examples:
130 0 $a **Concordato fra la S. Sede e l'Italia**
130 0 $a **Draft treaty establishing the European Union**
130 0 $a **Treaty of Mutual Cooperation and Security between the United States of America and Japan**

Additions to Access Points Representing Laws, Etc. (RDA 6.29.1.29). To differentiate similar access points of laws, and so on, from other laws, add the years of promulgation.

Examples:
110 1 $a Alabama. $t **Constitution (1901)**
110 1 $a American Samoa. $t **Laws, etc. (American Samoa code annotated: 2013)**

Additions to Access Points Representing Treaties. (RDA 6.29.1.30). Additions for differentiation of treaties are considered under single treaties, compilations, protocols, and associated matter. For a single treaty, add the date of the treaty as instructed in RDA 6.20.3. For a compilation of treaties, use the collective title of the treaties and a date inclusive of all treaty dates. When there is a separate protocol of a treaty, or an extension, and so on, construct the access point by combining the authorized point for the treaty, the terms "protocol," and the date of the protocol, and other details.

Examples:
130 0 $a Concordato fra la S. Sede e l'Italia $d **(1929 February 11)**
130 0 $a Convention Concerning International Expositions $d (1928). $k Protocols, etc. $d **1988 May 31**

Access point for Expressions of Legal works (RDA 6.29.2). To construct an access point for a particular expression, use the authorized access point for the legal work, followed by the appropriate element for the expression.

Example:
110 1 $a France. $t Code pénal. $l **Italian**
10 1 $a Soviet Union. $t Laws, etc. (Svod zakonov SSSR). $k Selections. $l **Spanish**

Variant Access Points for Legal Works and Expressions (RDA 6.29.3)

Use the variant form of the title as the basis for constructing the variant access point for a legal work. Combine the authorized access point for the person or corporate body and the variant title of the legal work to form the variant access point.

Example:

Authorized access point:	130 0 $a Draft treaty establishing the European Union $d (1984 February 14). $l French
Variant access point:	430 0 $a **Traité instituant l'Union européenne** $d **(1984 February 14)**
Variant access point:	430 0 $a **Traité d'Union européenne** $d **(1984 February 14)**

For bilateral treaties, add variant forms of the legal work, one for each treaty participant, in the form of authorized access point of the participant, followed by title of the treaty.

Example:

Authorized access point: 130 0 $a Tratado de Ancón $d (1883 October 20)

Variant access point: 410 1 $a Chile. $t Treaties, etc. $g **Peru**, $d **1883 October 20**

Variant access point: 430 0 $a **Ancon, Treaty of, 1883**

Variant access point: 410 1 $a Peru. $t Treaties, etc. $g **Chile**, $d **1883 October 20**

Authorized Access Points for Religious Works and Expressions (RDA 6.30)

For religious works other than sacred scriptures, theological creeds, and liturgical works, follow the general guidelines under RDA 6.27.1.

For sacred scriptures and theological creeds, confessions of faith, etc., use the preferred title of the work as the authorized access point. Several guidelines are provided for liturgical works associated with specific church bodies.

Examples:

130 0 $a **Qur'an**. $p **Sūrat al-Ikhlāṣ**
130 0 $a **Apocalypse of Esdras (Medieval version)**
130 0 $a **Bible**. $p Apocrypha. $l **Greek**. $s **Septuagint**. $f **1900**
130 0 $a **Bible**. $p **Old Testament**. $l **English. $s Rosenberg**
110 2 $a **Catholic Church**. $t **Evangeliarium (Ms. Codex Egberti)**
130 0 $a **Siddur (Sephardic)**
130 0 $a **Bible**. $p **Genesis**. $l **English**. $s **Authorized**. $f **2002**

Variant Access Points for Religious Works (RDA 6.30)

Use the variant form of the title as the basis for the variant form of a religious work, which follows the authorized access point representing the person or corporate body of the work. Make additions if important for differentiation.

Examples:

Authorized access point: 130 0 $a Siddur (Sephardic)

Variant access point: 410 2 $a Jews. $k Liturgy and ritual. $t **Daily prayers (Sephardic)**

Authorized access point: 130 0 $a Bible. $p Genesis. $l English. $s Authorized. $f 2002

Variant access point: 430 0 $a **Epochs of Moses**

Authorized Access Points for Official Communications (RDA 6.31)

Two major categories of official communications are covered in RDA 6.31: official communication of some type of governing body (e.g., head of state, head of government, head of an international body, etc.), and official communication from a head or official of a religious body (e.g., pope, patriarch, etc.).

Construct an authorized access point for official communication by the following combination:

Authorized access point for body + preferred title for the official communication

Examples:

110 1 $a **United States**. $b **President (1974-1977: Ford)**. $t **Executive** Order 11876

110 1 $a **United States**. $b **President (1861-1865: Lincoln)**. $t **Emancipation Proclamation**

110 2 $a **Catholic Church**. $b **Pope (1939-1958: Pius XII)**. $t **Fulgens corona**

110 1 $a **Constantinople (Ecumenical patriarchate).** $b **Patriarch (1835-1840: Grēgorios VI)**. $t **Patriarchikē kai synodikē enkyklios epistolē**

When there is a compilation of official communications by more than one holder of a specific office, construct the authorized access point by combining the authorized access point for the office (corporate body name), followed by the preferred title for the work.

Example:

100 1 $a **Ohio**. $b **Governor**. $t **Messages of the governor of Ohio, 1861-1925**

For an expression of official communication works, add to the authorized access point terms or a date, as instructed under the general guidelines for constructing authorized access points for expressions, in RDA 6.27.3.

Example:

710 22 $a **Catholic Church**. $b **Pope (1846-1878: Pius IX)**. $t **Ineffabilis Deus**. $l **Ojibwa**.

Variant Access Points for Official Communications (RDA 6.31.3)

Use the variant title as the basis of the variant access point by combining the authorized access point of the office, followed by the variant title.

Example:

Authorized access point:	110 2 $a Catholic Church. $b Pope (1073-1085: Gregory VII). $t Registrum. $k Selections. $l English
Variant access point:	410 2 $a Catholic Church. $b Pope (1073-1085: Gregory VII). $t **Correspondence of Pope Gregory VII**

DESCRIBING CONTENT

Thus far, we have covered work and expression attributes that relate to the "identify" user task as it is defined in FRBR and as it guides RDA. A number of attributes of works and expressions are defined to facilitate the "select a resource" user task. RDA focuses on these attributes by providing guidelines for the recording of elements typically used to select a resource that meets the user's information needs.

Elements describing content are associated with the intellectual content of the resource. With the exception of the subject of the resource (not currently covered in RDA, although there are placeholders for it), these elements are discussed in RDA Chapter 7. Not all elements are applicable to all types of resources.

In current cataloging practice using MARC structures, this information is typically recorded in bibliographic records. Some elements have MARC fields defined in both bibliographic and authority formats, possibly with a slight difference. It is possible that a particular implementation will enable the inclusion of this information as authority data relating to the work or expression, and, therefore, record this information in authority records; in such cases, all work-related information will be recorded in one work authority record, and, similarly, all expression-related information will be recorded in one authority record. Current practice is to record some of these elements in bibliographic records, with the examples below illustrating their use in MARC bibliographic records.

Elements describing the content of a work include the following:

- Nature of the content
- Coverage of the content
- Coordinates of cartographic content
- Equinox
- Epoch
- Intended audience
- System of organization
- Dissertation or thesis information

Elements describing the content as it relates to expressions include the following:

- Summarization of the Content
- Place and Date of Capture
- Language of the Content
- Form of Notation
- Accessibility Content
- Illustrative Content
- Supplementary Content
- Colour Content
- Sound Content
- Aspect Ratio
- Format of Notated Music
- Medium of Performance of Musical Content
- Duration
- Performer, Narrator, and/or Presenter
- Artistic and/or Technical Credit
- Scale
- Projection of Cartographic Content
- Other Details of Cartographic Content
- Award
- Note on Expression

Note that many of these elements are specific to a particular type of work, including cartographic materials and music. Not all elements will be discussed in detail below.

Nature of the Content (RDA 7.2)

The nature of the content is the specific character of the content of a resource. This element is similar to the form of the work (RDA 6.3). Examples here include spreadsheet, annual report, survey, and others. RDA instructs that this information be recorded if it is considered important for identification or for selection of a resource.

Example:

Nature of the content:	**technical report**
MARC (bibliographic):	500 $a **Technical report** for the US Department of Energy in Support of the National Climate Assessment
MARC (authority):	380 $a **Technical report**.

Coverage of the Content (RDA 7.3)

Coverage of the content is defined as the chronological or geographic coverage of the content of a resource. Examples may include the chronological coverage of a report or the geographic coverage of a map. This element is especially helpful when the coverage of the content is not evident by the title of the resource.

Examples (bibliographic):
522 $a **Includes map of Florence, Italy.**
513 $a Interim report; $b **2012-2013**.

Coordinates of Cartographic Content (RDA 7.4) [MARC bibliographic fields 034, 255 subfield $c]

Coordinates of cartographic content are the coordinates of the area covered in a map or atlas. These are typically expressed in longitude and latitude, or coordinate pairings. This element is usually recorded if the information is found on the resource. This information can be also entered as coded information in MARC bibliographic records (field 034).

Example (MARC bibliographic):
Coordinates of cartographic content: **W 1°08′ E 0°09′/N 54°13′ N 53°34′**
034 1 $b **389908** $d **W0010800** $e **E0000900** $f **N0541300** $g **N0533400**
255 $a Approximately 1:389,908 $c **(W 1°08′--E 0°09′/N 54°13′--N 53°34′)**

Intended Audience (RDA 7.7) [MARC bibliographic field 521]

Intended audience is the class of users for whom the content of a resource is intended. The element is recorded if it considered helpful to the user in identifying and selecting a resource.

Examples (bibliographic):

Intended audience:	**Grades 6-12**
MARC bibliographic:	521 8 $a **Grades 6-12.**
Intended audience:	**Board of Film Censors, Singapore: PG13 (Suitable for 13 and above)**

MARC bibliographic: 521 8 $a **Board of Film Censors, Singapore: PG13 (Suitable for 13 and above).**

Intended audience: **MPAA rating: PG for some mild rude language, humor, and scary images**
MARC bibliographic: 521 8 $a **MPAA rating: PG; for some mild rude language, humor, and scary images.**

System of Organization (RDA 7.8) [MARC bibliographic field 351]

The element of system of organization is used primarily for archival or other collections, and describes the system used to organize or arrange the collection materials.

Example (bibliographic):
351 $b **The Provost's Faculty Dinner Slide collection have been arranged chronologically, and are dated 1994 and 1996.**

Dissertation or Thesis Information (RDA 7.9) [MARC bibliographic field 502]

Defined as the work done as part of the requirements for an academic degree, this element of dissertation or thesis information is used to record the name of the degree, the name of the institution, and the year the degree was granted.

Examples (bibliographic):
Dissertation or Thesis information: **Thesis. M.S. University of Wisconsin, Madison, 1965.**
MARC bibliographic: 502 $a **Thesis** $b **M.S.** $c **University of Wisconsin, Madison** $d **1965**

Dissertation or Thesis information: **Master's .Harvard University, 2012**
MARC bibliographic: 502 $b **Master's** $c **Harvard University** $d **2012**

Dissertation or Thesis information: **Thesis. Ph.D. Harvard University, 2012**
MARC bibliographic: 502 $g **Thesis** $b **Ph.D.** $c **Harvard University** $d **2012**

Note that the formatting of this element when using MARC field 502 has changed from what many current records may include. LC-PCC PS 7.9

states that the LC practice is to use the pre-RDA punctuation and code the subelements as defined in MARC documentation, as illustrated in the above examples.

Summarization of the Content (RDA 7.10) [MARC bibliographic field 520]

Record a brief summary or abstract of the content of a resource if it is considered helpful for identifying and selecting a resource, or if the remaining description of the resource does not adequately describe its content.

Examples (bibliographic):

520 $a **Reviews the story of how women have helped shape America over the last fifty years through one of the most sweeping social revolutions in American history, in pursuit of their rights to a full and fair share of political power, economic opportunity, and personal autonomy.**

520 $a **FIFA 13 delivers the largest and deepest feature set in the history of the franchise. Five game-changing innovations create a true battle for possession, deliver freedom and creativity in attack, and capture all the drama and unpredictability of real-world football.**

520 $a **Burdened with the dark, dangerous, and seemingly impossible task of locating and destroying Voldemort's remaining Horcruxes, Harry, feeling alone and uncertain about his future, struggles to find the inner strength he needs to follow the path set out before him.**

Place and Date of Capture (RDA 7.11) [MARC bibliographic fields 033, 518]

Typically used for resources that are "captured" in film or recorded in other media, this element is used to record information about the place and the date of filming or recording. When recording the place of capture, include the studio or specific location, if this information is available, and the city. Record the date by providing the year, month, and day.

In a MARC bibliographic structure, this information can be recorded as free text in field 518 and/or as coded information in field 033.

Examples (bibliographic):

518 $o Filmed on location $p **Hydra Island, Greece**.

518 $a **Filmed and recorded live on location in Japan during Aerosmith's Fall 2011 tour**.

518 $o Recorded $p **Nrg Recording, Studio Barbarosa, and Red Star**.

518 $o Recorded $p **Kodak Hall** $d **2015 March 6.**
033 $a **20150306**
[Recorded on March 6, 2015]

033 00 $a **19890324** $b **4034** $c **D3**
[Recorded on March 24, 1989, in Dallas, Texas.]

Language of the Content (RDA 7.12) [MARC bibliographic fields 041, 546]

The language in which the content is expressed is recorded in the element of language of the content in accordance with the general instructions provided in RDA 6.11 (for language of expression) and RDA 3.20 (for programming language). LC-PCC PS 7.12 recommends recording not only the language of expression for the majority of the content, but also the languages of other content. In addition, the LC-PCC policy provides guidelines for the recording of the form of the language and for languages that constitute special cases such as Greek and Norwegian.

In a MARC bibliographic structure, this information can be recorded as free text in field 546 and/or as coded information in field 041.

Examples (bibliographic):
041 1 $a eng $a grc $h grc
546 $a **Greek text and English** translations on facing pages.
041 1 $a fre $a lat $h lat
546 $a **French and Latin** on opposite pages numbered in duplicate.
041 1 $a eng $a fre $a spa $j eng $j fre $j spa $h eng
546 $a **English, French or Spanish soundtracks with optional Spanish and French subtitles; optional English subtitles for the deaf and hard of hearing.**

In addition, in MARC bibliographic record, the language of the resource is recorded in position 35-37 (Lang) of the fixed field 008.

Form of Notation (RDA 7.13) [MARC bibliographic field 546]

The element of form of notation is used to record information about the script used to express the language of the content, the form of musical notation, the form of tactile notation, or the form of movement notation (choreography) used to express the content of a resource. A list of terms for musical notation, tactile notation, and movement notation is provided under the RDA guidelines for each type of form of notation.

Examples (bibliographic):
546 $a Mongolian $b (**Cyrillic and vertical script**).
546 $b In the original **neumatic notation**.
546 $b **Braille** with printed captions.
546 $b **Staff notation**.
546 $b **Mensural notation**.

Note that per LC-PCC PS 7.13, this element is core for LC when recording some scripts or the form of musical notation.

Accessibility Content (RDA 7.14) [MARC bibliographic fields 546, 500]

Content that assists those who have visual or hearing impairments is recorded in the accessibility content element. Examples include closed captioning and subtitles for spoken content, as long as the subtitles are in the same language as the primary content. If the subtitles are in a different language, this information is then recorded in the language of the content elements.

In a MARC bibliographic structure, the accessibility content is recorded either in field 546 (if it includes information about the language) or in field 500.

Examples (bibliographic):

Accessibility content:	**Closed captioned for the hearing impaired**
MARC bibliographic:	500 $a **Closed captioned for the hearing impaired.**
Accessibility content:	**Closed-captioned; English or Spanish dialogue**
MARC bibliographic:	546 $a **Closed-captioned; English or Spanish dialogue.**
Accessibility content:	**Subtitles for the deaf and hard of hearing**
MARC bibliographic:	546 $a **Subtitles for the deaf and hard of hearing.**

Illustrative Content (RDA 7.15) [MARC bibliographic field 300 subfield $b]

Illustrative content is defined as content that is meant to illustrate the primary content of the resource. Text and numerical data included in tables are not considered illustrations. Per RDA 7.15, do not record any decorative or minor illustrations that do not add any value to the content itself. Use the term "illustration" or "illustrations" to record the presence of illustrative content in a resource. Alternatively, in addition to the term "illustrations," more specific terms identifying the types of illustrations may be added if they are considered important for the identification and selection of the resource. A list of terms that can be used is included in RDA 7.15.1.3. In addition, there is an option to add the number of illustrations.

Examples (bibliographic):
300 $a xxi, 470 pages: $b **illustrations, maps**; $c 26 cm
300 $a 1 atlas (64 pages): $b color **illustrations**, color **maps**; $c 28 cm
300 $a 1 online resource (xvii, 280 pages, 32 unnumbered pages of plates): $b **illustrations, portraits**.
300 $a 334 pages: $b **illustrations**.; $c 24 cm
300 $a vi, 273 pages: $b **illustrations, 2 maps**; $c 29 cm

As stated in LC-PCC PS 7.15, the general LC practice is not to use the alternative guidelines to record specific types of illustrations and to only record "illustration" or "illustrations," although the term "maps" is used when maps are present in a resource. Illustrative content is a core element in LC's practice when describing children's resources.

Supplementary Content (RDA 7.16) [MARC bibliographic field 500, 504]

Content indented to supplement the primary content of a resource, such as bibliography, index, appendix, and so on, is recorded in the supplementary content element.

LC's practice (LCC-PC PS 7.16) is to record such supplementary content if it is important or if it is considered helpful for the identification and selection of the resource. The typical supplementary content that LC recommends recording includes bibliographical references, discographies, filmographies, indexes, appendices, and errata slips that have not been included in the publication. In addition, if it is considered important, record the location of the supplementary content within the resource, typically by page number. If the supplementary content is distributed throughout the resource and is not located all in one section of the resource, do not add this information. LC guidelines are specific about the format used to record bibliography information and indexes. The majority of cataloging agencies in the United States follow LC's formatting.

Examples (bibliographic):
504 $a **Includes bibliographical references and index.**

504 $a **Includes bibliographical references (pages 377-384) and index.**
500 $a **Includes index.**

Colour Content (RDA 7.17) [MARC bibliographic field 300]

Record the presence of color in the element of colour content. Ignore color present outside the content. Special guidelines are provided for still images, moving images, three-dimensional forms, and resources created for the visually impaired. Although the spelling "colour" is used in RDA examples, LC-PCC PS instructs that the term be spelled and used as "color."

Examples (bibliographic):
300 $a xxxiv, 842 pages: $b **color** illustrations; $c 29 cm
300 $a 1 online resource (x, 35 pages): $b illustrations (**some color**)
300 $a 5 videodiscs (DVD) (184 min.): $b **black & white**; $c 12 cm.
300 $a 1 film reel (100 min., 3,600 ft.): $b sound, **black and white**; $c 16 mm

Sound Content (RDA 7.18) [MARC bibliographic field 300 subfield $b]

The presence of sound in a resource other than a sound resource is recorded in the sound content element. When describing motion pictures or video recordings, record the term "sound" or the term "silent" in this element to indicate the presence or absence of sound.

Examples (bibliographic):
300 $a 1 DVD-video (approximately 128 min.): $b **sound**, colour; $c 12 cm
300 $a 2 videodiscs (76 min.): $b **silent**, black and white; $c 4 3/4 in

Aspect Ratio (RDA 7.19) [MARC bibliographic field 500]

The ratio of the width to the height of a moving image is recorded in the element of aspect ratio. Three possible terms are listed in RDA 7.19: full screen, wide screen, and mixed. Full screen is used when the ratio is less than 1.5:1, wide screen is used when it is 1.5:1 or greater, and mixed is used when there are multiple aspect ratios. Record the numerical ratio if it is known.

Examples (bibliographic):

Aspect ratio: **anamorphic wide screen 2.35:1**.

MARC bibliographic: 500 $a Dolby digital 5.1, **anamorphic wide screen 2.35:1**.

Aspect ratio: **wide screen 1.85:1**

MARC bibliographic: 500 $aDTS-HD Master Audio 5.1, **wide screen 1.85:1**.

Format of Notated Music (RDA 7.20) [MARC bibliographic field 500]

The musical or physical layout of the content of a resource, presented as a type of musical notation, is recorded in the element of format of notated music. For this, select an appropriate term from RDA 7.20.1.3. Examples include study score, piano score, part, choir book, and so on. Additional terms can be used if none of those listed in RDA is sufficient.

Examples (bibliographic):

Format of notated music: **Vocal score for male chorus and organ**

MARC bibliographic: 500 $a Vocal score for male chorus and organ.

The information in the above example could also be recorded as "other distinguishing characteristics" of the expression of a musical work (RDA 6.18.1.6).

Medium of Performance of Musical Content (RDA 7.21) [MARC bibliographic field 500]

The expression element of medium of performance of musical content is used to record the instrument(s) or voice(s) used to perform a piece of musical content. In contrast, the element of medium of performance of a musical *work* (RDA 6.15) is used to record the medium (instrument or voice, etc.) for which the work was created.

Examples (bibliographic):

500 $a **For solo voice and 2 part chorus with orchestra consisting of instruments indigenous to the Andean region**

500 $a **For 1 to 3 voices unaccompanied or with treble instrument accompaniment; some works for 3 solo voices, 4 voice chorus, and 4 instrumental parts.**

Duration (RDA 7.22)
[MARC bibliographic fields 300, 306, 500]

Duration is defined as the playing time or running time of the content of a resource. It also includes the performance time of a resource that includes notated music or notated movement. Abbreviated terms from RDA Appendix B.5.3 can be used when recording duration.

Examples (bibliographic):
500 $a Duration: **7:00:00.**
500 $a Duration: **15:00:00.**
306 $a **133000**
300 $a 7 audio discs (**8 hr., 30 min.**): $b CD audio, digital; $c 4 3/4 in.
306 $a 001831 $a 002504 $a 001508

Scale (RDA 7.25)
Core Element for Cartographic Materials
[MARC bibliographic field 255 subfield $a]

The element of scale is most commonly used for cartographic materials and is defined as the "ratio of the dimensions of an image or three-dimensional form contained or embodied in a resource to the dimensions of the thing it represents." In addition to cartographic materials, this element also applies to still images and three-dimensional forms. In general, RDA guidelines instruct that the scale be recorded in the form of a fraction expressed as a ratio, for example, "1:10,000," even if this is not the form in which the information appears on the resource itself. A scale 1:10,000 means that 1 unit of measurement (e.g., centimeter) of the map represents 10,000 units of measurement (e.g., kilometers) of the content it represents (e.g., a country represented on the map). The scale can be found on the resource, calculated, or estimated. If it is estimated, add the term "approximately" before the numeric scale.

Three elements of scale are described in RDA 7.25: the Horizontal Scale (RDA 7.25.3), the Vertical Scale (RDA 7.25.4), and Additional Scale Information (RDA 7.25.5).

Horizontal Scale (RDA 7.25.3) is defined as "the ratio of horizontal distances in the cartographic content of a resource to the actual distances they represent."

Examples:

Scale:	**1:700,000**
MARC bibliographic:	255 $a **Scale 1:700,000.**

255 $a **Scale 1:800,000. 1 cm = 8 km** $c (E 19°05′--E 30°30′/N 41°50′--N 34°45′).
255 $a **Scale 1:27,585. 1 inch represents 0.44 miles or 0.7 km**
255 $a **Scale approximately 1:150,000. 1 inch = 2.4 miles. 1 cm = 1.5 km** $c (E 23°30′--E 26°20′/N 35°43′--N 34°48′).
255 $a **Not drawn to scale.**

If more than one scale is present on the resource (e.g., one map, different scales), record the range of scale from smallest to largest, connecting them with a hyphen. If these values are not known, use the phrase "Scale varies." If more than one map is present and each map has its own scale, record the phrase "Scales differ." Alternatively, RDA 7.25.1.4 instructs that each scale be recorded separately. The LC practice (LC-PCC PS 7.25.1.4) instructs that the scales should be listed separately only if there are two scales and to not follow the given alternative when more than two scales are present.

Examples (bibliographic):
Two maps on one sheet:

Scale (1):	**Scale approximately 1:3,500**
MARC bibliographic:	255 $a **Scale approximately 1:3,500.**
Scale (1):	**Scale approximately 1:2,000**
MARC bibliographic:	255 $a **Scale approximately 1:2,000.**
Scale:	**Scale varies**
MARC bibliographic:	255 $a **Scale varies.**
Scale:	**Scales differ**
MARC bibliographic:	255 $a **Scales differ.**

Vertical Scale (RDA 7.25.4) is recorded, in addition to the horizontal scale, for relief models or three-dimensional cartographic materials; in such cases, it is considered a core element. Vertical scale is the scale of elevation or of the vertical dimensions of the cartographic content of a resource.

Additional Scale Information (RDA 7.25.5) is used to record any supplemental information about the scale of a resource, such as unusual scale information, errors in scale, or a direct quote of the scale statement on the resource.

Projection of Cartographic Content (7.26) [MARC bibliographic field 255 subfield $b]

The element of projection of cartographic content is used to record the "method or system used to represent the surface of the Earth or of a celestial sphere on a plane."

Examples:
Projection of cartographic content: **sinusoidal equal area projection**
MARC bibliographic: 255 $a Scale approximately 1:8,600,000; $b **sinusoidal equal area projection.**

Projection of cartographic content: **universal transverse Mercator projection**
MARC bibliographic: 255 $a Scale 1:100,000; $b **universal transverse Mercator projection** $c (W 121°37′30″-- W 121°00′00″/N 36°00′00″--N 35°30′00″).

Projection of cartographic content: **Conic projection**
MARC bibliographic: 255 $a Scale 1:4,752,000. 1 inch = 75 miles. Vertical exaggeration, 20 times; $b **Conic projection**, with two standard parallels $c (W 167°--W 14°/N 85°--N 40°).

Other Details of Cartographic Content (RDA 7.27)

Mathematical data or other features of cartographic content represented in a resource and not recorded in the coordinates, scale, or projection elements may be recorded in the other details of cartographic content element.

Example (bibliographic):
255 $a Scale 1:4,752,000. 1 inch = 75 miles. **Vertical exaggeration, 20 times**; $b Conic projection, w**ith two standard parallels** $c (W 167°--W 14°/N 85°--N 40°).

Award (RDA 7.28)
[MARC bibliographic field 586]

For an expression of a work that has received an award, special recognition, or prize by a granting body, record the award name and the year of the award if it is considered important for the identification and selection of the resource.

Examples:
Award: **Boston Globe/Horn Book Fiction Award Winner, 2014**
MARC bibliographic: 586 $a **Boston Globe/Horn Book Fiction Award Winner, 2014**

Award: **Caldecott Honor Book, 2013**
MARC bibliographic: 586 $a **Caldecott Honor Book, 2013**

586 $a **Academy Award Winner, 2015**: Best Picture, Best Cinematography, Best Original Screenplay, Best Director (Alejandro González Iñárritu); Academy Award Nominee, 2015: Best Supporting Actor (Edward Norton), Best Sound Mixing, Best Sound Editing, Best Supporting Actress (Emma Stone), Best Actor (Michael Keaton); Golden Globe Winner, 2015: Best Screenplay (Alejandro González Iñárritu), Best Actor in a Motion Picture - Musical or Comedy (Michael Keaton),; Golden Globe Nominee, 2015: Best Motion Picture - Musical or Comedy, Best Supporting Actor in a Motion Picture (Edward Norton), Best Supporting Actress in a Motion Picture (Emma Stone), Best Director (Alejandro González Iñárritu), Best Original Score (Antonio Sanchez).

Note on Expression (RDA 7.29)

The element of note on expression is used for any additional information relating to the content of any of the expression attributes or elements. Most often, changes in content characteristics of multipart monographs and serials are included in this element, such as changes in the language of an expression in some of the issues of a serial, changes in the presence of illustrations, and others.

Example:
Note on Expression: **Volume 2 lacks illustrations**
MARC bibliographic: 500 $a **Volume 2 lacks illustrations**.

NOTES

1. IFLA Study Group on the Functional Requirements for Bibliographic Records. (1998). *Functional Requirements for Bibliographic Records: Final Report* (UBCIM Publications, New Series Vol. 19). München, Germany: K.G. Saur. Retrieved from http://www.ifla.org/publications/functional-requirements-for-bibliographic-records (pp. 79–92) [Also available at www.ifla.org/VII/s13/frbr/frbr.htm (February 20, 2007) and in IFLA Working Group on Functional Requirements and Numbering of Authority Records. (2009). *Functional Requirements for Authority Data: A Conceptual Model* (IFLA Series on Bibliographic Control, Vol. 34). München, Germany: K.G. Saur.]
2. IFLA Study Group, 1998, p. 16.
3. IFLA Study Group, 1998, p. 18.
4. Music Library Association. (2011–). *Thematic Indexes Used in the Library of Congress/NACO Authority File*. Retrieved from http://bcc.musiclibraryassoc.org/BCC-Historical/BCC2011/Thematic_Indexes.htm.

Chapter 8

Resource Description and Access

Identifying Persons, Corporate Bodies, and Families

INTRODUCTION

This chapter covers RDA Section 3, Chapters 8 through 11, focusing on persons, families, and corporate bodies identified in the FR family model as the Group 2 entities. Chapter 8 covers general guidelines on identifying persons, corporate bodies, and families. Chapter 9 provides guidelines on identifying persons and constructing preferred access points to represent persons, Chapter 10 provides guidelines on identifying families and constructing preferred access points to represent families, and Chapter 11 provides guidelines on identifying corporate bodies and constructing preferred access points to represent corporate bodies.

As with the entities work, expression, manifestation, and item covered in chapters 6 and 7 of this text, the definitions of the entities persons, corporate bodies, and families are based on the FRBR family model, and, more specifically, the FRAD definitions (with some modifications). Although most RDA terminology for attributes comes from the FRBR and FRAD models, RDA terms for elements may be different, and may have specific meaning; therefore, we will start with the definitions of some important terms used in RDA Chapter 8 through 11.

Person is an individual or an identity established by an individual**.** The established identity can be by the individual alone or in collaboration with other individuals (e.g., two individuals establish a person's identity). This definition is broad enough to include humans, personas, fictitious characters, and nonhuman entities. Examples include Ariel (fictitious character from Disney), Koko (gorilla from the "Fine animal gorilla"), Nicole Foster (pseudonym used by a team of two writers).

Family is a group of two or more persons related to each other by birth, marriage, adoption, civil union, or by other such legal status, or who identify themselves as a family. The entity family was not included in the initial FRBR model; it was an addition with the publication of FRAD, mostly due to recognition by the archival community of families as a unique group of individuals acting as creators or contributors of content. An organization associated with a family is considered a corporate body. For example, the Jackson 5 is a corporate body formed by members of the Jackson family. "Jackson 5" is a separate entity from the Jackson family and from each individual family member.

Corporate body is defined as an organization or group of people and/or organizations that identifies itself by a name and acts as a unit. In other words, for an organization or group of people to be considered a corporate body, all of the following criteria should be met: it is an organization or group of people, it is identified by a specific name, and it acts (or has potential to act) as a unit. For example, the "Mills Blue Rhythm Band" is considered a corporate body because it meets all three criteria; in contrast, the group of concerned citizens in Springfield who came together to deliver a message to the mayor of Springfield is not a corporate body because it does not have a name by which it is identified.

Name denotes terms used for the names associated with persons, families, and corporate bodies. These include name, preferred name, and variant name.

> *Name* is a character, word, or group of characters and/or words by which a person, a family, or a corporate body is known. A person, family, or corporate body may be known by more than one name and more than one form for each name. For example, a person may be known as "Clemens Bonifacius," "P. C. Asbjørnsen," or "Peter Christen Asbjørnsen."
>
> *Preferred name* is the name among all names by which a person, family, or corporate body is known that is chosen to identify the person, family, or corporate body, and that serves as the base for the preferred access point to represent that person, family, or corporate body. In the above example, "P C Asbjørnsen" is the name chosen to represent this person and will be used as a basis to form the authorized access point to represent this person.
>
> *Variant name* is the name or the form of a name by which a person, family, or corporate body is known, but which has not been chosen as the preferred name to represent this person, family, or corporate body. Continuing with the same example, if "P C Asbjørnsen" is the preferred name for this person, "Clemens Bonifacius" and "Peter Christen Asbjørnsen" would be variant names. Variant names may include names found in resources associated with the entity, names found in reference resources, or names that a user may use to conduct their search.

Access point refers to a name, term, code, etc., used to represent a person, family, or corporate body. Two types of access points are defined in RDA: authorized access point and variant access point.

> *Authorized access point* is the standardized access point representing the entity, and its construction is based on the preferred name of the entity (i.e., the person, family, or corporate body). If necessary for differentiation, additional identifying elements are included in the authorized access point for the entity. (RDA 8.6)
>
> *Variant access point* is the alternate access point to that authorized access point that represents the entity. Each variant access point for a name, family, or corporate body is constructed using the variant form of the name of the entity. Additional elements may be added to the variant access point if it is considered necessary for identification of the entity. (RDA 8.7)

Data relating to these entities reflect entity attributes and are recorded as authority data, or as elements in authority records, when such structures are used to store this information. The objective of the recorded elements is to facilitate the following user tasks:

- ***find*** persons, families, and corporate bodies that match the user's search criteria. Although one will not find the actual person, one should be able to find data or elements used to represent the entity and relationships among entities;
- ***identify*** a person, family, or corporate body represented by the data as the one sought, or be able to distinguish between two entities with the same or similar names;
- ***understand*** the relationship between the name used to represent a person, family, or corporate body from the names by which they are known; and
- ***understand*** the reasons one name is chosen and recorded as the preferred name and the other(s) as variant.

The principle of differentiation states that data used in the description should differentiate the person, family, or corporate body from others, and the principle of representation states that the name or form of the name used as the preferred name of a person, family, or corporate body should be the most commonly found in resources associated with the person, family, or corporate body. These two principles ensure that RDA guidelines are designed to provide the necessary data that will meet the above objectives.

RDA 8.2 states that the preferred name or form of name to represent a person, family, or corporate body should be in the original language and script of the resources associated with the entity, but, in some cases, an alternative is given to use the language preferred by the agency creating the data. In these cases, the names should be taken from resources associated with the entities or reference sources in the language preferred by the agency.

Core Elements

RDA defines a number of core elements for a person, family, or corporate body. This means that, at the minimum, these core elements should be included in the description of each entity, if they apply and can be easily determined.

Core elements for persons, families, and corporate bodies are listed and discussed in more detail in the respective sections of this chapter.

RDA 8.4 instructs us to record the names in the language and script in which they appear in resources they are taken from. Alternatively, a transliterated form of the name can be recorded. Per LC-PCC PS 8.4, the transliterated form should be based on the *ALA-LC Romanization Tables: Transliteration Schemes for Non-Roman Scripts*, which has been approved by LC and the American Library Association.

General Guidelines For Recording Names (RDA 8.5)

Before we take a look at the guidelines for each element defined for persons, families, and corporate bodies, it will be useful to note some of the general guidelines offered in RDA 8.5:

- Capitalization of names follows the guidelines included in RDA Appendix A.2.
- Numerals expressed as numbers or words (e.g., III or Third) that are part of the name are recorded as they are found in resources. Ordinal numbers of meetings (events, conferences, etc.) are covered in RDA 11.6.1.
- Accents and other diacritics are recorded as they are found.
- If a name used by a person includes hyphens, record them as they appear. If the transliteration requires the use of hyphens, use them as they are determined by the transliteration system.
- Use RDA Appendix B.2 for the use of abbreviations in the names of persons, families, and corporate bodies.

Scope of Usage (RDA 8.8) [MARC authority field 677]

This element is used to record the type of work that is associated with the name when the person, family, or corporate body uses more than one name. This is more typical of persons who may use pseudonyms for one type of work and use their real names for another type of work. The element may also be used to record usage of a name in cataloging practice or based on rules from a specific set of standards.

Examples:
Person using "Harry Turtledove" for fiction and other works and "H.N. Turteltaub" for Byzantine history works:

100 1 $a Turtledove, Harry
372 $a Science fiction $a History $a Education $a Technical writing $2 lcsh
100 1 $a Turteltaub, H. N.
500 1 $a Turtledove, Harry
677 $a **Name used in Byzantine history scholarly works**
670 $a Justinian, 1998: $b CIP t.p. (H.N. Turteltaub) bk. jkt. (pseud. of well-known novelist who is also a respected scholar of Byzantine history)

Person using "A.D." and "Albert Dubois" for his works; also differentiated from a relative with similar name:

100 1 $a A. D. $ (Albert Dubois), $d 1839-
667 $a **Usage: A.D.; A. Dubois.** Not to be confused with his cousin, Albert Dubois (b. 1830), also a lithographer.

Person using both "Rudolf Charles" and his family name "Ablaing van Giessenburg":

100 1 $a Ablaing van Giessenburg, R. C. d', $d 1826-1904
500 1 $i Alternate identity: $a Charles, Rudolf, $d 1826-1904
667 $a **Do not confuse with his father**, R.C. (Rudolf Carel or Rudolph Charles) d'Ablaing baron van Giessenburg, 1804-1881, writer on economics
670 $a Nieuw Nederlandsch biografisch woordenboek, 1911-1937, via WWW, Feb. 14, 2014 $b (Ablaing van Giessenburg (Rudolf Charles d'; born April 26, 1826, Amsterdam; died March 13, 1904; established bookselling firm in 1850 under the name R.C. Meyer, librairie étrangère; **known by this name at the time, but later used his family name Ablaing van Giessenburg**; published Le testament de Jean Meslier, 1864; author of various works propagating the principles of free thought)

Date of Usage (RDA 8.9) [MARC authority field 677]

This is the range of date during which a particular name (in MARC authority field 1XX) can be used as a preferred name/authorized access point. This is important for name changes when each name is still valid and has limitations in usage.

Examples (authority):
100 1 $a Markey, Karen
400 1 $a Drabenstott, Karen Markey
677 $a Karen Markey changed name to Karen Markey Drabenstott **June 10, 1989**; changed name to Karen Markey **June 17, 2004.**

110 2 $a IBM Center for the Business of Government
510 2 $a IBM Endowment for the Business of Government
677 $a IBM Endowment for the Business of Government became IBM Center for the Business of Government in **July or Aug. 2003**

Status of Identification (RDA 8.10) [MARC authority field 008 position 33]

This element is used to record the status or the level of authentication of the data identifying the person, family, or corporate body. RDA provides three possible terms to record the status of identification: *fully established* (data are sufficient to fully establish an authorized access point), *provisional* (data are insufficient to fully establish an authorized access point), and *preliminary* (information was recorded using a description of the resource, but the resource itself was not available).

Libraries participating in the NACO are expected to fully establish authorized access points when entering records into the LC/NACO authority file, unless the information available at the time is insufficient.

In a MARC structure, this information is recorded in MARC authority field 008 position 33, which is labeled as "Auth status" in the OCLC display. Some preliminary records may also be entered in LC/NACO, but this not typical for authority records for persons.

Example:

Status of identification:	fully established
MARC authority:	008 831206nl azannaabn la aaa c
(OCLC display):	Auth status: **a**

Undifferentiated Name Indicator (RDA 8.11) [MARC authority field 008 position 32]

In most cases, RDA provides guidelines on how to differentiate authorized access points for entities having the same name or similar names, with the inclusion of additional elements that will create unique (differentiated) authorized access points. Sometimes, sufficient information cannot be found to distinguish the names. RDA 8.6 and 8.11 allow the use of the same name to represent entities. If the core elements are not sufficient to differentiate an access point, record the term "undifferentiated" (RDA 8.11.1.3).

This information is required when entering an authority record in the LC/NACO file and recorded in MARC authority field 008 position 32, labeled "Name" in OCLC, a value of "b" indicates undifferentiated.

Often, a record will be updated and separate authority records will be created for an undifferentiated name that has been differentiated. With the RDA guidelines that provide for additional elements to be used for authorized access points, many existing records created using previous standards have been revised. In this type of case, a note in MARC authority field 677 indicates that this differentiated name has been previously covered under an undifferentiated name:

667 $a **Formerly on undifferentiated name record n88682169**

Source Consulted (RDA 8.12) [MARC authority field 670]

One of the functional objectives of RDA is to understand the reasons one name is chosen and recorded as the preferred name and the other(s) as variant. This is typically done by including references to where the information was found, and, therefore, explaining why one name or form of a name was selected as the preferred name for the entity.

Although not an RDA core element, this element is an LC core element (LC-PCC PS 8.12), and, therefore, a required practice for all LC/NACO authority records. In MARC authority, field 670 is used to cite the source where the information was found; subfield $a is used to record the location where the title proper of the source is entered, and subfield $b is used to record where the information is found in the source and what information is found. Many authority records include all the information in subfield $a, without the use of subfield $b.

Examples (authority):
670 $a Family life, 1948: $b **credit frame (Florence M. King, M.S.; Assistant Professor of Home Economics, University of Illinois)**

670 $a Rituals for sacred living. c1999: $b **t.p. (Jane Alexander) jkt. (freelance journalist & writer specializing in body, mind & spirit)**

670 $a LinkedIn web site, 11 Sept. 2013 $b **(Jane Alexander, journalist and author, Taunton; professional writer for the last twenty-five years; has worked as writer and editor for several newspapers and magazines; has written over twenty books on natural health and wellbeing; has also ghost-written four books; a graduate in English language and literature, and applied linguistics)**

670 $a E-mail from author, 11 Sept. 2013 $b (Jane Elizabeth Alexander, born 3 January 1960; writer/journalist; wrote "Kind regards" under pseudonym Liz Williams)

670 $a Experimental physical chemistry by Farrington Daniels . . . and J. Howard Mathews . . . and John Warren Williams . . . 1941: $b **t.p. (John Warren Williams)**

670 $a OCLC, June 7, 2011 $b **(hdg: Williams, John Warren, b. 1898)**

As we see from the above example, sources consulted are not limited to published reference sources. Direct communication with a person, such as a phone call or an e-mail, are also considered sources consulted, and are recorded in this element.

Catalogers Note (RDA 8.13) [MARC authority field 677]

This element is used to record any information the cataloger has (decisions made, instructions, etc.), which will be helpful to those using, revising, or creating authority data and authorized access points for the particular entity or entities with the same or similar names. This element is not an RDA core element, but it is considered an LC core (LC-PCC PS 8.13). Currently, this element is intended for catalogers and other information professionals who are using, maintaining, or creating authority data.

Examples:
677 $a **Non-Latin script references not evaluated.**

667 $a **Cannot identify with Stephen Austin of Hertford, printer who was active 1859-1869--cf. BBTI, July 28, 2003**

667 $a **Cannot identify with: Australia. Dept. of the Parliamentary Library. Parliamentary Research Service**

Putting it All Together

In a MARC 21 environment, data about a person, family, or corporate body are recorded in authority records. The record below illustrates all authority data provided in a MARC 21 authority record for the person best known as Steve Jobs. MARC authority records use fixed field 008, position 10 (labeled as "Rules" in OCLC fixed-field display), value "z" for "other," and the code "rda" in subfield $e (description conventions) of field 040 (cataloging source) to identify RDA as the set of rules used to establish the entity's preferred name and authorized access point, appearing in field 1XX of the authority record. Variant names of the person appear in MARC fields 400, while other various characteristics of the person are recorded in fields 37Xs and sources consulted and cataloger's notes are recorded in fields 67Xs.

Rec stat c	Entered 19870924	Replaced	20140627140454.0
Type z	Upd status a	Enc lvl n	Source
Roman	Ref status a	Mod rec	Name use a
Govt agn	Auth status a	Subj a	Subj use a
Series n	Auth/ref a	Geo subd n	Ser use b
Ser num n	Name a	Subdiv tp n	Rules **z**

010 n 87883336
040 DLC $b eng $e **rda** $c DLC $d DLC $d DGW-L $d DLC
046 $f 19550224 $g 20111005
100 1 Jobs, Steve, $d 1955-2011
370 San Francisco, Calif. $c U.S. $v Wikipedia, Oct. 6, 2011 $u http://en.wikipedia.org/wiki/Steve_jobs
373 Apple Computer, Inc. $2 naf
374 Inventor $a Entrepreneur $a Executive
375 male
400 1 Jobs, Steven Paul, $d 1955-2011
400 0 Jiabosi, $d 1955-2011
400 1 Jia, Bosi, $d 1955-2011
400 1 賈伯斯, $d 1955-2011
667 Non-Latin script references not evaluated
670 Steve Jobs, c1988: $b p. 8, etc. (Steven Paul Jobs, b. Feb. 24, 1955)
670 WW in Amer., 1986-87 $b (Jobs, Steven Paul, 1955-)
670 Washington Post, Oct. 6, 2011 $b (Steve Jobs dies; Apple co-founder was 56; Jobs died Wednesday (Oct. 5, 2011); an original thinker

who helped create the Macintosh, one of the world's most influential computers, Mr. Jobs also reinvented the portable music player with the iPod, launched the first successful legal method of selling music online with iTunes, reordered the cellphone market with the iPhone and jump-started the electronic-tablet market with the iPad)

670 Tu jie Jiabosi, 2011: $b t.p. (賈伯斯 = Jiabosi = Jia Bosi = Steve Jobs)

IDENTIFYING PERSONS

RDA Chapter 9 provides guidelines on identifying persons. Part of this task is to provide instructions on how to record information for all elements representing attributes or characteristics of the entity person. Similar to chapters covering works and expressions, in Chapter 9, once all guidelines for recording the various core or additional elements for a person are covered, guidelines are offered on the construction of authorized and variant access points to represent a person. Theoretically, the authorized access point of a person recorded as authority data may then be linked through various relationships to their associated works and expressions (mainly recorded as authority data) and to their respective manifestations and items (recorded in bibliographic records).

The guidelines RDA Chapter 9 covers are the selection of preferred name(s) for persons, recording preferred and variant names and elements representing various attributes, and constructing authorized access points and variant access point for persons. In addition to Chapter 9, RDA Appendix F provides guidelines for special types of names, and should also be consulted.

Any source can be used for taking a name or names of a person.

Similar to other entities, RDA has defined a number of elements representing attributes of a person. Some of these are identified as RDA core elements. In addition, LC-PCC policy statements may identify some elements as LC/NACO core, even if they are not RDA core. These may be required elements if a library is participating in the NACO program or using LC/NACO authority files and following their practices, which is the case for the majority of US library cataloging.

Core Elements

The following elements for persons are RDA core elements, and, therefore, should be recorded when they are applicable and easily ascertained:

Preferred name for the person
Title of the person
(indicating royalty, nobility, ecclesiastical rank or office; a term of address for a person of religious vocation)

Date of birth
Date of death
Other designation associated with the person
(for a Christian saint, a spirit, a person named in a sacred scripture or an apocryphal book, a fictitious or legendary person, or a real nonhuman entity)
Profession or occupation
(if the name is not indicative that it represents a person)
Identifier for the person

The following elements are required if differentiation is necessary among persons with the same or similar names:

Title of the person
(another term indicative of rank, honor, or office)
Fuller form of name
Profession or occupation
Period of activity of the person
Other designation associated with the person

These elements and the elements discussed under the general guidelines, such as scope of usage, date of usage, status of identification, undifferentiated name indicator, source consulted, and cataloger's note may also be included in descriptions of person.

NAME OF THE PERSON (RDA 9.2)

Core Element: *Preferred Name for the Person*

The name of the person is defined as any word, character, or group of words and/or characters by which a person is known. Among these known names, two types of names are identified: the preferred name for the person, and the variant name for the person.

Preferred Name for the Person (RDA 9.2.2)
Core Element
[MARC authority field 100]

Preferred name for the person is the name or form of names selected to identify the person. The preferred name for the person is used as the basis for the construction of the authorized access point for this person.

To determine the preferred name for a person, RDA 9.2.2.2 instructs that first, the preferred sources of information in resources associated with the person be consulted, based on the RDA 2.2.2 guidelines; second, statements appearing anywhere on the resources associated with the person being consulted; and third, other sources, including reference sources, be consulted.

When choosing the preferred name, choose the name by which the person is most commonly known, including his or her real name, a pseudonym, a title, a phrase, or any other appellation (RDA 9.2.2.3). This guideline works well for resources where the name by which a person is most commonly known matches the name appearing in the sources listed in RDA 9.2.2.2. There are occasions where these two are not necessarily the same, but, due to the principle of representation (RDA 0.4.3.4), the most commonly known name is chosen as the preferred name. For example, while a former US President's name may appear in many resources as "James Earl Carter," the name or form of the name by which he is more commonly known and which is selected as the preferred name is "Jimmy Carter."

When a person's name appears in different variations or forms, choose the preferred name, following the instructions in RDA 9.2.2.5:

- If there is variation in the fullness of the name, select the form that is most commonly found. In choosing between "C.S. Lewis" and "Clive Staples Lewis," C.S. Lewis is chosen as the most commonly found form of the name. The form not chosen as preferred will be recorded as a variant name.
- If the name appears in different languages, choose the preferred name from sources that correspond to most resources. For example, if a name appears in Russian and English, and most resources the person's name is associated with are in English, choose the preferred form, based on the English resources. Exceptions are described for names appearing in Greek, Latin, and/or the native languages of persons. The names in the other languages are recorded as variant names.
- If the name appears in a script that is not the preferred script of the cataloging agency, use a transliterated form of the name based on the preferred name of the agency's transliteration schema. This applies when, for example, the language of the preferred name of a person is Greek and the name appears in the script of the language as "Νίκος Καζαντζάκης," but the preferred script of an agency in the United States is not Greek. Therefore, in this case, the transliterated form "Nikos Kazantzakēs," following the *ALA-LC Romanization Tables: Transliteration Schemes for Non-Roman Scripts*, is chosen.
- If the preferred name appears in different spellings not resulting from different transliterations, choose the spelling appearing in the first resource

received. This, of course, may result in selecting the spelling that is not the most commonly found.

When a person is known by more than one name, RDA 9.2.2.6 instructs us to use the name that is "clearly" the most commonly known, that is, the name most frequently used in associated resources, most frequently appearing in reference sources, or the latest name. The following cases are considered expeditions to this instruction:

- The person changed his or her name. In this case, choose as the preferred name the latest name or form of the name.
- The person has more than one identity. In this case, apply the guidelines for choosing the preferred name for each identity. If the person has a real name and a pseudonym or stage name, and only uses the pseudonym as a creator or contributor, choose the pseudonym as the preferred name. The names for each identity that have not been chosen as preferred are recorded as variant names for that identity. Note that establishing different identities means that a person will have more than one authorized access point.

RECORDING A NAME CONTAINING ONE OR MORE SURNAMES

Once a preferred name has been chosen to represent the person, one has to record it in the form necessary to serve as the basis for the authorized access point. This means that one or more parts of the name may have to be transposed. To do so, one needs to determine the form of the preferred name, for example, whether it includes a surname (last name), whether it includes a compound surname (which appears as if two or more surnames have been combined into one surname), a hyphenated surname, a surname and prefix combination, etc.

One Surname (RDA 9.2.2.9)

For names containing one surname, record the surname as the first element of the name. Follow the surname by a comma and add the other parts of the name (such as first name, middle name, or middle initial). If the name consists of a surname only, then record the surname alone.

Examples:
Preferred name as found: Ryan Thomas Skinner

Recorded preferred name: **Skinner, Ryan Thomas**
MARC authority: 100 1 $a **Skinner, Ryan Thomas**

Preferred name as found: Jon M. Conrad
Recorded preferred name: **Conrad, Jon M.**
MARC authority: 100 1 $a **Conrad, Jon M.**

Preferred name as found: Keller
Recorded preferred name: **Keller**
MARC authority: 100 1 $a **Keller** $c (Translator)

If the preferred name appears with terms of honor or other terms of address (e.g., Mr., Mrs., Ms., Miss, etc.), ignore them unless the name consists of a surname only or it is a name for a married person identified by the spouse's name and the address (e.g., Mrs. Jeremiah Oakland).

Example:
Preferred name as found: Mrs. J.S. Adams
Recorded preferred name: **Adams, J. S., Mrs.**
MARC authority: 100 1 $a **Adams, J. S.**, $c **Mrs.,** $d 1845-1885

For a surname consisting of an initial letter, the preferred name is recorded under the initial letter. Other parts of the name follow it.

Example:
Preferred name as found: Amber K.
Recorded preferred name: **K, Amber**
MARC authority: 100 1 $a **K, Amber**, $d 1947-

When a name does not contain a surname, but one part of it is used to identify the person and functions as a surname, record this part as the first element of the preferred name. For example, the name of the American boxer commonly known as Muhammad Ali (Cassius Marcellus Clay) would be recorded with "Ali" as the first element, functioning as a surname.

Example:
Preferred name as found: Muhammad Ali
Recorded preferred name: **Ali, Muhammad**
MARC authority: 100 1 $a **Ali, Muhammad,** $d 1942-

Names that contain a term indicating relationship (e.g., Junior, Sr., III, the 2nd) fall under two categories: Portuguese names and all other names. Record the term indicating the relationship as part of the surname when recording a Portuguese name. Record the term indicating the relationship after the surname, following a comma, for names in all other languages.

Examples:

Preferred name as found:	John Lewis Smith, Jr.
Recorded preferred name:	**Smith, John Lewis, Jr.**
MARC authority:	100 1 $a **Smith, John Lewis**, $c **Jr.**
Preferred name as found:	Joao Elias Abdalla Filho [Portuguese name, Filho is "son"]
Recorded preferred name:	**Abdalla Filho, Joao Elias**
MARC authority:	100 1 $a **Abdalla Filho, Joao Elias**
Preferred name as found:	Daniel S. Bowling, III
Recorded preferred name:	**Bowling, Daniel S., III**
MARC authority:	100 1 $a **Bowling, Daniel S.,** $c **III**, $d 1955-

Compound Surnames (RDA 9.2.2.10)

A name consisting of two or more proper names separated by a space or hyphen is considered a compound surname. Treat the compound surname as one element of the name, and record it as the first element of the preferred name. Follow the guidelines of RDA 9.2.2.9 to record preferred names containing compound surnames. Exceptions to these general guidelines include the following:

- If the person has a preference regarding the element to be listed first, record the preferred element first.
- If the person's preference is not known, record the same name as found in reference sources in the language of the country of residence of the person.
- If the person's name is unknown and there is no established usage in reference sources of the person's language or in the person's country of residence, consult the *Names of Persons: National Usages for Entry in Catalogues.*[1]
- If none of the above applies, record the first part of the surname as the first element of the preferred name.

Examples:

Preferred name as found:	Iain Duncan Smith
Recorded preferred name:	**Duncan Smith, Iain**
MARC authority:	100 1 $a **Duncan Smith, Iain,** $d 1954-

Preferred name as found: Simon Baron-Cohen
Recorded preferred name: **Baron-Cohen, Simon**
MARC authority: 100 1 $a **Baron-Cohen, Simon**

Preferred name as found: José Luis Rodríguez Zapatero
Recorded preferred name: **Rodríguez Zapatero, José Luis**
MARC authority: 100 1 $a **Rodríguez Zapatero, José Luis,** $d 1960-

Surnames with Separately Written Prefixes (RDA 9.2.2.11)

Some names contain one or more prefixes. Treat them as instructed in RDA 9.2.2.10 for compound surnames by recording as the first element the part of the name that is listed first in the person's language or country of residence. RDA Appendix F lists the common practices of such names in several languages. Make sure to consult Appendix F when dealing with names that contain separately written prefixes that fall under the category of articles and prepositions. For some languages, what is recorded as the first element depends on whether the prefix or preposition is alone or combined with an article.

Examples:
Preferred name as found: Paul R. La Chance [English]
Recorded preferred name: **La Chance, Paul R.**
MARC authority: 100 1 $a **La Chance, Paul R.**

Preferred name as found: Johann Wolfgang von Goethe [German with preposition only]
Recorded preferred name: **Goethe, Johann Wolfgang von**
MARC authority: 100 1 **Goethe, Johann Wolfgang von,** $d 1749-1832

If the prefix does not fall under any of the above categories (article, preposition, or a combination of the two), record the prefix as the first element of the preferred name.

If the prefix or preposition is combined or hyphenated with the surname, treat them as one, and enter it as the first element of the preferred name.

Example:
Preferred name as found: Janet MacDonald
Recorded preferred name: **MacDonald, Janet**
MARC authority: 100 1 $a **MacDonald, Janet**, $d 1950-

RECORDING NAMES CONTAINING A TITLE OF NOBILITY (RDA 9.2.2.14)

A person having a title of nobility is typically known by two names: his or her personal name (which may consist of a first and last name), and his or her title of nobility. RDA 9.2.2.14 provides guidelines on the recording of names that include a title of nobility. In such cases, the general guidelines of RDA 8.25 apply. The guidelines instruct that the proper name (the surname in most cases) should be recorded as the first element, depending on the type of name, as described in previous sections.

If the person is identified by his or her title of nobility rather than his or her personal name, record as the first element of the preferred name the proper name of the title of nobility, following the given pattern:

> Proper name of nobility, personal name in direct order, term of rank.
> For example,
> (1) Byron [proper name of nobility]
> (2) George Gordon Byron [personal name in direct order]
> (3) Baron (term of rank]
> à Byron, George Gordon Byron, Baron.

It should be noted that not all British titles are titles of nobility. Some of these titles are titles of honor, and, therefore, they are not treated the same way as the titles of nobility. In the case of titles of honor, select the first element of the preferred name based on the person's personal (family) name.

Examples:

Preferred name as found:	Christopher Bromhead Birdwood, 2nd Baron Birdwood
Recorded preferred name:	**Birdwood, Christopher Bromhead Birdwood, Baron**
MARC authority:	100 1 $a **Birdwood, Christopher Bromhead Birdwood,** $c Baron, $d 1899-1962
Preferred name as found:	Richard Briginshaw [also has a title of nobility Richard William Briginshaw, Baron Briginshaw but is commonly known by his personal name;]
Recorded preferred name:	**Briginshaw, Richard**
MARC authority:	100 1 $a **Briginshaw, Richard**
Preferred name as found:	Giovanni Antonio Petrucci conte di Policastro

Recorded preferred name:	**Policastro, Giovanni Antonio Petrucci, conte di**
MARC authority:	100 1 $a **Policastro, Giovanni Antonio Petrucci,** $c **conte di**, $d 1456-1486

RECORDING NAMES WITH NO SURNAME OR TITLE OF NOBILITY (RDA 9.2.2.14)

Not all names include a surname. These would be names consisting of forename (first name or given name), initials, letters, numerals, or phrases. In these cases, use the general guidelines in RDA 8.5, and follow RDA 9.2.2.9.2 to record as the first element the name under which the person is listed in reference sources. If the name includes a place, occupation, or other characteristic, include these as integral parts of the name.

Examples:

Preferred name as found:	Alexander de Villa Dei [forename with associated place of origin]
Recorded preferred name:	**Alexander, de Villa Dei**
MARC authority:	100 0 $a **Alexander**, $c **de Villa Dei**
Preferred name as found:	Leonardo da Vinci [forename with associated place of origin]
Recorded preferred name:	**Leonardo, da Vinci**
MARC authority:	100 0 $a **Leonardo**, $c **da Vinci**, $d 1452-1519
Preferred name as found:	Madonna [known by forename only]
Recorded preferred name:	**Madonna**
MARC authority:	100 0 $a **Madonna**, $d 1958-
Preferred name as found:	Kermit the Frog
Recorded preferred name:	**Kermit, the Frog**
MARC authority:	100 0 $a **Kermit**, $c **the Frog**

RECORDING NAMES CONSISTING OF INITIALS, OR SEPARATE LETTERS, OR NUMERALS (RDA 9.2.2.21)

When a person uses initials, letters, or numerals as the name by which they are identified, enter the initials, letters, or numerals in direct order as the preferred name for the person.

Examples:

Preferred name as found:	A.J.C.D. [poet signing with initials]
Recorded preferred name:	**A. J. C. D.**
MARC authority:	100 1 $a **A. J. C. D.,** $d 1848-1932

RECORDING NAMES CONSISTING OF A PHRASE

Sometimes, a person uses a phrase as his or her name. If this is the appellation by which the person is most commonly known, then this is chosen as the preferred name for the person. If the phrase does not include a forename, record it in direct order. The phrase can be an address followed by a forename, a phrase containing the name of another person, or a characterizing word or phrase.

Preferred name as found:	Miss Piggy
Recorded preferred name:	**Miss Piggy**
MARC authority:	100 0 $a **Miss Piggy**
Preferred name as found:	Uncle Ben
Recorded preferred name:	**Ben, Uncle**
MARC authority:	100 0 $a **Ben**, $c **Uncle**
Preferred name as found:	Amazing Delores [vocalist]
Recorded preferred name:	**Amazing Delores**
MARC authority:	100 0 **Amazing Delores**

If the name of the person includes a reference to another of the person's works, consider the phrase as the preferred name for the person and record it in direct order.

Preferred name as found:	Author of "A bride from the Rhineland"
Recorded preferred name:	**Author of A bride from the Rhineland**
MARC authority:	100 0 $a **Author of A bride from the Rhineland**

Variant Name for the Person (RDA 9.2.3)

Once a name or form of a name is chosen as the preferred name representing the person, the other names or forms of the name are considered variant names for the person. Recording variant names follows the same guidelines as for preferred names.

Variant name for a person is not an RDA core element, which means that it is up to the cataloger's judgment to decide whether to record the variant name or names for the person. Variant names are typically an important element to include for users. Although, in current practice, access points recorded in bibliographic records include the authorized access point representing a person, users are not always familiar with that name or the form in which it is presented. Allowing the user to search by any name or form of a name, and enabling the linking of these variant names to the preferred access point of the name, is very helpful to users. Variant names can be other names or forms of names by which a person is known, names or forms of names found in reference sources, or forms of names that result from different transliterations.

Variant names can be the real names of persons if pseudonyms or other names are used as the preferred names for the persons; they can also be secular names of persons of religious vocation using their religious names. In cases in which persons change names, the earlier and the later names of the persons, and the alternative linguistic forms of the names, are used as variant names.

Examples:

Preferred name:	Cruise, Tom
Variant name:	**Mapother, Thomas Cruise**, 1962-
MARC authority:	400 1 $a **Mapother, Thomas Cruise,** $d 1962-
Preferred name:	Confucius
Variant name:	**孔夫子**
MARC authority:	400 0 $a **孔夫子**
	400 0 $a K'oeng Foe-tse
	400 0 $a Kung-foo-tsze
	400 0 $a Kung-Kew
Preferred name:	Markey, Karen
Variant name:	**Drabenstott, Karen Markey** [earlier name]
MARC authority:	400 1 $a **Drabenstott, Karen Markey** $w nne
Preferred name:	Benedict XVI, Pope, 1927-
Variant name:	**Ratzinger, Joseph, 1927-**
MARC authority:	400 1 $a **Ratzinger, Joseph**, $d **1927-**

OTHER IDENTIFYING ATTRIBUTES FOR PERSON

RDA 9.2 provides guidelines on choosing and recording the preferred name for the person, which is used to form the basis of the authorized access point representing the person. Often, additional elements are necessary for identification and differentiation from other persons with the same or similar names. Such additional attributes are entered in the elements covered in RDA 9.3–9.18. A brief discussion of the differentiating attributes for the name of a person follows. Some of these elements are core, when it is necessary to identify or differentiate the person represented. Also, a number of these elements may be recorded as separate elements or as part of the authorized access point for the person.

Date Associated with the Person (RDA 9.3)
Core Element: *Date of birth, Date of death*
[MARC authority field 100 subfield $d, 046]

This element is used to record important dates associated with a person. It is not to be used for dates associated with the preferred access point (e.g., dates the name is valid). The two dates that are most commonly recorded, and are RDA core elements, are the dates of birth and death of the person. This means that if these dates are known, they must be recorded. Dates of birth are not necessarily part of the authorized access point, although they are one of the most commonly used elements for identification and differentiation among persons with the same or similar names. Dates associated with the person may be recorded as separate elements or as parts of the authorized access point for the person.

RDA 9.3.1.3 instructs us to record the dates according to the calendar of choice of each cataloging agency. Details in the Christian calendar are provided in RDA Appendix H. LC-PCC PS 9.3.1.3 states that the LC-PCC practice is to record dates in this element using the Gregorian calendar.

In addition to the year, the RDA optional addition allows the inclusion of more details, such as month and day, using the pattern [year] [month] [day], using the language of the cataloging agency to record the month. If the date is uncertain between two years, use the pattern "[year] or [year]." If the year is estimated, record it as "approximately [year]." Probable dates are recorded with the addition of a question mark, as "[year]?" For a range of years, record "[year]-[year]," and, for a range of centuries, use the form "[century]-[century]." RDA examples in 9.3 follow these patterns.

In a MARC authority structure, the date associated with the person is recorded in field 046 Special Coded Dates, which requires the recording of dates in a coded format, and field 100, when the date is part of the authorized access point. MARC documentation recommends the use of ISO 8601 *Representations of Dates and Times* to record dates and times in the pattern yyyy, yyyy-mm, or yyyymmdd in field 046. If another standard is used, the standard should be indicated in subfield $2.

Because RDA allows for questionable, approximate, and other dates that require different formatting, LC has developed a standard to accommodate this need, the Extended Date/Time Format (EDTF). Table 8.1 shows the LC-PCC PS 9.3.1.3 recommendations for the formatting of the optional addition and examples illustrating the different options using RDA formatting for regular dates and time recorded in field 100, and coded dates and time both in ISO 8601 and EDTF for use in field 046:

Table 8.1 RDA dates in ISO 8601 Date Scheme (No Need to Provide a source in $2)

Category	*RDA Presentation*	*ISO 8601 Coding in 046*
Single year:	1964	1964
Year/Month/Day:	1964 June 27	19640627
Early AD date:	65 AD	0065
BC date:	361 BC	-0360 (note there is a difference of one because the B.C. system has no year zero)
Century	20th century	19

RDA Dates in EDTF Date Scheme (provide "edtf" in 046 $2)

Category	*RDA Presentation*	*EDTF Coding in 046*
Probable date:	1816?	1816?
Approximate date:	Approximately 931	0931~
Known to be one of two years:	1666 or 1667	[1666,1667]

Date of Birth (RDA 9.3.2)
Core Element
[MARC authority field 100 subfield $d, 046 subfield $f]

Date of birth refers to the year a person was born. Sometimes, a more detailed date may be necessary for distinguishing persons with the same name and year of birth. Record the date of birth according to the general guidelines described above in the section on date associated with the person. Date of birth is core.

Examples:

Date of birth:	**1970**
MARC authority:	046 $f **19701120**
	100 1 $a Hall, Kevin, $d **1970-**
	670 Email from author, Apr. 7, 2014 $b (Kevin Dennis Hall; born Nov. 20, 1970)
Date of birth:	**1857**
MARC authority:	046 $f **1857** $g 1941~ $2 edtf

	100 1 $a Aasen, Oline, $d **1857**-approximately 1941 670 Dear Mama, c1993: $b p. 53 (Oline Aasen; b. June 15, 1857; d. about 1941 during German occupation of Norway)
Date of birth:	**approximately 1952-**
MARC authority:	046 $f **1952~** $2 edtf 100 1 $a Abbakar, Mahamat Hassan, $d **approximately 1952-**
Date of birth:	**1853 or 1854**
MARC authority:	046 $f **[1853,1854]** $g [1900,1901] $2 edtf 100 1 $a Ainhorn, Efrayim Tsevi, $d **1853 or 1854**-1900 or 1901
Date of birth:	**1900**
MARC authority:	046 $f **19000128** $g 19760824 100 1 $a Head, Michael, $d **1900**-1976 670 His Three hill songs, c1976: $b t.p. (Michael Head) cover p. 2 (Michael Dewar Head; b. Eastbourne, 1/28/1900; d. Capetown, South Africa, 8/24/76)
Date of birth:	**1956 November**
MARC authority:	046 $f **1956-11** 100 1 $a He, Ping, $d **1956 November-**
Date of birth:	1520?-
MARC authority:	046 $f **1520?** $2 edtf 100 1 $a Aiguino, Illuminato, $d **1520?-**

Date of Death (RDA 9.3.3)
Core Element
[MARC authority field 100 subfield $d, 046 subfield $g]

Date of death refers to the year a person died. Sometimes, a more detailed date may be necessary for distinguishing one person from another with the same name and year of death. Record the date of death according to the general guidelines described above in the section for date associated with the person. Date of death is core.

Examples:

Date of death: **approximately 1528**

MARC authority: 046 $f 1475~ $g **1528~** $2 edtf
100 1 $a Beer, Jan de, $d approximately 1475-**approximately 1528**

Date of death: **1956**
MARC authority: 046 $f 1871 $g **1956**
100 1 $a Heise, Robert Carl Wilhelm, $d 1871-**1956**

Date of death: **-1519 or 1520**
MARC authority: 046 $g **[1519,1520]** $2 edtf
100 1 $a A'raj, Muḥammad ibn 'Abd al-Wahhāb, $d **-1519 or 1520**

[*note in this example, there is no date of birth]*

Date of death: **1591**
MARC authority: 046 $f 1520~ $g **1591** $2 edtf
100 1 $a Brudieu, Joan, $d approximately 1520-**1591**

Date of death: **1594 or 1595**
MARC authority: 046 $f [1520,1521] $g **[1594,1595]** $2 edtf
100 0 $a Ratnāvalī, $d 1520 or 1521-**1594 or 1595**

Date of Activity of the Person (RDA 9.3.4) [MARC authority field 100 subfield $d, 046 subfields $s, $t]

Date of activity is another date recorded in this element. Date of activity can be a single date or a range of dates, and represents the period during which the person was active. Date of activity of the person is core if it is necessary to identify or differentiate the person from others with the same or similar names.

Examples:
Date of activity: active **approximately 1315**
MARC authority: 046 $s **1315~** $2 edtf
100 1 $a Abarqūhī, Shams al-Dīn Ibrāhīm, $d **active approximately 1315**
670 Allgemeines Künstler-Lexikon, 1992 $b (Beer, Jan de; b. ca. 1475; d. ca. 1528; Flemish painter, draughtsman)

Date of activity: **active 8th century-9th century**
MARC authority: 046 $s **07** $t **08**

100 0 $a Daosui, $d **active 8th century-9th century**
670 Chung-kuo jen ming ta tz'u tien, $b p. 1338 (Tao-sui; active around 785-807)

Date of activity: **active 1952-2006**
MARC authority: 046 $s **1952** $t **2006**
100 1 $a Green, Karen, $d **active 1952-2006**
670 Internet movie database WWW site, January 17, 2013 $b (Karen Green; actress; variant name: Karen Greene; cast member in films and television programs between 1952-2006)

Putting it All Together: Date Associated with the Person

Since RDA allows the recording of several dates associated with the person, let us summarize them with the following example.

046 $f **19111025** $g **19830408** $s **1952** $t **1982**

These dates are associated with a person who was born on October 25, 1911, and died on April 8, 1983. This person was active in his or her field between 1952 and 1982.

Title of the Person (RDA 9.4)
Core Element: *see conditions below*
[MARC authority field 100 subfield $c, 368 subfield $d]

Excluding terms of address that indicate gender or marital status, this element is used to record a word or a phrase indicating royalty, nobility, rank office, honor, or any other title. Title of the person is core if it indicates royalty, nobility, or ecclesiastical rank or office, or a term of address for a person of religious vocation. All other titles are core only when it is necessary to distinguish a person from another person with the same or a similar name. The title of the person can be recorded as a separate element or as part of the authorized access point representing the person. When a person has two titles, choose the highest title to add to the preferred name of the person.

Titles of Royalty (RDA 9.4.1.4)

Most royal persons are known by their first name and not by a surname. Therefore, recording their preferred names will most likely fall under the guidelines in RDA 9.2.2.20. The title is recorded the way it appears in reference sources, including the state or the people that is part of the title (e.g., King of England), in the language of the cataloging agency. LC-PCC PS 9.4.1.4 states that LC practice is to record both the title and state in English.

Examples:

Title of the person:	**King of England**
MARC authority:	046 $g 0955 100 0 $a Eadred, $c **King of England**, $d -955 368 $d **King of England**
Title of the person:	**Queen of Portugal**
MARC authority:	046 $f 17341217 $g 18160520 100 0 $a Maria $b I, $c **Queen of Portugal**, $d 1734-1816 368 $d **Queen of Portugal**
Title of the person:	**King of Thailand**
MARC authority:	046 $f 19271205 100 0 $a Bhumibol Adulyadej, $c **King of Thailand**, $d 1927- 368 $d **King of Thailand**

Consorts of Royals Persons (RDA 9.4.1.5)

To record the element consorts of royals, enter the appropriate title, the term "consort of," and the name of the royal. A consort is typically a wife, husband, or companion, in particular, the spouse of a reigning monarch.

Examples:

Title of the person:	**Queen, consort of Richard I, King of England**
MARC authority:	046 $f 1163~ $g 1230~ $2 edtf 100 0 $a Berengaria, $c **Queen, consort of Richard I, King of England**, $d approximately 1163-approximately 1230
Title of the person:	**Grand Duchess, consort of Dmitrii Ivanovich, Grand Duke of Vladimir and Moscow**
MARC authority:	046 $f [1352,1353] $g 14070607 $2 edtf 100 0 $a Evdokii͡a, $c **Grand Duchess, consort of Dmitrii Ivanovich, Grand Duke of Vladimir and Moscow**, $d 1352 or 1353-1407

Titles of Nobility (RDA 9.4.1.5)

If the title of a noble person was not recorded as the first element in the preferred name of the person (RDA 9.2.2.14), record the title of nobility in the language it was conferred (note: this is not in the language of the cataloging agency, as with the previous titles). Exceptions occur when a person with a title of nobility is best known by a family name (first element of his or her name is the surname). If the person is using his or her surname but is also known by the title of nobility, the guidelines instruct us to use the surname as the basis for the preferred name and to add the title of nobility in the authorized access point.

Examples:

Title of the person:	**Baron**
MARC authority:	100 1 $a Adrian, Edgar Douglas Adrian, $c **Baron**, $d 1889-1977 368 $d **Baron**
Title of the person:	**Baron**
MARC authority:	100 1 $a Byron, George Gordon Byron, $c **Baron**, $d 1788-1824 368 $d **Baron**
Title of the person:	**Earl of Cambridge**
MARC authority:	100 0 $a Richard, $c **Earl of Cambridge**, $d approximately 1376-1415 368 $d **Earl of Cambridge**
Title of the person:	**gróf**
MARC authority:	100 1 $a Esterházy, János, $c **gróf**, $d 1864-1905 368 $d **gróf**

Popes (RDA 9.4.1.6)

The term "Pope" is added as the title of the person for those who become a pope. The element can be recorded separately and also as part of the authorized access point.

Examples:

Title of person:	**Pope**
MARC authority:	100 0 $a Constantine, $c **Pope**, $d -715 368 $d **Pope**

Title of person: **Antipope**
MARC authority: 100 0 $a John $b XXIII, $c **Antipope**, $d 1370?-1419
368 $d **Antipope**

Bishops, etc. (RDA 9.4.1.7)

For ecclesiastical officials whose preferred names do not include surnames, record the highest titles acquired. As a core element, this information may be recorded as a separate element or as part of the authorized access point.

Title of person: **Bishop of Angers**
MARC authority: 100 0 $a Hubert, $c **Bishop of Angers**, $d approximately 980-1047
368 $d **Bishop of Angers**

Title of person: **Archbishop of Thessalonikē**
MARC authority: 100 0 $a Basilius Achridenus, $c **Archbishop of Thessalonikē**, $d - approximately 1169
368 $d **Archbishop of Thessalonikē**

Title of person: **Patriarch of Constantinople**
MARC authority: 100 0 $a Athanasios $b I, $c **Patriarch of Constantinople**, $d approximately 1230-approximately 1323
368 $d **Patriarch of Constantinople**

Title of person: **Cardinal**
MARC authority: 100 0 $a Bertrand de Deux, $c **Cardinal**, $d -1355
368 $d **Cardinal**

For a person whose preferred name includes a surname, RDA 9.4.1.7 instructs us to record the title in a separate element; however, this information is not included as part of the authorized name for the person.

Example:
Title of person: **Bishop of London**
MARC authority: 100 1 $a Fitzneale, Richard, $d approximately 1130-1198
400 0 $a Richard, $c Bishop of London, $d approximately 1130-1198
368 $d **Bishop of London** $s 1189 $t 1198

Fuller form of the Name (RDA 9.5)
Core Element: *for distinction*
[MARC authority field 100 subfield $q, 378 subfield $q]

A fuller form of a name is always an expansion of a name and not a different version of the name. Often, when the name or form of name chosen as the preferred name for a person includes initials or an abbreviated name, the fuller form of that part of the name (initials or abbreviation) is recorded in this element. The element can be recorded separately or as part of the authorized access point for the name. This element is core when it is necessary to differentiate between persons with the same or similar names. In such a case, this element is recorded as part of the authorized access point (MARC authority field 100). When it is not necessary for differentiation, it is recorded as a separate element (MARC authority field 378).

Fuller form of name:	**Karl Theodor Paul Polykarpos**
MARC authority:	100 1 $a Axenfeld, Th. $q **(Theodor)**, $d 1867-1930 378 $q **Karl Theodor Paul Polykarpos**

Fuller form of name:	**Johannes Ludwig Chrysostomus**
MARC authority:	100 1 $a Abineno, J. L. Ch. $q (**Johannes Ludwig Chrysostomus**), $d 1917- 378 $q **Johannes Ludwig Chrysostomus**

Fuller form of name:	**James Franklin**
MARC authority:	100 1 $a Bethune-Baker, J. F. $q (**James Franklin**), $d 1861- 378 $q **James Franklin**

In the first example, "Th." is an abbreviation of "Theodor," which is expanded in the fuller form of a name element. If "Theo" was chosen as the form of the name used for the preferred name, it would not be considered an abbreviation of "Theodor," but rather as a variant form of the name. Similarly, "Chris" is considered a variant form of "Christine" and "Jon" a variant form of "Jonathan," with neither considered an abbreviated form of either name.

Note that the fuller form of a name is enclosed in parentheses when it is part of the authorized access point for the name, following the preferred name after the addition of a comma.

Other Designation Associated with the Person (RDA 9.6)
Core Element: *for Christian saints and spirits*
[MARC authority field 368 subfield $c]

In addition to the more specific designations covered above, RDA 9.10 allows the recording of a broader category of designations associated with the person to be recorded as a separate element or as part of the authorized access point of the name. These designations include saints, spirits, persons named in sacred works, fictitious and legendary persons, and other designations, including designations indicating nonhuman entities. Only the subcategories of Christian saints and spirits are considered core, and, therefore, are also recorded in the authorized form of the name.

Other designation: **Spirit**
MARC authority: 100 0 $a Hilarion $c (**Spirit**)
368 $c **Spirit**

Other designation: **Spirit**
MARC authority: 100 1 $a Hitler, Adolf, $d 1889-1945 $c (**Spirit**)
368 $c **Spirit**

Other designation: **Saint**
MARC authority: 100 0 $a Kyriaki, $c **Saint**, $d active 3rd century
368 $c **Saint**

Other designation: **Fictitious character**
MARC authority: 100 0 $a Hulk $c (**Fictitious character**)
368 $c **Fictitious character**

Other designation: **Fictitious character**
MARC authority: 100 1 $a Simpson, Bart $c (**Fictitious character**)
368 $c **Fictitious character**

Other designation: **Fictitious character**
MARC authority: 100 0 $a Thomas, $c the Tank Engine (**Fictitious character**)
368 $c **Fictitious character**

Of the categories included under RDA 9.6 guidelines, spirits and nonhuman entities have generated discussions as to whether they would be appropriate to use as creators, contributors, or collaborators of works and expressions. For spirits, the content of the resource associated with them is often communicated via another person. For example, the spirit of Princess Diana is considered the author of a work communicated through Velera Kurleto or Christine

Toomey. In the case of other nonhuman entities, RDA allows their association with a resource to be that of a creator or cocreator of a work or collaborator of an expression of a work. Miss Piggy, a fictitious character from Jim Hensen's *Muppets*, has appeared as the author of works.

Examples:

Other designation: **Spirit**
MARC authority: 100 0 $a Diana, $c Princess of Wales, $d 1961-1997 $c (**Spirit**)
368 $c **Spirits** $2 lcsh

Other designation: **Fictitious character**
MARC authority: 368 $c **Fictitious characters** $c **Muppets (Fictitious characters)** $c **Swine** $2 lcsh
368 $c Pigs $2 lcac
375 $a female

Other designation: **Dogs**
MARC authority: 100 0 $a Rin-Tin-Tin $c (**Dog**)
368 $c **Dogs** $c **German shepherd dog** $2 lcsh

Gender (RDA 9.7) [MARC authority field 375]

A term for the gender of a person is recorded in this element. RDA 9.7 lists "male," "female," and "not known" as possible terms for this element, but other terms may also be used. This element, although not core, can be useful for identification or for finding associated resources by gender, for example, female actresses.

Examples:

Gender: **female**
MARC authority: 100 1 $a Bangerter, Geraldine Hamblin, $d 1924-
375 $a **female**

Gender: **male**
MARC authority: 100 1 $a Sansome, F. W. $q (Frederick Whalley), $d 1902-
375 $a **male**

Gender: **transgender**, **female, male**
MARC authority: 100 1 $a Arquette, Alexis
375 $a **Transgender people** $2 lcsh

375 $a **female** $s 2006
375 $a **male** $s 1969 $t 2006
400 1 $a Arquette, Robert

In the last example above, notice that the person was identified as male from birth until 2006 and as female since 2006. RDA does not specify the inclusion of dates for this element but such practice may provide useful information.

PLACE ASSOCIATED WITH THE PERSON

A number of different places can be associated with a person. When recording a place associated with a person, LC-PCC/NACO policy is to use the authorized access point of the place name. Therefore, the cataloger should be using the form that appears in the 151 MARC authority field for the name of a place in the name authority file, in which case the code "naf" should be recorded as the source for the name in MARC subfield $2. It is also possible to use LCSH for the place name (source should be recorded as $2 lcsh). If there is no authorized name for the place, establish one based on RDA chapter guidelines, without recording a source in subfield $2.

Place of Birth (RDA 9.8) [MARC authority 370 subfield $a]

Record the place of birth of the person if it is known.

Examples:

Place of birth:	**Los Angeles (Calif.)**
MARC authority:	370 $a **Los Angeles (Calif.)**
Place of birth:	**Malvern, Ark.**
MARC authority:	370 $a **Malvern, Ark.**

Place of Death (RDA 9.9) [MARC authority 370 subfield $b]

Record the place of death of the person if it is known.

Examples:

Place of death:	**Alhambra (Calif.)**
MARC authority:	370 $a Germany $b **Alhambra (Calif.)** $e Dawson (Yukon) $e Downey (Calif.) $2 naf

Place of death: **Willard (Utah)**
MARC authority: 370 $a Deerfield (N.H.) $b **Willard (Utah)** $2 naf

Country Associated with the Person (RDA 9.10) [MARC authority 370 subfield $c]

Record the country associated with a person, if known. This element is considered especially useful when a person is associated with a country that is not the place of his or her birth or death.

Country associated with person: **Nigeria**
MARC authority: 370 $c **Nigeria**

Country associated with person: **United States**
MARC authority: 370 $a Los Angeles (Calif.) $c **United States**

Country associated with person: **India**
MARC authority: 370 $c **India** $f Sivakasi, India

Place of Residence, etc. (RDA 9.11) [MARC authority 370 subfield $e]

Record the place of residence, if it is known, or an associated place, other than the place of birth or death. In a MARC authority structure, record the place of residence, if it is certain, in field 370, subfield $e. If the place of residence is uncertain, record it in subfield $f.

Place of residence, etc.: **Toronto, Ont.**
MARC authority: 370 $c England $e **Toronto, Ont.**

Place of residence, etc.: **St. John's (N.L.)**
MARC authority: 370 $e **St. John's (N.L.)**

Putting it All Together: Place Associated with a Person

There are different places associated with a person that can be provided using RDA guidelines. The following example and explanation provides an overview for place associated with the person:

Place of birth: Berclair (Miss.)
Place of death: Las Vegas (Nev.)
Country associated with the person: United States
Place of residence, etc.: Memphis (Tenn.)

Place of residence, etc.: Itta Bena (Miss.)
Place of residence, etc.: Indianola (Miss.)
MARC 21: 370 $a Berclair (Miss.) $b Las Vegas (Nev.) $c United States $f Itta Bena (Miss.) $f Indianola (Miss.) $2 naf

In the above example, the person was born in Berclair, Mississippi, between Itta Bena and Indianola, Mississippi; resided in Memphis, Tennessee, for a while but moved around; died in Las Vegas, Nevada. All associated places are in the United States.

Address of the Person (RDA 9.12) [MARC authority 371]

Any address associated with a person, including street address, e-mail address, or URL of a web site, is recorded in this element.

Example:
Address of the person: **Graceland, 3764 Elvis Presley Boulevard (Highway 51 South) Memphis, Tenn., 38116**
MARC authority: 371 $a **Graceland, 3764 Elvis Presley Boulevard (Highway 51 South)** $b **Memphis** $c **Tenn.** $e **38116**

Affiliation (RDA 9.13) [MARC authority 373]

The association between a person and an organization through employment, membership, cultural identity, etc., is recorded in the affiliation element. The form of the name of the organization recorded in the affiliation element should be in the preferred form of the name. Affiliation can be recorded as a separate element or as part of the access point.

Affiliation: **American Hospital Association**
MARC authority: 373 $a **American Hospital Association** $2 naf $t 1981
374 $a Librarians $2 lcsh

Affiliation: **St. Louis University. Department of Theology**
MARC authority: 373 $a **St. Louis University. Department of Theology** $2 naf
374 $a Church historians $2 lcsh

If the name of the affiliated organization was taken from the LC/NACO Name Authority File (naf), enter "naf" in MARC authority field 373, subfield 2, to indicate the source of the term.

Language of the Person (RDA 9.14) [MARC authority 377]

Although RDA instructs us to record in this element the language in which the person is writing for publication, in practice, the element is used to record the language in which a person creates or contributes to works and expressions. It is not necessarily the languages the person knows and speaks that are recorded, but the languages associated with works and expressions associated with the person.

Examples:

Language of the person: **English**
MARC authority: 377 $a **eng**

Language of the person: **Russian**
MARC authority: 377 $a **rus**

Language of the person: **Chinese**
MARC authority: 377 $a **chi**

It is typical practice to record the language code from the *MARC Code List for Languages* in MARC authority field 377, rather than the language term. This information is very useful for users who would like to find, for example, poets who wrote in Chinese.

Field of Activity of the Person (RDA 9.15) [MARC authority 372]

The field of activity of the person is defined as the field of endeavor, expertise, etc., in which a person is or was engaged. Best practice is to record a term from a controlled vocabulary, which, in LC-PCC's practice, is to use an LCSH term for the field of activity. In a MARC authority structure, add the source code for the vocabulary in subfield $2 of field 372.

Examples:

Field of activity: **Church history—Modern period, 1500-**
MARC authority: 372 $a **Church history—Modern period, 1500-** $2 lcsh
Field of activity: **Portuguese language**
Linguistics

MARC authority: 372 $a **Portuguese language** $a **Linguistics** $2 lcsh
Field of activity: **Travel photography**
MARC authority: 372 $a **Travel photography** $2 lcsh

Profession or Occupation (RDA 9.16)
Core Element: *see conditions below*
[MARC authority 374]

The profession or occupation of a person, defined as a person's vocation or avocation, is considered a core element when a person's name or appellation does not convey the idea that the subject in question is a person. In all other cases, the element is core when it is necessary to distinguish a person among others with the same or similar names. In general, it is a good practice to include this element and to use a controlled vocabulary as the source for the term, to allow for consistency in the user's ability to search by profession or occupation (for example, all poets writing in French).

Examples:
Profession or occupation: **Premiers (Canada)**
MARC authority: 374 **Premiers (Canada)** $2 lcsh

Profession or occupation: **Librarians**
MARC authority: 374 **Librarians** $2 lcsh

Profession or occupation: **Church historians**
MARC authority: 374 **Church historians** $2 lcsh

Profession or occupation: **Writer of hymns**
MARC authority: 374 **Writer of hymns**

Profession or occupation: **Booksellers and bookselling**
Type designers
Publishers and publishing
Bookbinders
MARC authority: 374 **Booksellers and bookselling** $a **Type designers** $a **Publishers and publishing** $a **Bookbinders** $2 lcsh

Putting it All Together: Field of Activity, Profession or Occupation, and Affiliation

Field of activity and profession or occupation are two elements that are interrelated. Field of activity describes what a person does, using abstract nouns or noun phrases, such as education or local history. Occupation or profession typically is a term describing a class of persons, such as teachers or historians. These two elements have the potential to allow for rich searches, separately or in combination with other elements. In the example below, we see an individual active in two fields, education (from 1958 until 1961) and real property: acting as a teacher and acting as a real-estate agent.

Field of activity:	Education; Real property
MARC authority:	372 $a Education $s 1958 $t 1961 $2 lcsh
	372 $a Real property $2 lcsh
Profession or occupation:	Teachers; Real estate agents
MARC authority:	374 $a Teachers $s 1958 $t 1961 $2 lcsh
	374 $a Real estate agents $2 lcsh

Often, a link is also made between the field, occupation, and affiliation. In the first example below, we see that this person served as a teacher at Santa Ana College, Butte Community College, and Bear River High School, teaching English as a second language:

Field of activity:	372 $a English as a second language $a Teaching
Affiliation:	373 $a Santa Ana College $a Butte Community College $a Bear River High School (Grass Valley, Calif.)
Profession or occupation:	374 $a Author $a Teacher

The second example shows a historian in the Abbots Langley Local History Society active in the field of local history:

Field of activity:	372 $a Local history $2 lcsh
Affiliation:	373 $a Abbots Langley Local History Society $2 naf
Profession or occupation:	374 $a Historians $2 lcsh

Biographical Information (RDA 9.17) [MARC authority 678]

A brief description of a person's life or history is recorded in the biographical information element. We must take care about potentially including private information about the person. Whenever possible, include information that relates to other identifying elements recorded about the person. Cite the source of information as instructed in RDA 8.12.1.3.

In a MARC authority structure, biographical information can be recorded in field 678, *biographical or historical data*, but most often we see it included in field 670, *source data found*, where in subfield $b one can include the data found:

678 0 $a **Early American cameraman and director, working primarily for the American Mutoscope and Biograph Company. He had a hand in creating more than 400 short subjects for AM&B. Several of his subjects stand out in their innovative use of camerawork, superimpositions, time-lapse photography and other effects then new to film-making. His 1902 film, Star Theatre, was named to the National Film Registry in 2002. Some sources indicate that his death date is unknown.**
670 $a **Russkiĭ biograficheskiĭ slovar', 1998-: $b (Anna Leopol'dovna, daughter of Russian princess Ekaterina Ioannovna and Grand Duke of Mecklenburg-Schwerin Karl; at birth was given name Elisabeth Katharina Christine von Mecklenburg-Schwerin; in 1733 was converted to Russian Orthodox religion and given name Anna Leopol'dovna, sometimes also called as Anna Karlovna, was princess regent of Russia from November 9, 1740 to November 25, 1741).**

Identifier for the Person (RDA 9.18)
Core Element
[MARC authority field 010, 026, 035]

A core element, identifier for the person is a string of characters that is uniquely associated with a person or a surrogate representation or description of a person (such as an authority record). As a unique string of characters, this element differentiates the person from other persons. Whenever possible, include the context of the identifier, that is, the organization creating and maintaining the identifiers. A person may be associated with more than one identifier, as the first example below illustrates; in this case, some of the identifiers form various authority records created by different organizations for Homer.

Examples:
Identifier for the person: **VIAF ID: 224924963**
BNF - 11907688
NSK-000016617

	PERSEUS-urn:cite:perseus:author.745.1 **LAC-0014F1326E** **DNB-11855333X**
Identifier for the person:	Library of Congress control number **n96107790**
MARC authority:	010 $a n **96107790**

Putting it All Together: Identifying Persons

As a conclusion on the elements identifying a person, the following is an example that covers all applicable elements in one record structure using MARC authority format.

RDA Element	*MARC Authority*
Identifier for the person:	010 n 78079487 $z sh 90005919
Dates associated with the person:	046 $f 19350108 $g 19770816
	053 0 ML420.P96 $c Biography
Preferred name (authorized AP):	100 1 Presley, Elvis, $d 1935-1977
Place of birth and death:	370 Tupelo, Miss. $b Memphis, Tenn.
Address associated with the person:	371 Graceland, 3764 Elvis Presley Boulevard (Highway 51 South) $b Memphis $c Tenn.
Profession or occupation:	374 Singer $a Guitarist $a Actor
Gender:	375 male
Fuller form of name:	378 $q Elvis Aron
Variant form of name:	400 1 Presley, Elvis Aron, $d 1935-1977
Variant form of name:	400 1 Crow, John, $d 1935-1977
Source consulted:	670 Operation Elvis, 1960.
Source, Biographical information:	670 Elvis disguised, c1980: $b in text (Elvis Presley called John Crow in his early days in the U.S. Army)
Source, Biographical information:	670 NUCMC data from Memphis State Univ. Lib. for his memorabilia, 1958-1981 $b (Elvis Presley, 1935-1977; full name generally recorded as Elvis Aron Presley, however gravestone reads Elvis Aaron Presley)

Source, Biographical information:	670 Grove music online, Jan. 8, 2008 $b (Presley, Elvis (Aaron) (Aron); b. Jan. 8, 1935, East Tupelo, MS, d. Aug. 16, 1977, Memphis; American rock and roll singer, guitarist, and actor)

ACCESS POINTS FOR PERSON

RDA 0.4.2 discusses its objectives, some of which, under the "responsiveness to user needs," state that a user should be able to "find the resources that correspond to the user's stated search criteria" and, most importantly, "find all resources associated with a particular person, family, or corporate body." In current practice, using MARC structures, we enable the user to find all resources associated with a particular person, with the use of bibliographic access points. For a person, these are the authorized access points representing the person, included in bibliographic records and linked to each corresponding authority record.

Use of the authorized access points, which are constructed based on RDA guidelines, ensures consistency. The authority data provided should be true representations (RDA 0.4.3.4) of the person's attributes, and should be sufficient (RDA 0.4.3.2) to uniquely identify the person and to differentiate (RDA 9.4.3.1) the person from others with the same or similar names.

The construction of the authorized access point representing a person (or points for persons represented by more than one name) is discussed in RDA 9.19 and in the following section of this chapter.

Authorized Access Point Representing a Person (RDA 9.19)

RDA 9.2–9.18 provides guidelines for attributes included in the description of a person for bibliographic purposes. Not all elements covered in RDA 9.2–9.18 will be used for the authorized access point representing a person; however, constructing the access point should be relatively easy once all data relating to a person are recorded in the various elements.

The examples below illustrate authorized access points for the person using MARC 21 formatting. Authorized access points for a person are recorded in MARC authority field 100. As an access point, these are also added in bibliographic records, more specifically in MARC bibliographic fields 100 (for creators), 600 (for the person as a subject of the work), and 700 (for contributors and collaborators). Subfield coding is the same for all three bibliographic fields. The examples include the authorized access point in the MARC authority 100 field, which is copied exactly into the bibliographic fields. The authorized access point is also called a "heading" in traditional library cataloging practice and MARC documentation.

General Guidelines (RDA 9.19.1)

There are typically three steps in the construction of an authorized access point for a person: (1) the preferred name of the person, (2) general additions required of all cases, and 3) additions required to resolve a conflict or conflicts.

Preferred Name (9.19.1.1)

Use the preferred name for the person, as guided in RDA 9.2.2, as the basis of the authorized access point for the person. Parts of the preferred name include the name, any numerals, and the title of the person. These are recorded in MARC authority 100 field, subfields $a, $b, and $c, respectively.

Examples (authority):
100 1 $a **Abernathy, Penelope Muse**
100 1 $a **Abbott, Mary**
100 1 $a **Dear, M. E.**
100 1 $a **Delany**, $c **Mrs.**
100 1 $a **Peck, George B.,** $c **Jr**.
100 0 $a **Alexander** $b **VI**
100 0 $a **A. M. R.**
100 0 $a **Ralph**, $c **Abbot of Battle**

General Additions

Add the following elements to the preferred name of a person, if applicable, even if it is not necessary to distinguish access points representing persons with the same or similar names:

- Title of royalty
- Title of nobility
- Title of religious rank

Add the following elements to the name when it is necessary to differentiate the access point of the person from others with the same or similar names:

- Date or birth and/or death
- Fuller name

- Period of activity and/or profession or occupation
- Other term of rank, honor, or office
- Other designation.

Title or Other Designation (RDA 9.19.1.2)

Add to the preferred name, if applicable:

- The title of royalty, in all cases it is applicable
- Nobility, in all cases it is applicable
- Religious rank, in all cases it is applicable
- The term "Saint," unless the person is a pope or emperor, empress, king, or queen
- The term "Spirit"
- Other designation associated with the person, such as a term indicating the person is documented in a sacred scripture or apocryphal book, the term "Fictitious character" or "Legendary character," or a term indicating the type, species, or breed for nonhuman subjects.

For names of persons that do not specify whether they represent a person, add to the name a term representing an occupation or profession (RDA 9.16) or a term indicating the fictitious or legendary nature of the entity (RDA 9.17). For a nonhuman entity, add to the name a term indicating the type or species (RDA 9.6.1.8).

Add the title after the preferred name, unless there is a need to add the fuller name of the person to the authorized access point (RDA 9.19.1.3). If the fuller form of the name is added, add the title after the fuller form of the name. The term "Spirit" is always entered at the end of the authorized access point.

Examples:
100 0 Alexander $b VI, $c **Pope**
100 0 Sidonius Apollinaris, $c **Saint**
100 0 Aeneas $c **(Legendary character)**
100 0 Ahhotep $b I, $c **Queen of Egypt**
100 1 Hasdeu, B. P. $q (Bogdan Petriceicu), $d 1838-1907 $c **(Spirit)**

Date of Birth and/or Death (RDA 9.19.1.3)

Add the date of birth and/or death if it is necessary for differentiation. Follow the guidelines in RDA 9.3.2 for birth date and RDA 9.3.3 for death date.

Examples:
100 1 $a Abell, Charles F., $d **1929-2011**
100 0 $a A. M. R. $q (Anna Maria Richards), $d **-1918**
100 0 $a Ralph, $c Abbot of Battle, $d **-1124**
100 1 $a Abernathy, Penelope Muse, $d **1951-**
100 1 $a Adams, John, $d **approximately 1730-approximately 1800**

Although this is not required in all cases, and is required only for differentiation, RDA provides the option of adding the date of birth and/or death even if it is not necessary for differentiation. LC-PCC PS 9.19.1.3 explains that the LC and PCC practice is to always add the dates when creating new authorized access points, if the dates are known, even if they are not needed for distinction. LC and PCC practice also provides an option to the cataloger to add both dates or a missing date (birth or death) to an existing authorized access point.

Fuller Name (RDA 9.19.1.4)

Add the fuller form of a name to the authorized access point if it is necessary to distinguish the person from others with the same or similar names, especially when the dates of birth or death are not known. Follow RDA 9.5 guidelines for the fuller name. LC-PCC practice is to add the fuller form of a name if part of the first or surname used in the preferred name is an initial or an abbreviation and if the cataloger considers the fuller form important for identification.

Examples:
100 0 $a A. M. R. $q **(Anna Maria Richards)**, $d -1918
100 1 $a Delany, $c Mrs. $q **(Mary)**, $d 1700-1788

Period of Activity and/or Profession or Occupation (RDA 9.19.1.5)

Add the period of activity of the person, or the profession, or the occupation, if needed, for differentiation among persons with the same or similar names. Add this information if no dates of birth and/or death or no fuller form of the name are available and are not used in the authorized access point for the person. Follow RDA 9.3.4 for guidelines on period of activity or RDA 9.16 for profession or occupation.

Example:
100 1 $a Dear, M. E. $q (Mary E.), $d **active 1848-1867**

Other term of rank, honor, or office (RDA 9.19.1.6)

Add the term indicating rank, honor, or office if it is part of the name and is needed for distinction from another with the same or similar name. Add this information if no dates of birth or death, or no period of activity, are known. RDA provides an option to include this information in the authorized access point, even if it is not necessary for distinction. LC and PCC practice for the optional addition is to leave it to the cataloger to determine if this information is helpful to users.

Examples:
100 1 $a Baker, Charles A. $c **(Captain)**
100 1 $a Sitwell, George Reresby, $c **Sir**, $d 1860-1943

Other Designation (9.19.1.7)

If none of the above additions to the preferred name are sufficient to uniquely distinguish the person, assign another designation, as instructed in RDA 9.6.1.9.

Examples:
100 1 $a Katz, Susan B. $c **(Of the National Institute of Standards and Technology)**
100 1 $a Chan, Vincent $c **(Member of the Har Gee Chans Reunion Committee 2014)**

Variant Access Points Representing a Person

Variant access points for a person are constructed by following the same guidelines as for the authorized access points for a person. The variant name is constructed like the preferred name, only using the variant name or variant forms of the name (following RDA 9.2.3). Additions to the variant name are made only if they are considered important for identification. The LC and PCC practice is to also make additions to the variant names if needed to resolve a conflict with another authorized access point or with another variant access point for the same person.

In a MARC authority environment, the variant access points for a person are recorded in field 400. Variant access points are never recorded in a bibliographic access point heading (e.g., fields 100, 600, or 700). Links are made from the authority data when a user enters a name or form of a name that is not the same as the authorized access point. The links from the search appear either as "see references," pointing to the authorized access point, or as automatic reformulations of the search to retrieved resources using the authorized access point instead.

Examples:

Authorized access point:	100 1 $a Ackerman, F. Eugene $q (Francis Eugene), $d 1888-1974
Variant access point(s):	400 1 $a **Ackerman, Francis Eugene**, $d **1888-1974**
	400 1 $a **Ackerman, Eugene,** $d **1888-1974**
Authorized access point:	100 1 $a Liu, Ping, $d 1980-
Variant access point(s):	400 1 $a **Liu, Fangjige,** $d **1980-**
	400 1 $a **Liu, Francis,** $d **1980-**
	400 0 $a **Liulangrenjian**, $d **1980-**
	400 1 $a **刘平**, $d **1980-**
Authorized access point:	100 1 $a Allen, Nicholas $c (Political scientist)
Variant access point(s):	400 1 $a **Allen, Nick**, $c **Dr**.
	400 1 $a **Allen, Nicholas**, $c **Dr.**
Authorized access point:	100 0 Abdullah, $c King of Saudi Arabia
Variant access point(s):	400 0 **'Abd Allāh ibn 'Abd al-'Azīz,** $c **King of Saudi Arabia**

400 0 **Abdullah, $c Prince, son of Ibn Sa'ūd, King of Saudi Arabia**
400 0 **Abdullah bin Abdul Aziz**, $c **King of Saudi Arabia**
400 0 **Abdallah ibn Abdulaziz, $c King of Saudi Arabia**
400 0 **'Abdullah ibn 'Abd al-'Aziz, $c King of Saudi Arabia**
400 0 **Abdullah bin Abdulaziz al-Saud, $c King of Saudi Arabia**
400 0 **Abdullah bin Abdul Aziz al-Saud, $c King of Saudi Arabia**
400 0 عبد الله، **$c** ملك السعودية

IDENTIFYING FAMILIES

The original FRBR model, as it was published in 1997, did not include the entity "family" in its Group 2 entities. This is mostly due to the fact that families were not considered to be the same as other entities responsible for creation, contribution, ownership, etc., of materials, or as a person or corporate body was under the *Anglo-American Cataloguing Rules*. Using families as entities responsible for content was not new for the archival community, however, which is reflected in the rules governing archival description, such as archives, personal papers, and manuscripts (*Archives, Personal Papers, and Manuscripts* (APPM)), or as the APPM's successor, *Describing Archives: A Content Standard* (DACS).

As discussed at the beginning of this chapter, family is defined in RDA as a group of two or more persons related by birth, marriage, adoption, civil union, or a similar legal status, or who present themselves as a family (RDA 8.1.2). RDA Chapter 10 provides guidelines for selecting the preferred names for families, recording the preferred and variant names for families and other additional attributes, and constructing authorized access points and variant access points to represent families.

Current practice is to use MARC 21 to record elements for these entities; this requires the recording of all elements for a family as authority data in authority records. However, information about the name, names, or forms of a name of a family can be taken from any source. Data describing family attributes (RDA elements) are recorded as authority data in a MARC environment. Authorized access points representing a family are recorded in MARC authority field 100 (same as for a person), with the first indicator taking a value "3" to indicate family name. Variant names representing a family are recorded in MARC authority field 400, with indicator 1 having a value of "3." The authorized access point representing a family may also be included in bibliographic records.

The general guidelines for identifying persons, families, or corporate bodies discussed at the beginning of this chapter apply to families, including language and script, and the elements status of identification, undifferentiated name indication, source consulted, and cataloger's note, and, therefore, are not discussed separately here.

Core Elements

Similar to other entities, RDA has defined a number of elements representing attributes of a family. Some of these are identified as RDA core elements. Core elements correspond to FRBR and FRAD attributes and relationships that are identified as important to support user tasks. In addition, LC-PCC policy statements may identify some elements as LC/NACO core, even if they are not RDA core. These may be required elements if a library is participating in the NACO program or using LC/NACO authority files and following their practices, which is the case for the majority of US library cataloging.

When describing families, the following are considered core elements, and, therefore, must be recorded if applicable:

- Preferred name for the family
- Type of family
- Date associated with the family
- Identifier for the family.

Elements required if necessary to differentiate among families with the same or similar names include the following:

- Place associated with the family
- Prominent member of the family.

Name of the Family (RDA 10.2)
Core Element: ***Preferred Name for the Family***

Similar to the name of the person, the name of the family is defined as a work, character, or group of words and/or characters by which a family is known. One of the known names or forms of a name is chosen as the preferred name for the family, while the other names or forms of a name are recorded as variant names for the family.

Preferred Name for the Family (RDA 10.2.2)
Core Element
[MARC authority 100]

The preferred name for the family is the name or form of the name chosen to identify the family and is used as the basis for the construction of the authorized access point representing the family.

CHOOSING THE PREFERRED NAME

Use preferred sources of information in the resources themselves to determine the preferred name (follow RDA 2.2.2). If this is not possible, use other formal statements within the resources associated with the family, and, as a last resource, use other sources, including reference sources. Choose as the preferred name, the name by which the family is commonly known, but, based on RDA 0.4.3.4, bear in mind that a well-known name or form of name in the language or script of the cataloging agency may be chosen instead in some cases. RDA 10.2.2.4 also instructs us to make an exception when a family is known to have a preference for one of its names that differs from the commonly used family name. In this case, follow the family's preference when selecting the first element of the preferred name for the family. The family name chosen as the preferred name can be a surname shared by the family members, such as the name of a royal house, or clan, among others.

Apply general guidelines from RDA 8.5 when recording the preferred name for a family.

Different Forms of the Same Name (RDA 10.2.2.5.4)

Because family names more often include a surname, RDA 10.2.2.5 directs us to the guidelines for a person in RDA 9.2.2.5.1–9.2.2.5.4, discussing the selection of the form of the same name based on fullness, language, names found in nonpreferred script, and different spellings.

Examples:

Name of family:	Borja
	Borjia
	Borgia
	Borges
Preferred name of family:	**Borgia**
MARC authority:	100 3 $a **Borgia** (Family: $d active 14th century-18th century)
Name of family:	Γαλάτης
	Galatēs
	Galatti
Preferred name of family:	**Galatēs**
MARC authority:	100 3 $a **Galatēs** (Family)
Name of family:	細川
	Hosokawa, Marquesses
	Hosokawa
	Hosokawa, Kōshaku
Preferred name of family:	**Hosokawa**
MARC authority:	100 3 $a **Hosokawa** (Family: $g Hosokawa, Katsumoto, 1430-1473)

Different Names for the Same Family (RDA 10.2.2.6)

The guidelines instruct us to choose the name by which a family is most commonly known if more than one name is found for the same family. The order of preference cited in RDA is, first, the most frequently found name in resources associated with the family, and, second, the name most frequently appearing in reference sources. All other names are recorded as variant names.

If a family changes its name, including changing it from one language to another, choose the name based on what appears in the associated resources. For example, choose the earlier name for resources associated with that name, but also choose the later name for resources associated with the new name (RDA 10.2.2.7).

Example of names for the same family:

Preferred name for the family:	**Zimmerman**
Variant forms of name:	Zemerman

	Zemmerman
	Zimerman
	Zimmer
	Zimmermon
Other Preferred name for the family:	**Simmerman**
	Timmerman
	Zimmerer

RECORDING THE PREFERRED NAME FOR THE FAMILY

The majority of family names chosen as the preferred name consist of a surname or a name that functions as a surname. In such cases, use the surname as the family name and record the surname as the first element of the preferred name for the family (RDA 10.2.2.9). Follow the same guidelines as for the preferred names of persons that consist of a surname in RDA 9.2.2.9. Also apply the same guidelines as for the preferred name of a person for compound names, surnames with prefixes written separately from the surname, and prefixes that are hyphenated or combined with surnames (RDA 9.2.2.10–9.2.2.12).

Examples:

Name of the family:	De los Ríos Amador
	Amador de los Ríos
Preferred name for the family:	Amador de los Ríos
MARC authority:	100 3 $a **Amador de los Ríos** (Family)

If the name of the family is based on a royal house, dynasty, etc., use that name to represent the family.

Examples:

Preferred name of family:	**Kamehameha**
MARC authority:	100 3 $a **Kamehameha** (Royal house: $d 1810-1872: $c Hawaii)
Preferred name of family:	**Romanov**
MARC authority:	100 3 $a **Romanov** (Dynasty: $d 1613-1917)

Variant name for the Family (RDA 10.2.3)

The names or forms of names for a family that have not been chosen as the preferred name for the family are recorded as the variant names for the family.

Variant forms include names or forms of names used by the family, names or forms of names found in reference sources, and forms of names resulting from a different transliteration of the same name. Record a name as a variant form if a different part of the name is used as the first element when recording the preferred name for the family. Also record as variant the names that are in different linguistic forms of the same name (same name, different language).

Examples:

Names of family:	Γαλάτης
	Galatēs
	Galatti
Preferred name for the family:	Galatēs
MARC authority:	100 3 $a Galatēs (Family)
Variant name for the family:	Γαλάτης
	Galatti
MARC authority:	400 3 $a Γαλάτης (Family)
	400 3 $a **Galatti** (Family)

Names of the family:	Zimmerman
	Zemerman
	Zemmerman
	Zimerman
	Zimmer
	Zimmermon
Preferred name for the family:	Zimmerman
Variant forms of name:	**Zemerman**
	Zemmerman
	Zimerman
	Zimmer
	Zimmermon
MARC authority:	400 3 $a **Zemerman** (Family)
	400 3 $a **Zemmerman** (Family)
	400 3 $a **Zimerman** (Family)
	400 3 $a **Zimmer** (Family)
	400 3 $a **Zimmermon** (Family)

OTHER IDENTIFYING ATTRIBUTES FOR FAMILY

A number of other attributes for families are defined and discussed in RDA 10.3–10.9. The RDA elements include type of family, date associated with the family, place associated with the family, prominent member of the family, hereditary title, language of the family, family history, and identifier for the family. These elements can be useful for identifying the family or for distinguishing the family from other families or entities with the same or similar names. Elements can be recorded separately, and some may be part of the authorized access point for the family. The construction of the authorized access point for the family—and, therefore, the determination of which elements will be used in the construction of the access point—is covered in RDA 10.11 and discussed later in the chapter.

Type of Family (RDA 10.3)
Core Element
[MARC authority 376 subfield $a]

Type of family is "a categorization or generic descriptor for the type of family." Examples include "family," "clan," "dynasty," "royal house," etc., with the most common type used being "family." Record the term for the type of family as a separate element or as part of the authorized access point.

Examples:

Type of family:	**Family**
MARC authority:	100 3 $a Gorgas (**Family**: $d 1853-: $c Ala.) 376 $a **Family**
Type of family:	**Royal houses** **Dynasty**
MARC authority:	100 3 $a Kamehameha (**Royal house**: $d 1810-1872: $c Hawaii) 376 $a **Royal houses** $2 lcsh 376 $a **Dynasty**
Type of family:	**Clan**
MARC authority:	100 3 $a Koteda (**Clan**: $d active fifteenth century-seventeenth century: $c Hirado-shi, Japan) 376 $a **Clan**

Date Associated with the Family (RDA 10.4)
Core Element
[MARC authority 046]

This element is used to record a significant date associated with the history of the family. The same guidelines apply here as with the date associated with the person (RDA 9.3); therefore, we see dates for when the family was active, starting and/or ending dates for the family, etc. Due to the vague instructions regarding "significant" date associated with the history of the family, it may be difficult to determine what dates to record in this element. For example, how does one determine the start date for a family, that is, does a family start at the time of marriage of a couple? Does it start when the first child of a couple is born? For historical families, such as royal families or dynasties, it may be easier to determine the dates associated with them. Often, dates associated with the family are based on resources associated with the family.

A date associated with the family is recorded in a separate element, and can also be recorded as part of the authorized access point for the family. As a core element, dates are recorded if available and are also part of the authorized access point for the family.

Examples:

Date associated with family:	**active 15th century-17th century**
MARC authority:	046 $s **14** $t **16** 100 3 Koteda (Clan: $d **active 15th century-17th century**: $c Hirado-shi, Japan)
Date associated with family:	**1872-1963**
MARC authority:	046 $s **1872** $t **1963** 100 3 $a Abdurahman (Family: $d **1872-1963**: $c South Africa)

Place Associated with the Family (RDA 10.5)
Core Element: ***for differentiation***
[MARC authority 370]

The place where a family resides or has resided in the past, or that the family is connected with, is recorded in the place associated with the family element. Recording of place names follows the same guidelines as for the place associated with a person, and follows guidelines in RDA Chapter 16. Use names for place from a controlled vocabulary, and record the source when possible.

RDA 10.5.1.3 instructs us to abbreviate the place name of larger geographic areas, as applicable. These abbreviations of names of countries, states, provinces, territories, etc., are listed in RDA Appendix B.11. The element is core if it is necessary to differentiate between families with the same or similar names. The place is recorded as a separate element or as part of the authorized access point representing the family.

Examples:

Place associated with family: country: **South Africa**

	residence: **Cape Town, South Africa**
MARC authority:	370 $c **South Africa** $e **Cape Town, South Africa**
Place associated with family:	residence: **Duxbury, Mass.**
MARC authority:	370 $e **Duxbury (Mass.)** 100 3 Bittinger (Family: $d 1824-1913: $c **Mass.**)
Place associated with family:	country: **Italy** place of origin: **Valencia, Spain**
MARC authority:	370 $c **Italy** $f **Valencia (Spain)** $2 naf

Prominent Member of the Family (RDA 10.6)
Core Element: ***for differentiation***
[MARC authority 376 subfield $b]

A prominent member of the family is a well-known individual who is a member of the family. Often, the family is distinguished from other families with the same or similar names by its prominent member. This element is core when it is necessary for differentiation. In this case, record the name of the prominent member in the form used as the authorized access point representing this prominent individual. Prominent members can be recorded as a separate element, as part of the access point, or both.

Examples:

Prominent member:	**Alexander VI, Pope, 1431-1503**
MARC authority:	100 3 Borgia (Family: $d active 14th century-18th century) 376 $b **Alexander VI, Pope, 1431-1503** $2 naf
Prominent member:	Pond, Bert, 1922-
MARC authority:	100 3 Pond (Family: $g **Pond, Bert, 1922-**) 376 $b **Pond, Bert, 1922-** $2 naf
Prominent member:	**Romney, George W., 1907-1995** **Romney, Lenore, 1908-1995**
MARC authority:	100 3 Romney (Family: $d 1931-: $g **Romney, George W., 1907-1995**) 376 Family $b **Romney, George W., 1907-1995** $b **Romney, Lenore, 1908-1995**

Prominent member: **Romney, Mitt**
Romney, Ann, 1949-
MARC authority: 100 3 Romney (Family: $d 1969-: $g **Romney, Mitt**)
376 Family $b **Romney, Mitt** $b **Romney, Ann, 1949-**

Notice that in the last two examples, the preferred family name of these two different families is the same. Also, two prominent members are recorded for each, although only one is used in the authorized access point for the family.

Hereditary Title (RDA 10.7) [MARC authority 376 subfield $c]

The element hereditary of the family is defined as a title of nobility, and so on, associated with a family. Record the title in direct order and in the plural form. Hereditary titles are those that are always held by a family member.

Example:
Hereditary title: **Dukes of Edinburgh**
MARC authority: 376 $c **Dukes of Edinburgh**

Language of the Family (RDA 10.8) [MARC authority 377]

The language the family uses for its communications is recorded in the element language of the family. The appropriate term or terms in the language preferred by the agency is used. In a MARC structure, preference often is given to codes for languages, like the *MARC Code List for Languages*.

Example:
Language of the family: **English**
MARC authority: 377 $a **eng**

Family History (RDA 10.9) [MARC authority 678]

A brief biographical sketch about the family and its members is recorded in the family history element. Information about the family that is included in other elements should be incorporated in the family history when possible.

Example:
678 0 The Sfondrati family were important political and religious leaders in Italy. $b **The Sfondrati family was founded by Francesco Sfondrati (1493-1550) and his wife Anna Visconti de Madrone (died 1535). The Sfondrati were of Spanish descent, and had lived in Cremona before settling in Milan. Francesco trained as a lawyer and taught at the University of Pavia. He became involved in politics, and was eventually made Count of Riviera di Lecco in 1537. After the death of his wife in 1538, Sfondrati entered service to the Church and became cardinal. Francesco and Anna had seven children. Of these, his sons Niccolò and Paolo were the most prominent. Like his father, Niccolò joined the Church, becoming a cardinal in 1583 and then being elevated to pope as Gregory XIV (1590-1591). Niccolò's brother, Paolo, was Baron of Valassina and Count of Riviera. Paolo's sons continued the family's legacy as political, military, and religious leaders: Ercole became Duke of Montemarciano, Francesco a general in the papal forces and marchese of Montafia, and Paolo Emilio a cardinal and papal secretary of state. The last male member of the family was Carlo Sfondrati, Count of Riviera (died 1788).**

Identifier for the Family (RDA 10.10)
Core Element
[MARC authority 010]

A core element, the identifier for the family is a string of characters that is uniquely associated with a family or a surrogate representation or description of a family (such as an authority record). As a unique string of characters, this element differentiates the family from other families. Whenever possible, include the context of the identifier, that is, the organization creating and maintaining the identifier. One family may be associated with more than one identifier.

Examples:

Identifier for the family:	*Library of Congress control number* **no2013141057**
MARC authority:	010 $a **no2013141057**

Putting it All Together: Identifying Families

As a conclusion on the elements identifying a family, the following example covers all applicable elements in one record structure, using MARC authority format.

RDA element	*MARC authority*
Identifier for the family:	010 no2014144171 024 7 305462998 (Personal) $2 viaf
Date associated with family:	046 $s 1685~ $2 edtf
Preferred name:	100 3 Ōkubo (Family: $d approximately 1685-: $g Ōkubo, Toshimichi, 1830-1878)
Place associated with family:	370 $e Higashiichiki-chō (Japan) $e Tokyo (Japan) $2 naf
Title and Prominent member:	376 Family $b Ōkubo, Toshimichi, 1830-1878 $c Kshaku
Variant name:	400 3 Ōkubo, Kōshaku (Family) 400 3 Ōkubo, Marquesses (Family) 400 3 大久保 (Family: $d approximately 1685-: $g Ōkubo, Toshimichi, 1830-1878)
Relationship:	500 1 $i Family member: $a Ōkubo, Toshimichi, $d 1830-1878 $w r
Cataloger's note:	667 SUBJECT USAGE: This heading is not valid for use as a subject; use a family name heading from LCSH.
Source consulted:	670 Hizōshashin, 2013: $b t.p. (大久保家 = Ōkubo-ke; family of: 大久保利通 = Ōkubo Toshimichi)
Source consulted & History:	670 Wikipedia, Japanese, Oct. 30, 2014 $b (大久保氏 = Ōkubo -shi; genealogy starting with 仲兵衛 = Chūbē at 市来郷 = Ichiki-gō, during Jōkyō era (1684-1687); accorded 侯爵 = Kōshaku [Marquess] title after Toshimichi was murdered)
Source consulted:	670 JTNDL in VIAF, Oct. 30, 2014 $b (hdg.: 大久保 (家) (東京都) = Ōkubo (Ke) (Tōkyō to); r)

ACCESS POINTS FOR FAMILY

Among the objectives stated in RDA 0.4.2 is to enable the user to find resources that correspond to the user's stated search criteria, and, more specifically, to find all resources associated with a family.

In current practice, using MARC structures, we enable the user to find all resources associated with a particular family with the use of bibliographic access points. For a family, these are the authorized access points representing the family, included in bibliographic records and linked to each corresponding authority record.

Use of the authorized access points, which are constructed based on RDA guidelines, ensures consistency. The authority data provided should be true representations (RDA 0.4.3.4) of the family's attributes and should be sufficient (RDA 0.4.3.2) to uniquely identify the family and differentiate the family from others with the same or similar names.

The construction of the authorized access point representing a family (or points for families represented by more than one name) is discussed in RDA 10.11 and in the following section of this chapter.

Authorized Access Point Representing a Family (RDA 10.11.1)

RDA 10.2–10.10 provides guidelines for attributes included in the description of a person for bibliographic purposes. Not all elements covered in RDA 10.2–10.10 will be used for the authorized access point representing a family; however, constructing the access point should be relatively easy once all data relating to the family are recorded in the various elements.

The examples below illustrate authorized access points for a family by using MARC 21 formatting. Authorized access points for a family are recorded in MARC authority field 100. As an access point, these are also added in bibliographic records, more specifically in MARC bibliographic fields 100 (for creators), 600 (for the family as a subject of the work), and 700 (for contributors and collaborators). Subfield coding is the same for all three bibliographic fields.

General Guidelines

When constructing an authorized access point for a family, use the preferred name for the family as the basis for the authorized access point for the family. Additions may be necessary if they are applicable, and should follow guidelines discussed in RDA 10.11.2–10.11.5 and in the following sections of this chapter. Follow the guidelines in RDA 10.2.2 and discussed above to record the preferred name as the basis of the authorized access point. In most cases, the preferred name of the family will be the chosen surname.

Examples:
100 3 $a **Sakakibara**
100 3 $a **Romanov**

100 3 $a **Kamehameha**
100 3 $a **Brewer**
100 3 $a **Sawyer**

General Additions

Additions made representing different families with same or similar names (even if it is not necessary to differentiate access points) include type of family (RDA 10.11.1.2) and date associated with the family (RDA 10.11.1.3).

Add the family type, following RDA 10.3, after the preferred name, enclosed within parentheses.

Add the date or dates associated with the family, as instructed in RDA 10.4, following the family type.

Examples (authority):
100 3 $a Sakakibara (**Clan**: $d **14th century-**: $c Jōetsu-shi, Japan)
100 3 $a Romanov (**Dynasty**: $d **1613-1917**)
100 3 $a Kamehameha (**Royal house**: $d **1810-1872**: $c Hawaii)
100 3 $a Brewer (**Family**: $g Brewer, John H. (John Hyrum), 1878-1950)
100 3 $a Sawyer (**Family**: $d **1862-1981**: $c Akron, Ohio: $g Sawyer, William T. (William Thomas), 1862-1953)

Additions for Differentiation

Additions made when necessary to differentiate authorized access points include place associated with the family (RDA 10.11.1.4) and prominent member of the family (RDA 10.11.1.5).

Add the name of the place associated with the family (based on RDA 10.5) only if it is necessary to distinguish among access points.

Add the prominent member of the family, using the form in the authorized access point for the person, if it is necessary to distinguish among access points. If a place associated with the family is not available, add the name of the prominent member to the authorized access point for the family.

Examples (authority):
100 3 $a Sakakibara (Clan: $d 14th century-: $c **Jōetsu-shi, Japan**)
100 3 $a Kamehameha (Royal house: $d 1810-1872: $c **Hawaii**)
100 3 $a Brewer (Family: $g **Brewer, John H. (John Hyrum), 1878-1950**)
100 3 $a Sawyer (Family: $d 1862-1981: $c **Akron, Ohio**: $g **Sawyer, William T. (William Thomas), 1862-1953**)

Alternatively, you may add the place associated with the family or the prominent member to the authorized access point representing the family if they are useful for identification.

Variant Access Points Representing a Family (RDA 10.11.2)

Any variant name or form of name is used as the basis for the construction of the variant access point(s) representing the family. Unlike authorized access points representing the family, variant access points are never included in bibliographic records.

In a MARC authority environment, the variant access points for a person are recorded in field 400. Links are made from the authority data when a user enters a name or form of a name that is not the same as the authorized access point. The links from the search appear either as "see references," pointing to the authorized access point, or as automatic reformulations of the search to retrieved resources using the authorized access point instead.

In constructing the variant access point, use the variant name for the family. Add the type of family within parentheses, following the variant name, based on RDA 10.3. Any other additions, such as date associated, place associated, or prominent member, are to be made if they are considered necessary for identification. Follow guidelines in RDA 10.11.1.3–10.11.1.5 in the order they appear in RDA.

Examples:

Authorized access point:	100 3 $a Romney (Family: $d 1931-: $g Romney, George W., 1907-1995)
Variant access point:	400 3 $a **Romney (Family: $d 1931-: Romney, Lenore, 1908-1998)**
Authorized access point:	100 3 $a Shijō (Family: $d 1894-)
Variant access points:	400 3 $a **Shijō, Danshaku (Family: $d 1894-)**
	400 3 $a **Shijō, Barons (Family: $d 1894-)**
	400 3 $a **四條 (Family: $d 1894-)**
Authorized access point:	100 3 $a Tsitseklēs (Family)
Variant access points:	400 3 $a **Zizecli (Family)**
	400 3 $a **Τσιτσεκλής (Family)**

IDENTIFYING CORPORATE NAMES

RDA defines a corporate body as an "organization or group of persons and/or organizations that is identified by a particular name and that acts, or may act, as a unit" (RDA 0.3.3 and 8.1). Based on this definition, a corporate body exists only if all of the following conditions are met:

- The entity is an organization or group of persons.
- The entity is identified by a particular name, that is, a specific appellation.
- The entity acts (or may act) as a unit.

If any of these conditions are not met, then the entity cannot be considered a corporate body. RDA states that a "particular name consists of words that are a specific appellation rather than a general description" (RDA 11.0).

Examples of corporate bodies include associations, institutions, nonprofit organizations, governments and government agencies, religious bodies, churches, meetings (such as athletic events, exhibitions, festivals, and conferences), and vessels (such as ships and spacecrafts).

The general guidelines for identifying persons, families, or corporate bodies discussed at the beginning of this chapter apply to corporate bodies, including language and script, status of identification, undifferentiated name indication, source consulted, and cataloger's note, and, therefore, are not discussed separately here.

Any source can be used to take the name or names of a corporate body.

Core Elements

Core elements, that is, those to be used at a minimum when describing a corporate body, are defined in RDA based on the FRBR and FRAD user tasks. Not all core elements will be used in the construction of the authorized access point representing the corporate body. Elements not identified as core may also be added, and other agencies may identify them as required elements. Core elements are recorded as separate elements, but may also be part of the authorized access point for the corporate body.

When recording elements for corporate bodies, the following are core elements, and, therefore, must be recorded if applicable:

- Preferred name for the corporate body
- Location of conference, etc.
- Date of conference, etc.
- Associated institution (for conferences, etc., if the institution's name provides better identification than the local place name or if the local place name is unknown or cannot be readily determined)
- Number of a conference, etc.
- Type of corporate body (for a body whose name does not convey the idea of a corporate body)
- Identifier for the corporate body.

Record the following elements if necessary to differentiate between corporate bodies with same or similar names:

- Location of headquarters
- Date of establishment
- Date of termination
- Period of activity of the corporate body
- Associated institution
- Other designation associated with the corporate body.

General guidelines as described under RDA Chapter 8 and in this chapter—such as those for language and script, capitalization, spacing, abbreviations, status of identification, undifferentiated name indication, source consulted, and cataloger's note—apply to corporate bodies.

For capitalization of the corporate body's name, consult RDA Appendix A.2. Record separate letters and initials without using spaces between them. Do not separate words where the corporate body does not. For example, do not separate the name "ExxonMobil."

NAME OF THE CORPORATE BODY (RDA 11.2)

The name of the corporate body is defined as a word, character, or a group of words and/or characters by which a corporate body is known. Under RDA guidelines, among the names by which the corporate body is known, one is selected as the preferred name for the corporate body, and the other names serve as the variant names.

In recording the name of a corporate body, use the general guidelines in RDA 8.5, including those for the use of RDA appendices.

Preferred Name for the Corporate Body (RDA 11.2.2) Core Element [MARC authority 110, 111, 151]

The preferred name for the corporate body is the name or form of the name chosen to identify the corporate body. The preferred name serves as the basis for the construction of the authorized access point representing the corporate body.

There are some differences in the treatment of corporate bodies in comparison to persons. When a person changes name, he or she is still considered the same person. The authorized access point is changed (in a MARC authority environment, this means that the existing authority record is revised to reflect the change). An individual may use more than one name, and, therefore, may have more than one authorized access point (e.g., when using a pseudonym and the real name). A corporate body changing names is considered a new corporate body. Therefore, a corporate body has only one authorized access point, and a name change will require the creation of a new description of the corporate body (in MARC authority, this means that a new authority record will be created).

CHOOSING THE PREFERRED NAME FOR CORPORATE BODIES

To determine the preferred name or form of the name for a corporate body, first consult the preferred source of information on the resources associated with the corporate body, as defined in RDA 2.2.2 (e.g., title pages of books, title frames for moving images, etc.). If this is not adequate to determine the preferred name, then consult formal statements in other locations of the resources associated with the corporate body. Last, consult any other source, including reference sources.

Per RDA 11.2.2.3, choose the name by which a corporate body is most commonly identified and record the name based on the general guidelines stated in RDA 8.5.

Example:

Name of corporate body:	Lower Hutt Women's Centre Women's Centre, Lower Hutt, N.Z.
Preferred name:	**Lower Hutt Women's Centre**
Name of corporate body:	Malaŵi Export Promotion Council M.E.P.C.
Preferred name:	**Malaŵi Export Promotion Council**

RDA 11.2.2.5 instructs us that if the same name appears in different forms on resources associated with the corporate body—including spelling variations, different languages, different names of an international organization, conventional name, etc.—choose the name that appears in the preferred sources of information. If more than one form appears in the preferred sources, choose the form most commonly found. If no name is commonly found, use a brief name that uniquely identifies the corporate body. The brief name can be an abbreviation or acronym, or may consist of initials. If the brief name is not sufficient to differentiate the corporate body from other bodies with the same or similar names, use the form of the name found in reference sources.

Variation in spelling: Choose the form on the first resource received.

Example:
Name of corporate body: Berks Summer Theatre
Berks Summer Theater
Preferred name: **Berks Summer Theatre**

LCC-PC PS 11.2.2.5.1 offers instructions for dealing with variations in spelling due to orthographic reform for corporate bodies located in countries of reform, such as in Greece, Netherlands, Indonesia, among others. In these cases, LC and PCC practice is to revise the name of the corporate body to conform to the reformed spelling.

Language variation: In the case of variation of the name as it appears in different languages, choose the name in the official language of the body (RDA 11.2.2.5.2). However, LC-PCC PS 11.2.2.5.2 states that if the name appears in more than one language and one of them is English, we must choose the English form of the name as the preferred name.

In a case where a country has more than one official language and one of them is the preferred language of the corporate body, choose that language for the preferred name. If, however, the preferred language of the corporate body is not one of the official languages or the official language of the corporate body is not known, use the form of the name in the language predominantly appearing in the resources associated with the body.

Examples:
Name of corporate body: Beogradski centar za ljudska prava
Belgrade Centre for Human Rights
Preferred name: **Beogradski centar za ljudska prava**

For international bodies (RDA 11.2.2.5.3) choose the language preferred by the cataloging agency, if one is determined. LC-PPC practice is to choose the name in the English form.

Examples:
International body names: Kommission der Europäischen Gemeinschaften
Commission des Communautés européennes
Commissione delle Comunità europee
Commission of the European Communities

	Comisión de las Comunidades Europeas
Preferred name:	**Commission of the European Communities**
MARC authority:	110 2 $a **Commission of the European Communities**
International body names:	Federación Internacional de Asociaciones de Bibliotecarios e Instituciones International Federation of Library Associations and Institutions Fédération internationale des associations de bibliothécaires et des bibliothèques Internationaler Verband der Bibliothekarischen Vereine und Institutionen Federació internacional d'associacions de bibliotecaris i de biblioteques
Preferred name:	International Federation of Library Associations and Institutions
MARC authority:	110 2 $a **International Federation of Library Associations and Institutions**

Conventional name: If an examination of reference resources in the language of the corporate body indicates that the most common form of the name is one other than the official name of the body (conventional name), choose the conventional name as the preferred name (RDA 11.2.2.5.4).

Examples:

Name:	Dudley Peter Allen Memorial Art Museum Allen Memorial Art Museum
Preferred name:	**Allen Memorial Art Museum**
MARC authority:	110 2 $a **Allen Memorial Art Museum**

Exceptions to 11.2.2.5.4, conventional name guidelines, include the following:

- Ancient and international bodies: use the name in the preferred language of the cataloging agency, if the body is well known with the name in that language. For example, *Augustinians*, not Augustiniáni.
- Religious orders: use the most known name in the language preferred by the cataloging agency. For example, *Archdiocese of Campinas*, not Arquidiocese de Campinas.
- Governments: use the conventional name of the area over which the government has jurisdiction. Governments exist in countries, states, provinces,

county, municipalities, etc. RDA Chapter 16 includes guidelines for the name of a jurisdiction. For example, *Belgium*, not Koninkrijk van België or Kingdom of Belgium.

- Conferences, congresses, meetings, etc.: use the form that includes the name of the associated body, if different names are used to refer to the conference; use the more specific name if a choice between a specific and a more general name of the series of events is known.
- Local places of worship: use the predominant name appearing in preferred sources of information associated with the body. If there is no preference, use the form of the person a church is dedicated or named after, a descriptive term for the church, or the name for the place in which the church is located. For example, *Saint Mary's Church*, *Chicago Illinois Temple*.
- Different names: sometimes, a corporate body may be known by different names at the same time, such as a nickname, but not different forms of the same name; in these cases, use the name most commonly found in resources associated with the corporate body.

Change of name (RDA 11.2.2.6): When a corporate body changes names, including from one language to another, choose the earlier name from the resources associated with that name; choose the later, newer name for resources associated with the new name.

Examples:

Earlier name:	Child & Family Research and Policy Unit
Later name:	Child & Family Research Centre
Preferred name:	**Child & Family Research and Policy Unit**
	Child & Family Research Centre
MARC authority:	110 2 $a **Child & Family Research Centre**
	110 2 $a **Child & Family Research and Policy Unit**

RECORDING THE PREFERRED NAME FOR THE CORPORATE BODY

Most preferred names of corporate bodies are recorded in the order they appear. Elements may be added or removed from a name. Subordinate bodies are often recorded under the parent or superordinate body.

In a MARC authority structure, the majority of corporate body–preferred names are recorded in field 110, and conferences, meetings, and other events are recorded in field 111. Although jurisdiction names are recorded in field 151, when they are part of a corporate body name, as the first element of the name, that name is recorded in field 110. Examples below illustrate data about corporate bodies as authority data.

Names Consisting of or Containing Initials (RDA 11.2.2.7)

Based on the most commonly known form of the name, record or omit full stops (period) and/or other punctuation marks as they appear on the preferred name for the corporate body. Do not add them if the name does not use these marks. When usage of full stops is uncertain, follow RDA's instruction to omit them.

Examples:

Name:	Unesco U.N.E.S.C.O
Preferred name:	**Unesco**
MARC authority:	110 2 $a **Unesco**
Name:	Americans for Music Libraries in Israel A.M.L.Y. A.M.L.I.
Preferred name:	**A.M.L.I.**
MARC authority:	110 2 $a **A.M.L.I.**

Initial Articles (RDA 11.2.2.8)

If an initial article is present in the preferred name of the corporate body, record it. The alternative guideline, followed by LC-PCC PS 11.2.28, instructs us to omit the initial article from the preferred name, unless the preferred name is indexed and accessed by the initial article. See RDA Appendix C for a list of initial articles in different languages. This guideline is mostly to accommodate the lack of nonfiling characters featured in MARC authority name fields.

Examples:

Name:	The Albert and Mary Lasker Foundation
Preferred name:	**Albert and Mary Lasker Foundation**
MARC authority:	110 2 $a **Albert and Mary Lasker Foundation**
Name:	Les Brigittines
Preferred name:	**Les Brigittines**
MARC authority:	110 2 $a **Les Brigittines** (Performance arts centre)

Terms Indicating Incorporation and Certain Other Terms (RDA 11.2.2.10)

In general, most terms or abbreviations indicating incorporation or ownership of the body, or phrases indicating type of incorporation, are omitted from the preferred name, unless the term is an integral part of the name or helps identify the entity as a corporate body. The term "company" does not indicate incorporation, and, therefore, should not be omitted. Terms such as "U.S.S." and "R.M.S.," used with names of ships, should be omitted.

Examples:

Name:	20/20 Multimedia, Inc.
Preferred name:	**20/20 Multimedia, Inc.**
MARC authority:	110 2 $a **20/20 Multimedia, Inc.**
Name:	U.S.S. Columbia
Preferred name:	**Columbia**
MARC authority:	110 2 $a **Columbia** (Spacecraft)
Name:	bce films & more GmbH
Preferred name:	**bce films & more GmbH**
MARC authority:	110 2 $a **bce films & more GmbH**

Number or Year of Convocation of a Conference, etc. (RDA 11.2.2.11)

Omit indication of year, number, etc. from the name of convocation, conference, meeting, congress, festival, exhibition, etc. The same applies to the name of a subordinate body.

Examples:

Name:	2nd Asian Yaws Conference
Preferred name:	**Asian Yaws Conference**
MARC authority:	111 2 $a **Asian Yaws Conference** $n (2nd: $d 1961: $c Bandung, Indonesia)
Name:	7th Mediterranean Conference on Information Systems
Preferred name:	**Mediterranean Conference on Information Systems**
MARC authority:	111 2 $a **Mediterranean Conference on Information Systems** $n (7th: $d 2012: $c Guimarães, Portugal)

Names Found in a Nonpreferred Script (RDA 11.2.2.12)

If the preferred name is in a script other than the preferred script of the cataloging agency, transliterate the name according to the scheme chosen by the agency. LC-PCC PS 11.2.2.12 states that the LC and PCC practice is to transliterate the name of a corporate body using the *ALA-LC Romanization Tables: Transliteration Schemes for Non-Roman Scripts.*

Examples:

Name:	Διεθνές Επιστημονικό Συνέδριο "Ο Ελληνισμός της Διασποράς"
Preferred name (transliterated):	**Diethnes Epistēmoniko Synedrio "Ho Hellēnismos tēs Diasporas"**
MARC authority:	111 2 $a **Diethnes Epistēmoniko Synedrio "Ho Hellēnismos tēs Diasporas"**
Name:	鰓類研究連絡会
Preferred name: (transliterated):	**Bansairui Kenkyū Renrakukai**
MARC authority:	110 2 $a **Bansairui Kenkyū Renrakukai**

RECORDING NAMES OF SUBORDINATE AND RELATED BODIES

Recording the preferred name of a subordinate body can fall under one of the following categories:

- The subordinate body has a distinctive name, and that name is sufficient to identify the corporate body. In this case, record the preferred name of the subordinate body directly as found, following the guidelines in RDA 12.2.2.4.
- The subordinate body or its name fall under one of the categories covered by the guidelines in RDA 11.2.2.14, including those whose name implies being part of another body, those whose name implies administrative subordination, those whose name does not convey the idea of a corporate body, etc.

Subordinate and Related Bodies Recorded Directly

Follow the guidelines in RDA 12.2.2.4 to record the preferred name of a subordinate and related body that has a distinctive name, which allows unique identification of the corporate body on its own, without the superordinate body.

Examples:	
Name:	World Bank, African Regional Studies Program Studies Program of the Africa Technical Department, World Bank World Bank. Africa Regional Office. Technical Department. Studies Program
Preferred name:	**Africa Regional Studies Program**
MARC authority:	110 2 $a **Africa Regional Studies Program**
Name:	Inter-Agency Technical Committee for Alaska United States. Inter-Agency Technical Committee for Alaska
Preferred name:	**Inter-Agency Technical Committee for Alaska**
MARC authority:	110 2 $a **Inter-Agency Technical Committee for Alaska**

Subordinate and Related Bodies Recorded Subordinately (RDA 11.2.2.14)

If the subordinate body or its name falls under one of the eighteen categories covered by the guidelines in RDA 11.2.2.14, including those whose name implies being part of another body, those whose name implies administrative subordination, those whose name does not convey the idea of a corporate body, etc., record the preferred name of the subordinate body as a subdivision of the higher or related body, after the preferred name of its superordinate or related body. Omit the name or abbreviated name of the higher body from the subordinate name (in other words, do not repeat it), unless the omission of the resulting name does not make sense. If in doubt, record the subordinate body directly without the use of the higher or related body.

Examples:	
Name:	BBC Architectural and Civil Engineering Department
Not preferred:	BBC Engineering. BBC Architectural and Civil Engineering Department
Preferred name:	**BBC Engineering. Architectural and Civil Engineering Department**
MARC authority:	110 2 $a **BBC Engineering**. $b **Architectural and Civil Engineering Department**

Name: National Museum Service of Trinidad and Tobago
Not preferred: Trinidad and Tobago. National Museum Service of Trinidad and Tobago
Preferred name: **Trinidad and Tobago. National Museum Service**
MARC authority: 110 1 $a **Trinidad and Tobago**. $b **National Museum Service**

Name Implies it is Part of Another Body (RDA 11.2.2.14.1)

Record the subordinate body subordinately under the higher or related body if the name of the subordinate body implies it is part of a higher body. Typically, the name will include terms such as division, section, branch, department, among others.

Examples:
Subordinate name: Division of Industrial Hygiene
Preferred name: **Ontario. Division of Industrial Hygiene**
MARC authority: 110 1 $a **Ontario**. $b **Division of Industrial Hygiene**

Subordinate name: Health Statistics Branch
Preferred name: **Western Australia. Health Statistics Branch**
MARC authority: 110 1 $a **Western Australia**. $b **Health Statistics Branch**

Name Implies Administrative Subordination (RDA 11.2.2.14.2)

Record the subordinate body subordinately under the higher or related body if the name of the subordinate body implies administrative subordination. Typically, the name will include terms such as committee, commission, executive, office, secretariat, working group, among others. For additional terms in various languages, see LC-PCC PS 11.2.2.14.2.

Examples:
Subordinate name: Commission on International Relations
Preferred name: **National Research Council (U.S.). Commission on International Relations**
MARC authority: 110 2 $a **National Research Council (U.S.)**. $b **Commission on International Relations**

Subordinate name: Sekretariat Negara
Preferred name: **Indonesia. Sekretariat Negara**
MARC authority: 110 1 $a **Indonesia**. $b **Sekretariat Negara**

Name is General in Nature or Simply Indicates Geographic, Chronological, or Numbered/Lettered Subdivision (RDA 11.2.2.14.3)

Record the subordinate body subordinately under the higher or related body if the name of the subordinate body is general in nature or simply indicates geographic, chronological, or numbered or lettered subdivision of the higher body. Typically, the name of the subordinate body will not include subject words, adjectives, or distinctive proper nouns.

Example:

Subordinate name:	Central Research and Statistics Division
Preferred name:	**Port Authority of New York and New Jersey. Central Research and Statistics Division**
MARC authority:	110 2 $a **Port Authority of New York and New Jersey**. $b **Central Research and Statistics Division**

Name does not Convey the Idea of a Corporate Body and does not Contain the Name of the Higher Body (RDA 11.2.2.14.4)

Record the subordinate body subordinately under the higher or related body if the name of the subordinate body does not convey the idea that it is a corporate body.

Example:

Subordinate name:	Technical Management Services
Preferred name:	**Cape Town (South Africa). Technical Management Services**
MARC authority:	110 1 $a **Cape Town (South Africa).** $b **Technical Management Services**

Name that Simply Indicates a Particular Field of Study of a University Faculty, School, College, Institute, Laboratory, etc. (RDA 11.2.2.14.5)

Record the subordinate body subordinately under the higher or related body of a university, school, etc., if the name of the subordinate body simply indicates a particular field of study.

Examples:

Subordinate name:	Matemaatikateaduskond [Faculty of Mathematics]
Preferred name:	**Tartu Ülikool. Matemaatikateaduskond**
MARC authority:	110 2 $a **Tartu Ülikool**. $b **Matemaatikateaduskond**

Subordinate name: School of Agricultural Engineering
Preferred name: **Ontario Agricultural College. School of Agricultural Engineering**
MARC authority: 110 2 $a **Ontario Agricultural College**. $b **School of Agricultural Engineering**

Name of Nongovernmental Body that Includes the Entire Name of the Higher or Related Body (RDA 11.2.2.14.6)

Record the subordinate body subordinately under the higher or related nongovernmental body if the name of the subordinate body includes the entire name of the superordinate body.

Example:
Subordinate name: Eton School Library
Preferred name: **Eton College. Library**
MARC authority: 110 2 $a **Eton College**. $b **Library**

Name of a Ministry or Similar Major Executive Agency (RDA 11.2.2.14.7)

Record the subordinate body subordinately under the higher or related body if the name is of a ministry or similar executive agency.

Example:
Subordinate name: Ministry of Public Works and Labour
Preferred name: **Burma. Ministry of Public Works and Labour**
MARC authority: 110 1 $a **Burma**. $b **Ministry of Public Works and Labour**

Name of Government Official or Religious Official (RDA 11.2.2.14.8)

Record the subordinate body subordinately under the higher or related body if the name is of a government official or a religious official. For additional information about government officials, see RDA 11.2.2.18, and for religious officials, see RDA 11.2.2.26 and relevant sections below.

Example:
Subordinate name: Governor
Preferred name: **Los Ríos (Ecuador). Governor**
MARC authority: 110 1 $a **Los Ríos (Ecuador).** $b **Governor**

Name of Legislative Body (RDA 11.2.2.14.9)

Record the subordinate body subordinately under the higher or related body if the name is of a legislative body. For additional information about legislative bodies, see RDA 11.2.2.19 and relevant section below.

Example:
Subordinate name: Territorial Legislature
Preferred name: **Alaska. Territorial Legislature**
MARC authority: 110 1 $a **Alaska**. $b **Territorial Legislature**

Name of Constitutional Convention (RDA 11.2.2.14.10 and 11.2.2.20)

Record the subordinate body subordinately under the higher or related body if the name is of a constitutional convention. For additional information about a constitutional convention, see RDA 11.2.2.20.

Example:
Subordinate name: Constitutional Convention
Preferred name: **Philippines. Constitutional Convention**
MARC authority: 110 1 $a **Philippines**. $b **Constitutional Convention**

Name of Court (RDA 11.2.2.14.11 and 11.2.21)

Record the subordinate body subordinately under the higher or related body if the name is of a court. For additional information about a court, see RDA 11.2.2.21.

Example:
Subordinate name: Court of Appeals
Preferred name: **Idaho. Court of Appeals**
MARC authority: 110 1 $a **Idaho**. $b **Court of Appeals**

NAME OF PRINCIPAL SERVICE OF THE ARMED FORCES OF A GOVERNMENT (RDA 11.2.2.14.12 AND 11.2.2.22)

Record the subordinate body subordinately under the higher or related body if the name is of principal service of the armed forces of a government. For additional information, see RDA 11.2.2.22.

Example:
Subordinate name: Royal Canadian Air Force
Preferred name: **Canada. Royal Canadian Air Force**
MARC authority: 110 1 $a **Canada.** $b **Royal Canadian Air Force**

NAME OF EMBASSY, CONSULATE, etc. (RDA 11.2.2.14.12 AND 11.2.2.23)

Record the subordinate body subordinately under the higher body. For additional information, see RDA 11.2.2.23.

Example:
Subordinate name: Botschaft [embassy]
Preferred name: **Germany. Botschaft (India)**
MARC authority: 110 1 $a **Germany.** $b **Botschaft (India)**

Name of Delegation to an International or Intergovernmental Body (RDA 11.2.2.14.14 and 11.2.2.24)

Record the subordinate body subordinately under the higher body. The delegation representing one country is recorded under the preferred name of the country, in the language preferred by the country represented. For additional information, see RDA 11.2.2.24.

Example:
Subordinate name: Delegation to Bangladesh
Preferred name: **European Commission. Delegation to Bangladesh**
MARC authority: 110 2 $a **European Commission.** $b **Delegation to Bangladesh**

Name of Council, etc., of a Single Religious Body (RDA 11.2.2.14.15 and 11.2.2.25)

Record the subordinate body subordinately under the higher body. For additional information, see RDA 11.2.2.25.

Example:
Subordinate name: North Dakota Conference
Preferred name: **Methodist Episcopal Church. North Dakota Conference**

MARC authority: 110 2 $a **Methodist Episcopal Church**. $b **North Dakota Conference**

Name of Religious Province, Diocese, Synod, etc. (RDA 11.2.2.14.16 and 11.2.2.27)

Record the subordinate body subordinately under the higher body. For additional information, see RDA 11.2.2.27.

Example:
Subordinate name: Hiera Synodos
Preferred name: **Orthodoxos Ekklēsia tēs Hellados. Hiera Synodos**
MARC authority: 110 2 $a **Orthodoxos Ekklēsia tēs Hellados.** $b **Hiera Synodos**

Name of Central Administrative Organ of the Catholic Church (RDA 11.2.2.14.17 and 11.2.2.28)

Record the subordinate body subordinately under the higher body. For additional information, see RDA 11.2.2.28.

Example:
Subordinate name: Congregatio Sancti Officii
Preferred name: **Catholic Church. Congregatio Sancti Officii**
MARC authority: 110 2 $a **Catholic Church.** $b **Congregatio Sancti Officii**

Name of Papal Diplomatic Mission, etc. (RDA 11.2.2.14.18 and 11.2.2.29)

Record the subordinate body subordinately under the higher body. For additional information, see RDA 11.2.2.29.

Example:
Subordinate name: Apostolic Nunciature in Ethiopia
Preferred name: **Catholic Church. Apostolic Nunciature (Ethiopia)**
MARC authority: 110 2 $a **Catholic Church.** $b **Apostolic Nunciature (Ethiopia)**

Direct or Indirect Subdivision (RDA 11.2.2.15)

Often, corporate bodies have more than one level in their hierarchy or chain of subordination. Sometimes, this creates very long strings of subordinate bodies under the higher body. RDA 11.2.2.15 instructs us to record the subordinate body's name as a subdivision under the first larger body that can be recorded directly under its own name, and to leave out any intermediate bodies, as long as the name of the lower body is not used by another unit with the same corporate body. For example, in the hierarchy

American Crystal Sugar Company
Personnel and Industrial Relations Department
Corporate Communications Office

we are unlikely to see another subordinate unit, other than the Personnel and Industrial Relations Department, to have a unit called Corporate Communications Office. Therefore, the lowest body, Corporate Communications Office, is recorded after the highest unit, and the intermediate Personnel and Industrial Relations Department is omitted. The preferred name of the body representing the lowest subordination is "American Crystal Sugar Company. Corporate Communications Office." The same process may result in the omission of a number of intermediate units.

In the second example, in the hierarchy
Kansas
Department of Human Resources
Division of Staff Services
Research and Analysis Section
Management and Program Information Unit

the lowest unit "Management and Program Information Unit" is recorded last. Looking at one level above it, we need to ask, can there be a "Management and Program Information Unit" under another subordinate body within the organization? In this case, it is determined that this is the only possible unit for such a subordinate body, and, therefore, "Research and Analysis Section" can be omitted. Going one level above, we examine whether there could be a "Research and Analysis Section" under another unit besides the "Division of Staff Services." In this case, because it is possible to have such a unit under other subordinate bodies of the Department of Human Resources, the "Division of Staff Services" is recorded and not omitted. The resulting preferred name for the lowest subordinate body is "Kansas. Department of Human Resources. Division of Staff Services. Management and Program Information Unit."

Example:
Subordinate body: Charitable Solicitation Branch
Hierarchy: North Carolina
Department of Health and Human Services
Division of Facility Services
Charitable Solicitation Branch
Preferred name: **North Carolina. Charitable Solicitation Branch**
MARC authority: 110 1 $a **North Carolina.** $b **Charitable Solicitation Branch**

Although this guideline offers some advantages to cataloging, it may not always be intuitive to users who are not aware of the guidelines and library practices. Inclusion of all levels as a variant name helps alleviate the access issue.

Joint Committees, Commissions, etc. (RDA 11.2.2.16)

The preferred name of a joint committee with membership from two or more different, independent corporate bodies is recorded directly under its preferred name. Variant names may be recorded for each of the independent corporate bodies, with the name of the joint committee recorded as subordinate under each.

Example:
Joint committee: Joint Legislative Water Committee
Independent bodies: Oklahoma House of Representatives
Oklahoma Senate
Preferred name for joint committee: **Oklahoma. Legislature. Joint Legislative Committee on Water**
MARC authority: 110 1 $a **Oklahoma**. $b **Legislature**. $b **Joint Legislative Committee on Water**

Conventional Names for State and Local Units of US Political Parties (RDA 11.2.2.17)

Record the local and state units under the name of the party. Omit from the subordinate body any indication of the location, state, or name of the party.

Example:
Local unit: Indiana Republican State Central Committee

Preferred name: **Republican Party (Ind.). State Central Committee**
MARC authority: 110 2 $a **Republican Party (Ind.).** $b **State Central Committee**

Government Officials (RDA 11.2.2.18)

RDA 11.2.2.18 covers preferred name for a government official, including the following:

Head of State, Head of Government, etc. (RDA 11.2.2.18.1), e.g., governor
Ruling executive bodies (RDA 11.2.2.18.2), e.g., junta ruler
Head of international intergovernmental bodies (RDA 11.2.2.18.3), e.g., secretariat
Governors of dependent or occupied territories (RDA 11.2.2.18.4), e.g., governor
Other officials (RDA 11.2.2.18.5), e.g., audit officer

When considering government officials, we are not considering necessarily the person, but the holder of the office. Therefore, in this case it is considered a corporate body and not a person. A separate entity exists for the individual as a person, with a complete set of authority data describing the elements applicable to the person. The two entities, the official as corporate body and the person, are linked through the statement of the relationship between the two, according to RDA chapters on recording relationships (Chapter 30 for person and Chapter 32 for corporate bodies) and chapter 9 of this text. In some instances, the person may hold more than one government office, and, therefore, may have more than one corporate body name.

Example:
Person: Carter, Jimmy, 1924-
Government official: **Georgia. Governor (1971-1975: Carter)**
United States. President (1977-1981: Carter)
MARC authority: 110 1 $a **Georgia**. $b **Governor (1971-1975: Carter)**
110 1 $a **United States**. $b **President (1977-1981: Carter)**

The preferred name of a government official is typically formulated by recording the jurisdiction and adding the title of the office as the subordinate body, in the language of the agency creating the data. For each person holding the office, add within parentheses the years of reign and the name of the person in brief form, in the language of the preferred name for the person. If the person's reign spans across nonconsecutive periods, create a separate preferred name for each period.

Example:

Government official:	Great Britain Prime Minister Baldwin
Preferred name:	**Great Britain. Prime Minister (1923: Baldwin)** **Great Britain. Prime Minister (1924-1929: Baldwin)** **Great Britain. Prime Minister (1935-1937: Baldwin)**
MARC authority:	110 1 $a **Great Britain**. $b **Prime Minister (1923: Baldwin)** 110 1 $a **Great Britain**. $b **Prime Minister (1924-1929: Baldwin)** 110 1 $a **Great Britain**. $b **Prime Minister (1935-1937: Baldwin)**
Government official:	Army Service Forces, Office of the Surgeon General
Preferred name:	**United States. Surgeon-General's Office**
MARC authority:	110 1 $a **United States**. $b **Surgeon-General's Office**

Legislative Bodies (RDA 11.2.2.19)

Record the name of a legislature, legislative committee or subordinate unit, and successive legislature under the preferred name for the jurisdiction it legislates. If the legislature has more than one chamber, record the preferred name of the chamber as a subdivision of the preferred name for the legislature.

Examples:

Legislature:	Parliament of Kenya
Preferred name:	**Kenya. Parliament**
MARC authority:	110 1 $a **Kenya**. $b **Parliament**.
Chamber:	National Assembly Senate
Preferred name:	**Kenya. Parliament. National Assembly** **Kenya. Parliament. Senate**

MARC authority: 110 1 $a **Kenya**. $b **Parliament**. $b **National Assembly**
110 1 $a **Kenya**. $b **Parliament**. $b **Senate**

The legislative committee or subcommittee preferred name is recorded as a subdivision of the preferred name of the legislature or chamber, except in the case of United States, where RDA exception instructs us to record the committee or subcommittee as a subdivision of the committee to which it is subordinate.

Example:
U.S. exception, record under committee
Subcommittee: Committee on Agriculture, Nutrition, and Forestry
Preferred name: **United States. Congress. Senate. Committee on Agriculture, Nutrition, and Forestry**
MARC authority: 110 1 $a **United States.** $b **Congress**. $b **Senate**. $b **Committee on Agriculture, Nutrition, and Forestry**

Other cases, record under legislature, not under committee
Subcommittee: Sub-Committee of the Standing Committee on Agriculture on Farm Credit Arrangements.
Preferred name: **Canada. Parliament. House of Commons. Sub-Committee of the Standing Committee on Agriculture on Farm Credit Arrangements.**
MARC authority: 110 1 $a **Canada**. $b **Parliament**. $b **House of Commons**. $b **Sub-Committee of the Standing Committee on Agriculture on Farm Credit Arrangements.**

For successive legislatures numbered consecutively, record the ordinal number and inclusive years enclosed within parentheses:

Successive legislature: **United States. Congress (41st, 2nd session: $d 1869-1870)**
MARC authority: 110 1 $a **United States**. $b **Congress** $n **(41st, 2nd session: $d 1869-1870)**

Religious Official (RDA 11.2.2.26)

Record the preferred name of the religious body and the title of the official under the authorized access point for religious jurisdiction. The brief form of the name of the incumbent of an office and his or her related dates may be added within parentheses, similar to the pattern followed for government officials.

Examples:

Religious official: Pope Pontian
Preferred name: **Catholic Church. Pope (230-235: Pontian)**
MARC authority: 110 2 $a **Catholic Church**. $b **Pope (230-235: Pontian**)

Religious official: Grēgorios VI, Patriarch of Constantinople
Preferred name: **Constantinople (Ecumenical patriarchate). Patriarch (1835-1840: Grēgorios VI)**
MARC authority: 110 1 $a **Constantinople (Ecumenical patriarchate).** $b **Patriarch (1835-1840: Grēgorios VI)**

Variant Name of the Corporate Body

A variant name of a corporate body is the name or form of name not chosen as the preferred name for the corporate body. Record the variant name according to the general guidelines under RDA 8.5. Record a variant name if it is a name or form of a name used by the corporate body that is found in reference sources or that results from a different transliteration of the name.

Examples:

Preferred name: Church Council of Greater Seattle. Task Force on Southern Africa
Variant name: **Task Force on Southern Africa (Church Council of Greater Seattle)**
Church Council of Greater Seattle. Task Force on South Africa
MARC authority: 410 2 $a **Church Council of Greater Seattle**. $b **Southern Africa Task Force**
410 2 $a **Church Council of Greater Seattle**. $b **Task Force on South Africa**

Preferred name: Ginn and Company
Variant name: **Ginn & Co.**
Xerox Corporation. Ginn and Company
MARC authority: 410 2 $a **Ginn & Co.**
410 2 $a **Xerox Corporation**. $b **Ginn and Company**

Preferred name: Church of Jesus Christ of Latter-day Saints
Variant name: **Corporation of the President of the Church of Jesus Christ of Latter-Day Saints**
MARC authority: 410 2 $a **Corporation of the President of the Church of Jesus Christ of Latter-Day Saints**

When a corporate body changes its name, it is treated as a new body. Relationships to new and old names are recorded based on the guidelines in RDA Chapter 32. A discussion on recording these relationships may be found in chapter 9 of this text.

When the preferred name of a corporate body consists of or includes initials, acronyms, or abbreviations, record the full version (expanded name) as a variant name; if the preferred name is the full form, record the name consisting of or including initials, acronyms, or abbreviations as the variant name of the body.

Examples:
Preferred name: K. J. P. Synod Hospital
Variant name: **Khasi Jaintia Presbyterian Synod Hospital**
MARC authority: 410 2 $a **Khasi Jaintia Presbyterian Synod Hospital**

Preferred name: Türkiye Jokey Kulübü
Variant name: **T.J.K**
MARC authority: 410 2 $a **T.J.K**

If the preferred name of a corporate body has one or more linguistic forms, record these other forms as variant names of the body. Also include variations due to script.

Examples:
Preferred name: Syllogos Architektonōn Nomou Achaias (SANA)
Variant name: **Architects Association of the Achaia Prefecture**
Σύλλογος Ερχιτεκτόνων Νομού Αχαίαε (ΣΑΝΑ)
MARC authority: 410 2 $a **Architects Association of the Achaia Prefecture**
410 2 $a Σύλλογος Ερχιτεκτόνων Νομού Αχαίαε (ΣΑΝΑ)

Preferred name: Intergovernmental Oceanographic Commission
Variant name: **Comisión Oceanográfica Intergubernamental**
Commission océanographique intergouvernementale

MARC authority: 410 2 $a **Comisión Oceanográfica Intergubernamental**
410 2 $a **Commission océanographique intergouvernementale**

Any other variant names or variant forms of the name of a corporate body may be recorded as variant names if considered important for identification or useful for access.

Examples:
Preferred name: Komisi Nasional Indonesia Untuk Unesco
Variant name: **Indonesia. Komisi Nasional Untuk Unesco.**
MARC authority: 410 1 $a **Indonesia**. $b **Komisi Nasional Untuk Unesco.**

OTHER IDENTIFYING ATTRIBUTES FOR CORPORATE BODY

RDA 11.2, as covered in the above section of this chapter, provides guidelines for the recording of the preferred name of the corporate body, which then serves as the basis of the authorized access point. Additional attributes may be recorded about the corporate body that are necessary and useful for the identification of the corporate body and for differentiation between corporate bodies with the same or similar names. RDA 11.3–11.12 guidelines, covered below, provide us with instructions on additional elements representing these attributes. This information is recorded as separate elements, some of which may be also recorded as part of the authorized access point representing the corporate body. Elements may be core elements, core for certain categories, or core only if necessary for differentiation. This means that it is often up to the person creating the data to decide if it necessary or helpful to record some of these elements.

Elements used to differentiate corporate bodies with the same or similar preferred names include place associated with the corporate body, date associated with the corporate body, associated institution, and other designation associated with the corporate body.

Place Associated with the Corporate Body (RDA 11.3)
Core Element: *for conferences, and so on; otherwise, only if necessary for differentiation*
[MARC authority 370]

This element is used to record a place of significance associated with the corporate body. Place may include the location of a conference, meeting, etc., the location of an organization's offices, headquarters, etc., or any other place. The place is recorded as a separate element or as part of the authorized access point for the corporate body. Use RDA Chapter 16 for instructions on how to record the name of the place, and RDA Appendix B for abbreviated names of countries, states, and other regions. A brief discussion on identifying places is also available at the end of this chapter.

Place of the conference, meeting, etc.—for example, the location where the conference is held—is a core element, and must be recorded if known. If a particular conference meeting is held in more than one place, record the names of each of the places.

Place of headquarters, and others, is a core element only if it is necessary for differentiation, although it may be useful for identification of the corporate body. Record the latest place associated with a corporate body during its lifetime, if the place has changed.

Examples:
Place of CB: Riva, Italy
MARC authority: 370 $e **Riva (Italy)** $2 naf
111 2 $a International Semantic Web Conference $n (13th: $d 2014: $c **Riva, Italy**)

Note that, in the above example, the place is a core and is also recorded as part of the authorized access point for the conference.

Place of CB: London, England
MARC authority: 370 $e **London (England)** $2 naf
110 2 $a Eastern Art Gallery (Publishing company)

Note here that the element is core only if necessary for differentiation. The cataloger has decided to include the element, although not necessary for differentiation; it is not used in the authorized access point for the CB.

Place of CB: Akron, Ohio
MARC authority: 110 2 $a Goodyear Tire and Rubber Company
no 370 field

Note here that the place of the headquarters is not recorded since it is not a core element, not necessary for differentiation, and, in the view of the cataloger, not important to record for identification.

Place of CB: Sacramento, Calif.
MARC authority: 370 $e **Sacramento, Calif.**

110 1 $a California. $b Legislature. $b Senate. $b Select Committee on Manufactured Homes and Communities

Here, although the place associated with the CB is part of the preferred name and authorized access point, the more specific place is also recorded in a separate element.

Place of CB: Atlanta, Georgia, United States
MARC authority: 370 $c **United States** $e **Atlanta (Ga.)** $2 naf
110 2 $a Coca-Cola Foundation

Date Associated with the Corporate Body (RDA 11.4)
Core Element: *for conferences, etc.; otherwise, only if necessary for differentiation*
[MARC authority 046]

A significant date associated with the history of a corporate body, such as when it was established, when a meeting was held, the end of its lifespan, etc., is recorded in the date associated with the corporate body element. This is a core element for conferences, meetings, etc., which means that it should be recorded, if known, and should also be made a part of the authorized access point.

Specific dates identified in RDA 11.4 include date of establishment, date of termination, date of a conference or meeting, etc., and period of activity of a corporate body. Record the date using the preferred calendar of the agency creating the data.

Examples:
Core for conference, meetings, etc.

Date associate with CB: 1896
MARC authority: 046 $s **1896** $t **1896**
111 2 Olympic Games $n (1st: $d **1896**: $c Athens, Greece)

Date associate with CB: 2012 July 27-2012 August 12
MARC authority: 046 $s **20120727** $t **20120812**
111 2 $a Olympic Games $n (30th: $d **2012**: $c London, England)

Date associate with CB: 2010 November 05
MARC authority: 046 $s **20101105** $t **20101105**
111 2 $a CERL Seminar $n (11th: $d **2010**: $c Royal Library of Denmark)

Core if necessary for differentiation

Date associate with CB: 1718-1887
MARC authority: 046 $s **1718** $t **1887**
110 2 $a Yale College (1718-1887)

Date associate with CB: 1887-
MARC authority: 046 $s **1887**
110 2 $a Yale University

Not core

Date associate with CB: 1984 [established]
MARC authority: 046 $s **1984**
110 2 Coca-Cola Foundation

Associated Institution (RDA 11.5)
Core Element: *for conferences, and similar events, under conditions; other cases for differentiation only*
[MARC authority 373]

An institution commonly associated with the corporate body is recorded in this element. It is a core element for conferences, meetings, etc., if the associated institution is better for identification than the place of the conference, meeting, etc., or if the place is not known. For all other corporate bodies, the associated institution is core only if necessary for identification of the corporate body, and if the institution is a better element for identification than the place associated with the corporate body or if the place is not known. Record the associated institution using the preferred name of the institution. This is recorded as a separate element, and may be recorded as a part of the authorized access point representing the access point.

Examples:

Core for conference, meetings, etc.

Associated Institution: **SPIE (Society)**
MARC authority: 373 $a **SPIE (Society)** $2 naf
111 2 $a Medical Imaging (Conference: **SPIE (Society)**) $d (2013: $c Lake Buena Vista, Fla.)

Associated Institution: **University of Birmingham**
Wellcome Trust (London, England)
MARC authority: 373 $a **University of Birmingham** $a **Wellcome Trust (London, England)** $2 naf

111 2 $a Medicine and the Workhouse Conference $d (2008: $c Birmingham, England)

Number of a Conference, etc. (RDA 11.6)
Core Element: *for conferences, and other similar events*
[MARC authority 111]

This is a core element for corporate bodies that fall under the category of conferences, meetings, exhibitions, etc., and is used to record the sequencing of the conference or other event in a series of conferences and other events. Record the ordinal number of the event in the form preferred by the agency creating the data.

Although RDA 11.6 instructs us to record the data as a separate element as part of the authorized access point for the conference, the current MARC authority structure allows us to record the number only in the field for the name access point (authorized or variant).

Examples:

Number of conference:	**5th**
MARC authority:	111 2 $a International Conference on Pairing-Based Cryptography $n (**5th**: $d 2012: $c Cologne, Germany)
Number of conference:	**17th**
MARC authority:	111 2 Olympic Winter Games $n (**17th**: $d 1994: $c Lillehammer, Norway)

Other Designation Associated with the Corporate Body (RDA 11.7)
Core Element: *if needed to convey the idea of corporate body or for differentiation*
[MARC authority 368]

This element is used to record a designation associated with a corporate body, which can be a word, phrase, or abbreviation that indicates incorporation or legal status (e.g., Inc.), or a term used to differentiate the corporate body from other entities, including corporate bodies, persons, or families. Information recorded in this element includes the following:

- type of corporate body (e.g., organization, church, radio station, etc.);
- type of jurisdiction (e.g., county, state, ecclesiastical principality); or
- other designation (e.g., place, date, or institution associated with the corporate body). LC-PCC PS 11.7 instructs us to record the other designation in English.

Type of corporate body is core for any body with a preferred name that does not convey the idea of corporate body. For all corporate bodies, other designation is core when it is necessary to differentiate the corporate body from other entities with the same or similar names.

Examples:

Type of corporate body:	**Sporting event** **Sports tournaments**
MARC authority:	368 $a **Sporting event** 368 $a **Sports tournaments** $2 lcsh 111 2 $a Olympic Winter Games $n (17th: $d 1994: $c Lillehammer, Norway)
Type of corporate body:	**Congresses and conventions**
MARC authority:	368 $a **Congresses and conventions** $2 lcsh 111 2 $a Ada-Europe International Conference on Reliable Software Technologies $n (19th: $d 2014: $c Paris, France)

Language of the Corporate Body (RDA 11.8) [MARC authority 377]

The language a corporate body uses for its communications is recorded in this element. RDA instructs us to use a term from a controlled vocabulary. Current practice is to use a code from the *MARC Code List for Languages*. Similar to the language of the person, this element for corporate bodies will allow searching for corporate bodies communicating in a particular language, if the language terms are recorded consistently.

Examples:

Language of CB:	**German**, **ger**
MARC authority:	377 $a **ger** 111 2 $a Medialität, Unmittelbarkeit, Präsenz - die Nähe des Heils im Verständnis der Reformation (Conference) $d (2010: $c Erlangen, Germany)
Language of CB:	**English**, **eng**
MARC authority:	377 $a **eng** 110 2 $a Chartoff Productions (Firm)

Address of the Corporate Body (RDA 11.9) [MARC authority 371]

The address of a corporate body's headquarters or offices, an e-mail address, or the URL for a corporate body's web site is recorded in this element. This is not a core element, and it is not recorded as part of an access point.

Examples:

Address of the CB:	**1250 6th St #101, Santa Monica $c Calif. 90401**
MARC authority:	371 $a **1250 6th St #101** $b **Santa Monica $c Calif.** $e **90401** 110 2 $a Chartoff Productions (Firm)
Address of the CB:	**https://www.google.com**
MARC authority:	371 $u **https://www.google.com** 110 2 $a Google (Firm)

Field of Activity of the Corporate Body (RDA 11.10) [MARC authority 372]

The field in which a corporate body is engaged, and the corporate body's area of responsibility, activity, jurisdiction, etc., is recorded in this field. The best practice is to record a term from a controlled vocabulary. In most cases, for data created in the United States, an appropriate term from the *Library of Congress Subject Headings* is used. In the MARC authority environment, the code "lcsh" is entered in subfield $2 of MARC authority field 372 to indicate the source of the term.

Examples:

Field of activity of the CB:	**Motion picture studios**
MARC authority:	372 $a **Motion picture studios** $2 lcsh 110 2 $a Chartoff Productions (Firm)
Field of activity of the CB:	**Knowledge organization**
MARC authority:	372 $a **Knowledge organization** 111 2 $a ISKO UK Biennial Conference $n (2nd: $d 2011: $c London, England)

Corporate History (RDA 11.11) [MARC authority 678]

Record any information on the history of the corporate body in this element.

Examples (authority):

678 $a **AQA provides external academic quality assurance for all New Zealand universities via a five-yearly cycle of audits.**

678 $a **Dedham Bank; Dedham, Mass.; in 1835 became Dedham National Bank; in 1935 merged with 5 other banks to form Norfolk County Trust; in 1976 Norfolk County Trust became part of BayBanks; taken over in 1996 to form: Bank Boston Corp.; in 1999 to become FleetBoston Financial Corp.; and in 2003 taken over by Bank of America**

Identifier for the Corporate Body (RDA 11.12) [MARC authority 010]

A string of characters that uniquely identifies the corporate body or a representation of the corporate body (e.g., an authority record) is recorded in the identifier for the corporate body. The identifier can be used to differentiate corporate bodies from each other. Record the identifier along with the context of the identifying agency.

Example:

Identifier for the CB:	LCCN - **n 50056077**
MARC authority:	010 $a **n 50056077**
Identifier for the CB:	LAC - **0000K8576E**
	DNB - **004735099**
	FRBNF**118621695**

Putting it All Together: Identifying a Corporate Body

As a conclusion on the elements identifying a corporate body, the following is an example that covers all applicable elements in one record structure, using MARC authority format.

RDA element	*MARC authority*
Identifier for CB:	010 $a n 81024714 $z sh 85028743
	040 $b eng $e rda
Date associated with CB:	046 $s 1896
Preferred name:	110 2 $a Columbia University
Type of CB:	368 $a Universities and colleges $2 lcsh
Place associated with CB:	370 $e New York (N.Y.) $2 naf
Address of CB:	371 $u http://www.columbia.edu/
Field of activity:	373 $a Education $2 lcsh

Variant name of CB:	410 2 Ko-lun-pi-ya ta hsüeh 410 2 Kolumbiĭskiĭ universitet 410 2 Panepistēmion Columbia 410 2 Université de Columbia 410 2 Columbia University in the City of New York
Relationship (see Chapter 9):	510 2 Columbia College (New York, N.Y.) $w a
Source consulted:	670 Tsopanakēs, A.G. To dikaiōma tou anthrōpou epi tēs glōseōs kai hē pneumatikē kai politikē eleutheria, 1955: $b t.p. (Panepistēmiou Columbia) 670 Rapport de l'etude sur la promotion et la prestation . . . 1989: $b t.p. (Université de Columbia) 670 Protokoly T͡Sentral'nogo komiteta i zagranichnykh grupp Konstitut͡sionno-demokraticheskoĭ partii, 1905-seredina 1930-kh gg., 1998: $b p. preceding t.p. (Bakhmet'evskiĭ arkhiv Kolumbiĭskogo universiteta. Columbia University) 670 Columbia College, WWW home page, viewed May 23, 2014: $b History of Columbia College (In 1896, Columbia College in the City of New York was renamed Columbia University in the City of New York, with the undergraduate school retaining the name Columbia College. In 1897, the Morningside campus opened its doors.)
History of CB:	678 Columbia University was founded 1754 as King's College. In 1784, the name changed to Columbia College, followed by a 1896 reorganization as Columbia University.

ACCESS POINTS FOR CORPORATE BODIES

One of the objectives stated in RDA 0.4.2 is to enable the user to find resources that correspond to the user's stated search criteria, and, more specifically, to find all resources associated with a corporate body.

In current practice, using MARC structures, we enable the user to find all resources associated with a particular corporate body through the use of authorized access points in bibliographic records, each linked to their corresponding authority record.

Use of the authorized access points, which are constructed based on RDA guidelines, ensures consistency. The authority data provided should be true representations (RDA 0.4.3.4) of the attributes for a corporate body and sufficient (RDA 0.4.3.2) to uniquely identify the body and differentiate it from others with the same or similar names.

The construction of the authorized access point representing a corporate body is discussed in RDA 11.13 and in the following section of this chapter.

Authorized Access Point Representing a Corporate Body

RDA 11.2–11.12 provides guidelines for attributes included in the description of a person for bibliographic purposes. Not all elements covered under these guidelines will be used in the authorized access point representing a corporate body.

The examples below illustrate authorized access points representing the corporate body using MARC 21 formatting. Authorized access points for a corporate body are recorded in MARC authority fields 110 and 111. As an access point, these are also added in bibliographic records, more specifically in MARC bibliographic fields 110, 111 (for creators), 610, 611 (for the body as a subject of the work), and 710, 711 (for contributors and collaborators). Subfield coding is the same for all three bibliographic fields.

General Guidelines

When constructing an authorized access point for a corporate body, use the preferred name for the body as the basis for the authorized access point representing the corporate body. Additions may be necessary if they are applicable and if they follow guidelines discussed in RDA 11.12.2–10.11.8 and in the following sections of this chapter.

General Additions

Additions to the preferred name in formulating the authorized access point may include the type of the corporate body, the associated institution, the date and place associated with the corporate body, other designation for the corporate body, and the date, place, and number for the conference, meeting, etc.

Type of Corporate Body (RDA 11.13.1.2)

Add a term to indicate the type of corporate body, if necessary, to distinguish between corporate bodies with the same or similar names. LC-PCC PS 11.13.1.2 instructs us to record the type of corporate body for all corporate bodies whose preferred names consist of initials or abbreviations.

Examples (authority):
110 2 $a Interlink **(Firm)**
110 2 $a Harmonica Hotshots **(Musical group)**
111 2 $a DGCI **(Conference)** $n (18th: $d 2014: $c Siena, Italy)
110 2 $a Apollo 11 **(Spacecraft)**

Place Associated with the Body (RDA 11.13.1.3)

Add the name of the place associated with the corporate body that needs differentiation from other bodies with the same or similar names. Include name of country, state, province, etc., as appropriate. LC-PPC PS instructs us to revise the data in this element when a corporate body changes location or the place changes name. As an option, RDA states that the place can be added to the authorized access point if it is deemed helpful in the identification of the corporate body.

Examples (authority):
110 2 $a Abingdon Church **(Gloucester County, Va.)**
110 2 $a NIST Cloud Computing Program **(U.S.)**
110 2 $a Austin High School **(Austin, Tex.)**
110 2 $a France Bleu Breizh Izel (Radio station: **Brittany, France**)
110 2 $a KIDO (Radio station: **Boise, Idaho**)

Associated Institution (RDA 11.13.1.4)

Add the name of an associated institution to the authorized access point if it is necessary to differentiate the corporate body from other bodies. Add the name of an institution that is commonly associated with the corporate body, as the addition of the institution is preferred over the addition of a local place associated with the corporate body. Optionally, add the name of the associated institution if it is determined that it will assist in the identification of the corporate body.

Examples (authority):
110 2 $a Alchemy, Manchester Museum (**University of Manchester**)

110 2 $a Chemical Conservation and Research Laboratory (**Government Museum** (Chennai, India))

Date Associated with the Corporate Body (RDA 11.13.1.5)

Add the date associated with the corporate body if it is necessary for differentiation among bodies, and if the place or associated institution is not available. As an optional addition, include the date if it is deemed necessary for identifying the corporate body.

Examples (authority):
110 2 $a Sally (Schooner: **1799 December 19**)

Type of Jurisdiction (RDA 11.13.1.6)

Add the jurisdiction to the preferred name of the corporate body with jurisdiction, if it is necessary for differentiation among corporate bodies. The term is added to the name of the government, but not in the case of a city or a town.

Examples (authority):
110 2 $a Adirondack Park Agency **(N.Y.)**
110 1 $a Arizona. $b Superior Court **(Yavapai County)**

Other Designation Associated with the Body (RDA 11.13.1.7)

If none of the above additions results in a differentiated authorized access point for the corporate body (RDA 11.13.1.2–11.13.1.6), add an appropriate designation to the authorized access point.

Examples (authority):
111 2 $a World Cup **(Rugby football)**
110 2 $a New Jersey (Battleship: BB-62)

Number, Date, and Location of a Conference, etc. (RDA 11.13.1.8)

For a particular instance of a conference, meeting, etc., add the number, date, and location, if known. For the name representing an entire series of conferences, meetings, etc., do not add this information.

Examples (authority):
series of conferences: 111 2 $a Medical Image Understanding and Analysis (Conference)

individual event: 111 2 $a Medical Image Understanding and Analysis (Conference) $n **(18th: $d 2014: $c London, England)**

Variant Access Points Representing a Corporate Body

Any variant name or form of name is used as the basis for the construction of the variant access point(s) representing the corporate body. Unlike authorized access points representing the corporate body, variant access points are never included in bibliographic records.

In a MARC authority environment, the variant access points for a person are recorded in field 410 or 411. Links are made from the authority data when a user enters a name or form of a name that is not the same as the authorized access point. The links from the search appear either as "see references," pointing to the authorized access point, or as automatic reformulations of the search to retrieved resources using the authorized access point instead.

In constructing the variant access point, use the variant name for the corporate body. Make additions to the variant name if necessary for identification.

Examples (authority):

Authorized access point: 110 2 $a International Social Security Association

Variant access point: 410 2 $a **Jamʻīyah al-Dawlīyah lil-Ḍamān al-Ijtimāʻī**

410 2 $a **International Social Insurance Conference**

410 2 $a **Asociación Internacional de la Seguridad Social**

410 2 $a **Association internationale de la sécurité sociale**

410 2 $a **Conférence internationale de la mutualité et des assurances sociales**

Authorized access point: 111 2 International Space Conference of Pacific-Basin Societies

411 2 $a **Conference of Pacific-Basin Societies, International Space**

411 2 $a **ISCOPS (Conference)**

411 2 $a **International Conference of Pacific-Basin Societies**

411 2 $a **Space Conference of Pacific-Basin Societies**

IDENTIFYING PLACES

In RDA, Section 4 serves as a placeholder for guidelines to describe the FRBR entities concept, object, event, and place. The only entity place is covered briefly in RDA. Chapter 16 guidelines for selecting the preferred name; recording the preferred names, variant names, and other attributes of places for use typically as names for governments, as additions to the names of corporate bodies and conferences, and as additions to titles of works; and noting places associated with persons, families, or corporate bodies. Therefore, a brief discussion is included here.

Two elements are defined in in RDA Chapter 16: name of place and identifier of place.

NAME OF THE PLACE (RDA 16.2)

The name of the place is defined as a word, character, or group or words or characters by which a place is known. Two categories of names are defined: preferred name of the place and variant name of the place.

Preferred Name for the Place (RDA 16.2.2)

The preferred name for the place is the name or form of the name chosen to represent the place. The preferred name is also used as the conventional name of a government, an addition to the name of a family, a corporate body, a conference, etc., or a work, and to record a place associated with a person, family, or corporate body.

Although RDA identifies gazetteers and other reference sources in the language preferred by the cataloging agency or issued in the jurisdiction (if the name is for jurisdiction) as sources of information for the preferred name, LC -PCC PS 16.2.2 provides a list of resources for names of places in different parts of the world. For example, for names in the United States, the preferred name for the place should be based on the names found in United States Board on Geographic Names (BGN) Geographic Names Information System (GNIS). In addition, a number of LC-PCC policies are offered for selecting and recording the preferred name for the place.

RDA guidelines provide the following instructions:

- Select the form of the name in the language preferred by the cataloging agency or in the official language of the jurisdiction.
- Record the name most commonly found in gazetteers or other reference resources.

- Transliterate a name found in a script not preferred by the cataloging agency.
- For name changes, follow guidelines in RDA Chapters 10 and 11 for family and corporate names, respectively.
- Record the name of the country in which the place is located, except for places in (1) Australia, Canada, United States, the former Union of Soviet Socialist Republics, or former Yugoslavia for which the name of the larger jurisdiction (e.g., country) is not recorded but the name of the place is qualified by the name of the state, republic, or province in which the place is located; abbreviate the place of the larger place following the instructions in RDA Appendix B11; (2) England, Northern Ireland, Scotland, and Wales, for which the name of the larger jurisdiction is not recorded (e.g., United Kingdom). England, Northern Ireland, Scotland, or Wales is recorded as part of the preferred name for the place.
- For places within a city, qualify the name of the place with the name of the city.

Examples:
Name of place: Montreal, Quebec, Canada
Preferred name for the place: **Montreal (Quebec)**

Name of place: Florence, Tuscany, Italy
Preferred name for the place: **Florence (Italy)**

Name of place: Shanghai, China
Preferred name for the place: **Shanghai (China)**

Name of place: Melbourn, Cambridgeshire, England, United Kingdom
Preferred name for the place: **Melbourn (England)**

Name of place: French Quarter, New Orleans, Louisiana, United States
Preferred name for the place: **French Quarter (New Orleans, La.)**

Variant Name for the Place (RDA 16.2.2)

Variant name for the place is a name or form of the name by which a place is known but is different from the preferred name for the place.

Variant names are recorded for (1) names of places whose preferred name begins with an initial article. The variant name in this case is recorded without the initial article; (2) the expanded form of the name if an abbreviation or initials are used as the preferred name; (3) the abbreviated form or initials if the expanded form is used as the preferred name; (4) an alternative linguistic form of a name that is different from the form used as the preferred name; or (5) any other variant name considered important for identification or access.

Examples:

Preferred name for the place:	Austria
Variant name for the place:	**German Austria** **Österreich**
MARC21 (authority):	151 $a Austria 451 $a **German Austria** 451 $a **Österreich**
Preferred name for the place:	Soviet Union
Variant name for the place:	**Rusiyah** **USSR**
MARC21 (authority):	151 $a Soviet Union 451 $a **Rusiyah** 451 $a **USSR**
Preferred name for the place:	Heilbronn (Germany)
Variant name for the place:	**Heilbronn a. N. (Germany)**
MARC21 (authority):	151 $a Heilbronn (Germany) 451 $a **Heilbronn a. N. (Germany)**

There are no guidelines for the construction of access points to represent the place but a reference to RDA 11.13.1.1 for guidelines to construct access points using place names as conventional names for governments.

NOTES

1. International Federation of Library Associations and Institutions. (1996). *Names of Persons: National Usages for Entry in Catalogues* (4th revised and enlarged ed., UBCIM Publication—New Series Vol. 16). *München*, Germany: K. G. Saur.

2. Library of Congress. (2007, October). *MARC Code List for Languages* (2007 ed.). Retrieved from http://www.loc.gov/marc/languages/langhome.html.

3. Society of American Archivists. (1989). *Archives, Personal Papers, and Manuscripts* (2nd ed.). Chicago, IL: Society of American Archivists.

4. Society of American Archivists. (2007). *Describing Archives: A Content Standard.* Chicago, IL: Society of American Archivists.

Chapter 9

Resource Description and Access

Recording Relationships

One of the areas of emphasis for both the FR family models and RDA is making relationships among entities more explicitly stated. The reason for this is not that relationships were not recorded in previous practice using AACR2 as the standard of description; rather, it is that AACR2 did not discuss them as relationships and did not always make all relationships explicitly recorded. Often, relationships existed implicitly within the data created using AACR2.

AACR2, based on the objects of the catalog defined by Cutter,[1] included rules for the provision of access points so that a user would be able to (paraphrased here to match FRBR and RDA terminology):

- *find* all resources in a given collection by a person, family, or corporate body;
- *find* all resources in a given collection if the title of the work or manifestation, or the subject of the work, are known.

These relationships were then recorded as access points, in most cases authorized access points, in bibliographic records. These may have included the relationship between a work and its creator, via a "main entry access point," the relationship between an expression and a work, via the uniform title access point, etc. Relationships were also recorded in authority records, such as the relationship between the authorized names of a person or the authorized access point for a corporate body and the variant name(s) of a corporate body. Figure 9.1 illustrates how relationships are recorded in an AACR2/MARC environment.

With RDA, the emphasis is on identifying and recording relationships between entities. RDA does not impose specific record structures, as AACR2 did, or impose the use of a particular encoding system. Figure 9.2 illustrates the recording of entity relationships and selected data elements for

Authority record for the person

100 1_ Colet, John, ‡d 1467?-1519
400 1 $a
670 ....

Authority record for the work

100 1_ Colet, John, ‡d 1467?-1519 $t Ioannes Colet in Ecclesiasticam Divi Dionisii Hierarchiam
400 1 $a
670 ...

Authority record for the expression

100 1_ Colet, John, ‡d 1467?-1519 $t Ioannes Colet in Ecclesiasticam Divi Dionisii Hierarchiam. ‡l English
400 1 $a
670 ...

Bibliographic record (work, expression, manifestation)

100 1_ Colet, John, ‡d 1467?-1519.
240 10 Ioannes Colet in Ecclesiasticam Divi Dionisii Hierarchiam. ‡l English
245 10 John Colet on the ecclesiastical hierarchy of Dionysius : ‡b a new edition and translation with introduction and notes / ‡c introduction, annotations, and edited text by Daniel T. Lochman ; translation and comments on Colet's Latin by Daniel J. Nodes.
264 _1 Leiden ; ‡a Boston : ‡b Brill, ‡c 2013.
300 xv, 379 pages ; ‡c 24 cm.
336 text ‡2 rdacontent
337 unmediated ‡2 rdamedia
338 volume ‡2 rdacarrier
490 1_ Studies in medieval and Reformation traditions, ‡x 1573-4188 ; ‡v v. 171
490 1_ Texts & sources ; ‡v 4
504 Includes bibliographical references (pages [367]-376) and index.
600 00 Pseudo-Dionysius, ‡c the Areopagite. ‡t Ecclesiastical hierarchy.
650 _0 Theology ‡v Early works to 1800.
600 04 Dionysius, ‡c Areopagita, ‡c Pseudo-, ‡d ca. 500 na Chr.
700 1_ Lochman, Daniel T., ‡e editor of compilation.
830 _0 Studies in medieval and Reformation traditions ; ‡v v. 171.
830 _0 Studies in medieval and Reformation traditions. ‡p Texts & sources ; ‡v 4.

Figure 9.1 Relationships in an AACR2/MARC environment (excerpt records).

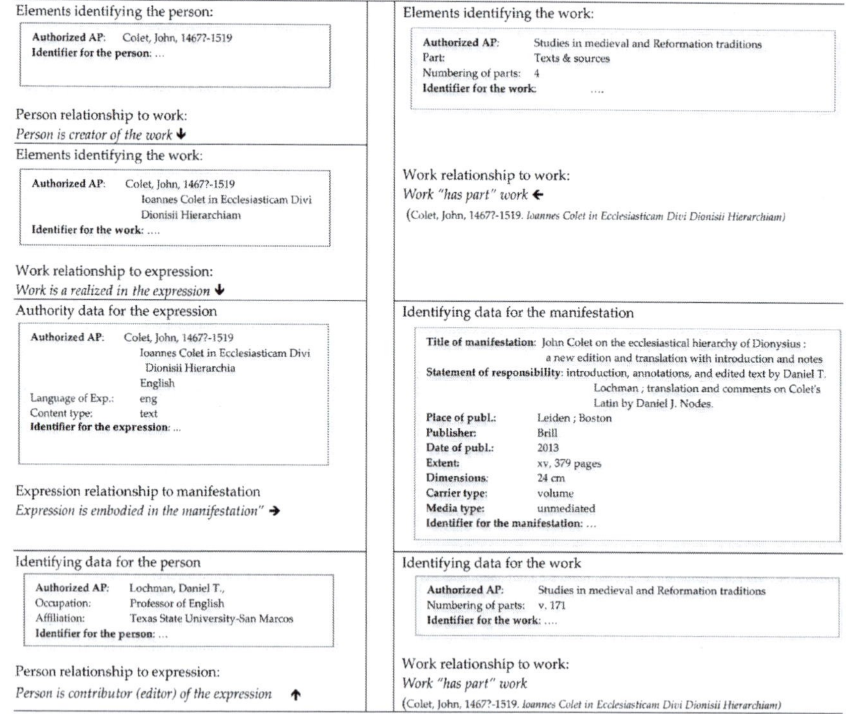

Figure 9.2 Entity relationships in RDA (selected elements are illustrated; AP = access point).

each entity. For simplification purposes, relationships are indicated as one-directional (e.g., *Person is creator of work*), although in FR family of models and RDA they two-directional (e.g., *Person is creator of work* and *Work has creator person*; *Work is realized in expression* and *Expression realizes work*).

RDA guidelines instruct us to record relationships by recording either the identifier or the authorized access point for the related entity. In many cases, RDA also instructs us to add appropriate relationship designators to authorized access point for the related entity, particularly when indicating relationship to a person, family, or corporate body. A relationship designator indicates the nature of the relationship that exists, for example, between a work and a person (e.g., "author" for the creator of a work that is primarily textual; "composer" for the creator of a musical work). A number of relationship designators have been established in RDA for the purpose of indicating the nature of the relationships that exist between the entities:

Appendix I: Relationship designators for relationships between a resource and persons, families, and corporate bodies associated with the resource
Appendix J: Relationship designators for relationships between works, expressions, manifestations, and items
Appendix K: Relationship designators for relationships between persons, families, and corporate bodies
Appendix L: Relationship designators for relationships between concepts, objects, events, and places
Appendix M: Relationship designators for subject relationships.

RECORDING PRIMARY RELATIONSHIPS BETWEEN WORKS, EXPRESSIONS, MANIFESTATIONS, AND ITEMS

RDA's emphasis on relationships is evidenced by the fact that RDA Chapters 17 through 30 are dedicated to the discussion about and recording of various relationships, along with instructions for recording those relationships. These relationships include (1) primary relationships between work, expression, manifestation, an item; (2) work, expression, manifestation, or item relationships to person, family, or corporate body; (3) subject relationship; (4) work, expression, manifestation, or item relationships to work, expression, manifestation, or item; and (5) person, family, or corporate relationships to person, family, or corporate body.

PRIMARY RELATIONSHIPS

Primary relationships are the first set of relationships discussed in RDA Chapter 17. These exist among the Group 1 entities (meaning between a work and its expression(s)), between an expression and its manifestation(s), and between a manifestation and its item(s), as Figure 9.3 illustrates below.

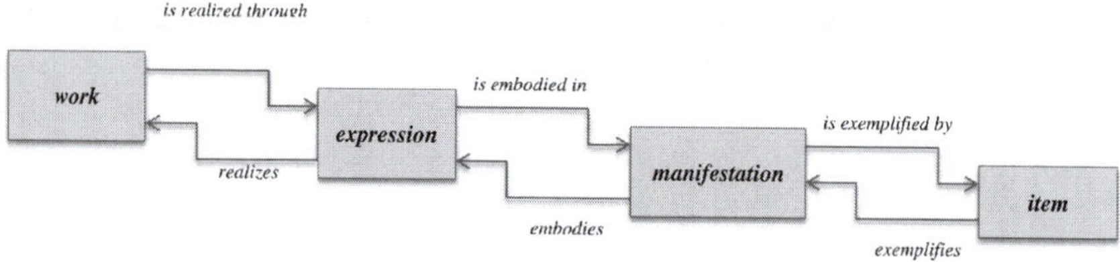

Figure 9.3 FRBR Group 1 entity relationships.

The following primary relationships are defined: work is realized through its expression or expressions; the expression, in turn, is embodied in a manifestation or manifestations; and each manifestation is then exemplified by one or multiple items. These relationships are reciprocal and therefore inverse relationships also exist: item is an exemplar of a manifestation; manifestation is the embodiment of an expression; and expression is the realization of a work.

In RDA terms, these relationships are important for the support of the functional objectives and goals, and by recording the primary relationships, a user is able to

- *find* all resources that embody a particular work or a particular expression; and
- *find* all items that exemplify a particular manifestation.

Therefore, in order to make sure that the data meet the above functional objectives, the data created using RDA should reflect the primary relationships. RDA Chapter 17 instructs us to record these primary relationships by means of three methods: using identifiers, using authorized access points, and creating a composite description. An explanatory note is provided to alert users to the limitations of encoding schemas in recording primary relationships, which includes MARC 21. The note states that "[s]ome encoding standards may not have a design that is suitable for recording the primary relationships. In these cases, primary relationships are not explicitly recorded though they may be inferred from other data elements in composite descriptions."[2] Therefore, LC-PCC PS 17.0 instructs us not to "apply Chapter 17 in the current implementation scenario." This is mostly due to the fact that MARC 21 is not designed to allow for explicit recording of primary relationships and therefore, in our current cataloging practice and implementation of RDA in a MARC environment, we have other ways to record this information in order to implicitly show relationships by implementing composite descriptions as they are described in RDA 17.4.2.3 and briefly discussed in this chapter. For example, the core primary relationship "work manifested" is indicated by including some form of the authorized access point for the work. This could be the authorized access point of the creator in MARC bibliographic field

1XX combined with the preferred title of the work in bibliographic field 240 or 245 $a (often the title proper of the manifestation is identical to the preferred title of the work).

Identifiers for the Work, Expression, Manifestation, or Item (RDA 17.4.2.1)

An identifier is a unique string of characters associated with the work, expression, manifestation, or item, and it is used to differentiate each entity from any other entity. Guidelines for recording the identifier of a work are covered in RDA 6.8, of an expression in RDA 6.13, of a manifestation in RDA 2.15, and of an item in RDA 2.20, and they are described in chapters 6 and 7 of this text.

There may be different identifiers for each entity. Each identifier may be associated with a particular context. For example, in the Library of Congress Name Authority File (LC-NAF) the record number (LCCN, recorded in MARC authority field 010) for a work is an identifier for the representation of the work. In the current MARC environment, typical of many libraries, especially in the United States, identifiers are recorded in authority records for works and expressions. Identifiers for manifestations are recorded in the MARC bibliographic records. For example, an ISBN number, which is an identifier of a manifestation, is recorded in MARC bibliographic field 020. Although these identifiers are recorded in authority or bibliographic records, they typically do not indicate primary relationships. It is possible that, when adding an authorized access point for the work in the bibliographic record, one may embed the identifier that directly links the string of the authorized access point for the work with the authority record representing the work, thus serving as a relationship to the work. Similarly, this is possible for expressions.

Examples:

Identifier of work:	**LCCN no 00077615**
MARC authority:	010 $a **no 00077615**
Work, authorized access:	100 1 $a García Márquez, Gabriel, $d 1927-2014. $t Amor en los tiempos del cólera
Identifier of expression:	**LCCN n 86061892**
MARC authority:	010 $a **n 86061892**
Expression, authorized access:	100 1 $a García Márquez, Gabriel, $d 1927-2014. $t Amor en los tiempos del cólera. $l English
Identifier of manifestation:	**ISBN 9780739328057** (paperback)

MARC bibliographic:	020 $a **9780739328057** (paperback)
Manifestation, title, statement of responsibility:	245 10 $a Love in the time of cholera / $c Gabriel García Márquez; translated from the Spanish by Edith Grossman.
Identifier of item:	**09679893254**
MARC holdings:	876 $a **09679893254**

Authorized Access Point Representing the Work or Expression (RDA 17.4.2.2)

RDA 17.4.2.2 instructs us to provide authorized access points representing the work or the expression. The construction of authorized access points for work is covered in RDA 6.27.1–6.27.2 and for expression is given in RDA 6.27.3.

Example of current structure:

MARC bibliographic

Creator:	100 1 $a **Dickens, Charles**, $d **1812-1870**.
Preferred title of work:	240 10 $a **Great expectations**.
Language of expression:	$l **Spanish**
Title of manifestation:	245 10 $a Grandes esperanzas / $c Charles Dickens; Benito Pérez Galdós, traducción.

MARC authority

Preferred access point for work:	100 1 $a **Dickens, Charles,** $d **1812-1870**. $t **Great expectations.**
Preferred access point for expression:	100 1 $a **Dickens, Charles,** $d **1812-1870.** $t **Great expectations.** $l **Spanish**

As this example illustrates, there is an implicit relationship between the work by Dickens, the expression of the text in Spanish, and the embodiment of the expression in the manifestation. This relationship is implied with the use of the authorized access point representing the work in the bibliographic record as an access point, the addition of the language of the expression in the access point, and the title of the manifestation, the statement of responsibility, and other elements (not included here).

In the current MARC structure, authorized access points are established as authority data, but are also recorded in bibliographic records as access points to serve as relationships and as ways to find resources. A combination of MARC bibliographic fields may be necessary to record an authorized access point representing a work or an expression. For example, if there is a creator as part of the authorized access point, the single or first creator's authorized access point is recorded in MARC bibliographic field 100, 110, or 111, and the work's preferred title is recorded in field 240 or 245 (if the preferred title of the work is the same as the title of the manifestation). Additional creators appear in field 700, 710, or 711. If there is no person, family, or corporate body associated with the creation of the work, then the work's authorized access point includes the preferred title for the work, which is recorded in MARC bibliographic field 130 or 245 (if the preferred title for the work is the same as the title of the manifestation).

Similarly, for an expression, the language of the expression and other distinguishing characteristics of the expression are added to the authorized access point of the work to formulate the authorized access point representing the expression.

Links to a work or an expression are also recorded in MARC bibliographic fields 7XX.

Examples:

MARC authority, work:	100 1 $a García Márquez, Gabriel, $d 1927-2014. $t Amor en los tiempos del cólera. $l English
MARC bibliographic, work:	100 1 $a **García Márquez, Gabriel,** $d **1927-2014**. 240 10 $a **Amor en los tiempos del colera.**
MARC authority, expression:	100 1 $a García Márquez, Gabriel, $d 1927-2014. $t Amor en los tiempos del cólera. $l English
MARC bibliographic, expression:	100 1 $a **García Márquez, Gabriel**, $d **1927-2014**. 240 10 $a **Amor en los tiempos del colera.** $l **English**
MARC authority, work:	130 0 $a Beowulf
MARC bibliographic, work:	130 0 $a **Beowulf**
MARC authority, expression:	130 0 $a Beowulf. $l English $s (Alexander). $f 2001
MARC bibliographic, expression:	130 0 $a **Beowulf**. $l **English** $s **(Alexander)**. $f **2001**
MARC bibliographic:	245 00 $a Sustainable happiness: $b live simply, live well, make a

difference / $c edited by Sarah van Gelder and the staff of YES! Magazine.

In the last example, we see only the presence of a MARC bibliographic field 245 $a, which implicitly states (or makes one assume) that the title of the manifestation is also the title of the work.

Composite Description (RDA 17.4.2.3)

A composite description is the use of one or multiple elements combined to describe a work realized in an expression, which is embodied in a manifestation with the description of the manifestation. A composite description is the current practice for one record structure, using MARC bibliographic, to record elements describing a work, expression, manifestation, and, often, item. The following example illustrates composite description in current practice (where W = work, E = expression, M = manifestation):

E, language of expression:	041 eng
W, creator of work:	100 1 $a Covey, Sean.
M [W], title of manifestation:	245 10 $a Sammy and the pecan pie / $c Sean Covey; illustrated by Stacy Curtis.
M, edition of manifestation:	250 $a First edition.
M, place, publisher, date:	264 1 $a New York: $b Simon & Schuster Books for Young Readers, $c [2013]
M&E, extent, dimensions, illustrative content	300 $a 1 volume (unpaged): $b color illustrations; $c 19 cm.
E, content type:	336 $a text $2 rdacontent
E, content type:	336 $a still image $2 rdacontent
M, media type:	337 $a unmediated $2 rdamedia
M, carrier type:	338 $a volume $2 rdacarrier
E, language of expression:	546 $a In English.
W, intended audience:	521 1 $a Ages 2-6.
W, content:	520 $a Sammy Squirrel and his twin sister, Sophie, usually get along but lately it seems everything is going her way.

RECORDING RELATIONSHIPS TO PERSONS, FAMILIES, AND CORPORATE BODIES (RDA CHAPTER 18)

RDA Chapter 18 provides basic guidelines for recording relationships to persons, families, or corporate bodies associated with a resource, and sets the stage for Chapters 19 through 22, which discuss the recording of relationships to Group 2 entities for work (Chapter 19), expression (Chapter 20), manifestation (Chapter 21), and item (Chapter 22), individually.

Throughout Chapters 18 through 22, the term resource is used when discussing a relationship to a person, family, or corporate body. "Resource" is a general term used to refer to a work, expression, or item (RDA 18.1.3) and can be a single entity (e.g., single work), an aggregated entity (e.g., an anthology of five works), or a component of an entity (e.g., one article from a journal, one song from an album).

Core Elements (RDA 18.3)

When recording the relationship of a resource to a person, family, or corporate body, the only core element or required relationship to be recorded is that to the creator of the resource. If more than one creator is named, core is considered the creator with the principal responsibility (as such is indicated or discerned); if no one creator is considered to have the principal responsibility for creating the work, the first creator listed on the resource is considered core. In addition to the creator, if any other person, family, or corporate body is associated with the work, and their name is included in the authorized access point for the work, consider that person, family, or corporate body as core.

In addition to the identifier and the authorized access point for the person, family, and corporate body, a third element, the relationship designator, identifies the relationship that is recorded with the identifier or the authorized access point for the person, family, or corporate body.

Recording Relationships to Persons, Families, or Corporate Bodies Associated with a Resource (RDA 18.4)

To record relationships to persons, families, or corporate bodies associated with a resource, RDA 18.4.1 instructs us to record either the identifier or the authorized access point for the person, family, or corporate body, or both. RDA also instructs us to add the appropriate relationship designator to the authorized access point for the person, family, or corporate body.

In the LC-PCC practice, relationship designators follow the *PCC Guidelines for the Application of Relationship Designators in Bibliographic Records*, with an instruction to use MARC 1XX/7XX subfield $e, or $j, as appropriate. Per MARC definitions, subfield $e is used when the responsibility or role of the person, family, or corporate body is known; subfield $j is used as attribution information when the responsibility or role of the person, family, or corporate body is unknown, uncertain, fictitious, or pseudonymous.

LC and PCC policy and practice is to record the relationship using the method of recording the authorized access point of the entity with the addition of the relationships designator. Examples below illustrate the use of authorized access points to record the relationships.

Authorized Access Points for Persons, Families, or Corporate Bodies (RDA 18.4.1.2)

Current practice is to follow RDA 18.4.1.2 and record the relationship to person, family, or corporate body by providing an authorized access point representing the person, family, or corporate body, by following the instructions in RDA 9.19 for persons, 10.11 for families, and 11.13 for corporate bodies, and by paying attention to the guidelines of when a corporate body can be considered a creator.

Examples (bibliographic):

One creator:

100 1 $a **Vérant, Samantha**, $e author.

111 2 $a **Annual Conference on Experimental and Applied Mechanics** $d (**2014**: $c **Greenville, SC**)

100 3 $a **Hunt (Family**: $g **Hunt, Gavine Drummond, 1794-1889)**

110 1 $a **United States.** $b **Army**. $b **Corps of Engineers.** $b **New Orleans District.**

More than one creator:

100 1 $a **Zucolotto, M. Elizabeth**, $e author.

700 1 $a **Fonseca, Ariadne do Carmo**, $e author.

700 1 $a **Antonello, Loiva Lízia**, $e author.

Change in Responsibility (RDA 18.4.2)

Provide additional access point to indicate relationship to persons, families, or corporate bodies when there is a change in responsibility between the parts of a multipart monograph (e.g., between volumes of a resource with multiple volumes), between journal parts or issues, and between different iterations of an integrated resource.

An additional access point for the person, family, or corporate body due to change of responsibility depends on whether the change is considered important enough to access the resource and whether the change in responsibility results in a new work and, therefore, requires a new description. If the latter is the case, then do not record the authorized access point for the changed, new responsibility.

Relationship Designator (RDA 18.5)

A designator indicating the nature of the relationship between the resource and a person, family, or corporate body is added to the authorized access point representing the responsible body. RDA Appendix I provides a list of terms to be used as relationship indicators and instructs us to use additional concise terms if no term from this list is appropriate. LC-PCC practice is to follow the *PCC Guidelines for the Application of Relationship Designators in Bibliographic Records*[3,4] and use MARC 1XX/7XX subfield $e or $j as appropriate. More than one designator may be used if multiple responsibilities are assumed by the same person, family, or corporate body.

LC-PCC PS 18.5.3.1 instructs us to provide an authorized access point in the bibliographic record for an illustrator in all cases of resources intended for children, with the addition of the relationships designator "illustrator" in MARC 700 subfield $e. This means that the relationship designator is considered required for children's illustrated resources, but not for all others.

Examples (bibliographic):

100 1 $a Pinto, Américo, $e **author**.
100 1 $a Loveless, Lydia, $d 1990- $e **composer**, $e **performer**.
100 1 $a Egerton, M., $d active 1824-1827, $e **author**, $e **illustrator**.
710 2_ $a National Research Council (U.S.). $b Transportation Research Board, $e **issuing body**.
710 2_ $a Airport Cooperative Research Program, $e **sponsoring body**.
710 1_ $a United States. $b Federal Aviation Administration, $e **sponsoring body**.

Last, RDA 18.6 states that a note can be added in the description of a resource that explains the relationship between the resource and a person, family, or corporate body.

LC-PCC PS 25.0 provides extensive instructions for the construction of authorized access points for series. A series is considered as a work, and when a work is created and then produced or published under the umbrella of a series, the relationship between the two works is recorded. This relationship is a whole-part relationship, as mentioned above in the discussion on numbering parts. Since this is a very common relationship between works, a brief discussion is warranted on authorized access points for series, information included in a series authority record, and recording of the relationship between a work and its series in a bibliographic record.

RECORDING RELATIONSHIPS OF PERSON, FAMILY, AND CORPORATE BODY ASSOCIATED WITH A WORK (RDA CHAPTER 19)

RDA Chapter 19 covers the relationship that exists between a person, family, or corporate body and the work, which, in most cases, constitutes the creator relationship.

Creator (RDA 19.2)
Core element
[MARC bibliographic 100, 110, 111, 700, 710, 711]

Creator is the person, family, or corporate body responsible for the creation of the work. There can be single responsibility or joined responsibility in the creation of a work. In a joint responsibility, the creators can either perform the same roles (e.g., all of them are authors, or all of them are composers) or they can perform different roles (e.g., one is the composer of the music and the other, the writer of the lyrics).

Creator is a core element. If there is more than one creator, only the one with principal responsibility for the creation of the work or the one first named on the preferred source of information of the resource is core. The remaining creators are not core, but it is a best practice to include other creators. There is no limit on how many creators can be recorded for a particular work, but sometimes those creating the data will make judgments based on both the importance of the creator and how helpful this information is for access, and will take into consideration maintenance issues (each creator requires authority data creation to be able to construct the authorized access point representing them).

Corporate Body As Creator (RDA 19.2.1.1.1)

Special attention is needed in considering a corporate body as the creator of a work, in addition to paying attention to the definition of a corporate body. There are only certain categories of types of works and corporate body responsibilities that qualify a corporate body as the creator of a work. Only under these categories can a corporate body's authorized access point appear in the 110 or the 111 field. In all other cases, the corporate body is not considered a creator, and, therefore, the access point for the corporate body is recorded in MAC bibliographic fields 710 and 711.

If the work falls under the following categories and a corporate body bears the responsibility for the work, then the corporate body is considered the creator of the work:

- Works of an administrative nature, including the body's policies, procedures, etc., various directories of staff, units, and other components, and lists of its own resources, for example, catalogs or inventories.
- Recorded collective thought of a corporate body, including report of a committee, standards of an organization, etc.
- Recorded hearing of a legislative body, government, judicial body, etc.
- Recorded collective activity of a conference, meeting, etc., such as proceedings of a conference.
- Recorded collective activity of a performing group, "where the responsibility of the group goes beyond that of mere performance, execution, etc."
- Cartographic works created by a corporate body, beyond the publishing or distribution responsibilities.
- Legal works by a body of jurisdiction, such as laws, decrees, bills, regulations, constitutions, court rules, and charges to juries, indictments, court proceedings, and court decisions.
- Named individual works of art created by two or more artists acting as a corporate body.

Government and Religious Officials as Creators (RDA 19.1.1.2)

Government and religious officials are considered creators in two cases: for official communications of heads of different types of government, and for official communications of popes, bishops, etc.

Any other communication by the individual holding the official position is considered the responsibility of the individual person, and, therefore, the access point used will be the authorized access point representing the person, not the corporate body.

Persons or Families as Creators of Serials (RDA 19.1.1.3)

In the case where a person or persons or a family or families are responsible for the content of the entire serial publication, and not just for an article in it or a particular issue, the person or the family is considered the creator of the serial. RDA 19.1.1.3 offers a list of cases in which this is applicable.

Recording Creators (RDA 19.2.1.3)

To record the relationship to a work, record the authorized access point representing the person, family, or corporate body in accordance with the guidelines in RDA 18.4. The examples below illustrate different cases. The MARC field 245, which includes the title of the manifestation and the statement of responsibility, is also included in the examples to offer the context for recording the creator.

Examples:

Creator:	**Building Bridges Seminar (11th: 2012: King's College London)**
MARC bibliographic:	111 2 $a **Building Bridges Seminar** $n **(11th:** $d **2012:** $c **King's College London)**
Context:	245 10 $a Death, resurrection, and human destiny: $b Christian and Muslim perspectives: a record of the Eleventh Building Bridges Seminar convened by the Archbishop of Canterbury, King's College London and Canterbury Cathedral, April 23-25, 2012 / $c David Marshall and Lucinda Mosher, editors.
Creator:	**Miss Piggy, author.**
MARC bibliographic:	100 0 $a **Miss Piggy,** $e **author.**
Context:	245 14 $a The diva code: $b Miss Piggy on life, love, and the 10,000 idiotic things men [strike through] frogs do / $c by Miss Piggy as told to Jim Lewis.
Creator:	**Saint-Germain, comte de, -1784 (Spirit), author.**
MARC bibliographic:	100 1 $a **Saint-Germain,** $c **comte de,** $d **-1784** $c **(Spirit),** $e **author**.
Context:	245 13 $a El séptimo rayo / $c Saint Germain.
Creator:	**Means, Barbara, 1949- , author.** **Bakia, Marianne, author.** **Murphy, Robert, 1962- , author.**
MARC bibliographic:	100 1 $a **Means, Barbara,** $d **1949-,** $e **author**. 700 1 $a **Bakia, Marianne,** $e **author**. 700 1 $a **Murphy, Robert,** $d **1962-,** $e **author**.
Context:	245 10 $a Learning online: $b what research tells us about whether, when and how / $c Barbara Means, Marianne Bakia, Robert Murphy, Center for Technology in Learning, SRI International.
Creator:	**Catholic Church. Pope (1216-1227: Honorius III), author.**
MARC bibliographic:	110 2 $a **Catholic Church.** $b **Pope (1216-1227: Honorius III)**, $e **author**.

Context:	240 10 $a Correspondence. $k Selections 245 10 $a Onorio III e la Sardegna, 1216-1227 / $c a cura di Mauro G. Sanna.
Creator:	**University of Maine at Farmington, author.**
MARC bibliographic:	110 2 $a **University of Maine at Farmington,** $e **author**.
Context:	245 10 $a Administration, Faculty and Staff Directory / $c University of Maine at Farmington.
Creator:	**Chicago Library Club, issuing body.**
MARC bibliographic:	110 2 $a **Chicago Library Club,** $e **issuing body.**
Context:	245 14 $a The Chicago Library Club. 246 3 $a [Constitution] 500 $a Includes officers, constitution, and members for 1893.

No creator associated with the resource:

Creator:	[none]
MARC bibliographic:	[no 1XX]
Context:	245 00 $a Himalayan passages: $b Tibetan and Newar studies in honor of Hubert Decleer / $c edited by Benjamin Bogin and Andrew Quintman.

Corporate body not considered a creator:

Creator:	[none]
MARC bibliographic:	[no 1XX]
Context:	245 00 $a Pioneer Venus VideoGraphics / $c Ames Research Center; videographics system, Dick Shoup; Pioneer Venus graphics, Damon Rarey; Xerox, Palo Alto Research Center.

Other Person, Family, or Corporate Body Associated with a Work (RDA 19.3)
Core element
[MARC bibliographic 700, 710, 711]

This element defines a person, family, or corporate body associated with the work, but not as a creator. The element is core only if the name of the other person, family, or corporate body associated with the work is used in the construction of the authorized access point for the work. Record other persons, families, or corporate bodies if they are considered important for access, using the authorized access point representing the person, family, or corporate body.

Different categories of associations with a particular type of work are discussed in RDA 19.3.

One of these categories includes the persons who are engaged in the correspondence with the originator, honorees of festschrifts (works created in honor of persons, families, etc.), directors, cinematographers, etc., involved in moving images, sponsoring bodies, hosts of exhibitions, etc.

Examples:

Other person assoc. with work:	Chanock, Martin.
MARC bibliographic:	700 1 $a **Chanock, Martin**.
Context:	245 00 $a For Martin Chanock: $b essays on law and society / $c editors, Stephen Ellmann, Heinz Klug and Penelope Andrews. 500 $a Proceedings of symposium in honor of Martin Chanock.
Others assoc. with work:	700 1 $a **Druyan, Ann,** $d **1949-** $e **director**, $e **writer**, $e **bibliographic antecedent.** 700 1 $a **Pope, Bill,** $d **1952-** $e **cinematographer**, $e **director**. 700 1 $a **Braga, Brannon,** $e **director**. 710 2 $a **Cosmos Studios,** $e **production company.** 710 2 $a **Fuzzy Door Productions (Firm),** $e **production company**.
Context:	245 00 $a Cosmos: $b a spacetime odyssey / $c Cosmos Studios; Fuzzy Door Productions; written and directed by Ann Druyan; directed also by Brannon Braga and Bill Pope.

This element also includes other persons, families, or corporate bodies associated with legal works including various legal decrees, administrative regulations, court rules, constitutions, charges, etc., of nonjurisdictional bodies, law reports, court report citations, judicial decisions, treaties, etc. In all of the cases listed in RDA 19.3, record the authorized access point of the body responsible for the resource but not qualifying to be considered the creator of the work.

Lastly, this element applies to other persons, families, or corporate bodies associated with religious works, only in the case of theological creeds, confessions of faith, etc., accepted by one or more denominations. These works include officially accepted texts of religious observance, books including required prayers, calendars for religious observances, readings for services, devotions, hymns, etc.

In all of these cases, record the authorized access point for the church, denominational body, or specific body within a church, applying the RDA guidelines to record other persons.

Examples:

Other corporate body:	710 1 $a **United States**. $b **Congress**. $b **Senate**. $b **Committee on Foreign Relations**, $e **issuing body**.
Context:	245 14 $a The protocol amending the Tax Convention with Spain: $b message from the President of the United States transmitting the protocol amending the Convention Between the United States of America and the Kingdom of Spain for the Avoidance of Double Taxation and the Prevention of Fiscal Evasion with Respect to Taxes on Income and its Protocol, signed at Madrid on February 22, 1990.
Other corporate body:	710 2 $a **Practising Law Institute,** $e **sponsoring body**.
Context:	245 10 $a 16th annual real estate tax forum / $c co-chairs, Leslie H. Loffman, Sanford C. Presant, Blake D. Rubin.
Others assoc. with work:	700 1 $a **Temple, Leofric**, $d **1819-1891.**
	700 1 $a Mew, George.
Context:	245 10 $a Reports of cases, argued and determined in the Court of Criminal Appeal: $b from Michaelmas term, 1848, to Michaelmas term, 1851 / $c by Leofric Temple, of Lincoln's Inn, Esq. and George Mew, of the Middle Temple, Esq., barristers-at-law.

RECORDING RELATIONSHIPS OF PERSONS, FAMILIES, OR CORPORATE BODIES ASSOCIATED WITH AN EXPRESSION (RDA CHAPTER 20)

In RDA Chapter 20, the term "contributor" is used to refer to a person, family, or corporate body contributing to an expression. Contributors may include translators, illustrators, editors, performers, music arrangers, etc. Contributors are recorded for a particular expression, for a work that has more than one expression, or for an accompanying resource to the primary work commentary, supplement, epilogue, etc.

LC-PCC PS 20.2.1.3 considers contributors as core for illustrators of children's resources, requiring the recording of the authorized access point for the first illustrator of all children's illustrated resources. For multiple illustrators, cataloger's judgment is necessary. For any other contributor, PCC practice is to add the authorized access point representing the contributor only if it is necessary for identification.

Relationship designators may be added to all contributors by using terms from RDA Appendix I as applicable to creators and other bodies associated with the work. Contributors are not necessary in the statement of responsibility to be recorded in an authorized access point. In addition to the statement of responsibility, a contributor can be taken from a note included in the description of the resource, especially when it relates to the expression.

Examples:

Contributor:	700 1 $a **Urban, Helle**, $e **illustrator**.
Context:	245 10 $a Little Halloween / $c Denise Brennan-Nelson; illustrated by Helle Urban.
Contributor:	700 1 $a **Zipes, Jack**, $d 1937- $e **translator**. 700 1 $a **Dezsö, Andrea**, $e **illustrator**.
Context:	245 14 $a The Original Folk and Fairy Tales of the Brothers Grimm: $b the complete first edition / $c [Jacob Grimm, Wilhelm Grimm; translated by] Jack Zipes; [illustrated by Andrea Dezsö].
Contributor:	700 1 **Jeffers, Chike**, $d **1982-** $e **editor**.
Context:	245 00 Listening to ourselves: $b a multilingual anthology of African philosophy / $c edited by Chike Jeffers; foreword by Ngũgĩ wa Thiong'o.
Contributor:	700 1 **Reale, Giovanni**, $e **writer of afterword.** 700 1 **Lio, Eugenio,** $e **interviewer.** 700 1 **Nesi, Edoardo,** $d 1964- $e **interviewer.** 700 1 **Battiato, Franco,** $e **interviewer.** 700 1 **Consoli, Carmen,** $d 1974- $e **interviewer.**

700 1 **Buttafuoco, Pietrangelo,** $e **interviewer.**
700 1 **Eco, Umberto,** $e **interviewer.**
700 1 **Gnoli, Antonio,** $e **interviewer.**
700 1 **Ghezzi, Enrico,** $e **interviewer.**
700 1 **Veronesi, Sandro,** $d 1959- $e **interviewer.**
700 1 **Morante, Laura,** $d 1956- $e **interviewer.**
700 1 **Sgarbi, Vittorio,** $e **interviewer.**
700 1 **Merlo, Francesco,** $e **interviewer.**

Context: 245 10 Se hai una montagna di neve tienila all' ombra: $b un viaggio nella cultura italiana / $c Elisabetta Sgarbi; interviste integrali di Edoardo Nesi, Euginio Lio . . . postfazione di Giovanni Reale.

Contributor not considered important:

Contributor: [none]

Context: 245 10 Exploring climate change through science and in society: $b an anthology of Mike Hulme's essays, interviews and speeches / $c Mike Hulme; with a foreword by Matthew C. Nisbet.

RECORDING RELATIONSHIPS OF PERSONS, FAMILIES, OR CORPORATE BODIES ASSOCIATED WITH A MANIFESTATION (RDA CHAPTER 21)

Chapter 21 provides guidelines for the recording of relationships between a person, family, or corporate body and a manifestation. Typically, these are in the role of producer of unpublished resources, publisher, distributor, and manufacturer, although other associations are possible. Record these if it is necessary or useful for access. These relationships are not core elements.

RDA instructs us to record the relationships as authorized access points for the producer, publisher, etc., or as identifiers, following guidelines set in RDA 18.4. Since current practice holds that the identifier is not used for recording relationships, the second option that data creators have is to record relationships as authorized access points representing the person, families, or corporate bodies associated with the manifestation. In a MARC environment, these would be recorded in the 700, 710, 711 bibliographic fields, with the possible addition of the relationship designation.

Example:

264 2 $a Port Washington, NY: $b Distributed by Entertainment One Film USA LLC
710 2 $a **E1 Entertainment (Firm)**, $e **film distributor**.

Although this is an option, most commonly we see the name of the producer of an unpublished work, the publisher, distributor, or the manufacturer recorded in the manifestation elements for the publisher's name and not as authorized access points representing the producer, publisher, etc. In such cases, the information is recorded in the MARC bibliographic field 264, subfield $b. It is typical for a manifestation to be associated with a number of persons or corporate bodies, but not to have these recorded.

Other persons, families, or corporate bodies associated with a manifestation, but not in the role of producer, publisher, manufacturer, or distributor, may include designer, platemaker, etc. These roles too are recorded only if they are considered important for access.

RECORDING RELATIONSHIPS OF PERSONS, FAMILIES, OR CORPORATE BODIES ASSOCIATED WITH AN ITEM (RDA CHAPTER 22)

RDA Chapter 22 offers guidelines for the recording of the relationships that exist between a person, family, or corporate body and the item, typically having the role of the owner, custodian, or other person associated with the item, such as a curator, and so on. RDA instructs us to record these relationships if they are considered important for access, again in the form of identifiers or authorized access points, following the guidelines in RDA 18.4.

Often, evidence of famous owners of an object, or of an autograph on a book by an important author, scholar, etc., is deemed important and recorded in the form of an authorized access point with the addition of an appropriate relationship designation.

Examples:

710 2 $a **Ashmolean Museum**, $e **current owner.**
700 1 $a **Sollins, Susan,** $e **curator.**

Again, a number of persons, families, or corporate bodies may be associated with an item, but in most cases these are not recorded.

RECORDING RELATIONSHIPS BETWEEN WORKS, EXPRESSION, MANIFESTATIONS, OR ITEMS (RDA CHAPTER 24)

Chapter 24 should not be confused with the recording of primary relationships among works, expressions, manifestations, and items, as covered in RDA Chapter 17. The primary relationship exists among the Group 1 entities deriving from the same work. Chapter 24 provides guidelines for the recording of relationships that exist between one work and a related work, an expression and a related expression, among manifestations, and among items.

A related work can be an adaptation of, a commentary on, or a sequel to the work described. A related expression can be a translation or a revised edition of the work described. A related manifestation can be different embodiments of that described work (e.g., a print and an electronic embodiment of the same expression of a work). A related item can be an item used as the basis for the production of the items described.

Recording the relationships between works, expressions, manifestations, and items supports the following FRBR-based RDA-defined functions of a catalog, stating that a user should be able to:

- *find* works, expressions, manifestations, and items that are related to those represented by the data retrieved in response to the user's search, and
- *understand* the relationship between two or more works, expressions, manifestations, or items.

Even so, the recording of these relationships is not core in RDA, and, therefore, they are not required.

There are different types of bibliographic relationships that exist between resources. Barbara Tillett, in her work on bibliographic relationships, established a taxonomy of bibliographic relationships that has been cited frequently and used widely. Some common relationships relating to the FRBR Group 1 entities of work, expression, manifestation and item include the following:

- Work—*derivative relationship*: a relationship between Work A and Work B, on which Work A is based. In other words, Work A is based on Work B but with some modifications that result in a new work. Examples include adaptations, abridgements, change in mode of issuance, etc.
- Work—*whole-part and part-whole relationship*: a relationship between a work and its components and vice versa. For example, an article contained in a journal, a book and its contained chapters, or the relationship between Tolkien's *The Lord of the Rings* and *The Two Towers.*
- Work—*accompanying relationship*: a relationship between a work and another work that accompanies it. For example, a software program and its accompanying handbook, a textbook and its accompanying teacher's guide.
- Work—*sequential relationship*: a relationship between work issued in a sequence, in a chronological or numerical order. For example, a journal and the resulting new journal continuing the earlier one, the relationship

between Tolkien's *The Fellowship of the Ring*, *The Two Towers*, and *The Return of the King*.

- Expression—*derivative relationship*: a relationship between Expression A and Expression B, when Expression B is based on Expression A. For example, the relationship between a translation and the original expression, revisions of expressions, different musical arrangements of the same work, etc.
- Expression—*descriptive relationship*: a relationship between an expression and another that describes it. For example, a review of particular translation.
- Manifestation—*equivalent relationship*: a relationship between a manifestation and its reproduction, which does not result in any difference in the expression embodied.
- Item—*accompanying relationship*: a relationship between two items that are brought together in the same container. For example, two manifestations packaged together, such as books bound together after their publication.

Per RDA 24.4, there are three methods for recording these relationships: identifiers, authorized access points, and descriptions. A description is typically a note providing details about the relationship, and it can be structured (following a certain format) or unstructured (free text). The relationship between related works and the relationships between related expressions can be represented by an identifier, an authorized access point, or a description; the relationships between manifestations and between items can be represented by an identifier or a description, not by an authorized access point.

Recording Identifiers (RDA 24.4.1)

RDA instructs us to record the identifier of the related work (RDA 6.8), expression (RDA 6.13), manifestation (RDA 2.15), or item (RDA 2.19). LC-PCC and current practice, especially in the MARC 21 environment, is to not record the identifier alone when recording the relationship between works, expressions, manifestations, and items, due to limitations of linking relationships in MARC.

Recording Authorized Access Points (RDA 24.4.2)

The most common method for recording relationships between works and between expressions in current practice is recording both, the authorized access point representing the work or part(s) of the work and the authorized access points representing the expression as authority data, following RDA 6.27.1 and 6.27.3, respectively. Authorized access point of related work and expressions can also be recorded in bibliographic records.

Recording a Description (RDA 24.4.3)

A relationship between works, expressions, manifestations, and items can be recorded in a descriptive note, which may provide more details on the nature of the relationship. The description may be structured—which means that it uses RDA elements, and, therefore, its order and content are governed by the RDA guidelines for that particular element (as is its structure, like ISBD, if implemented)—or unstructured—which means that the description is entered as free text without using formalized elements, following the order of guidelines to formulate the content of the description, but using a regular sentence structure. These notes are commonly recorded in a bibliographic record when using MARC.

Examples (bibliographic):

Structured description, indicating relationship:

Related manifestation	500 $a Reprint. Originally published: Scoundrels, eccentrics and originals: Victoria, BC: Greater Victoria Public Library, 2013.
Related work:	500 $a Adaptation of: Le passe-muraille / Marcel Aymé.
Related expression:	500 $a Translation of: The prince and the pauper.

Unstructured description, indicating relationship:

Related manifestation:	500 $a "This Dover edition...is a republication of the work originally published in 1971 by the McGraw-Hill Book Company, New York"—Copyright page.
Related work:	500 $a Originally released as a motion picture in 1935.

Relationship Designator (RDA 24.5)

A relationship designator can be added to the authorized access point of the entity, using a list of terms from RDA Appendix J. These are a little different from the relationship designators from RDA Appendix I, and are added to the authorized access points representing a person, family, or corporate body, where the designation is a term indicative of the role of the body. Relationship designators in Appendix J indicate how, for example, Work A is related to Work B. Terms may include phrases such as "continued by," "adaptation of," "evaluated in," "container of," and other such terms. These relationships between works and between expressions are recorded as authority data in the authorized access point for the related work or related expression, but may also be used in bibliographic records as access points.

Example (authority):

Work (authority):	130 0 $a Girl with the dragon tattoo (Motion picture: 2011)
Related work (authority):	500 1 $i **Motion picture adaptation of (work):** $a Larsson, Stieg, $d 1954-2004. $t Män som hatar kvinnor $w r
Related work (authority):	530 0 $i **Remake of (work):** $a Män som hatar kvinnor (Motion picture) $w r

Numbering of Parts (RDA 24.6)

This section of RDA 24 covers mostly the whole-part relationship between a work and a part or parts of a work. The guidelines are applicable for any work that has parts or for any aggregate work (a work consisting of works), but the most common cases are serials or series and their parts (issues or articles). RDA 24.6 focuses on the recording of the numbering of the parts, rather than how to record the whole-part relationship.

The numbering of the parts can use any system of numbering (letters, numbers, chronology, etc.). Record the numbering as it appears on the source of information, following general guidelines about numbering in RDA 1.8. Abbreviate the terms associated with the numbering based on the instructions in RDA Appendix B.

Examples (bibliographic):

830 0 $a Advances in consciousness research; $v **v. 90**.

830 0 $a Routledge research in information technology and society; $v **16**.

Examples (authority)

100 1 $a Handel, George Frideric, $d 1685-1759. $t Acis and Galatea, $n **HWV 49a**

100 1 $a Arwaker, Edmund, $d -1730. $t Vision. $n **Part 2**

100 1 $a Leeuwen, Simon van, $d 1625 or 1626-1682. $t Censura forensis. $n **Part 1, Book 5.** $l English

Other Elements

Source consulted is a core LC-PCC element when recording a relationship. A cataloger's note may be added to further explain the numbering of parts of a work.

RDA covers the relationships between works, between expressions, between manifestations, and between items in Chapters 25 through 28, respectively.

RECORDING RELATIONSHIPS BETWEEN WORKS (RDA CHAPTER 25)

RDA Chapter 25 provides guidelines for the recording of relationships that exist between works. Based on RDA instructions, a related work can be indicated by recording the identifier, the authorized access point, or a description.

Related Work (RDA 25.1)
Core LC element

RDA 25.1 does not offer detailed instructions other than to record the related work following RDA 24.4. Following the current practice of LC and most US libraries or libraries using MARC 21, record the authorized access point of the related work as authority data, and, to provide access, also record it in the bibliographic record, describing the resource at hand. In a MARC structure, the authorized access point of the related work is recorded in MARC authority 5XX field and in MARC bibliographic 7XX field. In both cases, the relationship designation can precede the authorized access point (in subfield $i).

Related work is a core element for LC practice and, therefore, for agencies following LC practice. LC-PCC PS 25.1 provides extensive instructions for the related work element.

Examples:

Work (authority):	110 2 $a Green Day (Musical group). $t American idiot (Musical)
Related work (authority):	510 2 $i **Musical theatre adaptation of (work):** $a Green Day (Musical group). $t American idiot (Album) $w r
Context (bibliographic):	245 00 $a Broadway Idiot: $b with Billie Joe Armstrong / $c director, Doug Hamilton; producer, Ira Pittelman; editor, Rob Tinworth; music, Green Day.

Related work (bibliographic):	710 2 $i **Adaptation of (work):** $a Green Day (Musical group). $t American idiot (Album)
Work (authority):	100 1 $a Lee, Harper. $t To kill a mockingbird
Related work (authority):	530 0 $i **Adapted as motion picture (work):** $a To kill a mockingbird (Motion picture: 1962) $w r
Context (bibliographic):	130 0 $a To kill a mockingbird (Motion picture: 1962) 245 10 $a To kill a mockingbird
Related work (bibliographic):	700 1 $i **Motion picture adaptation of (work):** $a Lee, Harper. $t To kill a mockingbird.

For examples of description as a method of recording relationships between works in a bibliographic record, consult RDA 24.6 and the respective section above in this chapter.

LC-PCC PS 25.1.1.3 provides extensive instructions on formulating structured descriptions using formal contents notes, recording relationships for works that are serials, and constructing authorized access points for parts of compilations of laws.

RECORDING RELATIONSHIPS BETWEEN EXPRESSIONS (RDA CHAPTER 26)

Chapter 26 provides guidelines for the recording of relationships between expressions. Follow the general RDA 24.4 guidelines for recording relationships between works, expressions, manifestations, and items as they apply to expressions.

Example (bibliographic):

Relationship recorded as an access point:

Context:	100 1 $a Chan, Lois Mai. 245 12 $a A guide to the Library of Congress classification / $c Lois Mai Chan.
Related expression:	500 $a "Based on the fourth edition of Immroth's Guide to the Library of Congress classification."

700 1 $i **Based on:** $a **Chan, Lois Mai.** $t **Immroth's Guide to the Library of Congress classification.**

Relationship recorded as a description:

Context (bibliographic): 100 1 Grygiel, Stanisław, $e author. 245 10 Discovering the human person: $b in conversation with John Paul II / $c Stansław Grygiel; translated by Michelle K. Borras.

Related expression (bibliographic): 500 **Expanded version of the Michael J. McGivney lectures delivered from March 18 to 21, 2013 at the John Paul II Institute for Studies on Marriage and Family, Catholic University of America, Washington, D.C.**

LC-PCC PS 26.1 specifies that related expression is an LC core element for most serials, and is therefore required. Record relationships between serials in MARC bibliographic 7XX with the addition of subfield $i for the relationship designation from RDA Appendix J. LC practice is not to record this relationship in a description (MARC bibliographic note field 5XX).

LC-PCC PS 26.1 also instructs us to record compilations as a content note (MARC bibliographic field 505) and provide authorized access points for each expression when both the original and the translation are present. Do not apply this policy to contributions such as introductions, or to anthologies of poems, conference proceedings, journals, collections of letters, etc.

RECORDING RELATIONSHIPS BETWEEN MANIFESTATIONS (RDA CHAPTER 27)

RDA Chapter 27 provides guidelines for recording relationships between manifestations. This element is an LC core only for reproductions (LC-PCC PS 27.1), defined in a broad way to include reproductions, republications, etc., which still represent the original content of the expression. Revisions that result in a different expression are not included here, and are covered under related expressions.

Examples (bibliographic):

Related manifestation: 775 08 $i **Reproduction of (manifestation):** $s **To kill a mockingbird (Motion**

	picture: 1962). $t **To kill a mockingbird** **$b High definition** $d **Universal City, CA: Universal Studios Home Entertainment, [2013]** $h **1 videodisc (130 min.): sound, color; 4 3/4 in.** $o **025192073717**
Related manifestation:	776 08 $i **Print version of (manifestation):** $a **Keates, J. S.** $t **Understanding Maps** $d **Hoboken: Taylor and Francis, ©2014** $z **9780582239272**

RECORDING RELATIONSHIPS BETWEEN PERSONS, FAMILIES, AND CORPORATE BODIES (RDA CHAPTER 29)

RDA Chapter 29 provides general guidelines for recording relationships between persons, between families, and between corporate bodies, applicable to RDA Chapters 30 through 32, which discuss each case separately in more detail.

Such relationships are important to record because they facilitate the FRBR-based user tasks defined in RDA, which stipulate that a user should be able to

- *find* persons, families, or corporate bodies that are related to the person, family, or corporate body represented by the data retrieved in response to the user's search; and
- *understand* the relationship between two or more persons, families, or corporate bodies.

Therefore, RDA 29.2 states that the data created using RDA should include "significant" relationships between related persons, families, and corporate bodies.

RDA does not define any of these relationships as core, but, as will be seen in the following sections, related person is a core element for LC/PCC for different identities, and related corporate body is a core element for LC and PCC for sequential relationships with immediately preceding and immediately succeeding corporate bodies; however, related families is not a core LC element.

RDA instructs us to use either the identifier or the authorized access point for the related person, family, or corporate body to record the relationship; however, as noted before, LC-PCC practice is not to record the identifier alone, and, in most cases, the current practice is to record the authorized form representing the related person, family, or corporate body with the addition of a relationship designator. These relationships are recorded exclusively as authority data and are not included in bibliographic descriptions.

Follow guidelines in RDA 9.19.1 for the construction of authorized access points for person, RDA 10.11.1 for families, and RDA 11.13.1 for corporate bodies. Record relationship designators using terms from RDA Appendix K to indicate the nature of the relationships between related persons, families, and corporate bodies. Terms from Appendix K include "alternate identity," "successor," etc.

As with other authority data, the element of sources consulted is core, and, therefore, it is required to cite the sources where the information regarding the relationship is found. In addition, the element of cataloger's note may be added if it is necessary to provide additional information that is considered important for future use, revision, or creation of new authority data.

Examples of recorded relationships are given in the respective discussions (given below) on persons, families, and corporate bodies.

RECORDING RELATIONSHIPS BETWEEN PERSONS (RDA CHAPTER 30)

The relationship(s) between a person and another person, family, or corporate body is discussed in RDA Chapter 30, based on the general guidelines provided in RDA Chapter 29. In current practice, this relationship is recorded as authority data, using the authorized access point of the related person, family, or corporate body, and in a MARC environment, it is recorded in a MARC authority field 5XX. A relationship designator may be added to the authorized access point to indicate the nature of the relationship. A list of terms to be used as relationship designator for the relationships between persons is available in RDA Appendix K. In a MARC environment, a term from RDA Appendix K for the relationship designation may be added in subfield $i (and also coded with $w nnnc when a field 663 is present).

The most common case is when a person has an alternate (more than one) identity; for example, a person using both a legal name and a pseudonym when associated with resources. Another case falling under this category is when a person not only uses a legal name but also holds an official or religious office, and, therefore, bears a name that is part of a corporate body's authorized access point.

LCC-PCC PS 30.1.1.3 has additional instructions for persons with different identities and instructs us to "follow the guidelines in the Descriptive Cataloging Manual Z1 sections for MARC fields 663 and 667." More information is available in the FAQ on personal names (http://www.loc.gov/catdir/cpso/pseud.pdf).

Examples (authority):

Person:	Roberts, Nora
Related person(s):	**Hardesty, Sarah, 1950-** **Robb, J. D., 1950-**
MARC:	500 1 $a **Hardesty, Sarah,** $d **1950-** $w nnnc 500 1 $a **Robb, J. D.,** $d **1950-** $w nnnc 663 $a For works of this author entered under other names, search also under: $b Hardesty, Sarah, 1950- $b Robb, J. D., 1950-

Notice that in the above example—due to the presence of field 663, which has an explanatory, structured link to the related persons—links from the two 500 fields for the related person access points are suppressed with the use of "$w nnnc" in order to publicly display only the reference from field 663, which provides additional helpful information to users.

Person:	Kane, Thomas L. (Thomas Leiper), 1822-1883
Related family:	**Kane (Family: Kane, Thomas L. (Thomas Leiper), 1822-1883)**
MARC:	500 3 $i **Descendants**: $a **Kane (Family:** $g **Kane, Thomas L. (Thomas Leiper), 1822-1883)** $w r
Person:	Cuomo, Mario M., 1932-2015
Related corporate body:	**New York (State). Governor (1983-1994: Cuomo)**
MARC:	110 1 $a **New York (State).** $b **Governor (1983-1994: Cuomo)**

Record an explanation to the relationship only if necessary for identification or clarification, following instructions in RDA Appendix E.

RECORDING RELATIONSHIPS BETWEEN FAMILIES (RDA CHAPTER 31)

The relationship(s) between a family and another person, family, or corporate body is discussed in RDA Chapter 31, based on the general guidelines provided in RDA Chapter 29. This relationship is recorded as authority data, using the authorized access point of the related person, family, or corporate body, and in a MARC environment, it is recorded in a MARC authority field

5XX. A term from RDA Appendix K for the relationship designation may be added in subfield $i (also coded with $w r when subfield $i is used).

Examples:

Family:	Pond (Family: $c Minn.)
Related person(s):	**Pond, Gideon H. (Gideon Hollister), 1810-1878** **Pond, Samuel W. (Samuel William)**
MARC:	500 1 $i **Family member:** $a **Pond, Gideon H.** $q **(Gideon Hollister)**, $d **1810-1878** $w r 500 1 $i **Family member:** $a **Pond, Samuel W.** $q **(Samuel William)** $w r
Family:	Fletcher (Family: 1884- Fletcher, Harvey, 1884-1981)
Related person:	**Fletcher, Harvey, 1884-1981**
MARC:	500 1 $i **Progenitor:** $a **Fletcher, Harvey,** $d **1884-1981** $w r

RECORDING RELATIONSHIPS BETWEEN CORPORATE BODIES (RDA CHAPTER 32)

The relationship between a corporate body and another person, family, or corporate body is discussed in RDA Chapter 32, based on the general guidelines provided in RDA Chapter 29. This relationship is recorded as authority data, using the authorized access point of the related person, family, or corporate body, and, in a MARC environment, it is recorded in a MARC authority field 5XX. A term from RDA Appendix K for the relationship designation may be added in subfield $i (also coded with $w r when subfield $i is used).

When a corporate body changes its name, it is considered a new corporate body, and, therefore, the two are considered related corporate bodies. The most common relationship of a corporate body is to its previous or subsequent existence. The second common relationship of a corporate body is to a related person who is also a government or religious official. These two entities are related, and the relationship is recorded in both the person's authority data as an individual with a related corporate body and in the authority data of the corporate body with a relationship to a person.

Examples (authority):

Corporate body (CB):	International Conference on Holography and Correlation Optics

Related CB: **International Conference on Holography, Correlation Optics, and Recording Materials**
International Conference on Correlation Optics
MARC: 511 2 $i **Predecessor:** $a **International Conference on Holography, Correlation Optics, and Recording Materials** $w r
511 2 $i **Successor:** $a **International Conference on Correlation Optics** $w r

Corporate body: Ferguson Publishing
Related CB: **Facts on File, Inc.**
MARC: 510 2 $i **Hierarchical superior:** $a **Facts on File, Inc.** $w r

Corporate body: Church of England. Diocese of Peterborough. Bishop (1638-1649: Towers)
Related person: **Towers, John, -1649**
Related CB: **Church of England. Diocese of Peterborough**
MARC: 500 1 $a **Towers, John,** $d **-1649**
510 2 $i **Hierarchical superior:** $a **Church of England.** $b **Diocese of Peterborough** $w r

NOTES

1. Cutter, C. A. (1904). *Rules for a Dictionary Catalog* (4th ed., rewritten). Washington, DC: Government Printing Office (pp. 11–12).
2. American Library Association, Canadian Library Association, & CILIP: Chartered Institute of Library and Information Professionals. (2010–). *RDA Toolkit: Resource Description and Access* (17.0). Retrieved from www.rdatoolkit.org.
3. Program for Cooperative Cataloging. (2014). *PCC Guidelines for the Application of Relationship Designators in Bibliographic Records.* Retrieved from http://www.loc.gov/aba/pcc/rda/PCC%20RDA%20guidelines/Relat-Desig-Guidelines.docx.
4. PCC Standing Committee on Training (SCT). (2015). *Training Manual for Applying Relationship Designators in Bibliographic Records.* Retrieved from http://www.loc.gov/aba/pcc/sct/documents/rel-desig-guide-bib.pdf.

Part IV

SUBJECT ACCESS AND CONTROLLED VOCABULARIES

STANDARDS AND TOOLS

Cataloging Policy and Support Office, Library of Congress. (1984–). *Subject Headings Manual*. Washington, DC: Cataloging Distribution Service, Library of Congress. Available in Cataloger's Desktop at http://www.loc.gov/cds/desktop/

Subject Cataloging Division, Library of Congress. (1975–). *Library of Congress Subject Headings*. Washington, DC: Cataloging Distribution Service, Library of Congress. Available in ClassificationWeb at http://classificationweb.net

Subject Cataloging Division, Library of Congress. (1914–1966). *Subject Headings used in the Dictionary Catalogs of the Library of Congress* (1st ed.–7th ed.). Washington, DC: Library of Congress.

U.S. National Library of Medicine. (April 6, 2015). *Medical Subject Headings*. Bethesda, MD: U.S. National Library of Medicine. Retrieved from www.nlm.nih.gov/mesh/

Bristow, B. A. (Ed.), and Farrar, C. A. (Assoc. ed.). (2014). *Sears List of Subject Headings* (21st ed.). Ipswich, MA: H. W. Wilson Company.

RECOMMENDED READING

Aitchison, J., Gilchrist, A., and Bawden, D. (2002). *Thesaurus Construction and Use: A Practical Manual* (4th ed.). New York, NY: Fitzroy Dearborn Publishers.

Bates, M. J. (1989). Rethinking subject cataloging in the online environment. *Library Resources & Technical Services, 33*(4), 400–12; Berman, S. (Ed.). (1985). *Subject Cataloging: Critiques and Innovations*. New York, NY: Haworth.

Chan, L. M. (1990). *Library of Congress Subject Headings: Principles of Structure and Policies for Application* (annotated version). Washington, DC: Library of Congress.

Chan, L. M. (1991). Functions of a subject authority file. In K. M. Drabenstott (Ed.), *Subject Authorities in the Online Environment: Papers from a Conference*

Program Held in San Francisco, June 29, 1987 (ALCTS Papers on Library Technical Services and Collections, No. 1). Chicago, IL: American Library Association.

Chan, L. M. (2005). *Library of Congress Subject Headings: Principles and Application* (4th ed.). Westport, CT: Libraries Unlimited.

Chan, L. M., and Hodges, T., revised by Martin, G. (1998). Subject cataloguing and classification. In M. Gorman (Ed.), *Technical Services Today and Tomorrow* (2nd ed.) (pp. 95–109). Englewood, CO: Libraries Unlimited.

Chan, L. M., Richmond, P., and Svenonius, E. (1985). *Theory of Subject Analysis: A Sourcebook*. Littleton, CO: Libraries Unlimited.

Coates, E. (1988). *Subject Catalogues: Headings and Structure*. London, England: Library Association.

Cutter, C. A. (1904). *Rules for a Dictionary Catalog* (4th ed., rewritten). U. S. Bureau of Education, Special Report on Public Libraries, Part II. Washington, DC: Government Printing Office.

Dunkin, P. S. (1969). What is it about? Subject entry. In P. S. Dunkin, *Cataloging U.S.A.* (pp. 65–95). Chicago, IL: American Library Association.

Foskett, A. C. (1996). *The Subject Approach to Information* (5th ed.). London, England: Library Association.

Hagler, R. (1997). *The Bibliographic Record and Information Technology* (3rd ed.). Chicago, IL: American Library Association.

Haykin, D. J. (1951). *Subject Headings: A Practical Guide*. Washington, DC: Government Printing Office.

Lancaster, F. W. (1986). *Vocabulary Control for Information Retrieval* (2nd ed.). Arlington, VA: Information Resources Press.

Landry, P., Bultrini, L., O'Neill, E. T., Roe, S. K., and International Federation of Library Associations. (2011). *Subject Access: Preparing for the Future*. Berlin, Germany: De Gruyter Saur.

Mann, T. (1993). *Library Research Models: A Guide to Classification, Cataloging, and Computers*. New York, NY: Oxford University Press.

Markey, K. (1984). *Subject Searching in Library Catalogs Before and After the Introduction of Online Catalogs* (OCLC Library, Information and Computer Science Series, No. 4). Dublin, OH: OCLC.

Miksa, F. (1983). *The Subject in the Dictionary Catalog from Cutter to the Present*. Chicago, IL: American Library Association.

Olson, H. A. (2002). *The Power to Name: Locating the Limits of Subject Representation in Libraries*. Dordrecht, The Netherlands: Kluwer Academic Publishers.

Olson, H. A., Boll, J. J., and Aluri, R. (2001). *Subject Analysis in Online Catalogs*. Englewood, CO: Libraries Unlimited.

O'Neill, E. T., and Chan, L. M. (December 2003). FAST (Faceted application of subject terminology): A simplified vocabulary based on the Library of Congress subject headings. *IFLA Journal, 29*(4), 336–42. Retrieved from www.ifla.org/IV/ifla69/papers/010e-ONeill_Mai-Chan.pdf

Principles of the Sears List of Subject Headings. (2004). In J. Miller (Ed.) and J. Goodsell (Assoc. ed.), *Sears List of Subject Headings* (18th ed.) (pp. xv–xxix). New York, NY: H. W. Wilson Company.

Prevost, M. L. (April 1946). An approach to theory and method in general subject heading. *Library Quarterly, 16*(2), 140–51.

Studwell, W. E. (1990). *Library of Congress Subject Headings: Philosophy, Practice, and Prospects*. New York, NY: Haworth Press.

Zeng, M. L., Žumer, M., and Salaba, A. (Eds.). (2011). *Functional Requirements for Subject Authority Data (FRSAD): A Conceptual Model* (IFLA Series on Bibliographic Control, Vol. 43). Berlin/München, Germany: De Gruyter Saur. Retrieved from http://www.ifla.org/publications/ifla-series-on-bibliographic-control-43

Chapter 10

Principles of Controlled Vocabularies and Subject Analysis

INTRODUCTION

In describing a resource, we represent both the inherent characteristics of the resource—such as titles, persons responsible for content creation, contribution, language and other expression attributes, and physical characteristics of manifestations and items—and the intellectual content of the work. The intellectual content of a resource is represented by determining what the content is about. Determining the topic of a resource is known as subject analysis or determining "aboutness." In addition to name and title access points, library catalogs and other retrieval systems provide subject access to resources through access points based on the subject content of the documents or other resources on which their descriptions are based and of which they are representative. Subject access points, like access points based on names and titles, serve the dual function of location and collocation.

FR Family Models and Subject Access

In the original FRBR model,[1] the topic of a work is expressed as a relationship with the entity *work*. As illustrated in Figure 10.1, a work can have as its subject any of the Group 1 entities (work, expression, manifestation, item), Group 2 entities (person, corporate body, and family—later added by FRAD[2]), a concept, an object, an event, or a place (labeled as Group 3 entities).

Published in 2011, the FRSAD,[3] introduced a more abstract model of subject data described in subject vocabularies, including controlled vocabularies such as lists of subject headings and thesauri. FRSAD introduced the terms *thema*, defined as anything that serves as a subject of a work, and *nomen*,

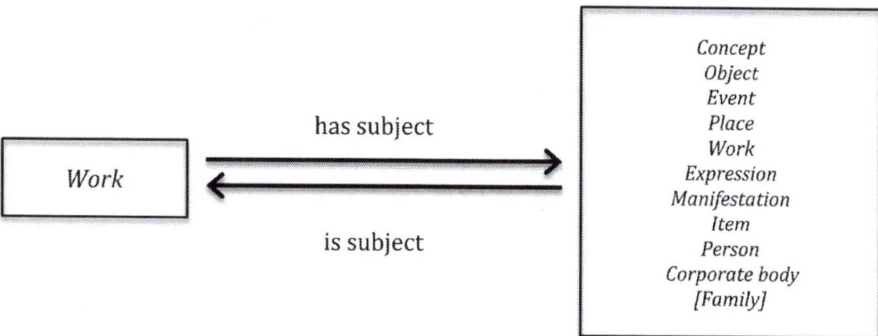

Figure 10.1 FRBR subject relationship.

defined as any sign or sequence of signs by which a *thema* is known, referred to, or addressed as. As illustrated in Figure 10.2, a work has as its subject a thema, which has a nomen or the name, symbol, or label for the term used to represent the subject.

The FRSAD model is meant for subject vocabulary development and provides much more flexibility to include any types of subjects to better serve the needs of particular subject vocabulary, instead of trying to impose a predefined set of subject types. For example, the *Library of Congress Subject Headings* (LCSH) includes types such as name, title, topical, chronological, and genre/form headings; the Art and Architecture Thesaurus (AAT) includes associated concepts, physical attributes, styles and periods, agents, activities, materials, and objects. In addition, FRSAD places more emphasis on the conceptual aspect, the thema, rather than the term used to represent it, the nomen.

RDA and the Subject Relationship

RDA Chapter 23 provides general guidelines on recording the subject relationship that exists between a work and subjects. Subject, in RDA, is defined

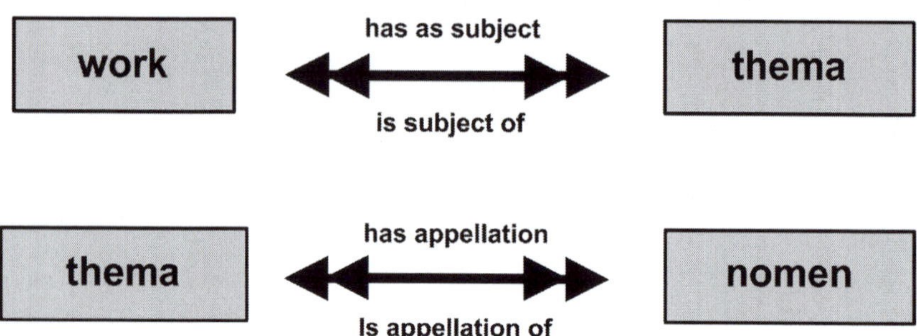

Figure 10.2 FRSAD subject relationship.

as any term, phrase, classification number, etc., that describes or indicates the aboutness of the work. Per RDA guidelines, this relationship is recorded in the core element "subject relationship." Information recorded in the subject relationships element may include: (1) the identifier for the subject; (2) the authorized access point representing the subject; and/or (3) a structured or unstructured description of the subject. Subject access points and classification numbers may be taken form an "identifiable subject system," which is any standard vocabulary, such as the LCSH or the DDC. Relationship designator may be used to indicate the nature of the relationship. RDA Appendix M provides a list of term to be used as relationship designators for subjects.

Examples:

Subject relationship (Identifier):	LCCN sh2009000250 (LCSH)
Subject relationship (Authorized access point):	Chocolate candy containers (LCSH)
Subject relationship (Description):	This resource discusses different types of containers used to store chocolate candy, food preservation aspects, appropriateness of each type of container, and potential health issues to consumers.

Subject Representation and Access

There are two ways of searching by subject in a library catalog or other information-retrieval systems: (1) through words in parts of the descriptions such as titles, notes (particularly contents notes), and/or the full text; and, (2) through words or phrases in the descriptions that have been specifically assigned as index terms.

The first approach is called *keyword* or *free-text* searching. The available access points are words in the title or note areas of a bibliographic or metadata record or, increasingly, in the full text. In an online catalog that offers keyword searching, the user may use as an access point almost any of the words in a title or other searchable field, such as a note. The advantage of keyword searching is that information may be retrieved in the author's own words, which often reflect the most current terminology in a particular subject field. The drawback is that when a user wishes to retrieve all information—or as much information as possible—on a given subject, he or she must search on all the synonyms for that subject.

The second approach is "controlled vocabulary" access. In this case, specific words or phrases designated as subject index terms are assigned to each bibliographic record; each term normally represents only one subject, and a given subject is normally represented by only one term. In other words, among possible synonyms, one term is chosen as the subject index term. The searcher who uses a particular controlled term is then able to retrieve all records bearing that term. A controlled vocabulary also differentiates homographs by distinguishing between words that have the same spelling, but different meanings. As in the case of name authority control, the principles of preferred and unique access points also apply to controlled vocabularies.

A controlled vocabulary system depends on a master list of predetermined terms that can be assigned to documents. For most library catalogs, manual or online, these are called *subject headings*; for many abstracting and indexing systems they are called *descriptors,* or perhaps simply *preferred* or *authorized* terms. Preferred terms are maintained in a *subject-headings list* or *thesaurus*, which lists the subject access terms to be used in the cataloging or indexing operation at hand. When there are synonymous terms for a given subject, these terms are included in the list as *lead-in* or *entry* terms, and references under them direct the searcher to the authorized term for the subject. Authorized terms that are related in meaning are also linked by references: the links from lead-in terms are called *use* references, and the links to related terms are, depending on the types of relationship, called broader term (BT), narrower term (NT), and related term (RT).

Subject-headings lists and thesauri require ongoing maintenance. This is accomplished through a control system, called *subject authority control*, which, for each term, documents the basis for decisions on the term, and on what links connect it with other terms. Reference and subject authority control are discussed in greater detail later in this chapter.

HISTORY OF SUBJECT ACCESS IN LIBRARY CATALOGS

Early library catalogs were primarily finding-lists providing author and catchword entries for each item along with a symbol indicating its location in the collection. The catchword entry played an important role in the evolution of subject headings. The catchword was usually the leading word in the title, but in cases where the leading word failed to express the subject content of a book, for example, *An Introduction to Physics*, another word from the title more indicative of the subject content, "Physics" in this example, was used as the entry word, that is, as an access point. This practice represented a step between the catchword entry and the true subject entry. Its use indicated that, by the middle of the nineteenth century, librarians had begun to be aware of the significance of the subject approach to library material.[4]

Depending on the type of catalog, subject access points may appear in different forms and configurations. When a subject access point contains terms from different levels of a hierarchy of subjects, it is called a *classed* or *classified entry*. When a subject access point contains the most specific word or phrase describing the subject, it is called a *specific and direct entry*.

The Classed or Classified Entry

The classed entry is probably the earliest form of subject access point. It begins with the term at the top of the hierarchy to which the subject being represented belongs, with each level in the hierarchy included in the subject heading so that a classed subject heading for "southern pines" would be:

Plants—Trees—Evergreens—Pines—Southern pines

When such access points are displayed systematically or hierarchically, they are collocated according to their subject relationships:

Plants—Trees—Evergreens—Pines
Plants—Trees—Evergreens—Pines—Southern pines
Plants—Trees—Evergreens—Pines—Southern pines—Longleaf pine

A subject catalog made up of classed entries is called a *classed catalog*. The order of progression of subjects is from the general to the specific. For most searches, using such a catalog effectively requires an accompanying alphabetical index listing individual terms, which allows the subject to be approached from any level of the hierarchy. Probably, when classed catalogs were in general use, almost all had accessible indexes. Furthermore, if a classed catalog were offered today, keyword searching would ease the access problem. In American libraries, the classed catalog as a public tool was replaced in the late nineteenth century by the dictionary or alphabetical catalog. However, as a working tool, the classed catalog was retained in the form of "shelflists" until the advent of the online catalog. A shelflist was arranged according to whatever classification system a given library used. The main difference between a shelflist and a classed catalog was that a shelflist contained only one record for each item, filed by its classification number. The classed catalog, on the other hand, included multiple access points for documents that dealt with more than one subject.

A variation on the classed catalog was the *alphabetico-classed catalog*, a hybrid of the classified approach and the alphabetical approach. In this form of catalog, the classed entries were arranged differently from those in the classified catalog. On each level of the hierarchy, the subject terms were arranged alphabetically rather than strictly by subject relationships. As a matter of fact, this is the arrangement adopted by most of the subject directories found on the Web today.

The Dictionary or Alphabetical Specific Catalog

An alphabetical specific entry is a controlled heading for a specific subject (without including terms for the higher levels of its subject hierarchy), for example, *Southern pines.* Cutter introduced this practice in the late nineteenth century. Entries are arranged in alphabetical order without regard to their subject relationships or hierarchical status; thus, subject collocation is sacrificed for quick and direct access. A later development than classed or alphabetico-classed catalogs, it quickly and almost completely replaced other catalog forms in American libraries.

The Online Catalog

In online retrieval systems, including library catalogs, the internal arrangement of the records is of no concern to the end users. What is important is the way retrieved records are displayed. Because the online catalog can display records based on words or text alphabetically or by class numbers, it provides the advantages of both the alphabetical and the classified catalogs. With the online catalog, the entry element of the subject heading is no longer a crucial issue in access and display. However, when libraries first put their catalogs online, their first step was to convert their existing records into machine-readable form. When new records were created, they were drawn up according to the same rules used in forming card catalog entries. As a result, the alphabetical specific headings that had been used in manual catalogs for a century were transferred to the online catalog with little structural change. Efforts to introduce changes that render subject headings more amenable to the online environment have been gradually implemented, and online capabilities now offer many possibilities for improved subject access.

SUBJECT VOCABULARIES

Prior to the making of standard lists for subject headings, catalogers in individual libraries assigned subject headings as they saw fit. With the increase in interlibrary loan operations and the introduction of centralized cataloging through the distribution of LC-printed cards, the advantages of having a standard list became apparent. Such a list would ensure consistency within the same library catalog as well as among catalogs of different libraries, thereby making retrieval easier for users who move from library to library as well as facilitating both interlibrary cooperation and the development of union catalogs.

In 1895, the first standard list for subject headings appeared. The *List of Subject Headings for Use in Dictionary Catalogs*, produced by an ALA committee of which Cutter was a prominent member, was based on Cutter's principles. It went through three editions (1895, 1898, and 1911). In the period 1910–1914, when LC began publishing its list under the title *Subject Headings Used in the Dictionary Catalogues of the Library of Congress*, which later changed to *Library of Congress Subject Headings* (LCSH), it was found unnecessary to continue the ALA list.

Once LC began distributing printed cards at the beginning of the twentieth century, the Library's practice soon became the de facto standard for cataloging in the United States. After the completion of the first printing of LC's subject-headings list in 1914, it became a standard tool for subject cataloging in American libraries. Details on LCSH are given in chapter 11 of this book.

LCSH and its predecessors reflected the practice of a large research collection, and neither were nor are always suited to medium-sized or small collections. Early on, the gap was filled by a list compiled by Minnie Earl Sears and first published in 1923 under the title *Subject Headings for Small Libraries*. It was renamed *Sears List of Subject Headings,* and has gone through twenty-one editions so far, with the most recent appearing in 2014. Despite the relatively greater ease of using subject headings from LC cataloging copy, the Sears list is still favored for general collections in many small and medium-sized American libraries. Lists of subject headings have also been developed for special fields. The best known among these are *Medical Subject Heading* (MeSH) or and FAST. Chapters 11 through 14 of this book discuss these standard lists and systems in detail.

Both LCSH and the Sears list adopted the principles of the dictionary catalog first propounded by Cutter. However, LCSH and the Sears list differ in many respects. Details on each are given in chapters 11 and 13, respectively.

CUTTER'S PRINCIPLES OF SUBJECT CATALOGING

The rules for subject headings in a dictionary catalog were first set forth by Cutter in his *Rules for a Dictionary Catalog*.[5] Writing on the subject approach, Cutter stated two objectives: (1) to enable a person to find a book of which the subject is known, and (2) to show what the library has on a given subject.[6] The first addresses the need to locate individual items; the second addresses the need to collocate materials on the same subject. It was on the basis of these needs that Cutter set forth his basic principles of subject entry. They are important because the impact of his principles on subject-heading construction and maintenance is still discernible today. The basic principles of subject headings are described below.

The User and Usage

For Cutter, the most important consideration in the cataloging of library materials was "the best interest of the user." He called this principle "the convenience of the public."[7] He felt that catalogers should be concerned with "the public's habitual way of looking at things" and that these habits should not be ignored, even if they occasionally demand a sacrifice of logic and simplicity. On this principle, the public's usage becomes an important determining factor in selecting the terms and the forms of subject headings.

The principle, though unassailable in intent, is the hardest of Cutter's recommendations to implement effectively in a system designed for wide general use. One cannot define "user" and "usage" because there is no such thing as a "typical library user." Users come into the library with different backgrounds and different purposes, and there has never been an objective way to determine how they approach the catalog or what their purposes are. As a result, in an attempt to follow Cutter's lead, catalogers have formed subject headings on the basis of what they assume to be the needs and habits of users. Recent studies on user behavior, using sophisticated methodology, have provided much more information regarding subject searching. However, because of the diversity of users and their background and interests, it is still impossible to define a "typical user."

Another approach to effective subject access is to attempt to develop a system that adheres to strictly formed principles, on the assumption that a logical and consistent system can be learned by its users. When one looks beyond Cutter's insistence on reflecting general usage, one finds that his early rules went a long way toward laying the groundwork for a logical and consistent subject access apparatus.

In current subject-heading systems, the most important factors that evolved over the years are (1) uniform and unique headings, (2) specific and direct entry, (3) consistency and currency in terminology, and (4) provision of cross-references. All of these apply, just as forcefully, to nonlibrary surrogate systems, as they do to library practice.

Uniform and Unique Headings

In order to show what a collection or a database has on a given subject, it must adopt a principle of *uniform headings*, that is, it must bring under one heading all the material dealing principally or exclusively with that particular subject. This principle is similar to that requiring a uniform heading for a given personal author. If a subject has more than one name ("ascorbic acid" and "Vitamin C," for instance), one must be chosen as the valid or authorized heading. In general, it is ideal that the term chosen is unambiguous and familiar to all users of the catalog. Similarly, if there are variant spellings of the same term, for example, "marihuana" and "marijuana," or different possible forms of the same heading, only one is used as the heading. Examples of variant heading forms might be "Air quality" versus "Air—Quality" or "Quality of air." One must be chosen, with the others listed as lead-in terms. However, in a few cases, duplicate access points are made for certain headings; for example, LC headings such as **United States—Foreign relations—Japan** and **Japan—Foreign relations—United States** may both be valid, although they are two forms of the same heading. The reason for duplicate access points is to provide access under both United States and Japan in manual catalogs. In online catalogs that provide searching on component parts of a heading, such duplicate access points have less value.

The converse of the principle of uniform headings is *unique headings*, which refers to the premise that the same term should not be used to represent more than one subject. If the same term must be used in more than one sense, as is often the case when different disciplines or fields of knowledge are involved, some qualification or clarification must be added so that it will be clear to the user which meaning is intended, for example, "Cold" and "Cold (Disease)."

Specific and Direct Entry

The principle of *specific entry* governs both how subject headings are formed (thesaurus construction and maintenance) and how they are assigned to documents (indexing or subject cataloging). Regarding formulation, the principle requires that a heading be as specific as (i.e., no broader than) the topic it is intended to cover. In application, it requires that a work be assigned the most specific heading that represents its subject content. Ideally, the heading should be coextensive with (i.e., no broader or narrower than) the subject content of the work. The rule for specific entry was set forth by Cutter in his *Rules for a Dictionary Catalog*:

> Enter a work under its subject headings, not under the heading of a class which includes that subject. . . . Put Lady Cust's book on "The Cat" under *Cat*, not under *Zoology* or *Mammals* or *Domestic animals*; and put Garnier's "Le fer" under *Iron,* not under *Metals* or *Metallurgy*.[8]

Cutter claimed that this rule is the main distinction between the dictionary catalog and the alphabetico-classed catalog. In an alphabetico-classed catalog, the subject "cats" would appear under a heading such as:

Zoology—Vertebrates—Mammals—Domestic animals—Cats

In this approach, the heading contains a series, or chain, of hierarchical terms beginning with, and therefore listed under, the broadest term, and leading to the most specific term. In other words, access is through the broadest term moving down the hierarchy to the term being sought. In the alphabetical approach, on the other hand, the subject is listed directly under its own name, in this case, "Cats." In other words, the major characteristic of the alphabetical approach is that its entries are both *specific* and *direct*.

Consistent and Current Terminology

It follows from what has been said above, particularly regarding the justifications for uniform headings, that the terminology in headings should be both consistent and current. Two elements are particularly important here: synonymy and changing usage. Choices among synonymous terms may require difficult decisions. By principle, common usage prevails when it can be determined. For example, a popular term is preferred to a scientific one in a general library and in standard lists of headings designed for general collections. Of course, the more specialized a library's collection and clientele, the more specialized its indexing terminology should be; special libraries, therefore, often develop their own thesauri or make extensive modifications of standard lists.

Changes in usage present many practical difficulties. A term may be chosen on the basis of common usage at the time it is established, but become obsolete later on. For emerging subjects, it often takes time for terminology to crystallize. For example, when computers first appeared, the Library of Congress (LC) subject heading chosen for them was "Electronic calculating machines"; this was later changed to "Computers." Even when the revision of thesauri or subject heading lists keeps pace with needed changes, updating obsolete vocabulary in catalog records poses a workload problem. This is one reason changes to more current terms were sometimes slow in implementation in manual catalogs. In many online catalogs and databases where the bibliographic and authority files are linked, updating is easier: once a heading is changed, every record that was linked to the old heading can be automatically linked to the new.

Cross-References

Three common types of *cross-references* are used in the subject heading structure: (1) the *see* (*or use*) reference, (2) the *see also* [or *BT*, *NT*, or *RT*] reference, and (3) the *general* reference.

See or Use References

To make sure that users who happen to consult the catalog under different names for (or different forms of the name of) a given subject will be able to locate material on it, *see* or *use* references are provided to lead them from the terms they have looked under to the authorized heading for the subject in question. These references guide users *from* terms that are not used as headings *to* the authorized headings.

See Also (Including BT, NT, and RT) References

This type of reference connects headings that are related in some way, either hierarchically or otherwise. Unlike the *see* reference, a *see also* reference relates headings that are all valid. The headings involved may overlap in meaning, but are not fully synonymous. If they were, they would not both be used in the catalog. By linking hierarchically related headings, *see also* (or BT for broader term and NT for narrower term) references guide the user to broader or more specific branches or aspects of a subject. By linking headings related nonhierarchically, *see also* (or RT for related term) references provide users with additional access points to material related to their interests.

General References

While a *specific* reference directs the user from the term being consulted to another individual heading, a *general* reference directs the user to a group or category of headings instead of to individual members of the group or category. It is sometimes called a blanket reference; an example is "**Exhibitions—Awards** *see also* the subdivision Awards under names of individual exhibitions." An obvious advantage of using general references is economy of space; they obviate the need to make long lists of specific references.

SYNTAX AND APPLICATION

The subject content of an information resource or a document may consist of

1. a single topic or concept, or multiple topics or concepts, treated separately in a work, for example, *Children; Children and young adults*;

2. aspect(s) of a topic or concept, for example, *Health care for children; Reading interests of children; Crimes against children*; and
3. two or more topics or concepts treated in relation to each other, for example, *Children in popular culture; Effects of violence on children.*

It is clear from this list that, except for single topics or concepts, the subject content of a work cannot always, or even often, be represented by a single word or a simple adjectival phrase. When this is the case, specificity (i.e., the degree to which words accurately represent content) must be achieved by other means. In this context, Mortimer Taube identified two types of specificity: "the specificity of a specific word or phrase and whatever degree of subdivision is allowed" and "the specificity achieved by the intersection, coordination, or logical product of terms of equal generality."[9]

The first type of specificity is an aspect of vocabulary design and the second type relates to application.

In many cases, a phrase is used to combine two or more general terms, either of which is broader than the resulting heading, for example, *Church and state*; *Intelligence testing for children*; *Fertilization of flowers; Effect of light on plants.* Another way to represent complexity is to use two or more separate terms without indicating the nature of their relationship; for example, a document might be assigned the two terms, *Flowers* and *Fertilization.* Such an approach leaves it to searchers to track down documents indexed with terms reflecting all aspects of the topics that interest them.

At the heart of the *syntax* concept is the representation of complex subjects through combination, or coordination, of terms representing different topics or different aspects or facets (defined as families of concepts that share a common characteristic[10]) of a topic. In other words, the term "syntax" refers to how words are put together to form phrases. In subject representation, while a single topic may be expressed with a single word or a phrase, a complex topic is almost always expressed in the English language with multiple words. When and how to combine individual words to represent multiple or complex topics in a document is a central issue in both the design of a vocabulary and in its application.

There are two aspects of syntax: term construction and application syntax. Term construction, that is, how words are chosen or put together to represent individual topics or concepts in the controlled vocabulary, is a matter of principle; in contrast, application syntax, that is, how terms are put together to reflect the contents of documents in the cataloging or metadata record, is a matter of policy, determined by practical factors such as user needs, available resources, and search engines and their capabilities.

For complex topics, term combination can occur at various stages in the process of information storage and retrieval:

1. during vocabulary construction;
2. at the stage of cataloging or indexing; or,
3. at the point of retrieval.

The first two approaches result in the presence of precombined index terms in the bibliographic or index records, a process called *precoordination*. The third approach results in such records containing single-concept terms only, a process called *postcoordination*. The terms *precoordination* and *postcoordination* refer to "when" single-concept terms are combined to form complex subjects. These concepts are discussed below.

Precoordination

Whether the combination of words and phrases to represent complex topics occurs in the vocabulary or is created by the cataloger or indexer, the result of either practice is having complex subject terms stored in the records. This practice is called precoordination.

In a precoordinate system, the combination of multiple topics or facets may take place either before the heading enters the vocabulary (an approach called *enumeration*) or before it is assigned to a document (an approach called *synthesis*). A totally enumerative vocabulary is by definition precoordinated. On the other hand, a faceted, controlled vocabulary—that is, a system that provides individual terms in clearly defined categories, or facets—may be applied either precoordinately or postcoordinately. A faceted scheme hence offers greater possibility for combinations.

When words or phrases representing different topics or different facets of a topic are precombined at the point of vocabulary construction, we refer to the process as *enumeration*. In an enumerative vocabulary, both single-concept terms and multiple-concept terms are included. In an enumerative list, prepositions or other devices (punctuation or the structure of the string) are used to show how the terms are interrelated within a heading, for example,

Single-concept terms	**Multiple-concept terms**
Books	Books and reading
Children	Children—Books and reading
Discrimination	Children—Health and hygiene
Health	Children—Nutrition
Hygiene	Children and motion pictures
Internet	Discrimination against people with disabilities

Reference services (Libraries)	Internet in library reference services
Motion pictures	Oil pollution of groundwater
Nutrition	Recorders (2) with plucked instrument
People with disabilities	Ensemble
Plucked instruments	Teenagers—Alcohol use
Popular culture	Teenagers—Books and reading
Reading	Violence in popular culture
Recorders	
Teenagers	
Violence	

Because it is not possible to list all combinations, there is no completely enumerative controlled vocabulary. Controlled vocabularies devised in early times tended to be partially enumerative. Many began as largely enumerative lists, but became less so as the volume of material to be covered increased and the subject matter treated became more complicated. Two examples of partially enumerative schemes are Library of Congress Subject Heading (LCSH) and *Sears List of Subject Headings*. In applying such lists, precoordinated headings, when available, are assigned to works on complex subjects, and new precoordinated headings are constantly established. In this approach, cataloging consists basically of finding the best match between the work being cataloged and the available precombined headings. With the use of prepositions and other connecting words, precoordinated headings are often made more expressive than what can be achieved by postcoordination. For example, the heading, **Effect of poison on plants** is more precise in meaning than combining the separate terms **Plants**, **Poison** with the Boolean operator *AND*.

The other approach, called *synthesis*, is to list the concepts and topics individually as single-concept subject headings or descriptors, which then can be combined by the indexer or cataloger during the process of indexing or cataloging or by the user when searching for complex subjects. When individual terms in the controlled vocabulary are divided into distinctive categories or facets, such as thing/object, place, time, and form, the list is called *faceted*.

Postcoordination

Because no system can be totally precoordinate, often complex topics are represented by assigning single-concept headings to bibliographic records, allowing the combination to take place at the point of retrieval. This concept is referred to as *postcoordination*. Postcoordination allows the user to combine the terms as appropriate at the point of searching. It can be easily seen that postcoordination is more flexible, allowing for infinite combinations of concepts. However, because it was not easy for the user to combine concepts in the book or card catalog, early cataloging practice tended to take the precoordinate approach. Postcoordination is favored in the online environment, because computer searching enables Boolean and other sophisticated operations. Other advantages of postcoordination include the ease in maintaining a vocabulary consisting of simple terms while allowing infinite combinations among the terms at retrieval.

Subject-heading lists typically contain both single-concept headings and enumerated complex headings, while thesauri contain single-concept terms, called *descriptors*, only. Subject vocabularies used in MARC records are typically precoordinated subject-heading strings, while controlled vocabularies used in online databases are mostly single-concept descriptors to be combined by the searcher as required.

SUBJECT AUTHORITY CONTROL

Any retrieval system offering both controlled terminology and a cross-reference apparatus must have a means of maintaining control over the vocabulary and the references. Librarians and other retrieval systems personnel have devised such a means, referred to as *authority control*. The principles of authority control in general and name authority control devices were discussed in chapters 8 and 9; subject authority control systems follow much the same pattern.

Subject authority systems have one main purpose: to ensure uniformity and consistency in subject-heading terminology and cross-references. To this end, headings are *established,* that is, authorized when they are used for the first time, and *subject authority records* are set up for them. Name and subject records in a library system may be kept in separate files or databases or in a combined name/subject authority file. Currently, LC's name and subject authority records can be searched through the same authorities interface at the Library's web site (http://authorities.loc.gov).

Subject Authority Record

A subject authority record contains the following information: the established heading; scope notes, if any; cross-references made from synonyms and those made to and from other headings; and the sources or authorities on which the decision on the heading form was based. For example, the authority record for the LC subject heading **International librarianship** contains the following data:

Established heading:	**International librarianship**
Scope note:	Here are entered works on the activities, cooperation, exchange, etc., in librarianship at the international level. Works on the study and analysis of the libraries and library systems of different countries are entered under Comparative librarianship.
Used-for (see) reference from:	Librarianship, International
Broader term reference:	International cooperation Library science
Related term reference:	Comparative librarianship Library cooperation
Narrower term reference:	Bibliography, International

Levels of Subject Authority Control

There are at least two levels of subject authority control: central and local. On the first level, a central agency—as in the case of the United States—the LC, the National Library of Medicine, or the H. W. Wilson Company—maintains the subject authority file, making changes to existing headings and cross-references as well as adding new ones.

On the local level, a library devises a subject authority apparatus that ensures conformity and currency of the subject headings and cross-references appearing in its own catalog. Most American libraries rely on one of the standard subject-headings lists, such as LCSH or the Sears list, and create local subject authority records only for headings not yet given in the standard list. In some libraries, newly established headings are simply recorded in a *subject-headings list*, along with necessary maintenance information. Local subject authority work then includes correcting erroneous headings and cross-references, updating obsolete headings, and adding or revising cross-references necessitated by new headings. The design and capabilities of a given online catalog system determine what methods of local subject authority control are best suited to that system.

Functions of a Subject Authority File

In the library setting, a subject authority file[11] serves a number of functions:

Cataloging. In subject cataloging, the subject authority file serves as the source of indexing vocabulary and as the means of verifying or validating headings assigned to individual cataloging records. With the subject authority file, a cataloger can ensure that the same heading is assigned to all works on a particular subject, and that each heading represents only one particular subject. Furthermore, by consulting the subject authority file, the cataloger can ensure that all headings assigned to cataloging records conform to the established forms.

Catalog maintenance. Even after cataloging records have been created, adjustments must be made from time to time as a result of heading changes. When existing headings are revised or new headings are added, cross-references are often affected and should be adjusted. The subject authority file, reflecting the most current status of headings and cross-references, serves as the source for verification and validation.

Retrieval. Enhanced retrieval must be considered the ultimate function of subject authority control, because the purpose of normalizing subject access points is to enable the user to retrieve relevant information.

There are two ways in which the subject authority file can aid the user in retrieval. First, the subject headings displayed in the subject authority file show the user the terminology and form of subject access points in the catalog. Second, the cross-references guide the user to related headings when the user's input terms fail to retrieve useful records. For either function, of course, the subject authority file must be available to the user.

GENERAL METHODS OF SUBJECT ANALYSIS

No matter what the subject access system within which a subject cataloger or indexer is working, subject analysis of a particular work or document involves basically three steps: (1) determining the overall subject content of the item being cataloged, (2) identifying multiple subjects and/or subject aspects and interrelationships, and (3) representing both of these concerns in the language of the controlled vocabulary at hand. These steps will now be discussed in greater detail.

1. The most reliable and certain way to determine the subject content is to read or examine the work in detail. Since this is not always practical for reasons of cost, catalogers usually have to use other means. Titles are sometimes but not always a fair indication of content. *An Introduction to Chemistry* is undoubtedly what its title implies, but *Tourist Attraction* is a novel rather than a travel book. Therefore, it is always advisable to look beyond the title for the subject content of the work. Other features of the work often provide information relating to content. These include abstracts, if any, tables of contents, chapter headings,

prefaces, introductions, indexes, book jackets, slipcases, and any other accompanying descriptive material—the latter two being particularly helpful in the case of nonprint materials. When these elements fail to provide a clear picture of what the work is about, external sources, such as bibliographies, catalogs, review media, and other reference sources, may prove helpful. Occasionally, subject specialists may have to be consulted, particularly when the subject matter is unfamiliar to the cataloger or indexer.

2. The next step is to identify the main and subsidiary subjects, including different aspects of the subject such as author's point of view, time, and place. A work may deal with several subjects separately, or deal with two or more subjects in relation to each other. The interrelationships of subjects in a work are called phase relations. Some examples of phase relations follow:

   Influence phase. The influence of one thing, one concept, or one person on another is a very common approach in scholarly works.

   Bias phase. Some works on a particular subject have a bias toward, or aimed at, a specific group of readers or audience; for example, *Fundamentals of Physical Chemistry for Premedical Students.*

   Tool or application phase. This relationship is particularly common among scientific or technical works; for example, *Chemical Calculations: An Introduction to the Use of Mathematics in Chemistry.*

   Comparison phase. This relationship is common in literary and social science studies.

3. The final step is to represent the content according to a particular system or scheme. The first two steps are the same in all subject analysis operations. The third step varies according to whether representation is through subject headings, indexing terms, or classification numbers. In many cases, the cataloger or indexer starts with a tentative wording or phrasing, and tries to match it in the tool being used.

ASSIGNING SUBJECT HEADINGS: GENERAL GUIDELINES

Although policies regarding subject-heading assignment may vary from library to library and from agency to agency, certain general practices are followed by most libraries and information agencies in the United States.

These are discussed below. For specific guidelines for assigning headings from a particular subject-headings list, catalogers and indexers should consult the following chapters in this book, the introduction to the subject list, and the cataloging manual of the system.

Levels of Subject Cataloging

The levels of indexing, that is, whether subject representation is provided for both parts and the comprehensive whole, depend on the policy of the indexing agency. In some cases, indexing is primarily at the work-as-a-whole level (such as in a monograph or a journal); in others, it is at the level of chapter or article content. In catalogs in American libraries prepared according to the *Library of Congress* (LC), Sears, or the National Library of Medicine Library, subject headings are assigned to each item to bring out the overall content of the work being cataloged. Occasionally, subject headings for parts of a work are also assigned. These are called *analytical* entries (for a component part such as a short story, play, or chapter) or *partial contents* entries (for a substantial portion of a work).

Headings for individual persons, families, corporate bodies, places, etc. are assigned if they are considered significant to the work as a whole.

Specific (Coextensive) Entry

The heading that represents precisely the subject content of the work is assigned as the primary subject heading, unless such a heading does not exist and cannot be established. In the absence of a coextensive heading, a broader or more general heading may be used. In such cases, the broader heading is the most *specific* authorized heading in the hierarchy that covers the content of the work. In many cases, several headings may be assigned in order to cover different aspects of a subject.

With a few exceptions, a general heading, which comprehends the specific primary heading, is not assigned as an additional heading to a work dealing with only the specific subject. For example, the subject heading **Science** is not assigned to a work on chemistry, which receives the heading **Chemistry**.

Number of Headings

The number of headings assigned to each work depends on the nature of its content, the structure of available headings, and the policies established by the cataloging agency. It is the policy of the LC, for example, to allow the assignment of up to ten subject headings for an individual item. The ideal situation is one in which one heading will suffice to express the subject of the work being cataloged. However, in many cases more than one heading may be required because the subject content of a particular work cannot be totally expressed in a single heading. Furthermore, headings are sometimes assigned to bring out secondary topics or concepts treated in the work.

Certain categories of works, such as general periodicals and individual works of fiction, are not usually given subject headings.

Multitopical and Multielement Works

For a multitopical or multielement work, more than one heading may be required; what is done in a given library or cataloging agency depends on the policy of the agency in question. The following guidelines reflect LC practice, and may be followed by libraries using LCSH or the Sears list.

A multitopical work (one that deals with two or three distinctive subjects or concepts separately) is assigned two or three separate headings, unless the two or three subjects constitute approximately the totality of a general subject; in the latter case, the heading for the general subject is used. For example, a book about Chinese and Japanese literature is assigned two headings, one for each literature, but a book about Greek and Latin literature is assigned the heading for classical literature. When a work deals with four or more subjects, all of which form parts of a larger subject, it is given a heading with regard to the larger subject, for instance, "**South America—Description and travel**" for a work about traveling in Argentina, Brazil, Chile, and Ecuador. When individual subjects in a work do not belong to a particular broad subject, they are given separate headings if there are no more than four; for more than four topics, the general practice is to use either several very general headings or a form heading only, for example, "**French essays**."

For a multielement work (one that features a single central topic considered from different aspects or containing various elements such as form, place, and time) the most desirable heading is one that brings out all of these aspects or elements. If such a heading is not available, a new heading may be established, or several headings may be used, as appropriate. Whether all of the concepts, aspects, and elements identified in the subject of a work should be represented in the catalog depends on the types of users for whom the catalog is intended. The main criterion is the potential value or usefulness of the headings for the users.

The methods and procedures outlined above represent general approaches to subject cataloging. Individual systems often have special policies or guidelines. These are discussed in the following chapters.

MARC CODING

MARC coding can be used to code both subject vocabulary information and the subject terms or headings assigned to represent the aboutness of a work.

Subject vocabulary information or subject authority data are recorded in authority records and therefore, in a MARC environment, MARC Authority Formats are used to code the information recorded to describe the thema and nomen entities and their attributes. Not all existing vocabularies use the FRSAD terminology or defined entities and attributes. In addition, not all subject vocabularies use the MARC authority record structures and encoding system to store information on each vocabulary term, including relationships.

In a MARC environment, assigned subject terms or subject headings representing the aboutness of the work are recorded in MARC bibliographic fields 6XX:

600 Personal name heading
610 Corporate name heading
630 Uniform title (or Authorized access point for work, expression, manifestation or item with no associated creator)
650 Topical heading
651 Geographic name heading
653 Index term - Uncontrolled
655 Index term - Genre/Form

Additional subject (6XX) fields have been defined in MARC. The majority of subject terms are topical headings. The first indicator in the 650 field indicates the "Level of subject":

—No information provided
0—No level specified
The level of the term could be determined but is not specified.
1—Primary
The term describes the main focus or subject content of the material.
2—Secondary

The subject term describes a less important aspect of the content of the material.

The second indicator in each 6XX field indicates the source vocabulary; for example, 0 indicates LCSH, 2 indicates MeSH headings. The complete list of predefined second indicator values include the following:

0 - Library of Congress Subject Headings
1 - LC subject headings for children's literature
2 - Medical Subject Headings
3 - National Agricultural Library subject authority file

4 - Source not specified
5 - Canadian Subject Headings
6 - Répertoire de vedettes-matière
7 - Source specified in subfield $2

When none of the vocabularies listed for values 0–6 is used, a 7 is used, which allows us to specify the source vocabulary in subfield $2.

NOTES

1. IFLA Study Group on the Functional Requirements for Bibliographic Records. (1998). *Functional Requirements for Bibliographic Records: Final Report* (UBCIM Publications, New Series Vol. 19). München, Germany: K. G. Saur. Retrieved from http://www.ifla.org/publications/functional-requirements-for-bibliographic-records.
2. Patton, G. E. (2009). *Functional Requirements for Authority Data: A Conceptual Model* (IFLA Series on Bibliographic Control Vol. 34). München, Germany: K. G. Saur. Retrieved from http://www.ifla.org/publications/functional-requirements-for-authority-data.
3. Zeng, M. L., Žumer, M., and Salaba, A. (Eds.). (2011). *Functional Requirements for Subject Authority Data (FRSAD): A Conceptual Model* (IFLA Series on Bibliographic Control Vol. 43). Berlin/München, Germany: De Gruyter Saur. Retrieved from http://www.ifla.org/publications/ifla-series-on-bibliographic-control-43.
4. Pettee, J. (1947). *Subject Headings: The History and Theory of the Alphabetical Subject Approach to Books*. New York, NY: H. W. Wilson Company (p. 151).
5. Cutter, C. A. (1953). *Rules for a Dictionary Catalog* (4th ed. rewritten). London, England: The Library Association (Original work published 1876).
6. Cutter, 1953 [1876], p. 12.
7. Cutter, 1953 [1876], p. 6.
8. Cutter, 1953 [1876], p. 66.
9. Taube, M. (October 1952). Specificity in subject headings and coordinate indexing. *Library Trends, 1*, 222.
10. Batty, D. (November 1998). WWW—Wealth, weariness or waste: Controlled vocabulary and thesauri in support of online information access. *D-Lib Magazine, 4*(11). Retrieved from www.dlib.org/dlib/november98/11batty.html.
11. Chan, L. M. (1991). Functions of a subject authority file. In K. M. Drabenstott (Ed.), *Subject Authorities in the Online Environment: Papers from a Conference Program Held in San Francisco, June 29, 1987* (ALCTS Papers on Library Technical Services and Collections No. 1). Chicago, IL: American Library Association.

Chapter 11

Library of Congress Subject Headings

INTRODUCTION

Library of Congress Subject Headings (LCSH) is a list of subject headings originally developed by the LC for use in its catalog descriptions. The list was begun in 1898, and first published in 1914 under the title *Subject Headings Used in the Dictionary Catalogues of the Library of Congress.*[1] Since then, it has become the standard list used by most large general libraries in the United States, as well as by many special libraries and some smaller libraries; it is also used in many libraries in other countries. The list has gone through many editions, and in its eighth edition the current title was adopted.

LCSH is essentially a subject authority list; in other words, it is a list of terms authorized by the LCs for use in its own subject cataloging. Libraries using LCSH for subject authority control rely on the list and follow LC policies and practices as de facto standards. Yet, for subject cataloging, there is no formal code of rules comparable to RDA guidelines for descriptive cataloging. In 1984, in response to the expressed need of the library community for a guide to subject cataloging, the LC began publishing its internal instructions for subject cataloging in *Subject Cataloging Manual: Subject Headings* (SHM), currently titled *Subject Headings Manual.*[2] This manual, initially available in print and now available as an online resource (part of Cataloger's Desktop), contains detailed instructions for establishing and assigning subject headings, but is not cast in the form of a subject cataloging code. In 1990, a document entitled *Library of Congress Subject Headings: Principles of Structure and Policies for Application*[3] was published. This document serves as a succinct statement of the principles and policies governing LCSH, with respect to both construction of subject headings and their application. In 1995, in recognition of the fact that this tool is used by libraries outside the LC itself, and based on a survey of a broader audience, a number of improvements were introduced to accommodate users not only within the LC, but also from all outside institutions. The following discussion is based on the SHM and its statement of principles and policies.

To use LCSH effectively, it is important to realize its scope: what it contains, and what it does not contain. Its most prominent feature is the set of headings authorized for use as subject access points in bibliographic records. It also contains many terms that are not authorized as headings, but that are included as lead-in (also called nonpreferred or entry) terms to help users as well as catalogers find the applicable authorized term for a topic at issue. Cross-references under the lead-in terms give directions to the associated authorized headings. However, not all authorized subject headings appear in LCSH: catalogers may derive headings from the Name Authority File or, acting under established policies, construct suitable headings on their own. In other words, many subject headings appearing in LC's bibliographic records are not listed in LCSH. These omissions include the following: (1) headings residing in the Name Authority File, (2) headings containing free-floating phrases such as . . . Metropolitan Area, . . . Region, and suchlike, (3) certain music headings, and (4) headings with free-floating subdivisions.

Many of the above resources are also available as free PDF files via the Library of Congress Acquisitions and Bibliographic Access web site.

FORMAT OF LCSH AND MARC CODING

From 1988 to 2014, the print version of LCSH was published annually, until the LC discontinued its print publications. Since 1986, the list has been available in electronic form, and is currently available on the World Wide Web (as part of *Classification Web* subscription-based tool, with select publications available as free PDF files via the LC web site) and is updated on a daily basis. *Subject Authorities* data sets are also available electronically via the LC Authorities interface or as linked-data data sets.

Subject Authority Records

Authorized headings appear in boldface type, for example, **Art**, **Berries**, **Business and education**, **Digital music players**, **Rural-urban relations**, etc. Each valid heading is followed by scope notes, cross-references, and subdivisions, if applicable. Entries appearing in lightface Roman are not to be used as subject headings: they are the lead-in terms (i.e., synonyms or variants of regular headings) followed by cross-references to the authorized headings (linking to the authorized heading entry for direct access). Examples of entries are shown below (underlined text indicates link to valid heading):

Adventure and adventurers—Computer games
USE Computer adventure games

Berries (*May Subd Geog*)
[SB381-SB386 (Culture)]
BT Fruit
Fruit-culture
RT Cookery (Berries)
SA *names of berries, e.g.* Strawberries
NT Amelanchier
Blueberries
Canned berries
Frozen berries
Huckleberries
Ornamental berries
Rubus
Berries—Harvesting (*May Subd Geog*)
Berries—Use in cooking
USE Cooking (Berries)
Berries—Varieties (*May Subd Geog*)

Computer adventure games *(May Subd Geog)*
[GV1469.22-.25]
UF Adventures and adventurers—Computer games
Adventure games, Computer
Games, Computer adventure
BT Adventure games
Computer games
SA *subdivision* **Computer games** *under subjects*
NT Dwarf Fortress (Game)
Island of Kesmai (Game)
Queen: The Eye (Game)

Fine arts
USE Art
Arts

Foreign relations
USE *subdivision* Foreign relations *under names of countries*
USE International relations

Games, Computer adventure
USE Computer adventure games

Subject Authorities are encoded according to MARC 21 authority formats. Each **main heading** or **main heading—subdivision** combination is represented by a separate authority record. The valid or authorized subject heading and the references are identified by specific tags. Each subdivision within a heading is identified by a subfield code. The field tags and subfield codes used in subject authority records are shown below.

Heading fields:
150 Heading—Topical term
151 Heading—Geographic name
155 Heading—Form/genre
180 Heading—General Subdivision
181 Heading—Geographic Subdivision
182 Heading—Chronological Subdivision
185 Heading—Form Subdivision

Common subfields:
$v Form subdivision
$x General subdivision
$y Chronological subdivision
$z Geographic subdivision

Tracing and References fields:
260 Complex see reference—subject
360 Complex see also reference—subject
450 See from tracing—Topical term
451 See from tracing—Geographic name
455 See from tracing—Genre/Form term
480 See from tracing—General Subdivision
481 See from tracing—Geographic Subdivision
482 See from tracing—Chronological Subdivision
485 See from tracing—Form Subdivision
550 See also from tracing—Topical term
551 See also from tracing—Geographic name
555 See also from tracing—Genre/Form term
580 See also from tracing—General Subdivision
581 See also from tracing—Geographic Subdivision
582 See also from tracing—Chronological Subdivision

585 See also from tracing—Form Subdivision

Common 4XX and 5XX subfields:
$i Relationship information
$w Control subfield
$4 Relationship code

Note fields:
667 Nonpublic general note
670 Source data found
675 Source data not found
680 Public general note
681 Subject example tracing note
688 Application history note

Field 150 includes form headings as well as topical headings. The MARC 21 authority record related to the heading **Computer adventure games** from the LC *Authorities* is shown below:

LC Control Number:	sh 85029475
LCCN permalink:	http://lccn.loc.gov/sh85029475
HEADING:	Computer adventure games
000	00653cz a2200229n 450
001	4681749
005	20120323071043.0
008	860211il anannbabn la ana
010	## $a sh 85029475
035	## $a (DLC)sh 85029475
035	## $a (DLC)28434
040	## $a DLC $c DLC $d DLC
053	#0 $a GV1469.22 $b GV1469.25
150	## $a Computer adventure games
360	## $i subdivision $a Computer games $i under subjects
450	## $a Adventure and adventurers $v Computer games
450	## $a Adventure games, Computer
450	## $a Games, Computer adventure
550	## $w g $a Adventure games
550	## $w g $a Computer games

(l = no attempt to code; # = blank; $ = subfield delimiter)

Subject Headings in Bibliographic Records

In the MARC bibliographic record, subject headings are identified by field tags, which include the following:

600 Personal name heading
610 Corporate name heading
630 Uniform title
650 Topical heading
651 Geographic name heading
655 Index term—Genre/Form

Subfield codes for fields 600, 610, and 630 are similar to those in fields 100, 110, and 130 in a name authority record. Subfield codes for fields 650, 651, and 655 are similar to those in fields 150, 151, and 155 in a subject authority record.

The LC and other libraries have also made use of field 653 *Index term—Uncontrolled* for additional subject entries that are not taken from LCSH or other subject lists/thesauri, nor constructed from other established subject/thesaurus-building rules.

MAIN HEADINGS: FUNCTIONS, TYPES, SYNTAX, AND SEMANTICS

Subject headings may be categorized into various types according to their functions. A *topical heading* represents a concept or object treated in a work. It reflects what the work is *about*. When headings are used to represent the physical or bibliographic form of the item being cataloged, they are called *form/genre headings*. A *form/genre heading* reflects what the work *is* rather than what it is *about*. Proper names may also be used as subject headings for works focusing on individual persons, corporate bodies, places, and other named entities. Headings for named entities established according to descriptive cataloging guidelines (e.g., RDA) always reside in the name authority file. Headings for named entities established according to subject cataloging conventions reside in the subject authority file if used only as subject headings, and in the name authority file as descriptive access points if necessary. SHM H405 lists named entities and the authority groups in which they belong.

Topical and Form Headings [MARC authority fields 150, 155; bibliographic fields 650, 655]

A topical or form heading may contain one or more words. A one-word heading represents a single object or concept, while a multiple-word heading may represent either a single concept or object or multiple concepts or objects. A heading may also carry a subdivision or subdivisions that bring out one or more aspects of the main subject. A heading containing more than one concept may appear either in the form of a phrase heading or a heading with subdivisions; this is called an *enumerated heading*, that is, a precombined complex heading in the list.

Syntax

On the basis of their syntactical structure, topical and form headings may be divided into two main categories: single-noun headings and phrase headings.

Single-Noun Headings

The simplest form of main heading consists of a noun or substantive, for example, **Cabbage**, **Cats**, **Economics**, **Poetry**, **Locomotion**, **Cataloging**, **Poor.** Some single-noun headings are followed by a qualifier, which is discussed in the section "Semantics" in this chapter.

Phrase Headings

When a subject or concept cannot be properly expressed by a single noun, a phrase is used. There are several patterns of phrase headings: adjectival, conjunctive, prepositional, inverted, and free-floating. These are discussed individually below:

Adjectival Phrase Headings. These are the most common type of phrase headings; they consist of a noun or noun phrase with an adjectival modifier. The adjectival modifier can be in one of several forms: a common adjective, a proper adjective, a geographic name, a noun modifier, or a noun in the possessive case, for example, **Alien films**, **Educational Web sites**, **Gospel singers**, **English literature**, **California sea lion**, **Library science**, **Cowper's glands**, **Carpenters' squares**, etc.

Conjunctive Phrase Headings. These headings consist of two or more nouns, noun phrases, or both, with or without modifiers, connected by the word *and*. This form serves two purposes: (1) to express a reciprocal relationship between two general topics discussed at a broad level from the perspectives of both topics, for example, **Literature and science**, **Church and social problems**, and so on; (2) to connect subjects that are often treated together in works because they are similar, opposite, or closely associated, for example, **Emigration and immigration**, **Open and closed shelves**, **Debtor and creditor**, **Children's encyclopedias and dictionaries**, **Bolts and nuts**, and so on.

Prepositional Phrase Headings. These headings consist of nouns, noun phrases, or both, with or without modifiers, connected by a preposition, for example, **Breach of contract**. Such phrase headings usually serve one of two purposes: (1) to express complex relationships between topics that cannot be represented by a single noun or a conjunctive phrase, for example, **Electric discharges through gases**, **Federal aid to youth services**, **Internet in earthquake relief**, and so on, or (2) to represent a concept or object that cannot be stated in English in any other way than by using a prepositional phrase, for example, **Boards of directors**, **Figures of speech**, **Fathers of children with disabilities**, among others.

Inverted Phrase Headings. In many cases, a phrase heading is inverted in order to bring a significant word into a prominent position as the entry element, for example, **Chemistry, Organic**; **Knowledge, Sociology of**; and so on. In older manual catalogs or single-entry listings or displays, the inverted form brought together headings containing the same initial word for the purpose of subject collocation. However, this inverted form is no longer used in newly established headings. SHM H306 instructs us to establish new topical or form headings in natural language form (not inverted), except for the majority of headings qualified by language, nationality, or ethnic group (see exceptions), for example, **Poets, Australian**; **Cooking, American**; and so on. On the other hand, **French poetry** is established in normal, natural language word order.

Free-floating Phrase Headings. A number of terms or phrases are designated as free-floating components, which may be combined with any heading within designated categories to form new phrase headings, for example:

> **[Name of city] Metropolitan Area**
> **[Name of city] Suburban Area**
> **[Name of geographic feature] Region**

The resulting combinations are usually not listed in LCSH.

> **New York Metropolitan Area**
> **Washington Suburban Area**
> **Mississippi River Region**

Semantics

In regard to semantics or terminology, LCSH is a controlled-vocabulary list, that is, a list that is designed to offer uniform and unique subject terminology.

A main heading represents a topic, which can be a thing, a concept, a process, an activity, a person, an organization, a geographic or jurisdictional entity, an event, a fictional construct, etc. Controlled-vocabulary builders, working on the principle of uniform headings and following accepted design principles, try to avoid using multiple terms that have the same meanings as valid headings; in LCSH, this is done by authorizing only one term from a set of synonyms as the valid heading.

A second design consideration, in accordance with the principle of unique headings, is to avoid headings that have more than one meaning. Many English words or phrases have more than one meaning. In constructing a controlled vocabulary, one method for solving the problem of multiple meanings is to choose an acceptable synonym that is unambiguous. Often, however, the most appropriate term for a topic may have multiple meanings. LCSH solves the problem of multiple meaning in part by adding a *qualifier* (a second term enclosed in parentheses) to resolve the ambiguity. Examples are **Cookies (Computer science)**, **Cold (Disease)**, and **Pool (Game)**.

A qualifier may also be used to provide context for obscure or technical terms, in which case it usually takes the form of the name of a discipline or of a category or type of things, for example, **Charge transfer devices (Electronics)**, **Chlorosis (Plants)**, and **Semantic integration (Computer systems)**.

Semantic confusion also arises with authorized terms that are close or overlapping in meaning to other authorized terms. This problem is resolved through the use of scope notes. Many headings in LCSH are provided with scope notes that (a) define the heading's scope, (b) specify the range of subject matter to which the heading applies in representing the topic of a resource, (c) distinguish between related headings, or (d) state which of several meanings of a term is the one to which a heading's use in subject representation is limited. The following examples are illustrative.

> **College graduates**
> Here are entered works on college graduates as a socioeconomic group. Works on college graduates in relation to their alma maters are entered under Universities and colleges—Alumni and alumnae.
>
> **Hairwork**
> Here are entered works on articles made of hair, such as wigs, switches, and so on.
>
> **Cellular control mechanisms**
> Here are entered works on the various mechanisms of cellular control such as structural control, biochemical control, cell differentiation,

and so on. Works on the control of the type and rate of cellular processes by regulation of the activity of specific genes controlling individual biochemical reactions are entered under Genetic regulation.

Headings for Named Entities [MARC authority fields 100, 110, 111, 130; bibliographic fields 600, 610, 611, 630]

Proper names are often needed as subject headings, and very few are listed in LCSH. The Name Authority File gives the established form for a large number of proper names, including names for persons, corporate bodies, and jurisdictions. Qualifiers are added as prescribed by RDA guidelines. Names used as subjects but not covered by RDA (e.g., names of geographic features) are established by the LC according to principles and policies compatible to those in RDA. These headings are listed in LCSH.

The following sections discuss three categories of name headings: personal names, corporate names, and geographic names.

Personal Names [MARC authority field 100; bibliographic field 600]

To facilitate retrieval, the same personal name heading is used for works *by* and *about* a person, for example, **Shakespeare, William, 1564–1616**; and **Austen, Jane, 1775–1817**. Personal name headings are established according to RDA, and are stored in the Name Authority File.

Certain types of personal name headings, including family name headings, headings for gods and goddesses, and headings for legendary and fictitious characters, are used only as subject headings. These are established and included in LCSH and the Subject Authority File. Examples are given below:

Bakewell family
Lincoln family
Baal (Canaanite deity)
Robin Hood (Legendary character)
Snoopy (Fictitious character)

Corporate Names [MARC authority field 110; bibliographic field 610]

Names of corporate bodies are used as subject headings for works that describe their origin and development and analyze and discuss their organization, function, and activities. Corporate name headings, established and stored in the Name Authority File, are used for this purpose. The most common types of corporate bodies are associations and firms, governments and their agencies, institutions, committees, and commissions, for example:

American Library Association
United States. Food and Drug Administration
Johns Hopkins University
University of Wisconsin—Madison. Arboretum

Geographic Names[4] *[MARC authority field 151; bibliographic field 651]*

Names of places and geographic features may appear as main headings or as subdivisions under topical or form headings. For a given place, the form of the geographic name should be the same when used in either position. There are two types of geographic names: jurisdictional and nonjurisdictional.

Jurisdictional Names. Geographic names, also called *jurisdictional headings*, which serve as subject as well as bibliographic access points are established according to RDA and stored in the Name Authority File. For example:

Madrid (Spain)
Athens (Ohio)

Nonjurisdictional Names. Nonjurisdictional geographic names, including names of natural geographic features, can be used as subject headings even though they are not used as bibliographic access points. Such names, established according to the policies discussed below, are listed in LCSH. If the name exists in more than one language form, English is generally preferred. Furthermore, in many cases, qualifiers are added in order to make the headings unique or compatible with jurisdictional headings.

Nile River
Great Smoky Mountains (N.C. and Tenn.)
Sepu Kangri (China)

Two types of qualifiers are used with geographic names: geographic and generic.

Geographic Qualifiers. The term *geographic qualifier* refers to the addition of the name of a larger geographic entity (normally the name of the country) to a place name. The descriptive cataloging rules governing jurisdictional names are followed for nonjurisdictional names as far as applicable. For places in certain countries, including Australia, Canada, Great Britain, Malaysia, and the United States, the name of the appropriate first-order political subdivision (i.e., state, province, constituent country, etc.) is used as the geographic qualifier, for example:

Sheep River (Alta.)
Ben Nevis (Scotland)
Albany (N.Y.)

The name of a natural feature generally does not require a geographic qualifier unless it is contained wholly within one or two jurisdictions, or when there are two or more entities bearing the same name, for example:

Amazon River
Himalaya Mountains
Ohio River Valley
Berkel River (Germany and Netherlands)
Table Rock Lake (Mo. and Ark.)
Ventana Wilderness (Calif.)
San Juan River (Colo.-Utah)
San Juan River (Colombia)
San Juan River (Nicaragua and Costa Rica)
Golden Triangle (Pittsburgh, Pa.)
Golden Triangle (Southeast Asia)

Generic Qualifiers. The names of many natural features contain a generic term, for example, **Ohio River** and **Baltic Sea**. If it is necessary to distinguish between headings and/or cross-references that have the same name and geographic qualifier, a generic qualifier is added to the nonjurisdictional name:

Big Bear Lake (Calif.) [heading for the city]
Big Bear Lake (San Bernardino County, Calif.: Lake) [heading for the lake in San Bernardino County]

Entry Element.[5] When a geographic name consists of more than one element, the elements are rearranged so that the distinctive portion of the name occurs in the initial position. Two situations account for the majority of inverted geographic names.

In the first situation, the inverted form is used when the name of a natural geographic feature consists of a generic term, such as "lake" or "valley," followed by the specific name, for example:

Fuji, Mount (Japan)
Superior, Lake
Mexico, Valley of (Mexico)

But, on the other hand, we also see geographic names that include a generic term in a noninverted, natural order of the name:

Rocky Mountains
Beaver Creek (McCreary County, Ky.)
Indian Lake (Ohio)

In the second situation, the inverted form is often used when the geographic heading consists of a geographic name preceded by a directional adjective, which is not an integral part of the proper name, for example:

Africa, Southern
California, Northern
Texas, East

But, here again, we see cases that do not follow the inverted from of the name:

South Africa
North Dakota
East China Sea

SUBDIVISIONS [MARC SUBFIELDS $V, $X, $Y, $Z]

A main heading may be subdivided by one or more of four kinds of subdivisions: form, topical, period, and geographic. In many cases, there may be several subdivisions following a main heading. The result is a string of elements, for example, **United States—History—Civil War, 1861–1865—Naval operations—Submarine**.

Most **heading—subdivision** combinations are specifically authorized by the LC as allowable subject strings. However, some commonly used form and topical subdivisions have been given a different status: they are of general application (under stated conditions), and are known as *free-floating subdivisions*. These are discussed later in this chapter.

Form Subdivisions [MARC subfield $v]

A form subdivision has been defined as an extension of a subject heading based on the bibliographic or physical form, or literary or artistic genre, in which the material in a work is organized and/or presented.[6] While a main heading normally expresses what the work is about, a form subdivision represents what it is, that is, what form the treatment of the subject takes.[7] Different works may deal with the same subject, but not be the same kind of work; in other words, they are in different bibliographical forms, for example:

Engineering—Examinations, questions, etc.
—Indexes
—Periodicals
Gardens—Pictorial works
—Poetry

Topical Subdivisions [MARC subfield $x]

In general, LCSH does not authorize any **topical heading—subdivision** combination where the subdivision represents a species, part, or kind of the subject represented by the main heading; in other words, by policy, there should be no authorized headings of the type, "Biology—Botany." Such a heading is characteristic of a classified catalog, and is against the principle of specific entry, which excludes genus-species or class-inclusion relationships. Typically, a topical subdivision limits the concept expressed by a main heading to a special subtopic; very often, a subdivision represents an activity or operation applied to or associated with the subject denoted by the main heading. For example, the heading **Agriculture—Accounting** means accounting as applied to the field of agriculture, and does not mean accounting as a kind or division of the subject agriculture. This type of topical subdivision is used extensively in LCSH.

Free-Floating Form and Topical Subdivisions

In order to ensure consistency and better control of subject strings, subdivisions and main headings may not be combined randomly. As a rule, each new combination of a subdivision with a main heading must be approved by an editorial committee at the LC before its use becomes authorized.

An exception to the rule stated above is a group of widely used subdivisions called *free-floating subdivisions*. This term refers to those form or topical subdivisions that may be used without prior authorization under a particular subject or name heading, where applicable and appropriate. Consequently, these **main heading—subdivision** combinations may be assigned as subject access points on bibliographic records without being listed in LCSH.

Free-floating subdivisions are listed either separately (apart from main headings) or under representative main headings called *pattern headings*, with the intention that these subdivisions may be combined with appropriate main headings in the same subject category at the time of application. There are four categories of free-floating subdivisions: those of general application, those to be used only under specific categories of headings, those controlled by pattern headings, and those indicated by "multiples."

Free-Floating Subdivisions of General Application

Form and topical subdivisions that are applicable to a large number of headings are designated as free-floating subdivisions of general application. Following are some examples of general free-floating subdivisions.

—Abstracts
—Examinations
—Lighting
—Literary collections
—Periodicals—Indexes
—Software
—Study and teaching

Under each subdivision in the free-floating subdivisions lists in SHM, instruction is given as to the kinds of headings to which the particular subdivision is applicable. For example, the subdivision **—Lighting** is applicable only under main headings representing vehicles, structures, buildings, rooms, installations, etc.

Free-Floating Subdivisions under Specific Types of Headings

Many subdivisions are authorized for use as free-floating subdivisions under specific categories of main headings only. Separate lists of free-floating subdivisions have been established and published in SHM10 for use with the following categories of main headings: classes of persons; ethnic groups; names of corporate bodies; names of persons; names of places; and names of bodies of water, streams, etc. The following headings, although not listed in LCSH, are valid headings that were constructed using these free-floating subdivisions.

Actors—Political activity
Asian-Americans—Race identity
American Library Association—Employees
Hong Kong (China)—Description and travel
Milton, John, 1608-1674 —Political and social views
Bush, George W. (George Walker), 1946—Inauguration, 2001
Colorado River (Colo.—Mexico)—Navigation

Free-Floating Subdivisions Controlled by Pattern Headings

Certain form or topical subdivisions are common in a particular subject field. Instead of authorizing them heading-by-heading and repeating them under each heading within the same category, they are listed under a chosen heading in the category. This chosen heading then serves as a *pattern heading* of subdivisions for headings in that category. The applicable subdivisions are displayed under the pattern heading in LCSH and in the Subject Authority File. Topical and form subdivisions listed under a pattern heading may be transferred and used with another heading in the same category, even though the combination does not appear in LCSH. For example, under **English language**, the pattern heading for languages, the subdivision—**Pronoun** is listed. Therefore, the combination **Japanese language—Pronoun** may be used, even though the combination does not appear in the list as such.

Table 11.1 shows the pattern headings designated for each subject category. For example, headings for individual corporate bodies may be subdivided according to the patterns listed in the table.

Catholic Church (as model for Christian denominations)
United States. Congress (for legislative bodies)
United States. Army (for armies of other countries)
United States. Navy (for navies of other countries)
Harvard University (for individual educational institutions)

As with other elements of LCSH, the provisions under pattern headings are under continual review. Therefore, the latest version of LCSH, available in ClassificationWeb, or the latest update of SHM should be consulted for complete and current lists of subdivisions under pattern headings.

Free-Floating Subdivisions Indicated by "Multiples"

Certain subject headings carry "multiple subdivisions," a device naming a few examples as suggestions for analogous subdivisions, for example:

Birth control—Religious aspects—Buddhism, [Christianity, etc.]
Vietnam War, 1961-1975—Foreign public opinion—Austrian, [British, etc.]

In both of these examples, the subdivision and the terms given in square brackets serve as examples of similar subdivisions that may be used without prior authorization, for example:

Vietnam War, 1961-1975—Foreign public opinion—French

Table 11.1 Pattern Headings in LCSH

Subject Field	*Category*	*Pattern Heading(s)*	
RELIGION	Religious and monastic orders	Jesuits	H 1186
	Religions	Buddhism	H 1185
	Christian denominations	Catholic Church	H 1187
	Sacred works (including parts)	Bible	H 1188
HISTORY AND GEOGRAPHY	Colonies of individual countries	Great Britain—Colonies	H 1149.5
	Legislative bodies (including individual chambers)	United States. Congress	H 1155
	Military services (including armies, navies, marines, etc.)	United States—Armed Forces United States. Air Force United States. Army United States. Marine Corps United States. Navy	H 1159
	Wars	World War, 1939–1945 United States—History—Civil War, 1861–1865	H 1200
SOCIAL SCIENCES	Industries	Construction industry retail trade	H 1153
	Types of educational institutions	Universities and colleges	H 1151.5
	Individual educational institutions	Harvard University	H 1151
	Legal topics legislation	Labor laws and	H 1154.5
THE ARTS	Art	Art, Italian Art, Chinese Art, Japanese Art, Korean	H 1148
	Groups of literary authors (including authors, poets, dramatists, etc.)	Authors, English	H 1155.2
	Literary works entered under author	Shakespeare, William, 1564–1616. Hamlet	H 1155.6
	Literary works entered under title	Beowulf	H 1155.8
	Languages and groups of languages	English language French language Romance languages	H 1154
	Literatures (including individual genres)	English literature	H 1156
	Musical compositions	Operas	H 1160
	Musical instruments	Piano Clarinet	H 1161

Table 11.1 Pattern Headings in LCSH *(cont...)*

Subject Field	*Category*	*Pattern Heading(s)*	
SCIENCE AND TECHNOLOGY	Land vehicles	Automobiles	H 1195
	Materials	Concrete Metals	H 1158
	Chemicals	Copper Insulin	H 1149
	Organs and regions of the body	Heart Foot	H 1164
	Diseases	Cancer Tuberculosis	H 1150
	Plants and crops	Corn	H 1180
	Animals	Fishes Cattle	H 1147

Source: Subject Headings Manual, H1146.

Chronological Subdivisions [MARC subfield $y]

Chronological (also called period or time) subdivisions are used with headings for the history of a place or subject. Certain subject areas—such as history, politics and government of individual countries, music, art, and national literatures—lend themselves particularly to historical or chronological treatment. Many chronological subdivisions are listed individually under the appropriate headings in LCSH. Those unique to specific places or topics are generally not free-floating. On the other hand, chronological subdivisions by century, as well as a few specific dates, have been established as free-floating subdivisions under certain categories of main headings, for example:

Under headings for art:

—10th century
—11th century
—12th century
—13th century

etc.

Under topical headings:

—History—To 1500
—History—16th century
—History—17th century
—History—18th century
—History—19th century
—History—20th century
—History—21st century

Under headings for Christian denominations:

> **—History—Modern period, 1500-**
> **—History—1965-**

These subdivisions may be used under individual corporate name headings or topical headings to which the free-floating subdivision**—History** can be assigned appropriately, for example, **Friendship—History—18th century**. However, if the resulting heading conflicts with an enumerated heading containing an established chronological subdivision in LCSH, the latter takes precedence. In other words, the free-floating chronological subdivisions may be used when they do not contradict enumerated headings. Chronological subdivisions in LCSH appear in various forms. Examples are given below.

1. The name of a monarch, a historical period, or an event followed by dates:
   American literature—Revolutionary period, 1775-1783
   France—History—Louis XIV, 1643-1715
   United States—History—Civil War, 1861-1865
2. The preposition "to" followed by a date:
   French literature—To 1500
3. Dates alone:
   China—Civilization—1976-2002
   Greece—History—1453-1821
4. The name of the century:
   Japanese fiction—19th century
   United States—History—20th century
5. An inverted "noun, adjective" heading:
   Architecture, Ancient
   Architecture, Baroque
   Architecture, Medieval
   Architecture, Renaissance
   Architecture, Rococo
   Architecture, Romanesque

The modifiers in these noun/adjective headings in fact denote both period and subject characteristics. They are generally not considered to be true chronological subdivisions, and, therefore, are interfiled alphabetically with other subdivisions that have no period connotation.

Frequently, both broad period subdivisions and period subdivisions covering lesser epochs or specific events falling within the broad periods are listed under the same main heading. However, they are not commonly used together for the same work; the heading closest to the period treated in the work being cataloged is the one chosen.

Great Britain—History—Norman period, 1066-1154
—History—Medieval period, 1066-1485
—History—1066-1687
—History—Angevin period, 1154-1216
—History—Plantagenets, 1154-1399
—History—13th century
—History—14th century
—History—Wars of the Roses, 1455-1485

For example, the heading **Great Britain—History—Norman period, 1066-1154** is assigned to a work such as *The Reign of William Rufus and the Accession of Henry the First*, while the heading **Great Britain—History—1066-1687** is used with a work covering the history of England from 1200 to 1640.

Geographic Subdivisions [MARC subfield $z]

A geographic subdivision[11] indicates the origin or the locality of the main topic, and may be used after subjects that lend themselves to geographical treatment (i.e., that show variations when treated in or with regard to different places). Headings that may be subdivided by place carry the designation (*May Subd Geog*) immediately after their listing in LCSH. This information also appears in the name and subject authority records.

Geographic subdivision is essentially accomplished by inserting the name of a place, for example, a city, a province, a country or other political entity, a region, or a geographic feature, into a subject-heading string; there are, however, established conventions governing form of geographic name and citation order within the string.

A main heading or a main heading—subdivision combination may be subdivided by place either *directly* or *indirectly*, depending on the place in question.

Direct Geographic Subdivision

With *direct* geographic subdivision, the name of the place follows the heading or another subdivision immediately, without the interposition of the name of a larger geographic entity, for example:

Music—Africa
Education—Curricula—Japan

Art—Great Britain
Education, Elementary—United States

Indirect Geographic Subdivision

With *indirect* geographic subdivision, the name of a larger geographic entity, normally the name of a country, is interposed between the main heading and the place in question (e.g., **Music—Austria—Vienna**). Indirect subdivision has the effect of gathering material on a particular subject under the name of the larger geographic entity. With a few exceptions, geographic names are entered indirectly after a heading when the place in question falls wholly within a country, for example:

Charities—Italy—Florence
Cities and towns—France—Brittany
Municipal government—Spain—Castilla y León
Rural development projects—Kenya—Coast Province
Wool industry—Government policy—Italy—Naples (Kingdom)

Exceptions are made when the larger divisions of certain countries are entered directly without the name of the country as an intervening element. These exceptional countries are the following:

Country	**Divisions**
Canada	Provinces
Great Britain	Constituent countries
United States	States

For example:

Agriculture—Florida
Music—British Columbia
Geology—Scotland

In addition, the names of the following cities are assigned directly: Jerusalem, Washington, D.C., and Vatican City (since it is treated as a country). For example,

Rabbis—Jerusalem

When the place in question falls within a division (called a first-order political division) in one of the exceptional countries, the name of the first-order political division, instead of the name of the country, is used as the intervening element in an indirect geographic subdivision, for example:

Music—British Columbia—Vancouver
Geology—Scotland—Highlands
Minorities—Missouri—Saint Louis

No more than two levels of geographic subdivision are used within a given heading, for example:

Horse breeders—Kentucky—Lexington
[*not* Horse breeders—Kentucky—Fayette County—Lexington]

In local subdivision, the latest name of any entity whose name has changed during the course of its existence is always used, regardless of the form of the name appearing in the work cataloged. For example, the heading **Banks and banking—Congo (Democratic Republic)—Kinshasa** is assigned to a work about banks in Leopoldville.

Similarly, local subdivision reflects the present territorial sovereignties of existing nations, regardless of whatever past territorial division is described in the work being cataloged. For a region or jurisdiction that existed in the past under various sovereignties, it is the name of the country currently in possession (as long as the region or jurisdiction is located wholly within that country) that is used. For instance, the heading **Education—France—Alsace** is assigned to a work about the status of education in Alsace in 1910, when it belonged to Germany.

When subdividing indirectly, if the geographic qualifier of the subordinate entity is identical to the name of the country or the name of the first-order political subdivision of an exceptional country, the geographical qualifier is omitted to avoid redundancy, for example:

Yangtze River (*China*) [as a main heading]
[*but*] **Stream measurements—China—Yangtze River**

Guadalajara (*Spain: Province*) [as a main heading]
[*but*] **Transportation—Spain—Guadalajara** (*Province*)

When the qualifier and the country subdivision are not identical, the qualifier is retained, for example:

Great Lake (*Tas.*) [as a main heading]
Boats and boating—Australia—Great Lake (*Tas.*)

In summary, the following places are entered *directly*:

1. Countries or larger geographic entities;
2. The first-order political divisions of Canada, Great Britain, and the United States;
3. Any jurisdiction or region that does not lie wholly within a single existing country or within a first-order political subdivision of Canada, Great Britain, and the United States, including: (a) historic kingdoms, empires, etc., for example, **Diplomatics—Holy Roman Empire**; and (b) geographic features and regions, such as continents and other major regions, bodies of water, mountain ranges, and so on, for instance, **Europe**; **Sahara**; **Great Lakes**; **Mexico, Gulf of**; **Rocky Mountains**; and **Nile River Valley**;
4. Islands or groups of islands situated some distance from land masses, even if they do not represent autonomous political rules, for instance, **Geology—Falkland Islands**;
5. The cities of Jerusalem and Washington, D.C., for example, **Museums—Washington (D.C.)**;
6. Vatican City.

The following places are entered *indirectly*:

1. Places below the level of the first-order political divisions of Canada, Great Britain, and the United States;
2. Places of the following types when they fall wholly within one of the other countries:
   - subordinate political jurisdictions, such as provinces, districts, counties, cities, and so on, with the exceptions noted above;
   - historic kingdoms, principalities, etc., for example, **Jesuits—Italy—Naples (Kingdom)**;
   - geographic features and regions, such as mountain ranges, bodies of water, lake regions, watersheds, metropolitan areas, and so on;
   - islands situated within the territorial limits of the country in question.

Order of Subdivisions

The citation order (i.e., the order in which elements are strung together in a heading) normally follows the patterns below:

1. When the string begins with a geographic heading, the elements are generally arranged in the following citation order:

[Place]—[Topic]—[Time]—[Form]

For example:

England—Civilization—17th century—Sources
Great Britain—Court and courtiers—History—16th century—Sources
United States—History—Civil War, 1861-1865—Sources—Juvenile literature

2. When the string begins with a topical heading, one of the following citation orders is used:

a. **[Topic]—[Place]—[Topic]—[Time]—[Form]**
[When (*May Subd Geog*) follows the main heading but not the topical, period, or form subdivision]

For example:

Farm buildings—Kentucky—Fayette County—Heating and ventilation
Nobility—Great Britain—History—16th century—Sources

b. **[Topic]—[Topic]—[Place]—[Time]—[Form]**
[When (*May Subd Geog*) follows the topical, period, or form subdivision]

For example:

Farm buildings—Specifications—Kentucky—Fayette County
Art—Collectors and collecting—United States—History—20th century—Exhibitions

CROSS-REFERENCES

Cross-references are provided in the catalog for two purposes: (1) to guide the users from their search terms to valid headings, and (2) to link related headings. In LCSH, the main types of relationships among subject headings expressed by cross-references are equivalence, hierarchy, and association.

Equivalence Relationships [MARC authority field 45X]

USE references direct searchers from the unauthorized or nonpreferred terms they may have chosen to the authorized or valid headings for the subject in question. *USE* terms include synonyms, alternative spellings (including singular and plural forms), alternative endings, changed or cancelled headings, abbreviations and acronyms, phrases in different word orders, and, occasionally, opposite terms that are often treated together in works. Examples of *USE* references are shown below.

Archeology
  USE **Archaeology**
Electronic calculating-machines
  USE **Computers**
German hymns
  USE **Hymns, German**
Hothouses
  USE **Greenhouses**
Illiteracy
  USE **Literacy**
Nonlinear logic
  USE **Fuzzy logic**
UFOs
  USE **Unidentified flying objects**

In LCSH, reciprocal entries appear under the valid headings with the symbol "UF" (used for) preceding the nonpreferred terms, for example:

Archaeology
  UF Archeology
Computers
  UF Electronic calculating-machines
  [former heading]
Fuzzy logic
  UF Nonlinear logic
Greenhouses
  UF Hothouses
Hymns, German
  UF German hymns
Literacy
  UF Illiteracy
Unidentified flying objects
  UF UFOs

Hierarchical Relationships [MARC authority field 55X]

Hierarchical references indicate topics that are either broader or narrower in scope than the one in question. Two symbols are used for these purposes: BT and NT, for example:

Poetry

BT Literature
NT Children's poetry
Lyric poetry
Odes

Lyric poetry

BT Poetry
NT Ballads
Dithyramb
Odes
Sonnets

Odes

BT Lyric poetry
Poetry

Sonnets

BT Lyric poetry

Headings connected by the BT or NT references are all valid headings. Each heading is connected to the heading or headings on the level immediately above or below it in the appropriate hierarchy or hierarchies. Therefore, there is no direct link between the heading **Poetry** and the heading **Sonnets** or **Dithyramb**. However, this policy may be relaxed where the hierarchies are not well or clearly defined. For instance, the heading **Odes** is linked to both **Poetry** and **Lyric poetry**. In MARC authority records, the broader topics are traced in field 55X in the record for the narrower topic.

Associative Relationships [MARC authority field 55X]

The symbol RT (related topic) is used to link headings that are related in concept, but not in a hierarchical sense. Such references are usually made for the following types of relationships: headings with meanings that overlap to some extent, headings representing a discipline and an object studied, and headings representing persons and their fields of endeavor. Examples are shown below.

Aliens

RT Immigrants

Entomology

RT Insects

Law
RT Jurisprudence
Legislation

Physicians
RT Medicine

In LCSH, as well as in MARC authority records, instructions for RT references are provided under both terms involved, for example:

Aliens
RT Immigrants

Immigrants
RT Aliens

Medicine
RT Physicians

Physicians
RT Medicine.

General References

In addition to the references discussed above, there is a type of general or blanket reference, represented by the symbol SA (see also), which refers from one heading to a group of headings or to subdivisions used under other headings, for example:

Courts of last resort
SA names of individual supreme courts

Cranberries—Diseases and pests
SA names of pests, for example, **Cranberry root-worm**

Atlases
SA subdivision **Maps** under names of countries, cities, etc., and under topics

The following entry, taken from LCSH, illustrates the different types of cross-references associated with the heading **Library education**.

Library education
UF Librarians—Education
Library science—Study and teaching
BT Professional education

RT Library schools
SA subdivision **Study and teaching** under special subjects, for example, **Book selection—Study and teaching**
NT Interns (Library science)
Library education (Continuing education)
Library institutes and workshops

In explanation, the cross-references mean that: (1) "Librarians—Education" and "Library science—Study and teaching" are synonymous terms not used as valid headings for the concept represented by the subject heading **Library education**; (2) **Professional education**—a valid heading—represents a broader concept; (3) **Library schools** represents a concept related to the heading **Library education**, but not in a hierarchical sense; (4) as a subdivision, **—Study and teaching** is used under specific subjects relating to library education; and, (5) **Interns (Library science)**, **Library education (Continuing education)**, and **Library institutes and workshops** represent narrower topics. The example below shows the MARC authority record for the heading **Computers**.

MARC Authority Record for the Heading Computers
000 01239cz a2200361n 450
001 4681824
005 20120323071051.0
008 860211il anannbabn lb ana
010 $a sh 85029552
035 $a (DLC)sh 85029552
035 $a (DLC)28509
040 $a DLC $c DLC $d DLC
053 0 $a QA75.5 $b QA76.95 $c Mathematics
053 0 $a TK7885 $b TK7895 $c Electrical engineering
150 $a Computers
360 $i headings beginning with the word $a Computer
450 $a Automatic computers
450 $a Automatic data processors
450 $a Computer hardware
450 $a Computing machines (Computers)
450 $a Electronic brains
450 $w nne $a Electronic calculating-machines
450 $a Electronic computers
450 $a Hardware, Computer
550 $w g $a Computer systems
550 $w g $a Cybernetics
550 $w g $a Machine theory

550 $a Calculators
550 $a Cyberspace
680 $i Here are entered works on modern electronic computers first developed after 1945. Works on present-day calculators, as well as on calculators and mechanical computers of pre-1945 vintage, are entered under $a Calculators.
681 $i Note under $a Calculators

ASSIGNING LCSH: PRECOORDINATION VERSUS POSTCOORDINATION

When a precoordinate heading that would suit a particular work is not enumerated in LCSH, a heading may be constructed by combining elements according to appropriate procedures. Especially since the mid-1970s, the LC has relied more on synthesis than enumeration for precoordinate complex headings. This development is consistent with the progress taking place in the field of indexing. As Svenonius states, "Probably the most significant development in index language construction in the twentieth century is the move from largely enumerative index languages to largely synthetic ones."[12]

Synthesis, or constructing subject-heading strings, is achieved in LCSH mainly through the use of free-floating subdivisions, a device that allows the combination of a main term with terms representing common aspects of subjects, without requiring that each combination be authorized. Typically, such synthesized headings do not appear in the list. Thus, many highly complex headings appear in bibliographic records, but not in LCSH, for example:

France—History—Revolution, 1789-1799—Literature and the revolution
Lawyers—United States—Discipline—Cases
Social sciences—Study and teaching (Graduate)—United States
Teenagers—Books and reading—United States

Synthesis renders a precoordinate subject indexing system much more flexible because it allows many more possible combinations than an enumerative system can accommodate.

When cataloging a work on a complex subject for which there is no coextensive heading and for which one cannot be synthesized, subject catalogers at the LC and those at cooperating libraries have two options. They may either propose a new heading as required for the work being cataloged (a procedure currently preferred) or choose to use several existing headings (i.e., take the postcoordinate approach) if the topic in question appears to be new, but is judged to be not yet discrete and identifiable.

ASSIGNING LCSH: SPECIAL MATERIALS

General guidelines for assigning subject headings are discussed in chapter 10. The LC has also established policies regarding subject-heading assignment for specific types of works. Some of the most common types are discussed below. The examples shown follow the format of the print version of LCSH, where the subdivisions are preceded by the symbol dash (—) rather than by the MARC codes.

Electronic Resources

There are no specific overall guidelines or policies regarding subject headings assigned to electronic resources. There are, however, subdivisions used specifically with electronic resources of various types. A number of subdivisions are used to indicate the electronic form, for example:

—Computer games
—Databases
—Juvenile software
—Software

Examples of subject headings containing these subdivisions are shown below.

Nickel takes on teasing: a clickable social skill story
1. **Social skills—Study and teaching (Elementary)—Juvenile software.**
2. **Teasing—Prevention—Juvenile software.**

FreeBooks4Doctors: promoting free access to medical books
1. **Medical literature—Databases.**
2. **Medicine—Databases.**

Stanley. Wild for sharks!
1. **Sharks—Juvenile software.**
2. **Computer games—Juvenile software.**
3. **Sharks—Interactive multimedia.**

The following subdivisions, on the other hand, are used for works *about* specific types of electronic resources; in other words, they are topical subdivisions, not form subdivisions:

—Computer network resources
—Computer programs
—Computer simulation

For example:

> *European history highway: a guide to Internet resources* / Dennis A. Trinkle and Scott A. Merriman, editors
> 1. **Europe—History—Research.**
> 2. **History—Computer network resources.**
> 3. **Internet.**

There are no special subdivisions designating Internet resources or Web resources. The subdivision—**Databases** is not used under subjects for electronic resources that are essentially textual in nature and that do not fit the definition of a database (i.e., a collection of logically interrelated data stored together in one or more computerized files, usually created and managed by a database management system[13]). Such materials include articles, conference proceedings, literary works, reference-type works, and so on. Many Web resources are of such nature and, as a result, are assigned subject headings similar to those assigned to print materials. Examples of subject headings assigned to Internet and Web resources are shown below:

> *Reclaiming the Everglades: South Florida's natural history, 1884–1934* / University of Miami Library, Florida International University Libraries, and Historical Museum of Southern Florida
> 1. **Nature conservation—Florida—Everglades.**
> 2. **Everglades (Fla.)—History.**
>
> *The Angry Kid series*
> 1. **Animated films—Catalogs.**

Examples of subject headings assigned to works *about* electronic resources are shown below:

> *Database and data communication network systems: techniques and applications* / edited by Cornelius T. Leondes
> 1. **Distributed databases.**
> 2. **Computer networks.**
>
> *Microsoft Office XP step by step courseware* / Microsoft Corporation
> 1. **Business—Computer programs.**
>
> *Online ecological and environmental data* / Virginia Baldwin, editor
> 1. **Environmental sciences—Computer network resources.**

2. **Environmental sciences—Databases.**

Rules of play: game design fundamentals / Katie Salen and Eric Zimmerman
1. **Computer games—Design.**
2. **Computer games—Programming.**

Literature

There are two main types of works in the field of literature[14]: (1) literary works and (2) works *about* literature. A literary work may consist of a collection of works by two or more authors, or an individual work or a collection of works by one author. A work about literature may focus on literature in general, in a particular language or from a particular nationality, on a particular period and/or genre of literature, on a particular author, or on a particular work. Subject headings are assigned to bring out various aspects of a work, including language, nationality, genre or form, theme, character, authorship, and so on.

Anthologies and Collections of Literary Works by Two or More Authors

For an anthology or collection of works by two or more authors, one or more literary form headings with appropriate subdivisions are assigned:

Literature—Collections
[for an anthology of world literature not limited to any language or genre]

Drama, Medieval
[for an anthology or collection of Medieval drama not limited to a particular language or nationality; note that the subdivision—**Collections,** is not used]

American drama—20th century
[for a collection of twentieth-century American plays]

In each of these cases, the literature heading represents the form or genre rather than the subject content of the work. The subdivision—**Collections** is not free-floating, and may be used with a given heading only when so listed in LCSH. The distinction between a collection of and a discussion of literature is indicated by adding to the latter the subdivision—**History and criticism**, for example, **French literature—20th century—History and criticism.**

If a collection is organized around a particular theme, additional topical headings with appropriate literary form subdivisions are also assigned. The following are examples of literary anthologies and collections:

The Norton anthology of modern and contemporary poetry / edited by Jahan Ramazani, Richard Ellmann, Robert O'Clair
1. **American poetry—20th century.**
2. **English poetry—20th century.**
3. **American poetry—19th century.**
4. **English poetry—19th century.**

Anthology of African American literature / Keith Gilyard, Anissa Wardi
1. **American literature—African American authors.**
2. **African Americans—Literary collections.**

Works Written by Individual Authors

Headings representing major literary genres, for example, **American drama** or **German fiction**, are *not* assigned to individual literary works, except in the case of literary works for children, which do receive form headings. In other words, the heading **American fiction—19th century** is not assigned to Mark Twain's *The adventures of Tom Sawyer*, nor is the heading **English poetry—19th century** assigned to Tennyson's *In memoriam*. In the case of collected works by one author, a literary form heading is assigned only when the form is highly specific, for example, **Allegories**, **Fables**, **Fairy tales**, **Radio stories**, **Amateur theater**, **Carnival plays**, **Children's plays**, **College and school drama**, **Didactic drama**, **Radio plays, Concrete poetry,** and **Sonnets, American**. The literary form heading is also assigned when it combines a theme with the literary form (e.g., **War poetry**) or when it combines in one heading a nationality or language and a highly specific genre, for example, **Sonnets, American**; **Love stories, French**.

For a drama or poem featuring a specific theme or based on the life of a real person, a topical heading in the form of the topic or the personal name with the subdivision—**Drama** or—**Poetry** is used.

If a collection of works in various forms by an individual author centers around a particular theme, a topical heading with the subdivision—**Literary collections** is used, for example:

In a house by the sea / Sandy Gingras
1. **Seaside resorts—Literary collections.**
2. **Vacation homes—Literary collections.**
3. **Beaches—Literary collections**.

For a collection of novels or stories by an individual author, the form subdivision—**Fiction** is assigned only under an identifiable topic, for example:

Automobile racing—Fiction.

For an individual novel or story, one or more topical headings with the subdivision—**Fiction** may be assigned. In addition, many libraries, including the LC, assign genre/form headings to selected works. These headings come from a separate controlled vocabulary entitled *Guidelines on Subject Access to Individual Works of Fiction, Drama, Etc.*,[15] for example:

The virtues of war : A novel of Alexander the Great / Steven Pressfield
1. **Alexander, the Great, 356-323 B.C.—Fiction.**
2. **Greece—History—Macedonian Expansion, 359-323 B.C.—Fiction.**

[Genre/form heading:
Biographical fiction.
War stories.]

Henry V / edited by John Crowther
1. **Henry V, King of England, 1387-1422—Drama.**
2. **Great Britain—History—Henry V, 1413-1422—Drama.**

[Genre/form heading:
Historical drama.]

Sequoyah / Robert J. Conley
1. **Sequoyah, 1770?-1843—Fiction.**
2. **Cherokee Indians—Fiction.**
3. **Kings and rulers—Fiction.**

[Genre/form heading:
Biographical fiction.]

Works about Literature in General

Works about literature in general are assigned appropriate headings regarding the approach, type, or form of literature treated in the work, for example:

Literature—History and criticism
[for histories of literature in general and works evaluating the character and qualities of works of literature]

Criticism
[for works on the principles of literary criticism, not used with a work of criticism]

Poetics
American fiction—20th century—History and criticism
Drama—20th century—Congresses
Poetry, Modern—19th century—Bibliography

Works discussing the relationship between literature and other subjects are given headings such as **Literature and technology**, **Literature and science**, **Music and literature**, and **Religion and literature**.

Discussions about particular themes in literature are assigned **[Subject** or **theme] in literature** in addition to other appropriate literature headings, for instance:

> **Politics in literature**
> [for a study of political themes in twentieth-century American fiction, assign this heading in addition to
> **American fiction—20th century—History and criticism**]
> **Soldiers in literature**
> **War in literature**

A discussion about a particular place or person as a theme or character in literature, fiction, drama, poetry, etc., is given the heading **[name of person** or **place** in RDA form**]—In literature** (a free-floating subdivision), for instance:

> **Shakespeare, William, 1564-1616—In literature**
> **New York (N.Y.)—In literature**

It is easy to confuse the situations in which the heading **[Name of person or place]—Drama** or **[Name of person or place]—Poetry** is used with those in which the heading **[Name of person or place]—In literature** is appropriate. The former is used for a drama or poem featuring the person or place named as a character, while the latter is used for a discussion of (i.e., a work *about*) the person as a character or the place as a subject in literature. Following are examples of works about literature:

> *Humanism and machinery in Renaissance literature* / Jessica Wolfe
> 1. **English literature—Early modern, 1500-1700—History and criticism.**
> 2. **Humanism in literature.**
> 3. **Machinery in literature.**
> 4. **Mechanics in literature.**
> 5. **Renaissance—England.**
> 6. **Humanists—England.**

> *Nation & novel: The English novel from its origins to the present day* / Patrick Parrinder
> 1. **English fiction—History and criticism.**
> 2. **National characteristics, English, in literature.**

3. **Nationalism and literature—Great Britain.**
4. **Nationalism in literature**.

Plotting early modern London: new essays on Jacobean City comedy / edited by Dieter Mehl, Angela Stock, Anne-Julia Zwierlein
1. **English drama—17th century—History and criticism.**
2. **English drama (Comedy)—History and criticism.**
3. **City and town life in literature.**
4. **London (England)—In literature.**

Works about Individual Authors: Biography and Criticism

A work about an individual author is assigned a personal name heading in RDA form, with or without a subdivision. For subdivisions, consult the list for free-floating subdivisions under names of persons.

Kafka, Franz, 1883-1924
Thoreau, Henry David, 1817-1862—Political and social views
Goethe, Johann Wolfgang von, 1749-1832—Dramatic works

[Note that this heading, assigned to works *about* Goethe's plays, is different from the heading **Goethe, Johann Wolfgang von, 1749-1832—Drama**, which is assigned to plays featuring Goethe as a character.]

The subdivision—**Biography** is not used under the name of a person, including literary authors. However, a subdivision denoting a biographical approach such as—**Correspondence** or—**Interviews** may be assigned. In addition, a second heading representing the class of persons to which the author belongs is also assigned, for example:

Edgar Allan Poe / by Aaron Frisch
1. **Poe, Edgar Allan, 1809-1849—Juvenile literature.**
2. **Authors, American—19th century—Biography—Juvenile literature.**

Conversations with Jack Kerouac / edited by Kevin J. Hayes
1. **Kerouac, Jack, 1922-1969—Interviews.**
2. **Authors, American—20th century—Interviews**.
3. **Beat generation—Interviews.**

Critical works without biographical information are assigned the personal name heading with the subdivision—**Criticism and interpretation** and/or another more specific subdivision designating criticism, for example:

Shakespeare / by Mark Van Doren ; introduction by David Lehman
1. **Shakespeare, William, 1564-1616 —Criticism and interpretation.**

Mark Twain: the fate of humor / James M. Cox
1. **Twain, Mark, 1835-1910—Criticism and interpretation.**
2. **Twain, Mark, 1835-1910—Humor.**
3. **Humorous stories, American—History and criticism.**

Works about Individual Works

For a work that contains criticisms or commentaries on another work, including literary works, the preferred title of the work commented on is assigned, in addition to other appropriate headings. If the work commented on is of known authorship, a [**Name. Title**] subject heading is used:

Temporal circumstances: form and history in the Canterbury tales / Lee Patterson
1. **Chaucer, Geoffrey, d. 1400—Criticism and interpretation—History.**
2. **Chaucer, Geoffrey, d. 1400. Canterbury tales.**
3. **Tales, Medieval—History and criticism.**
4. **Christian pilgrims and pilgrimages in literature.**

Charlotte Brontë's Jane Eyre / Harold Bloom, editor
1. **Brontë , Charlotte, 1816-1855. Jane Eyre.**
2. **Governesses in literature.**

For a work about a foreign title, the preferred title consists of the author's name and the title in the original language, regardless of the language in which the criticism is written, for example:

Thomas Mann's death in Venice: a reference guide / Ellis Shookman
1. **Mann, Thomas, 1875-1955. Tod in Venedig.**
2. **Mann, Thomas, 1875-1955—Criticism and interpretation.**

For a work about another work of unknown authorship, the subject heading consists of the title alone, for example:

Atlantic monthly

For a work about an anonymous classic or a sacred work, the subject heading is in the RDA form of the preferred title, for example:

Arabian nights
Beowulf
Chanson de Roland
Nibelungenlied
Pearl (Middle English poem)

Biography

Collective Biography

When a work consists of four or more life histories, it is generally considered a collective biography.[16] The heading **Biography** is assigned to a collective biography not limited to a place or a specific class of persons. When the persons treated in a collective biography belong to a specific period, a period subdivision is added, for example, **Biography—20th century**. When the persons are from a particular place, the subject heading consists of the name of the place with the subdivision **—Biography**, for example, **Illinois—Biography**. In addition, topical headings are assigned as appropriate. Examples of general collective biography are shown below.

> *Oxford dictionary of national biography: in association with the British Academy: from the earliest times to the year 2000* / edited by H.C.G. Matthew and Brian Harrison
> 1. **Great Britain—Biography—Dictionaries.**

> *The presidents, first ladies, and vice presidents: White House biographies, 1789–2005* / Daniel C. Diller and Stephen L. Robertson
> 1. **White House (Washington, D.C.)—History.**
> 2. **Presidents—United States—Biography.**
> 3. **Presidents' spouses—United States—Biography.**
> 4. **Vice-Presidents—United States—Biography.**

When the persons belong to a particular ethnic group or a particular profession or subject field, the appropriate term for the members of that group with the subdivision**—Biography** is used as the subject heading, for example:

Arabs—Biography
Chinese Americans—Biography
Artists—Biography
Authors, English—19th century—Biography
Dentists—Biography
Physicists—Biography

The subdivision **—Biography** is also used under names of corporate bodies and historical events, periods, etc., for example:

> **United States. Army—Biography**
> **United States—History—Revolution, 1775-1783—Biography**

When the required term referring to a special class of persons is not available in LCSH, an established subject heading consisting of the name of the relevant subject or discipline with the subdivision **—Biography** (not free-floating in this case), as listed in LCSH, is used, for example:

> **Art—Biography**
> [for all kinds of people associated with art, including artists, dealers, collectors, museum personnel, etc.]

If the work contains lists of works of authors active in particular fields as well as biographical information about those authors, the subdivision **—Bio-bibliography** is used under names of countries, cities, etc., and under subjects, for example:

> **California—Bio-bibliography**
> **English literature—Early modern, 1500-1700—Bio-bibliography**
> **American literature—Asian American authors—Bio-bibliography—Dictionaries**

This subdivision is not used with names of individual persons.

Individual Biography

For the biography (including autobiographical writings such as diaries and correspondence) of an individual, three types of headings may be assigned: (1) the name of the biographee, (2) a class-of-persons heading, and (3) other appropriate headings.

1. The name of the biographee in RDA form is assigned. If the biography focuses on a specific aspect of the person's life, an appropriate subdivision taken from the list "Free-Floating Subdivisions Used under Names of Persons"[17] is added. Note that the subdivision**—Biography** is not used under names of individual persons.

> **Freud, Sigmund, 1856-1939—Correspondence**
> **Gandhi, Mahatma, 1869-1948—Political and social views**
> **Twain, Mark, 1835-1910**

2. In addition to the personal name heading, a *class-of-persons* heading in the form of **[Class of persons]—[Place]—[Subdivision indicating type of biographical work]** is assigned. This practice in effect violates the general principle of *not* assigning a general heading and a specific heading encompassed in the general heading to the same work. The doubling (i.e., assigning both a specific heading and a general heading to the same work) is done for the purpose of collocating biographies of persons in the same field or with similar characteristics. For example, a biography of the basketball player Michael Jordan is assigned the following headings:

> *Michael Jordan: basketball player* / Mike McGovern
> 1. **Jordan, Michael, 1963-**
> 2. **Basketball players—United States—Biography.**

A biography of Barbara Bush is assigned the following headings:

> *Reflections: life after the White House* / Barbara Bush
> 1. **Bush, Barbara, 1925-**
> 2. **Bush, George, 1924-**
> 3. **Presidents' spouses—United States—Biography.**

3. For a partial biography or a biography that includes material about the field in which the biographee was involved, an additional topical heading or headings may be assigned to bring out the subject, for example:

> *Tony Blair: the making of a world leader* / Philip Stephens
> 1. **Blair, Tony, 1953-**
> 2. **Labour Party (Great Britain)—Biography.**
> 3. **Prime ministers—Great Britain—Biography.**
> 4. **Great Britain—Politics and government—1997-2007.**

For a work about a statesman, ruler, or head of state that contains information about his or her personal life, three types of headings are assigned: (1) the personal name heading with applicable subdivision(s), (2) the class-of-persons heading with appropriate subdivision(s), and (3) a heading for the event or period of the country's history in which the person was involved, for example:

> *Elizabeth I: always her own free woman* / edited by Carole Levin, Jo Eldridge Carney, and Debra Barrett-Graves
> 1. **Elizabeth I, Queen of England, 1533-1603.**
> 2. **Queens—Great Britain—Biography.**
> 3. **Great Britain—History—Elizabeth, 1558-1603.**

If the work contains mainly biographical material, the first two types of headings are assigned:

> *True myths: the life and times of Arnold Schwarzenegger: from pumping iron to governor of California* / Nigel Andrews
> 1. **Schwarzenegger, Arnold.**
> 2. **Motion picture actors and actresses—United States—Biography.**
> 3. **Governors—California—Biography.**

If the work presents the history of the jurisdiction for the period or events in which a statesman or ruler participated, but contains less than 20 percent biographical material, the class-of-persons heading is omitted, for example:

> *Blair's wars* / John Kampfner
> 1. **Blair, Tony, 1953- —Influence.**
> 2. **Great Britain—Foreign relations—1997-**
> 3. **Great Britain—Military policy.**
> 4. **Great Britain—Foreign relations—United States.**
> 5. **United States—Foreign relations—Great Britain.**

Corporate headings, such as **Great Britain. Sovereign (1660-1685: Charles II)**, which are used in descriptive cataloging as access points, are not used as subject entries. Instead, the personal name heading and the appropriate heading for the history of the period are used.

Subject Headings for Children's Literature

LC List of Juvenile Headings

The LC also developed a special list of subject headings for children's literature. In 1965, the library initiated the Annotated Card (AC) Program for children's materials, with the purpose of providing more appropriate and extensive subject cataloging for juvenile titles through more liberal application of subject headings and through the use of headings more appropriate to juvenile users. In some cases, existing LC subject headings were reinterpreted or modified in order to achieve these purposes; in other cases, new headings were created. The result was a separate list of subject headings that represented exceptions to the master list of LC headings. It was first published in 1969 as *Subject Headings for Children's Literature*. Beginning with the eighth edition of LCSH, the list, entitled *AC Subject Headings*, was included in the print version of LCSH, where it preceded the master list. The *Children's Subject Headings* is now available as part of the subscription-based ClassificationWeb tool (classificationweb.net). Subject authority records for children's headings are included in the authority file, and may be searched and viewed in LC's Web Authorities service (authorities.loc.gov). In application, this list must be used in conjunction with the master list.

Subject Cataloging of Children's Materials

In LC cataloging records for materials intended for children up through age fifteen (or the ninth grade), two sets of subject headings are assigned: (1) regular headings implying juvenile nature or with juvenile subdivisions, and (2) alternative headings (children's subject headings) for children's materials. These are discussed below:

Regular Headings Implying Juvenile Nature or with Juvenile Subdivisions

Topical or nonfictional juvenile materials are assigned appropriate topical headings with juvenile subdivisions such as **—Dictionaries, Juvenile**; **—Juvenile films**; **—Juvenile humor**; **—Juvenile literature** (used only for nonliterary works); **—Juvenile sound recordings** (not used with musical sound recordings); and **—Juvenile software**.

Juvenile belles lettres are assigned juvenile literary form headings such as **Children's plays** and **Children's poetry**. In addition, topical headings with juvenile literary form subdivisions (**—Juvenile drama, —Juvenile fiction, —Juvenile poetry**) are assigned to bring out themes, places, etc. This method is commonly used when children's materials are integrated into the general collection of the library.

Children's and Young Adults' Cataloging Program (CYAC)

For libraries that maintain separate collections and/or catalogs for children, alternative headings consisting of regular LCSH without juvenile subdivisions are provided in LC cataloging records. These headings are supplemented by headings from the *Children's Subject Headings*, which contain additional headings designed for use with children's materials, and which are not in LCSH or are different in form from those found in LCSH.

For juvenile belles lettres, topical headings with literary form subdivisions are assigned more liberally than in the case of adult materials, in order to provide topical access to such materials. Many topical headings, which are not generally used with adult literature, are assigned to juvenile fiction and drama.

In CIP, information prepared by the LC and found on the verso of the title page in most trade books, including children's materials, children's subject headings are enclosed in brackets; these headings may or may not differ from the regular headings. In MARC records, children's headings are identified by the second indicator 1 in 6XX fields.

Examples of subject headings assigned to children's materials are shown below. Children's subject headings are enclosed in brackets.

A season of hope / by Lauren Brooke
1. **Horses—Juvenile fiction.**
2. **Fathers and daughters—Juvenile fiction.**
3. **Heartland (Imaginary place)—Juvenile fiction.**
[Horses—Fiction.
Fathers and daughters—Fiction.
Heartland (Imaginary place)—Fiction.]

A apple pie / Gennady Spirin
1. **Nursery rhymes.**
2. **Alphabet rhymes.**
3. **Children's poetry.**
[Nursery rhymes.
Alphabet.]

Horsing around: jokes to make ewe smile / by Diane L. Burns . . . [et al.]; pictures by Brian Gable
1. **Animals—Juvenile humor.**
2. **Wit and humor, Juvenile.**
[Animals—Humor.
Jokes.
Riddles.]

The American heritage children's science dictionary
1. **Science—Dictionaries, Juvenile**.
[Science—Dictionaries.]

Bunny day / photographs by Michael Scott
1. **Easter—Juvenile fiction.**
2. **Infants—Juvenile fiction.**
[Easter—Fiction.
Babies—Fiction.]

1001 facts about insects / written by Laurence Mound . . . [et al.]
1. **Insects—Miscellanea—Juvenile literature.**
[Insects—Miscellanea.]

NOTES

1. Library of Congress, Catalog Division. (1910–1914). *Subject Headings used in the Dictionary Catalogues of the Library of Congress.* Washington, DC: Government Printing Office, Library Branch.

2. Library of Congress, Subject Cataloging Division. (1984). *Subject Cataloging Manual: Subject Headings* (prelim. ed.). Washington, DC: Library of Congress.

3. Chan, L. M. (1990). *Library of Congress Subject Headings: Principles of Structure and Policies for Supplication.* Washington, DC: Library of Congress.

4. *Subject Headings Manual*, H690.

5. *Subject Headings Manual*, H690.

6. Chan, 1990, p. 17.

7. Chan, 1990, p. 27.

8. Library of Congress, Cataloging Policy and Support Office. (1989–). *Free-floating Subdivisions: An Alphabetical Index.* Washington, DC: Library of Congress, Cataloging Distribution Service.

9. *Subject Headings Manual*, H1095.

10. *Subject Headings Manual*, H1100, H1103, H1105, H1110, H1140, H1145.5.

11. *Subject Headings Manual*, H830.

12. Svenonius, E. (1990). Design of controlled vocabularies. In A. Kent (Ed.), *Encyclopedia of Library and Information Science* (Vol. 45, Supp. 10). New York, NY: Marcel Dekker (p. 88).

13. *Subject Headings Manual*, H1520.

14. *Subject Headings Manual*, H1155.2, H1155.4, H1155.6, H1155.8.

15. Association for Library Collections & Technical Services, Cataloging and Classification Section, Subject Analysis Committee, Subcommittee on the Revision of the Guidelines on Subject Access to Individual Works of Fiction. (2000). *Guidelines on Subject Access to Individual Works of Fiction, Drama, etc.* (2nd ed.). Chicago, IL: American Library Association.

16. *Subject Headings Manual*, H1330.

17. *Subject Headings Manual*, H1110.

Chapter 12

FAST (Faceted Application of Subject Terminology)

INTRODUCTION

The phenomenal growth of digital resources and the emergence of numerous metadata schemes for their description have spurred a reexamination of the ways in which subject data might be efficiently and effectively provided for these resources. There is a need, particularly, for subject access methods that can handle large volumes of materials without requiring as much effort and cost as is needed for providing access to traditional library materials.

In 1998, OCLC began exploring a new approach to subject vocabulary while in the process of searching for a subject access system that would optimize the use of technology for DC metadata records. In keeping with the premises of the DC, it was determined that a subject vocabulary suitable for the Web environment should have the following functional requirements:[1]

- It should be simple in structure (i.e., easy to assign and use) and easy to maintain;
- It should provide optimal access points; and,
- It should be flexible and interoperable across disciplines and in various knowledge discovery and access environments, not the least among which is the OPAC.

In creating a new subject schema, two key decisions were required: (1) defining the semantics (the choice of vocabulary); and, (2) formulating the syntax (precoordination vs. postcoordination). Regarding the semantics, OCLC decided to retain the vocabulary of LCSH. By adapting its vocabulary, compatibility with LCSH is ensured. As a subject vocabulary, LCSH offers several advantages:[2]

- It is a rich vocabulary covering all subject areas, easily the largest general indexing vocabulary in the English language;
- It provides synonym and homograph control;
- It contains rich links (cross references) among terms;
- It is a de facto universal controlled vocabulary, and has been translated or adapted as a model for developing subject heading systems by many countries around the world;
- It is compatible with subject data in MARC records;
- With a common vocabulary, automated conversion of LCSH to the new schema is possible; and,
- The cost of maintaining the new schema is minimized since many of the changes to LCSH can be incorporated into the new schema.

While the rich vocabulary and semantic relationships in LCSH provide subject access beyond the capabilities of keywords, its complex syntax has often proven a stumbling block to wider use. Such complexity also runs counter to the basic premises of simplicity and semantic operability of the DC. For these reasons, OCLC decided to devise a simplified syntax using the LCSH vocabulary. The resulting scheme would be a controlled vocabulary built on the terminology and relationships already established in LCSH. In application, syntax would be separated from semantics, with the result that the application process would be simplified, but the richness of vocabulary in LCSH would be retained. The resulting schema would be much easier to use and maintain. Furthermore, with the change, computer technology could be used to greater advantage in both the assignment and the maintenance of subject data, as well as in subject authority control.

DEVELOPMENT

This new method, called Faceted Application of Subject Terminology or FAST,[3] is based on the existing LCSH vocabulary, but applied with a simpler syntax than that currently used by libraries following LC application policies. The development of FAST is a collaborative effort between OCLC and the LC.

FAST was developed as a response to the needs to be (1) simple to learn and use; (2) friendly for faceted navigation; and (3) designed for modern needs.

While an LC subject heading may contain elements representing different facets (i.e., topical, geographic, chronological, form, and name), or aspects of the main heading, in FAST, for the sake of simplicity and semantic interoperability, headings belonging to different facets are assigned as separate headings. In this sense, FAST is a postcoordinate scheme based on distinctive facets. By separating the facets, FAST is more in line with the basic premises and characteristics of the DC.

Since many FAST users are not expected to be trained subject catalogers, automated authority control must play a significant role in ensuring the quality of the subjects assigned. The application rules could be greatly simplified by fully establishing all headings in the new schema, thus eliminating most of the rules for heading construction and greatly simplifying authority control. In summary, the FAST schema is

- based on the LCSH vocabulary;
- designed for the Web environment;
- a postcoordinated faceted vocabulary;
- usable by people with minimal training and experience; and,
- amenable to automated authority control.

FACETING OF SUBJECT-RELATED ELEMENTS

FAST consists of seven subject facets and one form/genre facet. Headings in the subject facets reflect what the work being cataloged or indexed is about. Form/genre headings represent what a work is. The facets include the following:

- Personal names
- Corporate names
- Geographic names
- Events
- Titles
- Time periods
- Topics
- Form/Genre

Most of the headings are derived from LCSH or are adopted from LCSH headings. Complex LCSH headings that combine more than one facet are deconstructed into discrete FAST headings, each containing one facet. In some cases, faceting requires the creation of new FAST headings with no LCSH equivalent. For example, the faceting of the LCSH heading **United States—History—Civil War, 1861–1865** has resulted in the creation of a new event facet in FAST, **American Civil War, 1861–1865**.

Examples of the differences in heading formulation and assignment between LCSH and FAST are shown below:

Title: *Bank consolidation and small business lending: it's not just bank size that matters*

LC subject headings:

Small business—United States—Finance.
Bank loans—United States.
Bank mergers—United States.

FAST headings:

Topical: **Small business—Finance**
Bank loans
Bank mergers
Geographic: **United States**

Title: *Alcohol and aging*

LC subject headings:

Alcoholism—United States—Psychological aspects.
Older people—Alcohol use—United States.
Aging—United States.

FAST headings:

Topical: **Alcoholism—Psychological aspects**
Older people—Alcohol use
Aging
Geographic: **United States**

Title: *Churches of Florence*

LC subject headings:

Church architecture—Italy—Florence.
Florence (Italy)—Buildings, structures, etc.
Florence (Italy)—Church history.

FAST headings:

Topical: **Church architecture**
Buildings and structures
Geographic: **Italy—Florence**
Form: **Church history**

Title: *Economic & financial review*

LC subject headings:

Finance—United States—Periodicals.
Banks and banking—United States—Periodicals.
United States—Economic policy—1993–2001—Periodicals.
United States—Economic policy—2001—Periodicals.

FAST headings:
Topical: **Finance**
Banks and banking
Geographic: **United States**
Period: **Since 1993**
Form: **Periodicals**

Topics

Topical headings consist of topical main headings, which may be subdivided by topical subdivisions. Except for the fact that each heading contains elements belonging to the same facet only, the FAST topical headings look very similar to the established form of LCSH topical headings, for example:

Banks and banking
Electronic contracts
Hospitals—Administration—Data processing
Music and tourism
Nuclear reactors—Shutdown
Older people—Abuse of—Investigation
Space vehicles—Orbital assembly
Teenagers—Sleep
Web archives

A difference between LC and FAST practice is that all free-floating topical subdivisions in LCSH are part of the established form of the FAST heading and all "multiple" subdivisions are expanded. However, rather than establishing all possible combinations, only those that have actually been used will be established. For example, headings based on the following heading with multiple subdivisions are fully established in the Subject Authority File.

In LCSH:
Love—Religious aspects—Buddhism, [Christianity, etc.]

In FAST:
Love—Religious aspects—Buddhism
Love—Religious aspects—Christianity
Love—Religious aspects—Islam
Love—Religious aspects—Hinduism
Etc.

Geographic Names

Unlike LCSH, in which place names used as main headings appear in direct order (e.g., Paris (France)) but take the indirect form (—France—Paris) when used as subdivisions, all FAST geographic names are established and used in indirect order, except for top-level headings such as names of continents and most countries. Furthermore, first-level geographic names are limited to those from the MARC Code List for Geographic Areas.[4] This approach results in a hierarchical structure, from larger areas to those within them, for all geographic names. The following examples illustrate the differences between geographic headings in LCSH and in FAST:

LCSH	FAST
Los Angeles (Calif.)	**California—Los Angeles**
Tokyo (Japan)	**Japan—Tokyo**
Morgan line	**Europe—Morgan line**
Worcester County (Md.)	**Maryland—Worcester County**
Cochabamba (Bolivia : Dept.)	**Bolivia—Cochabamba (Dept.)**
Coventry (England)	**England—Coventry**
Great Lakes (North America)	**Great Lakes**
Italy	**Italy**
Chinatown (San Francisco, Calif.)	**California—San Francisco—Chinatown**

The last example above shows that FAST allows a three-level construction in formulating geographic headings. Three-level headings are limited to the following types of places:

- City sections
- Neighborhoods
- Interchanges
- Sites within a city
- Geographic features within a city
- Bays and similar bodies of water that are not associated with top-level bodies of water
- Bridges and tunnels within a city or closely associated with a city
- Other manmade structures within cities

Examples:

Ohio—Columbus—German Village
British Columbia—Victoria—Point Ellice Bridge

Minnesota—Minneapolis—Loring Park
Ontario—Lake Rosseau—Portage Bay

An advantage of the hierarchical structure is scalability. For applications where detailed geographic representation for local places is not required, first-level geographic headings may be sufficient and second- and third- level headings could be eliminated.

Events

FAST facet event is used for named events, such as meetings (named conference, congresses, etc.), military conflicts, sporting events, exhibitions, festivals, natural disasters, expeditions, and trials.[5] Some events may require a qualifier for the location of the event, but recurring events do not require a qualifier unless the event is always held in the same location. Other qualifiers that may be used include event type and date of event. Examples of event headings include the following:

Olympic Games
April Events (Bulgaria : 1925)
Vietnam War (1961–1975)—Peace
Paris Peace Conference

Qualifiers also may be used to indicate the nature of the event or for conflict resolution, for example:

Rose Bowl (Football game)
DIET (Event)
Tour de France (Bicycle race)

Time Periods

FAST chronological headings reflect the actual time periods of coverage for the resources. All chronological headings are expressed as either a single numeric date or as a date range. For example, the default time period associated with the period **Wars of the Huguenots, 1562–1598**, would be 1562 to 1598. However, in reducing this subdivision to simply a date range, the name of the war is lost. To prevent this loss of information and access point, period subdivisions with topical terms are established as event headings as well. For instance, the subdivision Wars of the Huguenots (1562–1598) is represented as both an event heading **Wars of the Huguenots, 1562–1598** and a chronological heading **1562–1598**, ensuring that both the period and event aspects are retained in the appropriate facets. Furthermore, since a chronological heading should reflect the actual time period covered, a work covering only a single battle (e.g., one that occurred in 1565) would be assigned a chronological heading that is limited to that single year. In addition, LC chronological headings with established periods are also retained. Examples of chronological headings include the following:

To 1500
1914–1918
1945
1942–1945
Since 1987
221 B.C.–220 A.D.
From 500 to 570 million years ago [Corresponding to the Cambrian period]

Names of Persons, Corporate Bodies, and Titles

Other than headings for places, headings for other types of proper names (including persons, corporate bodies, and uniform or preferred titles) that have been used as subject headings are extracted from MARC records prepared by the LC and OCLC member libraries. These headings are derived from LCSH containing such names, which in turn are based on the headings found in the Name Authority File,[6] a file maintained by the LC. For information about the types and forms of proper name headings (authorized access points representing persons, families, or corporate bodies), see discussions in chapter 8 of this book.

Examples of proper name headings and uniform titles used as FAST subjects include the following:

Charles II, King of France, 823–877
Einstein, Albert, 1879–1955
Teresa, Mother, 1910–1997
American Library Association
United Nations
Birds (Motion picture)
Beowulf
Dead Sea scrolls
Protestantische Ethik und der Geist des Kapitalismus (Weber, Max)

Form/Genre

Form data are treated as a distinct facet. All free-floating subdivisions taken from LCSH are established as separate form/genre headings. Other FAST form/genre headings are identified by extracting form subdivisions from enumerated and assigned topical and geographic headings in MARC records. For example,

Bibliography—Catalogs Biography—Dictionaries Catalogs
Controversial literature
Directories
Records and correspondence
Rules
Slides
Statistics
Textbooks
Translations

FAST AUTHORITY FILES

The FAST authority files are derived from unique LC topical and geographic subject headings assigned to records in OCLC's WorldCat and from headings appearing in the Name Authority File. The FAST authority files are built from LCSH headings extracted from MARC records in OCLC's WorldCat, and then broken into FAST facets. For example, the LCSH heading **France—History—Wars of the Huguenots, 1562–1598—Pamphlets** results in the following FAST headings:

Event: **Wars of the Huguenots (France : 1562–1598)**
Topical: **History**
Geographic: **France**
Period: **1562–1598**
Form: **Pamphlets**

Because of its wide acceptance, the MARC 21 format for authority data[7] was adopted for the creation of FAST authority records. Following is an example of a FAST authority record with MARC 21 field tags:

LDR 00000nz a2200037n 45 0
001 fst00953532
003 OCoLC
005 20041024193304.0

008 041024nn anznnbabn || ana d
016 7_ $a fst00953532 $2 OCoLC
040 $a OCoLC $b eng $c OCoLC $f fast
053 0 $a RC683 $b RC683.5
150 $a Heart $x Diseases $x Diagnosis
688 $a LC (2014) Subject Usage: 296 (299)
688 $a WC (2014) Subject Usage: 2,314 (2,353)
750 0 $a Heart $x Diseases $x Diagnosis $0 (DLC)sh 85059654

MODULAR APPROACH

FAST adopts a modular approach toward maintaining its term lists. This means that each facet forms a distinct and discrete group of headings in a separate file. These lists may be used together or separately. In a particular application, some facets may not be required. For example, in indexing a collection of naturally occurring objects, the chronological and personal name headings may not be applicable.

Furthermore, one or more of the facets may be used with other standard lists; for instance, topical headings from FAST may be used with geographic headings from the *Getty Thesaurus of Geographic Names* (TGN).[8]

FAST HEADINGS IN MARC BIBLIOGRAPHIC RECORDS

FAST headings assigned to resources are included in the following MARC bibliographic record subject and genre/form fields:

600 Personal name
610 Corporate name
611 Event name
630 Title (Uniform/Preferred)
648 Chronological term
650 Topical term
651 Geographic name
655 Form/Genre

The second indicator denotes the subject vocabulary where the terms are found. For FAST headings, the second indicator takes the value "7" with the addition of subfield 2, with values "$2fast." Following is an example of FAST headings in a MARC 21 bibliographic record.

650 7 $a Dragons. $2 fast $0 (OCoLC)fst00897397
650 7 $a Fairies. $2 fast $0 (OCoLC)fst00919878
650 7 $a Magic. $2 fast $0 (OCoLC)fst01005468
651 7 $a England $z London. $2 fast $0 (OCoLC)fst01204271
651 7 $a Solar system $z Halley's comet. $2 fast $0 (OCoLC) fst01241058
648 7 $a 1700-1799 $2 fast
655 7 $a Fantasy fiction $2 gsafd
655 7 $a Historical fiction $2 gsafd
655 7 $a Fiction. $2 fast $0 (OCoLC)fst01423787

NOTES

1. Chan, L. M., Childress, E., Dean, R., O'Neill, E. T., and Vizine-Goetz, D. (2001). A faceted approach to subject data in the Dublin Core Metadata Record. *Journal of Internet Cataloging, 4*(1/2), 35–47.

2. ALCTS/CCS/SAC/Subcommittee on Metadata and Subject Analysis. (1999). *Subject Data in the Metadata Record: Recommendations and Rationale.* Retrieved from http://www.ala.org/alcts/resources/org/cat/subjectdata_record.

3. OCLC Research. (October 14, 2014). *FAST (Faceted Application of Subject Terminology).* Retrieved from http://fast.oclc.org/.

4. Library of Congress, Network Development and MARC Standards Office. (April 7, 2008). *MARC Code List for Geographic Areas.* Retrieved from www.loc.gov/marc/geoareas/gacshome.html.

5. Chan, L. M., and O'Neill, E. T. (2010). *FAST: Faceted Application of Subject Terminology: Principles and Application.* Santa Barbara, CA: Libraries Unlimited.

6. Library of Congress. (December 7, 2012). *Library of Congress Authorities.* Retrieved from http://authorities.loc.gov.

7. Library of Congress, Network Development and MARC Standards Office. (1999). *MARC 21 Format for Authority Data: Including Guidelines for Content Designation.* Washington, DC: Cataloging Distribution Service, Library of Congress.

8. J. Paul Getty Trust. (2000). *Getty Thesaurus of Geographic Names Online.* Retrieved from http://www.getty.edu/research/tools/vocabularies/tgn/.

Chapter 13

Sears List of Subject Headings

INTRODUCTION

In the early 1920s, because neither LCSH nor the earlier ALA list (described in chapter 11) was judged suitable for the access needs of small and medium-sized general libraries, Minnie Earl Sears developed a new list with smaller libraries in mind. Recognizing the advantages of compatibility in creating her list, she decided to follow the general principles that underlie LCSH, with certain exceptions to meet the particular needs of small libraries. Therefore, although the Sears list she created is not an abridgment of LCSH, it is similar in principle, format, and structure.

The first edition of Sears' *List of Subject Headings for Small Libraries* appeared in 1923. Since then, the list has gone through many editions, the most recent being the twenty-first.[1] Sears was responsible for the first three (1923, 1926, and 1933). With the sixth edition (1950), the title was changed to *Sears List of Subject Headings*.

Today, the Sears list is used widely by school libraries and small public libraries in the United States. Thus, the Sears and the LCSH lists together serve as the two standard lists for subject headings for general libraries in the United States.

Throughout the history of the Sears list, its editors have followed the general principles set forth by Minnie Earl Sears, which is, maintaining close parallels with LCSH, with variations and modifications as appropriate for smaller libraries. Recent editions of the Sears list also have incorporated headings from the LCSH for Children's Literature, with a few exceptions where Sears headings are in a slightly different form. The variations, however, do not affect basic structure and principles. These are the principles of alphabetical specific headings first enunciated by Charles A. Cutter: specific and direct entry, common usage and literary warrant, uniformity (i.e., uniform headings), and syndetic devices.[2] Such variations, as there are, usually occur in the following areas: terminology (e.g., **Social work** instead of *Social service*), spelling (e.g., **Archeology** instead of *Archaeology*), word order (e.g., **Colleges and universities** instead of *Universities and colleges*), and a lower degree of specificity (e.g., combining closely related headings such as *Art, Greek* and *Art—Greece* into **Greek Art** only).

In format, the Sears list resembles the display format of LCSH (also the print version). Headings and their subdivisions used as subject access points in a catalog are printed in boldface type. Those printed in lightface roman type are nonpreferred terms; they are synonymous terms or variant forms of authorized headings and are followed by *USE* references for the terms that are used as headings.[2] Sample entries are shown below (UF refers to "used for").

Biological rhythms 571.7
UF Biological clocks
Biology—Periodicity
Biorhythms
BT **Cycles**
NT **Jet lag**

Computer music 786.7
BT **Music**
RT **Computer sound processing**
Electronic music
Conundrums
USE **Riddles**
Cookery, American
USE **American cooking**

Digital libraries 025.00285
UF Electronic libraries
Virtual libraries
BT **Information systems**
Libraries
Electronic libraries
USE **Digital libraries**

Except for very general subject headings, each valid heading in Sears is followed by one or more classification numbers taken from the Abridged DDC. Since the Sears list is designed for use in small libraries, the corresponding

DDC numbers are seldom carried out more than four places beyond the decimal point. Following common practices in controlled vocabularies, related terms are included under each heading, and the relationships among headings are indicated by commonly used symbols.

The following sections of this chapter discuss and explain the basic technical features of the Sears list. The topics covered are main headings, cross-references, subdivisions, classes of headings omitted from the list, and subject headings for biography and literature. Readers should note that, because the Sears list is a close parallel to LCSH, much of what is said about it repeats or overlaps with what was said in chapter 11 about LCSH. This repetition is useful in that many readers will need all pertinent information on the Sears list gathered in one chapter.

Sears headings consist of single nouns, compounds, adjective-noun phrases, and prepositional phrases. The list contains cross-references, and provides for subdivisions of headings. Many terms that can be used in subject cataloging according to the Sears list do not appear explicitly in the list, but must be supplied by catalogers. All of these topics are discussed and explained below.

MAIN HEADINGS

Topical Headings

Topical headings consist of words or phrases representing concepts or objects that depict the content of the works being cataloged. They can be in the form of single-noun headings, phrase headings, or compound headings.

Single-Noun Headings

Most of the broad fields of knowledge, concepts, and concrete objects are represented by headings consisting of single nouns, for example, **Chemistry**; **Education**; **Law**; **Democracy**; **Books**; **Rocks**; **Water**; and so on. When a noun has more than one meaning, a qualifier is added in parentheses to limit the heading to one concept or object, for example, **Bridge (Game)** or **Masks (Sculpture)**. The choice of the singular or the plural form depends on the term involved. In general, abstract concepts are represented by the singular noun, for example, **Credit**, while concrete objects are represented by the plural, for example, **Books**. Actions are also expressed in singular terms, for example, **Dining**. Sometimes, both the singular and the plural forms of a noun are used as headings. In such cases, they carry different meanings, for example, **Essay** (the technique) and **Essays** (the works), or **Art** (for visual arts) and **Arts** (for arts in general).

Phrase Headings

Phrase headings are used when a subject or concept cannot be properly or precisely expressed by a single noun. Types of phrase headings include compound headings, adjectival headings, and prepositional phrase headings.

Compound Headings. Compound headings consist of two nouns or noun phrases connected by the word *and*. They are used mainly for the following purposes: (1) to connect topics or concepts that are usually treated together in works, for example, **Scouts and scouting**, **Clothing and dress**, or **Cliff dwellers and cliff dwellings**; (2) to connect opposite subjects that are usually treated together in works, for example, **Debtor and creditor** or **Open and closed shop**; and (3) to express a relationship between two concepts or things, for example, **Church and education** or **Philosophy and religion**.

Adjectival Headings. The most common type of adjectival headings consists of a noun or noun phrase with one or more adjectival modifiers, for example, **English language**, **Space flight**, **Air-cushion vehicles**, **College students**, **Children's songs**, and so on. In the past, inverted adjectival headings were used, but these have been revised in later editions to appear in the direct, natural language order.

Prepositional Phrase Headings. Some concepts are expressed by nouns or noun phrases connected by prepositions that express their relationships, for example, **Cooking for the sick, Electricity in agriculture, Religion in the public schools,** or **Devotional literature for children**.

Form Headings

A form heading describes the form or genre of the work rather than its subject content. In other words, a form heading represents what the work *is* rather than what it is *about*. In the Sears list, form refers to the intellectual form, such as literary and artistic genres and forms of presentation, rather than the physical form, such as sound recordings or motion pictures. Examples of form headings include the following:

Book reviews
Children's poetry
Children's songs
Indexes
Short stories

Headings such as **Sound recordings** and **Motion pictures** are used for works *about* sound recordings or motion pictures, and suchlike. The scope note found under the particular heading indicates the usage, for example:

Sound recordings (May subdiv. geog.) **621.389; 780.26**

is used for general materials and for materials on sound recordings that emphasize the content of the recording rather than the format. Materials about the format are entered under the format, for example, **Compact discs.** Materials about the equipment or the process by which sound is recorded are entered under **Sound—Recording and reproducing**.

SA types of sound recordings, e.g., **Compact discs** and types of music with the subdivision *Sound recordings*, e.g., **Opera—Sound recordings** [to be added as needed]
(SA refers to "*see also.*")

Geographic Headings

Geographic names, that is, both jurisdictional names and names representing geographic features, may appear as main headings or as subdivisions. Only a few geographic headings, for example, **North America**, **United States**, **Ohio**, **Chicago (Ill.)**, and **Rocky Mountains**, appear in the Sears list as examples or to show cross-references and subdivisions. Others are to be added by the cataloger as needed. They are formulated according to Resource Description and Access RDA, for example, **Thailand**, **Tokyo (Japan)**, and **Mississippi River**.

Name Headings

Names of persons, families, corporate bodies, literary and artistic works, etc., may also be used as subject headings for works about them. Only a few name headings are included in the list, for example, **Napoleon I, Emperor of the French, 1769–1821**; **Shakespeare, William, 1564–1616**; and **Lincoln family**. Other names are to be added as needed.

The form of a personal heading and its cross-references are established according to RDA, in order that works written by and about the same person can be collocated in the catalog. The name authority record established for a person as an author serves to determine the form of both author and subject headings for that person. If a person whose name is required as a subject heading has not appeared as an author in the catalog, a name authority record should be established according to the same procedure as in descriptive cataloging.

Examples of names of persons as subject headings include the following:

Boone, Daniel, 1734-1820
Bush, George, 1924-
Madonna, 1958-

By way of exception, a few personal headings are included in the list. For example, **Jesus Christ** is included because of its unique subdivisions; **Shakespeare, William, 1564–1616** is included as a "key" to show subdivisions that may be used under names of other voluminous authors (in other words, it serves as a "pattern" heading); and **Napoleon I, Emperor of the French, 1769–1821—Drama** is included because it is used as an example under the heading **Drama.**

CROSS-REFERENCES

Cross-references are used for two reasons: first, to guide users who consult the catalog under terms that are not used as subject headings to those terms that are and, second, to call users' attention to materials related to the topics being consulted. Cross-references also help catalogers select the most appropriate headings for the work being cataloged. While a heading may appear many times in the catalog, each reference is made only once, regardless of how many times the heading involved has been assigned to bibliographic records. Cross-references appear in three forms: specific *see* references, specific *see also* references, and general references. When any heading in the Sears list has cross-references associated with it, coded instructions appear under the heading to indicate what should be done. These instructions are described and explained in the following sections.

Specific *See* References

Specific *see* references appear under unauthorized terms, and indicate that another term should be used. In the Sears list, instruction for making *see* references, indicated by a preceding UF (used for), is given after the authorized heading. The symbol UF means that references are to be made **from** the terms that follow **to** the heading immediately above it, for example:

Physicians
UF Doctors

Modern history
UF History, Modern

This means that in the printed Sears list, the lead-in terms "Doctors" and "History, Modern" are followed by references, indicated by the symbol *USE* to the authorized headings **Physicians** and **Modern history** respectively, for example:

Doctors
  USE **Physicians**

History, Modern
  USE **Modern history**

It also means that if a cataloger is adding a record to the catalog using the subject heading **Physicians** for the first time, he or she should check to ensure that the catalog includes a USE reference to **Physicians** from the lead-in term "Doctors."

In general, USE references are made from synonymous or near-synonymous terms and from inverted forms that are not used as subject headings. Occasionally, a USE reference is made from a more specific term that is not used as a heading to the more general term that is used, for example:

Cooking utensils
  USE **Kitchen utensils**

Specific *See Also* References

A *see also* reference connects a heading to a related heading or headings; such a reference is made only when the library has material listed under both headings. A *see also* reference is made for one of two purposes: to refer from a general subject to more specific parts of it (a downward hierarchical reference), and vice versa. A *see also* reference may also connect two related headings of more or less equal specificity (a same-level reference).

See also references, indicated by the symbols NT (narrow term), BT (broader term), and RT (related term) are listed directly under appropriate headings. In addition, reverse instructions are given under the headings referred to. For instance, for the headings **Bees,** Sears shows the following:

Bees
  BT **Insects**
  RT **Beekeeping**
    Honey

Beekeeping
  BT **Agriculture**
  RT **Beehives**
    Bees

Honey
BT **Food**
RT **Bees**

Insects
BT **Animals**
NT **Ants**
Bees
Etc.

General References

A general reference, in the form of SA, covers an entire category or class of headings rather than an individual heading. This device is used to save space in both the subject headings list and in the library catalog. A general explanation or direction is given instead of a long list of individual headings, for example:

Dogs
SA types of dogs, e.g., **Guide dogs**; and names of specific breeds of dogs [to be added as needed]

Electronic musical instruments
SA types of instruments, e.g., **Synthesizer (Musical instrument)** [to be added as needed]

Rivers
SA names of rivers [to be added as needed]

Army
USE **Armies**
Military art and science
and names of countries with the subhead Army, e.g., **United States. Army** [to be added as needed]

Examples of Cross-References

Following is an example of the different types of cross-references required for a particular heading.

Carving (Decorative arts) (May subdiv. geog.) **731.4; 736**
UF Carving (Arts)
SA types of carving, e.g., **Wood carving** [to be added as needed]
BT **Decorative arts**

NT **Wood carving**
RT **Sculpture**

Under the terms and headings referred to and from the authorized heading **Carving (Decorative arts)**, there are reciprocal references pointing back to the heading, as follows:

Carving (Arts)
USE **Carving (Decorative arts)**

Decorative arts
NT **Carving (Decorative arts)**

Wood carving
BT **Carving (Decorative arts)**

Sculpture
RT **Carving (Decorative arts)**

SUBDIVISIONS

In the Sears list, many general subjects are subdivided to indicate their specific aspects or to provide a subarrangement for a large number of works on the same subject. There are several types of subdivisions: subject or topical; form; period or chronological; and place, local, or geographic.

Subject or Topical Subdivisions

A subject or topical subdivision added to a main heading brings out a specific aspect or characteristic of the general subject, for example:

English language—Business English
English language—Dialects
English language—Etymology
Education—Curricula
Education—Finance

Form Subdivisions

A form subdivision expresses the intellectual or literary form of the work being cataloged, for example:

Animals—Poetry
Chemistry—Dictionaries

Chicago (Ill.)—Maps
Motion pictures—Catalogs
Sports—Fiction

Because many form subdivisions and some topical subdivisions are so common that they are applicable to many subjects, they are not enumerated under each heading with which they may be used, but instead are listed together in the introduction to the Sears list. These subdivisions are equivalent to the free-floating subdivisions in LCSH. Because these common subdivisions may be used under subject headings where applicable, the following combinations may be assigned by the cataloger, even though they are not actually so listed:

Librarians—Biography
Libraries—Directories
Piano music
Discography
Railroads—Maps
Space sciences—Periodicals

In addition to the list of common subdivisions mentioned above, instructions for the use of these subdivisions are also provided in the list itself under the appropriate terms, for example:

Bibliography
SA subjects and names of persons and places with the subdivision *Bibliography*, e.g., **Agriculture—Bibliography**; **Shakespeare, William, 1564-1616—Bibliography**; **United States—Bibliography**; etc. [to be added as needed]

Maps
SA types of maps, e.g., **Road maps**; subjects with the subdivision *Maps*, e.g., **Geology Maps**; and names of countries, cities, etc., and names of wars with the subdivision *Maps* [to be added as needed]

It should be noted that some of the subdivisions represent the physical form or medium of the work, for example,**—Computer software**;**—Data-bases**; and**—Sound recordings**. However, they are used as topical subdivisions for works *about*, not as form subdivisions for works *in*, these forms. Thus, the heading **Opera—Sound recordings** is assigned to a work *about* operatic sound recordings, not the recordings themselves.

Geographic Subdivisions

Many works deal with a subject with regard to a specific locality. For a subject that lends itself to such treatment, the Sears list authorizes geographic subdivisions; such authorization is indicated by a parenthetical statement (e.g., May subdiv. geog.) following the main heading. For example, a heading such as **Flowers** (May subdiv. geog.) indicates that the following headings, though not listed, are valid as subject entries:

Flowers—United States
Flowers—Hawaii
Flowers—Honolulu (Hawaii)

Period or Chronological Subdivisions

National history lends itself to chronological treatment. In the Sears list, chronological or period subdivisions are provided under the history of the United States and other countries about which American libraries are likely to have sizeable collections. Period subdivisions appear as further subdivisions under the subdivision**—History**.

United States—History—1600-1775, Colonial period
United States—History—1689-1697, King William's War
United States—History—1755-1763, French and Indian War
United States—History—1775-1783, Revolution
United States—History—1861-1865, Civil War

Japan—History—0-1868
Japan—History—1868-1945
Japan—History—1945-1952, Allied occupation
Japan—History—1952-

Even though **United States** is a key heading, the period subdivisions listed under it may not be used under headings of other countries, because each country has a unique history and the period subdivisions appropriate to one country may not apply to other countries.

Key Headings for Subdivisions

Many subdivisions are applicable to headings in a particular category. Instead of enumerating these subdivisions under each heading in the category, one heading is chosen as the "key" heading under which typical subdivisions are listed; in other words, they are analogous to pattern headings in LCSH. The following headings serve as the key patterns for subdivisions in Sears:

Table 13.1 Key Headings for Subdivisions

Category	*Key Heading*
Authors	**Shakespeare, William, 1564–1616**
Ethnic groups	**Native Americans**
Languages	**English language**
Literature	**English literature**
Places	**United States**
	Ohio
	Chicago (Ill.)
Public figures	**Presidents—United States**
Wars	**World War, 1939–1945**

The subdivisions listed under them may be used, whenever appropriate, with other headings in the same categories. For example, the subdivisions listed under **World War, 1939–1945** may be used with the heading for another war, for example, **Persian Gulf War, 1991—Causes.**

Order of Subdivisions

When a subject heading contains multiple subdivisions, the order of the subdivisions within the string follows the practice of LCSH:

[Topical]—[Geographic]—[Chronological]—[Form]
[Geographic]—[Topical]—[Chronological]—[Form]

An example of this is:

American literature—Southern States—Bibliography
United States—Civilization—1960–1970—Periodicals

HEADINGS TO BE ADDED BY THE CATALOGER

Sears contains the headings that are most commonly used in small libraries, and is not intended to be an exhaustive list of subject headings. Personal names, corporate names, and other proper names are potential subject headings because many works are written about individual persons, institutions, places, events, and so on. However, it is not practical or even possible to include in the subject headings list all possible names that may become subjects of works. Headings needed in cataloging, but not listed, may be added, according to specific instructions.[3] The "SA" references in the list provide instructions on creating headings in areas most frequently needed, for example:

> **Tools** (May subdiv. geog.)
> SA types of tools [to be added as needed]
> **Trees** (May subdiv. geog.)
> SA types of trees, e.g., **Oak** [to be added as needed], in the singular form

As a result, any catalog using the Sears list will likely show many assigned subject headings that do not appear in the list. Furthermore, when new names are needed as subject headings, the cataloger must derive the appropriate form. Most names that do not appear in the subject list are proper names for persons, families, places, or corporate bodies. In addition, certain types of common names may also be added as needed. Such headings are created by the cataloger according to descriptive cataloging rules or by following established headings in the same subject category or as shown in examples.

The arrays given below list the categories of headings that are not in Sears, but are likely to be needed in addition to headings in the list:

Topical Subjects

1. Types of common things—foods, tools, sports, musical instruments, etc. (e.g., **Carrots, Spinach**, **Pork**, **Hammers**, **Badminton**, **Harpsichord**, etc.).
2. Types of plants and animals—fruits, flowers, birds, fishes, etc. (e.g., **Grapefruit**, **Carnations**, **Swallows**, **Trout**, **Kangaroos**, etc.).
3. Types of chemicals and minerals (e.g., **Chlorite**, **Glycine**, **Potassium**, **Topaz**, etc.).
4. Types of enterprises and industries (e.g., **Horse industry**, etc.).
5. Types of diseases (e.g., **Measles**).
6. Names of organs and regions of the body (e.g., **Kidney**, **Legs**, etc.).
7. Names of languages, language groups, and national literatures (e.g., **Turkish language**, **Austrian literature**, etc.). **English language** and **English literature** serve as key headings for subdivisions.
8. Names of ethnic groups and nationalities (e.g., **Oneida Indians**, **Belgians**, **Germans**, etc.). **Native Americans** serves as the key for subdivisions under ethnic group or native people.
9. Names of wars, battles, treaties, etc. (e.g., **Waterloo, Battle of, 1815**; or **Portsmouth, Treaty of, 1905**). The heading **World War, 1939–1945**

serves as the key for subdivisions under any war, and in some cases under individual battles.

Geographic Headings

1. Names of political jurisdictions—countries, states, cities, provinces, etc. Very few geographical or place names are listed as such in Sears. Those that are included serve as key headings for treatment of analogous headings. Geographical or place names fall into several different categories, as described below.
   a. Countries (e.g., **India**, **Belgium**, etc.). A number of countries are included to show their unique period subdivisions. The heading **United States** serves as a key heading for topical and form subdivisions. The subdivisions (except period subdivisions, which are not transferable) under **United States** may be used with names of other countries, for example, **India—Geography** or **Belgium—Population**.
   b. States (e.g., **Colorado**, **Wyoming**, etc.). **Ohio**, as a key state, is listed with subdivisions that can be used under names of other states.
   c. Provinces, etc. (e.g., **Scotland**, **Ontario**, **British Columbia**, etc.).
   d. Cities (e.g., **San Francisco (Calif.), Athens (Ga.), Dijon (France)**, etc.). The name of the country or the state (if in the United States) is added to the name of a local place, in accordance with RDA guidelines for geographic names. For subdivisions, **Chicago (Ill.)** serves as the key city.
2. Groups of states, groups of countries, alliances, etc. (e.g., **Baltic States**).
3. Names of geographic features—regions, mountain ranges, island groups, individual mountains, individual islands, rivers, river valleys, oceans, lakes, etc.
   a. Mountain ranges and individual mountains (e.g., **Smokey Mountains**, **Mont Blanc**, etc.).
   b. Island groups and individual islands (e.g., **Virgin Islands**, **Jamaica**, etc.).
   c. River valleys and individual rivers (e.g., **Ohio Valley**, **Mississippi River**, etc.).
   d. Regions, oceans, lakes, etc. (**Indian Ocean**, **Kentucky Lake**, etc.).

Names

Works about individual persons, corporate bodies, and other works are assigned as subject headings in the form of name or uniform title headings. These headings are established according to descriptive cataloging rules so that they are compatible with headings used as primary and added access points.

1. Personal names—individual persons and families. (The heading for the name of a family consists of the family name followed by the word **family**, e.g., **Kennedy family**, **Brontë family**, etc.)
   a. **Shakespeare, William, 1564–1616** serves as the key for subdivisions under voluminous authors and under other individual persons, as appropriate.
   b. **Presidents—United States** serves as the key heading for subdivisions under presidents, prime ministers, governors, etc., and in some cases under names of individual presidents, prime ministers, etc.
2. Corporate names—names of associations, societies, government bodies, religious denominations, business firms, performing groups, colleges, libraries, hospitals, hotels, ships, etc.
   a. Names of associations, societies, clubs, etc. (e.g., **American Chemical Society**, **American Library Association**, etc.).
   b. Names of government bodies (**United States. Navy**; **California. Legislature**; etc.).
   c. Names of religious denominations (e.g., **Methodist Church**, etc.).
   d. Names of institutions: colleges, libraries, hospitals, etc. (e.g., **Smith College**, **Florida State University**, **New York Public Library**, **Massachusetts General Hospital**, etc.).
   e. Names of hotels, retail stores, ships, etc. (e.g., **Christina (Ship)**, etc.).
3. Preferred titles—anonymous literary works, newspapers, periodicals, sacred scriptures, motion pictures, etc.

SUBJECT HEADINGS FOR SPECIAL TYPES OF MATERIALS

Certain types of library materials require special treatment; of these, the most common are biography and literature.

Subject Headings for Biography

Collective Biography

A work containing biographies of more than three persons is treated as a *collective biography*. A subject heading covering the entire group is assigned, instead of individual personal headings. Various kinds of collective biographies are discussed below:

General Biography. If a collective biography is not limited to any geographic area, time period, or subject field or a particular class of people (e.g., Van Loon's *Lives*), the general form heading **Biography** is assigned. For a work *about* biography, the heading **Biography as a literary form** is used. For biographical reference works that are arranged in dictionary form, for example, *Webster's Biographical Dictionary* or *International Who's Who*, the heading **Biography—Dictionaries** is used.

Local Biography. When a collective biography contains lives of people from a particular geographic area or a specific ethnic group, for example, *Who's Who in Australia*, *Canadian Who's Who*, and *Who's Who among African Americans*, the subject heading is in the form of the geographic or ethnic name with the subdivision**—Biography** or**—Biography—Dictionaries**:

Australia—Biography—Dictionaries
Canada—Biography—Dictionaries
African Americans—Biography

Classes of Persons. When a collective biography contains lives of persons of a particular subject field or a class, a subject heading is assigned in the form of the term representing the members of the field or the class, for example, **Chemists**, **Explorers**, **Philosophers**, **Sailors**, and so on. In some cases, the heading may be divided geographically, for example, **Actors—United States**, **Composers—Germany**, **Statesmen—Great Britain,** and so on. In other cases, the adjective form is used, for example, **American poets** and **English dramatists**.

When there is no appropriate term to represent the members of a field, or when the name of the class or group refers to the subject in general rather than to individuals, the heading assigned is in the form of the name of the field or group with the subdivision**—Biography**:

Baseball—Biography
France—History—1789-1799, Revolution—Biography
Women—Biography

Individual Biography

For a biography of one, two, or three individuals, the name of each individual is assigned as a subject heading; the form of the heading should agree with the established heading of the same person used as the main or added entry in descriptive cataloging. A biography of Robert F. Kennedy, for example, is assigned the following heading:

Kennedy, Robert F., 1925–1968—Biography

A biography of two or three of the Kennedy brothers would be assigned headings under the name of each.

Frequently, when the biography of a person also contains material about the field in which the person is concerned, a second subject heading representing the subject field is added. For example, if the biography of President John F. Kennedy contains a substantial amount of material on his administration, a second heading **United States—History—1961–1974** is assigned in addition to the personal heading.

For persons about whom there is a large amount of material, subdivisions are used for subarrangement. The heading **Shakespeare, William, 1564–1616** serves as the "key" for subdivisions to be used under other voluminous authors when there is a large amount of material. The subdivisions listed under the heading **Presidents—United States** may be used under headings for individual presidents, prime ministers, and other rulers. In small libraries, for most individual biographies, the personal name alone without any subdivision is sufficient as the heading.

For autobiographical writings in addition to autobiographies—including journals, memoirs, and letters—a subject heading identical to the author entry is often assigned. This is important in searching because it allows the separate retrieval of works *by* and *about* the person.

The headings used with collective biographies are not assigned to individual biographies. For example, the heading **Musicians** or **Musicians—United States** is not used with a biography of Billy Joel. However, a reference is made from the collective heading to the individual headings, for example:

> **Musicians** (May subdiv. geog.)
> SA types of musicians and names of individual musicians [to be added as needed]

Subject Headings for Literature

There are two distinctive categories of works in the field of literature: (1) works *about* literature, and (2) literary works or specimens. These receive different treatment in subject cataloging.

Works about Literature

These works, in which literature *is* the subject, are treated like other works with subject headings representing the content and the scope of the works, for example:

> **Literature**
> [with or without subdivisions depending on the scope]

American literature
[use **English literature** as the key for subdivisions]
Drama
German drama—History and criticism
Essay
English essays—History and criticism

Many of the more general literature headings are subdivided for special aspects. These may be used when appropriate. In addition, the general subdivisions listed in the Sears introduction may also be used when appropriate. Note that the subdivision—**History and criticism**, instead of—**History**, is used with literature headings.

The headings discussed above do not apply to works about individual authors or about works written by them. A work about an individual author or about his or her works is assigned a heading in the form of the author's name, for example, **Dickens, Charles, 1812–1870**. The heading for Shakespeare serves as a key for subdivisions used with voluminous authors.

In addition to headings representing literary forms or genres, topical headings are also assigned to bring out the themes of the works. Headings for topics in literature are assigned according to the pattern shown under the following heading:

Literature—Themes: 809
SA subjects, racial and ethnic groups, and classes of persons in literature, for example, **Dogs in literature**; **Women in literature**; etc. and names of persons, families, and corporate bodies with the subdivision *In literature*, for example **Napoleon I, Emperor of the French, 1769-1821—In literature** [to be added as needed]

Literary Works

In these works, literature is the *form* rather than the *subject*. There are two categories of literary works: collections of works of more than one author, and single or collected works by individual authors.

Collections of Works of More Than One Author. A literary form heading (e.g., **Essays**; **American drama—Collections**; etc.), is assigned to a collection of works of more than one author. To differentiate a topical heading from a form heading containing the same term, the singular form is used as the topical heading (for a work *about* the literary form) and the plural form, when there is one, is used as the form heading (for literary collections). When there is no acceptable plural form of a noun, the subdivision—**Collections** is added, for example:

Subject heading	*Form heading for collections*
Essay	**Essays**
Short story	**Short stories**
Literature	**Literature—Collections**
Spanish literature	**Spanish literature—Collections**
Poetry	**Poetry—Collections**
English poetry	**English poetry—Collections**

Topical and geographic headings are often assigned to collections of novels, poems, and plays to bring out predominant topics, places, persons, or historical events. To distinguish between factual accounts of these topics and aspects from literary or imaginative works, the subdivisions—**Fiction**, —**Poetry**, or—**Drama** are added to the latter, for example:

Basketball—Fiction
United States—History—1861-1865, Civil War—Fiction
[for a work such as *Gone with the Wind* by Margaret Mitchell]
Lincoln, Abraham, 1809-1865—Drama
[for a work such as *Abe Lincoln in Illinois* by Robert E. Sherwood]
Napoleon I, Emperor of the French, 1769-1821—Poetry

Works by Individual Authors. For collected or individual works by individual authors, no literary form heading is assigned if the works are in one of the major forms such as drama, fiction, and poetry. However, for collected works in a minor form such as parodies, satire, and short stories by an individual author, headings similar to those used with collections by more than one author are assigned as instructed. The scope note under a particular heading gives instruction regarding its applicability to collected and/or individual works, for example:

Drama: 808.2; 808.82
Use for general materials on drama, not for individual works. Collections of plays are entered under **Drama—Collections**, **American drama—Collections**, **English drama—Collections**, etc.

English drama: 822
Use for general materials about English drama, not for individual works.

Short stories: 808.83
Use for collections of short stories by one author or by several authors.

Science fiction: 808.3; 808.83
May be used for individual works, collections, or materials about fiction based on imagined developments in science and technology.

For example, **English drama** is not assigned to a play written by Shakespeare, nor **American fiction** to Hemingway's novel *The Old Man and the Sea*. On the other hand, E. A. Poe's *Selected Tales*, a collection of short stories, is assigned the heading **Short stories**. Minor literary forms are not listed under the national adjectives.

In the eighteenth edition of Sears, many form or genre headings were added to enhance access to individual works of fiction, poetry, drama, and other imaginative works, based on the *Guidelines on Subject Access to Individual Works of Fiction, Drama, Etc.*,[4] issued by the ALA. The assignment of minor literary form and genre headings (such as **Ballads**, **Horror fiction**, and **Science fiction**) to individual works of literature is in keeping with the ALA *Guidelines*.

NOTES

1. Bristow, B. A. (Ed.), and Farrar, C. S. (Assoc. Ed.). (2014). *Sears List of Subject Headings* (21st ed.). Ipswich, MA: H. W. Wilson Company.
2. For a discussion of these principles, see "Principles of the Sears List," in *Sears List of Subject Headings*.
3. Bristow and Farrar, (2014). p. xl.
4. Association for Library Collections & Technical Services, Cataloging and Classification Section, Subject Analysis Committee, Subcommittee on the Revision of the Guidelines on Subject Access to Individual Works of Fiction. (2000). *Guidelines on Subject Access to Individual Works of Fiction, Drama, etc.* (2nd ed.). Chicago, IL: American Library Association.

Chapter 14

Medical Subject Headings

INTRODUCTION

Library of Congress Subject Headings (LCSH) and *Sears List of Subject Headings* are not the only systems of subject cataloging used in American libraries and information agencies. There are many others that, for the most part, are designed for special subject fields. This chapter discusses *Medical Subject Headings* (MeSH) as an example of a specialized subject vocabulary.

MeSH is the system designed and used by the NLM for assigning MeSH or indexing terms to books and journal articles in the biomedical sciences. It has gained considerable acceptance outside of NLM and is now widely used by both health sciences libraries and the abstracting and indexing services that serve the field.

BRIEF HISTORY

In the 1940s, a subject authority file on cards was established at NLM for use in its bibliographies and catalogs.[1] Its headings followed the patterns set by LCSH, but were not quite the same. Early on, NLM had two access systems—one for citations to medical books and one for indexing journal articles. In the early 1950s, NLM decided to integrate the two by constructing a thesaurus of MeSH to be used by both NLM catalogers and indexers of journal literature for both *Index Medicus* and its online version MEDLINE. In 2010, the NLM Catalog and the Journals Database were merged, integrating the MEDLINE indexing information of all journals and other resources in PubMed and other National Center for Biotechnology Information (NCBI) databases into the NLM Catalog. Through this catalog, one can access over

1.4 million journals, books, audiovisual materials, computer software products, electronic resources, and other materials indexed by using MeSH terms.[2]

MeSH was originally based on Library of Congress Subject Heading LCSH, but has departed considerably from it. Over the years, MeSH has become an increasingly faceted system so that most searching is done using postcoordination. This is true particularly when MeSH functions as an indexing tool for a large set of biomedical resources.

The first official publication of the medical subject headings list appeared in 1954 under the title *Subject Heading Authority List Used by the Current List.* Beginning in 1960, the list has been published under the title *MeSH.*[3]

MeSH is available online, and MeSH descriptors and qualifiers, as well as Supplementary Concept Records (SCR), are available to download in XML, ASCII, or MARC formats. The print version of the *Medical Subject Headings—Index Medicus Supplement*, with the alphabetic list and tree structures—ceased publication with the 2007 edition. The *Annotated Alphabetic List*, *MeSH Tree Structures*, and *Permuted MeSH* ceased with the 2003 editions.[4] The 2015 edition of MeSH contains 27,455 descriptors.

STRUCTURE OF MeSH

MeSH descriptors, also called MeSH headings, are organized into categorized lists called "tree structures" that show hierarchical relationships among terms. The publication *Tree Structures*[5] consists of a categorical arrangement placing each heading in relationship to other headings that represent similar areas and concepts. A system of "tree numbers" (each consisting of a capital letter followed by one or more digits) is used to reflect the hierarchies.

The tree structures first appeared in 1963 (in the second edition of MeSH) with thirteen main categories. There are currently sixteen main categories:

A. Anatomy
B. Organisms
C. Diseases
D. Chemicals and Drugs
E. Analytical, Diagnostic, and Therapeutic Techniques and Equipment
F. Psychiatry and Psychology
G. Phenomena and Processes
H. Disciples and Occupations
I. Anthropology, Education, Sociology and Social Phenomena
J. Technology, Industry, Agriculture
K. Humanities
L. Information Science

M. Named Groups
N. Health Care
V. Publication Characteristics
Z. Geographic Locations

Each category is subdivided into one or more subcategories, with headings arranged hierarchically. Each heading is accompanied by the full tree number providing the location of the heading in the "tree." If a topic represented by a given heading belongs in more than one subcategory, that heading may appear in several places in the *tree structures*. When a concept appears in more than one hierarchy, it is assigned multiple tree numbers. For example, the descriptor **Asthma** appears in the following "trees":

Respiratory Tract Diseases [C08]
  Bronchial Diseases [C08.127]
    Asthma [C08.127.108]
      Asthma, Exercise-Induced [C08.127.108.110]

Respiratory Tract Diseases [C08]
  Respiratory Hypersensitivity [C08.674]
    Asthma [C08.674.095]
      Asthma, Exercise-Induced [C08.674.095.110]

Immune System Diseases [C20]
  Hypersensitivity [C20.543]
    Hypersensitivity, Immediate [C20.543.480]
      Respiratory Hypersensitivity [C20.543.480.680]
    Asthma [C20.543.480.680.095]
      Asthma, Exercise-Induced [C20.543.480.680.095.110]

The tree structures provide a classificatory approach to medical subjects,[6] manifesting hierarchical principles and providing a logical basis for cross-references.

TYPES OF MeSH TERMS

MeSH contains the following types of records:[7] **Descriptors** (main headings), **Qualifiers**, **Geographics**, and **SCR**. **Publication Characteristics (publication types)**, essentially genre terms, are also included. SCR are not used for cataloging. These concepts are mapped to MeSH headings, which is what catalogers use.

Descriptors

Descriptors, also called *main headings*, represent main topics. Most descriptors are topical, in the form of single words or phrases. Examples are:

Acrylic Resins
Asthma
Blood Pressure
Nurses
Nurses' Aides
Nursing Administration Research
Pediatrics
Pulmonary Circulation
Respiratory System
Therapeutics
Thermal Conductivity
Vinyl Compounds

Some phrase headings are inverted in order to collocate significant terms, for example:

Nurses, Male
Respiration, Artificial
Respiratory Therapy Department, Hospital
Therapy, Computer-Assisted

The following examples show the authority records for the descriptors **Asthma** and **Blood Pressure**:

MeSH Heading	Asthma
Tree Number	C08.127.108
Tree Number	C08.381.495.108
Tree Number	C08.674.095
Tree Number	C20.543.480.680.095
Annotation	note specifics; ASTHMA, CARDIAC see DYSPNEA, PAROXYSMAL is also available; in historical literature consider indexing "phthisic" here; "phthisis" probably goes under TUBERCULOSIS, PULMONARY
Scope Note	A form of bronchial disorder with three distinct components: airway hyper-responsiveness (RESPIRATORY HYPERSENSITIVITY), airway

	INFLAMMATION, and intermittent AIRWAY OBSTRUCTION. It is characterized by spasmodic contraction of airway smooth muscle, WHEEZING, and dyspnea (DYSPNEA, PAROXYSMAL).
Entry Term	Asthma, Bronchial
Entry Term	Bronchial Asthma
See Also	Anti-Asthmatic Agents
Allowable Qualifiers	BL CF CI CL CN CO DH DI DT EC EH EM EN EP ET GE HI IM ME MI MO NU PA PC PP PS PX RA RH RI RT SU TH UR US VE VI
Unique ID	D001249

MeSH Heading	Blood Pressure
Tree Number	E01.370.600.875.249
Tree Number	G09.330.553.400.114
Annotation	general; note specifics; "arterial" pressure = BLOOD PRESSURE and not also ARTERIES unless a specific artery; pressure within a specific vessel: coordinate vessel / physiol (IM) + BLOOD PRESSURE (NIM); do not add SYSTOLE; DIASTOLE; or PULSE unless particularly discussed; with diseases coordinate IM with disease / physiopathol (IM), not / blood (IM): Manual 23.28; blood pressure vs HYPERTENSION & HYPOTENSION: Manual 23.27+
Scope Note	PRESSURE of the BLOOD on the ARTERIES and other BLOOD VESSELS.
Entry Term	Diastolic Pressure
Entry Term	Pulse Pressure
Entry Term	Systolic Pressure
See Also	Hypertension
See Also	Hypotension
Allowable Qualifiers	DE GE IM PH RE
Unique ID	D001794

Qualifiers

A *qualifier*, formally called a *subheading*, is used to qualify a main heading by specifying one of its aspects. Qualifiers are used with descriptors to collocate those documents concerned with a particular aspect of a subject. Not every qualifier is suitable for use with every main heading. The list of Qualifiers by Allowable Category (also known as AQ list) contains sixty-two topical categories that can be used in conjunction with MeSH descriptors. The following example from the AQ list shows select allowable qualifiers under headings relating to "general drugs and chemicals":[8]

D LIST—General Drugs and Chemicals
AA /analogs
AD /admin
AE /adv eff AG /agon AI /antag AN /anal BL /blood CF /csf
CH /chem
CL /class
CS /chem syn
CT /contra
DU /diag use

Example of authority record for a qualifier (Record type = Q): **administration & dosage analysis**

Subheading	administration & dosage
Record Type	Q
Entry Version	ADMIN
Abbreviation	AD
Scope Note	Used with drugs for dosage forms, routes of administration, frequency and duration of administration, quantity of medication, and the effects of these factors.
Annotation	subhead only; for routes of administration, timing, amounts of doses; not for "dosage" in Romance languages (/analysis) ; see MeSH scope note in Introduction; indexing policy: Manual 19.8.2; DF: /admin or /AD
Online Note	search policy: Online Manual; use: main heading/AD or AD (SH) or SUBS APPLY AD
History Note	66; used with Category D 1966-90 forward
Date of Entry	19731227
Revision Date	20030722
Date Established	19660101
Unique ID	Q000008

Publication Characteristics

Qualifiers for publication characteristics, also known as type of publication, indicate what the item *is*, that is, its genre, rather than what it is *about*. Examples include the following:

Abbreviations
Abstracts
Atlases
Congresses
Directory
Handbooks
Indexes
Periodicals
Popular Works

A list of publication characteristic terms is available in *Publication Types, with Scope Notes*,[9] and these terms are also listed in Category V of the MeSH Tree Structures. The following is an example of a MeSH record for the *caricatures* publication type term:

MeSH Heading	Caricatures
Tree Number	V01.185.500
Tree Number	V02.700.074
Annotation	this heading is used as a Publication Type. Used by catalogers only; caricatures as a subject are indexed under main heading CARICATURES AS TOPIC; Publication Type CARTOONS is also available
Scope Note	Works portraying in a critical or facetious way a real individual or group, or a figure representing a social, political, ethnic, or racial type. The effect is usually achieved through distortion or exaggeration of characteristics. (Genre Terms: A Thesaurus for Use in Rare Book and Special Collection Cataloguing, 2d ed)
History Note	2008(1997)
Date of Entry	19960621
Unique ID	D019492

Geographics

Geographics include continents, regions, countries, states, and other geographic subdivisions. They are listed in Category Z of the tree structures, but do not appear in the alphabetical list. Examples include the following:

Afghanistan
Africa
Africa, Eastern
Africa, Central
Hawaii Hebrides
Honduras
Hong Kong
New South Wales
New York
New York City
New Zealand
Pacific Islands
Pacific Ocean
Rhode Island
Romania
Rome

The following is an example of a MeSH record for *Puerto Rico*:

MeSH Heading	Puerto Rico
Tree Number	Z01.107.084.900.750
Tree Number	Z01.639.880.750
Annotation	an island in the Greater Antilles in the West Indies; for Puerto Rico as a geog entity (as in epidemiol articles) & for Puerto Ricans in Puerto Rico; for Puerto Ricans living in the United States as an ethnic group, coord PUERTO RICO / ethnol (NIM) + HISPANIC AMERICANS (IM)
Scope Note	An island in the Greater Antilles in the West Indies. Its capital is San Juan. It is a self-governing commonwealth in union with the United States. It was discovered by Columbus in 1493 but no colonization was attempted until 1508. It belonged to Spain until ceded to the United States in 1898. It

	became a commonwealth with autonomy in internal affairs in 1952. Columbus named the island San Juan for St. John's Day, the Monday he arrived, and the bay Puerto Rico, rich harbor. The island became Puerto Rico officially in 1932. (From Webster's New Geographical Dictionary, 1988, p987 & Room, Brewer's Dictionary of Names, 1992, p436)
Allowable Qualifiers	EH EP
Date of Entry	19990101
Unique ID	D011647

Entry Vocabulary

There are three categories of entry vocabulary: *see* references, *see also* (or *see related*) references, and *consider also* references.

1. Entry terms, or *see references*, include cross-references from synonyms or closely related terms to descriptors. In searches, they may be used interchangeably with preferred descriptors. *See* references indicate that information related to the term in question is found under its *descriptor*, that is, the authorized term for the subject. Not all such terms are synonyms of the descriptors to which they refer. They are, however, designed to lead from a user's entry term to valid headings, and are made from synonyms, near-synonyms, abbreviations, alternate spellings, and other alternate forms. Because of their narrow focus, some terms are not useful as subject headings and are listed instead as cross-references. Examples include the following:

AORTA/radiography see **AORTOGRAPHY**
HYPERTENSION see **BLOOD PRESSURE, HIGH**
NURSERY SCHOOLS see **SCHOOLS, NURSERY**
RESPIRATORS see **VENTILATORS, MECHANICAL**
VIDINE see **CHOLINE**
BAREFOOT DOCTORS see **COMMUNITY HEALTH AIDES**

2. *See also* or *see related* references indicate the presence of other headings that relate to the topic conceptually, but do not occur in the same subcategory of the MeSH Tree Structures. *See also* references are made regularly between an organ and a procedure (e.g., **Aorta,** see also **Aortography**); between an organ and a physiological process (**Bone and Bones,** see also **Osteogenesis**); between a physiological process and a related disease (**Blood Pressure,** see also **Hypertension**); and between an organ and a drug acting on it (**Bronchi,** see also **Bronchoconstrictor Agents**).

3. *Consider also* references are used primarily with anatomical descriptors. They refer to other descriptors that relate to the topic linguistically, that is, to groups of descriptors beginning with a common stem rather than to a single descriptor, for example:

Brain	consider also terms at **CEREBR**- and **ENCEPHAL**-
Heart	consider also terms at **CARDI-** and **MYOCARDI-**
Kidney	consider also terms at **GLOMERUL-, NEPHR-, PYEL-,** and **RENAL**

MeSH Heading	Nails
Entry Term	Fingernails
Entry Term	Toenails
Consider Also	consider also terms at ONYCHO-
Entry combination	abnormalities: Nails, Malformed

In the above example, entry terms *Fingernails* and *Toenails* are not used as headings when assigning subject headings to resources to represent their topics. The heading **Nails** is used for both or either entry term(s). MeSH also recommends considering terms that start with the term onycho- , for example, Onychophagia. Last, MeSH indicates in "Entry Combination" that the qualifier *abnormalities* cannot be used with the heading Nails. Instead, the term **Nails, Malformed** should be used.

CATALOGING INSTRUCTIONS

In 1998, the NLM installed the Voyager Integrated Library System. One of the components of Voyager is LocatorPlus, NLM's OPAC. LocatorPlus is available at http://locatorplus.gov. Since then, NLM has harmonized its cataloging and indexing practices in order to facilitate cross-file searching through the NLM Gateway. The NLM also made a decision to stop using the traditional subject-heading strings on its internal bibliographic records. However, on request from many users, NLM now reconstructs heading strings on those records that are distributed to bibliographic utilities and other licensees.

In addition to LocatorPlus, NLM introduced an alternative search interface in 2004: the NLM Catalog (available at www.ncbi.nlm.nih.gov/nlmcatalog). It provides access to NLM bibliographic records for journals, books, audiovisual materials, computer software, electronic resources, and other materials. In 2010, the NLM Catalog and the Journals Database were merged, including the MEDLINE indexing information about the journals in PubMed and other NCBI databases.

MeSH's introduction, "Use of Medical Subject Headings for Cataloging,"[10] sets out specific instructions regarding its cataloging practices, including how to construct subject-heading strings. These are summarized below.

Assigning Main Headings

As is true for other controlled vocabularies, catalogers and indexers are instructed to find and use the most specific MeSH descriptor or heading that is available to represent the main focus of the work. Additional descriptors or headings may then be assigned to bring out secondary topics and to enhance access.

For example, resources concerning streptococcus pneumoniae will be found under the descriptor Streptococcus pneumoniae rather than the broader term Streptococcus, while another resource referring to a new streptococcal bacterium, which is not yet in the vocabulary, will be listed directly under Streptococcus. Accordingly, the user may consult the trees to find additional subject headings that are more specific than a given heading, and broader headings as well. For example, under Abnormalities, there are specific abnormalities:

Congenital Abnormalities C16.131
Abnormalities, Drug Induced C16.131.042
Abnormalities, Multiple C16.131.077
Congenital Abnormalities C16.131.162
Skin Abnormalities C16.131.831

Assigning Two or More Main Headings

If the topic in question contains more than one concept or facet, catalogers may employ one or more of the three following methods:

1. using two or more main headings;
2. using a precoordinated main heading;
3. using a main heading and a subheading, including topical, geographic, form, or language subheadings.

If a publication deals with two or more subjects that are subordinate to a broad heading, up to three separate, specific headings are assigned. If more than three subjects are involved, the broad heading encompassing the individual specific topics in the tree structure is assigned. If the specific subjects are not within a tree, as many specific headings as necessary are assigned.

Representation of Complex Subjects

In applying MeSH, complex subjects can be represented in three ways:

1. Postcoordination: Using two or more separate descriptors, leaving it to the searcher to infer the connection. For example, jejunal enteritis may be expressed by assigning separately the terms **Jejunum** and **Enteritis**.
2. Precoordination at the point of indexing: using qualifiers in conjunction with appropriate descriptors. For example, a deficiency of monoamine oxidase may be indexed as **Monoamine Oxidase/deficiency**. The direct linkage of the qualifier to the descriptor to which it relates avoids the possibility of false coordination that may occur if two descriptors are used to represent a single concept.
3. Precoordination in the vocabulary: MeSH includes many precoordinated descriptors for frequently encountered subjects. When a descriptor-qualifier combination is available, it is assigned in preference to using two separate descriptors. For example, if MeSH has a precoordinated descriptor such as Heart Surgery, the indexer or cataloger uses this rather than a descriptor-qualifier combination.

Assigning Precoordinated Headings

As noted earlier, if a precoordinated main heading is available, it is used instead of two or more separate headings; for example, the phrase heading **NURSING RESEARCH** takes precedence over the two separate headings **NURSING** and **RESEARCH**. However, two headings are assigned for public health research, **PUBLIC HEALTH** and **RESEARCH,** because there is no phrase heading for the topic research in public health.

Assigning Topical Subheadings

Under a particular main heading, the cataloger or indexer may assign only those topical subheadings included in the allowable qualifier list for that heading. These can be found in the MeSH heading record in the MeSH Browser.

In cataloging a particular work for which more than three topical subheadings are applicable to a given main heading, multiple headings containing the main heading and appropriate topical subheadings are assigned. When more than three topical subheadings are applicable, the main heading is assigned without topical subheadings.

Geographic Locations

In NLM's Web-based catalogs, main headings, or main heading and topical subheading combinations, are not qualified by geographic, form, or language terms. This is because geographic descriptors and publication types (PTs), previously known as form divisions, are carried in separate fields. Retrieval is accomplished postcoordinately by using either main headings or main heading/topical subheading combinations.

On the other hand, in distributed records, geographic locations are included in the subject headings, for example:

> **650** _2 **$a** Hepatitis, Viral, Human **$x** prevention & control **$z** Minnesota.
> **650** _2 **$a** Needs Assessment **$z** Minnesota.

Language

MeSH headings in the LocatorPlus record do not contain language subfields in the subject string, since this information is encoded in the MARC 21 language field (041). They are, however, included in distributed records, for example:

> **650** 12 **$a** Medicine **$v** Dictionary **$x** English.
> **650** 12 **$a** Medicine **$v** Dictionary **$x** French.

Publication Types (PTs)

PTs, formerly known as "form subheadings," are used to indicate the form of the overall publication. Not all available PTs are used in cataloging. Those that are used fall into two categories: form divisions and genres.

PTs Used as Form Divisions

These may be added as form subdivisions in a subject-heading string (MARC 21 650 subfield $v in distributed records or MARC 21 field 655 (Genre/Form) in LocatorPlus). Examples include the following:

> **Bibliography Biography Case Report**
> **Collected Works Congresses Dictionary Laboratory Manuals**
> Etc.

An example of this is:

> In LocatorPlus:
> 650 12 $a Kidney Diseases
> 655 _7 $a **Congresses** $2 mesh

On distributed records:
650 12 $a Kidney Diseases $v **Congresses**

PTs Used as Genres

These are not added to subject-heading strings, but are assigned separately in MARC 21 field 655 on distributed records and in field 659 (a locally defined field) in LocatorPlus. Examples include the following:

Academic Dissertations
Almanacs
Book Reviews
Festschrift
Newspaper article
Posters
Practical Guideline
Etc.

For example:

In LocatorPlus:
650 12 $a Renal Dialysis
659 _7 $a **Practice Guideline** $2 mesh

In distributed records:
650 12 $a Renal Dialysis
655 _7 $a **Practice Guideline** $2 mesh

Because the descriptive and coded portions of a bibliographic record contain the physical format information pertinent to each item, such information is not part of the MeSH subject string.

CATALOGING EXAMPLES

The following examples illustrate the cataloging of medical publications using MeSH headings. LC subject headings are shown for the purpose of comparison. MARC 21 encoding is also used to illustrate how MeSH headings are encoded in a MARC environment.

The respiratory system / David Petechuk. 2004
MeSH subject heading:
1. **Respiratory System**
2. **Respiratory Tract Diseases**

MARC 21 bibliographic:

650 2 $a **Respiratory System.**

650 2 $a **Respiratory Tract Diseases.**

[LC subject headings:

1. **Respiratory organs—Diseases.**
2. **Respiratory organs.**
3. **Respiration**.]

Children, ethics, and modern medicine / Richard B. Miller. 2003

MeSH subject headings:

1. **Ethics, Clinical**
2. **Pediatrics**
3. **Ethics, Medical**

MARC 21 bibliographic:

650 2 $a **Ethics, Clinical**.

650 2 $a **Pediatrics**.

650 2 $a **Ethics, Medical**.

[LC subject headings:

1. **Pediatrics—Moral and ethical aspects**.
2. **Medical ethics**.
3. **Children—Diseases—Treatment—Moral and ethical aspects**.]

Introduction to human anatomy and physiology / Eldra Pearl Solomon. 2003

MeSH subject headings:

1. **Anatomy**
2. **Physiology**

MARC 21 bibliographic:

650 2 $a **Anatomy.**

650 2 $a **Physiology.**

[LC subject headings:

1. **Human physiology**.
2. **Human anatomy**.]

Running in place: how the Medicaid model falls short, and what to do about it / Eliot Fishman. 2002

MeSH subject headings:

1. **Medicaid—organization & administration**
2. **Medicaid—economics**
3. **Models, Economic—United States**
4. **State Government—United States**

MARC 21 bibliographic:

650 2 $a **Medicaid** $x **organization & administration**.

650 2 $a **Medicaid** $x **economics**.
650 2 $a **Models, Economic** $z **United States**.
650 2 $a **State Government** $z **United States**.

[LC subject headings:

1. **Medicaid**.
2. **Medical policy—United States**.]

The psychodynamics of addiction / edited by Martin Weegmann and Robert Cohen. 2002

MeSH subject headings:

1. **Behavior, Addictive—psychology**

MARC 21 bibliographic:

650 2 $a **Behavior, Addictive** $x **psychology**.

[LC subject headings:

1. **Compulsive behavior**.
2. **Compulsive behavior—Treatment**.]

The clinical interview of the child / Stanley I. Greenspan, with Nancy Thorndike Greenspan. 2003

MeSH subject headings:

1. **Interview, Psychological—child**
2. **Interview, Psychological—infant**

MARC 21 bibliographic:

650 2 $a **Interview, Psychological** $x **child**.
650 2 $a **Interview, Psychological** $x **infant**.

[LC subject headings:

1. **Mental illness—Diagnosis**.
2. **Interviewing in child psychiatry**.
3. **Child psychology**.]

NLM records its subject terms in a "deconstructed" or faceted form. Topical terms and topical subheadings are in MARC 650 $a and $x fields, geographic terms and their topical subheadings are in MARC 651 $a and $x fields, and PTs/Genres are in MARC 655 fields.

NOTES

1. Mehnert, R., and Hoffmann, C. F. B. (1986). The National Library of Medicine. In A. Kent (Ed.), *Encyclopedia of Library and Information Science* (Vol. 41, Supp. 6). New York, NY: Marcel Dekker.

2. National Center for Biotechnology Information. (2013). *The NCBI Handbook* (2nd ed.). Bethesda, MD: National Center for Biotechnology Information. Retrieved from http://www.ncbi.nlm.nih.gov/books/NBK143764/.

3. National Library of Medicine (U.S.). (August 6, 2014a). *Medical Subject Headings: Preface.* Retrieved from http://www.nlm.nih.gov/mesh/intro_preface.html#pref_hist.

4. National Library of Medicine (U.S.). (September 8, 2014b). *Medical Subject Headings.* Retrieved from http://www.nlm.nih.gov/mesh.

5. National Library of Medicine (U.S.). (August 6, 2014c). *Medical Subject Headings: MeSH Tree Structures.* Retrieved from http://www.nlm.nih.gov/mesh/intro_trees.html.

6. Gullion, S. L. (1983). Cataloging and classification: Classification and subject cataloging. In L. Darling, D. Bishop, and L. A. Colaianni (Eds.), *Handbook of Medical Library Practice* (4th ed.). Chicago, IL: Medical Library Association.

7. National Library of Medicine (U.S.), 2014a.

8. National Library of Medicine (U.S.). (August 7, 2014d). *Medical Subject Headings: Qualifiers by Allowable Category—2015.* Retrieved from http://www.nlm.nih.gov/mesh/topcat.html.

9. National Library of Medicine (U.S.). (August 6, 2014e). *Medical Subject Headings: Publication Characteristics (Publication Types)—Scope Notes.* Retrieved from www.nlm.nih.gov/mesh/pubtypes.html.

10. National Library of Medicine (U.S.). (August 6, 2014f). *Medical Subject Headings: Use of Medical Subject Headings for Cataloging.* Retrieved from http://www.nlm.nih.gov/mesh/catpractices.html.

Part V

ORGANIZATION OF LIBRARY RESOURCES

STANDARDS AND TOOLS

Cutter, C. A., Jones, K. E., Swanson, P. K., and Swift, E. M. (1969). *Cutter–Sanborn Three-figure Author Table* (Swanson–Swift revision). Chicopee, MA: H. R. Huntting Company.

Cutter, C. A., Swanson, P. K., and Swift, E. M. (1969). *C. A. Cutter's Three-figure Author Table* (Swanson–Swift revision). Chicopee, MA: H. R. Huntting Company.

Dewey, M., and Mitchell, J. S. (2011). *Dewey Decimal Classification and Relative Index* (Ed. 23). Dublin, OH: OCLC, Online Computer Library Center, Inc.

Dewey, M., and Mitchell, J. S. (2012). *Abridged Dewey Decimal Classification and Relative Index* (Ed. 15). Dublin, OH: OCLC, Online Computer Library Center, Inc.

Library of Congress. (January 2, 2002). *Library of Congress Classification Weekly List 01.* Retrieved from http://www.loc.gov/catdir/cpso/wlc02/awlc0201.pdf.

Library of Congress. (n.d.). *Classification Web.* Retrieved from http://www.loc.gov/cds/classweb/.

Library of Congress. (n.d.). *Classification Web: World Wide Web Access to Library of Congress Classification and Library of Congress Subject Headings.* Retrieved from www.classificationweb.net/.

Library of Congress, Cataloging Distribution Service. (2014). *Cataloger's Desktop.* Retrieved from https://desktop.loc.gov/jsp/login.jsp.

Library of Congress, Cataloging Policy and Support Office. (1901–). *Classification.* Washington, DC: Library of Congress.

Library of Congress, Cataloging Policy and Support Office. (1995). *Subject Cataloging Manual: Shelflisting* (2nd ed.). Washington, DC: Library of Congress.

Library of Congress, Cataloging Policy and Support Office. (2008). *Subject Cataloging Manual: Classification* (2008 ed.). Washington, DC: Library of Congress.

National Library of Medicine (U.S.). (2014). *NLM Classification 2014.* Retrieved from www.nlm.nih.gov/class/.

OCLC, Online Computer Library Center. (2011). *Webdewey.* Retrieved from www.dewey.org/webdewey/.

RECOMMENDED READING

Broughton, V. (2004). *Essential Classification*. New York: Neal–Schuman.

Chan, L. M. (1999). *A Guide to the Library of Congress Classification* (5th ed). Englewood, CO: Libraries Unlimited.

Chan, L. M., and Mitchell, J. S. (2003). *Dewey Decimal Classification: Principles and Application* (3rd ed.). Dublin, OH: OCLC Online Computer Library Center.

Comaromi, J. P. (1976). Conception and development of the Dewey decimal classification. *International Classification,* 3, 11–15.

Comaromi, J. P. (1976). *The Eighteen Editions of the Dewey Decimal Classification*. Albany, NY: Forest Press Division, Lake Placid Education Foundation.

Comaromi, J. P. (1981). *Book Numbers: A Historical Study and Practical Guide to their Use*. Littleton, CO: Libraries Unlimited.

Dewey, M., and Mitchell, J. S. (2011). Introduction to the Dewey decimal classification. In *Dewey Decimal Classification and Relative Index* (Ed. 23) (pp. xli–xlv). Dublin, OH: OCLC, Online Computer Library Center, Inc.

Dewey, M., and Mitchell, J. S. (2012). Introduction to the Dewey decimal classification. In *Abridged Dewey Decimal Classification and Relative Index* (Ed. 15) (pp. xxxix–liv). Dublin, OH: OCLC, Online Computer Library Center, Inc.

Dunkin, P. S. (1969). Where does it go? Call numbers. In P. S. Dunkin, *Cataloging U.S.A.* (pp. 96–137). Chicago, IL: American Library Association.

Foskett, A. C. (1996). *The Subject Approach to Information* (5th ed.). London, England: Library Association.

Koch, T., and Day, M. (January 28, 1999). *The Role of Classification Schemes in Internet Resource Description and Discovery*. Retrieved from www.ukoln.ac.uk/metadata/desire/classification/.

LaMontagne, L. E. (1961). *American Library Classification with Special Reference to the Library of Congress*. Hamden, CT: Shoe String Press.

Lehnus, D. J. (1980). *Book Numbers: History, Principles, and Application*. Chicago, IL: American Library Association.

Marcella, R., and Maltby, A. (2000). *The Future of Classification*. Aldershot, England: Gower.

Mitchell, J. S., and Vizine-Goetz, D. (2007). *Moving Beyond the Presentation Layer: Content and Context in the Dewey Decimal Classification (DDC) System*. Binghamton, NY: Haworth.

Palmer, B. I. (1971). *Itself an Education: Six Lectures on Classification* (2nd ed.). London, England: Library Association.

Ranganathan, S. R., and Palmer, B. I. (1959). *Elements of Library Classification: Based on Lectures Delivered at the University of Bombay in December 1944 and in the School of Librarianship in Great Britain in December 1956* (2nd ed., revised and rewritten). London, England: Association of Assistant Librarians, Section of the Library Association.

Satija, M. P. (2013). *The Theory and Practice of the Dewey Decimal Classification System*. Oxford: Chandos Pub.

Singh, S. (2011). *The Theory and Practice of the Dewey Decimal Classification System*. New Delhi: Isha Books.

Chapter 15

Classification and Categorization

DEFINITION

Classification, broadly defined, is the process of organizing knowledge into some systematic order. It has been considered the most fundamental activity of the human mind. The essential act of classification is the multistage process of deciding on a property or characteristic of interest, distinguishing things or objects that possess that property from those that lack it, and grouping things or objects that share a common property or characteristic into a class. Other essential aspects of classification are establishing relationships among classes and making distinctions within classes to arrive at broader and finer divisions. Those who devise and use library classification schemes do much the same thing. The classification of library materials can thus be seen as a special application of a much more general human intellectual activity.

Library classification, in particular, has been defined as "the systematic arrangement by subject of books and other material on shelves or of catalogue and index entries in the manner that is most useful to those who read or who seek a definite piece of information."[1] Although this definition covers what may be done in-house to serve the needs of a specialized audience, library classification traditionally has involved labeling materials in a collection according to the provisions of an inclusive, usually hierarchically arranged, scheme. The labels, called notations, are usually found in the form of numerals or letters or a combination of both, and serve a dual function: to arrange items in a logical order on library shelves and to provide a systematic display of bibliographic entries in printed catalogs, bibliographies, and indexes. It should be noted here that "logical order" is not the same for every circumstance. In any collection, the most appropriate basis for determining groups varies according to the needs of the collection. For example, library materials may be grouped by author, physical form, size, date of publication, or subject. In modern library classification systems, subject is the predominant characteristic for grouping.

In addition to shelving and display, classification is used as a tool for collection management, for example, facilitating the creation of specialized branch libraries and the generation of discipline-specific holdings lists. In OPACs, classification also serves a direct retrieval function because class numbers can be used as access points to MARC records.

In today's teeming information world, classification may have a wider role to play, a fact that has been recognized by many in the library community. In 1999, the Association of Library Collections and Technical Services (ALCTS) Subcommittee on Metadata and Subject Analysis recommended that subject access through classification be extended to other metadata records by including class numbers, but not necessarily item numbers, from existing classification schemes in metadata records for Web resources.[2] In the same year, its related committee, the ALCTS Subcommittee on Metadata and Classification, identified seven functions of classification: location, browsing, hierarchical movement, retrieval, identification, limiting/partitioning, and profiling.[3] With the rapid growth of networked resources over the last decades, the enormous amount of information available on the Web has cried out for systematic organization. In some cases, classification systems have been called into play. Many library portals that initially offered only alphabetical listing and/or keyword searching adopted a directory approach based on broad subject categorization schemes when their collections of electronic resources became voluminous and unwieldy.[4,5] In parallel, many Web designers turned to classification as a supplementary navigational tool, so that subject categorization devices that are similar to broad classification schemes have become fairly popular among Web information providers. However, not many such devices provide the rigorous hierarchical structure and careful conceptual organization found in traditional classification schemes. In both milieus, some of the adopted schemes are based on existing classification systems, such as the DDC and the Library of Congress Classification (LCC); others are the fruit of in-house labor.

The reason for the turn toward more systematic subject control lies in the fact that subject categorization defines narrower domains within which term searching can be carried out more efficiently, and, thus, enables the retrieval of more relevant results. In fact, combining subject categorization with term searching has proven to be an effective and efficient approach in resource discovery and data mining. In this regard, classification or subject categorizing schemes function as information filters, used "to quickly eliminate large segments of a database from consideration of a query."[6] Furthermore, classification schemes can also serve as switching mechanisms across different languages and different controlled vocabularies.[7]

In the library context, *classification* as a term refers both to the development of schemes for the systematic display of all aspects of the various fields of knowledge and to the art of arranging books or other objects in conformity with such schemes. In other words, it is used both for the creation of a classification scheme and for its application. For clarity in discourse, the people who are involved in these two processes are given different names. The inventor or creator of a classification scheme or a person who is engaged in the theory of classification is called a *classificationist*, while the person who applies such a scheme is referred to as a *classifier*.

BASIC CONCEPTS

The traditional ideas of library classification were borrowed from the logical or philosophical principles of classification. Classification begins with the universe of knowledge as a whole, and divides it into successive stages of classes and subclasses with chosen characteristics, also called *facets*, as the bases for each stage. For a broad subject area, called a main class, the progression is from general to specific, forming a hierarchical or "tree" structure in which each class is a *species* of the class on the preceding level and a *genus* to the one below it. The array of classes on each level, usually mutually exclusive and totally exhaustive categories, form a coordinate relationship to one another and are collocated according to the affinity of their relationships. Classification according to hierarchical principles, with biological taxonomy as the prevailing model, was in a particularly active stage of development during the latter part of the nineteenth century. The DDC and the LCC, the most widely used library classification systems today, both originated at that time and reflect the general intellectual climate of the era. Each would be seriously out of date by now were it not for the fact that each organization, OCLC's Dewey Services and LC's Policy and Standards Division, are conscientious about undertaking revisions and issuing updates.

With a particular hierarchy, the basis for division within a class into subclasses and sub-subclasses may vary considerably from subject to subject. For example, architecture can be classified according to schools and styles, periods, or types of buildings. Literature can be divided by language, genre/form, or period. Each characteristic is called a *facet*. Figure 15.1 illustrates the division of literature in DDC based on the three facets named above.

800	Literature		
810-890	**Literatures of specific languages and language families**		
810	American literature in English		
820	English & Old English literatures		
	821	English poetry	
		821.3	Elizabethan period, 1558-1625
		821.5	Queen Anne period, 1702-1745
		821.8	Victorian period, 1837-1899
	822	English drama	
		822.3	Elizabethan period, 1558-1625
		822.5	Queen Anne period, 1702-1745
		822.8	Victorian period, 1837-1899
	823	English fiction	
	824	English essays	
	825	English speeches	
	826	English letters	
	827	English humor and satire	
	828	English miscellaneous writings	
830	German & related literatures		
840	French & related literatures		
850	Italian, Romanian & related literatures		
860	Spanish, Portuguese, Galician literatures		
870	Latin & Italic literatures		
880	Classical & modern Greek literatures		
890	Other literatures		

Figure 15.1 Division of literature in DDC.

The coordinate elements on each level or stage of division form an *array*, for example, **American literature, English literature, German literature**, and so on. The term *chain* refers to a string of subjects, each of which represents a different level in the hierarchy, for example, **Literature—English literature—English poetry—Elizabethan poetry**. There is not always a built-in or natural order of the characteristics or facets in each class. For example, although language is a natural first-order division for literature, the next divisions could be first by form and then by period, or equally reasonably the other way around; similarly, as many readers presumably would like to see Victorian novels, drama, poetry, and so on in close array as would like to see English poetry arranged chronologically. The original designers of classification systems made what they considered appropriate decisions on principles of division, class by class; then, they and their successors tried to maintain consistency within each class as to how facets were determined and developed. Order of facets is called *citation order*.

Traditional library classification schemes tend to list all subjects and their subdivisions and provide readymade symbols for them. Such a scheme is referred to as *enumerative* classification. Among existing library classification schemes, LCC is considered the most fully enumerative.

Modern classification theory, on the other hand, places emphasis on *facet analysis* and *synthesis*—the *analysis* (or breaking up) of a subject into its component parts and the *synthesis* (or reassembling) of those parts as required by the document to be represented. Instead of enumerating all subjects in a hierarchical structure, modern theory argues that a classification scheme should identify the basic components of subjects and list under each discipline, or main class, the elements or aspects that are topically important within that class. Each class has its own class-specific *facets*. For instance, the class Education might have a facet for Persons Taught, a facet for Subjects Taught, a facet for Educators, a facet for Methods of Instruction, a facet for Educational Institutions, and so on. In addition, recurring or common facets, such as form divisions, geographical divisions, and chronological divisions, are listed separately for application to all classes. In applying such a scheme, the act of classification essentially consists of identifying appropriate component facets and synthesizing (i.e., combining) them according to a predetermined *citation formula*. A system based on these principles is called a *faceted* or *analytico-synthetic classification*. An example is the Colon Classification (CC).[8]

Some classification systems provide minute details under each class or subject, while others provide broad subject divisions only. The former are referred to as close classification, and the latter as broad *classification*.

NOTATION

Each classification scheme adopts a system of symbols to represent its classes and divisions. The purpose of such a device, called *notation*, is to furnish a brief designation of subjects (and sometimes their relationships as well) and to provide a sequential order for arrangement of library materials, particularly for shelf location.

In some classification systems, the notation consists of all letters; in others, all numbers; and in still others, a combination of both. A *pure notation* is one in which only one type of symbol is used: an example is the notation of DDC, which consists of Arabic numerals. A system that employs more than one type of symbol is called a *mixed notation*: an example is the combined letters and Arabic numerals in the notation of LCC.

A *hierarchical notation* is one that reflects the structural order or hierarchy of the classification, while an *expressive notation* is one that expresses relationships among coordinate subjects. The notation used with DDC is hierarchical, and that of the Universal Decimal Classification (UDC) is both hierarchical and expressive. The notation of LCC is neither. Another feature of some notation schemes is internal *mnemonics*, or aids to memory. In this context, the term means that when a given topic recurs in the scheme, it is represented consistently by the same symbol. For example, in DDC, poetry is represented by the number *1*, hence, 81*1* (American poetry), 83*1* (German poetry), 84*1* (French poetry), and so on. Correspondingly, *3* often pertains to Germany, and *4* to France.

COMPONENTS OF A CLASSIFICATION SCHEME

A classification scheme consists typically of the following components:

Schedule: the entire sequence of class numbers and captions arranged in class number order;

Tables: consisting of additional numbers used in conjunction with numbers from the schedule;

Index: a list of index terms with corresponding class numbers; and

Additional documentation: an introduction, a manual, a set of instructions on use, a glossary, etc.

HOW TO CLASSIFY

Classifying and assigning subject headings both begin with the same intellectual process: determining the subject content and identifying the principal concepts in the work under consideration. This process was described in the chapter on subject cataloging. Much of what was said in that chapter applies here, but the two processes are not fully parallel. One difference, of course, is that while in subject cataloging the content of a work is represented by verbal terms, in classification it is captured by notation (based, of course, on verbal terms in classification schedules) that carries the meaning. A more important difference is that, because in American libraries classification was traditionally used mainly as a shelving or location device, only one class number is chosen for each work; in subject cataloging, on the other hand, any number of subject headings may be assigned to a work. (Of course, where classification is considered a major retrieval device, as in libraries with a classed catalog or bibliographies arranged by classification numbers, two or more different classification numbers may also be assigned to a given work, with one of them being used as an indication of shelf location.)

Choosing a Number: General Guidelines

If the subject, or overall content, of the work in hand focuses on a clearly defined topic, classifying it is a relatively simple operation. One needs simply to choose the appropriate number from the scheme being used. However, a work may deal with more than one topic, or more than one aspect of a topic: different topics may be treated together as parts of a broader topic; they may be brought together by the author because they are affinitive topics considered separately; they may be treated in terms of their relationship to each other; or, finally, they may be treated from an interdisciplinary point of view. Faceted classification schemes such as the UDC or CC provide for combining class numbers to bring out every topic or aspect treated in a multitopical work. However, such combinations are not always possible with traditional schemes such as DDC or LCC; classifiers working in traditional situations often have to choose one number from two or more numbers that represent the different topics or aspects treated in the work.

The use of each classification system involves certain unique procedures, and, for DDC, LCC, and the NLM classification, these procedures are discussed in detail in later chapters. The following discussion focuses on some of the general principles and guidelines that apply to the classification of library resources in general.

1. Consider Usefulness

When a work can be classed in more than one number in a scheme, consider where it will be most useful to the users.

2. Make Topic the Primary Consideration

Topic should be mainly considered when the classification scheme allows alternatives, in general, class by topic, then by place, time, and form, except in literature, where language and literary form are what matter most.

3. Use the Most Specific Number Available

Class a work in the most specific number that will contain it. There may not be an exact number for every topic encountered, however. When there is no specific number for the work, place it in the next most specific category above it, depending on which scheme is used. For example, classify a history of Chicago in the number for Chicago, if available; if not, place it in the number for the next larger geographic unit, that is, the county, state, or country for which the scheme makes provision.

4. Do Not Classify from the Index Alone

The index or indexes that accompany each classification scheme provide help in locating specific class numbers. However, the chosen number should always be checked in the schedules to ensure that the topic of the work being classified has been placed properly in the overall structure of the scheme and that the instructions in the schedules restricting or elaborating the use of the number have been observed.

Choosing a Number: Multitopical Works

There is no hard and fast rule for the choice of a number for a multitopical work. The following guidelines[9,10,11] are generally applicable.

1. Determine the Dominant Topic or the Phase Relations

Dominant Topic. Classify under the dominant topic, if one can be determined. If the topics are treated separately, a ready indication of preponderance may be the amount of space devoted to each. Another gauge is the author's apparent intention or purpose.

Phase Relations. The situation with a work in which the different topics are viewed in relationship to each other is more complicated. In such a case, an analysis of the relationship may help to determine the emphasis of the work. The interrelationships among topics treated in a work known as *Phase relations* were discussed earlier in the chapter on subject cataloging. In classification, the following considerations apply:

Influence Phase. Classify a work about the influence of one thing or person on another under the topic or person being influenced.

Bias Phase. Classify a work on a particular subject written with a "bias" toward, or aimed at, a specific group of readers (e.g., *Fundamentals of Physical Chemistry for Premedical Students)* under the topic (physical chemistry), not the element to which it is "biased" (premedical or medical sciences).

Tool or Application Phase. Classify a work such as *Chemical Calculations: An Introduction to the Use of Mathematics in Chemistry* under the topic (chemistry) instead of the tool (mathematics).

Comparison Phase. Classify under the topic emphasized or under the first topic.

Note: It should be stressed that the preceding are only *general* guidelines. If a work on the influence of one topic or one person on another clearly places emphasis on the topic or person exerting the influence, it should be classed with that topic or person. Similarly, if a work on a topic written for a specific group of readers is of little value to other readers, it should be classed under the number reflecting the intended readers.

2. Class under First Topic

If the dominant topic cannot be ascertained—for instance, when works treating two or three topics separately or in comparison do not give any indication of preponderance—class under the first topic treated, unless instructed otherwise in the scheme. In DDC, *first* means the one coming first in the schedules. For example, a work dealing equally with Judaism (296) and Islam (297) would be placed in 296. Without such specific instructions, *first* may mean the topic treated first in the work.

3. Class under Broader Topic

Class under the broader topic a work dealing with two or three topics that are subdivisions of a broader topic and that together constitute the major portion of that topic, for instance, choosing the number for classical languages for a work about Greek and Latin. Likewise, for a work dealing with four or more topics, all of which are divisions of a broader topic, class under the number that covers them all; for example, use the number for chemistry (540) for a work about physical (541), analytical (543), inorganic (546), and organic (547) chemistry.

CALL NUMBERS

To distinguish individual bibliographic items on the same subject, an *item number* (also called *book number*) is added to the class number to form a "call number" as a location symbol for the item in the library's collection. The term "call number" probably originated from the fact that in the earlier days most libraries had closed stacks, and a library user would have to "call" for a book from the collection by means of its unique number.

Many libraries have adopted the principle of unique call numbers. In this practice, each item in the library is assigned a number different from any other call number in the collection. In this sense, the call number serves as the true address of the item. The call number consists of the class number followed by one or more elements based on the bibliographic characteristics of the item, such as the author's name, the title, the edition, the date of publication, the volume number, and suchlike.

There are various ways of composing a call number, depending on the size of the collection and the classification system used. The procedures for assigning call numbers are discussed in the following chapters on individual classification schemes.

MARC CODING FOR CLASSIFICATION AND ITEM NUMBERS

In *MARC 21 Format for Bibliographic Data*, the following fields contain data relating to call numbers based on classification systems discussed in this book:

050 Library of Congress call number
Indicators:
First—Existence in LC collection
(blank) No information provided
A call number assigned by an organization other than LC
0 Item is in LC
1 Item is not in LC
Second—Source of call number
0 Assigned by the Library of Congress (LC)
4 Assigned by agency other than LC
Subfield codes:
$a Classification number (R)
$b Item number (NR)
$3 Materials specified (NR) The part of the described materials to which the field applies
$6 Linkage (NR)
$8 Field link and sequence number (R)

060 National Library of Medicine (NLM) call number
Indicators:
First—Existence in NLM collection
(blank) No information provided
A call number assigned by an organization other than LC
0 Item is in NLM
1 Item is not in NLM
Second—Source of call number
0 Assigned by NLM
4 Assigned by agency other than NLM
Subfield codes:
$a Classification number (R)
$b Item number (NR)
$8 Field link and sequence number (R)

080 Universal Decimal Classification number
Indicators:
First—Type of edition
0 Full edition
1 Abridged edition

Second—Source of call number
(blank) No information provided
0 Assigned by LC
4 Assigned by agency other than LC
Subfield codes:
$a Classification number (R)
$b Item number (NR)
$x Common auxiliary subdivision (R)
$2 Edition number (NR)
$6 Linkage (NR)
$8 Field link and sequence number (R)

082 Dewey Decimal call number
Indicators:
First—Type of edition
0 Full edition
1 Abridged edition
Second—Undefined
(blank) Undefined
Subfield codes:
$a Classification number (R)
$b Item number (NR)
$2 Edition number (NR)
$6 Linkage (NR)
$8 Field link and sequence number (R)

090-099 Local call numbers

MODERN LIBRARY CLASSIFICATION SYSTEMS

Many library classification systems have been developed in modern times, some for general collections and others for specialized subject collections. The following chapters discuss in detail the major systems used by American libraries and make brief presentations of the salient characteristics of a number of other classification systems and of information on their conception and development.

NOTES

1. Maltby, A. (1975). *Sayers' Manual of Classification for Librarians* (5th ed.). London, England: Andre Deutsch (p. 15).

2. ALCTS/CCS/SAC/Subcommittee on Metadata and Subject Analysis. (1999). *Subject Data in the Metadata Record: Recommendations and Rationale.* Retrieved from http://www.ala.org/alcts/resources/org/cat/subjectdata_record.

3. ALCTS/CCS/SAC/Subcommittee on Metadata and Classification. (1999). *Final Report.* Retrieved from www.ala.org/alcts/mgrps/camms/cmtes/sac/inact/metadataandclass/metadataclassification.

4. Waldhart, T. J., Miller, J. B., and Chan, L. M. (2000). Provision of local assisted access to selected internet information resources by ARL academic libraries. *Journal of Academic Librarianship, 26*(2), 100–09.

5. Korfhage, R. R. (1997). The matching process. In *Information Storage and Retrieval.* New York: Wiley (pp. 79–104).

6. Chan, L. M. (2001). Exploiting LCSH, LCC, and DDC to retrieve networked resources. In A. M. Sandberg-Fox (Ed.), *Proceedings of the Bicentennial Conference on Bibliographic Control for the New Millennium: Confronting the Challenges of Networked Resources and the Web.* Washington, DC: Library of Congress (p. 164).

7. Chan (2001), p. 164.

8. Ranganathan, S. R. (1963). *Colon Classification* (6th ed., reprinted with amendments). Bombay, India: Asia Publishing House.

9. Dewey, M., and Mitchell, J. S. (2011). Introduction to the Dewey decimal classification. In *Dewey Decimal Classification and Relative Index* (Ed. 23) (pp. xli–xlv). Dublin, OH: OCLC, Online Computer Library Center, Inc.

10. Dunkin, P. S. (1969). *Cataloging U.S.A.* Chicago, IL: American Library Association (pp. 116–22).

11. Merrill, W. S. (1939). *Code for Classifiers* (2nd ed.). Chicago, IL: American Library Association (pp. 3–7).

Chapter 16

Dewey Decimal Classification

HISTORY

The Beginning

In 1876, the publication of a pamphlet entitled *A Classification and Subject Index for Cataloguing and Arranging the Books and Pamphlets of a Library* marked the beginning of the DDC, which was soon adopted by many libraries in the United States and later by libraries around the world. Today, in its twenty-third edition (2011), the DDC is the most widely used library classification system in the world.[1] The scheme has been translated into more than thirty languages, including Arabic, Chinese, French, German, Greek, Hebrew, Icelandic, Italian, Korean, Norwegian, Russian, Spanish, Swedish, and Vietnamese. It is used in more than 20,000 libraries in 135 countries. In the United States, DDC users include academic, public, special, and school libraries.

DDC was conceived as a classification of knowledge for the purpose of organizing a library. Melvil Dewey (1851–1931), the founder of the system named after him, was an assistant librarian at Amherst College when he developed the scheme. In the Preface to the first edition (1876), Dewey states that the system was developed early in 1873, as a result of several months' study of some hundreds of books and pamphlets and of over fifty personal visits to various American libraries.

The 1876 edition, consisting of merely forty-four pages and published anonymously, contains a brief Preface outlining Dewey's principles, the schedules for ten main classes subdivided decimally to form a total of 1,000 categories numbered 000–999, and an alphabetical subject index. The division of the main classes was based on an earlier classification system (1870)

Table 16.1 Classification Systems of Bacon, Harris, and Dewey

Bacon		*Harris*	*Dewey*
[Original]	*[Inverted]*		
		Science	
History (Memory)	Philosophy	Philosophy Religion Social and political science Natural sciences and useful art	General works Philosophy Religion Sociology Philology Science Useful arts
		Art	
Poesy (Imagination)	Poesy	Fine arts Poetry Pure fiction Literary miscellany	Fine arts Literature
		History	
Philosophy (Reason)	History	Geography and travel Civil history Biography	History Biography
		Appendix	
		Miscellany	

devised by W. T. Harris, who, in turn, had based his scheme on an inverted order of Francis Bacon's classification of knowledge.[2] Bacon divides knowledge into three basic categories (history, poesy, and philosophy), corresponding to the three basic faculties of the human mind (memory, imagination, and reason). The classifications of Bacon, Harris, and Dewey are compared in Table 16.1.

In his new classification scheme, Dewey introduced two new features: relative location and relative index. Prior to Dewey's publication, books in libraries were numbered according to the chronological order in which they were acquired, and that order determined their locations on the shelves. Such a practice meant that each book had a fixed location. The Dewey system, on the other hand, numbers books in terms of their relationship to one another, without regard to the shelves or rooms where they are placed. Relative location allows infinite interposition; new and reclassified books can be placed with others on the same subject. In the relative index, Dewey brings together, under one term, the locations in the scheme of a subject that, in many cases, fall in several fields of study and are scattered under different numbers.

Early Editions

The second edition (1885) of DDC, a considerable expansion from the 1876 edition, contained a number of relocations—that is, shifts of subjects from certain numbers to other numbers. This edition set the notational pattern for all subsequent editions. It was also in this edition that Dewey laid down his famous injunction of the "integrity of numbers." Being a pragmatist and a realist, Dewey was fully aware that a system that changed substantially from edition to edition would not be acceptable to librarians, because changes, particularly relocations, necessitate reclassification—a labor-intensive operation. Therefore, in the Preface to the second edition, Dewey declared that the numbers may be considered "settled," and henceforth there would be expansions when necessary, but as few relocations as possible. This policy had a stabilizing effect on subsequent revisions of DDC, particularly in the early editions. Nonetheless, in order to cope with new developments in knowledge, certain major changes could not be avoided.

Dewey himself supervised DDC revision through its thirteenth edition, working until his death in 1931. His interest in simplified spelling was reflected in the early schedules, for example, Filosofy and Geografy.

The fourteenth edition followed the editorial policies that had governed work on earlier editions: expansion in detail as required, but little change in basic structure. The expansion, however, had not always been balanced, and there were many underdeveloped areas.

Fifteenth Edition

With the fifteenth edition, it was decided that a new approach was necessary in order to give the scheme a more even structure and to keep up with new developments in knowledge, particularly in science and technology. Several innovations were introduced: details were cut back until all subjects reflected more or less equal degrees of subdivision; a large number of subjects were relocated; the index was pruned drastically; and the simplified spelling used in earlier editions was discontinued. The magnitude of the changes was considerable, for instance, some 31,000 entries in the fourteenth edition were reduced to 4,700 in the fifteenth edition.

After the publication of the fifteenth edition in 1951, it soon became clear that the changes were too much for practicing librarians, most of who refused to accept the new edition and continued to use the fourteenth. Criticism of the fifteenth edition was fierce and vehement. Many critics even pronounced the system "dead."

Sixteenth Edition and Later Editions

The sixteenth edition, under the editorship of Benjamin A. Custer, appeared in 1958. This edition reflected a return to the former policy of detailed enumeration, but incorporated some of the innovative features of the fifteenth edition, such as standard spelling, current terminology, and a pleasing typographical presentation.

The seventeenth through nineteenth editions, also under the editorship of Custer, continued to develop along similar lines. Attempts were made to keep pace with knowledge while maintaining "integrity of numbers" to the greatest reasonable extent.

Edition 20, under the editorship of John P. Comaromi, assisted by Julianne Beall, Winton E. Matthews, Jr., and Gregory R. New, appeared in 1989. The classification, by then, had grown into a four-volume set. A classifiers' manual, which was first issued as a separate publication after the appearance of Edition 19, was incorporated into Edition 20, following the index. Edition 21, begun under the leadership of Comaromi and continued under the editorship of Joan S. Mitchell, appeared in 1996. Edition 22 was published in 2003 and Edition 23 in 2011. Among the topics updated in Edition 23 include Orthodox Church and Islam in the Religion class, graphic and decorative arts in the Fine Arts class, and computer science in the Computer science, knowledge & systems class.

Under the direction of Mitchell, DDC underwent considerable internationalization, resulting in the adoption and translation of the scheme into many languages around the world. In recent editions, American biases in the treatment of certain subjects such as religion and law have been gradually removed to render the system more useful and useable outside of the United States.

PUBLICATION OF THE CLASSIFICATION

Versions of DDC

The DDC is issued in two versions: full and abridged.[3] After the publication of the second edition of DDC in 1885, it became obvious that a short form of the classification would be better suited to the needs of small and slowly growing libraries. Accordingly, an abridged edition of the scheme, about two-fifths the size of the full edition, was issued in 1894. In the beginning, the abridged edition was revised when the need arose; later, it was considered desirable to follow each full edition with an abridged edition. The present abridged Edition 15 (2012) accompanies the full Edition 23 (2011).

From its first appearance, the abridged edition has been designed specifically for small collections: the elementary and secondary school libraries, small public libraries with collections not expected to grow beyond 20,000 titles, and other relatively small collections of a general nature. It is used by most of the school libraries and many small libraries in the United States, and is also widely used in other countries, particularly in Great Britain, Canada, and Australia.

The numbers in the abridged version are based on those in the full edition. They are shorter and do not represent the complexities of topics to the extent expressed by the full numbers.

Formats of DDC Schedules

Until 1993, DDC was published in a print format only. Since then, it has been issued in electronic forms as well. WebDewey, the current electronic format, was based on two earlier versions of machine-readable DDC: Electronic Dewey (a DOS version) and Dewey for Windows. The current Web-based version was first released by OCLC in 2000, and was available through "OCLC Connexion," the interface for online cataloging at OCLC. Currently, WebDewey is a parallel of the full Edition 23, but is updated continuously, and the Abridged WebDewey contains the content of abridged Edition 15. Both are available through OCLC Connexion and the WebDewey interface, available at www.dewey.org.[4]

REVISION

Current Procedures for Revision

An editorial team, consisting of the Editor-in-Chief and assistant editors, oversees, and is responsible for, DDC revision. The editorial office is a part of the Bibliographic Access Divisions at the LC. OCLC, the publisher of DDC, has a contractual arrangement with the LC for the editorial work. Between these two organizations is a group called the Decimal Classification Editorial Policy Committee, composed of practicing librarians and library educators, which advises both the editors and OCLC concerning matters relating to the revision of DDC; the Committee examines proposed revisions and makes appropriate recommendations. The DDC editorial office is located in the Decimal Classification Division at the LC, which is responsible for assigning DDC numbers to LC cataloging records. The close proximity of the editorial staff and DDC classifiers ensures consistency and a great degree of coordination between the revision and the application of the system.

The print version of DDC was issued at approximately seven- to ten-year intervals. DDC 23 is the last edition to be published in print. Between the publications of the editions, the schedules and tables are regularly reexamined. Revisions of existing numbers and index entries, and provisions for new subjects, are made as required. This policy, called "continuous revision," was adopted after the publication of Edition 19 in order to ensure currency of the scheme. Results of continuing editorial work are incorporated into WebDewey immediately.

Forms of Revision

Revisions usually take the following forms:

Expansion

This method is used to introduce new subjects as well as to provide more minute and specific subdivisions under existing subjects. The numerical notational system of DDC is such that new subjects can only be introduced as subdivisions under existing subjects. This is a reasonable approach since new subjects seldom emerge totally independent of existing knowledge, but usually appear as an offspring or outgrowth of an existing field. For existing knowledge, as library material proliferates, more minute subdivisions of existing topics are also required.

Reduction and Discontinuation

Occasionally, existing subdivisions that are rarely used are discontinued, and the subtopics are classed with the more general topic. In rare cases, a table or an entire section in the schedule may be eliminated. In Edition 22, for instance, the entire Table 7 Persons was removed in favor of direct use of notation already available in the schedules and in notation -08 from Table 1. The class number 607.22 representing the topic technology historical research in Edition 22 was discontinued and the topic was included in the broader number for technology research, 607.2 in Edition 23.

Relocation

In each edition, a number of existing topics are moved to different locations (i.e., numbers) in the scheme. Relocation is usually an attempt to meet one of the following goals:

1. To eliminate dual provisions when two or more numbers have the same meaning or overlap to a large extent. For example, before Edition 22, the topic Motion pictures, radio, television was represented by both 306.485 and 302.234. In Edition 22, 306.485 was eliminated; all material on the subject is now classed in 302.234. All topics in Table 2 -992 of Edition 22 were relocated to -9952 in Edition 23.
2. To make room for new subjects when there is no available number. For example, in Edition 18 of DDC, Antarctica was moved from the area notation -99 to -989 in order that -99 could be used for Extraterrestrial worlds. In general, a number vacated as a result of relocation is not reused until

a later edition. However, in this case, the urgency to accommodate the Extraterrestrial worlds outweighed this policy of "starvation."

3. To provide uniformity of development for parallel subjects.
4. To reflect realignment of fields of knowledge. A new subject that had been introduced as a subdivision under an existing subject may turn out to belong more properly in a different field of knowledge. For example, Astronautics, which was originally placed in 629.1388 (as a subdivision under Aeronautics) was moved to 629.4 (as one of the "other branches" of engineering).
5. To rectify an improper placement by moving the topic to where it more accurately belongs. For example, in Edition 18, Yiddish language and literature, formerly in 492.49 and 892.49 (as subdivisions of Hebraic languages and literature), respectively, were relocated to 437.947 and 839.09 (as branches of Germanic languages and literatures), respectively.

Extensive Revisions

In each edition, selected classes, divisions, or sections undergo extensive revision. The main outline remains basically the same, but selected portions are reworked and expansions are provided for new topics. Examples include 370 Education, 580 (Plants (Botany)), and 590 (Animals (Zoology)) in Edition 21. Class 200 Religion was revised extensively during a two-edition span (Editions 21 and 22) in order to reduce Christian biases.

Completely Revised Schedules

A completely revised schedule, previously called a "phoenix schedule," represents the most drastic form of revision. With this method, an entire schedule, such as 780 (Music) in Edition 20 and 340 (Law) in Edition 18, is reconstructed without regard to previous divisions. The policy of integrity of numbers is suspended, and the editors are not hampered by notational constriction in rearranging existing subjects and inserting new subjects. As a result, massive relocations occur within that schedule. In recent editions, the following schedules have been revised completely:

301-307	(Sociology), 324 (The political process), and -41 and -42 (area notation for Great Britain in Table 2) in Edition 19
780	(Music) and -711 (area notation for British Columbia in Table 2) in Edition 20
570	(Biology and life sciences) in Edition 21

There is no completely revised schedule in Edition 22 or 23.

New Schedules

Occasionally, the schedule for a particular subject is completely reworked and moved to a new location, so that there is no conflict with the old schedule. An example of a new schedule is the 004-006 (Data processing and Computer science) revision that was developed and published separately between Editions 19 and 20. The new schedule was eventually incorporated into Edition 20.

BASIC PRINCIPLES

Classification by Discipline

To say that classification groups together materials on the same subject is an oversimplification. In fact, both the DDC and the LCC, the two major systems in use in the United States, are classifications by discipline. The division of main classes and subclasses is based on academic disciplines, or fields of study, rather than on subject. Such division means that the same subject may be classed in more than one place in the scheme. For example, the subject "family," depending on the author's approach and perspective, may be classed in ethics, religion, sociology, social customs, family planning, home economics, or genealogy.

In DDC, knowledge was initially divided into ten main classes that mirrored the recognized academic divisions of Dewey's time: General works, Philosophy, Theology, Sociology (later Social sciences), Philology, Natural science, Useful arts, Fine arts, Literature, and History (see Table 16.1). Some of these are not considered disciplines today, but rather areas of study, each of which includes several academic disciplines. Based on the curriculum of a modern university, one would group such fields as Philosophy, Languages, Fine arts, and Literature as disciplines under the area of Humanities, in parallel with other areas of study such as Social sciences and Physical sciences, each of which also contains various disciplines. In DDC, however, Philosophy, Languages, Literature, etc., remain as coordinate subjects with Social sciences, Pure sciences, and Technology/Applied sciences. This fact alone makes the scheme somewhat uneven in the extent to which its basic organization of knowledge matches what prevails in the world today. Furthermore, over the last hundred years, the advancement of knowledge in different fields has varied considerably in both quantity and velocity, so that some classes, such as 100 Philosophy and 400 Language, have remained fairly stable throughout successive editions while others, such as 500 Science and 600 Technology, have undergone tremendous development and expansion. Thus, disparity in treatment from class to class has been compounded. Table 16.2 shows the current distribution of topics over the system.

Table 16.2 Outline of DDC, Second Summary

Second Summary *The Hundred Divisions*			
000	Computer science, knowledge & systems	500	Science
010	Bibliographies	510	Mathematics
020	Library & information sciences	520	Astronomy
030	Encyclopedia & books of facts	530	Physics
040	[Unassigned]	540	Chemistry
050	Magazines, journals & serials	550	Earth sciences & geology
060	Associations, organizations & museums	560	Fossils & prehistoric life
070	News media, journalism & publishing	570	Biology
080	Quotations	580	Plants (Botany)
090	Manuscripts & rare books	590	Animals (Zoology)
100	Philosophy	600	Technology
110	Metaphysics	610	Medicine & health
120	Epistemology	620	Engineering
130	Parapsychology & occultism	630	Agriculture
140	Philosophical schools of thought	640	Home & family management
150	Psychology	650	Management & public relations
160	Philosophical logic	660	Chemical engineering
170	Ethics	670	Manufacturing
180	Ancient, medieval & eastern philosophy	680	Manufacture for specific uses
190	Modern western philosophy	690	Construction of buildings
200	Religion	700	Arts
210	Philosophy & theory of religion	710	Area planning & landscape architecture
220	The Bible	720	Architecture
230	Christianity	730	Sculpture, ceramics & metalwork
240	Christian practice & observance	740	Graphic arts & decorative arts
250	Christian pastoral practice & religious orders	750	Painting
260	Christian organization, social work & worship	760	Printmaking & prints
270	History of Christianity	770	Photography, computer art, film, video
280	Christian denominations	780	Music
290	Other religions	790	Sports, games & entertainment
300	Social sciences, sociology & anthropology	800	Literature, rhetoric & criticism
310	Statistics	810	American literature in English
320	Political science	820	English & Old English literatures
330	Economics	830	German & related literatures
340	Law	840	French & related literatures
350	Public administration & military science	850	Italian, Romanian & related literatures
360	Social problems & social services	860	Spanish & Portuguese, Galician literatures

Table 16.2 Outline of DDC, Second Summary *(cont...)*

Second Summary *The Hundred Divisions*			
370	Education	870	Latin & Italic literatures
380	Commerce, communications & transportation	880	Classical & modern Greek literatures
390	Customs, etiquette & folklore	890	Other literatures
400	Language	900	History
410	Linguistics	910	Geography & travel
420	English & Old English languages	920	Biography & genealogy
430	German & related languages	930	History of ancient world (to ca. 499)
440	French & related languages	940	History of Europe
450	Italian, Romanian & related languages	950	History of Asia
460	Spanish & Portuguese, Galician	960	History of Africa
470	Latin & Italic languages	970	History of North America
480	Classical & modern Greek languages	980	History of South America
490	Other languages	990	History of other areas

Consult schedules for complete and exact headings.
Source: Dewey decimal classification, Edition 23 (retrieved from Web Dewey) or DDC 23 (Web Dewey)

Structural Hierarchy

Each of the ten *main classes* is divided into ten *divisions*, and each division is divided into ten *sections*, with further subdivisions made as required. Each level, divided on a base of ten because of the notational system, is subordinate to the level above it, thus forming a hierarchical structure that progresses from the general to the specific. The ten main classes (Edition 23) include the following:

000 Computer science, information & general works
100 Philosophy & psychology
200 Religion
300 Social sciences
400 Language
500 Science
600 Technology
700 Arts & recreation
800 Literature
900 History & geography

In general, arrangement is first by discipline, then by subject (with various levels of subject subdivisions), then by geographic and/or period specification, and then by form of presentation. Exceptions to this pattern are found in Literature (800) and in History (900). In the 800 class, arrangement of belles-lettres is first by the discipline (literature), then by original language, then by literary form, and then by period of composition. In the 900 class, geography and history of individual continents are arranged first by place, then by period, topic, and form.

NOTATION SYMBOLS

Dewey adopted a pure notation based on Arabic numerals: each topic in the scheme is represented by a number expressed in Arabic numerals only, with decimal expansion as needed, for example, 030, 150, 346.73046956, and so on. Such a notation has the advantages of being widely recognized and of transcending most language barriers.

Main classes and divisions in DDC are organized around a base of ten, a characteristic of the Arabic numeral system. Main classes are numbered 0 through 9, as shown in Table 16.2. Further divisions and subdivisions follow the decimal principle, for example:

5 Science
51 Mathematics
52 Astronomy and allied sciences
53 Physics
54 Chemistry and allied sciences
etc.

For such numbers to be considered sequential, there must be a leading decimal. However, to make its notation easier to grasp, DDC uses three-digit numbers for its main classes, for the divisions of main classes, and for major sections of those divisions; zeros are put in as fillers in the numbers for main classes, so each contains at least three digits. Thus, we have 500 for the main class Science, and 510 for one of its major branches, Mathematics. When more than three digits are needed to specify a topic, a decimal point is placed after the third digit, giving numbers such as 512.56 and 512.546. In sequential arrangement and shelving, as decimal numbers, 512.546 precedes 512.56.

Notational Hierarchy

The DDC notation reflects the hierarchical order of the classification, showing the relationship between each level of knowledge and its superordinate and subordinate elements. Each of the ten main classes is divided into ten divisions represented by the second position in the notation. Thus, in 500 (Sciences & mathematics), 510 through 590 are used for the major branches of science, for example, 510 (Mathematics), 520 (Astronomy & allied sciences), 530 (Physics), 540 (Chemistry & allied sciences), and so on. Each division, in turn, is divided into ten sections, represented by the number in the third position of the notation, for example:

510	Mathematics
511	General principles of mathematics
512	Algebra
513	Arithmetic
514	Topology
540	Chemistry and allied sciences
541	Physical chemistry
542	Techniques, procedures, apparatus, equipment, and materials
543	Analytical chemistry

The system allows further subdivision into various degrees of specificity by means of a continued decimal notation. The decimal point is always placed after the third digit, followed by as many digits as required by the subject matter. The notation never *ends* with a zero after the decimal point, since a terminal zero after a decimal point has no value.

As the classification progresses from the general to the specific, each level of division is indicated by the addition of one new digit. The following example illustrates the hierarchical structure present in both the notation and the classificatory categories, carried to three digits beyond the decimal point:

500	Natural sciences and mathematics
510	Mathematics
516	Geometry
516.3	Analytic geometries
516.37	Metric differential geometries
516.375	Finsler geometry

There are, however, a few exceptions to the hierarchical structure, as is the case for Life Science, Biology (570), Plants (Botany) (580), and Animals (Zoology) (590); most scientists would consider it more reasonable to make botany and zoology subtopics under biology rather than coordinate topics. Nevertheless, the intention, in general, is that the classificatory structure be hierarchical and, as such, be reflected in the notation.

Mnemonics

In assigning numbers to subjects, the Dewey system frequently uses consistent numbers for recurring subjects. For example, Italy is regularly represented by the notation 5, which recurs in numbers related to that country: 945 (History of Italy); 914.5 (Description of Italy); 450 (Italian language); 554.5 (Geology of Italy); 195 (Italian philosophy); and 035 (General encyclopedic works in the Italian language). In literature, the number 1 represents poetry, thus, 821 (English poetry); 851 (Italian poetry); 895.11 (Chinese poetry); etc. This device helps readers memorize or recognize class numbers more easily. Furthermore, it has enabled the system to develop from an enumerative system to a more nearly analytico-synthetic scheme in which many elements in a class number can be readily isolated and identified.

In the earlier editions, the mnemonic device was used most prominently in the following areas: form divisions, geographical divisions, languages, and literature. As the analytico-synthetic nature of the system increased, the mnemonic device became standard practice for some aspects of the system.

Enumeration versus Synthesis

DDC began as a basically enumerative system, in that the numbers for individual subjects, including compound and complex subjects, were listed as such in the scheme. In the second edition, however, the table for form divisions was introduced; also, there was the provision that certain numbers in the scheme were to be divided like certain other numbers, particularly those pertaining to geographic subdivision. Thus, a limited amount of synthesis, or number building, existed from the early editions.

In Edition 17, an areas table for geographic subdivisions was introduced. Then, in Edition 18, more tables were added. The tables provide numbers for frequently occurring subtopics or aspects that may be used with base numbers representing main topics throughout the schedules.

EVALUATION

A great deal has been written about the merits and the weaknesses of the DDC. Following is a brief summary of some of the opinions.

Merits

1. The DDC is a practical system. The fact that it has survived many storms in more than 130 years, and is still the most widely used classification scheme in the world today, attests to its practical value.
2. Relative location was an innovation introduced by Dewey, even though it is now taken for granted.
3. The relative index brings together different aspects of the same subject scattered in different disciplines.

4. The pure notation of Arabic numerals is universally recognizable. People from any cultural or language background can adapt to the system easily.
5. The self-evident numerical sequence facilitates display and shelving.
6. The hierarchical nature of the notation expresses the relationships between and among the class numbers. This characteristic particularly facilitates online searching and browsing. The searcher can broaden or narrow a search by reducing or adding a digit to the class number.
7. The classification structure and notation progresses from the general to the specific and renders the scheme particularly suitable for organizing electronic resources for browsing and navigating.
8. The use of the decimal numbering system enables infinite expansion and subdivision.
9. The mnemonic nature of the notation helps users navigate within the system.
10. The continuous revision and publication of the schedules at regular intervals ensures the currency of the scheme.

Weaknesses

1. An Anglo-American bias is particularly obvious in 900 (Geography and history), and 800 (Literature). Furthermore, 200 (Religion) shows a heavy bias toward American Protestantism. However, such biases have been gradually removed from recent editions.
2. Related disciplines are often separated, for example, 300 (Social sciences) from 900 (Geography and history); and 400 (Languages) from 800 (Literature).
3. The proper placements of certain subjects have also been questioned; for example, Library science in general works (000s), Psychology as a subdivision under Philosophy (100s), and Sports and Amusements in The arts (700s).
4. In 800, literary works by the same author are scattered according to literary form, when most scholars would prefer to have them grouped together.
5. The base of ten limits the hospitality of the notational system by restricting the capacity for accommodating subjects on the same level of the hierarchy to nine divisions.
6. The different rate of growth in various disciplines has resulted in an uneven structure. Some classes, such as 300 (Social sciences), 500 (Natural sciences), and 600 (Technology), have become overcrowded.
7. Even though an existing subject can be expanded indefinitely by virtue of the decimal system, no new numbers can be inserted between coordinate numbers (e.g., between 610 and 620), even when required for the

accommodation of new subjects. The present method of introducing a new subject is to include it as a subdivision under an existing subject.

8. While the capacity for expansion is infinite, it also results in lengthy numbers for specific and minute subjects. The long numbers have been found inconvenient, particularly when the system is used as a shelving device.

ASSIGNING CALL NUMBERS

A call number based on the DDC consists of two parts: the *class number* and the *book* or *item number*. The class number reflects the main subject content of the item. The book or item number consists of one or more elements based on bibliographic characteristics such as the name of the author and/or the title of the item. The construction of the DDC call number is discussed below.

CLASS NUMBERS

The class number may be derived from the full edition or the abridged edition.

As a result of the influence of modern classification theory, DDC has become less enumerative and increasingly analytico-synthetic or faceted in recent editions. Many numbers that can be assigned to resources are not listed as such in the schedules. Instead, they must be built from base numbers found in the schedules and numbers in the tables. The discussion below illustrates how class numbers enumerated in the schedules are expanded as needed through notational synthesis—in other words, by what is called *number building*—in the full and abridged editions of DDC.

NUMBER BUILDING: FULL EDITION

The discussion and examples in this section are based on the full edition. A similar discussion based on the abridged edition is given later in this chapter. The *main* or *base* number is always taken from the schedules. The additional elements may come from either the schedules or the tables, or both, and are added to the base number. (In this context, "added" means "tacked onto," not added in the arithmetical sense.) The order of the elements in each case is determined by instruction in the schedules or tables. In building a number, the decimal point is first removed. After the process of synthesis is completed, a decimal point is inserted after the third digit.

Combining Schedule Numbers

Adding an Entire Number to a Base Number

A bibliography of physics **016.53**

1. The main number for bibliographies and catalogs of works on specific subjects or in specific disciplines with a note to "add to base number 016 notation 001-999" the number for the specific subject 016
2. The number for Physics 530
3. The subject number added to the base number 016.530
4. The resulting number with a decimal point after the third digit and the removal of the terminal 0 after the decimal point 016.53

Taxation of cork industry **336.278 674.9**

1. Base number for Taxes on products, services, and industries, with instruction to add 001-999 336.278
2. Number for Cork products 674.9
3. (2) added to (1) 336 278 674 9
4. With decimal point inserted 336 2786749

Adding a Fraction of a Number or Fractions of Numbers to a Base Number

A general Russian periodical **057.1**

1. Number for all serial publications as indicated in the index 050
2. Number in schedule for serial publications in Slavic languages, with instruction: "Add to base number 057 the numbers following 037 in 037.1-037.9" 057
3. The number in the sequence for Russian 037.1
4. The number following 037 added to (2) 057 1
5. With decimal point inserted 057.1

Fractures of the rib cage bones **617.15**

1. Base number for Fractures: "Add to base number 617.15 the numbers following 611.71 in 611.711-611.718" 617.15
2. The number for the chest bones in the Sequence 611.712
3. The number following 611.71 added to (1) 617 15 2
4. With decimal point inserted 617.152

Photographs of scientific subjects	**779.95**
1. Base number for photographs with instruction: "Add to base number 779 the numbers following 704.94 in 704.942-704.949"	779
2. The most appropriate number in the sequence Iconography of other specific subjects, with instructions: "Add to base number 704.949 notation 001-999"	704.949
3. The number for Science	500
4. (3) added to (2)	704 949500
5. The number following 704.94 added to (1)	779 9500
6. With decimal point inserted and terminal 0s removed	779.95

Adding Notation(s) from the Tables to a Base Number

In Edition 23 of DDC, there are six tables:

Table 1. Standard Subdivisions
Table 2. Geographic Areas, Historical Periods, Biography
Table 3. Subdivisions for the Arts, for Individual Literatures, for Specific Literary Forms
  Table 3A. Subdivisions for Works by or about Individual Authors
  Table 3B. Subdivisions for Works by or about More than One Author
  Table 3C. Notation to be Added Where Instructed in Table 3B, 700.4, 791.4, 808-809
Table 4. Subdivisions of Individual Languages and Language Families
Table 5. Ethnic and National Groups
Table 6. Languages

Notations from all tables, except 3 and 4, may be used throughout the entire schedules. Notations from Table 1 may be used wherever applicable. Notations from Tables 2, 5, and 6 are used only when instructed. However, notations from Tables 2 and 5 may also be added, according to instructions, to -09 and 089, respectively, in Table 1; the results are, then, used as standard subdivisions, that is, they may be used whenever appropriate.

Tables 3 and 4 apply only to certain schedules: Table 3 to the 800s and parts of 700s, and Table 4 to 420–490. These, too, are used only when specifically instructed.

All notations from the tables are preceded by a dash, indicating that these are not complete class numbers, but must be used in conjunction with main numbers from the schedules. In some cases, a notation from one table may be added to one found in another table, and the combination is then attached to the appropriate main number from the schedules to form a complete class number.

Table 1: Standard Subdivisions

After a specific class number has been chosen for a work, the classifier should consider whether further specification concerning the bibliographic form or the author's approach is desirable, that is, whether any of the standard subdivisions is applicable. Table 1 lists nine categories of standard subdivisions, which are further subdivided into more detailed specifications. All notations for standard subdivisions begin with a 0, for example, -01, -07154.

Notations from tables are never used alone, or as main numbers. With the exception of -04, the classifier does not need any specific instruction in the schedules in order to add the notations for standard subdivisions, unless there is a specific instruction to the contrary. Appropriateness and applicability are the general guides. For example, for a journal of inorganic chemistry, the standard subdivision -05 (for serial publications) is added to the base number 546 (inorganic chemistry) to form the number 546.05 (journal publication on the topic of inorganic chemistry).

Standard subdivision notations and their meanings are given in Table 1. However, under certain numbers in the schedules, a few standard subdivisions may be listed when these subdivisions have special meanings or when extended notation is provided for the subject in question. For example under 610 (Medicine and Health), the standard subdivisions -06 (i.e., 610.6) and -07 (i.e., 610.7) have extended meanings, such as 610.696 (Medical relationships) and 610.73 (Nursing and services of allied health personnel).

The standard subdivision -04 is reserved for special topics that have general application throughout the regular subdivisions of certain specific subjects. Therefore, it varies from subject to subject and is to be used only when the special topics are spelled out in the schedules, for example, the subdivisions .04-.049 found under 331 (Labor economics).

Before adding a standard subdivision to a base number, the classifier should remove all the terminal zeros that are used as fillers in the base number. Therefore, standard subdivision -03 added to the base number 100 results in 103, not 100.03. A journal of library science is classed in 020.5, not 020.05.

However, there are exceptions to this rule. In many cases, notations beginning with -0, -00, or even -000 have been assigned meanings other than those for standard subdivisions. In these cases, the classifier is instructed to use more than one zero for standard subdivisions, for example:

320 Political science (Politics and government)
.01-.09 Standard subdivisions
[Hence, 320.03 for an encyclopedia of political science]
338 Production
.001-.008 Standard subdivisions
[Hence, 338.005 for a journal of production]
620 Engineering and allied operations
.001-.009 Standard subdivisions
[Hence, 620.009 for a history of engineering]

When a standard subdivision (e.g., 507) or a span of standard subdivisions (e.g., 516.001-.009) is specifically named in the schedules, it is understood that the sub-subdivisions to these standard subdivisions may be used (e.g., 507.4 for science museums, or 516.0076 for review and exercises in geometry) unless there are contrary instructions in the schedules.

Certain standard subdivision concepts, particularly for geographical treatment, are displaced to nonzero numbers. For example, insurance in France is represented by the number 368.944 (Insurance in France) instead of 368.00944. When zeros are to be removed, there are clear indications and/or directions in the schedules.

Although standard subdivisions may be applied wherever they are appropriate, there are certain restrictions on their use. In addition to specific restrictions appearing in the schedules relating to individual numbers (e.g., 362.[09] *do not use; class in* 362.9), certain general restrictions are set forth in the "Introduction" to DDC:[5]

1. The classifier should not add standard subdivisions when they are redundant. In other words, for a history of the United States, do not add -09 to 973, which already means history of the United States. Likewise, it is redundant to add -03 to 423, which already means a dictionary of the English language.
2. Standard subdivisions should be added to the number chosen for a work only when the content of the work is equivalent to the whole, or "approximately the whole," meaning of the number. In other words, standard subdivisions are not used when the work in hand deals with a subject more specific than the content of the number, that is, when the subject represented in the work does not have its own specific number. For example, a history of classification systems is classed in 025.4309, but a history of the Russian Library-Bibliographical Classification, which does not have its own number, is classed in 025.43 instead of 025.4309. In other words, the standard subdivision is not added unless the content of the work being classified covers the whole, or approximately the whole, of the subject

represented by the main number. This is called the "approximate-the-whole" rule. In the case of multiterm headings of class numbers, instructions are provided with regard to the addition of standard subdivisions; for example, under the number 514.32 Systems and spaces [in Topology], there is the note: Standard subdivisions are added for either or both topics in heading. In this example, both "systems" and "spaces" are considered to "approximate-the-whole."

3. With a few exceptions noted below, the classifier should not add one standard subdivision to another standard subdivision, unless there are specific instructions to do so. When two or more standard subdivisions are applicable to a work, choose one. In choosing a standard subdivision, observe the table of preference found at the beginning of Table 1 (Vol. 1, p. 186), for example, 020.7 for *Journal of Education for Librarianship*, rather than 020.5 or 020.705. On the other hand, the use of more than one standard subdivision is allowed in the following cases:
   a. With standard subdivision -04 (Special topics) because of its unusual nature as a *standard* subdivision.
   b. With standard subdivisions that have extended meanings, for example, 610.7305 for a journal of nursing, although both -073 and -05 appear to be standard subdivisions. The subdivision -073 under the number 610 has been given an extended meaning, and there is a specific instruction in the schedule to add further standard subdivisions.
   c. With standard subdivision concepts that have been displaced to non-zero numbers, for example, 368.944068 (Management of insurance in France).

Furthermore, standard subdivisions may be extended by adding notation from other tables when so instructed; when this is the case, the resulting number is treated as an extended standard subdivision. For example, notation 3-9 from Table 2 may be added to standard subdivision -09 to specify treatment of the main topic by specific continents, countries, etc. Thus, the notation -769 may be added to the standard subdivision -09 to form -09769 for treatment of a topic in Kentucky. The following examples show the application of standard subdivisions:

The use of computers in education worldwide	370.285
1. Education	370
2. Standard subdivision for computer applications from Table 1	-0 285
3. (2) added to (1) (without terminal zero) with decimal point inserted	370.285

Management of welfare services — 361.0068

1. Social problems and social welfare with indication of an extra zero for standard subdivisions — 361.0
2. Standard subdivision for management from Table 1 — -068
3. (2) added to (1) with decimal point inserted — 361 . 0068

Table 2: Geographic Areas, Historical Periods, Persons

Notation from Table 2, providing representation of geographic areas, historical periods, and persons relating to the main subject, may be used with numbers throughout the schedules as instructed. It is used in the following ways.

1. Used directly when so noted with numbers from the schedules

Geology of Iceland — 554.912

1. Geology, with instruction to add area notation 4-9 to base number 55 — 55
2. Area notation for Iceland from Table 2 — -4 912
3. (2) added to (1) with decimal point inserted — 554.912

A journal of higher education in Japan — 378.5205

1. Higher education, with instruction to add to base number 378 notation 4-9 from Table 2 — 378
2. Area notation for Japan — -52
3. (2) added to (1) as instructed — 378 52
4. Standard subdivision for serial publications — -05
5. (4) added to (3) — 378.5205

Emigration from Italy to New York City — 325.245097471

1. Base number for emigration from specific continents, countries, localities — 325 2
2. Area notation for Italy — -45
3. (2) added to (1) as instructed — 325 245
4. Standard subdivision for New York City — -097471
5. (4) added to (3) — 325.245097471

North Dakota education law — 344.7840702632

1. Labor, social service, education, cultural law in specific jurisdictions and areas — 344.3 -.9

2. Area notation -784 for North Dakota added to base number 344	344 784
3. Education law	344.07
4. (2) and (3) combined as instructed under 344.3-.9	344 78407
5. Special form division for collected laws as listed under 342-347	- 02632
6. (5) added to (4)	344.7840702632

2. Used through interposition of notation -09 from Table 1

Under -093-099 in Table 1, there is an instruction to add area notation 3-9 from Table 2 to base number -09, for example, -0973, for historical, geographical, and persons-treatment of a subject with regard to the United States. Once an area number is added to -09, the entire combination (e.g., -0973) becomes a standard subdivision. Since -09 is a standard subdivision and can be added to any number from the schedules as desired, virtually every number in the DDC system can be subdivided geographically. However, when direct geographic subdivision is provided as illustrated above, it takes precedence over the use of -09 and its subdivisions.

Shopping centers in the United States	381.110973
1. Number for Shopping centers, with no direct provision for geographic subdivision	381 11
2. Standard subdivision for United States	- 0973
3. (2) added to (1)	381.110973
Paper industry in England	338.4767620942
1. Number for Paper industry as constructed under Paper industry on p. 334	338 476762
2. Standard subdivision for England	- 0942
3. (2) added to (1)	338.4767620942

3. Used when so noted with numbers from other table

American Chemical Society	540.6073
1. Number for Chemistry	540
2. Standard subdivision from Table 1 for national organizations	0 60
3. Area notation -73 for the United States from Table 2 added to (2) as instructed	- 0 6073
4. (3) added to (1)	540.6073

American Physical Society	530.06073
(Similar to the example above, except that the number 530 requires two 0s for standard subdivisions)	

A history of descriptive research in Library Science in Great Britain	020.723
1. Number for library and information science	020
2. Standard subdivision for descriptive research	- 0 723
3. Standard subdivision for historical and geographical treatment of Great Britain	- 0941
4. (2) added to (1) (Since the classifier has been advised not to add one standard subdivision to another one, (2) is chosen over (3) according to the order of precedence for standard subdivisions.)	020.723

4. Used with another number from Table 2

Foreign relations between Japan and Great Britain	327.41052
1. Base number for foreign relations between specific nations as listed under 327.3-327.9	327
2. Area notation for Japan	- 52
3. Area notation for Great Britain	- 41
4. As instructed, add area notation for one nation to the base number, add 0 and to the result, and add area notation for the other nation. The order of the area notations is determined by the emphasis of the work. If Japan is emphasized.	327 52041
5. If Great Britain is emphasized.	327 41052
6. "If emphasis is equal, give priority to the nation or region coming first in Table 2."	327.41052

Table 3: Subdivisions for the Arts, for Individual Literatures, for Specific Literary Forms

Notation from Table 3 is used, when applicable, with the base numbers for individual literatures identified by an asterisk (*) under 810-890, and also with specific instructions under 808-809 and certain numbers in the 700s in the schedules. Number building for literature and music calls for the most complex procedures in the DDC system. The application of Table 3 is discussed later in this chapter, under "Classification of Literature."

Table 4: Subdivisions of Individual Languages and Language Families

Notations from Table 4 are used with base numbers for individual languages identified by an asterisk (*) under 420-490 in the schedules. The classifier's first task is to identify the language in hand.

Verbs in the German language	435.6
1. Base number for German language	43
2. Subdivision for verbs from Table 4	-56
3. (2) added to (1) with decimal point inserted	435.6

Bilingual dictionaries are a special case. Since a bilingual dictionary involves two languages, the classifier must first determine which language is to be used as the base number. Instructions for choosing the base number are given under -32–39 in Table 4. If the entry words are given in only one language with equivalent words in the second language, the number for the first language is used as the base number, for example:

A German-French dictionary	433.41
1. Base number for the German language	43
2. Subdivisions for bilingual dictionaries	-32–39
3. Language notation for the French language from Table 6	-41
4. (3) added to (2) and (1)	433.41

A bilingual dictionary containing entry words in both languages is classed as instructed, usually with the number for the language lesser known to the users as the base number.

An English-Spanish, Spanish-English dictionary	463.21
1. Base number for Spanish as "more useful" for English-speaking users	46
2. Subdivision for bilingual dictionaries	- 32–39
3. Languages notation (-21) for English from Table 6 added to the subdivision for dictionaries (-3) in Table 4	- 3 21
4. (3) added to (1) with decimal point	463.21

As instructed under -32–39 in Table 4 (Vol.1, p. 655), "If classification with either language is equally useful, give priority to the language coming later in 420-490."

A German-French, French-German dictionary	443.31
1. Base number for French, since it is greater than the number for German, i.e., 43	44
2. Subdivision for bilingual dictionaries	- 32-39
3. Language notation (-31) for German from Table 6 added to the subdivision for dictionaries (-3) in Table 4	-3 31
4. (3) added to (1) with decimal point	443.31

Table 5: Ethnic and National Groups

Notations from Table 5 are used with those numbers from the schedules and other tables to which the classifier is instructed to add ethnic and national groups' notation.

Social groups among the Hindis	305.89143
1. Base number for ethnic and national groups with instruction to add notation 05-9 from Table 5	305 8
2. Notation for Hindis from Table 5	- 9143

Decorative arts of the Chinese	745.089951
1. Base number for decorative arts	745
2. Standard subdivision for treatment among specific ethnic and national groups with instruction to add notation 05-9 from Table 5	- 089
3. Notation for Chinese from Table 5	- 951

Table 6: Languages

Notations from Table 6 represent the language aspect, or facet, of a main subject, and are used with base numbers from the schedules. They are added as instructed, a procedure similar to that employed with Tables 2 and 5.

A French Bible	220.541
A Swahili Bible	220.596392
The Old Testament in French	221.541
The Old Testament in Swahili	221.596392
The Book of Job in French	223.10541
The Book of Job in Swahili	223.10596392
A general Japanese periodical	059.9 56

Classification of Literature

In classifying literature, the subject or topical aspect is secondary to language, literary form, and period, which are the main facets of literature. Other facets include style, mood, themes, and subjects. In general, the DDC numbers for works by or about individual authors reflect primary facets only, while those for collection and criticism of more than one author bring out other facets as well.

Citation Order

With a few exceptions, the citation order for the different facets in a class number for literature is the following:

1. The main class, *Literature,* is represented by the base number.
2. Language is the second element in the number, for example, 82- for English literature, 891- for Chinese literature, and so on. When the work is not limited to any language, a zero is used to fill the second digit, for example 80- for world literature.
3. Literary form is the third element. Mnemonics are employed, for example, -1 for poetry, -2 for drama, and so on. Hence, 821 for English poetry, 891.2 for Chinese drama, and 820 for English literature not limited to a particular form.
4. Period, if applicable, follows literary form, for example, 811.1 (colonial American poetry).
5. For literature written by more than one author and works about such literature, standard subdivisions, with rather elaborate sub-subdivisions for feature and theme, are represented as further sub-divisions under -08 (collections) and -09 (history and criticism).

The citation order varies when a collection by more than one author is not limited to a particular language/nationality or a literary form.

Examples

In DDC, number-building for literature, particularly literature of specific languages, is more complex than in other situations involving number building. Table 3 is devised for use with numbers in the 700 and 800 classes as instructed. It contains three parts:

Table 3A. Subdivisions for Works by or about Individual Authors
Table 3B. Subdivisions for Works by or about More than One Author
Table 3C. Notation to be Added Where Instructed in Table 3B, 700.4, 791.4, 808-809

Fortunately, very detailed instructions for carrying out the process are provided in the DDC manual (Vol. 1, pages 162–67), with brief step-by-step instructions printed at the beginning of Table 3 (Vol. 1, pages 616–17). These should be studied carefully. The following examples illustrate the many possible combinations of facets in classifying literature. The examples are divided by various types of literary works and works about literature: (1) collections of literature by more than one author, (2) works about literature, (3) works written by individual authors, (4) works about individual authors, and (5) works about individual works.

1. Collections of literature by more than one author

An anthology of world literature	808.8
A collection of nineteenth-century literature (Facet: Period)	808.80034
1. Base number for a collection of literature from specific periods	808.800
2. Standard subdivision for early nineteenth century from Table 1	-09034
A collection of Christmas literature (Facet: Feature/theme)	808.80334
1. Base number for a collection of literature displaying specific features	808.80
2. Notation from Table 3C for themes relating to holidays	-334
A collection of nineteenth-century poetry (Facets: Form plus Period)	808.81034
1. Base number for a collection of poetry from a specific period	808.810
2. Period notation from Table 1	-09034
A collection of Christmas poetry (Facets: Form plus Feature/theme)	808.819334
1. Base number for a collection of poetry displaying specific features	808.819
2. Notation from Table 3C for holidays	-334
An anthology of Spanish literature (Facet: Language)	860.8
1. Base number for Spanish literature	86
2. Subdivision for collections from Table 3B	-08

A collection of eighteenth-century Spanish literature (Facets: Language plus period)	860.8004
1. Base number for Spanish literature	86
2. Notation from Table 3B for collections of literary texts in more than one form, with instruction to add from Table 3C	- 0 800
3. Notation from Table 3C for specific periods	- 01 - 09
4. Notation for the eighteenth century from the period table for Spanish literature in the schedule (Vol. 3, p. 795)	4

A collection of Spanish poetry (Facets: Language plus Form)	861.008
1. Base number for Spanish literature	86
2. Notation from Table 3B for a collection of poetry	- 1 008

A collection of eighteenth-century Spanish drama (Facets: Language plus Form plus Period)	862.408
1. Base number for Spanish literature	86
2. Notation from Table 3B for drama of specific periods	- 21 - 29
3. Notation for the eighteenth century from period table for Spanish literature	4
4. Notation for collections of literary texts	08

A collection of American Christmas poetry (Facets: Language plus Form plus Feature/theme)	811.0080334
1. Base number for American literature	81
2. Collections of poetry featuring holidays (Tables 3B and 3C)	1 0080334

A collection of nineteenth-century American Christmas poetry (Facets: Language plus Form plus Period plus Feature/theme)	811.3080334
1. Base number for American literature	81
2. Poetry (Table 3B)	11 - 19
3. Nineteenth century (period table for American literature)	3
4. Collections featuring holidays (Tables 3B and 3C)	- 080334

2. Works about literature

Using examples similar to those listed above, one may build the following numbers for works about literature:

A history of world literature	809
A study of nineteenth-century literature	809.034
A study of Christmas literature	809.93334
A study of nineteenth-century poetry	809.1034
A study of Christmas poetry	809.19334
A history of Spanish literature	860.9
A study of eighteenth-century Spanish literature	860.9004
A study of Spanish poetry	861.009
A study of eighteenth-century Spanish drama	862.409
A study of American Christmas poetry	811.009334
A study of nineteenth-century American Christmas poetry	811.309334

3. Works written by individual authors

Because DDC classes literature by form, the works of an individual author may be classed in different numbers if the author wrote in different literary forms.

The notation for works written by individual authors contains the following facets: Literature (8), language, form, and period, for example,

The Adventures of Huckleberry Finn by Mark Twain (Novel)	813.4
The Celebrated Jumping Frog of Calaveras County, and Other Stories by Mark Twain	813.4
Essays by G. K. Chesterton	824.912
The Heart of Midlothian by Sir Walter Scott (Novel)	
The Lady of the Lake by Sir Walter Scott (Poems)	821.7

Selected and collected works by individual authors are classed according to literary forms in the same numbers as individual works without the use of -08, the subdivision notation for collections by more than one author, for example,

Short Stories by Sir Walter Scott	823.7
Selected Tales by Edgar Allen Poe	813.3

When the collected works are in different forms, the problem is, then, which number to use. In general, the number for the predominant form is chosen, for example:

The Annotated Waste Land, with T. S. Eliot's Contemporary Prose	821.912
Emerson's Prose and Poetry : Authoritative Texts, Contexts, Criticism	814.3

When no predominant form can be determined, or when the collection includes works in a variety of forms, the number -8 for Miscellaneous writings (from Table T3A) further subdivided by period and ending in -09 is used, for example:

The Wit and Wisdom of Mark Twain	818.409
Stories, Poems, and Other Writings, by Willa Cather (American Novelist, 1874-1947)	818.309
The Sayings of Sir Walter Scott	828.709
The Best of Oscar Wilde: Selected Plays and Literary Criticism	828.809

In DDC, literary authors do not receive individual unique class numbers as in the LCC. Authors writing in the same form and the same period share the same number. For example, all late-nineteenth century American novelists are assigned the number 813.4. The only exception to this rule is Shakespeare *as a dramatist*, to whom the unique number 822.33 has been assigned. In many libraries, fiction in English is not classified. Instead, it is assigned the letter *F* and subarranged alphabetically by author.

4. Works about individual authors

Works *about* an individual author are classed in the same number as assigned to the author's works, as instructed in Table 3A (vol. 1, p. 617), for example:

Ezra Pound: A Collection of Critical Essays	811.52
A Study of the Sonnets of Shakespeare	821.3
Aldous Huxley: A Study	823.912
An Essay on the Genius and Writings of Pope	821.5

In literature, it is often difficult to separate biography and criticism of an author. Therefore, they are usually both classed in the 800s, for example:

Henry James: a Study of the Short Fiction	813.4
The Selected Letters of Ralph Waldo Emerson	814.3
In the Footsteps of Hans Christian Andersen	839.8136

Note that the standard subdivision -0924 for individual biography is not used.

5. Works about individual works

Individual works and works about them are classed in the same numbers, as instructed in Table 3A. The subdivision -09 is not used, for example:

A critical study of Thackeray's *Vanity Fair*	823.8
A study of Marlowe's *Doctor Faustus*	822.3

Segmentation Mark

Dewey numbers assigned from the full edition by the LC and many other libraries carry a segmentation mark (a slash (/) or a prime mark (')). It is used to indicate the end of an abridged number (as provided in the abridged edition), for example, 025.2/1, 823/.7, and 338.4/76661097409041. This practice facilitates the assignment of abridged DDC numbers when full numbers for the same works are available.

NUMBER BUILDING: ABRIDGED EDITION

It is a characteristic of the abridged edition to provide a broad classification without minute details. Thus, in many cases, the classifier will find that the abridged edition does not supply a number for a subject as specific as the content of the work being classified. When this is the case, the classifier should choose the most specific base number that the edition provides.

The abridged edition does, however, provide for a certain degree of notational synthesis, or number building, as it, like the unabridged DDC, is a partially analytico-synthetic scheme. For number building in the abridged edition (as in the full), the main or base number is always taken from the schedules. To begin with, all decimal points are removed. Additional elements may come from either the schedules or the tables, or both. The order of the elements in each case is determined by instructions in the schedules or tables. After the process of number building is completed, a decimal point is inserted after the third digit.

It is assumed that those who use the abridged DDC edition and have little interest in the full edition may turn directly to this section without studying what was said above about notational synthesis in the previous section on the full edition. This section has, therefore, been written to stand more or less alone, and so, necessarily, much of what was said above is repeated here.

Combining Schedule Numbers

Adding an Entire Number to a Base Number

Bibliography of adult education	016 . 374
1. The number for a subject bibliography with the instruction: "Add to base number 016 notation 001-999," meaning any class number can be added to 016 to obtain the number for a bibliography of that subject	016
2. Adult education	374
3. (2) added to (1) with decimal point inserted	016.374

Adding a Fraction of a Number to a Base Number

An Interpretation of the Old Testament	221.6
1. Number for the Old Testament with a note under 221.1-221.9: "Add to base number 221 the numbers following 220 in 220.1-220.9"	221
2. The number in that range meaning an interpretation	220.6
3. The number following 220 added to (1)	221.6

Adding Notation(s) from the Tables to a Base Number

In the abridged edition, there are four tables:

Table 1. Standard Subdivisions
Table 2. Geographic Areas and Persons
Table 3. Subdivisions for Individual Literatures, for Specific Literary Forms
Table 4. Subdivisions of Individual Languages

Notations from Table 1 are applicable throughout the schedules wherever appropriate. Those from Table 2 also apply to all classes, but can be used only when instructed. Table 3 applies only to the numbers 810–890 and is used only when specifically instructed. Likewise, Table 4 applies to the numbers 420–490 and is also used only when specifically instructed.

All notations from the tables are preceded by a dash, indicating that these are not complete class numbers, but must be used in conjunction with numbers from the schedules. In some cases, a notation from one table may be added to one from another table, and the combination is then used with the appropriate base number from the schedules.

Table 1: Standard Subdivisions

After a specific number has been chosen for a work, the classifier should then consider whether further specification concerning the bibliographic form or the author's approach is desirable, that is, whether any of the standard subdivisions is applicable. Table 1 lists nine categories of standard subdivisions, which are further subdivided into more detailed specifications. All notations for standard subdivisions begin with a 0, for example, -01 and -075.

Notations from tables are never used alone or as main numbers. With the exception of -04, the classifier does not need any specific instruction in the schedules in order to add the notations for standard subdivisions. Appropriateness and applicability are the general guide. For example, for a journal of inorganic chemistry, the standard subdivision -05 (for serial publications) is added to the base number 546 to form the number 546.05.

The standard subdivision -04 is reserved for special topics that have general application throughout the regular subdivisions of certain specific subjects, for example, 604, and its subdivisions. Therefore, it varies from subject to subject, and is to be used only when the special topics are spelled out in the schedules.

In adding a standard subdivision to a base number, first remove all the zeros used as fillers. When this is done, for instance, standard subdivision -03 added to the base number 100 results in 103, not 100.03. A journal of library science is classed in 020.5, not 020.05.

However, there are exceptions to the single-zero rule. In many cases, notations beginning with 0 have been assigned meanings other than those for standard subdivisions. In these cases, the classifier is instructed to use more than one zero for standard subdivisions, for example:

300 Social sciences
Use 300.1-300.9 for Standard subdivisions
[Hence, 300.3 for an encyclopedia of social sciences]
551.7 Historical geology
.7001-.7009 Standard subdivisions
[Hence, 551.7007 for education and research in historical geology]
620 Engineering and allied operations
620.001-.009 Standard subdivisions
[Hence, 620.005 for a journal of engineering]

When a standard subdivision (e.g., 507) or a span of standard subdivisions (e.g., 516.001-.009) is specifically named in the schedules, it is understood that the sub-subdivisions to these standard subdivisions may be used when applicable (e.g., 507.4 for science museums, or 516.0076 for review and exercises in geometry), unless there are contrary instructions in the schedules.

Although standard subdivisions may be applied wherever they are appropriate, there are certain restrictions on their use. In addition to restrictions appearing in the schedules relating to specific numbers (e.g., *do not use* 362.09; *class in* 362.9), certain general restrictions are set forth in the Introduction to the abridged edition:[6]

1. The classifier should not add a standard subdivision when it is redundant, i.e., when the subdivision means the same as the base number. Therefore, for a history of the United States, do not add -09 to 973, which already means history of the U.S.
2. The classifier should not add one standard subdivision to another standard subdivision unless there are specific instructions to do so. When two or more standard subdivisions are applicable to a work, choose one according to the table of preference, which is found at the head of Table 1, e.g., choosing -068 over -09 and choosing -09 over -05.
3. Unless there are instructions in the schedules permitting their use, the classifier should be cautious about adding a standard subdivision to the number chosen for a work that deals with a subject more specific than the content of the number, i.e., when the subject represented in the work does not have its own specific number. For example, a history of special libraries is classed in 026.0009, but a history of medical libraries, which does not have its own number, is classed in 026, instead of 026.0009. In other words, the standard subdivision is not added unless the content of the work being classified covers the whole, or approximately the whole, of the subject represented by the main number. This is called the "approximate-the-whole" rule.

When the caption of a number contains two topics, instruction is provided as to whether standard subdivisions may be added to both topics, to either topic, or to one of the topics only, for example:

327.1 **Foreign policy and specific topics in international relations**
Standard subdivisions are added for foreign policy

005.74 **Data files and databases**
Standard subdivisions are added for either or both topics in heading

Certain standard subdivision concepts, particularly for geographical treatment, are displaced to nonzero numbers. For example, political campaigns in the United States are classed in 324.973 instead of being classed in 324.0973. In such cases, the full range of standard subdivisions may be added further, for example, maps of American political campaigns, 324.973022.

Table 2: Geographic Areas and Persons

Area notation specifies the historical or geographical treatment of a subject, and may be used with numbers throughout the schedules as instructed. It is used in the following ways:

1. Directly when so noted with numbers from the schedules

Geology of Latvia	554.796
1. Base number for regional geology; instruction to add notation from Table 2	55
2. Area notation for Latvia from Table 2	- 4 796
3. (2) added to (1) with decimal point inserted	554.796

Postage stamps from Japan	**769.56952**
1. Base number for postage stamps: historical geographic, persons treatment; instruction to add notation from Table 2	769 569
2. Area notation from Table 2 for Japan	- 52
3. (2) added to (1) with decimal point inserted	769.56952

A history of Thailand	**959.3**
1. Base number for general history of specific countries. Cf. note under 930-990 to add notation from Table 2 to base number 9	9
2. Area notation for Thailand from Table 2	- 59 3
3. (2) added to (1) with decimal point inserted	959.3

2. Through the interposition of notation -09 from Table 1

In Table 1, under -093-099, there is an instruction to add area notation 3-9 from Table 2 to base number -09, for example, -0973 for historical and geographical treatment of a subject with regard to the United States. The combination is then treated as one standard subdivision. Since -09 is a standard subdivision, and, therefore, can be added to any number from the schedules when appropriate, virtually every number in the DDC system can be subdivided geographically, unless there is specific instruction in the schedules not to use the standard subdivision under the particular number.

Economic geology of Germany	553.0943
1. Base number for economic geology	553
2. Standard subdivision for geographic treatment from Table 1	09
3. Germany from Table 2	43
4. (3) added to (2)	0943
3. (4) added to (1) with decimal point inserted	553.0943

When direct Table 2 geographic subdivision is provided from the schedules, it takes precedence over the use of -09 and its subdivisions.

Table 3: Subdivisions for Individual Literatures, for Specific Literary Forms

Notation from Table 3 is used with the base numbers for individual literatures according to add notes found under subdivisions of individual literatures in 810-890 in the schedules. It is not used for individual literatures that lack instructions to add from Table 3. A number for literature usually contains the following elements:

1. The main class, *Literature*, is represented by the base number 8.
2. *Language* is the second element, for example, 82- for English literature, 891.7 for Russian literature, and so on. When the work is not limited to any language, the -0- is used to fill the second digit, for example, 80- for world literature.
3. *Literary form* is the third element. Mnemonics are employed, for example, -1 for poetry, -2 for drama, and so on; hence, 821 (English poetry), 891.72 (Russian drama), etc. When the work covers more than one form, the -0 is used, for example, 820, English literature not limited to any particular form.
4. A standard subdivision when applicable, for example, 830.5 (a journal of German literature) is the fourth element.

Different types of literary works are classified in the following ways:

Collections of literature by more than one author

An Anthology of World Literature **808.8**

An Anthology of World Drama **808.82**

1. Base number for a collection of literary texts in specific forms from more than one literature 808.8
2. The number following 808 meaning drama - 2
3. (2) added to (1) 808.82

An Anthology of English Literature **820.8**

1. Base number for English literature 82
2. Notation for collections of literary texts from Table 3 - 0 8

An Anthology of French Poetry **841.008**

1. Base number for French literature 84
2. Notation from Table 3 for a collection of poetry by more than one author - 1 008

Works about literature

A History of World Literature	**809**
A Study of World Drama	**809.2**
1. Base number for a critical appraisal of literature in specific forms	809
2. Number following 808 in 808.1-808.7 meaning drama, i.e., 808.2	- 2
A History of English Literature	**820.9**
1. Base number for English literature	82
2. Notation from Table 3 for a history of more than one form by more than one author	- 0 9
An Outline of French Literary History	**840.90002**
1. Base number for French literature	84
2. Notation from Table 3 for history, description, appraisal of literature in more than one form by more than one author	- 0 9
3. Standard subdivision from Table 1 for an outline, with two extra zeros as instructed under -09 in Table 3	0002

Works written by individual authors. In DDC, literature is classified by form; works by a given author who writes in different literary forms are classed in different numbers according to their forms. Standard subdivisions are not used with works by individual authors.

Poems by Henry Wadsworth Longfellow	811
Ivanhoe by Sir Walter Scott	823
Charles Lamb's *Essays*	824

In many libraries, all fiction is grouped together without regard to language, and is assigned a simple notation *F* with the author's name or a *Cutter number* (see discussion on pages 634–642). Selected and collected works by individual authors are classed in the same numbers as individual works, for example:

Selected Poems by Edgar Allen Poe	811
Plays by Christopher Marlowe	822

When the collection contains works in various forms, the number for the predominant form or the form by which the author is best known is chosen, for example:

The Writings of Mark Twain	813
Selected Prose and Poetry by Ralph Waldo Emerson	814

By way of exception, William Shakespeare as a dramatist receives a unique number, 822.3; dramatic works written by him and works about him are classed in this number.

Works about individual authors. Works about individual authors are classed in the same numbers as the works written by them, as instructed in Table 3. The standard subdivision -09 is not used.

A Study of Longfellow's Poems	811
Commentary on Homer's Iliad	883
A Critical Appraisal of Sir Walter Scott's Novels	823

Table 4: Subdivisions of Individual Languages

Notation from Table 4 is used with base numbers for individual languages that are identified by an asterisk (*) under 420-490 in the schedules.

A Dictionary of the Russian Language	**491.73**
1. Base number for Russian	491.7
2. Notation for dictionaries from Table 4	- 3
English Word Origins	**422**
1. Base number for English	42
2. Notation for etymology from Table 4	- 2

Classification of Biography

Under 920 in the schedules, several methods of classing biographies of specific classes of persons are presented.

The preferred treatment is to class both individual and collected biographies of persons associated with a specific subject with the subject, using standard subdivisions notation -092 from Table 1, for example:

A Biography of Melvil Dewey	020.92
Biographical Directory of Librarians in the United States and Canada	020.92
A Biography of Abraham Lincoln	973.7092
Presidents of the United States	973.092

Note that biographies of heads of states are classed in the numbers for the history of their periods instead of in the number for political science.

Some libraries may find it desirable to use one of the optional methods:

1. Class both individual and collected biographies of persons associated with a specific subject in 920.1-928, for example:

A Biography of Melvil Dewey	920.2
Biographical Directory of Librarians in the United States and Canada	920.2
A Biography of Abraham Lincoln	923
Presidents of the United States	923

2. Class all individual biographies regardless of subject orientation in 92 or B, and all collected biographies regardless of subject orientation in 92 or 920 without subdivision, for example:

A Biography of Melvil Dewey	92 or B
Biographical Directory of Librarians in the United States and Canada	92 or 920
A Biography of Abraham Lincoln	92 or B
Presidents of the United States	92 or 920

3. Class individual biographies of men in 920.71 and of women in 920.72.

ITEM OR BOOK NUMBERS

One of the functions of a class number is to provide a shelf-location mark for a physical item in a library. In this capacity, the shelf mark for each item must be unique. Because many books are on the same subject and share the same class number, additional elements are added to the class number to create unique shelf marks, generally referred to as "call numbers." A call number contains the class number plus one or more of the following: an item number (based on the main entry), a work mark (usually based on the title of the work), a date, and a volume or issue number.

In cataloging records prepared by the LC, the DDC number does not include the item number. Also, when DDC is used for the purpose of organizing Web resources, the item number is generally omitted.

Several kinds of item or book numbers, also referred to as author notation (or Cutter numbers), may be employed with DDC class numbers. The simplest form, used by many small school, public, and church libraries, is the initial based on the main entry, in most cases the author's last name, for example:

512	822.3
D	M

For slightly larger collections, more letters from the main entry or author's last name may be used, hence:

512	822.3
Dic	Mar

An extreme of this method is to use the author's complete surname, for example:

512	822.3
Dickenson	Marlowe

However, this device is clumsy, and is used by very few libraries, in spite of its ability to distinguish between authors' names that begin with the same letters.

Cutter Numbers

Most libraries use a device called Cutter numbers, named after its designer, Charles Ammi Cutter. Developed originally for use with the Cutter Expansive Classification, it is now widely used with the DDC. A simplified form is used with the LCC and is described in chapter 17.

In the Cutter number system, the author number is derived by combining the initial letter or letters of the author's last name with numbers from a numerical table that was designed to ensure an alphabetical arrangement of names, for example, D556 (Dickens), D557 (Dickenson), and D558 (Dickerson). This device provides a shorter author number that is also easier to arrange and to read on the shelves.

There are three Cutter tables: *Two-Figure Author Table*,[7] *Three-Figure Author Table*,[8] and the *Cutter-Sanborn Table*,[9] listed in the order of increasing detail. The following instruction is based on the *Three-Figure Author Table*. A Dewey Cutter Program is made available by OCLC to download. The program provides automatic creation of Cutter numbers using OCLC Four-Figure Cutter Tables (Cutter Four-Figure Table and Cutter-Sanborn Four-Figure Table).[10] The Cutter number is constructed according to the following procedures:

1. In the Cutter table, locate the first few letters of the author's surname or corporate name, which is the *main entry* of the work. Use only the boldface letters shown in the combination and the Arabic numbers next to it, for example:

Dewes	514
Dewey	515
Dewil	516

Based on the above figures, the Cutter number for Melvil Dewey is *D515*.

Certain letters in the alphabet appear more frequently as initial letters of names. In order to keep the Cutter numbers short, two letters are used in a combination for names beginning with a vowel or the letter *S*, and three letters are used for names beginning with the letters *Sc*, for example:

813.54	813.54	813.54	813.54
Ed98	Sch56	Sm64	V896

2. Where there is no Cutter number in the table that fits a name exactly, use the first of the two numbers closest to the name, for example, *T325* for Thackeray, based on:

Thacher	325
Thad	326

3. Cutter numbers are treated decimally. Therefore, when required, any number can be extended by adding extra digits at its end. For example, if *Sm52* has been assigned to Benjamin Smith and *Sm53* has been assigned to Charles Smith, and a Cutter number must be provided for Brian Smith, the number Sm525 can then be used. The filing order is Sm52, Sm525, Sm53. The number 5 or 6 is often chosen as the extra digit in order to leave room on both sides for future interpolation.

For the same reason, although the tables provide many numbers ending in the numeral 1, it is advisable to add a digit and not to use a Cutter number ending in 1, because it places a limit on expansion. For example, use L5115 instead of L511 for David Lee. Furthermore, avoid using zero, because it is easily confused with the letter *o*, and, if possible, use some means to distinguish the number 1 from the letter *l*, such as substituting the lowercase script form (*l*) for the latter.

4. When two authors classified in the same number share the same Cutter number in the table, assign a different number for the second author by adding a digit, for example, M315 for Heinrich Mann and M3155 for Thomas Mann. If Thomas Mann has been assigned the number M315 before a number for Heinrich Mann is required, the number M3145 then can be used for the latter.

5. Names beginning with Mc, M', and Mac are treated as though they were all spelled Mac. The apostrophe is ignored, that is, O'Hara being treated as Ohara.

6. When the main entry is under title, the Cutter number is based on the first word (disregarding initial articles) of the title. *Encyclopaedia Britannica* is assigned En19. Therefore, it is more accurate to state that the Cutter number is derived from the main entry of the work, which may or may not be a personal author.

7. An exception is made for biographies. In order to group all biographies of a person together, the Cutter number is based on the name of the biographee instead of the main entry. For example, all biographies of Napoleon are grouped in the Cutter number N162. In many libraries, this practice is extended to include works about corporate bodies, particularly firms and institutions.

Unique Call Numbers

As mentioned above, when two or more authors with the same last name write on the same subject, they are assigned different author or Cutter numbers, for example, D557 for David Dickenson and D558 or D5575 for Robert Dickenson. When the same author has written more than one work on a particular subject, further devices—work marks, edition marks or dates of publication, and copy and volume numbers—are added to create unique call numbers. These are discussed below.

Work Mark

A *work mark* (sometimes called a *work letter*) is added to the Cutter number to distinguish different titles on the same subject by the same author. Work marks usually follow the Cutter number directly, and consist of the first letter or letters (in lower case) from the first word (disregarding initial articles) in the title. The following examples show the pattern.

512
D557i *Introduction to Algebra* by D. Dickenson

512
D557p *Principles of Algebra* by D. Dickenson

512
D557pr *Progress in Algebra* by D. Dickenson

813.4
J233a *The Ambassadors* by Henry James

813.4
J233am *The American* by Henry James

813.4
J233p *The Portrait of a Lady* by Henry James

In some cases, when books in a series by the same author on the same subject all begin with the same word, it is customary to use the first letter from each key word in the titles, for example:

738.2
H324ce Hayden's *Chats on English China*

738.2
H324co Hayden's *Chats on Old China*

738.2
H324cr Hayden's *Chats on Royal Copenhagen Porcelain*

Practices in assigning work marks vary slightly from library to library, as there are no definitive rules concerning this aspect of cataloging. The approach shown in the examples here represents one of various alternatives, and should not be taken as the *only* method.[11] Nonetheless, work marks illustrate the basic function of the call number, which is to provide a unique symbol for each item of library material and to ensure a logical arrangement of works that share the same class number.

Work marks are particularly important in cases where many items are classed under the same number, for example, B (Biography) and F (Fiction). Work marks for biographies and literary works therefore merit special consideration.

Cutter Numbers for Biography

In order to group all biographies of the same person together on the shelf, the Cutter number is taken from the name of the biographee instead of the author. All biographies of George Washington are cuttered under W277, and the work mark is then taken from the first letter of the main entry—which is usually the author's surname. The work mark *a* is used for all autobiographical writings in order to place such works before biographies written by other people. A biography written by an author whose surname begins with the letter *a* is then assigned two letters as the work mark, for example, W277ad (for Adams, etc.). When there is more than one autobiographical work, an arbitrary Arabic number may be added to the work mark. For example:

W277a	Washington, George. *Autograph Letters and Documents of George Washington Now in Rhode Island Collections*
W277a1	Washington, George. *Affectionately Yours, George Washington: A Self-Portrait in Letters of Friendship*, edited by T. J. Fleming
W277a2	Washington, George. *Last Will and Testament of George Washington of Mount Vernon*
W277ad	Adams, R. G. *Five Radio Addresses on George Washington*
W277b	Bellamy, F. R. *The Private Life of George Washington*

W277d	Delaware. Public Archives Commission. *George Washington and Delaware*
W277h	*Honor to George Washington and Reading about George Washington*

Cutter Numbers for Literary Works

In the DDC, critical appraisals and biographies of individual authors are classed in the same numbers as those assigned to their works; thus, they share the same class number and Cutter number. It is then the function of the work mark to distinguish the works written *by* and those written *about* an author. In this area particularly, libraries vary in their practices. For example, some libraries use an additional Cutter number for works about individual authors. There are, as yet, no standards or rules in this regard. The following is presented as an example of a workable mechanism. In many libraries, the practice outlined in this section also applies to philosophers and artists when works written by and about them are classed in the same numbers.

Works by Individual Authors

These are assigned work marks taken from the titles, for example:

821.5	Pope, Alexander
P8115d	*The Dunciad*
P8115ep	*An Epistle from Mr. Pope to Dr. Arbuthnot*
P8115es	*An Essay on Criticism*
P8115ess or P8115esm	*An Essay on Man*
P8115r	*The Rape of the Lock*

Biography and Criticism of Individual Authors

Since critical appraisals and biographies of an individual author share the same class number and Cutter number with the author's works, they require special work marks if the library does not wish to interfile these two categories of works. The most common device is to insert the letter *z* between the Cutter number and the work mark, for example:

P8115zc	Clark, D. B. *Alexander Pope*
P8115zr	Russell, J. P. *Alexander Pope: Tradition and Identity*

With the use of the letter *z*, works *about* Pope will be filed after works written *by* him. The letter *z* in this case is followed by the regular work mark based on the main entry. In this way, the letter *z* alone is reserved for any title by the author with the first word beginning with the letter *z*, for example:

833.912
M317z Mann, Thomas. *Der Zauberberg*
M317z*l* Lehnert, Herbert. *Thomas-Mann-Forschung*

In some libraries, serial publications devoted to the study of an individual author are assigned the work mark *zz* so that these publications will be filed after other critical works about the author, for example, M317zz for *Blätter der Thomas Mann Gesellschaft.*

As an alternative of using the letter *z* as a work mark for works about an author, a second Cutter number based on the main entry of the work may be used, for example:

821.5
P8115 Clark, D. B.
C547 *Alexander Pope*

821.5
P8115 Russell, J. P.
R914 *Alexander Pope: Tradition and Identity*

Works about Individual Works

If the library wishes to have individual works and the critical works about them stand together on the shelf, work marks may be used as a device for such an arrangement. The capital letter *Z* is inserted between the work mark for the work criticized, and the work mark is based on the critic's surname, for example:

821.5
P8115dZs Sitter, J. E. *The Poetry of Pope's Dunciad*
P8115dZw Williams, A. L. *Pope's Dunciad: A Study of Its Meaning*

This practice may be extended to include translations of literary works, if one wishes to have the original work and the translations stand together, for example:

833.912 Mann, Thomas
M317b *Bekenntnisse des Hochstaplers Felix Krull*
M317bE *Confessions of Felix Krull, Confidence Man*

The letter E stands for an English translation. In some libraries, the letter *x* is used as a work mark for an author's collected works, and the letter *y* for works such as bibliographies and concordances of individual authors, for example:

821.5	Pope, Alexander
P8115xb	*Complete Poetical Works*, edited by H. W. Boynton
P8115xd	*Poetical Works*, edited by H. Davis
P8115ya	Abbott, E., comp. *A Concordance to the Works of Alexander Pope*

The only problem with this practice is that an individual work with a title beginning with the letter *z* would then be separated from other individual works. An alternative is to use the letter *a* as a work mark for collected works, similar to the treatment of autobiographies. In this case, collected works of an author would precede individual works, an arrangement preferred by many libraries. Bibliographies and concordances would then be treated like other works about the author.

The works written *by* and *about* an individual author are therefore arranged in the following order:

- Collected works (arranged by date or by editor)
- Individual works (arranged alphabetically by title)
- Original text
- Translations (subarranged alphabetically by language and then by translators' names)
- Critical appraisals (subarranged alphabetically by the critics' names)
- General critical appraisals not limited to a single work (subarranged by the critics' names)
- Serial publications devoted to the study of the author

For example:

833.912	Mann, Thomas
M317a	*Gesammelte Werke*
M317t	*Der Tod in Venedig* M317tE *Death in Venice*
M317z	*Der Zauberberg* M317zE *The Magic Mountain*
M317zZm	Miller, R. D. *The Two Faces of Hermes: A Study of Thomas Mann's Novel, "The Magic Mountain"*
M317ze	Eichner, H. *Thomas Mann*
M317zs	Schroter, K. *Thomas Mann*
M317zz	*Blätter der Thomas Mann Gesellschaft*

It should be noted that, in filing, capital letters precede lowercase letters. Shakespeare constitutes a special case because of the large number of editions and translations of his works and of works about him. In DDC, he has been given a special class number, 822.33. Since no other author shares that class number, it would be redundant to base the Cutter number on his name. Therefore, a special scheme of Cutter numbers based on his titles has been developed. It appears in the DDC schedules following the class number 822.33.

In the case of anonymous classics, the Cutter number is based on the preferred title, and the work mark may be taken either from the title of the version being cataloged, or from the editor, translator, or the person most closely associated with the edition, for example:

821.1	Pearl (Middle English poem)
P316c	*The Pearl*; with an introductory essay by S. P. Chase
P316g	*Pearl*; edited by E. V. Gordon
P316zk	Kean, P. M. *The Pearl: An Interpretation*

For various versions of the Bible, it would be redundant to cutter under title, since the class number already represents the Bible, its parts (i.e., the Old and New Testaments), or individual books. The Cutter number is then based on the name of the version, the name of the editor, or, lacking such, on the name of the publisher.

For libraries with large collections of other sacred scriptures, a similar arrangement may be used.

Edition Mark

Many works appear in different editions, which share the same class and Cutter numbers. In order to create a unique call number for each edition, an edition mark in the form of a number is usually added after the work mark or a date under the Cutter number, for example:

025.431 D515d17	025.431 D515d18	025.431 D515d19	025.431 D515d20

or

025.431 D515d 1965	025.431 D515d 1979	025.431 D515d 1989	025.431 D515d 2003

Some libraries use dates as edition marks for all works; others use both methods in the same catalog. The choice of method in each case depends on appropriateness; for instance, dates are usually used when editions are not numbered. When there is more than one edition of a work within a year—as is often the case with literary works—a letter is added arbitrarily to the date, for example, 1976a, 1976b, 1976c, and so on.

Copy and Volume Number

When a work is published in more than one volume or when the library has more than one copy of a work, a volume or copy number, or in some cases both, is added to the call number on the physical volume, in order to provide a unique address for each item in the collection, for example:

025.431	025.431
D515d19	D515d20
v.2	v.1
	copy 2

The copy designation does not appear in the bibliographic record, since the record represents the entire work rather than an individual copy. The volume number may or may not appear there, depending on whether the record has been created for that particular volume or for the entire work. In more recent years, many libraries do not include copy number in the call numbers due to the use of unique bar codes to identify each copy in an online catalog.

Prefixes to Call Numbers

When a particular item is to be shelved in a special location or out of its ordinary place, a prefix may be added to the call number. The most commonly used prefix is the letter *R* for books in the reference collection, for example:

R
031
En19

Prefixes are also used for large-size books, books in special collections, and nonprint materials.

MARC CODING

In a MARC environment, bibliographic field 082 is used in MARC 21 for coding the DDC number. The first indicator is used to identify the type of

Dewey edition used to classify the work, with the edition number indicated in subfield 2. Indicator 2 indicates the type of agency assigning the class number.

The most commonly used subfields are $a for the classification number, $b for item number (including Cutter number, work mark, etc.), and $2 for DDC edition number.

The alternate field 092 may also be used by cataloging agencies contributing records to OCLC's WorldCat that are not the LC, the Library and Archives Canada (NLC), or other national agencies. OCLC Bibliographic Formats defines indicator 1 of field 092 the same as in MARC 21 field 082. Indicator 2 is not defined.

Examples:

Using DDC full edition:
813.4

J233p *The Portrait of a Lady* by Henry James
082 0# $a 813.4 $b J233p $2 23
092 0 $a 813.4 $b J233p $2 23

Using DDC abridged edition:
124
W887t *Teleology* by Andrew Woodfield

092 1 $a 124 $b W887t $2 15

NOTES

1. Dewey, M., and Mitchell, J. S. (2011). *Dewey Decimal Classification and Relative Index* (Ed. 23). Dublin, OH: OCLC, Online Computer Library Center, Inc (p. xxxix).

2. Maltby, A. (1975). *Sayers' Manual of Classification for Librarians* (5th ed.). London, England: Andre Deutsch (p. 121).

Note: John Phillip Comaromi, on the other hand, argued that Hegel provided the philosophic underpinnings of Harris's and Dewey's classification systems. [Comaromi, J. P. (1976). *The Eighteen Editions of the Dewey Decimal Classification.* Albany, NY: Forest Press Division, Lake Placid Education Foundation (p. 29).]

3. Dewey, M., and Mitchell, J. S. (2012). *Abridged Dewey Decimal Classification and Relative Index* (Ed. 15). Dublin, OH: OCLC, Online Computer Library Center, Inc.

4. OCLC, Online Computer Library Center. (2011). *Webdewey* [Subscription service]. Available from www.dewey.org/webdewey/.

5. Dewey, M. (2011). Introduction. In M. Dewey, and J. S. Mitchell (Eds). *Dewey Decimal Classification and Relative Index* (Ed. 23) (pp. xli–xlv). Dublin, OH: OCLC, Online Computer Library Center, Inc.

6. Dewey, M. (2012). Introduction. In M. Dewey, and J. S. Mitchell (2012). *Abridged Dewey Decimal Classification and Relative Index* (Ed. 15) (pp. xxxix–liv). Dublin, OH: OCLC, Online Computer Library Center, Inc.

7. Cutter, C. A., Swanson, P. K., and Swift, E. M. (1969). *C. A. Cutter's Two-figure Author Table* (Swanson-Swift revision). Chicopee, MA: H. R. Huntting Company.

8. Cutter, C. A., Swanson, P. K., and Swift, E. M. (1969). *C. A. Cutter's Three-figure Author Table* (Swanson-Swift revision). Chicopee, MA: H. R. Huntting Company.

9. Cutter, C. A., Jones, K. E., Swanson, P. K., and Swift, E. M. (1969). *Cutter-Sanborn Three-figure Author Table* (Swanson-Swift revision). Chicopee, MA: H. R. Huntting Company.

10. OCLC, Online Computer Library Center. (2014). *Dewey Cutter Program* [Software program]. Available from http://www.oclc.org/support/services/dewey/program.en.html.

11. See also:

Comaromi, J. P. (1981). *Book Numbers: A Historical Study and Practical Guide to their Use*. Littleton, CO: Libraries Unlimited.

Lehnus, D. J. (1980). *Book Numbers: History, Principles, and Application.* Chicago, IL: American Library Association.

Chapter 17

Library of Congress Classification

INTRODUCTION

During most of the nineteenth century, the LC collection was organized according to a system devised by Thomas Jefferson. When the Library moved into its new building in 1897, however, the Jeffersonian system was found to be inadequate for a collection that had grown to over one and a half million pieces. Two other classification systems, the DDC and Charles A. Cutter's Expansive Classification (EC), had emerged during the last few decades of the nineteenth century and were in use in many other libraries in the nation, but neither was considered suitable for the LC. It was decided to construct a new system, to be called the *Library of Congress Classification* LCC, and work began on its development.

From the beginning, individual classes were developed by different groups of specialists working under the direction of J. C. M. Hanson and Charles Martel. The schedules, each of which contained an entire class, a subclass, or a group of subclasses, were published separately. Thus, unlike most other classification systems, LCC was not the product of one mastermind. Indeed, it has been called "a coordinated series of special classes."[1]

Today, the LCC consists of twenty-one classes displayed in over forty separately published print schedules and a large database. Its provisions are continually updated, and information on additions and changes is made widely available to the library community. Although LCC was originally designed expressly for the LC collection, it has been adopted by most large academic and research libraries, as well as by some large public libraries. During the 1960s, in particular, there was a trend among academic libraries previously using DDC or other systems to switch to LCC. There were several reasons for the trend: (1) the basic orientation of LCC toward research libraries; (2) the economic advantage offered by LC cataloging services—libraries can simply adopt whole call numbers as they appear on LC cataloging records; and (3) the increasing ease with which many libraries can bring up full LC MARC records online and add them to their own catalog databases. The fact that LCC is used in so many libraries has had some impact on its development; LC catalogers no longer focus solely on the Library's own needs as they revise and expand the schedules.

In the early stages of Web environment, the potential of using LCC as a tool for organizing Internet resources has also been considered and experimented with.[2,3] An early example of using LCC in a portal was the CyberStacks(sm) system on the Iowa State University web site.[4]

HISTORY

From its earliest days, the two persons primarily responsible for the design and logistics of the new LCC were J. C. M. Hanson and Charles Martel. They chose Cutter's Expansive Classification (EC) as their chief guide, with considerable modification of the EC notation. Some of the early parallels, particularly for Class Z (Book Arts in Cutter; Bibliography and Library Science in LCC) were very close. Figure 17.1, a comparison of Cutter's outline and Hanson's first outline, shows how much the two schemes resembled each other in broad divisions.

For notation, it was decided at the outset to adopt a three-element pattern: first, single capital letters for main classes (H for Social sciences, P for Language and literature, Q for Science, etc.) with one or two capital letters for their subclasses (H for General works on social sciences, HA for Statistics, QD for Chemistry, etc.); second, Arabic integers from 1 to 9999 for subdivisions; and third, Cutter numbers (letter/number strings read decimally) for individual books.[5] Gaps were left for future expansion. Before many decades, parts of the schedules became crowded as knowledge developed. To accommodate new topics, decimal expansion of the original integers was allowed in some cases, and so was the use of Cutter numbers for some topical subdivisions. More recently, three capital letters have been used for some subclasses (KBM for Jewish law and DAW for History of Central Europe).

Class Z was chosen as the first schedule to be developed because its subject matter included the bibliographical works necessary for work on all the other schedules. The LC adopted the Class Z draft in 1898, although the schedule was not published until 1902. From the beginning, the LCC schedules have been developed and published separately, each on its own timetable. The first schedule to be published was Class E–F, *America, History and Geography* (1901). A full system outline appeared in 1904, by which time the classification of Classes D, E–F, M, Q, R, S, T, U, and Z had been completed, and work was underway on Classes A, C, G, H, and V. By 1948, all but

Cutter's Outline	*Hanson's First Outline*
General works	Polygraphy; Encyclopedia; General Periodicals; Societies
Philosophy	Philosophy
Religion	Religion; Theology; Church history
Christianity	
Historical sciences	Biography; and studies auxiliary to history
Biography	General history; periods; and local
History	America; history and geography
Geography and travel	Geography and allied studies
Social sciences	Political science
Demotics, Sociology	Law
Civics	Sociology
Legislation	Women; Societies; clubs, etc.
	Sports and amusements
	Music
	Fine arts
Sciences and Arts	Philology; Literature
Natural history	
Botany	Science; Mathematics; Astronomy; Physics; Chemistry
Zoology	Natural history, general; Geology
	Zoology; Botany
Medicine	Medicine
Useful arts. Technology	Useful arts; Agriculture
Constructive arts	Manufactures
Fabricative arts	Engineering
Art of War	Military and Naval science; light houses; lifesaving; fire extinction
Recreative arts. Music	Special collections
Fine arts	
Language	
Literature	
Book arts	Bibliography (Book arts)

Figure 17.1 Cutter's outline and Hanson's first outline. *Source:* Immroth, J. P. (1971). *A Guide to the Library of Congress Classification*, 2nd ed., pp. 20–21. Littleton, CO: Libraries Unlimited.

one schedule had been completed and published; the exception was Class K (Law). The first schedule of this class, KF (United States law), was published in 1969, and schedules for other subclasses of law have appeared since.

Early 2013, the LC announced that it had ceased print publications of its standards and documentation and was transitioning to online-only publications. At that point, the LCC schedules consisted of forty-one print volumes. At present, the most current edition of each print volume is publicly available online in PDF form, and annual updates are made available through LC's web site for free. The most updated version of the LCC schedules is available electronically at the web site ClassificationWeb.net. This site includes both the LCC and LCSH, with links between many of the class numbers and their LCSH equivalents. In addition, it displays correlations among LCC, LCSH, and OCLC's WebDewey as they are found in LC bibliographic records.

BASIC PRINCIPLES AND STRUCTURE

Overall Characteristics

Like the other classification systems originating in the nineteenth century, the LCC is basically a classification by discipline. Main classes, established to accommodate all subject areas represented in the LC collection, correspond to major academic areas or disciplines. Main classes are divided into subclasses, which in turn reflect individual disciplines or their branches. Classes or subclasses are then further subdivided by topic and/or by form, place, or time. The structure of LCC, therefore, is hierarchical, progressing from the general to the specific. One striking difference between LCC and most other modern classification systems is that it is essentially an enumerative scheme; most subject subdivisions are listed in highly specific detail, and compound or multifaceted subjects are specifically listed as such in the schedules. Even many common divisions, including those for form, are also individually listed under their applicable subjects. Such detailed enumeration means that relatively little notational synthesis, or number building, is required. There are many tables, but these are included mainly as a device for saving space in the schedules; they are usually used for pinpointing specific numbers within a range of numbers given after a caption in a schedule. Thus, tables in LCC have quite a different purpose from those in the DDC and other systems, where numbers can be quite literally "built." LCC's degree of enumeration is only one way in which it differs dramatically from DDC. Another is that, because of the use of letters as notation for representing main classes and subclasses, there is room for a substantially larger number of classes and subclasses to be included.

Although a detailed schema, LCC was not designed as a universal system (i.e., a system that details all existing subjects), but rather as one specifically tailored to LC needs. In other words, it was based on the "literary warrant" of the materials already in, and being added to, the LC itself. To a considerable extent, this fact partly explains the seemingly uneven distribution of LCC notation, especially its preponderance in history and other social sciences.

Figure 17.2 shows the current LCC classes.

Main Classes

The rationale for the arrangement of LCC's main classes was explained by Charles Martel,[6] one of the persons responsible for the original planning and supervision of the development of the system. The class of general works (A), not limited to any particular subject, leads the scheme. It is followed by the class containing philosophy and religion (B), which sets forth theories about human beings in relation to the universe. The next classes in the sequence, history and geography (C–G), cover such concepts as the human abode and the source of humanity's means of subsistence, humans as affected by and affecting their physical milieu, and the mind and soul of humanity in transition from primitive to advanced cultures. The next group, classes H–L, deals with the economic and social evolution of human beings. Classes M–P (music, fine arts, and language and literature) concern human aesthetic and intellectual development and states. Classes B–P form the group of the philosophico-historical and philological sciences. The second large group, Classes Q–V, embraces the mathematico-physical, natural, and applied sciences. Bibliography, which in many libraries may be distributed throughout different subject classes, shares the same class (Z) with librarianship.

Because different persons were responsible for the development of the individual classes, a given class may display unique features. The use of tables and the degree and method for notational synthesis often vary from schedule to schedule. However, certain features are shared by all schedules: the overall organization, the notation, the method and arrangement of form and geographic divisions, and many tables. (These will all be discussed in detail later in the chapter.) The organization of divisions within a class,

A	General works
B	Philosophy. Psychology. Religion
C	Auxiliary Sciences of History
D	World History and History of Europe, Asia, Africa, Australia, New Zealand, etc.
E	History of the Americas
F	History of the Americas
G	Geography. Anthropology. Recreation
H	Social Sciences
J	Political Science
K	Law
L	Education
M	Music and Books on Music
N	Fine Arts
P	Language and Literature
Q	Science
R	Medicine
S	Agriculture
T	Technology
U	Military Science
V	Naval Science
Z	Bibliography. Library Science. Information Resources (General)

Figure 17.2 LCC main classes and subclasses.

subclass, or subject originally followed a general pattern, often called Martel's seven points. Briefly, these are (1) general form divisions; (2) theory/philosophy; (3) history; (4) treatises or general works; (5) law/regulation/state-relations; (6) study and teaching; and (7) special subjects and subdivisions of subjects. Subsequent additions and changes have clouded this pattern to some extent, but it is generally still discernible. Since the development of the K (Law) schedules, legal topics relating to specific subjects have been moved to Class K.

Subclasses

Each of the main classes, with the exception of E and F, is divided into subclasses that represent disciplines or major branches of the main class. Class Q, for example, is divided into the following subclasses:

Q	Science (general)
QA	Mathematics
QB	Astronomy
QC	Physics
QD	Chemistry
QE	Geology
QH	Natural History (General)—Biology (General)
QK	Botany
QL	Zoology
QM	Human anatomy
QP	Physiology
QR	Microbiology

Divisions

Each subclass is further divided into divisions that represent components of the subclass. For example, the subclass chemistry has the following divisions:

QD	*Chemistry*
1-65	General
	Including Alchemy
71-142	Analytical chemistry
146-197	Inorganic chemistry
241-441	Organic chemistry
415-436	Biochemistry
450-801	Physical and theoretical chemistry
625-655	Radiation chemistry

701-731 Photochemistry
901-999 Crystallography

Each of the divisions, in turn, has subdivisions specifying different aspects of the subject, such as form, time, place, and more detailed subject subdivisions. Figure 17.3 shows a portion of the subdivisions under Inorganic chemistry.

QD	*Chemistry*
146-197	Inorganic chemistry
	Cf. QD475 Physical inorganic chemistry
	Cf. QE351 Mineralogy
146	Periodicals, societies, congresses, serial publications
147	Collected works (nonserial)
148	Dictionaries and encyclopedias
149	Nomenclature, terminology, notation, abbreviations
	History
149.5	General works
149.7.A-Z	By region or country, A-Z
150	Early works through 1800
	General works, treatises, and advanced textbooks
151	1801–1969
151.2	1970–2000
151.3	2001-
151.5	Elementary textbooks
152	Addresses, essays, lectures
152.3	Special aspects of the subject as a whole
152.5.A-Z	Special topics, A-Z
	Mathematics
	Reaction mechanisms, see QD502.5
152.5.M38	Study and teaching. Research
153	General works
153.5	Outlines, syllabi, etc.
154	Problems, exercises, examinations
155	Laboratory manuals
155.5	Handbooks, tables, formulas, etc.
156	Inorganic synthesis
	Electric furnace operations
	Cf. QD277, Electric furnace operations (Organic)
157	Nonmetals
161	General works
162	Gases
163	Chemistry of the air
	Cf. TD881 + , Air pollution
165	Halogens: Bromine, chlorine, fluorine, iodine
167	Inorganic acids
	Cf. QD477, General theory of acids and bases

Figure 17.3 Portion of subdivisions under inorganic chemistry.

QD	*Chemistry*
169.A-Z	Other, A-Z
169.C5	Chalcogenides
	Heavy water, see .W3
169.W3	Water
	Cf. GB855+, Natural water chemistry
	Metals
	Cf. TN600 +, Metallurgy
171	General works, treatises, and textbooks
172	By group, A-Z
172.A3	Actinide elements
172.A4	Alkali metals
172.A42	Alkaline earth metals
172.I7	Iron group
172.M4	Magnesium group
172.P8	Platinum group
172.P88	Precious metals
172.R2	Rare earth metals
172.S6	Spinel group
172.S93	Superheavy elements
	Cf. QC796.2 Nuclear physics
172.T52	Titanium group
172.T6	Transition metals
172.T65	Transplutonium elements
172.T7	Transuranium elements

Figure 17.3 *Continued*

NOTATION

Symbols

As mentioned earlier, the LCC uses a mixed notation of letters and Arabic numerals to construct call numbers. Main classes are represented by a single letter, for example, K (Law), N (Fine arts), and Q (Science). Most subclasses are represented by double or triple letters, for example, QD (Chemistry), DJK (History of Eastern Europe), and KFF (Law of Florida). Classes E and F, the earliest classes to be developed, have not been divided into subclasses.

An interesting feature of LCC notation is that, in most schedules, the single letter stands for the class as a whole as well as for its first subclass; this subclass usually involves general works relating to the subject as a whole, but sometimes is the most prominent subclass, which is narrower in scope. For example:

Class H: Social Sciences
  Subclass H: Social Sciences (General)
Class N: Fine arts
  Subclass N: Visual arts

Class P: Language and literature
Subclass P: Philology. Linguistics

Divisions within subclasses are represented by Arabic numbers from 1 to 9999 (as integers) with possible decimal extension, and/or with further subdivision indicated by Cutter numbers (a combination of a capital letter and one or more numerals). An item number (also in the form of a Cutter number) and, in most cases, the year of publication completes the call number. Typical forms of LC call numbers are:

		Class number
DJK	SD	One, two, or three capital letters
7	207	Integer 1 to 9999
.5		Possible decimal extension
.H36	.P57	*Item number*
2004	2004	*Year of publication*

		Class number
HD	N	One, two, or three capital letters
9651	6530	Integer 1 to 9999
.9		Possible decimal extension
.D6	.N6	Cutter number for further subdivision of subject
D69	H64	*Item number*
2004	2003	*Year of publication*

No LC call number contains more than two Cutter numbers. Call numbers for certain types of maps and atlases, however, may contain three letter-number combinations that appear to be triple Cutter numbers.

An important characteristic of LCC notation is that it is not hierarchical beyond the class/subclass level. In other words, the notation does not necessarily reflect whatever general/specific relationships are inherent in the scheme itself. For this reason, there has been some criticism of LCC's nonhierarchical notation.[7] On the other hand, the absence of notational hierarchy can be viewed as an advantage for LCC. For one thing, most of its class numbers are thereby relatively brief, and are thus easily manageable for shelving purposes. For another, LCC notation is remarkably hospitable, in part because relationships are largely ignored.

Hospitality

A classification system with its notation is said to be *hospitable* if it can readily accommodate expansion. Compared with the Dewey system, especially, the LCC notation stands out for its hospitality. One reason is that, from the beginning, generous notational provisions were made for future expansion. At the class level, the alphabet provides a broad base for division by major subject area or discipline—broad enough that not all letters are used, with I, O, X, and Y not yet assigned to any subjects, and thus available for later or specialized use. At the subclass level, generous gaps have been left between two-letter combinations, and these too are available for future expansion or specialized use. An example of specialized use is found in the LCC-based NLM Classification; it has adopted the vacant letter W for Medicine and the unused span QS–QZ for Preclinical sciences. Finally, there is the option of interpolating three-letter combinations to denote new subclasses.

Within subclasses, expansion is usually achieved by using vacant numbers, but when this is not feasible, two other methods can be used: decimal extension and Cutter numbers. Regarding decimal extensions, the absence of hierarchy allows their use for coordinate subjects or even for subjects broader than those represented by shorter numbers. For Cutter numbers, their alphabetical base and broad decimal extensibility make them especially suitable for alphabetical arrangement of subtopics or for geographic subdivision.

Mnemonics

LCC lacks the mnemonic aids found in some other systems. There is some use of mnemonics in Class A, where the second letter for the subclass is taken from the name of the subject covered, for example, A*C* for Collections, A*E* for Encyclopedias, A*S* for Societies, and so on.

EVALUATION OF THE LCC

The LCC[8,9,10] has both strong and weak points, both supporters and detractors. Ideally, someone making decisions on a classification system for a *new* collection would look for one with provisions most suitable for the nature and size of that collection. A medical library, for instance, is best organized by a classification system with deeply detailed provisions for medical topics. Other considerations include the availability of cataloging copy (i.e., of ready-to-use records) and frequency of update of provisions. For existing collections already classed by one system or another, one thing can be said with some force: there must be strong reasons for change, because accomplishing a change is very demanding in terms of personnel and other resources. In this context, the following lists of LCC's merits and weaknesses may be helpful.

Merits

1. The LCC is a practical system that has proven to be satisfactory. "It is a triumph for pragmatism."[11]
2. It is based on the literary warrant of the resources in the LC collection, and of those in academic and research libraries that are members of SACO, a subject authority cooperative.
3. It is largely an enumerative system that requires minimal notational synthesis, or number building.
4. Each schedule was developed by subject specialists rather than by "generalists."
5. Its notation is compact and hospitable.
6. There are frequent additions and changes, stemming for the most part from what is needed in the day-to-day cataloging work at LC and cooperating libraries, and these are made readily available to the cataloging community.
7. The need for reclassification of large blocks of material is kept to a minimum because, to ensure stability of class numbers, few structural changes have been made over the years. (This advantage is also a disadvantage: see point 6 under "Weaknesses," below.)

Weaknesses

1. The LCC's scope notes are inferior to those of the DDC, not providing enough detail.
2. There is much national bias in emphasis and terminology.
3. Too few subjects are seen as compounds. Multitopical or multielement works for which specific provisions have not yet been made cannot be classified with precision.
4. Alphabetical arrangements are often used in place of logical hierarchies.
5. There is little clear and predictable theoretical basis for subject analysis.
6. As a result of maintaining stability, parts of the classification are obsolete in the sense that structure and collocation sometimes do not reflect current conditions.

THE SCHEDULES: REVISION AND PUBLICATION PATTERNS

Revision

Revisions and expansions of LCC take place continuously. Changes are the responsibility of the Policy and Standards Division (PSD) of the LC, with assistance from catalogers at the LC as well as those of cooperating libraries.

Additions and changes often originate with catalogers who become aware of subjects not previously provided for, or who discover anomalies as they attempt to find classification placements for new materials. Proposals are reviewed regularly, and, if approved, they are incorporated into the ClassificationWeb LCC schedules.

APPLYING THE LCC INSTRUCTIONS AND EXAMPLES

The LCC is highly enumerative, with little need for synthesis. There are, however, many places in the schedules where the classifier needs to use tables, and the application rules for these must be learned. Furthermore, in some cases, use of Cutter numbers with LCC is quite complex.

The following instructions and examples are based on LCC schedules H, P, Q, and S. They cover such matters as characteristics of arrays of numbers within classes or subclasses, types of LCC tables, the special Cutter number table used with LCC, Cutter numbers as part of class numbers, double and successive Cutter numbers, and Cutter number variations such as "A" and "Z" Cutter numbers. The focus is on understanding how LCC works in order to use it according to LC policies and practices. In most collections classified by LCC, a large number of new records originate from LC itself; it is generally considered important that records prepared locally should be consistent and compatible with LC practice. Only if this is the case can the full advantage of using LC cataloging copy be realized.

LCC Schedules

To use LCC efficiently, one must be familiar with the format and physical characteristics of the schedules. As noted earlier, the old print version comprised over forty separately published schedules, while the current electronic version consists of a large database of class number entries and an index. The print schedules have similar format, with the following elements found in most of them: (1) a preface; (2) a synopsis of the subclasses; (3) an outline of the major divisions within subclasses; (4) the main array of provisions giving all details except those that need to be extrapolated through the use of tables; (5) any applicable tables; and (6) an index.

Class Numbers

The primary task in classifying according to any system is the same as it is in subject cataloging: identifying the subject content of, and the principal concepts in, the work in hand. The next task is to express that content (even when multiple concepts are involved) as accurately as possible within the provisions of the classification system with which one is working. Given the structure and nature of LCC, most subjects can be found enumerated in the schedules, with whatever form, period, geographic, and topical subdivisions as provided; thus, no notational synthesis is required. In other cases, there are tables to be used as directed, usually within a range of numbers listed in the main schedule or subdivisions by means of Cutter numbers. Finding the optimal classification placement often requires judicial use of whatever indexes are available, careful attention to any scope notes or other placement directions pertaining to the subject at issue, and persistent study of the list of captions preceding and following what one has selected as a starting point. It may involve using a table or constructing complicated Cutter numbers.

Figure 17.4, taken from the schedule for Class Q, Science, shows typical divisions of a scientific subject, and also illustrates the possible helpfulness of "cf." and "see" references. As can be seen from Figure 17.4, the numbers QC120–129.5 contain form, period, and geographic divisions of the subject, Descriptive and experimental mechanics. A journal on this subject is classed in QC120, and a current treatise on the subject is classed in QC125.2. Numbers beginning with QC133 provide topical divisions of the subject, such as Dynamics, Motion, and so on. Each of the topical divisions may have its own subdivisions, depending on literary warrant. More elaborate subdivisions appear under Fluids and Fluid mechanics than under Dynamics; thus, a handbook on Fluid mechanics is classed in QC145.3. When no form divisions are provided under a particular subject, the number designated for General works is used for all forms; a handbook on Dynamics is, therefore, classed in QC133.

Cutter Numbers

As mentioned earlier, the Cutter number is used in LCC for two purposes: as a further extension of the class number (as part of subfield $a, e.g., $a HD9651.9.D6 $b D69 2004) and as an item or book number. A Cutter number consists of a capital letter followed by an Arabic number; the number is read decimally and the decimal point precedes the letter, for example, .T7, .T7324, .T745, .T8, and so on. The decimal feature of Cutter numbers is important, because it allows for infinite interpolation on the decimal principle.

Because, in most cases, subject provisions in LCC are developed in greater detail than those in the Dewey system, not as many items are likely to be assigned the same class number. Therefore, the elaborate Cutter tables used with DDC are not needed for constructing LCC item numbers. Instead,

QC Physics

Descriptive and Experimental Mechanics

For theoretical and analytical mechanics see *QA801–939*
Cf. *QC71.82–73.8* Force and energy (General)
Cf. *QC176–176.9* Solid state physics
Cf. *TA349–359* Applied mechanics

QC120	Periodicals, societies, congresses, serial publications
QC121	Collected works (nonserial)
QC121.6	Dictionaries and encyclopedias
QC121.8	Nomenclature, terminology, notation, abbreviations
	History
	For general history of mechanics see *QA802*
QC122	General works
QC122.2.A-Z	By region or country, A-Z
QC123	Early works through 1800
	General works, treatises, and advanced textbooks
QC125	1801–1969
QC125.2	1970–
QC127	Elementary textbooks
QC127.3	Popular works
QC127.4	Juvenile works
QC127.6	Addresses, essays, lectures
	Study and teaching. Research
QC128	General works
QC129	Problems, exercises, examinations
QC129.5	Laboratory manuals
QC131	Special aspects of the subject as a whole
	Dynamics. Motion
	Cf. *QA843–871* Analytic mechanics
QC133	General works, treatises, and textbooks
QC133.5	Juvenile works
QC135	Kinematics
QC136	Vibrations
	Cf. *QA865–867.5* Analytic mechanics (Dynamics)
	Cf. *QA935–939* Vibrations of elastic bodies
	Cf. *QC231* Sound
	Cf. *TA355* Engineering
QC137	Inertia
	Including Mach's principle
	Velocity. Speed
	Cf. *QC233* Velocity of sound
	Cf. *QC407* Velocity of light
QC137.5	General works, treatises, and textbooks
QC137.52	Juvenile works
	Fluids. Fluid mechanics
	Including liquids
	Cf. *QA901–930* Analytic mechanics
	Cf. *TA357–359* Applied fluid mechanics
QC138	Periodicals, societies, congresses, serial publications

Figure 17.4 Divisions of a subject: Class Q, Science: QC, Physics.

QC139	Dictionaries and encyclopedias
QC140	Nomenclature, terminology, notation, abbreviations
QC141	History
QC142	Early works through 1500
	General works, treatises, and textbooks
QC143	1501–1700
QC144	1701–1800
QC145	1801–1969
QC145.2	1970–
QC145.24	Juvenile works
QC145.26	Addresses, essays, lectures
QC145.28	Study and teaching
QC145.3	Handbooks, tables, formulas, etc.
QC145.4.A-Z	Special properties of liquids, A-Z
QC145.4.A25	Acoustic properties
QC145.4.C6	Compressibility
QC145.4.D5	Diffusion
QC145.4.E45	Electric properties
QC145.4.E9	Expansion
QC145.4.M27	Magnetic properties
QC145.4.O6	Optical properties

Figure 17.4 *Continued*

a relatively simple Cutter table, shown in Figure 17.5,[12] is used. Since the table provides only a general framework for the assignment of numbers, the symbol for a particular name or work is constant only under a particular class number. Each entry must be added to the existing entries in the shelf-list in such a way as to create unique call numbers and preserve alphabetical order in accordance with filing rules.

Cutter Number as Part of Class Number

In Figure 17.3, under QD149.7, the caption "By region or country, A-Z" indicates that Cutter numbers are to be used for geographic division of the subject, History of inorganic chemistry. In Figure 17.4, QC145.4 carries the caption "Special properties of liquids, A-Z." This means that individual properties are represented by Cutter numbers after the main class number. For example, the class number for the subject of expansion of fluids contains the following elements:

QC	Double letters for the subclass, Physics
145.4	Arabic number meaning special properties of liquids
.E9	Cutter number for expansion

1. ***After initial vowels***

for the second letter:	**b**	**d**	**l-m**	**n**	**p**	**r**	**s-t**	**u-y**
use number:	**2**	**3**	**4**	**5**	**6**	**7**	**8**	**9**

2. After the initial letter *S*

for the second letter:	**a**	**ch**	**e**	**h-i**	**m-p**	**t**	**u**	**w-z**
use number:	**2**	**3**	**4**	**5**	**6**	**7**	**8**	**9**

3. After the initial letters ***Qu***

for the second letter:	**a**	**e**	**i**	**o**	**r**	**t**	**y**
use number:	**3**	**4**	**5**	**6**	**7**	**8**	**9**

for initial letters ***Qa-Qt***
use numbers: **2–29**

4. After other initial ***consonants***

for the second letter:	**a**	**e**	**i**	**O**	**r**	**u**	**y**
use number:	**3**	**4**	**5**	**6**	**7**	**8**	**9**

5. For ***expansion***

for the letter:	**a-d**	**e-h**	**i-l**	**m-o**	**p-s**	**t-v**	**w-z**
use number:	**3**	**4**	**5**	**6**	**7**	**8**	**9**

Letters not included in the table are assigned the next higher or lower number, as required by previous assignments in the particular class.

The arrangements in the following examples illustrate possible applications of this table:

Vowels		**S**		**Q**		**Consonants**	
IBM	.I26	Sadron	.S23	*Qadduri	.Q23	Campbell	.C36
Idaho	.I33	*Scanlon	.S29	*Qiao	.Q27	Ceccaldi	.C43
*Ilardo	.I4	Schreiber	.S37	Quade	.Q33	*Chertok	.C48
*Import	.I48	*Shillingburg	.S53	Queiroz	.Q45	*Clark	.C58
Inman	.I56	*Singer	.S57	Quinn	.Q56	Cobblestone	.C63
Ipswich	.I67	Stinson	.S75	Quorum	.Q67	Cryer	.C79
*Ito	.I87	Suryani	.S87	Qutub	.Q88	Cuellar	.C84
*Ivy	.I94	*Symposium	S96	*Qvortrup	.Q97	Cymbal	.C96

[The Cutter numbers marked by the asterisk (*) reflect the adjustments made to allow for a range of letters on the table, e.g., l–m, or for letters not explicitly stated, e.g., h after an initial consonant.]

Figure 17.5 Cutter table. *Source: Classification and Shelflisting Manual,* G 63 Cutter numbers.

Cutter Number as Item Number

Each call number contains an item number generally based on the main entry of the work. Its main purpose is to distinguish different works on the same subject that have been given the same class number. If the Cutter number taken from the table has already been assigned to another work, it is adjusted for the work being classified. The following example illustrates the assignment of Cutter number for authors writing on the same topic:

	Barro, Robert J.
HB172.5.B37	*Money, expectations, and business cycles : essay in macroeconomics*
	Barron, John M.
HB172.5.B375	*Macroeconomics*
	Baumol, William J.
HB172.5.B38	*Macroeconomics: principles and policy*

According to the Cutter table, names beginning with Bar- are assigned the Cutter number .B37. In this case, because .B37 has already been assigned to Barro, the Cutter number assigned to Barron was adjusted as .B375.

If the same author has written more than one work on a subject, the Cutter numbers are adjusted in a similar manner. Because .B37 has been assigned to Barro's *Money, expectations, and business cycles*, his other book, *Macroeconomics*, arriving in the library after the first book, was then assigned the number .B36, to maintain the alphabetical sequence by title:

	Barro, Robert J.
HB172.5.B36	*Macroeconomics*
HB172.5.B37	*Money, expectations, and business cycles: essays in macroeconomics*

In order to place a translation of a work with the original text, the call number of the original work with an extension of the item number is assigned to the translation, for example:

	Remmert, Reinhold
QA331.R46	*Funktionentheorie* [original work in German]
QA331.R4613	*Theory of complex functions* [an English translation of the above title]

The Table for Translations[11] (see Figure 17.6) is used unless there are specific instructions for subarranging translations in the schedules.

.x	Cutter number for original work
.x12	Polyglot
.x13	English translation
.x14	French translation
.x15	German translation
.x16	Italian translation
.x17	Russian translation
.x18	Spanish translation

Figure 17.6 Translations. *Source: Classification and Shelflisting Manual,* G 150 Translations/Texts in parallel languages.

In Figure 17.6, the letter x represents the Cutter number assigned to the original work. The Arabic numerals representing languages may be adjusted to accommodate translations in languages other than the ones shown in the table. For instance, for a Bulgarian translation, one may use .x13 if the original work is in English or .x125 if the original is in a language other than English.

Double Cutter Numbers

When a class number includes a Cutter number as a subdivision, a second Cutter number is added as the item or book number, resulting in a double Cutter number.

For example, a work about computer security is assigned the following call number:

> *Techniques and applications of digital watermarking and content protection* / Michael Arnold, Martin Schmucker, Stephen D. Wolthusen. 2003
>
> QA Double letters meaning Mathematics
> 76.9 Arabic number meaning topics about Computers
> .A25 First Cutter number for the topic Access control; computer security
> A76 Item number for the main entry under Arnold
> 2003 Date of publication

Note that only one decimal point, preceding the first Cutter number, is required for double Cutter numbers. (The first decimal in the call number above results from numerical expansion of the schedule notation, and thus is not part of the Cutter sequence.)

Call numbers for biography often contain double Cutter numbers, one for the biographee and one for the biographer, for example, a biography of LeBron James, by Lew Freedman:

LeBron James : a biography / Lew Freedman 2008

GV	Double letters for Recreation and leisure
884	Arabic number meaning a biography associated with basketball
.J36	First Cutter number for James
F74	Second Cutter number for Freedman
2008	Date of publication

In rare instances, both Cutter numbers may be extensions of the class number, and the call number will then not include an item number.

Successive Cutter Numbers

Successive Cutter numbers are a series of consecutive Cutter numbers (e.g., .F3, .F4, .F5) or decimal extensions of a Cutter number (e.g., .F32, .F33, .F34, .F35) in an established sequence. They are used when certain works are to be grouped on the shelves in an established order. An example is the additional digits for a translation (e.g., 14, French) attached to an item number. Frequently in the schedules and in the tables, there are instructions to use successive Cutter numbers. They are used most frequently in tables for internal subarrangement (see examples in the section "Tables for Internal Subarrangement").

A and Z Cutter Numbers

Under a class number, a span of Cutter numbers at the beginning or at the end of the alphabetical sequence is, in some cases, assigned special meanings. These spans are called "A" Cutter numbers and "Z" Cutter numbers, respectively. The "A" Cutter numbers are used most frequently for form divisions such as periodicals or official publications, for example:

QC	PHYSICS
174.4	Quantum statistics
174.4.A1	Periodicals, societies, congresses, serial publications
174.4.A2	Collected works (nonserial)
174.4.A6-Z	General works, treatises, and textbooks

The Cutter numbers .A1 and .A2 are used for serial publications and nonserial collected works. The numbers A3-.A5 are not used at present. A treatise on quantum statistics by an author named Adams, which is normally assigned the Cutter number .A3 according to the Cutter table, will receive a Cutter number greater than .A6.

The "Z" Cutter numbers are often assigned to special divisions of the subject, such as biography and criticism of a literary author, or corporate bodies associated with the subject.

UA ARMIES:	ORGANIZATION, DISTRIBUTION, ETC.
	By region or country
	Europe
	France
	Army
	Artillery
705.A1-.A5	Documents
.A6-.Z4	General works
.Z5	Bataillons d'artillerie à pied
.Z6	Regiments. By number and author

Dates in Call Numbers

Dates in LC call numbers serve two functions. A date may be part of the class number; at various points in the schedules, there are dates listed explicitly, or there are instructions about using them. A date may also be part of an item number; the date of publication or copyright is now added to the Cutter numbers for all monographs and to later editions of serials.

Date as Part of Class Number

The following example shows a case in which a date is called for as part of a class number.

Rainbow's end: the crash of 1929 Maury Klein. 2003

HB	Economic theory
3717	History of crises
1929	Date of the crisis

In such cases, the item number and date of publication follow the first date to complete the call number, that is, HB3717 1929 .K54 2003.

Date of Publication in Item Numbers

The date of publication is added to an item number for all monographic publications (including most types of nonprint materials) and to later editions of serials. An example is shown below.

Economic growth / Robert J. Barro, Xavier Sala-i-Martin. 2nd ed. c2004

HD	Industries. Land use. Labor
75.5	Mathematical models
.B37	Item number based on the main entry, Barro
2004	Date of publication

Since different editions of the same work receive the same class and item numbers, they are distinguished by dates of publication.

	Reagan, Nancy
E878.R43A3 1989	*My turn : the memoirs of Nancy Reagan* (Random House, c1989)
E878.R43A3 1990	*My turn : the memoirs of Nancy Reagan* (Thorndike Press large print edition, 1990)
	Heyne, Paul T.
HB171.5.H46 1990	*The economic way of thinking*. 6th ed. 1990
HB171.5.H46 2003	*The economic way of thinking*. 10th ed. 2003

If different dates are shown in the work, the date to be used in the call number is based on the imprint or copyright date given in the "publication, distribution, etc." area in the bibliographic record.

If there is more than one edition of the same work published in the same year, a lowercase letter (called a *work letter*) is added to the date. The work letters are assigned in the following manner:

[date]	Original work
[date]a	A facsimile or photocopy edition, the date being that of the original
[date]b	A variant edition published in the same year
[date]c	Another variant edition
etc.	

For supplements and indexes, the designations *Suppl., Suppl. 2*, etc., and *Index, Index 2,* etc., are added after the date.

TABLES

Tables represent recurring patterns of subdivision. Those familiar with other classification systems will find a basic difference between LCC tables and those used in other systems. The tables in the Dewey system, for instance, provide additional segments to be *attached* to a main class number, extending it lengthwise to render it more specific. In LCC, with the exception of those for subdivisions that are represented by Cutter numbers, the tables are a device for locating the desired number within a range of numbers given in the schedule. Usually, the number given in the table is *added* (in the arithmetic sense) instead of being attached to the base number from the schedule. The base number is normally given in the schedule under the class number or numbers for which the table is to be used.

There are two types of tables in LCC: tables of general application and tables of limited application. Tables of general application include (1) the biography table (G320), (2) the translation table mentioned earlier (G150), and (3) geographic tables (G300 & G302) based on Cutter numbers. These tables were initially used with only a few schedules, but are now applicable throughout the schedules, whenever called for. In turn, there are two kinds of LCC tables that are limited in their application: one applies to a whole class or subclass, and the other (referred to as "tables for internal subarrangement") is used with specific spans of numbers. These tables are applied only according to specific directions in the schedules. Tables appear either in the schedules or in the *Classification and Shelflisting Manual.*[13]

Tables of General Application

Several tables for general application are discussed with illustrations below.

Tables for Geographic Division by Means of Cutter Numbers

Two methods for geographic subdivision are used in LCC. One is through regular class numbers within the schedules; the other is through the use of tables containing Cutter numbers.

Regions and Countries Table (G300). The Regions and Countries Table provides alphabetical arrangement of countries by means of Cutter numbers. It is used whenever the schedule gives the instruction "By region or country, A-Z." This table is found in *Classification and Shelflisting Manual.*[14]

Figure 17.7 shows portions of the table. The following examples illustrate its application.

Canada's federal marine protected areas strategy. c2005

QH	Natural history (general)
91.75	Marine parks and reserves: By region or country, A-Z
.C2	Canada (according to "Regions and Countries Table")
C36	Cutter number for the main entry under the title, *Canada's federal . . .*
2005	Date of publication

Abyssinia *see* Ethiopia		Great Britain	G7
Afghanistan	A3	Greece	G8
Africa	A35	Greenland	G83
Africa, Central	A352	Grenada	G84
Africa, East	A353	Salvador	S2
Africa, Eastern	A354	Samoa	S23
Africa, French-Speaking West	A3545	United States	U6
Caribbean Area	C27	Vatican City	V3
Caroline Islands	C275	Venezuela	V4
Caucasus	C28	Vietnam	V5
		Zimbabwe	Z55

Figure 17.7 Regions and countries (portions).

Micro enterprise development in Ghana / by Richard Jinks Bani. 2003

HD	Industries. Land use. Labor
2346	Small business. Medium-sized business: By region or country, A-Z
.G4	Ghana (according to "Regions and Countries Table")
B36	Cutter number for the main entry, Bani
2003	Date of publication

Although the table is applied universally, the Cutter number assigned to a particular country may sometimes vary under different class numbers, depending on what already exists in the shelf-list. For example, although .U6 is the Cutter number listed in the table for the United States, the following example displays that .U5 is assigned instead.

Abortion—murder or mercy? : analyses and bibliography / Francois B. Gerard (compiler). 2001

HQ	The family. Marriage. Woman
767	Abortion
.5	By region or country, A-Z
.U5	United States
A2655	Cutter number for the main entry under title, *Abortion . . .*
2001	Date of publication

The *Table of American States and Canadian Provinces (G302)* contains an alphabetical list of the states and regions of the United States and provinces in Canada, and is used when the instruction "By state, A-W" or "By province, A-Z" appears under numbers assigned to the United States or Canada in the schedule. The table is found in *Classification and Shelflisting Manual*.[15] The following examples illustrate its use.

The state of North Dakota: economic, demographic, public service, and fiscal conditions : a presentation of selected indicators / by Randal C. Coon, F. Larry Leistritz. 2003

HC	Economic history and conditions
107	United States, by region or state
.N9	North Dakota (according to the table "American States and Canadian Provinces")
C66	Item number based on the main entry, Coon
2003	Date of publication

Industry and society in Nova Scotia: an illustrated history / Jim Candow, editor. 2001

HC	Economic history and conditions
117	Canada (the seventh number in the range HC111-120 assigned to Canada in the main schedule, chosen according to Table H15 in the schedule), by state, etc., A-Z
.N8	Nova Scotia (according to the table "American States and Canadian Provinces")
I53	Item number based on the main entry under title: *Industry and . . .*
2001	Date of publication

Biography Table

When works about a person, including autobiography, letters, speeches, and biography, are classed in a number designated for individual biography, they are subarranged according to the biography table. This table (G320, reproduced in Figure 17.8) contains extensions (in the form of successive Cutter numbers) of the Cutter number (represented by .x in the table) assigned to the individual or biographee.

.x	Cutter number for the biographee
.xA2	Collected works. By date
.xA25	Selected works. Selections. By date including quotations
.xA3	Autobiography, diaries, etc. By date
.xA4	Letters. By date
.xA5	Speeches, essays, and lectures. By date including interviews
.xA68-Z	Individual biography, interviews, and criticism. By main entry Including criticism of selected works, autobiography, quotations letters, speeches, interviews, etc.

Figure 17.8 Biography.

Application of the biography table results in double Cutter numbers: the first Cutter number (shown as .x in the table) is for the biographee and the second is taken from the table. The use of "A" Cutter numbers for autobiographical writings in this table results in works written by the biographee to be filed before works written by other people about him or her. The table is found in *Classification and Shelflisting Manual*.[16] The following example illustrates the use of the biography table.

The autobiography of William Sanders Scarborough: an American journey from slavery to scholarship / edited and with an introduction by Michele Valerie Ronnick; foreword by Henry Louis Gates, Jr. c2005

E	History: United States
185.97	Elements in the population—African Americans—Individual biography
.S28	First Cutter number for Scarborough
A3	Second Cutter number (for autobiography) from the Biography Table
2005	Date of publication

Tables of Limited Application

Tables Applicable to an Individual Class or Subclass

Many LCC schedules contain tables that apply to an entire class or subclass only. Examples include the author tables used throughout the schedules for Class P, Language and literature; the form tables used in the schedules of Class K, Law; and the geographic tables in Class H, Social sciences, and in Class S, Agriculture. These may be Cutter tables, numerical tables, or a combination of both.

In using a table that contains Cutter numbers, the appropriate Cutter number, adjusted if necessary, is simply attached to the main number from the schedule.

In applying a numerical table, the following steps should be followed:

1. Find the range of numbers in the schedule within which the subject being represented falls, and note its base number.
2. Determine the appropriate table to be applied to the specific range of numbers.
3. Select the number in the table that represents the specific subject or aspect appropriate to the item being classified, and fit the number (usually by simple substitution or addition) into the range of numbers from the schedule.

Geography tables in Class S. An example of numerical tables is the "Geographical Distribution Tables" in Class S, Agriculture. A portion of Table S2 is reproduced in Figure 17.9. The following example illustrates the application of Table S2.

> *Development of forest resources in the European part of the Russian Federation* / by A.I. Pisarenko . . . [et al.]. 2001
>
> SD Forestry
> 207 Number for a history of forestry in Russia
> .D48 Cutter number for the main entry under the title, *Development of . . .*
> 2001 Date of publication

The number SD207 is determined by following the steps outlined below:

1. In Schedule S, the numbers SD145-245 have been assigned to the history of forestry subdivided geographically.
2. These class numbers are to be used with Table S2 for specific countries.
3. The number 63, meaning Russia (General Works), from Table S2 is added to the base number 144, as given in the schedule.

Geography tables in Class H. The "Tables of Geographical Divisions" in Class H consist of a group of ten tables (Tables H1–H10) providing detailed geographic divisions. They are used with spans of numbers given in the main schedules, with specific instructions indicating which table is to be used in a particular case. For example, to classify a work about the standard of living in Asia and Europe, the first step is to find the appropriate class number or numbers in the schedule:

S2	
	America
	North America
1–2	Canada
3–4	Mexico
5–6	Central America
7–8	West Indies
33	Europe
35–36	Great Britain. England
37–38	Wales
59–60	Norway
61–62	Portugal
63–64	Russia. Soviet Union. Russia (Federation)

Figure 17.9 Geography (portions of S2) from Class S.

HD	INDUSTRIES. LAND USE. LABOR
	Labor. Work. Working class
	Cost and standard of living
6981-7080	By region or country. (Table H1 modified)

The instruction indicates that numbers from "Table H1 modified" are to be added to HD6980. A portion of Table H1 is reproduced as Figure 17.10. (The term "modified" refers to variations from the table, noted in the schedule.) The number designated for Asia in Table H1 is 68. This number is added to the base number HD6980 (instead of 6981, which is the first number in the range, not the base number) to obtain the desired number, HD7048. Attaching the item number for the main entry and the date of publication yields the desired call number, HD7048.L58 2005. This number is analyzed below:

> *Living standards in the past : new perspectives on well-being in Asia and Europe* / edited by Robert C. Allen, Tommy Bengtsson, and Martin Dribe. 2005

HD	Industries. Land use. Labor
7048	Cost and standard of living in Asia
.L58	Cutter number for the main entry under the title, *Living . . .*
2005	Date of publication

Since the schedule does not provide for period subdivision, the chronological aspect of the book is not represented in the class number.

The following example illustrates the use of Table H19 (Table for Industries and Trades) in Class H. In the schedule for Class H, chemical industries are given the span of numbers HD9650-9660, with the instruction to use Table H19 (Table for Industries and Trades (10 nos.)). A work about the Dow Chemical Company in the United States, written by Jack Doyle, is classed in HD9651.9 .D6D69 2004.

> *Trespass against us : Dow Chemical & the toxic century* / Jack Doyle. 2004

HD	Industries. Land use. Labor
9651	Second number (according to Table H19) in the range HD 9650-9660 assigned to chemical industries—United States in the schedule
.9	By firm, A-Z (1.9.A-Z in Table H19)
.D6	Cutter number for Dow Chemical
D69	Cutter number for the main entry, Doyle
2004	Date of publication

H1	Tables of Geographical Divisions
1	America. Western Hemisphere
	North America
2	General works
	United States
3	General works
4	Northeastern States. New England
5	Middle Atlantic States. Middle States
15	Canada
15.25	Saint Pierre and Miquelon Islands
	Asia
68	General works
	Middle East. Near East
68.2	General works
	Caucasus
68.215	General works
68.22	Armenia

Figure 17.10 Geographical divisions (portions of H1) in Class H.

Author tables in Class P. The author tables in Class P present special features because provision has to be made for a large number of related works. Their use is illustrated below. Works written by and about an individual literary author are classed together in LCC. Each author is assigned a range of numbers, a number, or a Cutter number. The literature tables used with authors, originally published in the appropriate schedules of Class P, have been revised, renumbered, and published together in a separate volume entitled *Library of Congress Classification: P-PZ: Language and Literature Tables*. These tables provide patterns for subarrangement of works by and about literary authors. The following examples illustrate the use of author tables in Class P.

> *The Chicago of Europe, and other tales of foreign travel* / Mark Twain; edited and introduced by Peter Kaminsky. 2009
>
> PS American literature
> 1302 Third number ("2" in Table P-PZ31 modified) in the range of 1300–1348 assigned to Clemens, Samuel Langhorne (Mark Twain) for selected works
> .K28 Item number based on the name of the editor, Kaminsky, as instructed in Table P-PZ31
> 2009 Date of publication

> *The adventures of Huckleberry Finn* / Mark Twain; foreword by Azar Nafisi; introduction and notes by R. Kent Rasmussen. 2014
>
> PS American literature

1305 Number (within the range of 5–22 designated for separate works by an author with 49 numbers in Table P-PZ31) assigned specifically to *The adventures of Huckleberry Finn*
.A1 Cutter number (according to Table P-PZ41, "Table for Separate works (1 no.)"), meaning the text of the work arranged by date (if no editor is given)
2014 Date of publication

Selected stories and poems of Edgar Allan Poe. 2009
PS American literature
2602 Third number (2) in the range 0–49 in Table P-PZ31 for selections fitted into the range of numbers PS2600–2648 assigned to Poe in the schedule
2009b Date of publication, with the letter b to indicate a variant edition published in the same year

No Cutter number is assigned to this work because the author's name, Poe, is already implied in the class number, and no editor is given.

The following examples illustrate the application of Table P-PZ32 for Alexander Pope, an author assigned nineteen numbers.

The Dunciad : in four books / edited by Valerie Rumbold. 1999
PR English literature
3625 Number assigned to *Dunciad* in the schedule (within the range of numbers (25-30) for separate works according to Table P-PZ32, i.e., PR3625-3630 for Pope)
.A2 Text arranged by editor (according to Table P-PZ41, Table for Separate Works (1 no.))
R86 Item number based on the name of the editor, Rumbold
1999 Date of publication

More solid learning : new perspectives on Alexander Pope's Dunciad / edited by Catherine Ingrassia, Claudia N. Thomas. c2000
PR English literature
3625 Number for *Dunciad*
.M67 Cutter number (within the range of .A7-Z for criticism according to Table P-PZ41) based on the main entry under the title: *More . . .*
2000 Date of publication

Tables for Internal Subarrangement

Tables designed for use with specific spans of numbers are scattered throughout the schedules. Such tables are used for subarrangement within a span of numbers, and may contain form, period, geographic, and/or subject elements. They range from a few lines of instructions to several pages.

Table 17.11 contains an example of tables for internal subarrangement from Class H, found under HE215–300. For example, a work about transportation and communications in Canada is classed in HE215. In Table H1 (partially reproduced in Figure 17.7), Canada is assigned the number of 15, which is to be added to the base number HE200 shown in Figure 17.11 to form the number HE215. Adding the item number results in HE215.A15T7a, which is analyzed below:

> *Annual report to Parliament* / Transportation Safety Board of Canada. 199?-
>
> HE Transportation and communications
>
> 215 Number for Canada, resulting from adding the number 15 from Table H1 to the base number 200
>
> .A15 First Cutter number meaning serial publications from internal table HE215/1 for 1-number countries (i.e., countries that have been assigned one Cutter number each)
>
> T7 Second Cutter number for the main entry, Transportation safety . . .
>
> a Work letter for a serial publication

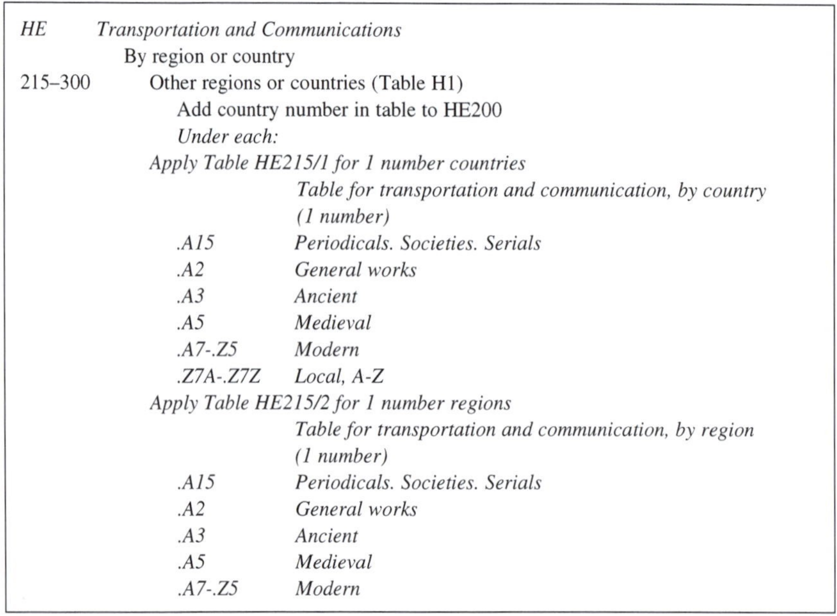

HE *Transportation and Communications*
By region or country
215–300 Other regions or countries (Table H1)
Add country number in table to HE200
Under each:
Apply Table HE215/1 for 1 number countries
Table for transportation and communication, by country (1 number)
.A15 *Periodicals. Societies. Serials*
.A2 *General works*
.A3 *Ancient*
.A5 *Medieval*
.A7-.Z5 *Modern*
.Z7A-.Z7Z *Local, A-Z*
Apply Table HE215/2 for 1 number regions
Table for transportation and communication, by region (1 number)
.A15 *Periodicals. Societies. Serials*
.A2 *General works*
.A3 *Ancient*
.A5 *Medieval*
.A7-.Z5 *Modern*

Figure 17.11 Internal (HE).

A general work on the same subject is classed in HE215.A2:

> *Weather and transportation in Canada* / edited by Jean Andrey and Christopher Knapper. c2003
>
> HE Transportation and communications
>
> 215 Number for Canada, resulting from adding the number 15 from Table H1 to the base number 200
>
> .A2 Cutter number meaning general works from internal table HE215/1 for 1-number countries
>
> W43 Second Cutter number for the main entry under the title, *Weather . . .*
>
> 2003 Date of publication

Some internal tables are simple, containing only two or three numbers. An example is the table under HD3616.A-Z shown in Figure 17.2. Figure 17.12 contains a small table (using successive Cutter numbers, .x, .x2, .x3, .x4). Note that the first Cutter number in the small table is .x (e.g., .C2 for a periodical on industrial policy in Canada) instead of .x1 (.C21), because the use of a Cutter number ending in the digit '1' limits the possibility of interpolation, and is, therefore, generally avoided. Furthermore, the digit 1 is used to introduce a successive Cutter number for a translation, for example, .C214 for a French translation and .C215 for a German translation of a work assigned the Cutter number .C2.

An example of applying the small internal table is shown below:

> *Between public and private: readings and cases on Canada's mixed economy* / edited by Diane Jurkowski, George Eaton. c2003
>
> HD Industries. Land use. Labor
>
> 3616 Industrial policy by region or country
>
> .C23 Cutter number (.C2 for Canada according to the Regions and Countries Table) with the successive number (3) for public policy based on the internal table under 3616.A-Z
>
> B48 Item number based on the main entry under the title, *Between . . .*
>
> 2003 Date of publication

HD	*Industries. Land Use. Labor*
	Industry
	Industrial policy. The state and industrial organization
3616.A-Z	By region or country, A-Z
	Under each country (except the United States):

Figure 17.12 Internal (HD).

.x	*Periodicals. Societies. Serials*
.x2	*History*
.x3	*Public policy*
.x4A-.x4Z	*Local, A-Z*

Figure 17.12 *Continued*

In many cases, call numbers are constructed by using a combination of different types of tables. An example is given below.

> *Working across boundaries: collaboration in public services* / Helen Sullivan and Chris Skelcher. 2002
> HD Industries. Land use. Labor
> 4148 Public policy regarding state industries and public works
> .S85 Cutter number for the main entry, Sullivan
> 2002 Date of publication

In this example, the main number HD4148 is constructed as follows:

1. Locate the appropriate range of numbers in the schedule:
   HD4001-4420.7 Industry
   Industrial policy. The state and industrial organization. State industries. Public works. Government ownership
   By region or country
   Other regions or countries (Table H9)
   Add country number in table to HD4000
2. Consult Table H9 for the numbers assigned to Great Britain:
   141-150
3. Consult the internal table HD4001/1 for 10 number countries, under HD4001-4420.7:
   8 Public policy
4. Choose the eighth number in the range 141-150: 148
5. Add 148 to 4000: 4148

MARC CODING

In a MARC environment, bibliographic field 050 is used in MARC 21 for coding the LCC number. The first indicator is used to identify whether the item is contained in the LC collections. Indicator 2 indicates the agency assigning the class number, with 0 indicating that LC assigned the class number and 4 indicating that an agency other than LC assigned the class number.

The most commonly used subfields are $a for the classification number and $b for the item number (including Cutter number and date).

The alternate field 090 may also be used by cataloging agencies contributing records to OCLC's WorldCat that are not the LC, the Library and Archives Canada (NLC), or other national agencies. OCLC Bibliographic Formats does not define either indicators.

Examples:

The Chicago of Europe, and other tales of foreign travel / Mark Twain; edited and introduced by Peter Kaminsky. 2009

PS
1302
.K28
2009

050 00 $a PS1302 $b .K28 2009
090 $a 813.4 $b J233p $2 23

Between public and private: readings and cases on Canada's mixed economy / edited by Diane Jurkowski, George Eaton. ©2003

HD
3616
.C23
B48
2003

050 _0 $a HD3616.C23 $b B48 2003
090 $a HD3616.C23 $b B48 2003

NOTES

1. Maltby, A. (1975). *Sayers' Manual of Classification for Librarians* (5th ed.). London, England: Andre Deutsch (p. 175).
2. Vizine-Goetz, D. (1999). *Using Library Classification Schemes for Internet Resources*. OCLC Internet Cataloging Project Colloquium Position Paper. Retrieved from http://staff.oclc.org/~vizine/Intercat/vizine-goetz.htm.
3. Koch, T. (1999). *The Role of Classification Schemes in Internet Resource Description and Discovery*. Retrieved from http://www.ukoln.ac.uk/metadata/desire/classification/index.html.
4. CyberStacks(sm). (August 24, 1998). *Welcome to CyberStacks(sm)!* Retrieved from http://www2.iastate.edu/~cyberstacks/.
5. Hanson, J. C. M. (1929). The Library of Congress and its new catalogue: Some unwritten history. In W. W. Bishop and A. Keogh (Eds.), *Essays Offered to Herbert*

Putnam by his Colleagues and Friends on his Thirtieth Anniversary as Librarian of Congress: 5 April 1929. New Haven, CT: Yale University Press (pp. 186–87).

6. LaMontagne, L. E. (1961). *American Library Classification with Special Reference to the Library of Congress*. Hamden, CT: Shoe String Press (p. 254).

7. Maltby, 1975, p. 180.

8. Maltby, 1975, pp. 187, 174–89.

9. Mills, J. (1967). *A Modern Outline of Library Classification*. London, England: Chapman & Hall, Ltd. (pp. 89–102).

10. Foskett, A. C. (1982). *The Subject Approach to Information* (4th ed.). Hamden, CT: Linnet Books (pp. 409–17).

11. Maltby, 1975, p. 187.

12. Library of Congress. (2013a). G055: Call numbers. In *Classification and Shelflisting Manual.* Retrieved from http://www.loc.gov/aba/publications/FreeCSM/G055.pdf.

13. Library of Congress. (2014a). *Classification and Shelflisting Manual.* Retrieved from http://www.loc.gov/aba/publications/FreeCSM/freecsm.html.

14. Library of Congress. (2014b). G300: Regions and countries table. In *Classification and Shelflisting Manual.* Retrieved from http://www.loc.gov/aba/publications/FreeCSM/G300.pdf.

15. Library of Congress. (2013b). G302: U.S. states and Canadian provinces. In *Classification and Shelflisting Manual.* Retrieved from http://www.loc.gov/aba/publications/FreeCSM/G302.pdf.

16. Library of Congress. (2013c). G320: Biography. In *Classification and Shelflisting Manual.* Retrieved from http://www.loc.gov/aba/publications/FreeCSM/G320.pdf.

Chapter 18

National Library of Medicine Classification and Other Modern Classification Schemes

INTRODUCTION

The preceding two chapters presented the two classification systems used by most of the general libraries in the United States, as well as by many other libraries around the world. This chapter discusses, in some detail, a system that was designed for a special library. It also describes, briefly, some additional library classification systems. These latter systems show how much classification schemes may differ from one another, and also illustrate many aspects of classification theory.

NLM CLASSIFICATION

Introduction

The NLM has developed its own classification system as well as its own indexing thesaurus—*Medical Subject Headings* MeSH, described in chapter 14. The NLM Classification is an example of a special-subject classification system that was expressly designed to be fully compatible with an extensive, existing general classification system. In this case, the general system is the LCC, which, as noted in chapter 17, was designed with many "empty spaces" in its notational array of main classes and major subclasses. What the original designers of the NLM Classification proposed was a classification scheme that would (1) follow LCC in both style of classification and general pattern of notation; (2) develop its own classification scheme for medicine and related subjects, fitting it into LCC's vacant Class W; and (3) develop its own scheme for the preclinical sciences, using LCC's vacant subclasses QS–QZ (in LCC main Class Q for Science). In response, the LC agreed with NLM that the main Class W and subclasses QS–QZ would be permanently excluded from LCC.

For any material in its collection that does not fall within either medicine or the preclinical sciences, NLM uses LCC as it stands, except for Class R (Medicine), subclasses QM (Anatomy), QP (Physiology), and QR (Microbiology), and Class Z (provisions for medicine-related bibliographies).

The resulting NLM Classification system has many advantages for a specialized medical library such as NLM. The classificational development of the subject matter that is its primary concern is fully under its control, while provisions for peripheral subjects are developed and kept up-to-date by outside specialists, in this case the LC staff. Yet the two parts of the system are fully compatible. More specifically, its advantages are the following: (1) currency in arrangement of medical material and in terminology; (2) compatibility in terminology with MeSh;[1] (3) compatibility in notation with LCC; (4) the presence of NLM call numbers in both the NLM Web catalog of all types of materials and LocatorPlus, its online public access catalog including holdings information; and (5) the presence of both NLM class numbers and LCC class numbers on most, if not all, LC MARC records for materials in health sciences. This dual provision of class numbers, which results from NLM's involvement in the Library of Congress LC cooperative cataloging program, is especially helpful to libraries with collections classified by both LC and NLM systems.

Brief History and Current Status

In the early 1940s, a survey at the US Army Medical Library (now the NLM) indicated the need for a specialized classification scheme for its books. In 1948, Mary Louise Marshall prepared a preliminary edition of such a scheme. This edition was modified and revised by Dr. Frank B. Rogers in 1950, and published in 1951 as the first edition of the *Army Medical Library Classification.*[2] The second edition was published in 1958 under the title *National Library of Medicine Classification*. The most recent print edition, the fifth edition, revised, was published in 1999.[3] Beginning with the 2002 edition, the *National Library of Medicine Classification* has been published only in electronic form,[4] and has been updated annually. Beginning with the 2006 edition, the NLM Classification has also been available in PDF form.

Although originally designed for the Army Medical Library (now the NLM), the NLM scheme is also used by most of the other major medical libraries in the United States and in many countries around the world.

Basic Principles and Structure

The NLM Classification comprises two major subject groups. The first group, divided into eight subclasses, QS–QZ, contains the preclinical sciences. The second group, Class W, contains twenty-seven subclasses within medicine and related subjects; these subclasses begin with the health professions in general, followed by public health and medical practice, then by diseases, physiological systems, medical specialties, hospitals, nursing, and the history of medicine. An outline of the first-order divisions of the NLM Classification is shown in Figure 18.1.

Within a particular schedule for a subclass and, in some cases, under a main subject, the numbers 1–39 generally are used for form divisions such as society publications, collected works, history, dictionaries and encyclopedias, tables and statistics, and atlases and pictorial works (e.g., WG 1-39). In the schedules for physiological systems, form divisions are followed by general divisions and then by division by organ. For example, a brief outline of subclass WI is given below:

DIGESTIVE SYSTEM

WI 1-150 Reference Works. General
  WI 101-113 Anatomy. Physiology. Hygiene
  WI 140-150 Diseases. Diagnosis. Signs and Symptoms
WI 200-250 Stomatognathic System. Esophagus
WI 300-387 Stomach
  WI 400-575 Intestines
  WI 400-480 Intestines (General)
  WI 500-512 Small Intestine
  WI 520-560 Large Intestine
  WI 575 Peritoneum
WI 600-650 Anus. Rectum
WI 700-770 Liver. Biliary Tract
WI 800-830 Pancreas
WI 900-970 Abdomen. Abdominal Surgery

Divisions by organ have priority over diseases, which are subsumed under the organ or region chiefly affected, regardless of special emphasis on diet, drug, or other special form of therapy.

Materials treating several subjects that fall into different areas of the classification are classed by emphasis. If no emphasis is apparent, they are classed with the first subject treated.

Notation

As mentioned earlier, it was planned from the beginning that the notation for the NLM Classification would be compatible with that for LCC, and that, for material that did not fall within the areas covered by its own system, NLM would use provisions from LCC proper.

PRECLINICAL SCIENCES

QS Human Anatomy
QT Physiology
QU Biochemistry. Cell Biology and Genetics
QV Pharmacology
QW Microbiology and Immunology
QX Parasitology
QY Clinical Pathology
QZ Pathology

MEDICINE AND RELATED SUBJECTS

W General Medicine. Health Professions
WA Public Health
WB Practice of Medicine
WC Communicable Diseases
WD Disorders of Systemic, Metabolic or Environmental Origin, etc.
WE Musculoskeletal System
WF Respiratory System
WG Cardiovascular System
WH Hemic and Lymphatic Systems
WI Digestive System
WJ Urogenital System
WK Endocrine System
WL Nervous System
WM Psychiatry
WN Radiology. Diagnostic Imaging
WO Surgery
WP Gynecology
WQ Obstetrics
WR Dermatology
WS Pediatrics
WT Geriatrics. Chronic Disease
WU Dentistry. Oral Surgery
WV Otolaryngology
WW Ophthalmology
WX Hospitals and Other Health Facilities
WY Nursing
WZ History of Medicine. Medical Miscellany
19th Century Schedule

Figure 18.1 Outline of the NLM Classification. *Source:* U.S. National Library of Medicine, *Outline of the NLM Classification,* www.nlm.nih.gov/class/OutlineofNLMClassificationSchedule.html.

One necessary condition for the implementation of these plans was that NLM would not use the LC schedules for Class R (Medicine) and subclasses QM–QR (Anatomy, Physiology, and Microbiology); another was that LC would not seek to develop class W or subclasses QR–QZ, which were, in a sense, "ceded" to NLM. Within these limitations, the NLM notational system is fully compatible with that of LCC.

Class Numbers

A typical NLM class number consists of one or two capital letters followed by an Arabic number of up to three digits with possible decimal extensions, for example, **W 1**, **QS 22.1**, **QY 350**, **W 40.1**, and **WK 700**. Triple capital letter combinations are used in classifying some nineteenth-century publications. Also, in some cases, Cutter numbers are used for subject subdivision. With respect to notational capacity, the NLM Classification allows a range of 1–999 integers under each main class or subclass, in contrast to the range of 1–9999 in LCC. The NLM Classification is a relatively broad classification system, leaving specificity in subject analysis to the MeSH system and its tree structures.

Cutter Numbers

NLM Cutter numbers, used primarily as item numbers and occasionally for subject subdivisions, differ from those used in LCC. The difference springs from the fact that there may be a large number of works written on any one of the topics enumerated in the NLM scheme for which the relatively simple Cutter number table used for item numbers in LCC does not suffice. Instead, NLM uses the more detailed *Cutter-Sanborn Three-Figure Author Table*[5] for item numbers. Even then, numbers from this table may need to be adjusted to accommodate the many books that are crowded into NLM's broad class numbers. Work letters—that is, the work mark, taken from the first word in the title, disregarding initial articles—are added to distinguish works on the same subject by the same author, and publication dates are routinely added to records for monographs, as they are in LCC. Illustrations of NLM item numbers appear in the cataloging examples in a later section of this chapter. Note that NLM does not use a period before the item number, even though the numbers are read decimally.

Examples of Cutter numbers used for subject subdivisions, where a simpler Cutter number scheme suffices, are given below.

QW MICROBIOLOGY. IMMUNOLOGY

138 Enterobacteriaceae

138.5 Specific organisms, A-Z

.E5 Enterobacter

.E8 Escherichia

.K5 Klebsiella

.P7 Proteus

.S2 Salmonella

.S3 Serratia

.S4 Shigella

.Y3 Yersinia

Cutter numbers are not used as item numbers for nonprint materials. Instead, the system uses a media code consisting of a serial number following a brief alphabetic notation representing type of material (e.g., IM for interactive multimedia, VC for videocassette, etc.).

Geographic Table

There is only one table in the NLM Classification system: Table G for geographic subdivisions, which is based on a modified Cutter pattern. The world is divided into ten regions, each of which is assigned a capital letter, as follows:

A—United States (Federal Government)
    AA1—United States (as geographical area)
D—Americas
F—Great Britain
G—Europe
H—Africa
J—Middle East and Asia
K—Australasia
L—Islands of the Pacific and Indian Oceans
M—International Agencies
P—Polar Regions

Within each region, subdivisions are provided for subordinate units, for example:

AA1—United States
AA4—Alabama
AA5—Alaska
AA6—Appalachian Region

FA1—Great Britain
FE5—England
FG9—Guernsey
FI7—Northern Ireland
FM2—Isle of Man
FS2—Scotland
FW3—Wales

M—International agencies (General or not listed below)
MA4—Allied Forces

MF6—Food and Agricultural Organization of the United Nations
MU5—United Nations
MU8—Unicef

Table G is used mainly with serial government publications and with hospital publications. However, there are some numbers in the schedules that expressly call for the use of Table G, for example:

QV PHARMACOLOGY
11 History (Table G)
11.1 General coverage (Not Table G)
32 Laws (Table G)
(Used for both monographs and serials)
32.1 General coverage (Not Table G)
(Used for both monographs and serials)

In these cases, the decimal extension .1 is used for material covering areas broader than any of the areas represented in Table G. A history of pharmacology in a particular geographic area is classed in QV 11 with a number from Table G (e.g., QV 11 AA1 for history of pharmacology in the United States), while a general history of pharmacology is classed in QV 11.1.

Index

There is a detailed index to the NLM schedules, with major terms chosen and updated annually to conform to those in MeSH. In the index, major terms are arranged alphabetically with subterms indented under them. Each major term or subterm is followed by a class number or range of numbers, including numbers from LCC. The example below shows these features:

Lasers
  Diagnostic use WB 288
  In dentistry (General) WU 26
  In surgery see Laser Therapy WO 511
  Physics QC 685-689.5
  Therapeutic use WB 480
  Used for other purposes, by subject
  See also special topics under Radiation, Nonionizing
  See also Holography

Classification of Special Types of Materials

Certain types of materials receive special treatment in the NLM Classification. These include bibliographies and related materials, serial publications, and early publications.

Bibliography

The call number for a bibliography in a topic listed in the NLM schedules begins with the letter Z, followed by the class number for the particular subject of the bibliography without a space between the "Z" and the other letter of the class number. A bibliography outside the scope of the NLM Classification is assigned a number from Class Z of the LCC. Examples of class numbers for bibliographies are shown below:

Z 7144.I8	A bibliography of isotopes
ZQT 35	A bibliography of biomedical mathematics
ZW 1	A bibliography of general medical serials
ZWB 100	A bibliography of works on medicine practice
ZWD 700	A bibliography of aviation medicine

Serial Publications

Serials are classified in the form number W 1, with the exceptions noted below:[6]

1. Government Administrative Reports or Statistics. Serial government publications that are administrative or statistical in nature are classed in W 2. Integrated reports of administrative and/or statistical information on several hospitals under government administration are also classed in W 2.
2. Hospital Administrative Reports or Statistics. Serial hospital publications that are administrative or statistical in nature, including reports of single government hospitals, are classed in WX 2.
3. Directories, Handbooks, etc. Certain publication types, such as directories, handbooks, among others, issued serially are classed in form numbers used also for monographs. For example, directories, whether monographic or serial in nature, are classed for the publication type Directory in form number 22 [for example, W 22; WX 22]. Numbers used for both types of publications are identified in the schedules with the parenthetical note "(Used for both monographs and serials)." The appropriate LC schedule is used for the above-defined publication types when their subjects fall outside the scope of the NLM Classification.
4. Bibliographies and Indexes. Serial publications of bibliographies or indexes are classed according to the instructions in the section on Bibliographies above.

Early Publications

1. Nineteenth-century titles

A "19th Century Schedule," which is a simplified version of the NLM Classification, is provided for the classification of works published during 1801–1913, except nineteenth-century bibliographies. This special schedule appears at the end of the NLM schedules. An excerpt from this special schedule is shown below:

QS	Anatomy
QS 22	Directories (Table G)
QSA	Histology
QSB	Embryology
WB	Practice of medicine
WB 22	Directories (Table G)
WBA	Popular medicine
WBB	Diagnosis

2. Early printed books

Books published before 1801 and Americana (early imprints from North, South, and Central America and the Caribbean islands) are classed in WZ 230–270, a section of the classification specially designed for such works.[7]

These books are arranged alphabetically by author under the classification number for the period during which they were printed. Reprints and translations of pre-1801 works are classified in WZ 290–292, and modern criticism of early works in WZ 294.

Cataloging Examples

Application of the NLM Classification system is illustrated in the following examples. Notice that all MARC records of medical literature prepared by NLM for the LC through its shared cataloging program contain both Class R (LCC) and Class W (NLM) numbers, as shown in some of the following examples.

Netter's cardiology / edited by Marschall S. Runge, George A. Stouffer, Cam Patterson. 2nd ed. c2010

WG	Cardiovascular system
120	Cardiovascular diseases
N474	Cutter number for the title, *Netter's . . .*
2010	Date of publication

[LC call number: RC667.N47 2010]

Microbiology / Vikas Bhushan . . . [et al.]. 4th ed. c2005

QW Microbiology and Immunology
18.2 Educational materials
M6216 Cutter number for the title, *Microbiology* . . .
2005 Date of publication
[LC call number: QR46.B465 2005]

How to read a paper : the basics of evidence-based medicine / Trisha Greenhalgh. 5th ed. 2014

WB Practice of Medicine
102 Clinical medicine
G813h Cutter number for the author, Greenhalgh, and work mark (h) for the title
2014 Date of publication
[LC call number: R118.6.G74 2014]

Medical publishing in 19th century America . . . / Francesco Cordasco. 1990

WZ History of medicine
345 Medical writing and publishing
C794m Cutter number for the author, Cordasco, and work letter (m) for the title
1990 Date of publication
[LC call number: Z473.C764 1990]

Paediatrics and child health / Mary Rudolf, Malcolm Levene. 2nd ed. 2006

WS Pediatrics
200 General works
L657p Cutter number for the first author, Levene, and work letter (p) for the title
2006 Date of publication
[LC call number: RJ45.R86 2006]

Women in medicine : career and life management / Marjorie A. Bowman, Erica Frank, Deborah I. Allen. 3rd ed. c2002

W Health Professions
21 Medicine as a profession
B787w Cutter number for the first author, Bowman, and work letter (w) for the title
2002 Date of publication
[LC call number: R692.B69 2002]

Cutter numbers are not assigned to audiovisual and locally accessed electronic resources.

Medicine is a man's game? : women physicians in the movies / Patricia E. Gallagher. 2014. (DVD, 61 min.)
W Health Professions
21 Medicine as a profession
DVD no.2 2014 DVD number assigned to videodisc

Moving medical innovations forward [electronic resource] *: new initiatives from HHS* / U.S. Department of Health and Human Services. [2005]
QY Clinical Pathology
4 General works

MARC Field 060

MARC21 field 060 is used to record the NLM call number. The first indicator is used to indicate whether the resource classified exists in the NLM collection, and the second indicator is used to indicate if the call number was assigned by the NLM or a different agency.

Two subfields have been defined in MARC 060 field: subfield a for the NLM class number, and subfield b for the Cutter number, work mark, and date.

Examples:

Paediatrics and child health / Mary Rudolf, Malcolm Levene. 2nd ed. 2006
WS 200 L657p 2006
060 00 $a WS 200 $b L657p 2006

How to read a paper : the basics of evidence-based medicine / Trisha Greenhalgh. 5th ed. 2014
WB 102 G813h 2014
060 00 $a WB 102 $b G813h 2014

Before prozac : the troubled history of mood disorders in psychiatry / Edward Shorter. 2009
QV 11 AA1 S559b 2009
060 10 $ QV 11 AA1 $b S559b 2009

OTHER MODERN LIBRARY CLASSIFICATION SYSTEMS

In addition to the library classification systems discussed previously, a number of other systems have been developed in modern times. The following account presents the salient characteristics of the most notable, along with information on their conception and development. They are listed in chronological order, by date of publication of their first editions.

Although some of the systems are no longer in use, they are included here not only because they are part of the history of librarianship, but also because they illustrate different ways of classifying bibliographical materials. In designing new retrieval schemes, an appropriate classification framework is one of the keys to effective design. A comparison of the different principles and structures that characterize the many classification systems can be a fruitful exercise.

Expansive Classification (EC; Charles Ammi Cutter, 1837–1903)

Brief History

Cutter first designed the EC for the Boston Athenaeum, where he was librarian. He later recognized its value as a general library classification system and, with certain modifications and refinements, made it available to other libraries by publishing it over the years 1891–1893.[8]

Cutter continued work on his seven-stage scheme, the first of which was intended for small libraries, and the seventh for a collection of ten million volumes. Unfortunately, he died before its completion. EC was adopted by a number of American libraries. However, perhaps because there has never been a mechanism or organizational support for updating the scheme, libraries have long ceased to adopt it. The latest survey, conducted in the 1970s, revealed that it was used then by only a dozen American and Canadian libraries, most of which were special or small public libraries.[9]

Basic Principles and Characteristics

The EC is perhaps best known today because it served as a model for the early development of the LCC. However, it presents several interesting features in its own right. The most striking is that the same basic organizational approach to recorded knowledge was developed at several levels of fullness. Cutter was very much aware of the fact that a village library and a national library have vastly different needs, so he decided to work out a system that could meet the needs of all sizes of libraries. EC was therefore prepared in seven versions, called classifications, in increasing fullness of detail. The first has eight main classes with rather broad subdivisions. The second has fifteen main classes, and the third through sixth have twenty-seven; these are shown in Figure 18.2. The idea of providing varying degrees of fullness to suit the needs of individual libraries is in keeping with Cutter's proposal of the full, medium, and short catalogs for libraries of different sizes.[10] A similar principle, followed to a lesser degree, was adopted by both the DDC (two versions, full and abridged) and the UDC (three versions, full, medium, and abridged).

In arranging the subdivisions of each main class, Cutter claims to have followed an evolutionary order; that is, placing the subdivisions of each subject in the order that evolutionary theory assigns to their appearance in creation. For example, Science in general proceeds from the molecular to the molar (a term used in physics, to denote the whole as distinguished from its constituent elements), from number and space, through matter and force, to matter and life. In Book arts, the subdivisions follow the history of the book from its production through its distribution, to its storage and use in libraries, ending with its description, that is, bibliography.

For notation, Cutter used capital letters for main classes and subdivisions, for example:

X	**Language**
XDG	Grammar
XDHZ	Parts of speech
XDI	Noun
XDIW	Adjective

The notation is thus kept shorter than that in a system using only Arabic numerals. However, it is not expressive.

For forms and geographic areas, Cutter devised two tables of common subdivisions, designated by Arabic numerals that were applicable throughout the system. The following lists, the first in its entirety and the second an excerpt, illustrate these tables.

Forms:	.1	Theory; Philosophy
	.2	Bibliography
	.3	Biography
	.4	History
	.5	Dictionaries; Encyclopedias
	.6	Yearbooks; Directories
	.7	Periodicals
	.8	Societies
	.9	Collections

For example, XDG.4 designates History of grammar.

A	General works
B	Philosophy
BR	Religion (except the Christian and Jewish)
C	Christian and Jewish religions
D	Ecclesiastical history
E	Biography
F	History
G	Geography and travels
H	Social Sciences
I	Sociology
J	Government; Politics
K	Legislation; Law; Woman; Societies
L	Science in general; Physical sciences
M	Natural history
N	Botany
O	Zoology
Q	Medicine
R	Useful Arts (technology)
S	Engineering; Building
T	Manufactures; Handicrafts
U	Defensive and preservative arts
V	Recreative Arts: Sports; Theatre
VV	Music
W	Fine Arts
X	Language
Y	Literature
Z	Book Arts

Figure 18.2 Outline of the EC.

Areas:	30	Europe
	32	Greece
	35	Italy
	45	England, Great Britain
	47	Germany
	80	America
	83	United States

For example, with IU denoting Schools, IU45 is for English schools and IU83 is for schools in the United States.

For subarrangement of books on the same subject, Cutter devised an extensive system of author or item numbers to be used with his classification. Ironically, this part of Cutter's achievement, which has become known as the Cutter number system, has survived the classification itself; it is now widely used with the Dewey and the NLM systems, and a version of it, considerably simplified, is used with the LCC.

Universal Decimal Classification (UDC)

Brief History

The UDC is an adaptation and expansion of the DDC. It was originally developed for the purpose of compiling a classified index to a universal bibliography that would list all publications, including books and articles in periodicals (*Répertoire bibliographique universel*). This project was initiated in 1895 by the Institut International de Bibliographie (IIB) in Brussels, which moved from Belgium to the Netherlands in 1931 and became the Fédération Internationale de Documentation (FID). Paul Otlet and Henri La Fontaine, two Belgian lawyers who were responsible for the initial development of UDC, decided to base the new system on DDC, which by the end of the nineteenth century had become a highly successful and widely known library classification system. Because much more detail and minute specifications are needed for indexing journal articles than were available in DDC, the Institute obtained Melvil Dewey's permission to expand and modify DDC to suit the purpose of a universal bibliography.

The first edition was in French; it was published between 1904 and 1907[11] under the title *Manual du Répertoire bibliographique universel.* A second French edition appeared in the 1920s, and a third in German in the 1930s. Belgium remains responsible for the French edition to the present day. The first English edition began appearing in the 1940s, and other language editions were produced in a range of levels of detail. Apart from the first three, no other complete edition has appeared in the form originally envisaged, but smaller editions in varying sizes have been produced over the years. At present, there are editions of varying sizes in about thirty-eight languages.[12]

By the 1930s, the project of the universal bibliography was abandoned, but the development of UDC as a general scheme for classification and indexing continued. It has been adopted widely in Europe (especially Eastern Europe), in South America, and in North Africa.

In the recent past, many changes have taken place both in the management of UDC and in the way in which UDC is maintained and published. In 1989, the FID found that the elaborate revision system that had long been in place had become too unwieldy and that revision was proceeding too slowly. The cost of maintaining the classification was also a concern. Therefore, an international Task Force was established to consider the future potential of the scheme and to make recommendations including, if that were the finding, the possible cessation of the classification.[13]

In 1990, the Task Force recommended that the scheme should continue, having found considerable enthusiasm from the results of its international survey. It recommended that a machine-readable database should be created, and that this should become a Master File from which all future versions should be created. It also proposed that this file should be limited to some 60,000 records, in order to make revision manageable, and that the unevenness of some of the classes should be rectified.

Soon afterward, in 1992, the UDC Consortium, consisting of UDC publishers, was formed. The Consortium collectively took over responsibility for the classification. At the same time, the FID relinquished its sole responsibility for UDC and became a partner in the new consortium. (FID itself ceased to exist in 2000.) The Consortium members are all publishers of the classification, in many cases standards organizations. Anyone who wishes to translate the scheme into a major world language must first become a member. Other language editions are produced under license.[14]

In order to create a machine-readable file as quickly as possible, the Consortium based their work on the 1985 Medium English Edition, published by the British Standards Institution (BSI), together with subsequent extensions and corrections. The Master Reference File was completed in 1992, the same year the Consortium came into being. This file, known as MRF, is the authoritative version of the classification. It is in English and is updated in the publication of the annual *Extensions and Corrections to the UDC*. The latest UDC MRF release in 2011 contains over 70,000 UDC classes. Published versions are the responsibility of the individual publisher, either by virtue of being a member of the Consortium or under license. The latest English two-volume standard edition was published in 2005. An online service, UDC Online, serves as a hub of UDC schemes in multiple languages, based on a collaboration between the UDC Consortium and UDC publishers in several countries. Since 2013, the English version of UDC has been published online by the UDC Consortium (The Hague). English UDC Online is a complete standard edition of the scheme on the Web with over 70,000 classes extended with more than 11,000 records of historical UDC data (cancelled numbers).[15]

UDC is continually reviewed, revised, corrected, and extended by the UDC Editorial Team. New and amended schedules are released annually. Changes may be proposed by UDC users, UDC publishers, or by members of the Editorial Team and UDC Advisory Board.

Revision of the classification not only has to contend with developments in knowledge and in classification theory, but also has to correct errors of previous revisers. For example, Table 1k-05, the Table of Persons, originally devised for use in Class 3—Social sciences, was later extended for use with Class 61—Medicine, and eventually became a table of general application. However, there were numerous places in the classification where persons were enumerated with an entirely different notation: revision was, therefore, needed to accommodate the new use of Table 1K-05. As with all other classification schemes, there is a constant struggle to establish a helpful order while maintaining a stable, predictable arrangement, because changes in a classification are very unpopular with the user community. For the most part, these problems are handled in three different ways: (1) an increased use of facet analysis, (2) the elimination of cross-classification, and (3) the use of the colon to handle interdisciplinary topics.

Revision is of two kinds. There is the creation of a totally new class, as has happened with such disciplines as Theology, Management, Biotechnology, Environmental science, and Tourism. However, there is also a constant "patching up," as has been undertaken with Education, Domestic science, and Architecture. In addition, the Area Table is continuously updated with the current policy being to remove all alphabetical extensions and to spell out areas with their own notation (e.g., in South America, the Middle East, the Indian Subcontinent, and Africa) and provide equal detail for all parts of the world. Details from non-English versions of the scheme are incorporated into the MRF; examples are the locally produced expansions for France, Estonia, and Macedonia.

There are some deviations from the original DDC base. For example, Language and Linguistics and Literature, which are separated in classes 400 and 800 in DDC, are collocated in UDC in Class 8. Management, seen as a generally applicable discipline, has a totally new and coherent class, located at 005. In the same manner, a new class Computer science was created at 004. The emptying of Class 4, formerly Language and Linguistics, has freed up space for a totally new class, and there is a proposal to use it for Psychology and Medicine. The latter class is in the process of a total reconstruction and revision. When a total revision is undertaken, it is a deliberate policy not to reuse the same numbers, so libraries that do not wish to alter their practices can continue to use the "old" notations.

Basic Principles and Characteristics

UDC follows the basic outline of the Dewey system in the majority of its main classes and major subdivisions: these are delineated in Figure 18.3. It is, thus, a general classification scheme covering all fields of knowledge. The DDC provisions, however, required extensive expansion in order to meet the needs of a system intended to serve as an indexing tool for a universal bibliography. In the subsequent proliferation of subject subdivisions, the progression is from general to specific, and division is based as far as possible on mutually exclusive classes. Efforts are also made to collocate related topics. This task is made more manageable than it would be in most other schemes because the synthetic nature of UDC permits notations from different parts of the scheme to be linked using a colon as the connecting symbol. Figure 18.3 shows the outline of the UDC.

Features of the UDC include the following:

1. it is a general classification covering the universe of information;
2. it is a classification designed for all bibliographic purposes, from shelf arrangement to the organization of resources on the Internet;
3. it is continuously being developed into a faceted classification from an enumerative one;
4. it is designed for bibliographic use, but is eminently suitable for library use;
5. it is an aspect classification in which a phenomenon is classed according to the concept or discipline in which it is considered; and,
6. it is an analytico-synthetic classification, permitting the expression of a compound concept by linking two separate concepts notationally.

Because of their differences in initial purpose and later development, there are several aspects in which UDC has moved a long way from DDC. Especially noticeable is that an attempt has been made to remove all national biases. However, a Western, or Occidental, viewpoint is still detectable, especially in Class 3 (Social sciences). In general, the bias is more likely to be European rather than American. Especially commendable in countering this is the revision of Class 2 (Religion), which now treats each major religion equally and provides sets of auxiliary tables that permit detailed specification. By arranging the various world religions in historical order, a logical and unbiased arrangement is achieved.

For notation, UDC followed DDC in adopting a base notation of Arabic numerals, including a decimal after the third digit; such notation is particularly advantageous for an international bibliographical system, because it is universally recognizable with virtually infinite possibilities for expansion. UDC notation departs from DDC notation in not requiring three-digit integers as base numbers; in other words, UDC does not use zeros as fillers. Every

0	Science and Knowledge. Organization. Computer Science. Information. Documentation. Librarianship. Institutions. Publications
1	Philosophy. Psychology
2	Religion. Theology
3	Social sciences
4	(vacant)
5	Mathematics. Natural sciences
6	Applied sciences. Medicine. Technology
7	The Arts. Recreation. Entertainment. Sport
8	Language. Linguistics. Literature
9	Geography. Biography. History

Figure 18.3 Outline of the UDC.

digit is considered a decimal, and the decimal point is inserted to break up the notation—normally after every third digit—rather than signifying the break between ordinal and decimal numbers. For example, Religion is represented by 2 instead of 200, as it is in DDC. Divisions and subdivisions of main classes are represented by additional digits, for example, 63 Agriculture, 633 Field crops, 633.1 Cereal, corn, grain. All revisions adhere to a strictly hierarchical notation, so it is immediately obvious that one concept is subordinate to another.

As noted above, because it serves as an indexing tool, UDC is required to have many more detailed subdivisions than a scheme designed mainly for shelving purposes. Perhaps for this reason, over the years, UDC has adopted modern classification theory more readily than DDC and has incorporated many of the features of a faceted scheme. This provides for a considerable degree of synthesis through combining subjects and concepts by means of auxiliary devices. There are common auxiliaries—such as form, period, and place—that apply to all classes, and special auxiliaries that apply to certain parts of the schedules. The distinguishing aspect of UDC's provisions for synthesis, however, is that topics and subtopics in disparate parts of the schedules can be combined, as required, by means of connecting symbols (called *facet indicators*) that not only provide links, but show the nature of the relationship. Figure 18.4 lists these facet indicators and their meanings. The examples that follow demonstrate that UDC notation is both hierarchical (i.e., capable of representing hierarchical relationships) and expressive (i.e., capable of representing associative relationships).

Symbol	*Meaning*
+	Combining two closely related topics, separated by the classification
/	Combining two or more consecutive numbers
:	Simple relationships between two subjects
::	Connecting symbol indicating the order of the component numbers in a compound number
=. . .	Language
(0 . . .)	Form
(1/9)	Place
(=. . .)	Ethnic group and nationality
" . . ."	Time
A/Z	Alphabetical subarrangement
-02	Properties
-03	Materials
-04	Processes, operations
-05	Persons
[. . .]	Denoting subordinate concepts
*	Connecting non-UDC concepts to a UDC number

Figure 18.4 Facet indicators in the UDC.

Following are examples of UDC numbers:

94(735.5 736.9)	History of Virginia and Kentucky
94(735.5)	History of Virginia
94(736.9)	History of Kentucky
026:61 (058.7)	Directory of medical libraries
026	Libraries
61	Medicine
(058.7)	Directory
61 (038) 111 131.1	Italian-English dictionary of medicine
61	Medicine
038	Dictionary
111	English
131.1	Italian
821.311 19	Twentieth-century Italian literature
821.311	Italian literature
"19"	Twentieth century

Example of a hierarchy:

(73)	United States of America (USA)
(734)	States of the northeastern USA
(734.7/.8 737.1/.6)	States bordering the Great Lakes
(734.7/.9)	Middle Atlantic states
(734.7)	New York (state)
(734.711 734.912)	Boroughs and counties of New York metropolitan area
(734.711)	New York metropolitan area within New York state
(734.711.1)	Borough of Manhattan (New York County Manhattan Island)
(734.711.2/.5)	Boroughs and counties of Long Island
(734.711.2)	Borough of Brooklyn (Kings County)

UDC is a powerful system, one that is particularly suited to the computer environment: retrieval algorithms can be written that can either refine or expand subject searches just through operations on the class numbers. It has the advantage of being able to capitalize on its hierarchical structure and its synthetic devices, and has made increasing use of facet analysis. Recent revisions are totally faceted. All revisions have their hierarchies clearly distinguished by the notation. Unlike DDC, it is able to adapt to different levels of need, from the highly complex technical environment to the children's library. In the English-speaking world, it is most often found in specialized situations, but, in other parts of the world, the reverse is the case; in countries such as Spain, Croatia, or Romania, it is universally used in public libraries. Because of its flexible structure, it is less likely to impose a rigid order in the component parts of a class number. This is not a problem online, but can create difficulties for shelf arrangement or for the ordering of bibliographical or other listings. In this respect, it is less attractive than DDC. The standard citation order, however, is the recommended one, and the recent addition of Common Auxiliary Tables for commonly recurring properties and activities goes a long way toward solving this problem.

Subject Classification (SC; James Duff Brown, 1862–1914)

Brief History

The SC, developed by James Duff Brown (1862–1914), has now faded into obscurity, but is worth consideration for its interesting features. The classification originated as a protest. Toward the end of the nineteenth century, the Dewey system, already widely used in the United States, was gradually gaining ground in Britain also. Brown, who was dissatisfied with the Dewey system because of its obvious American bias and other weaknesses, set out to devise a British system. The SC first appeared in 1906, with a second edition in 1917, three years after Brown's death. (The third (1939) edition was edited by J. D. Stewart.) Prior to his work on SC, Brown was responsible for two other schemes. The *Quinn-Brown Classification* (in collaboration with John Henry Quinn) was developed in 1849. It was modified by Brown and published in 1898 as the *Adjustable Classification*.[16]

Although SC had enough viability in its early years to merit the 1939 edition, in the end it failed to win over British libraries, and only a small number adopted it. Failure to keep the system up-to-date may have been the crucial factor in its obsolescence.

Basic Principles and Characteristics

In its arrangement of the main classes, SC follows an order of "scientific progression." Brown's theory was that, in the order of things, matter and force came first; they gave rise to life and then to mind. Finally, mind was followed by the making of its record. Figure 18.5 shows the SC outline.

Brown is most famous for his "one-place theory," which assumes that materials on a concrete subject are more useful grouped together in one place than scattered according to the author's standpoint or discipline. This is the major difference between his system and other schemes such as DDC and LCC. Although the subject Iron may be treated from such standpoints as Metallurgy, Mineralogy, Inorganic chemistry, Geology, Economics, and Industry, in SC, all materials on the subject Iron are grouped together with

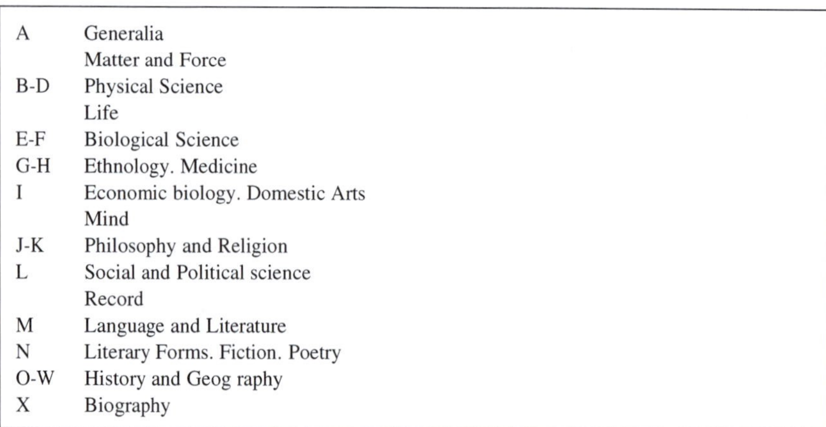

A	Generalia
	Matter and Force
B-D	Physical Science
	Life
E-F	Biological Science
G-H	Ethnology. Medicine
I	Economic biology. Domestic Arts
	Mind
J-K	Philosophy and Religion
L	Social and Political science
	Record
M	Language and Literature
N	Literary Forms. Fiction. Poetry
O-W	History and Geog raphy
X	Biography

Figure 18.5 Outline of the SC.

locations determined on the principle of placing each subject as near as possible to the science in which it is based. Hence, Iron is classed under Mineralogy, Apple under Botany, and Music under Acoustics, which is, in turn, a subdivision of Physics. Applications follow their theoretical base: Chemical technology under Chemistry, and Mining under Geology.

Brown adopted a simple mixed notation: main classes are represented by single capital letters, and subdivisions by Arabic numerals, for example:

N	Literary forms and texts
N000	Fiction
N100	Poetry
N110	Forms of poetry
N114	Lyric poetry—English

Brown also provided a Categorical Table for commonly used subdivisions; its provisions can be used throughout the scheme. Given this, limited notational synthesis is provided by combining the main number with a number from the Categorical Table (for the subdivision of subjects) representing form or other divisions, as shown below:

.0	Generalia
.00	Catalogs. Lists
.01	Monarchs. Rulers
.02	Subdivisions for rearrangement
.1	Bibliography
.2	Encyclopedias. Dictionaries
.10	History (for general use in all classes)

For example:

I229.10 History of gardening in England

Colon Classification (CC; Shiyali Ramamrita Ranganathan, 1892–1972)

Brief History

The CC was developed by S. R. Ranganathan, a prominent librarian from India who is considered by many to be the foremost theorist in the field of classification because of his contributions to the theory of facet analysis and synthesis. His writings on classification, the best known of which is *Prolegomena to Library Classification*,[17] form the basis of modern classification theory. The CC is a manifestation of Ranganathan's theory, which has had a major influence on all currently used classification and indexing systems. CC itself, however, has not been widely used, even in India.

The first edition of Colon Classification CC was published in 1933. The sixth edition[18] appeared in 1963 (reprinted with amendments from the 1960 version). Over the years, as Ranganathan refined and redefined his thinking about classification, each edition reflected the progress of his theory. Drastic changes took place between editions, and stability was sacrificed for the sake of keeping up with knowledge as well as with classification theory. Ranganathan died before completing the seventh edition.[19]

Basic Principles and Characteristics

In the CC, knowledge is divided into more or less traditional main classes; these are shown in Figure 18.6. However, the similarity between CC and other classification systems ends there.

CC is a faceted scheme. Each class is broken down into its basic concepts or elements according to certain characteristics, called *facets*. In isolating these component elements, Ranganathan identified five fundamental categories, often referred to as PMEST: Personality (entity in question), Matter (materials, substances, properties, etc.), Energy (operations, processes, activities, etc.), Space (geographical areas and features), and Time (periods, dates, seasons, etc.). When classifying a document, the classifier identifies the component parts that reflect every aspect and element of the subject content, then puts them together according to a structural procedure, called a *facet formula*, which has been individually designed for each main class. Thus, unlike enumerative classification schemes, CC does not list complete, readymade numbers in its schedules. A combination, or *synthesis*, of notation is tailored for each work in hand.

In addition to subject subdivisions in each main class, there are certain common subdivisions (called *isolates* in the CC system) that can be applied throughout the entire scheme. These include form and language isolates.

The basic ideas of facet analysis and synthesis had been present in earlier classification schemes, notably in the form divisions in Dewey's system, the common subdivisions and the local list in Cutter's classification, and the Categorical Table in Brown's classification, but it was left to Ranganathan to systematize and formalize the theory. The influence of this work is particularly apparent in the revision of UDC and the Bibliographic Classification (BC). In addition, revision of DDC, particularly in recent editions, shows increasing use of facet analysis and synthesis, most noticeably in the auxiliary tables added since Edition 18.

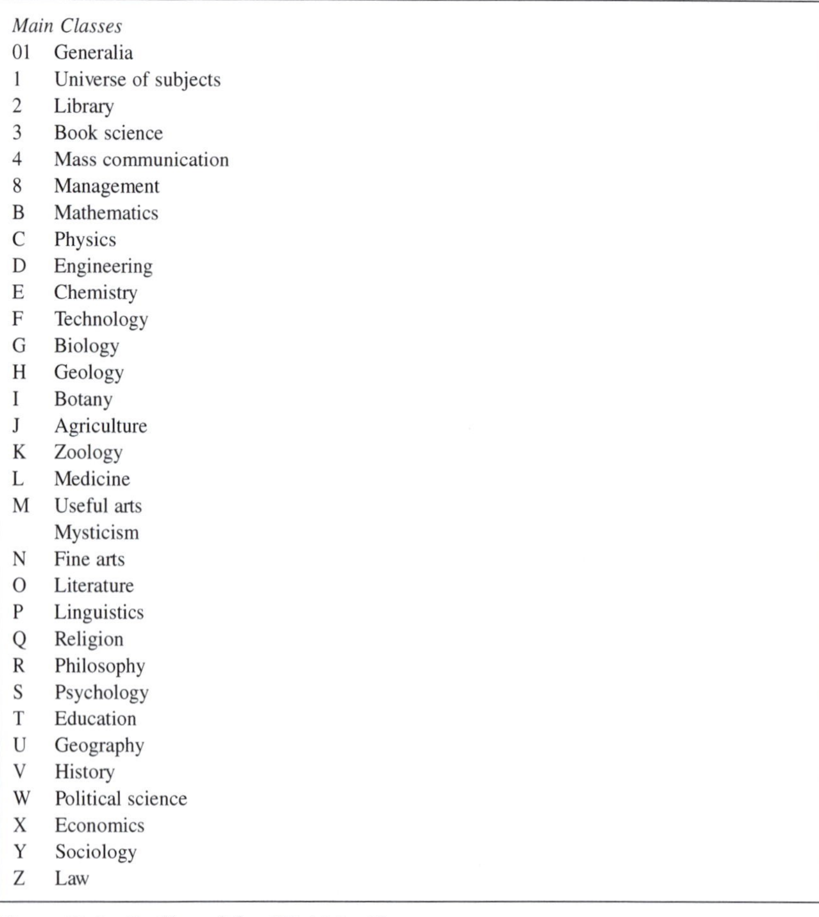

Main Classes

01	Generalia
1	Universe of subjects
2	Library
3	Book science
4	Mass communication
8	Management
B	Mathematics
C	Physics
D	Engineering
E	Chemistry
F	Technology
G	Biology
H	Geology
I	Botany
J	Agriculture
K	Zoology
L	Medicine
M	Useful arts
	Mysticism
N	Fine arts
O	Literature
P	Linguistics
Q	Religion
R	Philosophy
S	Psychology
T	Education
U	Geography
V	History
W	Political science
X	Economics
Y	Sociology
Z	Law

Figure 18.6 Outline of the CC, Main Classes.

Notation for the CC is extremely mixed and complex. It combines Arabic numerals, capital and lowercase letters, some Greek letters, brackets, and certain punctuation marks. The Generalia classes are represented by Arabic numerals.

Main classes are shown by capital letters of the Roman alphabet and certain Greek letters. Basic concepts and elements under each main class are represented mainly by Arabic numerals, for example:

L	Medicine
2	Digestive system
27	Large intestine
2721	Caecum

Common subdivisions, called common isolates, are shown in lowercase letters, capital letters, or Arabic numerals, for example:

4	Asia
5	Europe
52	Italy
5215	Sicily
r	Dry
u	Rainy
v	Monsoonish
L	1700-1799 A.D.
N	1900-1999 A.D.
Z	Future

In formulating a class number, certain punctuation marks are used as facet indicators to show the nature of the element being presented. The following meanings have been assigned to them:

(,) connecting symbol for Personality
(;) connecting symbol for Matter
(:) connecting symbol for Energy
(.) connecting symbol for Space
(‘) connecting symbol for Time

In Edition 7 of CC, additional connecting symbols were introduced, for example, (equal to) as in the space isolate 1 (Q,7) for the Muslim area of the world, where 1 means the world and Q,7 means Islam. Following are examples of CC class numbers:

Research in the cure of the tuberculosis of lungs by X-ray, conducted in India in 1950s

L,45;421:6;253:f.44'N5

L	Medicine
45	Lungs
421	Tuberculosis
6	Treatment
253	X-Ray
f	Research
44	India
N5	1950

Discharge of partnership in Indian Law

Z,44,315,7

Z	Law
44	India
315	Partnership
7	Discharge

Eradication of virus in rice plants in Japan (1971)

J,381;421:5.42'N7

J	Agriculture
381	Rice
421	Virus disease
5	Prevention
42	Japan
N7	1970s

Bibliographic Classification (BC; Henry Evelyn Bliss, 1870–1955)

Brief History

Henry Evelyn Bliss, a librarian in the College of the City of New York for nearly half a century, devoted more than thirty years of his life to the study of classification and to the development of the BC. The publication of the scheme took thirteen years, from 1940 to 1953. In the course of its development, Bliss also produced numerous articles and books on classification. Among his best-known works are *Organization of Knowledge and the System of the Sciences* (1929) and *Organization of Knowledge in Libraries and the Subject Approach to Books* (1933; 2nd ed., 1939). The latter embodies the theory on which his classification scheme was based, and includes an outline of the scheme.

Before the full schedules were published, an expansion of the outline appeared in a one-volume work entitled *A System of Bibliographic Classification* (1935).

Although BC was not widely adopted in the United States, it received much attention in Britain. In 1967, an abridged *Bliss Classification* was published there by the School Library Association. A Bliss Classification Association was formed in Britain, which has assumed responsibility for maintaining and updating the scheme. A second edition, entitled *Bliss Bibliographic Classification*,[20] under the editorship of J. Mills and V. Broughton, began publication in 1977 in separate volumes. Currently, not all schedules in the second edition have been published. As of 2007, thirteen of the twenty-three scheduled volumes were published.

Basic Principles and Characteristics

From the beginning, several principles guided Bliss's work. These are consensus, collocation of related subjects, subordination of special to general, gradation in speciality, and the opportunity for alternative locations and treatments.

Respecting **consensus**, Bliss asserted that "knowledge should be *organized in consistency with the scientific and educational consensus*, which is *relatively stable* and tends to become more so as theory and system become more definitely and permanently established in general and increasingly in detail."[21] He believed that such an order would be the most helpful to library users, and he tried to reflect scientific and educational consensus in arranging his main and subordinate classes.

The original BC was essentially an "aspect" classification—in other words, classification by discipline—in which information on individual "phenomena" is scattered over many disciplines and subdisciplines. For instance, Iron is subordinated variously to Chemistry, Chemical technology, Mineralogy, Mining, Industrial economics, and so on.

Bliss acted on his ideas of **collocation of related subjects** by bringing them into close proximity in his schedules. For example, certain pure sciences are collocated with the appropriate technology. This idea is similar to Brown's. However, Bliss did not carry it to the extremes Brown used in the SC. Bliss brought together only those pure sciences and technologies which are most likely to be used together.

In developing subclasses and subdivisions, Bliss followed the principle of **subordination of special to general** in bringing special subjects under comprehensive general subjects. In arranging coördinate topics under them, the principle of **gradation in speciality** was followed. The premise of this principle is that certain derivative subjects draw on the findings of other subjects. In a classification scheme, the subject that borrows from another is considered to be more specialized than the latter, and should follow it. For example, mathematics is a science that many other sciences draw on, and, therefore, it is placed at the very beginning of the classification.

Bliss recognized that, frequently, a subject may be placed with equal usefulness in two or more possible locations in the scheme. In order to render the system useful to the largest number of users, **alternative locations** are provided in the scheme for these subjects. For example, Economic history can be subordinated to General history or classed in Economics. There are a large number of alternative provisions in BC, and this feature is enhanced even further in the new edition. Alternative locations might involve placing Religion between History and the Occult or putting it at the end of the scheme, or concentrating all Technology together in Class U instead of subordinating the more science-oriented areas with the appropriate sciences (e.g., Chemical technology with Chemistry).

Bliss also realized that, in some cases, a body of material may be organized in different but equally useful ways. He made many provisions for **alternative treatment** in the schedules. A notable example is his four modes of classifying literature:

1. Separating literary history from texts;
2. Putting literary history and texts together;
3. Using (1) for modern literature and (2) for earlier literature;
4. Same as (3) except that modern texts are classed by form rather than by author.

In the new edition, referred to below as BC2,[22] the editors have taken into consideration advances in classification theory since Bliss's death, particularly explicit citation order and explicit filing order, and the principles of facet analysis based on Ranganathan's work. The second edition of BC adopts the facet analytical theory[23] developed by the members of the United Kingdom Classification Research Group. Thus, in BC2, S. R. Ranganathan's original five categories (Personality, Matter, Energy, Space, and Time) were expanded into a set of thirteen categories:

> **Thing—kind—part—property—material—process—operation—patient—product—by-product—agent—space—time**

In addition, a standard citation order, enabling combination between categories, also was developed, based on the principles of progression from general to special, increasing concreteness of terms, and pragmatic order derived from literary warrant and preferred arrangements of documents.[24]

While the main outline of the first edition was largely retained, many of the internal details have undergone radical revision. Each class has been given a fully faceted structure. Furthermore, the vocabulary has been thoroughly revised and greatly enlarged, as well as organized into explicitly named facets and arrays.

At the beginning of the scheme, the new edition provides classes for comprehensive works (called Generalia attributes, Generalia processes, and Generalia entities), but with the option of placing these works with the most suitable "aspect" or discipline. Many new subjects have been added, such as Media science, Recording and reproduction techniques, Data processing, and so on.

Bliss's notation was simple, with Generalia classes represented by Arabic numerals, subject classes by single capital letters, and subclasses and subdivisions by a combination of capital letters, for example:

U	Technology, useful arts
UE	Engineering
UHC	Construction techniques
UHV	Architecture, planning and building
UJ	Architectural practice and design

Bliss constantly emphasized the desirability of brief notation. The wide base provided by the use of the letters in the alphabet makes brevity more easily achievable, but, inevitably, entails a sacrifice of expressivity. (Many designers of classification schemes have made the same choice.) The new BC edition has retained most of the notational features of the original. In the earlier edition, lowercase letters and arbitrary symbols were also used, but these have been abandoned in the new edition.

Outline of Bliss BC

Figure 18.7 shows an outline of the current BC2 main schedules. Table 18.1 contains excerpts from auxiliary schedules in BC2.

The main features of BC2 are summarized as follows:[25]

- The main class order is based on closely argued theoretical principles; these include the principle of gradation supplemented by that of integrative levels, developed by Feibleman and others.
- Each main class, and every subclass demanding it (whatever its hierarchical level) is fully faceted; that is, the vocabulary is organized rigorously into clearly defined and easily grasped categories. For example, Human biology and medicine is organized into Types of persons, Parts and systems of

the person, Processes in the person, Actions on the person, and Agents of actions.

- A comprehensive and consistent citation order is observed throughout, making the position of any compound class highly predictable. For example, the citation order in medicine is the order of the facets listed above; thus, a work on nursing child victims of cancer would go under (Type of person) Pediatrics—(Processes)—Pathological—Cancer—(Actions on) Nursing. This reflects the Standard Citation Order in which, for any subject, the primary (first cited) facet is that reflecting the purpose of the subject (its defining system, end product, etc.) followed by its Types, Parts, Processes, Actions, and Agents—always in that order. Medicine is definable as the

Class	*Subject*
Introduction and Auxiliary schedules	
2/9	Generalia, Phenomena, Knowledge, Information science & technology
A/AL	Philosophy & Logic
AM/AX	Mathematics, Probability, Statistics
AY-B	General science, Physics
C	Chemistry, Chemical Engineering
D	Space & Earth sciences
	Astronomy
	Geology
	Geography
E/GQ	Biological sciences
E	Biology
	Biochemistry
	Genetics
	Virology
F	Botany
G	Zoology
GR	Agriculture
GU	Veterinary science
GY	Applied Ecology, Human environment
H	Physical Anthropology, Human biology, Health sciences
I	Psychology & Psychiatry
J	Education. Rev. ed.
K	Society (includes Social sciences, sociology & social anthropology)
L/O	History (includes Archaeology, biography and travel)
P	Religion, Occult, Morals and ethics
Q	Social welfare & Criminology. Rev. ed.
R	Politics & Public administration
S	Law
T	Economics & Management of economic enterprises
U/V	Technology, Engineering
W	Recreation, Arts, Music
X/Y	Language, Literature

Figure 18.7 Outline of the Bliss Bibliographic Classification (second edition).

study and treatment of biological processes in humans—hence the citation order in the above example.

- The filing order consistently maintains general-before-special. Thus, HMYNursing in general files before HQE Cancer in general, which files before HXO Pediatrics in general. The subject Children—Cancer—Nursing files after all of them at HXO QEM Y, being more specific. Note that the initial letter for this class (H) is dropped when combining subclasses.
- The notation is fully faceted and synthetic. Any class may be qualified by all the classes following it in citation order (and therefore filing before it). The notational base is very wide—thirty-five characters (1/9, A/Z). It is also purely ordinal, that is, it does not attempt the impossible task of always reflecting hierarchy. These two features produce classmarks that are

Table 18.1 Excerpts from Auxiliary Schedules in BC

Schedule	*Divisions*	
1. Common subdivisions	2EN	Nonbook materials
	2WHU	Government publications
	5V	Bibliographies
	6C	Research in the subject
	7	History (see Schedule 4)
	8	Places, localities in the subject
	9	Biography
1A. Persons	A CP JD NS RC	Persons in the subject
	AS	Relations to community, society
		Minority groups
		Families
		Refugees
		Regions by climate
2. Place	BAJ BC	Regions by land and resource use
	D	Urban
	O RB	Europe
	X Y	Asia
		China
		America
		U.S.A.
3. Language	G	American aboriginal languages Indo-European languages Germanic
	PB WB X	German, Dutch, English
3A. Ethnic Groups	BS	Europiforms
	G KY	American aborigines Northeast Asian
	L	groups Japanese
4. Periods of Time	DF EV FX	4000 BC000 AD1300
	GZ	1500
	Q	1900
	S	2000

exceptionally brief in relation to their specificity (number of compounded concepts defining the class). For example, the class of a work on the nurse as a caregiver for terminal patients and their families is exactly represented by the classmark HPK PEY FBG K. No other general scheme can approach this degree of specificity without significantly longer classmarks. No symbols other than numbers and letters are needed in BC2.
- Fully detailed alphabetical indexes to all classes are provided, using the economies of chain procedure.

Examples of Application

The following examples illustrate the application of BC2:[26]

Questionnaires on changes in marriage patterns among Muslims in France: KVF QSP BKC E7N

K	Society
K7N	Questionnaires
KCE	Social change
KPB K	Muslims
KQS	Marriage
KVF	France

Unemployment in rural communities in India: KVQ EOM MUR

KMU R	Rural communities
KOM	Unemployed persons
KVQ E	Indian society

Field studies of kinship in hunter-gatherer societies: KSX JPG 9V

K9V	Field studies
KPG	Kinship
KSX J	Hunter-gatherer societies

Community care policy: QEN AGP

Q	Social welfare
QAG P	Policy
QEN	Community care

The Common Auxiliary Schedules (from the BC2 volume Introduction and Auxiliary Schedules) are used to specify place, date, language, or form:

European child protection services: training pack for careers: QLJ JE8 D2F P

QLJ JE	Child protection services
8D	Europe
2FP	Multimedia

NOTES

1. National Library of Medicine (U.S.). (September 8, 2014a). *Medical Subject Headings*. Retrieved from http://www.nlm.nih.gov/mesh.

2. United States Army Medical Library. (1951). *Army Medical Library Classification: Medicine. Pre-clinical Sciences: QS-QZ, Medicine and Related Subjects: W* (1st ed.). Washington, DC: Government Printing Office.

3. National Library of Medicine (U.S.). (1999). *National Library of Medicine Classification: A Scheme for the Shelf Arrangement of Library Materials in the Field of Medicine and its Related Sciences* (5th ed., revised). NIH Publication no. 00-1535. Bethesda, *MD:* National Library of Medicine.

4. National Library of Medicine (U.S.). (April 29, 2014b). *NLM* Classification. Retrieved from www.nlm.nih.gov/class/.

5. Cutter, C. A., Jones, K. E., Swanson, P. K., and Swift, E. M. (1969). *Cutter-Sanborn Three-figure Author Table (Swanson-Swift revision).* Chicopee, MA: H. R. Huntting Company.

6. National Library of Medicine (U.S.). (April 29, 2014c). *NLM Classification Practices: Serial Publications.* Retrieved from http://www.nlm.nih.gov/class/nlm-classprac.html#Serial.

7. National Library of Medicine (U.S.). (April 29, 2014d). *NLM Classification Practices: Early Printed Books.* Retrieved from http://www.nlm.nih.gov/class/nlm-classprac.html#Early.

8. Cutter, C. A. (1891–1893). *Expansive Classification: Part 1: The First Six Classifications.* Boston, MA: C. A. Cutter.

9. Mowery, R. L. (Spring 1976). The Cutter classification: Still at work. *Library Resources and Technical Services*, 20, 154–56.

10. Cutter, C. A. (1904). *Rules for a Dictionary Catalog (4th ed., rewritten). U. S. Bureau of Education, Special Report on Public Libraries,* Part II. Washington, DC: Government Printing Office (p. 13).

11. McIlwaine, I. C. (2000). *The Universal Decimal Classification: A Guide to its Use. The Hague,* Netherlands: UDC Consortium (Chapter 1).

12. Slavic, A. (2004). UDC translations: A 2004 survey report and bibliography. *Extensions and Corrections to the UDC, 26, 58–80.*

13. McIlwaine, I. C. (1990). The work of the system development task force. In A. Gilchrist and D. Strachan (Eds.), *The UDC: Essays for a New Decade* (19–27). London, England: Aslib.

14. UDC Consortium. (2015a). *International UDC Seminar 2015: Classification and Authority Control.* Retrieved from www.udcc.org.

15. UDC Consortium. (2015b). *UDC Online*. Retrieved from http://www.udc-hub.com/.

16. Brown, J. D. (1898). *Adjustable Classification for Libraries, with Index.* London, England: Library Supply Company.

17. Ranganathan, S. R., assisted by M. A. Gopinath. (1967). *Prolegomena to Library Classification* (3rd ed.). London, England: Asia Publishing House.

18. Ranganathan, S. R. (1963). *Colon Classification* (6th ed., reprinted with amendments). Bombay, India: Asia Publishing House.

19. Ranganathan, S. R. (1987). *Colon Classification* (7th ed., revised and edited by M. A. Gopinath). Bangalore, India: Sarada Ranganathan Endowment for Library Science. [cf. Dhyani, P. (1988). Colon classification edition 7—An appraisal. *International Classification, 15*(1), 13.]

20. Bliss, H. E. (1977–). *Bliss Bibliographic Classification* (2nd ed., edited by J. Mills and V. Broughton, with the assistance of V. Lang). Boston, MA: Butterworths. [See also Bliss Classification Association. (2013). *Bliss Bibliographic Classification: Schedules* (2nd ed., edited by J. Mills and V. Broughton). London, England: Bowker-Saur, 1970–2000; K. G. Saur, 2001–. Retrieved from http://www.blissclassification.org.uk/bcsched.shtml.]

21. Bliss, H. E. (1939). *The Organization of Knowledge in Libraries* (2nd ed.). New York, NY: The H. W. Wilson Company (pp. 42–43).

22. Mills, J. (Spring 1976). The new Bliss classification. *Catalogue and Index*, 40(1), 3–6.

23. Bliss Classification Association. (2011). *The Bliss Bibliographic Classification.* Retrieved from http://www.blissclassification.org.uk/.

24. Bliss Classification Association. (2011).

25. Bliss Classification Association. (2007). *The Bliss Bibliographic Classification: History and Description.* Retrieved from http://www.blissclassification.org.uk/bchist.shtml.

26. Bliss Classification Association, 2011.

Appendix A

MARC Records

MARC BIBLIOGRAPHIC RECORDS

***CHINESE SYNTAX IN A CROSS-LINGUISTIC PERSPECTIVE*. 2015**
[text, monograph, edited work]

000	01888cam a2200433 i 4500
001	18173069
005	20150528134324.0
008	140602s2015 enk b 001 0 eng
010 __	$a 2014018513
020 __	$a 9780199945672 (paperback)
020 __	$a 9780199945658 (hardcover)
020 __	$z 9780199945665 (ebook)
050 00	$a PL1241 $b .C4858 2015
082 00	$a 495.15 $2 23
084 __	$a LAN009000 $2 bisacsh
245 00	$a Chinese Syntax in a Cross-linguistic Perspective / $c edited by Audrey Li, Andrew Simpson, and Wei-Tien Dylan Tsai.
264 _1	$a Oxford; $a New York: $b Oxford University Press, $c [2015]
300 __	$a xi, 446 pages; $c 25 cm.
336 __	$a text $2 rdacontent
337 __	$a unmediated $2 rdamedia
338 __	$a volume $2 rdacarrier
490 0_	$a Oxford studies in comparative syntax

520 __ $a “Chinese Syntax in a Cross-linguistic Perspective collects twelve new papers that explore the syntax of Chinese in comparison with other languages”—$c Provided by publisher.
504 __ $a Includes bibliographical references and index.
650 0 $a Chinese language $x Syntax.
650 _0 $a Chinese language $x Grammar, Comparative.
650 _0 $a Chinese language $x Comparison.
650 _0 $a Chinese language $x Foreign elements.
650 _0 $a Chinese language $x Influence on foreign languages.
650 _0 $a Comparative linguistics.
700 1_ $a Li, Yen-hui Audrey, $d 1954- $e editor.
700 1_ $a Simpson, Andrew, $d 1962- $e editor.
700 1_ $a Tsai, Wei-Tien Dylan, $d 1964- $e editor.

***GREEN LANTERN*. 2014**
[text, monograph, multiple authors]

000 03030cam a2200565 i 4500
001 18098882
005 20140806163608.0
008 140401s2014 nyua 6 000 1 eng
010 __ $a 2014008616
020 __ $a 9781401248161 (hardback)
050 00 $a PN6728.G74 $b V44 2014
082 00 $a 741.5/973 $2 23
084 __ $a CGN004080 $2 bisacsh
100 1_ $a Venditti, Robert, $e author.
245 10 $a Green Lantern. $n Lights Out / $c Robert Venditti, Justin Jordan, Van Jensen, Charles Soule, writers; Sean Chen, Brad Walker, Rags Morales, Billy Tan, Bernard Chang, Alessandro Vitti, Jon Sibal, Walden Wong, Drew Hennessy, Cam Smith, Rob Hunter, Marc Deering, Ryan Winn, artists; Dave Sharpe, Dezi Sienty, Taylor Esposito, letterers; Sean Chen, Jon Sibal & Alex Sinclair, collection cover artists.
246 30 $a Lights Out
264 _1 $a New York: $b DC Comics, $c [2014]
300 __ $a 1 volume (unpaged): $b color illustrations; $c 27 cm.
336 __ $a text $2 rdacontent
336 __ $a still image $2 rdacontent
337 __ $a unmediated $2 rdamedia

338 __ $a volume $2 rdacarrier
490 0_ $a The New 52!
520 __ $a "The epic event that will forever change the universe and the different color Lantern Corps forever! Relic has arrived and the universe with shiver in his wake. The lights of the Lanterns are fading as the emotional spectrum is being drained. It is up to Hal and the Green Lanterns to rally the other Corps together if they are going to survive. Many won't and others will change allegiances, but one thing is certain—nothing will ever be the same. This volume collects Green Lantern New Guardians #23-24, Green Lantern #23.1: Relic #24, Red Lanterns #24, Green Lantern Corps #24, Green Lantern Annual #2"—$c Provided by publisher.
655 _0 $a Graphic novels.
650 _7 $a COMICS & GRAPHIC NOVELS / Superheroes. $2 bisacsh
655 _7 $a Superhero comic books, strips, etc. $2 gsafd
700 1_ $a Jordan, Justin, $e author.
700 1_ $a Jensen, Van, $e author.
700 1_ $a Soule, Charles, $e author.
700 1_ $a Chen, Sean, $e illustrator.
700 1_ $a Walker, Brad $c (Comic book artist), $e illustrator.
700 1_ $a Morales, Rags, $e illustrator.
700 1_ $a Tan, Billy, $e illustrator.
700 1_ $a Chang, Bernard, $d 1972- $e illustrator.
700 1_ $a Vitti, Alessandro, $d 1978- $e illustrator.
700 1_ $a Sibal, Jon, $e illustrator.
700 1_ $a Wong, Walden, $e illustrator.
700 1_ $a Hennessy, Drew, $e illustrator.
700 1_ $a Smith, Cam, $e illustrator.
700 1_ $a Hunter, Rob, $d 1971- $e illustrator.
700 1_ $a Deering, Marc, $e illustrator.
700 1_ $a Winn, Ryan, $d 1976- $e illustrator.
700 1_ $a Sinclair, Alex, $e illustrator.

"FAIRING" THE FISCAL CRISIS. 2011

[text, monograph, legal work, corporate body authorship]

000 01275cam a2200301 i 4500
001 17220299
005 20131017144702.0

008 120321s2011 cau s000 0 eng
010 __ $a 2012379009
037 __ $b Senate Publications & Flags, 1020 N Street, B-53, Sacramento, CA 95814; phone 916-651-1538.
043 __ $a n-us-ca
050 00 $a KFC10 $b .F34 2011
086 __ $a L500.F2 2011 no.1 $2 cadocs
110 1_ $a California. $b Legislature. $b Joint Committee on Fairs Allocation and Classification.
245 10 $a "Fairing" the fiscal crisis: $b the future of fairs in California / $c Joint Committee on Fairs Allocation and Classification.
264 _1 $a Sacramento, CA: $b Senate Publications & Flags, $c [2011]
300 __ $a 86 pages; $c 28 cm
336 __ $a text $2 rdacontent
337 __ $a unmediated $2 rdamedia
338 __ $a volume $2 rdacarrier
500 __ $a "April 28, 2011, State Capitol, Sacramento, California."
500 __ $a Senate Publications & Flags stock no.: 1498-S.
650 _0 $a Fairs $x Law and legislation $z California.

***CONSTRUCTING COMMUNICATION*. 2014-**
[text, continuing resource, electronic resource]

000 01726cas a2200421 i 4500
001 17667766
005 20141110123214.0
006 m o d
007 cr $$$
008 130321c20149999dcuqx p o $ a0eng
010 __ $a 2013200742
012 __ $a -3-7-1411060115-p-----
022 0_ $a 2327-5243 $2 1
037 __ $b Communicandi.org, 5335 Wisconsin Avenue, NW, Suite 640, Washington, DC 20015
050 00 $a P87
082 10 $a 302.2 $2 23
130 0_ $a Constructing communication (Washington, D.C.)
210 0_ $a Constr. commun. $b (Washington, D.C.)
222 _0 $a Constructing communication $b (Washington, D.C.)
245 10 $a Constructing communication: $b a journal.

264 _1 $a [Washington, DC]: $b www.communicandi.org, $c [2014-]
310 __ $a Three to four times a year
336 __ $a text $b txt $2 rdacontent
337 __ $a computer $b c $2 rdamedia
338 __ $a online resource $b cr $2 rdacarrier
362 1_ $a Began with: Volume 1, Number 1 (2014)
588 __ $a Description based on: Volume 1, Number 1 (Spring 2014); title from browser title bar (communicandi.org, viewed Nov. 6. 2014).
588 __ $a Latest issue consulted: Volume 1, Number 1 (Spring
2014) (communicandi.org, viewed Nov. 6. 2014).
650 _0 $a Communication $v Periodicals.
859 40 $u http://www.communicandi.org

***CONGO*. 2012**
[map]

000 01935cem a2200457 i 4500
001 18134735
005 20140501143359.0
007 aj$canzn
008 140430t20121993fr bg a f 0 fre
010 __ $a 2014588677
020 __ $a 3282118501519
034 1_ $a a $b 1000000 $d E0120000 $e E0180000 $f N0040000 $g S0050000
045 __ $a d1993
050 00 $a G8700 2012 $b .C4
052 __ $a 8700
052 __ $a 8701
110 2_ $a Centre de recherche géographique et de production cartographique (Brazzaville, Congo)
245 10 $a Congo 1:1 000 000 (1 cm = 10 km): $b carte haute précision et lisibilité optimale: itinéraires pittoresques, patrimonie historique et naturel / $c réalisé et édité par l'Institut géographique national-France.
246 3_ $a Congo 1:1,000,000 (1 cm = 10 km)
246 18 $a Congo (1)
250 __ $a Édition 1 / $b mise à jour partielle de l'édition 1990, réalisée par le CERGEC en 1993.
255 __ $a Scale 1:1,000,000 $c (E 12°--E 18°/N 4°--S 5°).
264 _1 $a Paris: $b Institut géographique national, $c [2012?]

264 _4 $c ©1993
300 __ $a 1 map: $b color; $c 108 × 86 cm, folded to 24 × 11 cm.
336 __ $a cartographic image $b cri $2 rdacontent
337 __ $a unmediated $b n $2 rdamedia
338 __ $a sheet $b nb $2 rdacarrier
490 0_ $a Pays découverte du monde
500 __ $a Also shows roads.
500 __ $a Relief shown by shading and spot heights.
500 __ $a Title from panel.
500 __ $a Includes distance chart, index map to 1:200,000 sheets, and indexed ancillary map of "Carte administrative."
500 __ $a "85015."
651 _0 $a Congo (Brazzaville) $v Maps.
651 _0 $a Congo (Brazzaville) $x Administrative and political divisions $v Maps.
655 _7 $a Road maps. $2 lcgft
710 2_ $a Institut géographique national (France)

***THE PIANO CONCERTOS*. 2013**
[sound recording]

000 03016cjm a22006377i 4500
001 18372976
005 20141117093313.0
007 sd fsngnnmmned
008 141114p20132009nyumun$ efi $ zxx d
010 __ $a 2014626827
024 1_ $a 028947848905
028 02 $a B0018117-02 $b Decca
033 2_ $a 20090912 $a 20100308 $b 5754 $c L7
041 0_ $g eng
042 __ $a lccopycat
047 __ $a co $a rp
048 __ $b ka01 $a oa
050 00 $a SDC 43759
082 04 $a 784.2/62 $2 23
100 1_ $a Rachmaninoff, Sergei, $d 1873-1943, $e composer.
240 10 $a Piano, orchestra music
245 14 $a The piano concertos; $b Paganini rhapsody / $c Rachmaninoff.
246 30 $a Paganini rhapsody
264 _1 $a New York, NY: $b Decca, $c [2013]

264 _4 $c ℗2013
300 __ $a 2 audio discs (145 min., 55 sec.); $c 4 3/4 in.
306 __ $a 002613 $a 003928 $a 003245 $a 002448 $a 002241
336 __ $a performed music $b prm $2 rdacontent
337 __ $a audio $b s $2 rdamedia
338 __ $a audio disc $b sd $2 rdacarrier
344 __ $a digital $g stereo $2 rda
347 __ $a audio file $b CD audio $2 rda
500 __ $a Title from container.
511 0_ $a Valentina Lisitsa, piano; London Symphony Orchestra; Michael Francis, conductor.
500 __ $a Editions recorded: Hawkes and Son (concertos); Boosey & Hawkes (rhapsody).
518 __ $o Recorded $d 2009 September 12-13 (no. 1-2), 2009 December 6-7 (no. 3-4), 2010 March 8 (rhapsody) $p Studio 1, Abbey Road Studios, London.
500 __ $a Compact discs.
500 __ $a Program notes in English (11 pages) in container.
505 0_ $a Piano concerto no. 1 in F sharp minor, op. 1 (26:13) -- Piano concerto no. 3 in D minor, op. 30 (39:28) -- Piano concerto no. 2 in C minor, op. 18 (32:45) -- Piano concerto no. 4 in G minor, op. 40 (24:48) -- Rhapsody on a theme of Paganini: op. 43 (22:41).
650 _0 $a Concertos (Piano)
650 _0 $a Piano with orchestra.
650 _0 $a Rhapsodies (Music)
700 1_ $a Lisitsa, Valentina, $e performer.
700 1_ $a Francis, Michael $c (Conductor), $e conductor.
700 12 $i Contains (work): $a Rachmaninoff, Sergei, $d 1873-1943. $t Concertos, $m piano, orchestra, $n no. 1, op. 1, $r F♯ minor.
700 12 $i Contains (work): $a Rachmaninoff, Sergei, $d 1873-1943. $t Concertos, $m piano, orchestra, $n no. 2, op. 18, $r C minor.
700 12 $i Contains (work): $a Rachmaninoff, Sergei, $d 1873-1943. $t Concertos, $m piano, orchestra, $n no. 3, op. 30, $r D minor.
700 12 $i Contains (work): $a Rachmaninoff, Sergei, $d 1873-1943. $t Concertos, $m piano, orchestra, $n no. 4, op. 40, $r G minor.
700 12 $i Contains (work): $a Rachmaninoff, Sergei, $d 1873-1943. $t Rapsodie sur un thème de Paganini.

710 2_ $a London Symphony Orchestra, $e performer.
740 02 $a Paganini rhapsody.

HOIKUEN NO NICHIYŌBI. 2008

[videorecording, parallel titles, alternate graphic representation (script)]

000 02466cgm a2200529 i 4500
001 18507236
005 20150401112249.0
007 vd cvaizu
008 150226p20081997ja 090 vljpn
010 __ $a 2015368723
028 42 $a KKJS-79 $b Siglo
043 __ $a a-ja---
050 00 $a DVD 7226 (viewing copy)
066 __ $c $1
245 00 $6 880-01 $a Hoikuen no nichiyōbi = $b Sunday at the preschool; Megamisama karano tegami = Letter from a Goddess / $c kantoku Satō Makoto.
880 00 $6 245-01/$1 $a 保育園の日曜日 = $b Sunday at the preschool; 女神様からの手紙 = Letter from a Goddess / $c 監督佐藤真.
246 30 $6 880-02 $a Megamisama karano tegami
880 30 $6 246-02/$1 $a 女神様からの手紙
246 31 $a Sunday at the preschool
246 31 $a Letter from a Goddess
264 _1 $6 880-03 $a Tōkyō-to Nakano-ku: $b Kabushiki Kaisha, Shiguro, $c 2008.
880 _1 $6 264-03/$1 $a 東京都中野区: $b 株式会社シグロ, $c 2008.
300 __ $a 1 videodisc (90 min.): $b sd., col.; $c 4 3/4 in.
336 __ $a two-dimensional moving image $b tdi $2 rdacontent
337 __ $a video $b v $2 rdamedia
338 __ $a videodisc $b vd $2 rdacarrier
490 0_ $6 880-04 $a Satō Makoto eiga no shigoto = Sato Makoto complete works
880 0_ $6 490-04/$1 $a 佐藤真映画の仕事 = Sato Makoto complete works
490 0_ $6 880-05 $a Satō Makoto kantoku sakuhin = Sato Makoto film
880 0_ $6 490-05/$1 $a 佐藤真監督作品 = Sato Makoto film
538 __ $a DVD, NTSC, region ALL; Dolby digital.

500 __ $a "Sunday at the preschool" originally released in 1997; "Letter from a Goddess" originally released in 1998.
500 __ $a One sheet of "Feature documentary" inserted.
520 __ $a This documentary film is privately taken. Enjoyment of daily lives of preschool children where the director's child attend, and their parents' involvement were captured innocently.
650 _0 $a Documentary films.
650 _0 $a Preschool children $z Japan.
700 1_ $6 880-06 $a Satō, Makoto, $d 1957-2007.
880 1_ $6 700-06/$1 $a 佐藤真, $d 1957-2007.
710 2_ $6 880-07 $a Shiguro, Kabushiki Kaisha.

MARC AUTHORITY RECORDS

NAGY, IVAN
[person]

000 01144cz a2200217n 450
001 4979536
005 20140226110548.0
008 991112n$ azannaabn $n aaa c
010 __ $a nr 99036001
035 __ $a (DLC)nr 99036001
040 __ $a NN-PD $b eng $e rda $c NN-PD $d DLC
046 __ $f 19430428 $g 20140222
100 1_ $a Nagy, Ivan, $d 1943-2014
370 __ $a Debrecen (Hungary) $b Budapest (Hungary) $e Valldemosa (Spain)
372 __ $a Ballet $2 lcsh
373 __ $a American Ballet Theatre $2 naf $s 1968 $t 1978
374 __ $a Ballet dancers $2 lcsh
375 __ $a male
670 __ $a In a rehearsal room [MP] 1976: $b credits (Ivan Nagy; ballet dancer)
670 __ $a Concise Oxford dict. of ballet, 2nd ed., 1987 $b (Nagy, Ivan; b. Debrecen, Hungary, 28 Apr. 1943; principal dancer, American Ballet Theatre, 1968-1978)
670 __ $a New York times (online), viewed Feb. 26, 2014 $b (in obituary published Feb. 25: Ivan Nagy; b. Apr. 28, 1943, Debrecen; d. Saturday [Feb. 22, 2014], Budapest, aged 70;

lived in Valldemossa, Majorca; dancer of riveting noble presence who became one of American Ballet Theatre's most popular stars in the 1970s as an acclaimed partner to great ballerinas)

LOTHAIR II, KING OF ITALY
[person, royalty]

000	01814cz a2200217n 450
001	7775640
005	20130325175020.0
008	090128n$ azannaabn $a aaa
010 __	$a n 2009005403
040 __	$a DLC $b eng $e rda $c DLC $d DLC
046 __	$f 0926~ $g 0950 $2 edtf
100 0_	$a Lothair $b II, $c King of Italy, $d approximately 926-950
400 0_	$a Lothair $b II, $c King of Italy, $d ca. 926-950
400 0_	$a Lothair, $c of Arles, $d approximately 926-950
400 0_	$a Lothair $b II, $c King of Italy, $d approximately 926-950
400 0_	$a Lothair $b II, $c King of Italy, $d approximately 926-950
670 __	$a Wikipedia, Jan. 28, 2009 $b (Lothair II of Italy; Lothair II (926/8-22 November 950); often Lothair of Arles; King of Italy from 948 to his death; was of the noble Frankish lineage of the Bosonids; although he held the title of rex Italiae, he never succeeded in exercising power there; betrothed in 931 and married, 12 December 947, to the fifteen-year-old Adelaide; co-king with his father [Hugh of Provence] from 931); under List of Italian monarchs, Frankish Kingdom of Italy (781-963): Lothair II (945-950); succeeded by Berengar II of Ivrea jointly with his son Adalbert of Ivrea)
670 __	$a Biog.-bibliog. Kirchenlexikon WWW Homepage, viewed 08/20/2003 $b (Adeleheid, die Heilige, Kaiserin; b. ca. 931, daughter of King Rudolf II of Burgundy; d. Dec. 16, 999 in Kloster Selz (Elsass); widow of King Lothair of Italy; married German King Otto I; crowned Empress in 962 by Pope John XII; named a saint in 1097 by Urban II)
670 __	$a Kongekronologi for en del italienske regenter, viewed Jan. 28, 2009 $b (Lothair of Italy; 915-959; King of Italy

from 931 or 947; consort: Adelaide of Burgundy; ca. 931-999)
670 __ $a Kingdoms of Italy—Franks of Italy, viewed Jan. 28, 2009 $b (Lothair II of Arles)

MCALEXANDER FAMILY
[family]

000 01485cz a2200205n 450
001 9151077
005 20130211095016.0
008 121204n$ aznnnabbn $a ana c
010 __ $a no2012153664
100 3_ $a McAlexander (Family: $g McAlexander, Ulysses Grant, 1864-1936)
370 __ $e Fort Douglas, Utah
376 __ $a Family $b McAlexander, Ulysses Grant, 1864-1936
500 1_ $i Progenitor: $a McAlexander, Ulysses Grant, $d 1864-1936
670 __ $a McAlexander family photograph album, 1922-1926 $b (commanding officer over Fort Douglas in 1922)
670 __ $a Arlington Cemetery web site, via WWW, viewed Feb. 15, 2012 $b (McAlexander, father was Brigadier General Ulysses Grant McAlexander—commanding officer over Fort Douglas in 1922; was known as the "rock of the Marne"; wife May Skinner McAlexander (1865-1920))
670 __ $a Ancestry.com, viewed Feb. 15, 2012 $b (Ulysses Grant McAlexander married May Skinner McAlexander in 1887 in York, Ont.; one son, Perry Harlan McAlexander (1888-1952))
678 0_ $a The McAlexander family was an American military family. Ulysses Grant McAlexander (1864-1936), a career soldier, married May Skinner (1865-1920) in York, Ontario in 1887. They had one son, Perry Harlan McAlexander (1888-1952). Ulysses Grant McAlexander served as commanding officer at Fort Douglas, Utah in 1922.

BRITISH RAILWAYS
[corporate body]

000 02699cz a2200397n 450
001 1907055
005 20150417073807.0

008 800709n$ azannaabn $a ana
010 __ $a n 80085271
046 __ $s 19480101 $t 1964
110 2_ $a British Railways
410 2_ $a British Transport Commission. $b British Railways
510 2_ $i Hierarchical superior: $a British Transport Commission
510 2_ $i Mergee: $a Great Western Railway (Great Britain)
510 2_ $i Mergee: $a Kent & East Sussex Railway
510 2_ $i Mergee: $a London and North Eastern Railway
510 2_ $i Mergee: $a London, Midland and Scottish Railway Company
510 2_ $i Mergee: $a South Yorkshire Joint Railway
510 2_ $i Mergee: $a Southern Railway (Great Britain)
510 2_ $i Successor: $a British Rail (Firm)
670 __ $a Its Your British Railways, 1951.
670 __ $a Its Southern. Southern, as at 7 May 1973, 1973: $b map verso (British Rail)
670 __ $a BLAISE, 7-86 $b (British Railways; later name=British Rail)
670 __ $a Bonavia, M. R. British Rail, the first 25 yrs., c1981: $b pref. (British Railways; British Rail) p. 135 (abbreviated form "British Rail" standardized, 1965)
670 __ $a Mitchell, V. Branch line to Tenterden, 1985: $b p. 5 (Kent & East Sussex Railway became part of British Railways in 1948)
670 __ $a The South Yorkshire Joint Railway and the coalfield, 2002: $b p.79 (on 1 Jan. 1923, the LNER and the LMS took over running the line [until nationalization in 1948])
670 __ $a British Rail, the first 25 yrs., c1981: $b pref. (British Railways; British Rail) p.135 (abbreviated form "British Rail" standardized, 1965)
670 __ $a British Railways, 1948-73, 1986: $b page 343 (new name style, "British Rail," adopted in 1964)
670 __ $a British Railways Board, Annual report and accounts, 1964 (uses British Railways)
670 __ $a British Railways Board, Annual report and accounts, 1965 (uses British Rail; BR)
670 __ $a Wikipedia, Apr. 16, 2015 $b (British Railways formed by nationalization for the Big Four: Great Western Railway (GWR), London, Midland and Scottish Railway (LMS), London and North Eastern Railway (LNER), Southern Railway

(SR), named adopted Jan. 1, 1948) $u https://en.wikipedia.org/wiki/Big_Four_(British_railway_companies)

678 1_ $a British Railways formed by nationalization for the Big Four: Great Western Railway (GWR), London, Midland and Scottish Railway (LMS), London and North Eastern Railway (LNER), Southern Railway (SR), named adopted Jan. 1, 1948. The name British Rail was adopted in 1964.

INTERNATIONAL CONFERENCE ON CONVERGENCE INFORMATION TECHNOLOGY

[conference]

000 01970cz a2200289n 450

001 7671955

005 20121122051023.0

008 081001n$ azannaabn $a ana c

010 __ $a no2008143561 $z no2010121315 $z no2010121313

046 __ $t 2007

111 2_ $a International Conference on Convergence Information Technology

368 __ $a Conference

372 __ $a Information technology $2 lcsh

377 __ $a eng

411 2_ $a Conference on Convergence Information Technology, International

411 2_ $a ICCIT (Conference)

411 2_ $a International Conference on Convergent Information Technology

511 2_ $a ICHIT (Conference)

511 2_ $a International Conference on Computer and Information Technology (1998-)

511 2_ $w b $a International Conference on Computer Sciences and Convergence Information Technology

667 __ $a See also related access points for individual instances of this conference which include specific information about the number, date, or place of the individual conference

670 __ $a ICCIT 2007, c2007, via WWW, Oct. 1, 2008: $b PDF t.p. (ICCIT 2007; 2007 International Conference on Convergence Information Technology; Hydai Hotel, Gyeongju, Korea, 21-23 November, 2007) p. vii (second International Conference on Convergent Information Technology (ICCIT 07))

675 __ $a ICHIT 2008, c2008, via WWW, July 7, 2010: PDF t.p. (ICHIT 2008; 2008 International Conference on Convergence and Hybrid Information Technology; 28-29 August 2008, Daejeon, Korea); Fourth International Conference on Computer Sciences and Convergence Information Technology, c2009, via WWW, Aug. 11, 2010: PDF t.p. (Fourth International Conference on Computer Sciences and Convergence Information Technology; Seoul, Korea, 24-26 November 2009) cover (ICCIT 2009) p. xxviii (4th International Conference on Convergence Information Technologies)

Appendix B

One Work

The following group of records represents various manifestations and transformations of the same work, Jane Austen's *Pride and Prejudice*. The records are from the Library of Congress Online Catalog (unless otherwise indicated).

PRIDE AND PREJUDICE / JANE AUSTEN

[work, authority record]

000	07394cz a2200793n 450
001	5729278
005	20150707073839.0
008	020814n$ azannaabn $a aaa
010 __	$a n 2002041181
046 __	$k 1813
046 __	$k 1796 $l 1797
100 1_	$a Austen, Jane, $d 1775-1817. $t Pride and prejudice
370 __	$g Great Britain $2 naf
380 __	$a Novels $a Romance fiction $a Novels of manners $2 lcgft
380 __	$a Fiction $2 lcsh
400 1_	$a Austen, Jane, $d 1775-1817. $t Jane Austen's Pride and prejudice
400 1_	$a Austen, Jane, $d 1775-1817. $t Pride & prejudice
400 1_	$a Austen, Jane, $d 1775-1817. $t First impressions
500 1_	$i Dramatized as (work): $a Cox, Constance. $t Pride and prejudice
500 1_	$i Dramatized as (work): $a Hanreddy, Joseph. $t Pride & prejudice

500 1_ $i Dramatized as (work): $a Jerome, Helen, $d 1883-1958. $t Pride and prejudice
500 1_ $i Dramatized as (work): $a Jory, Jon. $t Darcy and Elizabeth
500 1_ $i Dramatized as (work): $a Jory, Jon. $t Pride and prejudice
500 1_ $i Dramatized as (work): $a Kendall, Jane, $d 1906- $t Pride and prejudice
500 1_ $i Dramatized as (work): $a MacKaye, Steele, $c Mrs., $d 1845-1924. $t Pride and prejudice
500 1_ $i Dramatized as (work): $a Macnamara, Margaret, $d 1874-1950. $t I have five daughters
500 1_ $i Dramatized as (work): $a Milne, A. A. $q (Alan Alexander), $d 1882-1956. $t Miss Elizabeth Bennet
500 1_ $i Dramatized as (work): $a Phelps, Pauline. $t Pride and prejudice
530 _0 $i Adapted as motion picture (work): $a Pride and prejudice (Motion picture: 1940)
530 _0 $i Adapted as motion picture (work): $a Pride & prejudice (Motion picture: 2003)
530 _0 $i Adapted as motion picture (work): $a Pride & prejudice (Motion picture: 2005)
530 _0 $i Adapted as television program (work): $a Pride and prejudice (Television program: 1980)
530 _0 $i Adapted as television program (work): $a Pride and prejudice (Television program: 1995)
500 1_ $i Adapted as (work): $a Strange, Joanna. $t Pride and prejudice
500 1_ $i Adapted as (work): $a Tarner, Margaret. $t Pride and prejudice
500 1_ $i Adapted as (work): $a West, Clare. $t Pride and prejudice
500 1_ $i Parodied as (work): $a Grahame-Smith, Seth. $t Pride and prejudice and zombies
500 1_ $i Parodied as (work): $a Lee, Tony, $d 1970- $t Pride and prejudice and zombies
500 1_ $i Sequel: $a Tennant, Emma. $t Pemberley
500 1_ $i Sequel: $a Tennant, Emma. $t Unequal marriage
500 1_ $i Derivative (work): $a Herendeen, Ann. $t Pride/prejudice
500 1_ $i Derivative (work): $a James, P. D. $t Death comes to Pemberley

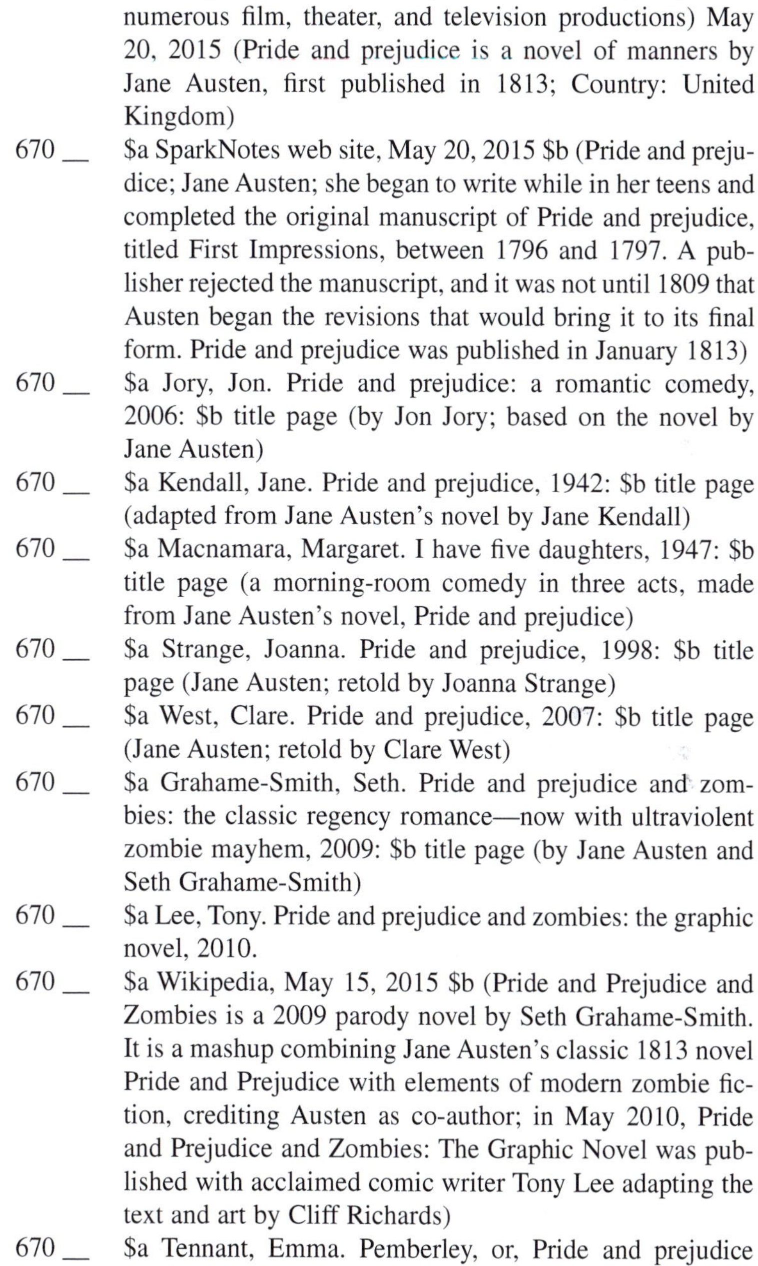

670 __ $a Austen, Jane. Jane Austen's Pride and prejudice, 2002.

670 __ $a Wikipedia, Nov. 30, 2012 $b (Pride and prejudice; novel by Jane Austen; first published in 1813; adapted in numerous film, theater, and television productions) May 20, 2015 (Pride and prejudice is a novel of manners by Jane Austen, first published in 1813; Country: United Kingdom)

670 __ $a SparkNotes web site, May 20, 2015 $b (Pride and prejudice; Jane Austen; she began to write while in her teens and completed the original manuscript of Pride and prejudice, titled First Impressions, between 1796 and 1797. A publisher rejected the manuscript, and it was not until 1809 that Austen began the revisions that would bring it to its final form. Pride and prejudice was published in January 1813)

670 __ $a Jory, Jon. Pride and prejudice: a romantic comedy, 2006: $b title page (by Jon Jory; based on the novel by Jane Austen)

670 __ $a Kendall, Jane. Pride and prejudice, 1942: $b title page (adapted from Jane Austen's novel by Jane Kendall)

670 __ $a Macnamara, Margaret. I have five daughters, 1947: $b title page (a morning-room comedy in three acts, made from Jane Austen's novel, Pride and prejudice)

670 __ $a Strange, Joanna. Pride and prejudice, 1998: $b title page (Jane Austen; retold by Joanna Strange)

670 __ $a West, Clare. Pride and prejudice, 2007: $b title page (Jane Austen; retold by Clare West)

670 __ $a Grahame-Smith, Seth. Pride and prejudice and zombies: the classic regency romance—now with ultraviolent zombie mayhem, 2009: $b title page (by Jane Austen and Seth Grahame-Smith)

670 __ $a Lee, Tony. Pride and prejudice and zombies: the graphic novel, 2010.

670 __ $a Wikipedia, May 15, 2015 $b (Pride and Prejudice and Zombies is a 2009 parody novel by Seth Grahame-Smith. It is a mashup combining Jane Austen's classic 1813 novel Pride and Prejudice with elements of modern zombie fiction, crediting Austen as co-author; in May 2010, Pride and Prejudice and Zombies: The Graphic Novel was published with acclaimed comic writer Tony Lee adapting the text and art by Cliff Richards)

670 __ $a Tennant, Emma. Pemberley, or, Pride and prejudice continued, 1993.

670 __ $a Tennant, Emma. An unequal marriage: Pride and prejudice continued, 1994.

670 __ $a Herendeen, Ann. Pride/prejudice, 2010: $b cover (Pride/prejudice: a novel of Mr. Darcy, Elizabeth Bennet, and their forbidden lovers) page 4 of cover (Jane Austen's most popular novel, Pride and prejudice; Ann Herendeen reimagines this classic love story)

670 __ $a Wikipedia, June 19, 2015 $b (Pride and Prejudice (1940 film), 1940 American film adaptation of Jane Austen's novel Pride and Prejudice, directed by Robert Z. Leonard; Pride & Prejudice: A Latter-Day Comedy, 2003 independent film adaptation of Jane Austen's novel set in modern-day Provo, Utah; Pride & Prejudice (2005 film), British romance film directed by Joe Wright and based on Jane Austen's novel of the same name; Pride and Prejudice (1980 miniseries), BBC miniseries, faithfully adapted by British novelist Fay Weldon from Jane Austen's novel of the same name; Pride and Prejudice (1995 TV series), six-episode 1995 British television drama, adapted by Andrew Davies from Jane Austen's 1813 novel of the same name)

670 __ $a Cox, Constance. Pride and prejudice, 1972: $b title page (a play: a new adaptation from the novel by Jane Austen)

670 __ $a Milne, A. A. Miss Elizabeth Bennet, 1936: $b title page (a play from "Pride and prejudice") page vii (dramatization of Pride and prejudice)

670 __ $a Phelps, Pauline. Pride and prejudice, 1941: $b title page (a comedy adapted from Jane Austen's book of the same name)

670 __ $a MacKaye, Steele, Mrs. Pride and prejudice, 1906: $b title page (a play, founded on Jane Austen's novel / by Mrs. Steele MacKaye)

670 __ $a Tarner, Margaret. Pride and prejudice, 1994: $b title page (Jane Austen; retold by Margaret Tarner

670 __ $a Hanreddy, Joseph. Pride & prejudice, 2010: $b title page (by Jane Austen; adapted for the stage by Joseph Hanreddy & J.R. Sullivan)

670 __ $a Jory, Jon. Darcy and Elizabeth, 2009: $b title page (a short romantic comedy adapted by Jon Jory from Pride and prejudice by Jane Austen)

670 __ $a James, P. D. Death comes to Pemberley, 2011: $b jacket flap (draws the characters of Jane Austen's beloved novel Pride and Prejudice into a tale of murder and emotional mayhem)

***PRIDE AND PREJUDICE* / JANE AUSTEN**

[expression, translation; authority record]

000	00704nz a2200169n 450
001	9855536
005	20150510122506.0
008	150509n$ azannaabn $a aaa c
010 __	$a no2015062058
046 __	$k 1957
100 1_	$a Austen, Jane, $d 1775-1817. $t Pride and prejudice. $l Polish $s (PrzedpeÅ,ska-Trzeciakowska)
377 __	$a pol
381 __	$a PrzedpeÅ,ska-Trzeciakowska
400 1_	$a Austen, Jane, $d 1775-1817. $t Duma i uprzedzenie
670 __	$a Her Duma i uprzedzenie, 2014: $b title page (Translated into the English by Anna PrzedpeÅ,ska-Trzeciakowska) title page verso (Original title, Pride and prejudice; Polish translation first copyrighted in 1957)

***PRIDE AND PREJUDICE* / JANE AUSTEN. 2014**

[composite record (manifestation, work, expression); bibliographic record]

000	01375cam a2200385 i 4500
001	17945895
005	20140311074656.0
008	131118t20142014mnu j 000 1 eng
010 __	$a 2013039364
020 __	$a 9781467732383 (pbk.: alk. paper)
020 __	$a 1467732389 (pbk.: alk. paper)
040 __	$a DLC $b eng $c DLC $e rda $d DLC
042 __	$a lcac $a pcc
043 __	$a e-uk-en
050 00	$a PR4034 $b .P7 2014
082 00	$a 823/.7 $2 23
100 1_	$a Austen, Jane, $d 1775-1817.
245 10	$a Pride and Prejudice / $c by Jane Austen.
264 _1	$a Minneapolis, MN: $b First Avenue Editions, $c [2014]
264 _4	$c ©2014
300 __	$a 408 pages; $c 22 cm.
336 __	$a text $2 rdacontent
337 __	$a unmediated $2 rdamedia

338 __ $a volume $2 rdacarrier
490 0_ $a First Avenue classics
650 _0 $a Sisters $z England $v Fiction.
650 _0 $a Young women $z England $v Fiction.
650 _0 $a Courtship $v Fiction.
650 _0 $a Social classes $z England $v Fiction.
651 _0 $a England $x Social life and customs $y 19th century $v Fiction.
655 _0 $a Domestic fiction.
655 _7 $a Love stories. $2 gsafd

PRIDE AND PREJUDICE / JANE AUSTEN. 2012
[composite record (manifestation, work, expression); bibliographic record]

000 01351cam a2200409 i 4500
001 17610677
005 20130524165038.0
008 130201s2012 nyu 000 1 eng
010 __ $a 2012464503
020 __ $a 9781435136564 (cloth)
020 __ $z 9781435141247 (ebook)
020 __ $a 9781435145030 (special edition)
043 __ $a e-uk-en
050 00 $a PR4034 $b .P7 2012b
082 00 $a 823/.7 $2 23
100 1_ $a Austen, Jane, $d 1775-1817.
245 10 $a Pride and prejudice / $c Jane Austen.
250 __ $a 2012 edition.
264 _1 $a New York, NY: $b Barnes & Noble: $b Sterling Publishing Co., Inc., $c 2012.
300 __ $a xvii, 325 pages; $c 22 cm
336 __ $a text $2 rdacontent
337 __ $a unmediated $2 rdamedia
338 __ $a volume $2 rdacarrier
650 _0 $a Gentry $z England $v Fiction.
651 _0 $a England $x Social life and customs $y 19th century $v Fiction.
650 _0 $a Social classes $z England $v Fiction.
650 _0 $a Young women $v Fiction.
650 _0 $a Mate selection $v Fiction.
650 _0 $a Courtship $v Fiction.
650 _0 $a Sisters $v Fiction.

655 _0 $a Domestic fiction.
655 _7 $a Love stories. $2 gsafd

PRIDE AND PREJUDICE AND ZOMBIES

[related work; adaptation; composite record (manifestation, work, expression); bibliographic record]

000 02341cam a2200409 a 4500
001 16448157
005 20140618094625.0
008 100907s2010 nyua 6 001 0 eng d
010 __ $a 2010282287
020 __ $a 9780345520685
020 __ $a 0345520688
050 00 $a PN6737.A87 $b G7 2010
082 00 $a 741.5/942 $2 22
100 1_ $a Grahame-Smith, Seth.
245 10 $a Pride and Prejudice and zombies: $b the graphic novel / $c Jane Austen and Seth Grahame-Smith; adapted by Tony Lee; illustrated by Cliff Richards.
260 __ $a New York: $b Del Rey, $c 2010.
300 __ $a 1 v. (unpaged): $b ill.; $c 26 cm.
520 __ $a "It is known as 'the strange plague' and its unfortunate victims are referred to only as 'unmentionables' or 'dreadfuls'. All over England, the dead are rising again, and now even the daughters of Britain's best families must devote their lives to mastering the deadly arts. Elizabeth Bennet is a fearsome warrior whose ability with a sword is matched only by her quick wit and even sharper tongue. But she faces her most formidable foe yet in the haughty, conceited, and somehow strangely attractive Mr. Darcy."—From publisher's description.
650 _0 $a Bennet, Elizabeth (Fictitious character) $v Comic books, strips, etc.
650 _0 $a Darcy, Fitzwilliam (Fictitious character) $v Comic books, strips, etc.
650 _0 $a Zombies $v Comic books, strips, etc.
650 _0 $a Social classes $z England $v Comic books, strips, etc.
650 _0 $a Families $z England $v Comic books, strips, etc.
650 _0 $a Sisters $v Comic books, strips, etc.
655 _0 $a Parodies.
655 _0 $a Graphic novels.

700 1_ $a Lee, Tony, $d 1970-
700 1_ $a Richards, Cliff.
700 1_ $a Austen, Jane, $d 1775-1817. $t Pride and prejudice.
856 42 $3 Publisher description $u http://www.loc.gov/catdir/enhancements/fy1108/2010282287-d.html
856 42 $3 Contributor biographical information $u http://www.loc.gov/catdir/enhancements/fy1108/2010282287-b.html

LIZZY BENNET'S DIARY / MARCIA WILLIAMS

[related work; inspired by Austen's work; composite record (manifestation, work, expression); bibliographic record]

000 02741cam a2200649 i 4500
001 17794459
005 20150210165716.0
008 130627r20142013maua j 000 1 eng d
010 __ $a 2013944006
020 __ $a 9780763670306 $q (lib. bdg)
020 __ $a 0763670308 $q (lib. bdg)
043 __ $a e-uk-en
050 00 $a PZ7.W6669 $b Liz 2014
082 00 $a [Fic] $2 23
100 1_ $a Williams, Marcia, $d 1945- $e author.
245 10 $a Lizzy Bennet's diary: $b 1811-1812 / $c discovered by Marcia Williams.
250 __ $a First U.S. edition.
264 _1 $a Somerville, Massachusetts: $b Candlewick Press, $c 2014.
264 _4 $c ©2013
300 __ $a 1 volume (unpaged): $b color illustrations; $c 24 cm
336 __ $a text $b txt $2 rdacontent
337 __ $a unmediated $b n $2 rdamedia
338 __ $a volume $b nc $2 rdacarrier
500 __ $a "Inspired by Jane Austen's Pride and Prejudice"—Cover.
520 __ $a An illustrated, scrapbook-style diary inspired by Jane Austen's classic imparts the events of "Pride and Prejudice" from Elizabeth Bennet's firsthand perspective.
600 10 $a Austen, Jane, $d 1775-1817. $t Pride and prejudice $v Fiction.
650 _0 $a Sisters $v Juvenile fiction.
650 _0 $a Courtship $v Juvenile fiction.

651 _0 $a England $x Social life and customs $y 19th century $v Juvenile fiction.
650 _0 $a Families $v Juvenile fiction.
650 _0 $a Diaries $v Juvenile fiction.
650 _0 $a Lift-the-flap books $v Specimens.
650 _1 $a Sisters $v Fiction.
650 _1 $a Courtship $v Fiction.
651 _1 $a England $x Social life and customs $y 19th century $v Fiction.
650 _1 $a Family life $v Fiction.
650 _1 $a Diaries $v Fiction.
650 _1 $a Lift-the-flap books.
650 _1 $a Toy and movable books.
700 1_ $a Austen, Jane, $d 1775-1817. $t Pride and prejudice.
775 08 $i Reproduction of (manifestation): $a Williams, Marcia, 1945- $t Lizzy Bennet's diary. $d London: Walker Books, 2013 $z 9781406346947

CELEBRATING PRIDE AND PREJUDICE / SUSANNAH FULLERTON

[related work; subject relationship, about work; composite record (manifestation, work, expression); bibliographic record]

000 03496cam a2200361 a 4500
001 17420650
005 20140319142641.0
008 120807s2013 mnua b 001 0 eng
010 __ $a 2012029595
020 __ $a 9780760344361 (hardback)
043 __ $a e-uk-en
050 00 $a PR4034.P73 $b H37 2013
082 00 $a 823/.7 $2 23
084 __ $a FIC004000 $a FIC019000 $2 bisacsh
100 1_ $a Fullerton, Susannah, $d 1960-
240 10 $a Happily ever after
245 10 $a Celebrating Pride and Prejudice: $b 200 years of Jane Austen's masterpiece / $c Susannah Fullerton.
264 _1 $a Minneapolis, MN: $b Voyageur Press, $c 2013.
300 __ $a 240 pages: $b color illustrations; $c 23 cm
336 __ $a text $b txt $2 rdacontent
337 __ $a unmediated $b n $2 rdamedia
338 __ $a volume $b nc $2 rdacarrier

500 __ $a "First published in the United Kingdom in 2012 by Frances Lincoln Limited under the title Happily ever after: a celebration Jane Austen's Pride and Prejudice"—T.p. verso.

520 __ $a "'Think only of the past as its remembrance gives you pleasure,' Elizabeth Bennet tells Fitzwilliam Darcy in one of countless exhilarating scenes in Pride and Prejudice by Jane Austen. The remembrance of Austen's brilliant work has given its readers pleasure for 200 years and is certain to do so for centuries to come. The book is incomparable for its wit, humor, and insights into how we think and act—and how our 'first impressions' (the book's initial title) can often be remarkably off-base. All of these facets are explored and commemorated in Celebrating Pride and Prejudice, written by preeminent Austen scholar Susannah Fullerton. Fullerton delves into what makes Pride and Prejudice such a groundbreaking masterpiece, including the story behind its creation (the first version may have been an epistolary novel written when Austen was only twenty), its reception upon publication, and its tremendous legacy, from the many films and miniseries inspired by the book (such as the 1995 BBC miniseries starring Colin Firth) to the even more numerous 'sequels,' adaptations, mash-ups (zombies and vampires and the like), and pieces of merchandise, many of them very bizarre. Interspersed throughout are fascinating stories about Austen's brief engagement (perhaps to the man who inspired the ridiculous Mr. Collins), the 'Darcin' pheromone, the ways in which Pride and Prejudice served as bibliotherapy in the World War I trenches, why it caused one famous author to be tempted into thievery, and much more. Celebrating Pride and Prejudice is a wonderful celebration of a book that has had an immeasurable influence on literature and on anyone who has had the good fortune to discover it"— $c Provided by publisher.

520 __ $a "As Pride and Prejudice turns 200, discover all the details of its creation, groundbreaking style, and tremendous, important legacy in this loving commemoration of Jane Austen's brilliant work"— $c Provided by publisher.

504 __ $a Includes bibliographical references (p. 226-231) and index.

505 0 $a Introduction — "My own darling child": The writing of Pride and Prejudice —"A very superior work": Reactions to Pride and Prejudice — "A truth universally acknowledged":

The famous first sentence — "Bright and sparkling": The style of Pride and Prejudice — "As charming a creature": The heroine, Elizabeth Bennet — "Mr Darcy ... is the man!": The hero, Fitzwilliam Darcy — "The female line": Her relations — "The same noble line": His relations — "Delighting in the ridiculous": Other characters — Pride and Prejudice goes overseas: The translations — "Pictures of perfection": Illustrating and covering — Pride and Prejudice — Did they all live happily ever after?: Sequels and adaptations — Bonnets and bosoms: Film and theatrical versions — Mugs and skateboards: Selling Pride and Prejudice — "Behold me immortal": Pride and Prejudice now and in the future — Bibliography — Index — Acknowledgments — Picture credits

600 10 $a Austen, Jane, $d 1775-1817. $t Pride and prejudice.
600 10 $a Austen, Jane, $d 1775-1817 $x Appreciation.
600 10 $a Austen, Jane, $d 1775-1817 $x Influence.
650 7 $a FICTION / Classics. $2 bisacsh
650 _7 $a FICTION / Literary. $2 bisacsh

***PRIDE & PREJUDICE* (MOTION PICTURE)**
[related work; motion picture; composite record (manifestation, work, expression); bibliographic record]

007 v $b d $d c $e v $f a $g i $h z $i s
024 3 $a 8886356074146
028 42 $a 43349 $b Universal Studios
041 1 $a eng $a tha $j chi $j eng $j ind $j tha $h eng
043 $a e-uk-en
082 04 $a 791.4372 $2 23
130 0 $a Pride & prejudice (Motion picture: 2005)
245 10 $a Pride & prejudice / $c Universal Pictures presents; in association with Studiocanal; a Working Title production; produced by Tim Bevan, Eric Fellner, Paul Webster; screenplay by Deborah Moggach; directed by Joe Wright.
246 3 $a Pride and prejudice
264 1 $a [Universal City, California]: $b Universal Studios Home Entertainment, $c [2013]
300 $a 1 videodisc (approximately 126 min.): $b sound, color; $c 4 3/4 in.
336 $a two-dimensional moving image $2 rdacontent
337 $a video $2 rdamedia

338 $a videodisc $2 rdacarrier
538 $a DVD; region 3; NTSC; anamorphic widescreen 2.35:1; Dolby Digital 5.1.
546 $a In English or Thai; with optional English, Indonesian, Cantonese and traditional Chinese subtitles.
511 1 $a Keira Knightley, Matthew Macfadyen, Brenda Blethyn, Donald Sutherland, Tom Hollander, Rosamund Pike, Jena Malone, Judi Dench, Kelly Reilly, Claudie Blakley, Peter Wight, Penelope Wilton, Simon Woods, Rupert Friend, Carey Mulligan, Talulah Riley.
508 $a Director of photography, Roman Osin; editor, Paul Tothill; music, Dario Marianelli.
500 $a Based on the novel by Jane Austen.
500 $a Originally released as a motion picture in 2005.
521 8 $a Board of Film Censors, Singapore: PG.
520 $a Mr. Bennet is an English gentleman living in Hartfordshire with his overbearing wife and 5 daughters. There is the beautiful Jane, the clever Elizabeth, the bookish Mary, the immature Kitty and the wild Lydia. Unfortunately, if Mr. Bennet dies their house will be inherited by a distant cousin whom they have never met. The family's future happiness and security is dependent on the daughters making good marriages. Life is uneventful until the arrival in the neighborhood of the rich gentleman Mr. Bingley, who rents a large house so he can spend the summer in the country. Mr Bingley brings with him his sister and the dashing, rich, but proud Mr. Darcy. Love soon buds for one of the Bennet sisters, while another sister may have jumped to a hasty prejudgment. For the Bennet sisters many trials and tribulations stand between them and their happiness.
600 10 $a Austen, Jane, $d 1775-1817 $v Film adaptations.
650 0 $a Bennet, Elizabeth (Fictitious character) $v Drama.
650 0 $a Darcy, Fitzwilliam (Fictitious character) $v Drama.
650 0 $a Social classes $z England $y 19th century $v Drama.
650 0 $a Young women $z England $y 19th century $v Drama.
650 0 $a Women $z England $x Social conditions $y 19th century $v Drama.
650 0 $a Courtship $z England $y 19th century $v Drama.
650 0 $a Sisters $v Drama.
650 0 $a Man-woman relationships $v Drama.
651 0 $a England $y 19th century $v Drama.

651 0 $a England $x Social life and customs $y 19th century $v Fiction.
655 7 $a Feature films. $2 lcgft
655 7 $a Fiction films. $2 lcgft
655 7 $a Romance films. $2 lcgft
655 7 $a Film adaptations. $2 lcgft
700 1 $a Wright, Joe, $d 1972- $e film director.
700 1 $a Bevan, Tim. $e film producer.
700 1 $a Fellner, Eric. $e film producer.
700 1 $a Webster, Paul. $e film producer.
700 1 $a Moggach, Deborah. $e screenwriter.
700 1 $a Knightley, Keira, $d 1985- $e actor.
700 1 $a Macfadyen, Matthew, $d 1974- $e actor.
700 1 $a Blethyn, Brenda, $d 1946- $e actor.
700 1 $a Sutherland, Donald, $d 1935- $e actor.
700 1 $a Hollander, Tom, $d 1967- $e actor.
700 1 $a Pike, Rosamund, $d 1979- $e actor.
700 1 $a Malone, Jena, $d 1984- $e actor.
700 1 $a Dench, Judi, $d 1934- $e actor.
700 1 $i Motion picture adaptation of (work) $a Austen, Jane, $d 1775-1817. $t Pride and prejudice.
710 2 $a Universal Pictures Company. $e production company.
710 2 $a Studio Canal. $e production company.
710 2 $a Working Title Films. $e production company.

Glossary

The following works were used in compiling this glossary:

The ALA Glossary of Library and Information Science. (1983). Heartsill Young, ed. Chicago: American Library Association.

Joint Steering Committee for Revision of AACR (American Library Association, Australian Committee on Cataloguing, British Library, Canadian Committee on Cataloguing, Library Association, & Library of Congress.) (1988). *Anglo-American cataloguing rules* (2nd ed., 1988 revision). M. Gorman & P. W. Winkler (Eds.). Chicago, IL: American Library Association.

IFLA Study Group on the Functional Requirements for Bibliographic Records. (1998). *Functional requirements for bibliographic records: Final report* (UBCIM Publications, New Series Vol. 19). München, Germany: K. G. Saur.

IFLA Working Group on Functional Requirements and Numbering of Authority Records. (2009). *Functional Requirements for Authority Data: A Conceptual Model* (IFLA Series on Bibliographic Control, Vol. 34). München, Germany: K.G. Saur.

Chan, L.M. (2005). *Library of Congress Subject Headings: Principles and Application*. 4th ed. Westport, Conn.: Libraries Unlimited.

Dewey, M., & Mitchell, J. S. (2011). *Dewey Decimal Classification and Relative Index* (Ed. 23). Dublin, OH: OCLC, Online Computer Library Center, Inc.

RDA: Resource Description and Access. (2010-). Developed in a collaborative process led by the Joint Steering Committee for Development of RDA (JSC). Chicago: American Library Association.

Please consult these works for definitions of terms not included in this glossary.

access point. A name, term, code, etc. that can serve as a search key in information retrieval. *See also* authorized access point; variant access point.

added entry. In AACR2 (Anglo-American Cataloguing Rules), the additional access point by which a cataloging record can be retrieved. *See also* main entry.

administrative metadata. A type of metadata providing information regarding the management of an information resource or object, such as when and how it was created, file type, and other technical information, as well as information regarding access.

alphabetical catalog. *See* dictionary catalog.

alphabetical specific catalog. A catalog containing subject entries based on the principle of specific and direct entry and arranged alphabetically. *See also* alphabetico-classed catalog; classed catalog; dictionary catalog.

alphabetico-classed catalog. A subject catalog in which entries are listed under broad subjects and subdivided hierarchically by topics. The entries on each level of the hierarchy are arranged alphabetically. *See also* alphabetical specific catalog; classed catalog; dictionary catalog.

analytical description. A record for a part of a larger resource for which a comprehensive record is also made.

analytico-synthetic classification. *See* faceted classification.

array. A group of coordinate subjects on the same level of a hierarchical structure, for example, oranges, lemons, limes, but not citrus fruit.

attribute. A term referring to characteristics of bibliographic entities identified in FRBR, FRAD, and FRSAD. RDA elements, subelements, and element types correspond to FR family attributes.

author number. *See* Cutter number.

authority control. The process of maintaining consistency in access points in a catalog.

authority file. A collection of authority records.

authority record. A record containing information relating to an authorized access point representing an entity, additional identifying information for the entity, variant access points, and sources consulted in the process of authority work. *See also* name authority record; subject authority record.

authorized access point. The standardized access point representing an entity.

bibliographic control. The operation or process by which recorded information is organized or arranged and thereby made readily retrievable. The term covers a range of bibliographic activities, including complete records of bibliographic items as published; standardization of bibliographic description; and provision of access through consortia, networks, or other cooperative endeavors.

bibliographic database. A collection of bibliographic records in machine-readable form.

bibliographic description. The description of a bibliographic resource, consisting of information, including title and statement of responsibility, edition, publication and manufacturing, physical description, notes of useful information, and standard numbers, that together uniquely identifies the resource. *See also* resource description.

bibliographic file. A collection of bibliographic records.

bibliographic record. A record containing details with regard to identification, physical and other characteristics, and subject access information of a bibliographic resource. In a catalog, it is also called a catalog record.

bibliographic resource. An information resource in tangible or intangible form that is used as the basis for bibliographic description.

bibliographic utility. A processing center or network providing services based on machine-readable cataloging data or metadata.

book number. *See* item number.

Boolean operations. Logical or algebraic operations, formulated by George Boole, involving variables with two values, such as Value 1 *and* Value 2; Value 1 *or* Value 2; and Value 1 but *not* Value 2. Used in information retrieval to combine terms or sets, for example, Children *and* Television; Children *or* Young adults; Children *not* Infants.

broad classification. (1) A classification scheme that does not provide for minute subdivision of topics. (2) Arrangement of works in conformity with the provisions of such a scheme. *See also* close classification.

call number. A composite notational system consisting of the class number, book, or item number, and sometimes other data such as the date, volume number, and copy number, which provides identification of an individual item and its shelf location. *See also* Cutter number; item number; work mark.

carrier. A container or physical medium in which data, sound, images, etc., are stored. *See also* container; media.

catalog. (1) A list of materials prepared for a particular purpose, for example, an exhibition catalog or a sales catalog. (2) In the narrower sense, a list of library resources contained in a collection, a library, or group of libraries, organized according to a definite scheme or plan.

catalog record. A basic unit in a catalog, containing cataloging data—bibliographic description, subject headings, and call number—of a particular resource.

centralized cataloging. The preparation of cataloging records by one agency to be used by other agencies or libraries. *See also* shared cataloging.

chain. A series of subject terms each from a different level of a hierarchy, arranged either from general to specific or vice versa.

characteristic of division. *See* facet.

conference. A meeting of individuals or representatives of various bodies for the purpose of discussing or acting upon topics of common interest.

collection. A group of resources.

container. Housing that can be separated from the resource being housed.

creator. A person, family, or corporate body responsible for the creation of a work.

preferred source of information. The part of a bibliographic recourse containing data as the preferred source based on which a resource description is prepared.

chronological subdivision. A subdivision showing the period or span of time treated in a work or the period during which the work appeared. Also called period subdivision.

CIP (Cataloging-In-Publication). A system of providing cataloging information within or along with the material it represents.

citation order. The order by which the facets or elements of a compound or complex subject are arranged in a subject heading or class number. *See also* close classification.

class. (1) (*noun*) A group of objects exhibiting one or more common characteristics, usually identified by a specific notation in a classification scheme; (2) (*verb*) To assign a class number to an individual work. *See also* classify; classification (2).

class entry. A subject representation consisting of a string of hierarchically related terms beginning with the broadest term and leading to the subject in question, in the form of a chain. *See also* direct entry.

class number. Notation that designates the class to which a given item belongs.

class-of-persons heading. A subject heading used with biographies that consists of the name of a class of persons with appropriate subdivisions, for example, Physicians—California—Biography; Poets, American—19th century—Biography. Also called biographical heading.

classed catalog. A subject catalog consisting of class entries arranged logically according to a systematic scheme of classification. Also called class catalog; classified subject catalog; systematic catalog. *See also* alphabetical specific catalog; alphabetico-classed catalog; dictionary catalog.

classification. A logical system for the arrangement of knowledge. *See also* class.

classification schedule. *See* schedule.

classificationist. A person who designs or develops a classification system or one who engages in the philosophy and theory of classification.

classifier. A person who applies a classification system to a body of knowledge or a collection of documents.

classify. (1) To arrange a collection of items according to a classification scheme; (2) To assign a class number to an individual item. *Also called* class.

close classification. (1) A classification providing for minute subdivision of topics; (2) Arrangement of works in conformity with the provisions of such a scheme. *See also* broad classification.

closed stacks. Parts or all of a collection not open for free access by users.

coextensive heading. A heading that represents precisely (not more generally or specifically than) the subject content of a work.

collective biography. A work consisting of two or more life histories. *See also* individual biography.

compiler. (1) One who produces a collection by selecting and putting together matter from the works of various persons or corporate bodies. (2) One who selects and puts together in one publication matter from the works of one person or corporate body.

completely revised schedule. Previously called a phoenix schedule, a term used in the Dewey Decimal Classification to refer to a completely new development of the schedule for a specific discipline. Except by chance, only the basic number for the discipline remains the same as in previous editions; all other numbers are freely reused.

composite description. A description that combines one or more elements identifying a work and/or its embodied expression in a manifestation with a description of the manifestation.

compound surname. A surname consisting of two or more proper names, connected with or without a hyphen, or conjunction, and/or preposition.

comprehensive description. A description that describes the resource as a whole.

content designation. A system of special codes (tags, indicators, and subfield codes) in a MARC 21 record used for the purpose of identifying a particular unit of information. *See also* tag; indicator; subfield code.

continuation. A supplement to, or a part issued in continuance of, a monograph, a serial, or a series.

contributor. A person, family, or corporate body contributing to an expression. For example, editors, translators, performers, and suchlike.

controlled vocabulary. In subject analysis and retrieval, the use of an authorized subset of the language as indexing terms. *See also* free-text.

conventional name. A name, other than the real or official name, by which a corporate body is more commonly known.

cooperative cataloging. *See* shared cataloging.

copy cataloging. The process of adapting an existing catalog record prepared by another library or agency. *See also* original cataloging.

core record. A Program for Cooperative Cataloging (PCC) standard record, combining RDA "Core," RDA "Core if," "PCC Core," and "PCC Recommended" elements applicable for the description of resource.

corporate body. An organization or group of persons that is identified by a particular name and that acts, or may act, as an entity. Examples include associations, institutions, business firms, nonprofit enterprises, governments, government agencies, religious bodies, local churches, and conferences.

cross-classification. Placing works on the same subject in two different class numbers when a given work deals with two or more subdivisions of a subject, with each subdivision representing a different characteristic of division. Such a situation creates the possibility of inconsistent classification. Example: a work on weaving cotton cloth deals with two subdivisions of textile technology, cotton (material) and weaving (process), and may be classed with either. *See also* citation order.

cross-reference. *See* reference.

Cutter number. A system combining letters and numerals devised by Charles A. Cutter for the purpose of distinguishing works on the same subject (or sharing the same classification number) by different authors. Also called author number. *See also* call number; item number.

delimiter. A code (represented by the symbol $, ǀ, or ‡) used to identify a subfield in a MARC 21 record.

description. *See* resource description.

descriptive cataloging. That part of cataloging consisting of the presentation of bibliographic description and the determination of access points through personal names, corporate names, and titles.

descriptive metadata. A type of metadata, consisting of data elements such as title, abstract, author, and keywords, describing an information resource or object.

dictionary catalog. A catalog in which all the entries (author, title, subject, series, etc.) and the cross-references are interfiled in one alphabetical sequence. The subject entries in a dictionary catalog are based on the principle of specific and direct entry. Also called an alphabetical catalog. *See also* alphabetical specific catalog; alphabetico-classed catalog; classed catalog.

direct entry. A subject representation containing the most specific word or phrase describing the subject. *See also* class entry.

direct subdivision. Geographic subdivision of subject headings by the name of a local place without interposition of the name of a larger geographic entity. *See also* geographic subdivision; indirect subdivision.

directory. In the MARC 21 record, a series of entries that contain the MARC tag, length, and starting location of each variable field within the record.

duplicate entry. Entry of the same subject heading in two different forms, for example, United States—Foreign relations—France, and France—Foreign relations—United States.

element. A word, character, or group of words and/or characters representing a distinct unit of bibliographic information.

encoding. The marking of the individual parts or elements of a record according to specific schemas to enable computer manipulation of the parts or elements for display and retrieval.

entry word. The first word (other than an article) in an access point, which determines the location of the record in the catalog. *See also* heading.

enumerative classification. A classification scheme or subject-headings system that lists subjects and their subdivisions and provides readymade class marks or compound headings for them. *See also* faceted classification.

expression. The intellectual or artistic realization of a *work* in the form of alphanumeric, musical, or choreographic notation, sound, image, object, movement, etc., or any combination of such forms (FRBR).

facet. A component (based on a particular characteristic) of a complex subject, for example, geographic facet, language facet, literary form facet.

facet analysis. The division of a subject into its component parts (facets). Each array of a facet consists of parts based on the same characteristic, for example, English language, French language, German language, and so on.

faceted classification. A classification scheme that identifies subjects by their component parts and requires fitting together the appropriate parts in order to provide a class mark for a work. For example, the Colon Classification is a faceted scheme, while the Dewey Decimal Classification is partially so. Also called analytico-synthetic classification. *See also* enumerative classification.

family. Two or more persons related by birth, marriage, adoptions, civil union, or other legal status, who present themselves as family.

field. A unit of data in a MARC record, identified by a three-character numeric tag.

field terminator. A symbol used to signal the end of a field in a MARC record.

fixed field. A field with a fixed (i.e., predetermined) length in a MARC record. *See also* variable field.

fixed location. System of marking and arranging library materials by shelf and book marks so that their absolute position in the room or tier and on the shelf is always the same.

form heading. A heading representing the literary genre, or physical, bibliographic, or artistic form of a work, for example, Encyclopedias and dictionaries; Essays; Short stories; String quartets.

form subdivision. A division of a class number or subject heading that brings out the form of the work, for example, –03 and –05 in Dewey Decimal Classification; —Dictionaries and Periodicals in Library of Congress Subject Headings.

FRAD. *see* Functional Requirements for Authority Data.

FRBR. *See* Functional Requirements for Bibliographic Records.

free-floating subdivision. A subdivision that may be used by a cataloger at the Library of Congress under any existing appropriate subject heading for the first time without establishing the usage editorially.

free-text. The use of natural language in information retrieval. *See also* controlled vocabulary.

FRSAD. *see* Functional Requirements for Subject Authority Data.

Functional Requirements for Authority Data (FRAD). A conceptual model that defines how bibliographic and authority entities are related. FRAD is an extension of the FRBR conceptual model, adding new entities, attributes, and relationships. New entities defined include (1) Family (which was incorporated in FRBR after the release of FRAD); (2) Name; (3) Identifier; (4) Controlled access point; (5) Rules; and (6) Agency.

Functional Requirements for Bibliographic Records (FRBR). A conceptual model that defines the bibliographic entities and the relationships among them. The three groups of entities are: (1) products of intellectual activities: work, expression, manifestation, and item; (2) persons and corporate bodies that are related to group 1 in terms of their role in the existence of the entities; and, (3) subjects of works, including concepts, objects, events, and places as well as the entities in groups 1 and 2.

Functional Requirements for Subject Authority Data (FRSAD). A conceptual model that defines the subject relationship between a work and what the work is about. Two entities are defined: (1) Thema, defined as any entity used as the subject of a work; and (2) Nomen, defined as any word, phrase, symbol, etc. by which a thema is known, referred to, or addressed.

general reference. A blanket reference to a group of headings rather than to a particular heading. *See also* specific reference.

geographic qualifier. The name of a larger geographic entity added to a local place name, for example, Cambridge (Mass.); Toledo (Spain).

geographic subdivision. A subdivision by the name of a place to which the subject represented by the main heading is limited. Also called local subdivision. *See also* direct subdivision; indirect subdivision.

half title. A title of a publication appearing on a leaf preceding the title page.

heading. A name, word, or phrase placed at the head of a catalog entry to provide an access point. *See also* access point; entry word.

hierarchy. The arrangement of disciplines and subjects in an order ranging from the most general to the most specific.

holdings. Items belonging to a library's collection.

imprint. Details regarding the publication and distribution of a printed item.

indicator. One of two character positions at the beginning of each variable data field in a MARC 21 record, containing values that interpret or supplement the data found in the field.

indirect subdivision. Geographic subdivision of a subject heading with the interposition of a larger geographic entity between the main heading and the local subdivision. *See also* direct subdivision; geographic subdivision.

individual biography. A work devoted to the life of a single person. *See also* collective biography.

integrity of numbers. The policy of maintaining the stability of numbers in a classification scheme. Such a policy is opposed to revision, especially when the relocation of a subject is involved.

International Standard Bibliographic Description (ISBD). An internationally agreed-upon standard format for representing bibliographic information.

International Standard Book Number (ISBN). An internationally agreed-upon standard number that identifies a book uniquely.

International Standard Serial Number (ISSN). An internationally agreed-upon standard number that identifies a serial publication uniquely.

item. (1) A document or set of documents in any physical form, published, issued, or treated as an entity, and as such forming the basis for a single bibliographic description. (2) A single exemplar of a *manifestation*; it represents the lowest entity in bibliographic relationships in the FRBR model.

item number. That part of a call number which designates a specific individual resource within its class. May consist of the author number and/or other elements such as a work mark, and an edition mark. An item number for a book is also called a book number. *See also* call number; Cutter number; work mark.

key heading. In Sears subject headings, a heading that serves as a model of subdivisions for headings in the same category.

keyword. A significant word in the title, subject-heading strings, notes, abstract, other parts of a record, or the text, that can serve as an access point in retrieval.

leader. Data elements (numbers or coded values identified by relative character position) that provide information for the processing of the MARC record.

literary warrant. (1) The principle that allows a category to exist in a classification or thesaurus only if a work exists for that category; (2) The use of an actual collection or holdings of a library or actual published works as the basis for developing a classification scheme or thesaurus.

local subdivision. *See* geographic subdivision.

machine-readable cataloging. *See* MARC.

main entry. In AACR2 (Anglo-American Cataloguing Rules) the primary access point. *See also* added entry.

main heading. In subject headings the first part of a heading excluding subdivisions.

manifestation. The physical embodiment of an *expression* of a *work*, representing the third level of FRBR entities.

MARC (Machine-Readable Cataloging). A system in which cataloging records are prepared in a format that enables the computer to recognize the elements and manipulate them for various purposes.

MARC record. A catalog record in machine-readable form.

media. The means used to convey the content of a resource.

metadata. A collection of structured information that provides details regarding the attributes of information items or resources for the purposes of facilitating identification, discovery, as well as management of such resources.

mixed notation. A notational system using a combination of two or more kinds of symbols, for example, letters and numerals.

mnemonics. Recurring concepts denoted by the same notational symbols in a classification scheme.

model heading. *See* pattern heading.

monograph. A bibliographic resource that is complete in one part or intended to be completed within a finite number of parts.

name. A word, character, or a combination of words and characters by which a person, family, or corporate body is known.

name authority file. A collection of name authority records.

name authority record. A record that shows a personal, corporate, or geographic authorized access point, cites the sources consulted in determining the choice of the preferred form for the access point representing the entity, the variant access points, and records additional identifying information for the entity. *See also* subject authority record.

network. (1) Two or more organizations engaged in a common pattern of information exchange through communications links, for some common objectives; (2) An interconnected or interrelated group of nodes.

notation. Numerals, letters, and/or other symbols used to represent the main and subordinate divisions of a classification scheme. *See also* mixed notation; pure notation.

notational synthesis. *See* number building.

number building. The process of making a class number more specific through addition of segments taken from auxiliary tables and/or other parts of the classification. *See also* synthesis.

online catalog. A catalog containing records encoded for access and display in an interactive mode.

open entry. An element within a cataloging record with a beginning but no ending date or number.

open stacks. A library or collection allowing users open access to the stacks.

organization. The method of arranging both surrogates and physical resources according to established orders: alphabetic (in most browsing lists or files), alphanumeric (in Library of Congress classification order), or numeric (Dewey Decimal Classification order).

original cataloging. The preparation of a cataloging record without the assistance of outside cataloging agencies. *See also* copy cataloging.

outsourcing. Having a specific task performed by an external agency or company.

pattern heading. A subject heading that serves as a model of subdivisions for headings in the same category. Subdivisions listed under a pattern heading may be used whenever appropriate under other headings in the same category. For example, Shakespeare, William, 1594–1616, serves as a pattern heading for literary authors; and Piano serves as a pattern heading for musical instruments. Also called model heading.

period subdivision. *See* chronological subdivision.

person. An individual or an identity established by an individual.

phoenix schedule. *See* completely revised schedule.

place. A location known by a name.

postcoordination. Combination of individual concepts into compound or complex subjects at the point of retrieval. *See also* precoordination.

precoordination. Combination of individual concepts into compound or complex subjects at the point of storage. *See also* postcoordination.

pure notation. A notational system using one kind of symbol only, for example, Arabic numerals or letters.

qualifier. A term (enclosed in parentheses) placed after a name heading or subject heading for the purpose of distinguishing between homographs or clarifying the meaning of the heading, for example, Paris (France); Mercury (Planet); PL/I (Computer program language); Mont Blanc (Freighter); Naples (Italy : Province). *See also* geographic qualifier.

record. A unit in a file or database. *See also* bibliographic record; catalog record; name authority record; subject authority record.

record terminator. A symbol used to signal the end of a MARC 21 record.

refer-from reference. An indication of the terms of access points *from* which references are to be made to a given access point. It is the reverse of the indication of a *see* or *see also* reference and is represented by the symbols *UF* (used for) or *x* (*see* reference from); and *BT* (broader term) and *RT* (related term), or *xx* (*see also* reference from). In the MARC authority record, these terms are stored in fields 4XX and 5XX.

reference. A direction from one access point to another. Also called cross-reference.

reference source. Any source, not limited to reference works, from which authoritative information may be obtained.

relative location. The arrangement of library materials according to their relations to each other and regardless of their locations on the shelves.

relocation. An adjustment in a classification system resulting in the shifting of a topic between successive editions from one number to another.

resource. An information resource, tangible or intangible, including a work, expression, manifestation or item. The term includes not only an individual entity but also aggregates and components of such entities (e.g., three sheet maps, a single slide issued as part of a set of twenty, an article in an issue of a scholarly journal).

resource description. The process or the product of creating a surrogate (a bibliographic or metadata record) or a brief representation containing essential attributes describing an information resource, based on established standards. *See also* bibliographic description.

schedule. The list containing the main part of a classification scheme, listing class numbers with captions and notes.

secondary entry. *See* added entry.

***see also* reference.** A reference from an access point or heading to a less-comprehensive or otherwise-related access point or heading.

***see* reference.** A reference from a term or name not used as the authorized access point to one that is used.

segmentation mark. A slash (/) or prime mark (') used to indicate the end of an abridged number (as provided in the abridged edition of Dewey Decimal Classification) in a Dewey class number assigned from the full edition.

shared cataloging. The preparation by one of several participating agencies or libraries of a cataloging record that is made available to the other participating agencies or libraries. Also called cooperative cataloging. *See also* centralized cataloging.

shelflist. A file of cataloging records arranged by call number.

specific entry. Entry of a work under a subject term that expresses its special subject or topic as distinguished from an entry for the class or broad subject that encompasses that special subject or topic.

specific reference. A reference from one access point to another. *See also* general reference.

standard subdivision. In Dewey Decimal Classification, a subdivision that represents a frequently recurring physical form (dictionaries, periodicals, etc.) or approach (history, research, etc.) applicable to any subject or discipline.

structural metadata. A type of metadata indicating how an item is structured, for example, how compound objects are put together or how pages are ordered to form chapters.

subdivision. The device of extending a subject heading by indicating one of its aspects—form, place, period, topic. *See also* form subdivision; geographic subdivision; chronological subdivision; topical subdivision.

subfield. A subunit within a field in a MARC 21 record.

subfield code. A two-character code identifying a subfield in the MARC 21 record, consisting of a delimiter (represented by $ or | or ‡) followed by a data element identifier (a lowercase alphabetic or numeric character).

subject. The overall content of a work; a word, phrase, classification number, etc. representing what the work is "about."

subject access point. An access point based on the subject of a resource.

subject analysis. The process of identifying the intellectual content of a work. The results may be displayed in a catalog or bibliography by means of notational symbols as in a classification system, or by verbal terms such as subject headings or indexing terms.

subject analytical entry. A subject entry made for a part of a work.

subject authority file. A collection of subject authority records.

subject authority record. A record of a subject heading that shows its established form, cites the sources consulted in determining the choice and form of the heading, and indicates the cross-references made to and from the heading. *See also* name authority record.

subject catalog. A catalog consisting of subject entries only; the subject portion of a divided catalog.
subject cataloging. (1) The process of providing subject access points to bibliographic records; (2) The process of assigning subject headings.
subject heading. The term (a word or a group of words) denoting a subject under which all material on that subject is entered in a catalog.
subject-to-name reference. A reference from a subject heading to a name access point for the purpose of directing the user's attention from a particular field of interest to names of individuals or corporate bodies that are active or associated in some way with the field.
superimposition. The policy of adopting a new catalog code while leaving headings derived from an earlier code unrevised.
surrogate record. A collection of essential data (such as creator, title, date, subject, location, etc.) regarding an information resource, assembled for the purpose of efficient access to and retrieval of the resource it represents.
syndetic device. The device used to connect related headings by means of cross-references.
synthesis. The process of composing a class number, subject heading, or indexing term by combining various elements in order to represent a compound or complex subject. *See also* number building.
table. A list in a classification scheme listing numbers to be combined with main numbers from the schedule. *See also* schedule.
tag. A three-character numeric code that identifies a field in a MARC 21 record.
thesaurus. A controlled-vocabulary list of indexing terms (descriptors) consisting of a subset of a natural language and cross-references from synonyms and related terms.
topical subdivision. A subdivision that represents an aspect of the main subject other than form, place, or period.
tracing. (1) The record of the headings under which an item is represented in a catalog; (2) The record of the references that have been made to a name or to the title of a resource that is represented in a catalog.
union catalog. A catalog representing the holdings of a group of libraries.
unique heading. An authorized access point that represents only one person, corporate body, or subject.
universal bibliographic control. The ideal of achieving universal bibliographic information exchange and sharing through standard bibliographic description of all publications in the world, each created and distributed by a national agency in the country of origin.
variable field. A field with variable length in a MARC record. *See also* fixed field.
variant access point. An access point other than the authorized access point representing an entity.
verso of the title page. The back side of the title page.
vocabulary control. The effort to standardize indexing terms by controlling synonyms and homographs and providing term relationships for the purpose of efficient and effective retrieval of information.

work. A distinct intellectual or artistic creation, representing the highest level in the FRBR conceptual model.

workform. A standardized framework or template for creating a catalog record by filling in data in appropriate places.

work mark. A part of call number based on the title of a work. *See also* item number; call number.

XML (eXtensible Markup Language). A markup language designed for Web documents to enable the inclusion of data about themselves *within* the document, that is, allowing the documents to carry with them specifications that guide their processing independent of any specific software application.

Bibliography

Aitchison, J., Gilchrist, A., and Bawden, D. (2002). *Thesaurus Construction and Use: A Practical Manual* (4th ed.). New York, NY: Fitzroy Dearborn Publishers.

ALCTS/CCS/SAC/Subcommittee on Metadata and Classification. (1999). *Final Report.* Retrieved from www.ala.org/alcts/mgrps/camms/cmtes/sac/inact/metadataandclass/metadataclassification

ALCTS/CCS/SAC/Subcommittee on Metadata and Subject Analysis. (1999). *Subject Data in the Metadata Record: Recommendations and Rationale.* Retrieved from http://www.ala.org/alcts/resources/org/cat/subjectdata_record

Alemu, G., Stevens, B., Ross, P., and Chandler, J. (May 24, 2012). *Linked Data for Libraries: Benefits of a Conceptual Shift from Library-specific Record Structures to RDF-based Data Models.* Paper presented at the 78th IFLA General Conference and Assembly, August 11–17, 2012, Helsinki, Finland (Meeting 92—New Futures for Bibliographic Data formats: Reflections and Directions—UNIMARC Core Activity). Retrieved from http://conference.ifla.org/past-wlic/2012/92-alemu-en.pdf

American Library Association. (1908). *Catalog Rules: Author and Title Entries* (American ed.). Chicago, IL: American Library Association.

———. (1941). *ALA Catalog Rules: Author and Title Entries* (preliminary American 2nd ed.). Chicago, IL: American Library Association.

———. (1949). *ALA Cataloging Rules for Author and Title Entries* (2nd ed.). C. Beetle (Ed.). Chicago, IL: American Library Association.

American Library Association, British Library, Canadian Committee on Cataloguing, Library Association, & Library of Congress. (1978). *Anglo-American Cataloguing Rules* (2nd ed.). M. Gorman and P. W. Winkler (Eds.). Chicago, IL: American Library Association.

American Library Association, Library of Congress, Library Association, & Canadian Library Association. (1967). *Anglo-American Cataloging Rules* (North American text). Chicago, IL: American Library Association.

American National Standards Institute. (1971). *American National Standard Format for Bibliographic Information Interchange on Magnetic Tape* (ANSI Z39.2-1971). New York, NY: ANSI. [Current edition: National Information Standards

Organization. (2014). *Information Interchange Format* (ANSI/NISO Z39.2-1994 [R2009]). Retrieved from http://www.niso.org/apps/group_public/download.php/12590/z39-2-1994%28r2009%29.pdf]

Anderson, D. (1974). *Universal Bibliographic Control: A Long Term Policy, A Plan for Action.* Pullach/Munich, Germany: Verlag Dokumentation.

Association for Library Collections & Technical Services, Cataloging and Classification Section, Subject Analysis Committee, Subcommittee on the Revision of the Guidelines on Subject Access to Individual Works of Fiction. (2000). *Guidelines on Subject Access to Individual Works of Fiction, Drama, etc.* (2nd ed.). Chicago, IL: American Library Association.

Association for Library Collections & Technical Services, Committee on Cataloging: Description & Access, Task Force on Metadata. (June 16, 2000). *Final Report* (CC:DA/TF/Metadata/5). Retrieved from www.libraries.psu.edu/tas/jca/ccda/tf-meta6.html

Attig, J. (June 1982). The USMARC formats—Underlying principles. *Information Technology and Libraries, 1*(2), 169–74.

Avram, H. D. (1975). *MARC: Its History and Implications.* Washington, DC: Library of Congress.

Bates, M. J. (1989). Rethinking subject cataloging in the online environment. *Library Resources & Technical Services, 33*(4), 400–12.

Batty, D. (November 1998). WWW—Wealth, weariness or waste: Controlled vocabulary and thesauri in support of online information access. *D-Lib Magazine, 4*(11). Retrieved from www.dlib.org/dlib/november98/11batty.html

Berman, S. (1977). The cataloging shtik. *Library Journal, 102*(11), 1251–53.

———. (Ed.). (1985). *Subject Cataloging: Critiques and Innovations.* New York, NY: Haworth.

Bibliographic Framework Initiative. (n.d.a). *BIBFRAME.org.* Retrieved from http://bibframe.org/

———. (n.d.b). *BIBFRAME.org Tools.* Retrieved from http://bibframe.org/tools/

Bliss Classification Association. (2007). *The Bliss Bibliographic Classification: History and Description.* Retrieved from http://www.blissclassification.org.uk/bchist.shtml

———. (2011). *The Bliss Bibliographic Classification.* Retrieved from http://www.blissclassification.org.uk/

———. (2013). *Bliss Bibliographic Classification: Schedules* (2nd ed., edited by J. Mills and V. Broughton). London, England: Bowker-Saur. Retrieved from http://www.blissclassification.org.uk/bcsched.shtml

Bliss, H. E. (1939). *The Organization of Knowledge in Libraries* (2nd ed.). New York, NY: The H. W. Wilson Company.

———. (1977–). *Bliss Bibliographic Classification* (2nd ed., edited by J. Mills and V. Broughton, with the assistance of V. Lang). Boston, MA: Butterworths.

Bourne, C. P., and Hahn, T. B. (2003). *A History of Online Information Services, 1963-1976.* Cambridge, MA: MIT Press.

Bristow, B. A. (Ed.), and Farrar, C. A. (Assoc. ed.). (2014). *Sears List of Subject Headings* (21st ed.). Ipswich, MA: H. W. Wilson Company.

British Museum, Department of Printed Books. (1936). *Rules for Compiling the Catalogues of Printed Books, Maps and Music in the British Museum* (rev. ed.). London, England: British Museum.

Broughton, V. (2004). *Essential Classification.* New York: Neal-Schuman.

Brown, J. D. (1898). *Adjustable Classification for Libraries, with Index.* London, England: Library Supply Company.

Bush, V. (1945). As we may think. *The Atlantic Monthly, 176*(1), 101–08. Retrieved from www.theatlantic.com/unbound/flashbks/computer/bushf.htm

Calhoun, K. (2006). *The Changing Nature of the Catalog and its Integration with Other Discovery Tools* (Prepared for the Library of Congress). Retrieved from www.loc.gov/catdir/calhoun-report-final.pdf

Caplan, P. (2003). *Metadata Fundamentals for All Librarians.* Chicago, IL: American Library Association.

Carpenter, M. (1985). Editor's introduction: "Mr. Panizzi to the Right Hon. the Earl of Ellesmere." In M. Carpenter and E. Svenonius (Eds.), *Foundations of Cataloging: A Sourcebook* (pp. 15–17). Littleton, CO: Libraries Unlimited.

Chan, L. M. (1990). *Library of Congress Subject Headings: Principles of Structure and Policies for Application* (annotated version). Washington, DC: Library of Congress.

———. (1991). Functions of a subject authority file. In K. M. Drabenstott (Ed.), *Subject Authorities in the Online Environment: Papers from a Conference Program Held in San Francisco, June 29, 1987* (ALCTS Papers on Library Technical Services and Collections, No. 1). Chicago, IL: American Library Association.

———. (1999). *A Guide to the Library of Congress Classification* (5th ed). Englewood, CO: Libraries Unlimited.

———. (2001). Exploiting LCSH, LCC, and DDC to retrieve networked resources. In A. M. Sandberg-Fox (Ed.), *Proceedings of the Bicentennial Conference on Bibliographic Control for the New Millennium: Confronting the Challenges of Networked Resources and the Web.* Washington, DC: Library of Congress.

———. (2005). *Library of Congress Subject Headings: Principles and Application* (4th ed.). Westport, CT: Libraries Unlimited.

Chan, L. M., Childress, E., Dean, R., O'Neill, E. T., and Vizine-Goetz, D. (2001). A faceted approach to subject data in the Dublin Core Metadata Record. *Journal of Internet Cataloging, 4*(1/2), 35–47.

Chan, L. M., and Hodges, T., revised by Martin, G. (1998). Subject cataloguing and classification. In M. Gorman (Ed.), *Technical Services Today and Tomorrow* (2nd ed.) (pp. 95–109). Englewood, CO: Libraries Unlimited.

Chan, L. M., and Mitchell, J. S. (2003). *Dewey Decimal Classification: Principles and Application* (3rd ed.). Dublin, OH: OCLC Online Computer Library Center.

Chan, L. M., and O'Neill, E. T. (2010). *FAST: Faceted Application of Subject Terminology: Principles and Application.* Santa Barbara, CA: Libraries Unlimited.

Chan, L. M., Richmond, P., and Svenonius, E. (1985). *Theory of Subject Analysis: A Sourcebook.* Littleton, CO: Libraries Unlimited.

Chu, H. (2003). *Information Representation and Retrieval in the Digital Age.* Medford, NJ: Information Today.

Coates, E. (1988). *Subject Catalogues: Headings and Structure*. London, England: Library Association.

Comaromi, J. P. (1976a). Conception and development of the Dewey decimal classification. *International Classification,* 3, 11–15.

———. (1976b). *The Eighteen Editions of the Dewey Decimal Classification*. Albany, NY: Forest Press Division, Lake Placid Education Foundation.

———. (1981). *Book Numbers: A Historical Study and Practical Guide to their Use*. Littleton, CO: Libraries Unlimited.

Crawford, W. (1989). *MARC for Library Use: Understanding Integrated USMARC*. Boston, MA: G. K. Hall & Co.

Cutter, C. A. (1891–1893). *Expansive Classification: Part 1: The First Six Classifications*. Boston, MA: C. A. Cutter.

———. (1953). *Rules for a Dictionary Catalog* (4th ed. rewritten). London, England: The Library Association. (Original work published 1876.)

Cutter, C. A., Jones, K. E., Swanson, P. K., and Swift, E. M. (1969). *Cutter-Sanborn Three-figure Author Table* (Swanson-Swift revision). Chicopee, MA: H. R. Huntting Company.

Cutter, C. A., Swanson, P. K., and Swift, E. M. (1969a). *C. A. Cutter's Three-figure Author Table* (Swanson-Swift revision). Chicopee, MA: H. R. Huntting Company.

———. (1969b). *C. A. Cutter's Two-figure Author Table* (Swanson-Swift revision). Chicopee, MA: H. R. Huntting Company.

CyberStacks(sm). (August 24, 1998). *Welcome to CyberStacks(sm)!* Retrieved from http://www2.iastate.edu/~cyberstacks/

Dewey, M., and Mitchell, J. S. (2011). *Dewey Decimal Classification and Relative Index* (Ed. 23). Dublin, OH: OCLC, Online Computer Library Center, Inc.

———. (2012). *Abridged Dewey Decimal Classification and Relative Index* (Ed. 15). Dublin, OH: OCLC, Online Computer Library Center, Inc.

Dhyani, P. (1988). Colon classification edition 7—An appraisal. *International Classification, 15*(1), 13.

Dublin Core Metadata Initiative. (November 7, 2005). *Using Dublin Core—Dublin Core Qualifiers*. Retrieved from http://dublincore.org/documents/2005/11/07/usageguide/qualifiers.shtml

———. (June 14, 2012). *DCMI Metadata Terms*. Retrieved from http://dublincore.org/documents/dcmi-terms

———. (2014). *History of the Dublin Core Metadata Initiative*. Retrieved from http://dublincore.org/about/history/

Dunkin, P. S. (1969). *Cataloging U.S.A.* Chicago, IL: American Library Association.

Ebenezer, C. (2003). Trends in integrated library systems. *VINE, 32*(4), 19–45.

Editeur. (2009a). *ONIX for Books* (ONIX 3.0). Retrieved from http://www.editeur.org/11/Books/

———. (2009b). *ONIX for Books: Product Information Format Specification, Release 3.0.* Retrieved from http://www.editeur.org/11/Books/

Foskett, A. C. (1996). *The Subject Approach to Information* (5th ed.). London, England: Library Association.

Freedman, M. J. (1977). Public libraries, the Library of Congress, and the National Bibliographic Network. *Library Journal, 102*(19), 2211–19.

Godby, C. J. (2012). *A Crosswalk from ONIX Version 3.0 for Books to MARC 21*. Dublin, OH: OCLC Research. Retrieved from http://www.oclc.org/research/publications/library/2012/2012-04.pdf

Google. (2012). *Google Books*. Retrieved from http://books.google.com/

Gorman, M. (2004). *The Concise AACR2* (4th ed.). Chicago, IL: American Library Association.

Gorman, M., and Hotsinpiller, J. (1979). ISBD: Aid or barrier to understanding? *College & Research Libraries, 40*(6), 519–26.

Gullion, S. L. (1983). Cataloging and classification: Classification and subject cataloging. In L. Darling, D. Bishop, and L. A. Colaianni (Eds.), *Handbook of Medical Library Practice* (4th ed.). Chicago, IL: Medical Library Association.

Hagler, R. (1997). *The Bibliographic Record and Information Technology* (3rd ed.). Chicago, IL: American Library Association.

Hahn, T. B. (1998). Pioneers of the online age. In T. B. Hahn and M. Buckland (Eds.), *Historical Studies in Information Science* (pp. 116–31). Medford, NJ: Information Today.

Hanson, J. C. M. (1929). The Library of Congress and its new catalogue: Some unwritten history. In W. W. Bishop and A. Keogh (Eds.), *Essays Offered to Herbert Putnam by his Colleagues and Friends on his Thirtieth Anniversary as Librarian of Congress: 5 April 1929*. New Haven, CT: Yale University Press.

Hardy, Q. (March/April, 2006). Can we know everything? *California [UC Berkeley Alumni Magazine], 117*(2). Retrieved from http://alumni.berkeley.edu/california-magazine/march-april-2006-can-we-know-everything/can-we-know-everything

Harold, E. R., and Means, W. S. (2004). *XML in a Nutshell* (3rd ed.). Sebastopol, CA: O'Reilly.

Hauben, M., and Hauben, R. (1998). Behind the Net: The untold history of the ARPANET and computer science. *First Monday, 8*(3). Retrieved from http://firstmonday.org/index

Haykin, D. J. (1951). *Subject Headings: A Practical Guide*. Washington, DC: Government Printing Office.

Hillmann, D. (November 7, 2005). *Using Dublin Core*. Retrieved from http://dublincore.org/documents/2005/11/07/usageguide/

IFLA Cataloguing Section and IFLA Meetings of Experts on an International Cataloguing Code. (2009). *Statement of International Cataloguing Principles*. München, Germany: K. G. Saur. Retrieved from http://www.ifla.org/publications/statement-of-international-cataloguing-principles

IFLA Cataloguing Section and ISBD Review Group, International Federation of Library Associations and Institutions. (2011). *International Standard Bibliographic Description (ISBD)* (Consolidated ed.; IFLA series on bibliographic control, Vol. 44). München, Germany: De Gruyter Saur. Retrieved from http://www.ifla.org/publications/international-standard-bibliographic-description

IFLA Study Group on the Functional Requirements for Bibliographic Records. (1998). *Functional Requirements for Bibliographic Records: Final Report* (UBCIM Publications, New Series Vol. 19). München, Germany: K. G. Saur. Retrieved from http://www.ifla.org/publications/functional-requirements-for-bibliographic-records [Also available at www.ifla.org/VII/s13/frbr/frbr.htm (20

Feb. 2007), and in IFLA Working Group on Functional Requirements and Numbering of Authority Records. (2009). *Functional Requirements for Authority Data: A Conceptual Model* (IFLA Series on Bibliographic Control, Vol. 34). München, Germany: K.G. Saur.]

IFLA Study Group on the Functional Requirements for Bibliographic Records, International Federation of Library Associations and Institutions. (2009). *Functional Requirements for Bibliographic Records, Final Report.* München, Germany: K. G. Saur. Retrieved from http://www.ifla.org/files/assets/cataloguing/frbr/frbr_2008.pdf

IFLA Working Group on Functional Requirements and Numbering of Authority Records (FRANAR), International Federation of Library Associations and Institutions. (2013). *Functional Requirements for Authority Data: A Conceptual Model.* München, Germany: K. G. Saur. Retrieved from http://www.ifla.org/files/assets/cataloguing/frad/frad_2013.pdf

IFLA Working Group on the Functional Requirements for Subject Authority Records (FRSAR), International Federation of Library Associations and Institutions. (2011). *Functional Requirements for Subject Authority Data (FRSAD): A Conceptual Model.* Berlin, Germany: De Gruyter Saur. Retrieved from http://www.ifla.org/files/assets/classification-and-indexing/functional-requirements-for-subject-authority-data/frsad-final-report.pdf

Immroth, J. P. (1971). *A Guide to the Library of Congress Classification* (2nd ed.). Littleton, CO: Libraries Unlimited.

International Conference on Cataloguing Principles. (1961). *Statement of Principles Adopted by the International Conference on Cataloguing Principles.* Retrieved from http://www.nl.go.kr/icc/paper/20.pdf

International Federation of Library Associations. (1974). *ISBD (M): International Standard Bibliographic Description for Monographic Publications* (1st standard ed.). London, England: IFLA Committee on Cataloguing. (And subsequent editions.)

International Federation of Library Associations and Institutions. (1996). *Names of Persons: National Usages for Entry in Catalogues* (4th revised and enlarged ed., UBCIM Publication—New Series Vol. 16). München, Germany: K. G. Saur.

———. (2007). *International Standard Bibliographic Description (ISBD)* (preliminary consolidated ed.). München, Germany: K.G. Saur.

International Organization for Standardization. (1973). Documentation: Format for bibliographic information interchange on magnetic tape: ISO 2709. Geneva, Switzerland: International Organization for Standardization.

———. (2003). *Information and Documentation—The Dublin Core Metadata Element Set* (ISO 15836: 2003). Available from http://www.iso.org/iso/iso_catalogue/catalogue_tc/catalogue_detail.htm?csnumber=37629

———. (2011). *Information and Documentation: Format for Information Exchange: ISO 2709:2008.* Geneva, Switzerland: International Organization for Standardization.

Intner, S. S., Lazinger, S. S., and Weihs, J. (2006). *Metadata and Its Impact on Libraries.* Westport, CT: Libraries Unlimited.

Jewett, C. C. (1853). *Smithsonian Report on the Construction of Catalogues of Libraries, and their Publication by Means of Separate, Stereotyped Titles, with Rules and Examples* (2nd ed.). Washington, DC: Smithsonian Institution.

Joint Steering Committee for Revision of AACR (American Library Association, Australian Committee on Cataloguing, British Library, Canadian Committee on Cataloguing, Library Association, & Library of Congress.) (1988). *Anglo-American Cataloguing Rules* (2nd ed., 1988 revision). M. Gorman and P. W. Winkler (Eds.). Chicago, IL: American Library Association.

———. (1998). *Anglo-American Cataloguing Rules* (2nd ed., 1998 revision). M. Gorman and P. W. Winkler (Eds.). Chicago, IL: American Library Association.

Joint Steering Committee for Revision of AACR (American Library Association, Australian Committee on Cataloguing, British Library, Canadian Committee on Cataloguing, Chartered Institute of Library and Information Professionals, & Library of Congress). (2002). *Anglo-American Cataloguing Rules* (2nd ed., 2002 revision). Chicago, IL: American Library Association.

———. (2005). *Anglo-American Cataloguing Rules* (2nd ed., 2005 revision). Chicago, IL: American Library Association.

J. Paul Getty Trust. (2000). *Getty Thesaurus of Geographic Names Online.* Retrieved from http://www.getty.edu/research/tools/vocabularies/tgn/

Kanellos, M. (September 11, 2006). The hard drive at 50: Half a century of hard drives, *CNET News.com.* Retrieved from http://www.zdnet.com/news/a-half-century-of-hard-drives/149491

Kilgour, F. G. (1977). Ohio College library center. In A. Kent, H. Lancour, and J. E. Daily (Eds.), *Encyclopedia of Library and Information Science* (Vol. 20, pp. 346–47). New York, NY: Marcel Dekker.

Koch, T. (1999). *The Role of Classification Schemes in Internet Resource Description and Discovery.* Retrieved from http://www.ukoln.ac.uk/metadata/desire/classification/index.html

Koch, T., and Day, M. (January 28, 1999). *The Role of Classification Schemes in Internet Resource Description and Discovery.* Retrieved from www.ukoln.ac.uk/metadata/desire/classification/

Korfhage, R. R. (1997). The matching process. In *Information storage and retrieval* (pp. 79–104). New York: Wiley.

LaMontagne, L. E. (1961). *American Library Classification with Special Reference to the Library of Congress.* Hamden, CT: Shoe String Press.

Lancaster, F. W. (1986). *Vocabulary Control for Information Retrieval* (2nd ed.). Arlington, VA: Information Resources Press.

Landry, P., Bultrini, L., O'Neill, E. T., Roe, S. K., and International Federation of Library Associations. (2011). *Subject Access: Preparing for the Future.* Berlin, Germany: De Gruyter Saur.

Laughead, G., Jr. (2008). *WWW-VL: History: Internet & W3 World-Wide Web.* Retrieved from http://vlib.iue.it/history/internet/

Lehnus, D. J. (1980). *Book Numbers: History, Principles, and Application.* Chicago, IL: American Library Association.

Library of Congress. (n.d.a). *Classification Web.* Retrieved from http://www.loc.gov/cds/classweb/

———. (n.d.b). *Classification Web: World Wide Web Access to Library of Congress Classification and Library of Congress Subject Headings.* Retrieved from www.classificationweb.net/

———. (n.d.c). *MODS: Metadata Object Description Schema*. Retrieved from www.loc.gov/standards/mods/

———. (1949). *Rules for Descriptive Cataloging in the Library of Congress Adopted by the American Library Association*. Washington, DC: Library of Congress.

———. (1974–1983). *Library of Congress Name Headings with References*. Washington, DC: Library of Congress.

———. (2000). *MARC 21 Specifications for Record Structure, Character Sets, and Exchange Media*. Retrieved from http://www.loc.gov/marc/specifications/spechome.html

———. (2002a). *Encoded Archival Description Tag Library, Version 2002. Appendix C: Encoded Examples*. Retrieved from http://www.loc.gov/ead/tglib/appendix_ca.html

———. (2002b). *Encoded Archival Description: Version 2002*. Retrieved from www.loc.gov/ead/

———. (January 2, 2002). *Library of Congress Classification Weekly List 01*. Retrieved from http://www.loc.gov/catdir/cpso/wlc02/awlc0201.pdf

———. (December, 2002). *Development of the Encoded Archival Description DTD*. Retrieved from www.loc.gov/ead/eaddev.html

———. (May 26, 2006). *Encoded Archival Description Tag Library, Version 2002: EAD Elements: <eadheader> EAD Header*. Retrieved from http://www.loc.gov/ead/tglib/elements/eadheader.html

———. (October 2007). *MARC Code List for Languages* (2007 ed.). Retrieved from http://www.loc.gov/marc/languages/langhome.html

———. (November 21, 2012). *Bibliographic Framework as a Web of Data: Linked Data Model and Supporting Services*. Retrieved from http://www.loc.gov/bibframe/pdf/marcld-report-11-21-2012.pdf

———. (December 7, 2012). *Library of Congress Authorities*. Retrieved from http://authorities.loc.gov

———. (2013a). G055: Call numbers. In *Classification and Shelflisting Manual*. Retrieved from http://www.loc.gov/aba/publications/FreeCSM/G055.pdf

———. (2013b). G302: U.S. states and Canadian provinces. In *Classification and Shelflisting Manual*. Retrieved from http://www.loc.gov/aba/publications/FreeCSM/G302.pdf

———. (2013c). G320: Biography. In *Classification and Shelflisting Manual*. Retrieved from http://www.loc.gov/aba/publications/FreeCSM/G320.pdf

———. (2014a). *Classification and Shelflisting Manual*. Retrieved from http://www.loc.gov/aba/publications/FreeCSM/freecsm.html

———. (2014b). G300: Regions and countries table. In *Classification and Shelflisting Manual*. Retrieved from http://www.loc.gov/aba/publications/FreeCSM/G300.pdf

———. (July 2014). *RDA in MARC*. Retrieved from http://www.loc.gov/marc/RDAinMARC.html

Library of Congress, Catalog Division. (1910–1914). *Subject Headings Used in the Dictionary Catalogues of the Library of Congress*. Washington, DC: Government Printing Office, Library Branch.

Library of Congress, Cataloging Distribution Service. (2014). *Cataloger's Desktop*. Retrieved from https://desktop.loc.gov/jsp/login.jsp

Library of Congress, Cataloging Policy and Support Office. (1984–). *Subject Headings Manual*. Washington, DC: Cataloging Distribution Service, Library of Congress. Available in Cataloger's Desktop at http://www.loc.gov/cds/desktop/

———. (1901–). *Classification*. Washington, DC: Library of Congress.

———. (1989–). *Free-floating Subdivisions: An Alphabetical Index*. Washington, DC: Library of Congress, Cataloging Distribution Service.

———. (1995). *Subject Cataloging Manual: Shelflisting* (2nd ed.). Washington, DC: Library of Congress.

———. (2008). *Subject Cataloging Manual: Classification* (2008 ed.). Washington, DC: Library of Congress.

Library of Congress, Subject Cataloging Division. (1914–1966). *Subject Headings Used in the Dictionary Catalogs of the Library of Congress* (1st ed.–7th ed.). Washington, DC: Library of Congress.

———. (1975–). *Library of Congress Subject Headings*. Washington, DC: Cataloging Distribution Service, Library of Congress. Available in ClassificationWeb at http://classificationweb.net

———. (1984). *Subject Cataloging Manual: Subject Headings* (prelim. ed.). Washington, DC: Library of Congress.

Library of Congress, Library and Archives Canada, British Library, & National Library of Canada. (2000–). *MARC 21 Format for Holdings Data: Including Guidelines for Content Designation*. Washington, DC: Cataloging Distribution Service, Library of Congress.

Library of Congress, Library and Archives Canada, National Library of Canada, & British Library. (1999–). *MARC 21 Format for Bibliographic Data: Including Guidelines for Content Designation*. Washington, DC: Cataloging Distribution Service, Library of Congress.

Library of Congress & National Library of Canada. (1999–). *MARC 21 Format for Authority Data: Including Guidelines for Content Designation*. Washington, DC: Cataloging Distribution Service, Library of Congress.

———. (2000–). *MARC 21 Format for Classification Data: Including Guidelines for Content Designation*. Washington, DC: Cataloging Distribution Service, Library of Congress.

Lubetzky, S. (1960). *Code of Cataloging Rules: Author and Title Entry*. Chicago, IL: American Library Association.

———. (1969). *Principles of Cataloging. Final Report. Phase I: Descriptive Cataloging*. Los Angeles, CA: Institute of Library Research, University of California.

———. (1985). Principles of Descriptive Cataloging. In M. Carpenter and E. Svenonius (Eds.), *Foundations of Cataloging: A Sourcebook* (pp. 104–12). Littleton, CO: Libraries Unlimited. (Original work published 1946.)

———. (2001). Cataloging rules and principles: A critique of the A.L.A. rules for entry and a proposed design for their revision. In E. Svenonius and D. McGarry (Eds.), *Seymour Lubetzky: Writings on the Classical Art of Cataloging* (pp. 78–139). Englewood, CO: Libraries Unlimited. (Original work published 1953.)

Maltby, A. (1975). *Sayers' Manual of Classification for Librarians* (5th ed.). London, England: Andre Deutsch.

Mann, T. (1993). *Library Research Models: A Guide to Classification, Cataloging, and Computers*. New York, NY: Oxford University Press.

MARC Development Office, Library of Congress. (1974). *Information on the MARC System* (4th ed.). Washington, DC: Library of Congress.

Marcella, R., and Maltby, A. (2000). *The Future of Classification*. Aldershot, England: Gower.

Markey, K. (1984). *Subject Searching in Library Catalogs Before and After the Introduction of Online Catalogs* (OCLC Library, Information and Computer Science Series, No. 4). Dublin, OH: OCLC.

McCallum, J. C. (February 23, 2013). *Disk Drive Prices*. Retrieved from http://jcmit.com/diskprice.htm

McIlwaine, I. C. (1990). The work of the system development task force. In A. Gilchrist and D. Strachan (Eds.), *The UDC: Essays for a New Decade* (19–27). London, England: Aslib.

———. (2000). *The Universal Decimal Classification: A Guide to its Use*. The Hague, Netherlands: UDC Consortium.

Meadow, C. (1988). Online database industry timeline. *Database, 11*(5), 23–31. Retrieved from http://www.infotoday.com/

Mehnert, R., and Hoffmann, C. F. B. (1986). The National Library of Medicine. In A. Kent (Ed.), *Encyclopedia of Library and Information Science* (Vol. 41, Supp. 6). New York, NY: Marcel Dekker.

Merrill, W. S. (1939). *Code for Classifiers* (2nd ed.). Chicago, IL: American Library Association.

Miksa, F. (1983). *The Subject in the Dictionary Catalog from Cutter to the Present*. Chicago, IL: American Library Association.

Mills, J. (1967). *A Modern Outline of Library Classification*. London, England: Chapman & Hall, Ltd.

———. (Spring 1976). The new Bliss classification. *Catalogue and Index, 40*(1), 3–6.

Mitchell, J. S., and Vizine-Goetz, D. (2007). *Moving Beyond the Presentation Layer: Content and Context in the Dewey Decimal Classification (DDC) System*. Binghamton, NY: Haworth.

Mowery, R. L. (Spring 1976). *The Cutter Classification: Still at Work*. Library Resources and Technical Services, 20, 154–56.

Music Library Association. (2011–). *Thematic Indexes Used in the Library of Congress/NACO Authority File*. Retrieved from http://bcc.musiclibraryassoc.org/BCC-Historical/BCC2011/Thematic_Indexes.htm

National Center for Biotechnology Information. (2013). *The NCBI Handbook* (2nd ed.). Bethesda, MD: National Center for Biotechnology Information. Retrieved from http://www.ncbi.nlm.nih.gov/books/NBK143764/

National Information Standards Organization (U.S.). (2001). *The Dublin Core Metadata Element Set* (ANSI/NISO Z39.85-2001). Bethesda, MD: NISO Press. Retrieved from http://www.niso.org/apps/group_public/download.php/6578/The%20Dublin%20Core%20Metadata%20Element%20Set.pdf

———. (2004). *Understanding Metadata*. Bethesda, MD: NISO Press. Retrieved from www.niso.org/standards/resources/UnderstandingMetadata.pdf

National Library of Medicine (U.S.). (1999). *National Library of Medicine Classification: A Scheme for the Shelf Arrangement of Library Materials in the Field of Medicine and its Related Sciences* (5th ed., revised). NIH Publication no. 00-1535. Bethesda, MD: National Library of Medicine.

———. (2014). *NLM Classification 2014*. Retrieved from www.nlm.nih.gov/class/

———. (April 29a, 2014). *NLM Classification*. Retrieved from www.nlm.nih.gov/class/

———. (April 29b, 2014). *NLM Classification Practices: Early Printed Books*. Retrieved from http://www.nlm.nih.gov/class/nlmclassprac.html#Early

———. (April 29c, 2014). *NLM Classification Practices: Serial Publications*. Retrieved from http://www.nlm.nih.gov/class/nlmclassprac.html#Serial

———. (August 6a, 2014). *Medical Subject Headings: MeSH Tree Structures*. Retrieved from http://www.nlm.nih.gov/mesh/intro_trees.html

———. (August 6b, 2014). *Medical Subject Headings: Preface*. Retrieved from http://www.nlm.nih.gov/mesh/intro_preface.html#pref_hist

———. (August 6c, 2014). *Medical Subject Headings: Publication Characteristics (Publication Types)—Scope Notes*. Retrieved from www.nlm.nih.gov/mesh/pubtypes.html

———. (August 6d, 2014). *Medical Subject Headings: Use of Medical Subject Headings for Cataloging*. Retrieved from http://www.nlm.nih.gov/mesh/catpractices.html

———. (August 7, 2014). *Medical Subject Headings: Qualifiers by Allowable Category—2015*. Retrieved from http://www.nlm.nih.gov/mesh/topcat.html

National Library of Medicine (U.S.). (September 8, 2014). *Medical Subject Headings*. Retrieved from http://www.nlm.nih.gov/mesh

Network Development and MARC Standards Office, Library of Congress. (n.d.). *BIBFRAME*. Retrieved from http://www.loc.gov/bibframe/

———. (November 1996). *The MARC21 Formats: Background and Principles*. Retrieved from http://www.loc.gov/marc/96principl.html

———. (1999). *MARC 21 Format for Authority Data: Including Guidelines for Content Designation*. Washington, DC: Cataloging Distribution Service, Library of Congress.

———. (July 27, 2004). *MARC 21 Concise Formats*. Retrieved from http://www.loc.gov/marc/archive/2000/concise/

———. (2005, May 3). *ONIX to MARC 21 Mapping*. Retrieved from www.loc.gov/marc/onix2marc.html

———. (December 4, 2007). *MARC 21 Specifications for Record Structure, Character Sets, and Exchange Media*. Retrieved from http://www.loc.gov/marc/specifications/

———. (2008). *MARC 21 Concise Formats*. Retrieved from http://www.loc.gov/marc/concise/

———. (April 7, 2008). *MARC Code List for Geographic Areas*. Retrieved from www.loc.gov/marc/geoareas/gacshome.html

———. (April 24, 2008). *MARC 21 Lite Bibliographic Format*. Retrieved from http://www.loc.gov/marc/bibliographic/lite/

———. (April 13, 2012). *MARC Records, Systems and Tools*. Retrieved from http://www.loc.gov/marc/marcservice.html

———. (June 11, 2013). *MADS: Metadata Authority Description Schema*. Retrieved from http://www.loc.gov/standards/mads/

———. (September 9a, 2013). *Understanding MARC Authority Records: Machine-readable Cataloging*. Retrieved from www.loc.gov/marc/uma/

———. (September 9b, 2013). *Understanding MARC Bibliographic: Machine-readable Cataloging*. Retrieved from www.loc.gov/marc/umb/

———. (April 28, 2014). *MARC 21 Format for Classification Data*. Retrieved from http://www.loc.gov/marc/classification/

———. (May 21, 2014). *MARCXML: MARC 21 XML Schema*. Retrieved from http://www.loc.gov/standards/marcxml/

———. (October 20a, 2014). *MARC 21 Format for Authority Data*. Retrieved from http://www.loc.gov/marc/authority/

———. (October 20b, 2014). *MARC 21 Format for Bibliographic Data*. Retrieved from http://www.loc.gov/marc/bibliographic/

———. (October 20c, 2014). *MARC 21 Format for Holdings Data*. Retrieved from http://www.loc.gov/marc/holdings/

———. (November 24, 2014). *MODS: Metadata Object Description Schema*. Retrieved from http://www.loc.gov/standards/mods/

———. (December 18, 2014). *MARC Standards*. Retrieved from http://www.loc.gov/marc/

OCLC. (n.d.) *OCLC-MARC Records: Record Structure*. Retrieved from http://www.oclc.org/content/dam/support/worldcat/documentation/records/subscription/1/1.pdf

———. (2011). *Webdewey* [Subscription service]. Available from www.dewey.org/webdewey/

OCLC. (2014a). *Dewey Cutter Program* [Software program]. Available from http://www.oclc.org/support/services/dewey/program.en.html

———. (2014b). *OCLC World Cat*. Retrieved from www.oclc.org/worldcat/open/

———. (2015a). *History of the OCLC Research Library Partnership*. Retrieved from http://www.oclc.org/research/partnership/history.html

———. (2015b). *OCLC Online Computer Library Center*. Retrieved from www.oclc.org/

———. (2015c). *WorldCat FCataloging Partners*. Retrieved from https://www.oclc.org/cataloging-partners.en.html

OCLC Research. (October 14, 2014). *FAST (Faceted Application of Subject Terminology)*. Retrieved from http://fast.oclc.org/

Olson, H. A. (2002). *The Power to Name: Locating the Limits of Subject Representation in Libraries*. Dordrecht, The Netherlands: Kluwer Academic Publishers.

Olson, H. A., Boll, J. J., and Aluri, R. (2001). *Subject Analysis in Online Catalogs*. Englewood, CO: Libraries Unlimited.

O'Neill, E. T., and Chan, L. M. (December 2003). FAST (Faceted application of subject terminology): A simplified vocabulary based on the Library of Congress subject headings. *IFLA Journal, 29*(4), 336–42. Retrieved from www.ifla.org/IV/ifla69/papers/010e-ONeill_Mai-Chan.pdf

Palmer, B. I. (1971). *Itself an Education: Six Lectures on Classification* (2nd ed.). London, England: Library Association.

Panizzi, A. (1985a). Mr. Panizzi to the Right Hon. the Earl of Ellesmere—British Museum, January 29, 1848. In M. Carpenter and E. Svenonius (Eds.), *Foundations of Cataloging: A Sourcebook* (pp. 18–47). Littleton, CO: Libraries Unlimited. (Original work published 1850.)

———. (1985b). Rules for the compilation of the catalogue. In M. Carpenter and E. Svenonius (Eds.), *Foundations of Cataloging: A Sourcebook* (pp. 3–14). Littleton, CO: Libraries Unlimited. (Original work published 1841.)

Patton, G. E. (2009). *Functional Requirements for Authority Data: A Conceptual Model* (IFLA Series on Bibliographic Control Vol. 34). München, Germany: K. G. Saur. Retrieved from http://www.ifla.org/publications/functional-requirements-for-authority-data

Pettee, J. (1947). *Subject Headings: The History and Theory of the Alphabetical Subject Approach to Books*. New York, NY: H. W. Wilson Company.

Prevost, M. L. (April 1946). An approach to theory and method in general subject heading. *Library Quarterly, 16*(2), 140–51.

Program for Cooperative Cataloging (PCC). (n.d.a.). *About the PCC*. Retrieved from http://www.loc.gov/aba/pcc/about/

———. (n.d.b.). *PCC Guidelines for the Application of Relationship Designators in Bibliographic Records*. Retrieved from http://www.loc.gov/aba/pcc/rda/PCC%20RDA%20guidelines/Relat-Desig-Guidelines.docx

Principles of the Sears list of subject headings. (2004). In J. Miller (Ed.) and J. Goodsell (Assoc. ed.), *Sears List of Subject Headings* (18th ed.) (pp. xv–xxix). New York, NY: H. W. Wilson Company.

The Prussian Instructions: Rules for the Alphabetical Catalogs of the Prussian Libraries (translated from the 2nd ed., authorized August 10, 1908, with an introduction and notes by A. D. Osborn). (1938). Ann Arbor, MI: University of Michigan Press.

Ranganathan, S. R. (1963). *Colon Classification* (6th ed., reprinted with amendments). Bombay, India: Asia Publishing House.

———. (1987). *Colon Classification* (7th ed., revised and edited by M. A. Gopinath). Bangalore, India: Sarada Ranganathan Endowment for Library Science.

———, assisted by Gopinath, M. A. (1967). *Prolegomena to Library Classification* (3rd ed.). London, England: Asia Publishing House.

———, and Palmer, B. I. (1959). *Elements of Library Classification: Based on Lectures Delivered at the University of Bombay in December 1944 and in the School of Librarianship in Great Britain in December 1956* (2nd ed., revised and rewritten). London, England: Association of Assistant Librarians, Section of the Library Association.

RDA: Resource Description and Access. (2010–). Developed in a collaborative process led by the Joint Steering Committee for Development of RDA (JSC). Chicago: American Library Association.

Reitz, J. M. (2004–2014). *ODLIS: Online Dictionary for Library and Information Science*. Retrieved from www.abc-clio.com/ODLIS/searchODLIS.aspx

Richmond, P. (1981). *Introduction to PRECIS for North American Usage*. Littleton, CO: Libraries Unlimited.

Satija, M. P. (2013). *The Theory and Practice of the Dewey Decimal Classification System*. Oxford: Chandos Pub.

Singh, S. (2011). *The Theory and Practice of the Dewey Decimal Classification System*. New Delhi: Isha Books.

Slavic, A. (2004). UDC translations: A 2004 survey report and bibliography. *Extensions and Corrections to the UDC, 26,* 58–80.

Society of American Archivists. (1989). *Archives, Personal Papers, and Manuscripts* (2nd ed.). Chicago, IL: Society of American Archivists.

———. (2007). *Describing Archives: A Content Standard*. Chicago, IL: Society of American Archivists.

Studwell, W. E. (1990). *Library of Congress Subject Headings: Philosophy, Practice, and Prospects*. New York, NY: Haworth Press.

Svenonius, E. (1985). Editor's introduction: "Smithsonian catalogue system [by] Charles C. Jewett." In M. Carpenter and E. Svenonius (Eds.), *Foundations of Cataloging: A Sourcebook* (p. 49). Littleton, CO: Libraries Unlimited.

———. (1990). Design of controlled vocabularies. In A. Kent (Ed.), *Encyclopedia of Library and Information Science* (Vol. 45, Supp. 10). New York, NY: Marcel Dekker.

Taube, M. (October 1952). Specificity in subject headings and coordinate indexing. *Library Trends, 1*, 222.

Taylor, A. G. (2004). *The Organization of Information* (2nd ed.). Englewood, CO: Libraries Unlimited.

———. (2006). *Introduction to Cataloging and Classification* (10th ed.). Westport, CT: Libraries Unlimited.

Tedd, L. (1994). OPACs through the ages. *Library Review, 43*(4), 27–37. Retrieved from http://www.emeraldinsight.com/loi/lr

Text Encoding Initiative. (September 16, 2014). *Example: <teiHeader> (TEI Header)*. Retrieved from http://www.tei-c.org/release/doc/tei-p5-doc/en/html/examples-teiHeader.html

Tillett, B. B. (1989). *Bibliographic Relationships: Toward a Conceptual Structure of Bibliographic Information Used in Cataloging* (Dissertation). Los Angeles, CA: UCLA.

———. (1991). A taxonomy of bibliographic relationships. *Library Resources and Technical Services, 35*(2), 150–58.

———. (2003). FRBR (Functional requirements for bibliographic records). *Technicalities, 23*(5), 1, 11–13. Retrieved from: www.loc.gov/cds/FRBR.html

UDC Consortium. (2015a). *International UDC Seminar 2015: Classification and Authority Control*. Retrieved from www.udcc.org

———. (2015b). *UDC Online*. Retrieved from http://www.udc-hub.com/

United States Army Medical Library. (1951). *Army Medical Library Classification: Medicine. Pre-clinical Sciences: QS-QZ, Medicine and Related Subjects: W* (1st ed.). Washington, DC: Government Printing Office.

U.S. National Library of Medicine. (April 6, 2015). *Medical Subject Headings*. Bethesda, MD: U.S. National Library of Medicine. Retrieved from www.nlm.nih.gov/mesh/

———. (April 29, 2015) *Outline of the NLM Classification.* Retrieved from www.nlm.nih.gov/class/OutlineofNLMClassificationSchedule.html

Vatican Library (Biblioteca Apostolica Vaticana). (1948). *Rules for the Catalog of Printed Books* (translated from the 2nd Italian ed. by the Very Rev. T. J. Shanahan, V. A. Schaefer, and C. T. Vesselowsky). W. E. Wright (Ed.). Chicago, IL: American Library Association.

Visual Resources Association Data Standards Committee. (2007). *VRA Core Cataloging Examples.* Retrieved from http://www.loc.gov/standards/vracore/schemas.html

———. (April 5, 2007). *VRA Core 4.0 Element Description and Tagging Examples.* Retrieved from http://www.loc.gov/standards/vracore/

Vizine-Goetz, D. (1999). *Using Library Classification Schemes for Internet Resources.* OCLC Internet Cataloging Project Colloquium Position Paper. Retrieved from http://staff.oclc.org/~vizine/Intercat/vizine-goetz.htm

Waldhart, T. J., Miller, J. B., and Chan, L. M. (2000). Provision of local assisted access to selected internet information resources by ARL academic libraries. *Journal of Academic Librarianship, 26*(2), 100–09.

WebCrawler. (2006). *About WebCrawler.* Retrieved from www.webcrawler.com/info.wbcrwl/search/help/about.htm

W3C. (January 26, 2015). *Extensible Markup Language (XML).* Retrieved from www.w3.org/XML/

Zeng, M. L., and Qin, J. (2008). *Metadata.* New York, NY: Neal-Schuman Publishers.

Zeng, M. L., Žumer, M., and Salaba, A. (Eds.). (2011). *Functional Requirements for Subject Authority Data (FRSAD): A Conceptual Model* (IFLA Series on Bibliographic Control, Vol. 43). Berlin/München, Germany: De Gruyter Saur. Retrieved from http://www.ifla.org/publications/ifla-series-on-bibliographic-control-43

Index

About the Author

Lois Mai Chan, professor emeritus at the School of Library and Information Science, University of Kentucky, Lexington, Kentucky, was the author of eight books and numerous articles and co-editor of two collections in the areas of knowledge organization and subject indexing. In 1989, Chan was awarded the Margaret Mann Citation for Outstanding Achievement in Cataloging and Classification given by the American Library Association. In 1992, she received the Distinguished Service Award from the Chinese-American Librarians Association. In 1999, Chan and Diane Vizine-Goetz were chosen for the Association for Library Collections & Technical Services' (ALCTS) Best of LRTS Award for the Best Article Published in 1998. In 2006, Chan received the Beta Phi Mu (International Honor Society for Library and Information Science) Award for distinguished service to education for librarianship. From 1986 to 1991, Chan served as the chair of the Decimal Classification Editorial Policy Committee. She served as a member of the IFLA Standing Committee on Knowledge Management and the IFLA Functional Requirements for Subject Authority Data (FRSAD) Working Group. Her research interests included knowledge organization, subject vocabulary, authority control, metadata, and organization and retrieval of Web resources.

Athena Salaba, associate professor at the School of Library and Information Science, Kent State University, Kent, Ohio, is the co-author of three books and a number of journal articles. She holds a Ph.D. in Library and Information Studies from the University of Wisconsin-Madison. Salaba served as the Co-chair and Secretary of the IFLA Working Group on the Functional Requirements for Subject Authority Records (FRSAR) and a member of the IFLA FRBR Review Group. She and Dr. Yin Zhang were the recipients of an IMLS grant to research the FRBR implementation in the development of effective library catalogs. Her research interests include organization of information, knowledge organization systems, and information-seeking behavior.